ANCIENT
TRADITION &

Translated by

A BOARD OF SCHOLARS

And Edited by

Prof. J. L. SHASTRI

Vol. 7

ANCIENT INDIAN TRADITION AND MYTHOLOGY SERIES

PURĀṆAS IN TRANSLATION

VOLUMES

ŚIVA 1-4

LIṄGA 5-6

BHĀGAVATA 7-11

GARUḌA 12-14

NĀRADA 15-19

KŪRMA 20-21

BRAHMĀṆḌA 22-26

AGNI 27-30

VARĀHA 31-32

BRAHMA 33-36

VĀYU 37-38

PADMA 39-48

VOLUMES UNDER PREPARATION

SKANDA

BHAVIṢYA

BRAHMAVAIVARTA

DEVĪBHĀGAVATA

KĀLIKĀ

MĀRKAṆḌEYA

MATSYA

VĀMANA

VIṢṆU

VIṢṆUDHARMOTTARA

THE
BHĀGAVATA-PURĀṆA

Translated and Annotated by
GANESH VASUDEO TAGARE
M.A., Ph.D
Maharashtra Education Service (Retd.)

PART I

MOTILAL BANARSIDASS PUBLISHERS
PRIVATE LIMITED • DELHI

First Edition: Delhi, 1976
Reprint: Delhi, 1979, 1986, 1992

ISBN: 81-208-0096-6

Also available at:
MOTILAL BANARSIDASS
41 U.A. Bungalow Road, Jawahar Nagar, Delhi 110 007
120 Royapettah High Road, Mylapore, Madras 600 004
16 St. Mark's Road, Bangalore 560 001
Ashok Rajpath, Patna 800 004
Chowk, Varanasi 221 001

UNESCO COLLECTION OF REPRESENTATIVE WORKS—INDIAN SERIES
This book has been accepted in the Indian Translation Series of the UNESCO Collection of Representative Works, jointly sponsored by the United Nations Educational, Scientific and Cultural Organization (UNESCO) and the Government of India

PRINTED IN INDIA

BY JAINENDRA PRAKASH JAIN AT SHRI JAINENDRA PRESS, A-45 NARAINA INDUSTRIAL AREA, PHASE I, NEW DELHI 110 028 AND PUBLISHED BY NARENDRA PRAKASH JAIN FOR MOTILAL BANARSIDASS PUBLISHERS PVT. LTD., BUNGALOW ROAD, JAWAHAR NAGAR, DELHI 110 007

PUBLISHER'S NOTE

The purest gems lie hidden in the bottom of the ocean or in the depth of rocks. One has to dive into the ocean or delve into the rocks to find them out. Similarly, truth lies concealed in a language that with the lapse of time has become obsolete. Man has to learn that language before he discovers that truth.

But he has neither the means nor the leisure to embark on that course. We have, therefore, planned to help him acquire knowledge by an easier course. We have started the series of *Ancient Indian Tradition and Mythology in English Translation*. Our goal is to universalize knowledge through the most popular, international medium of expression. The publication of the Purāṇas in English translation is the step towards that goal.

PREFACE

The present Volume contains the *Bhāgavata Purāṇa* Part I (Skandhas 1-3) in English translation. It is the seventh in the series of fifty Volumes on *Ancient Indian Tradition and Mythology*.

The project of the series was envisaged and financed in 1970 by Shri Sundarlal Jain, the veteran enterprizer in the field of Oriental Publication and the leading partner Messrs Motilal Banarsidas. Hitherto seven Volumes of the Series (that is, four Vols of *Śiva Purāṇa*, two Vols of *Liṅga Purāṇa*, completing both the *Purāṇas* and the present Vol. of the *Bhāgavata Purāṇa*, Part I, Skandhas 1-3) have been published and are ready for sale.

The present translation is based on the Sanskrit text of the *Bhāgavata Purāṇa*, published by Messrs Kṣemarāja Śrīkṛṣṇadass, Veṅkaṭeśvara Press, Bombay. This text, constructed on the collation of mss and supported by the oldest Commentator Śrīdhara Svāmin, is fairly accurate. But we have also recorded the translation of all the additional verses accepted as genuine in the authoritative commentaries of Rāmānuja and Madhva Schools, that are not found in the text of Śrīdhara Svāmin.

The *Bhāgavata Purāṇa* deals with a variety of subjects—geographical, historical, philosophical, religious and the like which need elucidation. This task could not be accomplished by a mere translation. We have, therefore, provided footnotes on these topics. On the philosophical verses, especially, we have recorded different interpretations of the commentators belonging to different schools of thought, viz. those of Śaṅkara, Rāmānuja, Madhva, Nimbārka, Vallabha and Caitanya (Gauḍīya School of Vaiṣṇavism) and also two eminent Marathi commentators—Kṛṣṇa Dayārṇava and Ekanātha. In the accomplishment of this task we have utilized the commentaries published in the Bhagavata Vidya Peeth Ahmedabad Edition and in the Vrindavana edition of this Purāṇa.

In order to help the reader understand the background of

the subject matter we have prefixed to this part a critical and comparative introduction which discusses, among other topics, the date, authorship, philosophy, religion and general characteristics of this Purāṇa. A brief note on the commentators has also been added to the introduction while a general index is thought to be included in the last Part of this work.

Before closing, it is our pleasant duty to put on record our sincere gratitude to Dr. S. K. Chatterjee, Dr. V. Raghavan, Dr. R. N. Dandekar, Shri K. R. Kripalani, and the authorities of the UNESCO for their kind encouragement and valuable help which render this work more valuable to scholars than it would otherwise have been. We must also thank the learned translator and annotator Dr. G.V. Tagare for his untiring zeal and sustained efforts in bringing out this Volume within scheduled time, in spite of untold obstacles.

Finally, we avail of this opportunity to state that any critical suggestion and advice for improvement are welcome and will receive proper consideration from us.

Editor

ABBREVIATIONS

Common and self-evident abbreviations such as Ch.(s)—Chapter (s), P.—Page, PP.—(Pages), V.—Verse, VV.—Verses, Ft. n—Foot-note, *Hist. of Ind. Phil.—History of Indian Philosophy* are not included in the list below.

The abbreviated form of the commentator's name is used for his commentary on the *Bhāgavata Purāṇa*.

ABORI.	*Annals of the Bhandarkar Oriental Research Institute*, Poona.
Agni P.	*Agni Purāṇa*.
AIHT.	*Ancient Indian Historical Tradition* by F.E. Pargiter.
ASD.	Apte's *Sanskrit-English Dictionary* (Motilal Banarsidass, 1963). "P" after ASD means the page No of the dictionary.
BDCRI.	*Bulletin of the Deccan College Research Institute*, Poona.
BG.	*The Bhagavad Gītā*.
Bh. P.	*The Bhāgavata Purāṇa*. Bhāgavata Vidyā Peeṭha Ahmedabad edition, 1965-1975 and the Veṅkaṭeśvara Edition used.
BM.	*The Bhāgavata Māhātmya* (*Padma Purāṇa Uttara Khaṇḍa*) Editor : Krishna Shankar Shastri, Ahmedabad, 1965.
BP.	Bhagavat Prasāda's *Bhakta-manorañjanī* (A com. on the Bh. P , Ahmedabad edition).
BPK.	*Bhāratīya Paurāṇika Kośa* (Marathi), Pub.: D.S. Yande and Co., Bombay, 1929.
CHI.	*Cambridge History of India* (Ed. E.J. Rapson).
Com.	Commentary.
DHM.	*A Classical Dictionary of Hindu Mythology* by John Dowson, Kegan Paul, London, 1928.
ERE.	*Encyclopaedia of Religion and Ethics* Ed. by Hastings.

Garuḍa P.	*Garuḍa Purāṇa* Ed. by Ramashankar Bhattacarya, Chowkhamba Varanasi 1964.
GD.	Gosvāmī Giridhara-lāla's *Bāla-prabodhinī*, a com. on the Bh.P. (*Śuddhādvaita* School).
GDAMI	*The Geographical Dictionary of Ancient and Medieval India* by Nundo Lal De, Luzac and Co, London, 1927.
GS	Gaṅgā Sahāya's *Anvitārtha-prakāśikā* : A com. on the Bh. P. (*Advaita* School).*
HDS	*History of Dharma Śāstra* by P. V. Kane, G.O.S. Class B., 6 : BORI Poona, 1930 onwards (References are to Volumes and pages).
HIL	*History of Indian Literature*, by M. Winternitz, 2nd Edn., Oriental Books Reprint Corporation, New Delhi, 1972.
IA	*Indian Antiquary*, Bombay.
IHQ	*Indian Historical Quarterly*, Calcutta.
JG	Jīva Gosvāmi's *Krama-sandarbha*, a Com. on the Bh. P. It represents the Bengal School of Vaiṣṇavism.
Kūrma P.	*Kūrma Purāṇa* Edt. by Ramashankar Bhattacārya, Indological Book House, Varanasi.
MBH.	*Mahābhārata* (Gita Press, Gorakhpur). References show the Parva No. or name (e.g. Vana, Mausala) the Ch. in that *parvan* and the verse No.
MNK.	Mahābharāta Nāmānukramaṇikā (Gita Press Gorakhpur).
Matsya P.	*Matsya Purāṇa* (Guru Mandal Grantha Mālā, Calcutta. Unless mentioned otherwise, the Purāṇas mentioned here belong to that Grantha Mālā).

*With the exception of Skandha X of the Bh. P., I have used the text of the Comm. as published in the Bhagavata Vidya-Peeth Ahmedabad's edition of the Bh. P. For Skandha X I have followed the text of the Comm. as found in the Vrindāvan Edition of the Bh. P

PCK	*Bhāratavarṣīya Prācīna Caritra Kośa*, by M. M. Siddheshvara Shastri Chitrav, Poona, 1968.
PG.	Puruṣottama Gosvāmi's *Subodhini-prakāśa* a Com. on the Bh. P. (*Śuddhādvaita* School).
PI	*Purāṇa Index*, by V.R. Ramchandra Dikshitar, (Referencs are to Volumes and Pages) Madras.
PSB.	*The Philosophy of the Śrīmad Bhāgavata*, by Siddheshvara Bhattacarya, Visva Bharati, Santiniketana, 1960 and 1962.
PSK.	*Prācīna Bhāratīya sthala Kośa*, by M.M. Siddheshvar Shastri Chitrav, Poona, 1969.
PYP.	*Pātañjala Yoga Pradīpa* (Gita Press, Gorakhpur).
RN	*Ṛju-nāmnī* Com. on the B. M. by Ramapratāp, Son of Brajalāl of Vijaypur (Śekhāvaṭ).
RR.	Rādhā Ramaṇa Gosvāmī's *Dīpinī*, a Com. on the Bh. P. (*Advaita* School).
RV	*Ṛg Veda Saṁhitā* (Both Aundha and Poona editions used).
SD.	Śuka Deva's *Siddhānta-pradīpa*, a com. on the Bh. P. (It represents the Nimbārka School of Vedānta).
SGAMI	*Studies in the Geography of Ancient and medieval India, by* D.C. Sircar (Motilal Banarsidass, 1971)
Śiva P.	*Śiva Purāṇa*, Pandit Pustakalaya, Kaśi, Samvat 2020.
ŚR.	Śrīdhara Svāmī's *Bhāvāratha Dīpikā*, the oldest Com. on the Bh. P. (*Advaita* School).
Vāyu P.	*Vāyu Purāṇa.*
VB.	Vallabhācārya's *Subodhinī*, a Com. on the Bh. P. (*Śuddhādvaita* School).
VC.	Viśvanātha Cakravarti's *Sārārtha-darśinī*, a Com. on the Bh. P. (Bengal school of Vaiṣṇavism).

VD.	Vaṁśīdhara's *Bhāvārtha-dīpikā-prakāśa*, a Com. on the Bh. P. (*Advaita* School).
Viṣṇu P. also VP.	*Viṣṇu Purāṇa* (Gita Press, Gorakhpur).
VJ.	Vijayadhvaja's *Padaratnāvalī*, a Com. on the Bh. P. (*Dvaita* School).
v.l.	A variant; a different reading.
VR.	Vīra-rāghava's *Bhāgavata Candrikā*, a Com. on the Bh.P. (*Viśiṣṭādvaita* school).
YSP.	*The Yoga Sūtras of Patañjali*, By J. H. Woods (Harvard Oriental Series).

Self-evident abbreviations e.g. *Hist. of Ind. Civilization* by R.K. Mukerjee are not included.

CONTENTS

INTRODUCTION

1. The Bh. P.—*A Purāṇa with Ten Characteristic Topics*

(1) *The Term Purāṇa*

The term *Purāṇa* usually occurs in close association with *itihāsa* in old Sanskrit literature.[1] Originally it connoted simply 'an old narrative'. The *Purāṇas* describe this term as 'that which lives from ancient times'[2] or 'the records of ancient events'[3]. To convey the same sense, Sanskrit lexicons derive the term *Purāṇa* grammatically as follows :[4]

(1) *Purā (pūrvasmin kāle) bhavam*[5] /
(2) *purā nīyate iti*

As a class of literature *Purāṇas* existed in Vedic times and are mentioned as such along with *Brāhmaṇas*, *Itihāsa* and *Nārāśaṁsī gāthā in the AV*[6] (*Athırva Veda*), in *Brāhmaṇas*[7] and in the *Tai. Ār.* (*Taittirīya Āraṇyaka*[8]). By the time of the *Chāndogya Upa.*, they were accorded the status of 'the fifth Veda', and formed a part of the syllabus of Vedic studies[9]. The use of *itihāsa* and *purāṇa* in a collective *dvandva* and in the singular number in these ancient works suggests that, possibly, there was one work or rather tract of literature called *Purāṇa*—a tradition recorded in the *Matsya*, *Padma* and *Skanda Purāṇas*.[10] As P.V. Kane shows,

1. *Baudhāyana Dharma Sūtra* 2.5.9.14.
   Taittirīya Brāhmaṇa 3.12.8.2.
2. *Vāyu P.* 1.123.
3. *Matsya P.* 53.63.
4. *Śabda-kalpa-druma* III. 179, vide also *Halāyudha Kośa* p.430.
5. *Pāṇini* 4.3.23; 2.1.49 or 4.3.105.
6. *AV.* XI.7.24; XV.6.11.
7. *Gopatha* I.2.10; *Śatapatha* 14.6.10.6.
8. *Tai. Ār.* 2.10.
9. *Āśvalāyanagṛhyasūtra* (3.3.1) states the inclusion of *itihāsa* and *Purāṇas in svādhyāya*.
   Chāndogya Upa. 7.1.7.
10. *Matsya P.* 53.4; *Purāṇam ekam evāsid asmin kalpāntare nṛpa* /— *Sakanda P.—Revā Māhātmya* 1.23.30 Patañjali in *Mahābhāsya* (I.p.9).

the *Āpastamba Dharma Sūtra* twice quotes verses from a *Purāṇa* and summarizes the view of a *Bhaviṣyat Purāṇa*.[1] The quotations show that *Purāṇas* in those days were versified compositions in archaic Sanskrit and that even in those times there was a *Purāṇa* called *Bhaviṣyat Purāṇa*.

(2) *Five characteristics of Purāṇas*

It appears that probably due to the pre-eminence of the war between Kauravas and Pāṇḍavas wherein the then contemporary Aryandom participated, the *Mahābhārata* with all its accretions came to be designated as *itihāsa* (history) and the rest of the ancient lore *purāṇa*. But both *itihāsas* and *purāṇas* are equally myth and history. It is presumed by scholars like M. Winternitz that 'similar to the *Vedic Saṁhitās* there existed one or several collections of *Itihāsas* and *Purāṇas*, made up of myths and legends.[2] During the *Brāhmaṇa* period, 'the recital of narrative poems formed a part of the religious ceremonies at the sacrificial and domestic festivals. Thus the daily recitation of legends of gods and heroes belonged to the preliminary celebration, which lasted a whole year, of the great horse-sacrifice'.[3] As shown by S. Bhattacarya[4] it was this sacrificial milieu which led to the formation of the following main topics dealt with in the *Purāṇas*, viz. (1) *sarga* (creation of the universe); (2) *pratisarga* (recreation after destruction or deluge); (3) *vaṁśa* (genealogy); (4) *manvantara* (the great periods of time with Manu as the primal ancestor) and (5) *vaṁśānucarita* (the history of the dynasties both the Solar and the Lunar). These topics formed an integral part of the 'definition' of the *purāṇas*, as given in the *Amara Kośa*.[5] But as G.V. Devasthali notes, 'the texts that have come down to us under the title *Purāṇa* hardly conform to this definition, since they contain either something more or

1. *Āpastamba Dh. S.* 1.6.19.13; 2.9.23.3-6; 2.9.24.6.
2. *HIL*. Vol. I. 313.
3. *Ibid*. Vol. I. 311.
4. *PSB*. Vol, I. Intro. iii-v.
5. *Amara Kośa* 1.6.5.

The Pañcalakṣaṇa verse (with minor variations) is found in a number of *Purāṇas* such as *Agni* P. 1.14, *Garuḍa P.* 1.2.27, *Kūrma P.* 1. 1. 12, *Matsya P.* 53.64, *Śiva P.—Vāyavīya saṁhitā* 1.41, *Vāyu P.* 4.10.11, *Viṣṇu P.* 3.6.25.

something less than the limitations set by it.'[1] The reasons were obvious. The process of Aryanisation of pre-Aryan masses and assimilation of foreign invaders like Greeks, Scythians, Hūṇas and others in the Hindu fold necessitated the creation of a literature which included non-Aryan beliefs, rituals, customs etc. and could shape the conduct and meet the worldly and spiritual needs of the masses. Hence the conglomeration of legends of gods, and tales of demons and snake-deities, old sages and kings of ancient times in Purāṇas. Some Purāṇas like *Agni*, *Garuḍa* and *Nārada* are ancient encyclopaedias of literature containing abstracts of works in Arts and Sciences, medicine, grammar, dramaturgy, music, astrology etc. Most of them are rich in *dharma-śāstra* material such as *ācāra* (religious duties), *āśrama-dharma* (duties pertaining to one's social class and stage in life), *dāna* (gifts), *prāyaścitta* (atonement for sins), *Śrāddha* (rituals pertaining to the death-anniversary), *Tīrtha* (holy places) etc.[2] They have amalgamated *āgamic Vaiṣṇavism* with early (*Vedic*) *Viṣṇuism* and *āgamic Śaivism* with the Vedic traditions. A number of them are rich in historical material, e.g. the *Vāyu*, *Brahmāṇḍa*, *Bhāgavata*. Hence they (the *purāṇas*) afford us far greater insight into all aspects and phases of Hinduism—its mythology, its idol-worship, its theism, its pantheism, its love of God, its philosophy and its superstition, its festivals and ceremonies and its ethics, than any other work.[3] Pargiter is not exaggerating when he calls *Purāṇas* as a popular encyclopaedia of ancient and mediaeval Hinduism, religious, philosophical, historical, personal, social and political.[4]

(3) *Mahāpurāṇas and the Bh. P.*

The *Purāṇic* literature consists of 18 *Mahāpurāṇas* and numerous *Upa-purāṇas*. The term *Mahāpurāṇa* for the 18 principal *Purāṇas* is of a very late origin, being found only in the

1. *The History and Culture of the Indian People*, Vol. III *The Classical Age*, p. 292.

2. For a detailed tabular statement of *dharma-śāstra* materials in *Purāṇas* vide P.V. Kane—*History of Dharma-Śāstra*, Vol. I., pp 164-167.

3. Winternitz—*HIL*. 1. 529.

4. *ERE* (*Encyclopaedia of Religion and Ethics*), Vol.X., p. 448.

Bh. P.[1] According to the Bh. P. 12. 13.4-8, the following are the names of the *Mahāpurāṇas* along with the number of *ślokas* as given below :

S. No.	*Names of the Purāṇas*	*No. af ślokas*
1.	Brahma	10,000
2.	Padma	55,000
3.	Viṣṇu	23,000
4.	Vāyu	24,000
5.	Bhāgavata	18,000
6.	Nārada	25,000
7.	Mārkaṇḍeya	9,000
8.	Agni	10,500
9.	Bhaviṣya	14,500
10.	Brahmavaivarta	18,000
11.	Liṅga	11,000
12.	Varāha	24,000
13.	Skanda	81,000
14.	Vāmana	10,000
15.	Kūrma	17,000
16.	Matsya	14,000
17.	Garuḍa	19,000
18.	Brahmāṇḍa	12,000

As P.V. Kane notes there is considerable divergence about the names of the 18 principal *purāṇas*. For example, the *Matsya-purāṇa* (chap.53) enumerates them as follows :-Brahma, Padma, Viṣṇu, Vāyu, Bhāgavata, Nārada, Mārkaṇḍeya, Āgneya, Bhaviṣya, Brahmavaivarta, Liṅga, Varāha, Skanda, Vāmana, Kūrma, Matsya, Garuḍa and Brahmāṇḍa. The *Viṣṇupurāṇa* (3.6) on the other hand, omits *Vāyu* from the above list and adds *Śiva*.[1] These Mahāpurāṇas have been classified by the *Padma Purāṇa* (*Uttara-khaṇḍa*, 263.81-4) into *Sāttvika*, *rājasa* and *tāmasa*. Viṣṇu, Nārada, Bhāgavata, Garuḍa, Padma and Varāha are *Sāttvika*; Brahmāṇḍa, Brahmavaivarta, Brahma, Vāmana and Bhaviṣya are *rājasa*; Matsya, Kūrma, Liṅga, Śiva, Agni and Skanda are *tāmasa*. The *Skanda Purāṇa*, however, differs. It states that 10 Purāṇas describe the glory of Śiva, 4 of Brahmā and 2

1. *Kane—Hist. of Dharma Śāstra*, Vol. 1, p. 161.

each of Devī and Hari (*Kedāra-khaṇḍa* 1). The *Matsya P.* (53.68-9) considers that the Agni Purāṇa is *Rājasa.*

Although the Bh.P. assigns for itself the fifth position in the list of *Mahāpurāṇas,*[1] it is acclaimed as the best and most important work by ancient and modern scholars. For example, according to Winternitz, this is indisputably the most famous *Purāṇa* work. Still it exerts a powerful influence on the life and thought of the innumerable adherents to the sect of the Bhāgavatas.[2] The last redactor of the Bh.P. calls it as "the ripe fruit entirely made of ambrosial juice of the wish-yielding tree called the Vedas, fallen from the mouth of a connoisseur (of sweet fruits) like Śuka".[3] The *Padma P.* states that Bh.P. explains what is actionlessness (*naiṣkarmya*) synthesized with spiritual knowledge, renunciation and devotion. By listening to it and contemplating on it, and through devotion, a man attains to Liberation.[4] According to Bopadeva, the *Vedas, Purāṇa* and *Kāvya* (Poetry) advise us like the Master, friend and beloved respectively. But the Bhāgavata synthesizes the function of these three (and guides us).[5] Numerous quotations can be given from old Indian writers. But it will be enough if it be submitted that eminent commentators belonging to different schools of the Vedānta are vying with each other to show that the Bh.P. supports their own school of philosophy. To wit, Śrīdhara (*Advaita*), Gaṅgā Sahāya (*Advaita*), Vīra-rāghava and Sudarśana Sūri (*Viśiṣṭādvaita*), Vijayadhvaja (*Dvaita*), Śuka-deva, (*Bhedābheda* or *Nimbārka*), Vallabha Giridhara (*Pūrṇādvaita*), Jīva Gosvāmī and Viśvanātha Cakravarti (Caitanya or Bengal School of Vaiṣṇavism) and a number of commentators in Sanskrit and regional lauguages have written excellent commentaries on the Bh.P. As Winternitz puts it, the extremely numerous Mss. and

1. Cf. *Viṣṇu* P. 3.6.20, *Padma* P. Ch. 115 but *Devī Bhāgavata* 1.3.17 assigns it the last position. Despite the claims of *Devī Bhāgavata* to be the real *Bhāgavata* and a *Mahā Purāṇa*, it is now generally conceded that our Bh. P. is the *Bhāgavata Mahā Purāṇa* in the traditional list, and not the *Devī Bhāgavata*. (H.C. Hazra—*JOR* XXI, pp. 63-5).

2. Winternitz—*HIL* (*History of Indian Literature*) I, 554.

3. *Bh. P.* 1.1.3.

4. *Padma P.—Bhāgavata Māhātmya* 6.83; cf. Bh. P. 12. 13. 18.

5. Bopadeva—*Harilīlā'mṛta*—1.9.

printed editions of the text, many commentaries on the work, bear witness to 'its enormous popularity and extraordinary reputation' of being the most famous epic in India.[1]

(4) *Ten characteristics of a Mahāpurāṇa*

As the Bh. P. is now generally regarded as a *Mahāpurāṇa* the old academic discussion about the claim of the *Devī-bhāgavata* as the real *Bhāgavata* is not taken up here. R.C. Hazra in his paper on *Devī-Bhāgavata* has already proved that it cannot be the real *Bhāgavata*, and it is much younger than the latter.[2] Due to the unsatisfactory nature of the *pañcalakṣaṇa* definition, the Bh.P. has made another attempt to redefine *Purāṇas*. As per Bh. P. 2.10.1, the following are the 10 characteristics of a *Purāṇa* :[3]

(1) subtle creation (*sarga*); (2) gross creation (*visarga*); (3) law and order—ensured by God (*sthāna*); (4) protection —welfare of all (*poṣaṇa*); (5) material lust for karmas (*ūti*); (6) the periods of Manus and history of that epoch (*manvantara*); (7) accounts of the deeds of the Lord (*īśānukathā*); (8) physical annihilation (*nirodha*); (9) liberation (*mukti*); (10) the last resort of the universe or the ultimate reality (*āśraya*). These characteristics occur with some variations in the Bh. P. 12.7.9-10. According to ŚR.'s commentary on these verses, the terms *vṛtti* and *rakṣā* are used for *sthāna* and *poṣaṇa* above; *vaṁśānucarita* stands for *īśānukathā*; *saṁsthā* includes *nirodha* and *mukti* of the second Skandha; *hetu* is substituted for *ūti* and *apāśraya* for *āśraya*. These ten characteristics constitute a *Mahāpurāṇa*.[4]

This is nothing but an elaboration of the original five characteristic topics of *Purāṇas*.

Thus, creation upto the formation of the cosmic egg was regarded as subtle and retained the old term *sarga*, while the gross creation of the fourteen worlds was called *vi-sarga*. The old term *Pratisarga* presuming dissolution of the universe, in-

1. Winternitz—*HIL*. I. 554-55.
2. Vide *JOR* XXI, pp. 49-79.
3. *atra sargo visargas' ca sthānaṁ poṣaṇam ūtayaḥ /*
manvantare'śānukathā nirodho muktir āśrayaḥ // Bh.P.2.10.1.
4. *Bh. P.* 12.7.9-10 A.

cludes the new terms *nirodha* (the periodic physical annihilation), and *mukti* (liberation) where from the point of *jīva*, it is the absolute annihilation of *saṁsāra*. *Hetu* i.e. *jīva* and *ūti* i.e. the material lust for *karmas*, are the cause of *sarga*, and can be included under *sarga*. For the protection and law and order (*poṣaṇa* and *sthāna* or *vṛtti* and *rakṣā*) of the world, God incarnates in the world in some family. Thus *īśānukathā*, *poṣaṇa* and *rakṣā* form a part of *Vaṁśānucarita*.[1] The object of the Bh.P. is to lead the *jīva* or *Hetu* to the realization of Brahman, who is the ultimate Reality, and the last resort (*āśraya* or *apāśraya*) of all. All the nine topics of the *Purāṇa* are meant for and lead to the tenth topic, viz., God-realization (*āśraya/apāśraya*).[2] The elaboration of the five topics to ten as found in the Bh. P., suggests the orientation of the Purāṇa literature from their mundane character to high metaphysics.[3]

(5) *The Bh. P. and its ten characteristic topics*

Traditionally, the *Skandha*-wise distribution of these topics is made as follows :

Name of the characteristic Topic	No. of the *Skandha*	No. of Chapters *in the Skandha*
1. *Sarga*	III	33
2. *Visarga*	IV	31
3. *Sthāna*	V	26
4. *Poṣaṇa*	VI	19
5. *Ūti*	VII	15
6. *Manvantara*	VIII	24
7. *Īśānucarita*	IX	24
8. *Nirodha*	X	90
9. *Mukti*	XI	31
10. *Āśraya*	XII	13

This distribution is supported by eminent authors like Bopadeva in his *Harilīlāmṛta*, Vallabha in his *Nibandha* (*Saprakāśa-Tattvārtha-dīpa-nibandha*) and old commentators like

1. Baldeva Upadhyaya—*Purāṇa-Vimarśa*, pp. 137-38.
2. *daśamasya viśudhyarthaṁ navānām iha lakṣaṇam*/—Bh. P. 2.10.2.
3. S. Bhattacarya—*PSB*. Vol. I. vi-vii.

Śrīdhara, Vīra-Rāghava, Vijayadhvaja and others. They have left out the Skandhas I and II. These traditional writers attach special significance even to the number of chapters in each *Skandha*.

Before criticizing the scheme, the traditional viewpoint is briefly stated :

Skandha-wise distribution of the Characteristic topics of the Bh. P.

(i) *Sarga*

'Sarga' is the (subtle) creation of the five elements (*bhūtas*), the objects of senses, sense organs and the mind, the ego and the principle of cosmic intelligence (*mahat*), due to the disturbance of the equilibrium of attributes (*guṇas*)[1]. Elsewhere, it is described as 'the evolution of the *mahat* through the disturbance of the equilibrium of the three *guṇas* constituting the Unmanifest (*avyākṛta* i.e. the primordial matter), of the threefold *Ahaṁkāra* (egoism from the *Mahat*) and (from the threefold Ahaṁkāra) of the five subtle elements, the (eleven) sense-organs (viz. the cognitive and conative organs and the internal organ—the mind), and the objects of these senses'.[2] This process of creation is described in various places in the Bh. P. (e.g. 2.5.20 ff), but traditionally the III Skandha is regarded to delineate creation. Creation is two-fold : (A) *alaukika* (Divine), (B) *laukika* (Worldly). (A) The Divine (*alaukika*) creation consists of 33 gods, whom the Lord in the form of *Yajña-Varāha* created for the protection of the world. The description of the Lord's Boar incarnation (in which he killed the demon Hiraṇyākṣa) is meant for this, and it represents the *Karma-Mārga* (Path of action). (B) The worldly (*laukika*) creation describes the evolution of the universe from the twenty-eight elements, the four subtle *bhūtas* and time. This teaching of Kapila (and his life) represents the Path of knowledge. The total No. of chapters in this Skandha is 33, which corresponds to the number of gods in the divine

---

1. *bhūta-mātrendriya-dhiyāṁ janmasarga udāhṛtaḥ|* *Bh. P.* 2.10.3.
2. *Bh. P.* 12.7.11.

creation and number of principles (*tattvas*) in the worldly creation.[1]

(ii) *Visarga*

In the Bh. P., *Visarga* is the gross creation produced by the *Virāṭ Puruṣa.*[2] Elsewhere it is described as 'the name of the collective creation, both mobile and immobile, of the above-mentioned causal principles fecundated by the Supreme Person, and brought about by the effects of past *karmas* of countless *jīvas*, proceeding from seed to seed.[3] *Visarga* is thus creation as proceeding from Brahmā. The contents of the IV Skandha deal with *Manvantaras*—the Svāyambhuva Manu and his genealogy—the sacrifice of Dakṣa (Chs 2-7), the Dhruva legend (Chs 8-11), and the allegorical story of Purañjana (Chs 13-29), and the Prācetas brothers. But a great authority like Bopadeva states 'the 4th Skandha of 29 chapters is called *Visarga* which is the production of effects (*kārya-sambhūtiḥ*).[4] This Skandha is divided in four parts (1) pertaining to a woman, viz. Satī (Śiva's consort), (2) about a child, viz. Dhruva, (3) concerning an adult, viz. King Pṛthu and (4) relating to the old persons who are to perform penance. This refers to Prācīnabarhiṣ. It is in this way that the IV Skandha is regarded as dealing with *Visarga.*

(iii) *Sthiti*

Sthiti is the triumph of the Lord in the maintenance of the (divine) law and order.[5] Elsewhere, it is called *Vṛtti*, and it implies professions or means that men adopt to maintain themselves. The means which men adopt are the result of their own nature and inherent tendencies due to the law of *Karma.*[6] As that law comes under God's influence, *Vṛtti* or

1. This discussion is based on Bopadeva's *Harilīlāmṛta*, and Vallabha's *Nibandha* and Krishna-Shankara Shastri's *Introduction to the third Skandha* of the Bhāgavata, Vidyā-peeṭh Edn. of the Bh. P.

2. Brahmaṇo guṇa-vaiṣamyād visargaḥ pauruṣaḥ smṛtaḥ/—*Bh. P.* 2.103.

3. *Ibid.* 12.7.12.

4. *Harilīlāmṛta* 4.1-2.

5. *Bh. P.* 2.10.4.

6. *Ibid.* 12.7.13.

Sthāna or *Sthiti* is the preservation of the created beings in their own states and moral laws by the Lord. The V Skandha gives the description of the terrestrial globe as the support of the entire creation, both mobile and immobile, and thus represents the characteristic *Sthiti*. Bopadeva in his *Harilīlāmṛta*, V Skandha, and his able commentator, Madhusūdana Sarasvatī take pains to show how the contents of the V Skandha demonstrate the characteristic *Sthāna* or the 'observation of limitations.[1] A Modern reader, however, wonders how legends of Priyavrata, Nābhi, Ṛṣabha and Bharata (Chs 1-15) followed by the geography of different mythological continents, the different heavenly bodies, and the *Śiśumāra cakra*, and different hells form an organic whole to be included under one characteristic called *Sthiti* or *Vṛtti*.

(iv) *Poṣaṇa*

Poṣaṇa is the protection and welfare of all by the Lord's grace.[2] It is called *Rakṣā* in Skandha XII,[3] and consists of the exploits of the incarnations of Lord Viṣṇu, appearing in every age according to the needs, in the form of birds, beasts, human beings, sages and gods, and in these incarnations, the enemies of the Vedas are killed. As usual Bopadeva staunchly supports the view that the contents of Skandha VI constitute the characteristic *Poṣaṇa* or *rakṣā* of a *Mahā Purāṇa*. *Puṣṭi* is Hari's grace towards His fallen devotees. The efficacy of Lord's name is illustrated by the liberation of Ajāmila, despite his sinful life (Chs 1-3), Indra-Vṛtra legend—Vṛtra, though a demon, was an ardent devotee of Viṣṇu in his former birth as Citraketu (Chs 7-17). The Skandha ends with the birth of *Marut* gods from Diti (Chs 18-19).[4]

The point at issue is, why this particular *Skandha* is to be called *Poṣaṇa* when legends showing the grace of the Lord abound all over the rest of the Skandhas of the Bh. P. The liberation of the king-elephant from the alligator in Skandha VIII, is a concrete example of such overlapping.

1. *Harilīlā* V.
2. *Bh. P.* 2.10.4.
3. *Ibid.* 12.7.14.
4. For details vide *Harilīlāmṛta* VI and Madhusūdana Sarasvatī's commentary on it.

(v) Ūti

Ūti is the desire for action (directed by) tendencies resulting from past *karmas*.[1] These tendencies are (1) evil, (2) good and (3) mixed in nature. Skandha VII is regarded as representing this characteristic. The evil tendencies are illustrated in Chs 1-5 wherein Hiraṇyakaśipu rules wickedly over the world, and maltreats his saintly son Prahlāda. The good tendencies are evinced in Chapters 6-10 where the pious life of Prahlāda, his advice to his Asura boy-friends, and the death of Hiraṇyakaśipu at the hands of Nṛsiṁha, and Prahlāda's praise of the Lord, are described. The mixed tendencies of human beings are to be controlled as per instructions given in the Smṛti-like Chapters 11-15, the last describing the previous birth of Nārada.[2]

As pointed out by ŚR. on 12.7.9, *ūti* corresponds to *hetu*. *Jīva* is doer of actions prompted by ignorance, which is the result of his past actions. He is, thus, the cause of the phenomenal world[3].

(vi) *Manvantara*

Manvantara consists of the account of the righteous path followed by Manus who observe the duty of protecting their subjects.[4] According to the Bh. P. 12.7.15, the period over which a six-fold group, viz., Manu, his sons, gods, Indra, the seven sages and an incarnation (partial manifestation) of Lord Hari, preside, is called *Manvantara*.[5] As ŚR. states in the introductory verses to Skandha VIII, this Skandha is devoted to the description, how in each *Kalpa*, this six-fold group headed by Manu practised and propagated the moral and spiritual order, and sustained the universe for the period of a *kalpa*. Hence *Saddharma* (True path of righteousness) is the charac-

1. *Bh. P.* 2.10.4.

2. Based on Krishna-Śaṅkara Śāstrī's *Introduction to Skandha* VII of the *Bh. P.*, Ahmedabad edition.

3. *hetur jīvo'sya sargāder avidyā-karma-kārakaḥ| Bh. P.* 12.7.18.

4. *Ibid.* 2.10.4.

5. *Manvantaraṁ Manur devā Manu-putrāḥ sureśvarāḥ|*
ṛṣayo 'ṁśāvatārāś' ca Hareḥ ṣaḍvidham ucyate|| Ibid 12.7.15.

teristic of the *Manvantara*.[1] We find here the history of all the fourteen Manus, even though the current Manvantara is the seventh.

Skandha VIII is alternatively called *dharma*. It follows *ūti* VII or *karma-vāsanā*, as it is *dharma* that eradicates the impression left by *karma* (*vāsanā*). Four topics of *dharma* are delineated here:

(1) Remembrance of Lord Hari. It is illustrated by the story of the Liberation of King-elephant-Gajendra (Chs 1-4)

(2) Gifts (*dāna*)—the distribution of the valuable finds emerged from churning of the sea, is an example of *dāna* (Chs 5-14).

(3) Self-dedication—as illustrated by the legend of Bali—(Chs 15-23).

(4) Propagation of *dharma* done by Lord Viṣṇu in His Fish incarnation—(Ch. 24).

Hence it is aptly called *Saddharma-Skandha* (the Skandha dealing with the path of righteousness).

The inclusion of *dharma* is not extraneous. *Jaya Maṅgalā* on Kauṭalīya *Arthaśāstra* (1-5) quotes an old definition of *Purāṇa* according to which *dharma* is an integral part of *Purāṇas*[2].

(vii) *Īśānukathā*

Īśānukathā is the life accounts of various manifestations of Hari, as well as those of His devotees.[3] It is called *vaṁśānucarita* in Bh. P. 12.7.16. *Vaṁśa* is the race extending over all the three divisions of time (viz. the past, present and future), of Kings of pure descent (from god Brahmā). A connected account of such kings and their descendants is denoted here as *Vaṁśānucarita*.[4] This supplements the characteristic called *poṣaṇa* above. As a matter of fact the whole Bh. P. consists of stories which can be labelled as *īśānukathā*.

In the introduction to Skandha IX, ŚR. states that this Skandha describes the genealogy of the 7th Manu Śrāddhadeva

1. ŚR. Intro. to Skandha VIII.

2. Vide Rajeśvara Śāstrī Dravid, 'Bhāratīya-rājanītau Purāṇa-pañcalakṣaṇam', *Purāṇa Patrikā* 4.1.236-44, July 1964, Varanasi.

3. *Bh. P.* 2.10.5.

4. *Ibid.* 12.7.16.

under two heads: (1) The Solar Race and (2) the Lunar Race. Śrāddhadeva Manu was the son of Vivasvān Āditya (identified with the physical Sun) and his sons and their male descendants from the Sūrya vaṁśa (the Solar race) and is described in Chs 1-13 of Skandha IX. Śrāddhadeva's daughter Ilā, was married to Budha, the son of Soma and the genealogy of the sons of Ilā is recorded in Chs 14 to 24. Rāma was born in the Solar race, and Lord Kṛṣṇa, in the Lunar race, though both are regarded as the descents of Viṣṇu, the Bh. P. being mainly concerned with Lord Kṛṣṇa, the traditional history from the earliest times to the birth of Kṛṣṇa, in Skandha IX is only a background for the full-fledged biography of Lord Kṛṣṇa in Skandha X.

(viii) *Saṁsthā or Pralaya*

Saṁsthā or Pralaya is of four types : *naimittika*, *prākṛtika*, *nitya* and *ātyantika*. The first three are included in *Nirodha* while the last comes under *Mokṣa*. According to ŚR., Skandha X constitutes *āśraya* as it deals with the life of Kṛṣṇa. Although described variously elsewhere, *nirodha* i.e. the destruction of wicked kings who caused decline of religion, is detailed in Skandha X, for spreading the great glory of Kṛṣṇa. The nine characteristics of a *Mahā-purāṇa* (such as *Sarga*, *visarga*) are contributory to the last characteristic. viz., *āśraya* (the last resort of the universe or the ultimate Reality). The embodiment of *āśraya* is Lord Kṛṣṇa whose life is described in Skandha X. The Skandha consists of 90 chapters. After description of Kṛṣṇa's incarnation in response to god Brahmā's prayer, the various *līlās* (sportive activities) of Kṛṣṇa mainly at Gokula, Mathura and Dvārakā are described here. The first 35 chapters, extol Kṛṣṇa's *līlās* while he stayed at Gokula and Vṛndāvana. After the deputation of Akrūra to bring Rāma and Kṛṣṇa to Mathura, 11 chapters are devoted to His *līlās* at Mathura. The rest of the chapters are concerned with founding of Dvārakā and Kṛṣṇa's *līlās* there.

The above summary of ŚR.'s introduction to Skandha X clarifies the following points :

(1) Skandha X mainly demonstrates the *āśraya* characte-

ristic, though *nirodha* is also found in Kṛṣṇa's destruction of wicked kings.

(2) All the other *Skandhas,* including Skandha XI, which represents the characteristic called *mukti* or Liberation, are subservient to *Skandha* X—even though Kṛṣṇa Himself teaches the spiritual path to Uddhava, in Skandha XI.

(3) *Nirodha* is also interpreted as control, and one masters it either by Yoga or by listening to the nectar-like *līlās* of Kṛṣṇa. As this Skandha extols the *līlās* of Kṛṣṇa, this demonstrates the characteristic called *nirodha.* As a result of this *nirodha,* one attains to liberation (*mukti*) which characteristic is found in Skandha XI. Skandhas X and XI thus bear close causal relation.

(ix) *Mukti* (Liberation)

Skandha XI constitutes the topic *mukti* or Liberation. It is the next stage after *nirodha*, so ably illustrated in Skandha X. *Mukti* or *Mokṣa* (Liberation) consists in abandoning the unreal form and staying established in the essential nature of Brahman.[1] *Mukti* and *nirodha* of Skandha 2.10.6 correspond to *Saṁsthā* in Bh.P. 12.7.17. Liberation is both of *jīva* and of God. When *jīva* becomes one with Brahman, it is the liberation of *jīva.* When God lays aside His roles in various incarnations etc., and becomes established in His own essential form, it is the liberation of God.

There are four groups of chapters. The 1st group of five *adhyāyas* is written to inspire one with aversion to the worldly life. The introductory story of the creation of iron pestle q the curse of sages like Viśvāmitra is intended to create that aversion. Nārada teaches the *Bhāgavata dharma* to Vasudeva, by reporting to him the conversation between Janaka and the nine sages. It contains all the topics concerning the nine-fold *bhakti,* its variations in different *Yugas*, God's incarnations, Draviḍa-deśa being a stronghold of *bhakti.*

The next part called *Jīva-sāyujya-Prakaraṇa*, consists of 24 chapters (Chs 6-29). It contains the dialogue between Kṛṣṇa and Uddhava, and is the kernal of this Skandha. We learn here

1. *Muktir hitvā 'nyathā rūpaṁ svarūpeṇa vyavasthitiḥ|* *Bh. P.* 2.10.6.

the different 'teachers' of Dattātreya, the details of *bhakti*, its philosophy and technique, the different manifestations of the Lord, the duties of different social classes in different stages of life (*varṇāśrama-dharma*), discussions of different *Yogas* including *bhakti*, the Sāṅkhya Philosophy, the technical details of the worship of God and importance of complete submission to Lord; and how *bhakti* is superior even to Liberation (*mukti*).

After teaching the *Bhāgavata dharma*, Kṛṣṇa deputes Uddhava to Badarikāśrama.

The 3rd part called *Brahma-mukti-Prakaraṇa* consists of two chapters. It deals with Kṛṣṇa's retirement from this world, and Arjuna's arrival to attend the funeral of all Yādava heroes and their wives; and Dvārakā is submerged in the sea.

(x) *Āśraya or Apāśraya*

Āśraya or *Apāśraya* is the final resort which is nothing but the absolute Brahman. Bh.P. 2.10.7 describes *āśraya* (asylum, resort) as 'that from which creation and dissolution (of the universe) are definitely known to emerge. It is also called the Supreme Brahman or the Supreme Soul'.[1] Elsewhere in Skandha XII. 7.19-20 it is called *apāśraya* (the ground). 'It stands for the (absolute) Brahman which is present in all the three states undergone by a *jīva* viz. wakefulness, dream and deep sleep, as well as in all substances which are the products of Māyā. It is also distinct from them. It runs through all the (nine) stages undergone by living organism, from entry into the womb in the form of a seed to death (as their substratum), and is also distinct from them (as their witness) even like the material of which substances are made or as a bare existence underlying names and forms'.[2]

In the introduction to Skandha XII, ŚR. states that this Skandha deals with the topic *āśraya* which is God. Out of the 13 chapters, chapters 1-6 give Śuka's narration to Parīkṣit and the rest form Sūta's discourse to the sages like Śaunaka. After recounting 'future' history of India of post-Kṛṣṇa period upto the ascension of Āndhras, and predicting the rule of Śūdra and Mleccha kings in future, Śuka prepares the mind of Parīkṣit to

1. *Bh. P.* 2.10.7.
2. *Ibid.* 12.7.19-20.

face death fearlessly. After discussing the Kali age, he assures him that if one concentrates on the Lord at the time of death, the Lord, the asylum of all (*Sarvasaṁśrayaḥ*) absorbs him in Himself.[1] In Ch.4, he describes the four kinds of dissolutions of the universe (*pralayas*)—out of which the ultimate one is *Mokṣa* or Liberation—and emphasizes that the Lord is the boat which can ferry one across the ocean of *Saṁsāra* and that the Lord's episodes are the panacea to all miseries.[2] It is the 5th chapter which seems to have given the name *āśraya* to this Skandha. In this Śuka briefly enunciates *Brahmavidyā* to Parīkṣit, and removes from him completely the fear of death. Parīkṣit was so much convinced that, in the beginning of the next (6th) chapter, he tells Śuka that he has accomplished his purpose in life,[3] and that he is not afraid of death as he has entered the fearless and all blissful state of one-ness with Brahman.[4] Finally he requests Śuka :

"Give me permission; I shall dedicate my speech (and other senses) to Lord Adhokṣaja. Having established in the Supreme Lord my mind which is rid of desires and other kindred tendencies, I shall give up life".

"My nescience has been removed through firm insight into *jñāna* and *vijñāna* (the knowledge of the Supreme Reality and its realization). You have shown to me the highest nature of the Almighty Lord, the safest asylum."[5]

He worshipped Śuka who left. After Śuka's departure, Parīkṣit fixed his mind firmly on the *Pratyagātman* and contemplated on the Supreme Spirit, remaining breathless like (the trunk of) a tree.[6] It was in this stage that Takṣaka bit him.

In the remaining chapters, Sūta tells how Vyāsa arranged the *Vedas* and composed the 18 *Purāṇas*. In chapters 8,9,10, he recounts the life of the sage Mārkaṇḍeya. Ch.12 gives a recapitulation of the 12 Skandhas of the Bh.P. The last chapter

1. *Bh. P.* 12.3.50.
2. *Ibid.* 12.4.37-40.
3. *Ibid.* 12.6.2.
4. *Ibid.* 12.6.5.
5. *Ibid.* 12.6.6-7.
6. *Ibid.* 12.6.9.

enumerates the number of verses in each *Mahāpurāṇa* and concludes with glory of the *Bhāgavata Purāṇa*.

It will thus be found that the importance of Chapters 3 to 6 has led these old commentators to designate the whole Skandha as *āśraya*.

The above traditional application of the 10 characteristics of a *Mahāpurāṇa* to Skandhas III to XII is broadly justifiable. But it leaves out the first two Skandhas though they are designated as *Adhikāra* and *Dharma* respectively by some writers. A cursory glance at the contents of the Bh.P. shows that there is so much overlapping and repetition of these topics beyond the Skandhas which are supposed to represent them. Thus we find *Īśānukathā* is spread over Skandhas II, III, V, VII, VIII, X, XI. The same can be said of *Poṣaṇa* or *Manvantara*, while Skandha II is an epitome of the Bh.P. with all its characteristics.

(6) *Concluding remarks*

In fact the Bh.P. is an epic of growth where such repetition, overlapping, looseness in organization of material is inevitable. To judge it as a scientific work preplanned and executed by one single author, is to show one's ignorance about the history and development of this form of literature. The Bh.P. itself states that there were three authors of the text—Vyāsa, Śuka and Sūta. But as Winternitz notes it, despite its manifold revisions, the Bh.P. bears the stamp of a unified composition.[1] It has incorporated the best of the Vedic tradition. The metaphysical and spiritual legacy of the Vedas and Upaniṣads is ably synthesized with the *āgamic* tradition of the *Pañcarātrins*, and embraced even non-Aryan tribes in its fold. As A.A. Macdonell[2] and Winternitz[3] state, it has exercised the most powerful influence in India and as such holds indisputably the most prominent position in Indian sacred literature.

But to justify the particular label of a Skandha throughout all its chapters and to attribute special significance even to the number of chapters in that particular Skandha,

1. *HIL.* Vol. I. 556.
2. A.A. Macdonell—*India's Past* p. 90.
3. *HIL.* Vol. I. 554.

is stretching an excellent epic on the *daśa-lakṣaṇa* bed of procrustes.

The claim of the author of the Bh.P. that it is a Mahāpurāṇa with ten characteristics is perfectly justifiable within the limits of its being an epic of growth.

2. *The Date and Authorship of the Bh.P.*

The date of the Bh.P. is still an open question. Various divergent views expressed so far may be summarised as below :

(1)	Burnouf, Wilson, Colebrooke	1300 A.D.[1]
(2)	R.G. Bhandarkar	200 years before Ānanda Tīrtha circa. 1000 A.D.[2]
(3)	S.N. Dasgupta	1000 A.D.[3]
(4)	S. Radhakrishnan	900 A.D.[4]
(5)	J.N. Farquhar	900 A.D.[5]
(6)	Eliot	800-900 A.D.[6]
(7)	D.S. Śāstrī	825-50 A.D.[7]
(8)	B.N.Krishnamurti Śarmā	800 A.D.[8]
(9)	A.N. Ray	550-650 A.D.[9]
(10)	Hazra	600 A.D.[10]
(11)	Dikshitar	300 A.D.[11]
(12)	R.N. Vyas	900 B.C.[12]
(13)	S.D. Gyani	1200-1000 B.C.[13]

Out of these, the 1st view was based on the slippery argument that as the Bh. P. is not mentioned by Rāmānuja (1017-1137 A.D.), it must have been composed after Rāmānuja, pro-

1. Quoted by Winternitz—*HIL*. Vol. I. 555-6.
2. *Vaiṣṇavism, Śaivism, Minor Religious Systems*, p. 49.
3. *A History of Indian Philosophy*, Vol. IV. p. 1.
4. *Indian Philosophy*, Vol. II, p. 667.
5. *An Outline of the Religious Literature of India*, p. 233.
6. *Hinduism and Buddhism*—Intro.
7. *Concise History of Vaiṣṇava Religion* (Marathi) p. 119.
8. *ABORI* XIV. i-ii, 1932-33, pp. 190-207.
9. *JRAS*, II. p. 79.
10. *NIA* Vol. I. 523-4.
11. *Purāṇa Index*, Vol. I. p. xxix.
12. *Synthetic Philosophy of the Bhāgavata* p. 35.
13. *NIA* Sept. 1942, p. 132.

bably by Bopadeva, the author of *Muktāphala* and *Hari-līlāmṛta.* As Bopadeva was a protege of Hemādri, a minister of Rāmacandrarāva Yādava of Devagiri (1271-1309), the Bh. P. must have been composed in the 13th Cent. A.D. But J.N. Farquhar[1] pointed out the untenability of the view, as Madhva who lived 50 years earlier than Bopadeva, used the Bh. P. as the basic text of the new sect founded by him. He further added that the Bh. P. was 'recognized as an authoritative work some centuries before Madhva wrote'. Madhva alias Ānanda Tīrtha (1197-1276 A.D.) regards the Bh. P. as the 5th Veda, and has written *Bhāgavata-tātparya nirṇaya* on the essence of the Bh. P.[2] The hollowness of the argument of the silence of Rāmānuja was proved when a quotation from *Vedastuti*, Bh. P. 10.8.7. was found in his *Vedānta-tattva-sāra.* And irrespective of Rāmānuja's mention of the Bh. P., we find the famous Arab Scholar Al Biruni (1030 A.D.), in his list of *Purāṇas*, clearly mentioning the Bh. P. of the Vāsudeva cult, assigning it the 5th place as in the *Viṣṇu Purāṇa*[3]. Due to the authoritative status of the Bh. P. at the time of Madhva, Bhandarkar proposed 10th Cent. A.D. as the date of the Bh. P.—a date accepted by S.N. Dasgupta, and Winternitz[4]. Pargiter places the Bh. P. in the 9th Cent. A.D.[5], on the detailed study of *Purāṇas*. As mentioned above, J.N. Farquhar and S. Radhakrishnan accept this date.

Attempts have been made to shift the date earlier still by referring to Gauḍapāda's Bhāṣya on the *Uttara Gītā* where he mentions the Bh. P., and quotes Bh. P. 10.14.4. But this Gauḍapāda is supposed to be a later author of the same name as that of Śaṅkara's spiritual grand-sire. On the contrary, it can be argued that the Bh. P. borrowed words and ideas from the *Māṇḍūkya Kārikās* of Gauḍapāda.[6] Plainly speaking, the Bh.P., as the source of quotations for the works of Śaṅkara and Gauḍapāda, has not been conclusively proved, as the Bh. P. can be said to be the borrower from Gauḍapāda or both might

1. *An Outline of the Religious Literature of India*, p. 231.
2. *History and Culture of Indian People*, Vol. V, p. 442.
3. Sachau—*Alberuni's India*, Vol. I, p. 131.
4. *HIL*. Vol. I., p. 556; also vide Vaidya *JBRAS*, 1925, pp. 144-48.
5. *AIHT* (Ancient Indian Historical Tradition), p. 80.
6. A. N. Ray—*BSOS*. VII. 107-111.

have quoted from a different common source. It is for this reason that the 2 verses common to *Māṭhara Vṛtti* and Bh. P. 1.8.52 and 1.6.35 are not taken as a conclusive evidence, for fixing the date of the Bh.P., even though the textual resemblance between the two is clear.[1] Hence the similarity between the legends in the Bh. P. and the Jātakas, though carefully shown by Gokuldas Dey,[2] cannot be regarded as an irrefutable evidence for determining the date of the Bh. P., as both the works might have independently borrowed from old Indian folk-lore and other traditional tales.

S.D. Gyani's date viz. 1200-1000 B.C. is untenable as the language of the Bh. P. is much more modern than the Vedic which is presumed to be then current in about 1200-1000 B.C.[3] Moreover, if Parīkṣit, to whom the Bh. P. was narrated, ruled in 900 B.C. as shown by Ray Chaudhari,[4] the Bh. P. cannot precede Parīkṣit.

We do not question the historicity of the discussion between Parīkṣit and Śuka about the glory of the former's grandsire (grand-mother Subhadrā's brother Kṛṣṇa) in 900 B.C. but the text before us is written in a language which is much more modern than the OIA of the 9th Cent. B.C. As the History of the text, as given in the Bh. P. shows, some members of the audience present at the dialogue between Śuka and Parīkṣit seem to have transmitted the 'proceedings' of that royal conference elaborately, resulting in the accretions of so many episodes in the generations that followed. But the historicity of the dialogue between Parīkṣit and Śuka (say in 900 B.C.) does not and cannot support 900 B.C. as the date of the present composition.

We have, however, an independent source of a definite date which can be regarded as *the lowest limit* of the date of

---

1. In fact *Māṭhara Vṛtti* on Kārikā 2 is the same as *Bh. P.* 1.8.52.
Yathā paṅkena paṅkāmbhaḥ surayā vā surākṛtam/
bhūta-hatyā tathaivemāṁ na yajñair mārṣṭum arhati//

2. G.D. Dey—*Significance and Importance of Jātakas*. Quoted by R.N. Vyas—*Synthetic Philosophy of Bhāgavata*, p. 30.

3. T. Burrow—*The Sanskrit Language*, p. 31.

4. *Political History of Ancient India from the Accession of Parīkṣit to the Extinction of the Gupta Dynasty*, p. 9, 1923.

the Bh.P. The *Nandī Sūtra*, a work of the Śvetambara Jaina canon, was composed by Devardhi Gaṇi, the president of the final redaction (*Vācanā*) of the Śvetāmbara Jaina Canon, held at Valabhī (Saurāṣṭra) in 980 or 993 after Vīra i.e. 453-466 A.D. or 512-525 A.D., as the *Hist. and Culture of the Indian People* Vol. III, p. 415, takes it.

In giving a list of heretical texts (*mithyā śruta* i.e. non-Jaina literature), the *Nandī Sūtra* gives the following list of works and authors (standing for their works) :

Bhārata (*Mahābhārata*), *Rāmāyaṇa*, *Kauṭalīya* (*Artha Śāstra*), *Kanaka-Sattari* (Īśvara Kṛṣṇa's *Sāṅkhya Kārikās*), Vaiśeṣika, Buddha-Vācanā, Kāpālika, Lokāyata, *Ṣaṣṭi Tantra*, *Māṭhara*, *Purāṇa Bhāgavata*, Patañjali etc.

The mention of the Bh. P., when the *Mahā-Bhārata* was simply known as *Bhārata*, and its mention after *Purāṇa*, are significant. This recognition of the Bh. P. in the list of famous non-Jaina works like the *Bhārata*, *Rāmāyaṇa*, *Kauṭalīya Artha Śāstra in* the Ardha Magadhi Jaina canon would have been possible only if the composition of the Bh. P. is presumed at least a century earlier than the last *Vācanā* of the Jaina canon at Valabhī in the 5th Century A.D. The mention of foreign tribes does not imply the conquest of a part of India by that tribe. In that case, the mention of Turks (Turuṣkas) in the list of foreign tribes in the Śvetāmbara Jaina canon will push the date of the canon 600 years later, to the post-Gazhanavi period, i.e. the earlier part of the 12th Cent. A.D. The fact of the matter is that people in Asia, Europe and North Africa have been visiting India as travellers, merchants, soldiers etc. since ancient times, long before some of them invaded India. Hence the mention of the Hūṇas in the list of the sinful races whom the Lord purifies by his grace[1] does not mean that the Bh. P. was composed after the Hūṇa invasion in the 5th Cent A.D.

Whoever may be the author of the Bh. P., it is a unique work. It is 'not only a magnificent epic singing the great deeds of Kṛṣṇa, but a scripture of the people to which the entire Hindu people from the Himālayas to the Vindhya and

1. *Bh. P.* 2.4.18 mentions the following tribes : Kirāta, Hūṇa, Āndhra, Ābhīra, Kaṅka, Yavana, Khaśa and others.

from Panjab to Bengal, turn for spiritual sustenance, a code of ethics constantly on the lips of all, from princes to peasants and a truly fine expression of poetic genius'.[1] Not that Vyāsa or Śuka are unhistorical, but objective and reliable evidence to assign the authorship of a particular part of the Bh. P. to a particular author is so meagre, that it will be sheer personal speculation to do so.

We have so far traced the mention of the Bh. P. in literary and other sources. But the Bh. P. is an epic of growth and as such, it is difficult to fix up the date(s) (and even authorship) of each part. An analysis of the text shows that it has amalgamated four traditions represented by the following lines of teachers :

(1) Viṣṇu→Brahmā→Nārada→Vyāsa→Śuka (*Bh. P.* 2.4.25; 2.9.5-7; 3.4.13.

(2) Nārāyaṇa→Nārada→Vyāsa→Śuka (*Bh. P.* 10.87.8, 47-48).

(3) Nārāyaṇa→Nārada→Prahlāda (*Bh. P.* 7.6.27-28).

(4) Saṅkarṣaṇa→Sanatkumāra→Sāṁkhyāyana → Parāśara→Bṛhaspati→Maitreya→Vidura (*Bh. P.* 3.8.2-9).

Out of these, the first three lines have Nārada as the common factor, though the Ist line starts from Viṣṇu and the next two from Nārāyaṇa—presumably bearing some relation with the Nārāyaṇīya section of the M. Bh. (*Mahā-Bhārata*). Assuming for the present that the first three traditions can be comprised under one 'Nāradīya' tradition, the 4th appears to be a distinct and different line of teachers.

We do not know when these different strands were amalgamated in the Bh. P., and as such it is hazardous to presume their existence or otherwise in the initial stage of the text and hence, to brand the verses expounding the teaching of the Saṅkarṣaṇa tradition as new or old, is rather uncritical.

The language of the Bh. P. is at places very archaic, showing the absorption of Vedic or Upanisadic passages,[2] use

---

1. Panikkar—*A Survey of Indian History*, p. 174.

2. Absorption of Vedic passages:

e.g. *the Puruṣa Sūkta* (*RV*. 10.90) in *Bh. P.* 2.6.15-30, 10.1.20; the description of *Virāṭ Puruṣa* in the *Aitareya Upa.* 1.4 and the *Bh. P.* 2.10.10ff.

The *Mantropaniṣad* in the *Bh. P.* 8.1.9-16 and *Īśa Upa.*

(i) *Viṣṇor nu kaṁ vīryāṇi pravocam—RV.* 1.154.5.

of Vedic words[1], and old metres, even though some modernisation at the time of redaction must have ironed out many of the archaisms. The prose passages in Skandha V show close similarity to prose passage in the *Brāhmaṇas*. Such passages and verses using archaic and older stage of SK. may be regarded as the original or the first stage of the *Bhāgavata*. The history of the Bh. P. as recorded in the present text shows that the *Mahābhārata*, (probably the *Harivaṁśa*) and the

---

and *Viṣṇor nu vīrya-gaṇanaṁ katamo'rhatīha*—*Bh.P.* 2.7.40).

(ii) *dvā suparṇā sayujā sakhāyā* (*RV.* 1.164.20, *AV.* 9.9.20.)
and *Suparṇāvetau sadṛśau sakhāyau,*
yadṛcchayaitau kṛtanīḍau ca vṛkṣe/
ekastayoḥ khādati pippalānnam
anyo niranno'pi balena bhūyān//—*Bh. P.* 11.11.6.

(iii) *bhidyate hṛdayagranthiś chidyante sarva-saṁśayāḥ/*
kṣīyante cāsya karmāṇi tasmin dṛṣṭe parāvare—*Muṇḍaka Up.* 2.2.8.
Bh. P. 1.2.21 and XI. 20.30 repeat this *verbatim*.

(iv) *avidyāyām antare vartamānāḥ svayaṁ dhīrāḥ paṇḍitaṁ manyamānāḥ/*
dandramyamāṇāḥ pariyanti mūḍhā andhenaiva nīyamānā yathāndhāḥ//
—*Kaṭha Upa.* 1.2.5; *Muṇḍaka Upa.* 1.2.8.
Cf. *Bh. P.* 7.5.31.

(v) *hantā cen manyate hantuṁ hatas' cen manyate hatam/*—*Kaṭha Upa.* 2.3.14.
Cf. *Bh. P.* 10.4.?2.

(vi) Vedic description of the fire-god:
catvāri śṛṅgā trayo'sya pādā dve śīrṣe sapta hastāso asya.
tridhā baddho ṛṣabho roravīti/—*RV.* 4.58.3.
namo dvi-śīrṣṇe tripade catuḥ-śṛṅgāya tantave/
saptahastāya yajñāya trayīvidyātmane namaḥ//—*Bh. P.* 8.16.31.

1. A number of Vedic words (sometimes with semantic change) are used. These references are to the *Bh. P.* e.g.
adabhra (1.3.4), *uktha* 'vital breath' ŚR. (1.15.6),
urukrama 'god with long strides' (2.3.20; 2.7.18; 3.9.8 etc.
śuṣma 'intoxication' (ŚR. on 7.12.32).
gopīthāya 'for protection' (ŚR. on 1.10.32).
apīcya 'beautiful' (ŚR. on 1.19.28; 10.47.2).
rādhas 'prosperity' *aiśvarya* (ŚR. on 2.4.14).
nṛmṇa 'conferring happiness' (ŚR. on 4.8.46).
carṣaṇī 'subjects', *prajā* (ŚR. on 10.21.2).

But even the old portion in the Bh. P. is, from language point of view, not as old as 900 B.C. when Parīkṣit is believed to have lived. This is not to deny the historicity to Parīkṣit or the Śuka's narration of Bhāgavata to him. The 'kernel' of the Bh. P. may be old but the extent text is much more modern than 900 B.C.

Viṣṇu Purāṇa were composed earlier than the Bh. P., and that Bh. P. must have freely borrowed materials from these in its early stage. But no attempt to reconstruct this stage has so far been made. Hence it is premature to state whether the Bh.P. was then a *pañca-lakṣaṇa* (possessing the five characteristic divisions of a) *Purāṇa*.

The most important phase is the middle one, in which the early nucleus of the Bh.P. was expanded into a *mahā purāṇa* of full-fledged ten characteristics (*daśa-lakṣaṇa*). Scholars generally assign the *Gupta era* to this stage. The last redactor of the Bh. P.—perhaps a Sūta—appears to be a Southerner who is proud of the southern region, its rivers, holy places etc. In Bh.P. 11.5.38-40 he mentions the Kāverī, the Tāmraparṇī, the Payasvinī the Kṛtamālā—all from Tāmil Naḍ—as the most holy rivers and the riparian population thereof ('those who drink their waters') become the devotees of Lord Vāsudeva[1]. In the Purañjana story, Purañjana, in the birth as a Vidarbha princess, marries a Pāṇḍya King and gives birth to seven Draviḍa kings[2] (Bh.P. 4.28.29-30). The elephant-king in the 8th Skandha was king Indradyumna of the Pāṇḍya country[3]. King Satyavrata of Draviḍa Deśa got the fish—the Fish-incarnation—while he was bathing in the river Kṛtamālā. Jāmbavatī in the *Harivaṁśa* has no *Draviḍa* as her son, but in Bh. P. 10.61.12 she gets one of that name. The description of hills and rivers in India begins from those in South India (Bh. P. 5.19). This Dravidian influence is noted in the *Padma* P.[4] wherein *bhakti* is allegorically regarded as a lady born in the Dravida country and was rejuvenated at Vṛndāvana. The last redactor or the Sūta seems to have incorporated the *Pañcarātra* system, *Smṛti* texts, popular beliefs and some folk lore to popularise the Bh. P. text. Some of these accretions might have crept in the post-Gupta era.

---

1. *Bh. P.* 11.5.38-40.
2. *Ibid.* 4.2 30.
3. *Ibid.* 8. 7.
4. *Padma P.*—Bhāgavata Māhātmya 1.48,50.

It appears that when these lines were written Bhāgavatism was not popular in Maharastra and Gujarat.

(1) *Antiquity of Bhāgavatism*

Though the Bh. P. was composed in Circa 400 A.D., Bhāgavatism or the Vāsudeva cult is, however, much older than the Bh. P. as can be seen from the following:

(1) From the time of Candra-Gupta II (A.D. 376-415) the Imperial Guptas called themselves as 'ardent devotees of Bhagavat' (*parama bhāgavata*). As a sect requires some time to attain to the status and patronage of the royalty, Bhāgavatism must be earlier than the 4th century A.D.

(2) Nanaghat Inscription (100 B.C.)[1] mentions Vāsudeva as a deity. It means that at that period, in Maharashtra, Bhāgavatism was a respectable sect.

(3) Heliodorus, the ambassador of the Indo-Greek king Antialkidas to the court of Kāśīputra Bhāgabhadra of Vidiśā (near Gwalior M.P.) has recorded in a Prākrit inscription on the shaft of the pillar (of *Garuḍa-dhvaja*) that *Bhāgavata* Heliodorus erected that *Garuḍa-dhvaja* in honour of *Devadeva Vāsudeva.* The inscription is in Brāhmī characters of 2nd century B.C.[2]

(4) An earlier stone inscription at Ghosundi (Rajasthan) Circa 200 B.C., refers to the erection of a pillar together with the wall round the temple (Pūjā-śilā-prākāra) of Vāsudeva[3].

(5) Megasthenes, the Greek ambassador who lived at the court of Candragupta Maurya (324-300 B.C.) found that the people of Śūrasena (Sourasenoi) region round Mathura, worshipped Heracles (Hari or Vāsudeva)[4].

(6) Quintas Curtius, a Greek historian of the 1st cent. B.C. records on the authority of Alexander's contemporary historians that the soldiers of Porus carried the effigy of Herakles (Hari-Vāsudeva) while fighting the Greeks[5]. The above two references show that Vāsudeva-worship was well-established from the North-West Frontier Province upto Magadha before 400 B.C.

---

1. Luder's Ins. No. 6—*Epigraphica Indica.*
2. D.C. Sircar—*Select Inscriptions*, pp. 90-91; also *Epigraphica Indica*—Luder's Ins. No. 669.
3. *Epigraphica Indica*—Luder's Ins. No. 6.
4. M.C. Crindle, pp. 140, 201.
5. A.K. Mujumdar—*Caitanya—His Life and Doctrine*, p. 23.

(7) The earliest reference to the devotion to and worship of Vāsudeva is found in the *Aṣṭādhyāyī* of *Pāṇini* (500 B.C.). The special formation of *Vāsudevaka*<Vāsudeva, 'a person whose object of *bhakti* is Vāsudeva'[1] shows that Vāsudeva was regarded as an adorable deity before Pāṇini. Patañjali clearly explains that this designation refers to Lord Vāsudeva and not merely to a Kṣatriya Prince[2].

This worship was prevalent among the people of the *Sātvata* tribe who are mentioned as neighbours of the Bharatas in the *Śatapatha Brāhmaṇa* (13.5.4.21) and as a southern tribe in the *Aitareya Brāhmaṇa* (8.3.14). But the probable date of the emergence of the Vāsudeva-worship or rather Kṛṣṇa-cult among them cannot, at the present state of our knowledge, be precisely defined. This is not to deny the historicity of Devakīputra Kṛṣṇa for which sufficient data has been presented by A.D. Pusalkar[3].

In passing, it may be noted that, due to the outstanding role as a Philosopher-King, of Vāsudeva Kṛṣṇa, *Vāsudeva* came to be looked upon as a type or a title, and Jainas presume that there were nine Vāsudevas out of whom Kṛṣṇa was one. There must have been some ground for this Jaina supposition, as Brahmanical Purāṇas record another Vāsudeva in East India—*Pauṇḍraka Vāsudeva*—a contemporary of Vāsudeo Kṛṣṇa, who was finally discomfited by Kṛṣṇa. The metaphysical *Vāsudeva* is derived from *vas*-to dwell-and means 'one who is immanent in the universe'. The Brahmanical tradition is unanimous in regarding Vāsudeva and Devakī as the father and mother of Kṛṣṇa.

3. *The Bh. P. and Pāñcarātra*

The *Pāñcarātra* is the name of an ancient Vaiṣṇavite system which deals with the knowledge (*rātra*) of (1) Ontology or Cosmology (*tattva*), (2) Liberation (*Mukti*), (3) devotion (*bhakti*), (4) Yoga, (5) the objects of senses (*vaiśeṣika*). The earliest reference to Pāñcarātra is in the *Śatapatha Brāhmaṇa* (13.6.1) and the sect is designated after 'the five-days conti-

1. *Vāsudevārjunābhyāṁ vuñ*/ 4.3.98.
2. *Mahābhāṣya on Pāṇ*. 4.3.98.
3. *Studies in Epics and Purāṇas*, pp. 84-111.

nuous sacrifice' (*Pañcarātra Sattra*) of Nārāyaṇa, the traditional author of the *Puruṣa Sūkta*. The philosophical connotation of this *Sattra* implies 'five-fold self-manifestation of God by means of His *Para, Vyūha, Vibhava, Antaryāmin* and *Arcā* forms. Normally the following ten topics are treated in the Pāñcarātra: (1) Philosophy, (2) Linguistic occultism (*Mantra-Śāstra*), (3) Theory of magical figures (*Yantra-Śāstra*), (4) Practical Magic (*Māyā-Yoga*), (5) *Yoga*, (6) Temple-building (*Mandira-nirmāṇa*), (7) Image-making (*Pratiṣṭhā vidhi*), (8) Domestic observances (*Saṁskāra, āhnika*), (9) Social rules (*varṇāśrama-dharma*), (10) Public festivals (*utsava*)[1].

Vedic tradition did not look upon with favour many activities of this non-Vedic sect, and prohibited their followers from even speaking with these 'sinners' as will be found in *Parāśara P.* (Purāṇa), *Kūrma P.*, *Bṛhan-Nāradīya P.*, *Agni P.* the *Viṣṇu*, *Hārīta*, *Bodhāyana* and *Yama Saṁhitās* and *smṛti*-commentators and writers on *dharma-śāstra* like Medhātithi (A.D. 825-900) and Hemādri (13th cent. A.D.)[2]. Śaṅkara on *Brahma Sūtra* 2.2.42 has refuted the *Vyūhavāda* (Doctrine of Emanations of Vāsudeva) of the Bhāgavatas i.e. *Pañcarātrins*. All these texts testify to the strong opposition to the *Pāñcarātra*-sect. The Pañcarātrins, however, patiently and tactfully infiltrated through orthodox Purāṇas and assimilated many Vedāntic concepts. Thus the *avatāra-vāda* was blended with *Vyūha-vāda* by the Pañcarātrins[3]. *Viṣṇu* P. is 'a work which was written by a pro-Vedic Pāñcarātra scholar of a comparatively late age with the deliberate intention of writing a religious book for the propagation of his sectarian views under the garb of a Purāṇa[4]. Yāmuna and Rāmānuja brilliantly advocated

---

1. F. Otto Schrader—*Introduction to the Pāñcarātra and the Ahirbudhnya Saṁhitā* (Adyar, 1916) pp. 24-26. Both the spellings *Pañcarātra* and *Pāñcarātra* are used by scholars to designate this sect.

I have retained Schrader's translation of technical terms in spite of the inadequacy of some of them.

2. Vide *A.K.* Majumdar—*Caitanya, His life and Doctrine*, pp. 26-27 and Kane's *Hist. of Dharma Śāstra*, II, 673 etc.

3. *History and Culture of Indian People*, Vol. III, pp. 423-24.

4. R.C. Hazra—*Intro. to Viṣṇu* p. translated by H.H. Wilson 3, Calcutta, 1961.

the Pāñcarātra philosophy as against Śaṅkara, and quoted the authority of *Viṣṇu* P. in rehabilitating Pāñcarātra and blended it with the *Vedānta*. 'Viṣṇu of Vedic Brahmanism, Nārāyaṇa of the Pāñcarātras, Kṛṣṇa-Vāsudeva of Sātvatas, Gopāla of a pastoral people (probably Ābhīras) all had been put in the melting pot from which originated the Bhāgavatism of the Gupta period, though originally *Vyūhavāda*, the central idea in the Pāñcarātra is absent from the Bhāgavatism of the Guptas[1].

In evaluating the opinions of these scholars, one must not lose sight of the historical perspective. Various views on Vāsudeva-Kṛṣṇa cult or Bhāgavatism and Pāñcarātra system ultimately lead to the following conclusions:

(1) Vāsudeva-Kṛṣṇa cult, the origin of Bhāgavatism, represents the Vedic tradition and was different from the Pāñcarātra system which, despite its professed connection with the *Pañcarātra Sattra* of Nārāyaṇa mentioned in the *Śatapatha Brāhmaṇa* was non-Vedic and was condemned as such along with *Pāśupatas* and other *āgamic* sects.

(2) Vāsudeva-Kṛṣṇa in the *Bhagavad-Gītā* mentions only *Sāṁkhya* and *Yoga* and is silent about *Pāñcarātra*. Its philosophy and even *avatāra-vāda* is different from that of the *Pāñcarātra* system and its *Vyūhavāda*.

As Schrader points out, the first mention of the *Pañcarātra* is found in the *Spanda-pradīpikā* of Utpala Vaiṣṇava of Kashmir (10th cent.A.D.) and this fixes the 8th century A.D. as the *terminus ad quem* of the original *Pāñcarātra Saṁhitās*[2].

(3) Though *Vyūhavāda* was absent from Bhāgavatism of the Gupta era, the process of amalgamation between the two sects began in that period.

As the final form of the Bh.P. took place by the Gupta Period, it is interesting to see how the Bhāgavatism in the Bh. P. and the Pāñcarātra systems were in the process of merging.

The Bh.P. has assimilated the following from the *Pāñcarātra system*:

(1) The doctrine of Emanation (Vyūha) is absorbed in the doctrine of Incarnation (*Avatāra*).

(2) The *tantric* method and procedure of the worship of

---

1. P.C. Bagchi in *History of Bengal*, Vol. I. 402-03.
2. Schrader—Op. Cit. p. 19.

the Lord is prescribed in the Bh.P.[1] The details of the procedure of such worship are given in Bh.P.XII.Ch.11. It is, however, worth noting that a votary who limits himself to idol-worship is regarded as the lowest type of votary[2].

(3) The Bh.P. adopted many stories from the *Viṣṇu P.*—a Pāñcarātra work.

They, however, differ mutually on the following points:

1. The Bhāgavata system, founded by Vāsudeva-Kṛṣṇa is unquestionably based on Vedic tradition. The Pāñcarātra system is based on non-Vedic—*āgamic*—tradition.

2. The Bhāgavata system (as seen from the *Bhagavad Gītā*) moves within the frame-work of *Varṇāśrama-dharma* but the portals of the Pāñcarātra were open even to foreigners.

3. The Bhāgavata system naturally attaches importance to the Vedic tradition as found in *dharma-sūtras*, but the *Pāñcarātrins* composed their own *Saṁhitās* (manuals).

4. The Bhāgavata *mantra* is : *Oṁ namo bhagavate Vāsudevāya* while the Pāñcarātrins adhere to their traditional *mantra* : *Oṁ namo Nārāyaṇāya.*

5. The Bh.P. gives prominence to *avatāra-vāda* (doctrine of incarnations) but the Pāñcarātrins stick to their Vyūha-vāda (doctrine of Emanations)[3].

The Fusion of Vāsudeva Kṛṣṇa, Viṣṇu and Nārāyaṇa ultimately gave a respectable status to Pāñcarātrins and today the form of worship, use of magical figures (*Yantra-śāstra*), temple-building, infusion of the Spirit in images, public festivals of the Pāñcarātrins have become as it were an integral part of Bhāgavatism due to the popular appeal of these externalities. The fusion of the two sects was practically complete before the composition of the Bh. P.

4. *The Teaching of the Bh. P.*

The present text of the Bh.P. is so full of various readings, additions, interpolations, abridgements, omissions etc. that it has

---

1. *Vidhino'pacared devaṁ tantro'ktena ca Keśavam /—Bh.* P. 11.3.47.
2. *arcāyām eva Haraye pūjāṁ yaḥ Śraddhayehate /*
   na tad-bhakteṣu cānyeṣu sa bhaktaḥ prākṛtaḥ smṛtaḥ //—Ibid. 11.2.47.
3. Schrader—*Introduction to Pāñcarātra*, pp. 35-42.

been possible for all the schools of the Vedānta to claim it as an authoritative text expounding the tennets of their particular school. Although I have incorporated in my translation and notes, the different interpretations of the philosophical verses in the Bh.P. as advocated by these Schools, the present section is based on the text followed by the oldest and the most famous commentator —Śrīdhara Svāmin (ŚR.). But even his text shows a confluence of two thought currents—(1) the Vedic, starting with *sūktas* like the cosmogonic enquiry in the *Nāsadīya Sūkta*, *Viṣṇu Sūktas* and the *Puruṣa Sūkta* and culminating in the wealth of philosophic ideas incorporated in the *Upaniṣads* and (2) the *āgamic*, consisting of the theories in the *Pāñcarātra* system, Tantrism and the intensely sublime devotional songs of *Āḷvārs*. The credit of the superb blending of these and other thought-currents in a homogeneous whole giving it 'a stamp of a unified composition'[1] goes to the last redactor—be it the Sūta Ugraśravas or somebody else.

The Bh.P. exhorts us 'to meditate upon the Supreme Truth or Reality or Supreme Lord (as ŚR. takes it) which is both immanent and transcendant. The universe originates from the Reality, is sustained therein and finally dissolves into the same Reality. But despite the continuation of the world-process, Reality is eternally established in its native grandeur, the world-process being due to the cosmic illusion'[2]. The Reality is variously designated as *Brahman*, *Paramātman* and *Bhāgavata*[3] and is non-dual consciousness[4]. This non-duality shows that the *Upaniṣadic* and *Purāṇic* reference to *pādas*[5] or grades or aspects of Reality should not be interpreted as internal differences in *Brahman*. The Supreme Truth of the Bh.P. is the transcendental state of existence (*turīya pāda*) or supratranscendental (*turīya-*

1. Winternitz—*HIL*. 1.556.

2. *Bh*. p. 1.1.1.

According to *Chāndogya Up*. (8.3.5), the term *Satya* signifies the existence of the individual Soul in *Brahman* (*Sati ayam iti*). ŚR. interprets it as 'the Supreme Person.'

3. *Bh*. P. 1.2.11.

4. *Ibid*. 1.2.11.

5. S. Bhattacarya has used the term 'grade' and based his classification on the basis of the *Tripād vibhūti-Mahānārāyaṇa Up*. I prefer the term 'aspect', as there can be no real gradation in the Absolute.

turīya) or the auspicious non-duality in the consciousness of the Supreme 'I' (*ātma-pratyaya-sāra*) of the *Upaniṣads*. It is Brahman which is "tranquil, eternal, above fear, pure consciousness, absolutely pure, of grand equipoise, transcendental, Supreme, beyond all description, not attainable by any activity, free from all afflictions, infinite bliss"[1].

In fact it is beyond delineation and may be stated as absolute existence (*sattā mātra*)[2]. At the time of his 'birth', when Kṛṣṇa manifested himself as four-armed Viṣṇu to Devakī, she, in her praise, identifies Kṛṣṇa, Viṣṇu, and *Brahman* and calls him 'the indescribable Reality, the unmanifest, Primordial cause, the Supreme *Brahman*, Pure consciousness transcending all *guṇas* and modifications, absolute existence, attributeless and devoid of activity'. This conception of the metaphysical Kṛṣṇa, identifying him as *bhagavān* or 'the third grade or aspect of Reality' is the contribution of the Bh.P. to the philosophy of religion. This aspect is 'pure bliss,' and *rāsa-krīḍā* is the purposeless sport, a child-like mirth of Kṛṣṇa, the Supreme Man, with his own shadows' or his 'own powers' in the form of cowherd women, though he was satisfied in his own blissful state[3].

The universe is the creation of the Māyā which emerged due to his consciousness of being alone, his desire to be many and to be born as many[4]. The Māyā, according to the Bh.P. includes *Prakṛti* and *Avidyā* and tries to explain the physical world and the subjective reaction of an individual to it. The evolution of *Prakṛti* into categories deserves notice. The *Bh.P.* refers to thirteen views about the number of categories such as nine, eleven, five etc., but it seems to accept twenty-five categories, twenty-four material ones (viz. *citta*, *ahaṁkāra*, *manas*,

1. *Bh. P.* 2.7.47-48.
2. *Ibid.* 10.3.24.
3. (a) *tābhir vidhūta-śokābhir bhagavān Acyuto vṛtaḥ |*
   vyarocatā'dhikaṁ tāta puruṣaḥ śaktibhir yathā || *Ibid.* 10.32.10.
   (b) *reme Rameśo Vraja-sundarībhir-|*
   yathārbhakaḥ sva-pratibimbhavibramaḥ|| *Ibid*, 10.33.17.
   (c) *reme sa bhagavān tābhir ātmārāmo'pi līlayā|* *Ibid*, 10.33.20.
4. *Ibid.* 3.2.23-25, 3.5.22.
   Cf. *Chāndogya Up*.6.1.3.
   tad aikṣata bahu syāṁ prajāyeya |

buddhi, five sense organs, five action-organs, five subtle elements and five gross elements)[1] *plus* one spiritual. But the Bh.P. looks at the categories from metaphysical point of view, reducing the cosmic evolution to two categories, viz., *puruṣa* and *Prakṛti* resolving ultimately the subject object duality into the non-dual Reality. And this non-dual Reality or consciousness has three features—pure being, pure knowledge and pure bliss.

(1) *The Absolute—the 4th aspect or grade of Reality*

The ultimate nature of the Supreme truth is immutable pure being, absolutely impersonal, actionless. As there is nothing beyond it[2], it may be called the Absolute. Being the perfect state of Self-sufficiency it is absolute, calm and free from attachment. It is the ultimate cause of the universe. Its eternal existence, during the creation, continuance and dissolution of the universe, and even after it, shows its perfection. In the Absolute, existence and bliss coalesce[3] wherein lies its intrinsic majesty.

(2) *Bhagavat—3rd aspect or grade of Reality*

Yogamāyā—The principle of plurality charged with divine majesty is the potency of the Absolute with which it plays with itself, and the universe is the Divine sport. When this divine activity assumes definiteness, the Absolute comes to be called *Bhagavat*—all bliss characterised by all powers[4]. Yogamāyā is innate with *Bhagavat*—the so-called third degree of Reality. The *Bh.P.* declares that Kṛṣṇa is Bhagavān Himself[5]. He is

1. *Pañcabhiḥ pañcabhir brahma caturbhir daśabhistathā/*
etac caturviṁśatikaṁ gaṇam prādhānikaṁ viduḥ// Bh.P. 3.26.11.

2. *vinācyutād vastu-taraṁ na vācyam/*
Sa eva sarvaṁ paramārthabhūtaḥ//— Ibid. 10.46.43.

3. *Satya-jñānā'nantānanda-matraika-rasa-mūrtayaḥ/*
aspṛṣṭa-bhūri-māhātmyā api hyupaniṣad-dṛśām// Ibid. 10.13.54.
In fact the whole description is important.

4. *tvaṁ pratyagātmani tadā bhagavatyananta*
ānanda-mātra upapanna-samasta-śaktau/ Ibid. 4.11.30.

5. *Kṛṣṇas tu bhagavān svayam/—Ibid.* 1.3.28.

the highest metaphysical reality who embodies the highest fulfilment of all spiritual aspirations, the *summum bonum* attained by observance of the supreme religion. He is the pivot of the Bhāgavata Philosophy.

The evolution and fusion of the Viṣṇu and Kṛṣṇa concepts and of their cults, is beyond the scope of this Introduction[1]. But the metaphysical Kṛṣṇa-concept is a happy blending of the Vedic and non-Vedic thought currents, the former developing out of Vedic philosophical hymns like the *Puruṣa* and *Viṣṇu sūktas* through *Brāhmaṇas* like the *Śatapatha*, and culminating in the Upaniṣadic concept of *Brahman* and *Purāṇic* concept of Mahā-Viṣṇu, and the latter, the *Āgamic* (e.g. *Pāñcarātra*) concept of Vāsudeva influenced by Tantrism and other popular beliefs. The historical Vāsudeva Kṛṣṇa presented to us is, according to the Bh.P., the eternal metaphysical *bhagavān Kṛṣṇa*—the so-called 'third degree of Reality.' The Bh.P. draws upon the Kṛṣṇa concept to preach 'a new religion—*Bhāgavata dharma*—most appropriate for the ignorant people of this dark iron age'[2]. Although all the *Skandhas* of the Bh.P. are woven in the texture of the Kṛṣṇa-concept, Skandha X characterised as *āśraya* embodies the complete personality of Kṛṣṇa, and the ultimate object of the nine characteristics (*lakṣaṇas*) of the Bh.P. is to lead to the 10th characteristic—the *āśraya*.

Rāsa-līlā

This identification of historical Vāsudeva Kṛṣṇa with the metaphysical *bhagavān* Kṛṣṇa raised a moral problem. The first critic was King Parīkṣit himself. He could not understand why Kṛṣṇa, the protector, propounder and upholder of mora-

1. A number of books and articles have been published on this topic. To mention a few: R.G. Bhandarker—*Vaiṣṇavism, Śaivism and other minor religious systems*, Strassburg 1913; A. Barth,—*Religions de l'Inde*, Paris 1914; J.E. Carpentier—*Theism in Mediaeval India*, London 1926; Bhagvan Das—*Kṛṣṇa*, Madras-Adyar 1929; H. Ray Chaudhari—*Materials for the Study of early history of the Vaishṇava sect*, Calcutta 1936; *The History and Culture of the Indian People, Vol. II* Bharatiya Vidya Bhavan, Bombay, 1953; J. Gonda—*Aspects of early Viṣṇuism*, Motilal Banarsidass, Delhi 1969, S. Bhattacarya—*The Philosophy of Śrīmad Bhāgavata, Śantiniketana*, 1960; S. Radhakrishnan—*Indian Philosophy*, Vol. I 1966 London.

2. S. Bhattacarya—*PSB* (*Philosophy of the Śrīmad Bhāgavata*). I. 73.

lity, acted otherwise by inflicting outrage on the wives of others when, as being the manifestation of *Bhagavān*, he should be self-contented[1].

In reply, Śuka made out the following points:

1. Extraordinary persons are not to be judged by the ordinary standards of morality, for they are like fire which consumes everything offered to it. One should not eat poison because Rudra drank up the *halāhala* (poison). The words of the great should be followed, not their deeds. Moreover, Kṛṣṇa being above egotism cannot be charged with having some interest in *Rāsa-līlā* either ways.
2. Metaphysically, Kṛṣṇa being the Inner Controller of all, abides in the bodies of Gopīs as well as of their husbands. Different persons are different bodies, assumed by the Lord, for the sake of Divine Sport.
3. This behaviour of Kṛṣṇa was an attractive device to induce ordinary people to spirituality[2].

According to Śrīdhara, the five chapters on the *Rāsalīlā* are intended for extinguishing carnal desires. Kṛṣṇa resorted to *Yoga-māyā* for the purpose of sport with the Gopīs[3]. He has already triumphed over the sex. As will be shown later, ŚR.'s explanation was correct.

Nimbārka presumes that Rādhā was the daughter of Vṛṣabhānu and a married wife of Kṛṣṇa and Gopīs were her attendants. There is no reference to Rādhā in the Bh. P., but Rādhā being the *raison-d'-etre* of some Vaiṣṇava sects, they have extorted Rādhā by acrobatic feats of grammar and logic,[4] from the text of the Bh. P. 10.30.28.

---

1. *Bh. P.* 10.33. 27-29.
2. *Ibid.* 10.33.30-37.
3. ŚR. on *Bh. P.* 10.29.33.
4. For example, *SD.*, on this verse, remarks :

   rādhā saha jātā asya tathā—tārakādibhya itac |

The difficulty is that the *sūtra* quoted, *tadasya sañjātaṁ tārakādibhya itac* (Pāṇini 5.2.36) is inapplicable. According to this, the derivation should have been *rādhā sañjātā asya* which is absurd. Moreover, the *ākṛti-gaṇa* mentioned here as *tārakādi* does not include *rādhā* (vide *Siddhānta Kaumudī* Venkateshvar Press Bombay, 1909, pp. 352, 767). The analogy of *tārakita, puṣpita, phalita* is not applicable to *rādhita*.

anayā'rādhito nūnaṁ bhagavān harir īśvaraḥ |
yanno vihāya Govindaḥ prīto yām anayad rahaḥ ||

Moreover, the social impropriety of playing *rāsa* with the maid-servants of one's wife is not exonerated by making the non-existent Rādhā, Kṛṣṇa's married wife.

The Śuddhādvaita School of Vallabha regards *rāsa* as the association with the metaphysical eternal Kṛṣṇa and not with the historical Vāsudeva Kṛṣṇa. Kṛṣṇa episodes at Vṛndāvana are symbolic. Thus, when the divine form of the Lord manifests himself in the mind of the devotee, it is the birth of Lord Kṛṣṇa. About the sports at Vṛndāvana it is explained:—With the annihilation of sins and God's grace the devotee, through various forms of devotion, develops in him *bīja-bhāva* (a spiritual disposition) due to the intensity of which the *guṇa*-reals are destroyed. By spiritual service (*sevā*), the *bīja-bhāva* becomes a *vyasana* (passion), and leads to the attainment of *Brahmabhāva* (becoming one with Brahman). Then Puruṣottama or Lord Nārāyaṇa manifests himself. The gross and subtle bodies of the devotees are destroyed and the devotee is endowed with a body suitable for *rāsa* or the Divine Sport. Then the devotee enters the region of *rāsa-līlā* that goes on eternally. This is *Mokṣa*. (Bālakṛṣṇa Bhaṭṭa—*Prameya Ratnākara* 39-44). This explanation is based on the text of the Bh. P. It will thus be found that the allegations of sexuality, social impropriety are beside the point with reference to his spiritual *rāsa-līlā*.

The Bengal School of Vaiṣṇavism has shown great ingenuity in regularising the relations between Kṛṣṇa and Gopīs. Briefly, the position taken by Jīva Gosvāmī is that Gopīs were Kṛṣṇa's legal wives—*Kṛṣṇa-vadhvaḥ* as the Bh. P. puts it, though Jīva adduces other authorities like the *Gopāla Tāpanī Upa*. But in the Bh. P. elsewhere (e.g. Bh. P. 10.29.20) Kṛṣṇa refers to their husbands (*patayaś ca vaḥ*). Viśvanātha Cakravartī states that Gopīs had two kinds of husbands, the Gopas, their human husbands, and Kṛṣṇa, their spiritual husband—a meeting with the spiritual husband transcends conventional moral standards[1]. S. Bhattacarya rightly criticizes:

1. Vide comms. of JG. and VC. on the *rāsa-pañcādhyāyī* (*Bh. P.* 10.29 to 33) and on Rūpa Gosvāmī's *Ujjvala-nīla-maṇi*. Also S. Bhattacarya —*PSB*. I. 103-108.

"The concept of Kṛṣṇa being their spiritual husband does not give him the license to exhibit amorous behaviour which stinks at the nose of ordinary beings."[1]

Rāsa-līlā—Significance

This brings us directly to the thorny yet much-discussed problem of Kṛṣṇa's behaviour during his *Rāsa-krīḍā*. The author of the Bh. P. clearly gives us to understand that it is the *bhagavān*, the metaphysical Kṛṣṇa, the "third degree of Reality" and not the historical Kṛṣṇa who participated in the Rāsa-līlā. The *rāsa-pañcādhyāyī* opens with the following verse. :

bhagavān api tā rātrīḥ śāradotphulla-mallikāḥ |
vīkṣya rantum manaścakre yogamāyām upāśritaḥ ||
—Bh. P. 10.29.1.

"Seeing that those nights were most delightful with full-blown jasmines of *Śarad* (Autumnal season), *Bhagavān* as he was, he decided to play (with the cowherd women) with the help of Yoga-māyā."

The author places before us the following points:

(i) It was the (third degree of) Reality—the metaphysical Kṛṣṇa (and not the historical Kṛṣṇa) who participated in the Rāsa-līlā.

(ii) Yogamāyā—the divine power of the Lord—was brought into play in this *rāsa*. Otherwise multiplication of the historical Kṛṣṇa each per Gopi would have been impossible.

(iii) The word *api* (even though) shows that though the Lord is Self-sufficient, self-complacent and self-satisfied (*ātmā-rāma*) he participated in the *rāsa* just to fulfill his promise at the time of *Kātyāyanī vrata*.

(iv) Yoga-māyā is the Principle of the divine sport. The whole affair is spiritual and the canons of morality of ordinary mortals are inapplicable in the spiritual world.

(v) ŚR. explains that *rāsa* is simply 'an ardent intensity or ovation' e.g. in Bh. P. 3.7.19.

rati-rāso bhavet tīvro pādayor vyasanārdanaḥ |

'The ovation of devotion to the feet of Kṛṣṇa becomes intense.'

---

1. S. Bhattacarya—*PSB*. p. 108.

(vi) The word *rantum* means simply 'playing'. It does not connote sexuality. S. Bhattacarya has pointed out parallelisms about the use of the verb √*ram*—'to play'—in Kṛṣṇa's play with boys also[1].

(vii) The historical as well as metaphysical Kṛṣṇas is depicted as being noted for self-control in sexual matters, be it with his wives, cowherd-women or others. In the *rāsa-pañcādhyāyī*, he is called the 'veritable annihilator of the god of love' (*sākṣān manmatha-manmathaḥ*[2]). He was self-satisfied in his own blissful nature, but he participated in the *rāsa* to please the Gopīs. (*ātmārāmo' pyarīramat*[3]/). He was not enamoured of Gopīs. When they felt they had secured him, he disappeared from the rāsa (Bh. P. 10.29.28). The Bh. P. certifies that Kṛṣṇa maintained control over himself in the company of *Gopīs* even though he mixed with them.[4] Even before *rāsa*, at the time of *Kātyāyanī vrata*, he passed the most crucial test of remaining above temptation in the presence of naked women[5]. Even his 16000 wives could not tempt him with all their dalliances[6]. Moreover the tender physical age of historical Kṛṣṇa at the time of *rāsa* is a factor against sexual

---

1. e.g. The use of *ram*—'to play,' in the context of boy friends :

(1) *tan mañju-ghoṣāli-mṛga-dvijākulam*
mahan-manaḥ-prakhya-payaḥ sarasvatā /
vātena juṣṭaṁ śata-patra-gandhinā
nirīkṣya rantum bhagavān mano dadhe //—Bh. P. 10.15.3.

The last line is comparable to the last line of *Bh. P.* 10.29.1.

vīkṣya rantum manaścakre /

(2) *reme ramā-lālita-pāda-pallavo*
grāmyaiḥ samaṁ grāmyavad īśa-ceṣṭitaḥ //—Bh. P. 10.15.19.

The Lord played with the rural boys like an ordinary man from the country.

reme rameśo vraja-sundarībhiḥ /
yathā'rbhakaḥ sva-prati-bimba-vibhramaḥ //—Ibid. 10.33.16.

The Lord played with the beauties of Vraja like a child playing with his reflection or shadow.

2. *Bh. P.* 10.32.2.
3. *Ibid.* 10.29.42.
4. *sa satyakāmo'nuratā' balā-gaṇaḥ /*
siṣeva ātmanyavaruddha-saurataḥ—Bh.P. 10.33.26.
5. Is it the influence of Tantrism on the Bh. P. here ?
6. *patnyas tu ṣoḍaśa-sahasram anaṅga-bāṇair /*
yasyendriyaṁ vimathituṁ karaṇair na śekuḥ//—Bh. P. 10.61.4.

allegations. The Jaina canon which gives so many details about Vāsudeva Kṛṣṇa does not mention *l'affaire* Rādhā or *rāsa-līlā*.

All this evidence shows that the author of the Bh. P. intended to depict a symbolic event about the metaphysical Kṛṣṇa—and not the involvement of the historical Kṛṣṇa (despite his self-control). The Bh. P. wishes to emphasize that the attachment of Gopīs may be physical but any strong feeling—say sexual love, hatred or affection—directed towards the Lord, leads to Mokṣa[1].

(3) *Paramātman* (*Viṣṇu*)

The concept Viṣṇu is evolved out of the Vedic concepts of the Cosmic Man and the Solar deity. He represents all-pervasive Reality, the original Person (*ādi-puruṣa*), the vital principle of life (*Paramātman*) animating physical body. By the time of the *Viṣṇu-Purāṇa*, Viṣṇu became a four-handed god combining majesty, martial character and grace. Historical Kṛṣṇa is originally regarded as a part of Viṣṇu (*Viṣṇu P.* 5.1.60), but gradually they fused together, and Kṛṣṇa emerged as Vāsudeva-Viṣṇu giving rise to the doctrine of the four Vyūhas—Saṅkarṣaṇa, Pradyumna and Aniruddha, all close relatives of historical Kṛṣṇa. This evolution shows a blending of Vedic and Tantric ideas enriching the imageries[2]. The Viṣṇu image to be meditated upon by sages is described in details in the Bh. P. 3.28.21-33. The mass of imageries about his physical features (*aṅga*), weapons (*āyudhas*), ornaments (*ākalpa*) and accessories (*upāṅgas*) shows the fusion of the Vedic and *āgamic* concepts was complete before the compo-

---

1. *Bh. P.* 7.1.28-29.

2. The *Bh.P.* 11.5. 20-30 traces the evolution of the Viṣṇu-concept and its fusion with that of Vāsudeva-Kṛṣṇa. The confluence of Vedic and Tantric forms of worship and the amalgamation of *Pāñcarātra* system with Vedic Viṣṇu is mentioned as follows :

taṁ tadā puruṣam martyā mahārājopalakṣaṇam |
yajanti veda-tantrābhyaṁ paraṁ jijñāsavo nṛpa ||
namaste vāsudevāya, namaḥ saṅkarṣaṇāya ca |
pradyumnāyā'niruddhāya tubhyaṁ bhagavate namaḥ ||
nārāyaṇāya ṛṣaye puruṣāya mahātmane |
viśveśvarāya viśvāya sarva-bhūtātmane namaḥ || *Bh. P.* 11.5. 28-30.

sition of the Bh.P. But the Bh.P. carefully explains these symbols of Viṣṇu in the light of its own conception of the structure of the Reality. Thus the Kaustubha jewel is his self-luminosity (*ātma-jyotis*)—the state of non-dual consciousness. *Vana-mālā* is his *ātma-māyā*. The ear-rings are the *Sāṁkhya* and the *Yoga* systems. The mystic significance of his weapons, and gestures (*mudrās*), and his paraphernalia (including attendants) are similarly explained, Viṣvaksena etc. being the presentation of the *Tantras* (Bh. P. 12.11.10-20).

(4) *4th aspect : Brahman—the First grade of Reality.*

The *Brahman* is the basis of the world process—emergence, continuance and dissolution. It has no beginning, middle and the end, no internality or externality[1]. It transcends the manifested and unmanifested forms. Though limitless and non-dual, immutable and eternal (First), it possesses diverse and heterogenous powers[2]. At the beginning of the cosmic process, Brahman, the source of plurality manifests itself as time, nature, destiny and other factors necessary for the cosmic process. It is then the abode of all mobiles and immobiles. When it withdraws the universe, it remains as the only residium capable of the whole game of creation and dissolution of the universe. This dynamism in Brahman to bring about the creation, destruction of the universe is called *Ātma-Māyā*.[3]

This *Ātma-Māyā* which is a principle of heterogeneity, is the expression of *Viṣṇu-Māyā* (the Divine Will). Impelled by the will of Divine Sport, it differentiates between two mutually contra-co-operative powers, viz., Māyā (Principle of materiality) and *cit-śakti* (Principle of divinity). Characterised by these contradictory yet co-operative potencies, Brahman, the sub-stratum of *Ātma-Māyā* becomes immanent in creation.

---

1. *na yasyādyantau madhyañ ca svaḥ paro nā'ntaraṁ bahiḥ /*
viśvasyāmūni yad yasmād viśvañ ca tad ṛtam mahat // Bh. P. 8.1.12.

2. *yasmin viruddhagatayo hyaniśam patanti*
vidyādayo vividha-śaktaya ānupūrvyāt /
tad brahma viśva-bhavam ekam anantam ādyam
ānanda-mātram avikāram aham prapadye / Ibid. 4.9.16.

3. *yathātma-māyā-yogena nānā-śaktyupabṛṁhitam /*
vilumpan visṛjan gṛhṇan bibhrad ātmānam ātmanā //
krīḍasyamogha-saṅkalpa ūrṇa-nābhir yathorṇute/ etc., *Bh. P.* 2.9.26-72

Brahman or God residing in creation, (*Pura*) is called *Puruṣa*. According to the Bh. P. 'neither god nor creation pre-existed the other, but both came simultaneously into existence'.[1]

(5) *The Grace Divine* (*Anugraha*)

This brings us to the concept of the Divine grace. According to the Bh. P., Bhagavān Kṛṣṇa was perfect bliss in which all powers consummated. This was the culmination of the Viṣṇu concept of the Vedas. The creation and dissolution of the universe is due to the Divine Will. So it is due to the Divine grace that man becomes attracted to the Lord and his faith in penance deepens;[2] his passion (*rati*) for the Lord intensifies and his devotion (*bhakti*) is selfless; Revelations both internal and external are an index of the divine grace. God is self-satisfied but his worship reflects back upon the worshipper[3] and enhances his inner qualities and makes him eligible to receive the divine grace.

Bhagavān is all bliss, i.e. all love. Divine grace is the radiation of the love of the Bhagavān on man. When our mental outlook is crystalized that Bhagavān is in all and expresses its universal friendliness (*maitrī*), the divine grace flows to him and beings bow to him automatically like water to the lower level[4]. The grace may assume a frowning appearance but the devotee knows that it is His real grace and prays for it[5].

(6) *Avatāra-Vāda* (*The Doctrine of Divine Incarnation*)

According to the Bh. P., the whole world-order is a divine *līlā*. (sport)—'the free unmotivated self-expression in a spatio-temporal order of his Supra-Spatial, Supra-temporal perfect self-enjoyment'[6] This *līlā-vāda* is closely associated with the

1. S. Bhattacarya—*PSB*. I. 213.
2. *Bh. P.* 3.9.38.
3. *Ibid.* 7.9.11.
4. *Ibid.* 4.9.47.
5. *Ibid.* 1.8.25.

The wives of the serpent Kaliya echo this sentiment—vide *Bh. P.* 10.16.34.

6. *History of Philosophy—Eastern and Western* I. 125.

avatāra-vāda[1]. In an *avatāra* (descent, incarnation) the Supreme Spirit, by virtue of its unique *Māyā*-potency, sportively descends from the plane of the absolute unity to the plane of the relative plurality, from the plane of infinity and eternity to the spatio-temporal plane, from the plane of non-dual changeless existence-consciousness-bliss to the plane of the diversities of changing conscious and unconscious imperfect existences, without losing its essential transcendental character. In his Com. on Bh. P. 11.4.2, ŚR suggests that the idea of *avatāra* has Vedic basis, and quotes ṚV. 1.154.1[2]. One of the main objects of the Bh. P. was to extol fully the deeds of various *avatāras*.[3] Although God and His incarnations are consubstantial, the Bh. P. classifies the incarnations as (1) *aṁśa*, (2) *kalā* and (3) *aṁśa-kalā*.

(i) *aṁśāvatāra* is a form of God possessing God's omniscience and omni-potence which may or may not be revealed, depending on the exigencies of the situation, e.g. Yajña, Vāmana.

(ii) *kalāvatāras* are God-filled empirical Souls, e.g. Gods[4] and Vyāsa, Datta, Kumāra among human beings.

(iii) *aṁśa-kalāvatāra* : Border cases between (i) and (ii) e.g. Ṛṣabha in Skandha V. This is an artificial category.

Avatāras are classified according to the *guṇa* which they dominantly represent e.g. Brahmā (*rajo-guṇa*), Viṣṇu (*sattva-guṇa*) Rudra, (*tamo-guṇa*), their main function is the creation, sustenance and destruction of the universe (Bh. P. 3.7.28).

From a temporal point of view, God assumes *Manvantarāvatāra* to superintendent the working of gods, men etc. in different *Manvantaras*, and also *Yugāvatāras* corresponding to different *Yuga*-epochs and *Kalpāvatāra* for each Kalpa. But according to the Bh. P., *Līlāvatāra* is the best[5], for in this

1. *Bh.P.* 1.1.18

2. In fact *Bh. P.* 2.7.40-41 and 11.4.2 use the same wording as in *ṚV.* 1. 154.1.

But it is worth noting that with the exception of Vāmana, the other descents, e.g. the fish, the tortoise, the boar are attributed to Prajāpati in *Śatapatha* and other *Brāhmaṇas*. For details vide *History and Culture of the Indian People*, Vol. III, 419-423.

3. *Bh. P.* 12.12.45.

4. *Ibid.* 4.14.22.

5. *Bh. P.* 2.6.45.

avatāra the Lord assumes any form—of man, animal, fish etc. —only to abide by the desire of the devotee[1]. In this he behaves like an ordinary man (e.g. Rāma's lamentation after Sītā's abduction) but restores the moral order, showers grace unto his devotees and departs leaving behind supreme glory.

(7) *Vyūha Vāda* (*The Doctrine of Emanations*)

As seen above, the Bhāgavata and the Pañcarātra sects were originally different and were treated as such till the time of Bāṇa (7th Cent. A.D.), and followers of the latter were roundly condemned as outcasts by *smṛtis*, *Purāṇas* and great *Smṛti*-annotators like Medhātithi. It is also held that Bhāgavatism in the Gupta period was different from the present Bhāgavatism which has assimilated the *Vyūha* doctrine, the *Tantric* method of worship, and other external rites from the *Pāñcarātra* system. But the Bh. P. shows that it could not properly digest even the *Vyūha Vāda* of the *Pāñcarātrins*. Bh. P. regards *vyūha* (emanation) as 'image of god' (*mūrti*)[2] which is thus similar to the concept of *aṁśāvatāra* and as a *Vyūhāvatāra* He protects the world in every *Kalpa*[3]. This doctrine is closely associated with the Kṛṣṇa cult as Kṛṣṇa Vāsudeva himself and his closest relatives, brother Balarāma alias Saṅkarṣaṇa, son Pradyumna and grandson Aniruddha, are the four *vyūhas* acknowledged as such by the Bh. P.[4] and the Pañcarātra sect.

The Bh. P. attempts to connect these *vyūhas* with the four modes of the *antaḥkaraṇa* of man (a Vedāntic concept) and the states of the empirical ego as follows :

Name of the Vyūha	*Mode of antaḥkaraṇa*	*State of the empirical ego* (*Witness of*:)
a. Vāsudeva	—*Citta* (or *buddhi*)— (ŚR. reserves *Citta* for Vāsudeva only).	Transcendental state.

---

1. *Ibid.* 10.59.25.
2. *aṅgopāṅgā'yudhā'kalpair bhagavāṁs tac catuṣṭayam /*
bibharti sma catur-mūrtir bhagavān harir īśvaraḥ // *Bh. P.* 12.11.23.
3. *evaṁ hyanādi-nidhano bhagavān harir īśvaraḥ /*
kalpe kalpe svam ātmānaṁ vyūhya lokān avatyajaḥ // *Ibid.* 12.11.50.
4. *vāsudevaḥ saṅkarṣaṇaḥ pradyumnaḥ puruṣaḥ svayam /*
aniruddha iti brahman, mūrti-vyūho'bhidhīyate // *Ibid.* 12.11.21.

b. Saṅkarṣaṇa	—*ahaṁkāra*	—	dreamless sleep
c. Pradyumna	—Nil in Bh. P., but ŚR. assigned *buddhi* (vide ŚR. on 3.26.21.)		Dream
d. Aniruddha	—*manas*	—	Waking state

This obviously conflicts with the Sāṅkhya theory of evolution, and the *lacuna* about Pradyumna is amended by ŚR. at a later date. The attempt of the Bh. P. to connect each *vyūha* with the particular category of creation proved inadequate, though it could do so in the case of the four states of empirical ego. One suspects the *Vyūha* concept to be a later grafting on the Kṛṣṇa cult. But once it was accepted, the *tāntrikas* described in rich details his limbs (*aṅgas*), accessories, e.g. vehicle, attendants (*upāṅga*), weapons (*āyudha*) and articles of dress and ornaments (ākalpa)[1]. The detailed descriptions of Vāsudeva, Saṅkarṣaṇa, Pradyumna and Aniruddha are really picturesque. Bh. P., however, carefully explains the metaphysical symbolism of each e.g. the Kaustubha gem represents (pure) consciousness of the Jīva, Vanamālā (garland of sylvan flowers), his Māyā, his sacred thread, the mystical syllable OM (A+U+M), ear-rings, the Sāṅkhya and Yoga systems[2]. As S. Bhattacarya notes, 'In fact the *doctrine of four* seems to have developed itself in different directions, giving rise to the *four* aspects of the great Personality, his *four* manifestations, the *fourfold* witnessing of the *four* states of empirical self and what not[3].

Later, the number of these *vyūhas* increased to nine and later to twelve manifestations but the doctrine of four Vyūhas has permanently influenced our religious imagination.

(8) *Path-ways to God-realization*

The Bh. P. does not merely advise us 'to meditate on the Supreme Reality' but delineates the different paths leading to the realization of that Reality, emphasizing at the same time its preference for the path of devotion. In explaining the

1. *Bh. P.* 12.11.2.
2. Vide *Bh. P.* 12.11. 10-20.
3. *PSB.* I. 199.

three paths, the Bh. P. has synthesized the best of the Vedic tradition with the teaching of Kṛṣṇa-Vāsudeva. Some Vaiṣṇava authors regard the Bh. P. as 'a commentary' on the *Bhagavad-Gītā*. Though there is a great deal of similarity in the teachings of Vāsudeva-Kṛṣṇa to Arjuna and to Uddhava as recorded in these two works, both are independent, even though the Bh. P. is chronologically later. The Bh. P. clearly states that a person should continue to perform the duties prescribed in the Vedas till he develops a feeling of dissociation or a liking for or faith in listening to the deeds of the Lord[1]. At the outset the Bh. P. declares its Vedic tradition by claiming to be 'the ripe fruit of the wish-yielding tree called the *Veda*'[2] and that 'a self-less and uninterrupted devotion to the Lord is the sublime religion[3]. He further defines religion as that which conduces to the devotion of the Lord.[4] Devotion is a spiritual discipline which immediately generates renunciation and motiveless spiritual knowledge[5]. And these arise simultaneously just as after the intake of a morsel of food satisfaction, nourishment and quenching of hunger take place simultaneously[6]. Commenting on this verse ŚR. points out that this triad of effects of the first morsel leads to a higher degree of satisfaction with the next morsel forming as it were a chain of causation. This is the significance of the statement of the Bh. P. that *bhakti* (devotion) leads to (higher plane of) devotion[7]. According to the Bh. P. the three *puruṣārthas* (objectives in human life), the ritualistic and spiritual teaching of the Vedas and their ancillaries like logic, all converge upon the need of self-dedication to the Supreme Person[8] and this 'self' in self-dedication includes whatever one does and regards as his own such as wife, children and one's own body[9]. This dedication purifies all our acts[10].

1. *Bh.P.* 11.20.9.
2. *Ibid.* 1.1.2.
3. *Ibid.* 1.2.6.
4. *Ibid.* 11.19.27.
5. *Ibid.* 1.2.7.
6. *Ibid.* 11.2.42.
7. *Ibid.* 11.3.31.
8. *Ibid.* 7.6.26.
9. *Ibid.* 11.3.28.
10. *Ibid.* 11.21.15.

Different people are attracted to God with variegated motives. They may concentrate their mind on him through sexual urge, hatred, fear, affection or kinship as well as through devotion or friendship but they ultimately become one with him[1], only that they should incessantly do so.[2] The cowherd-women attained God through sexual urge, Śiśupāla (Kṛṣṇa's cousin) through dire hatred, Kaṁsa through fear, Yudhiṣṭhira (the eldest Pāṇḍava) through friendship or affection, Vṛṣṇis through bloodrelationship, persons like Nārada through devotion[3]. But the highest type of devotion is the self-less meditation marked by the dominance of pure *Sattva* and it leads to the experience of divine ecstasy. Other types of devotion influenced by *rajas*, *tamas* or *sattva* mixed with other mental modes, are inferior types of devotion. Although the Bh. P. like the *Bhagavad Gītā* classifies devotion in three types according to the dominance of a particular *guṇa* like *sattva*, *rajas* and *tamas* (Bh. P. 3.29.7-10), ŚR. in his commentary on the above derives eightyone types of devotion. Madhusūdana Sarasvatī, Jīva Gosvāmi and Bopadeva have classified devotion in their own ways, but that discussion is beyond the scope of this Introduction.

(9) *The Path of devotion—Classification*

The Bh. P. has delineated in details the ninefold path of devotion. It consists of (1) *Śravana* (Listening), (2) *Kīrtana* (Chanting), (3) *Smaraṇa* (Remembrance, meditation), (4) *Pāda-sevana* (Serving the feet of the Lord), (5) *Arcana* (Worship), (6) *Vandana* (Prostration before God), (7) *Dāsya* (Service), (8) *Sakhya* (Friendship), (9) *Ātma-nivedana* (Self-dedication). This is treated as a continuous series in which one form merges into the next culminating in union with God, but as Jīva Gosvāmī asserts, even one form of devotion is efficacious enough to attain to Godhood[4]. A glance at the list

1. *Bh. P.* 7.1.29.
2. *Ibid.* 10.29.15.
3. *Ibid.* 7.1.30.

Bh. P. gives a positive verdict in favour of antagonistic type of devotion as being more efficacious than the devotion of softer feelings : *Ibid.* 7.1.26

4. Jīva Gosvāmī quotes in Saṭ Sandarbha (p. 545) what form of devotion led what devotee to the *summum bonum*—oneness with God—

of these forms shows its eclectic character. Most of them are found in the *Ṛgveda*[1], but the trinity beginning with *Pāda-sevana*[2] is the *Pāñcarātra* contribution, as they pertain to idol-worship. And the last three forms comprise the progressive journey of the spirit of submissiveness to God to the indissoluble tie of unity between the votary and his object of reverence[3], and as such are both means as well as ends[4],—*svayam phalarūpatā* as Nārada puts it.

With faith (*Śraddhā*) in the Lord, one should receive the Lord in his mind by listening to the name of the Lord and his sportive exploits. This annihilates all sins where traditional methods of expiation such as Vedic studies, donations etc. fail (*Bh. P.* 11.6.9). This *Śravaṇa* leads to *Kīrtana*, i.e. chanting of the Lord's name, forms and exploits. In this *Kali* age, *Kīrtana* leads to the highest stage (*Bh. P.* 11.5.36, 12.3.51). It yields the same spiritual fruit as was obtained by meditation in the *Kṛta* age, performance of sacrifices in the *Tretā* age and worship of the Lord in the Dvāpara age (*Bh. P.* 12.3.52). *Kīrtana* is the river of nectar of God's episodes which satiates the spiritual thirst of the listeners who thereby transcend human torments and passions[5].

The *Kīrtana*-form of devotion reaches deep into the heart which is then drowned in meditation. This is Remembrance (*Smaraṇa*) which is really God's presence in the depth of our hearts. It thoroughly washes out all inner impurities due to our past deeds, more effectively than could be achieved by any other means[6].

---

(1) *Śrī-Viṣṇoḥ Śravaṇe Parīkṣid abhavad*
(2) *Vaiyāsakiḥ kīrtane* / (3) *Prahlādaḥ smaraṇe,*
(4) *tadaṅghri-bhajane Lakṣmīḥ,* (5) *Pṛthu pūjane* /
(6) *Akrūras tvabhivandane,* (7) *Kapi-patir dāsye'tha*
(8) *sakhye'* (*A*) *rjunaḥ* /
(9) *sarvasvātma-nivedane Balir abhūt Kṛṣṇā'ptir eṣāṁ param* //

1. H.D. Velankara—*Bhakti in the Ṛgveda* (Marathi—Kauśik Lectures) Poona.
2. S. Bhattacarya traces this to the Puruṣa-sūkta in the *Ṛgveda*—*PSB.* II. 127-28.
3. *Ibid*, II. 176.
4. *Bhakti Sūtra*, 30.
5. *Bh. P.* 4.29.40, 10.83.3.
6. *vidyā-tapaḥ-prāṇa- nirodha-maitrī-tīrthābhiṣeka-vratadāna-japyaiḥ / nā'tyanta-śuddhiṁ labhate'ntarātmā yathā hṛdisthe bhagavatyanante* //—*Ibid.* 12.3.48.

Through continued remembrance, the devotee is led to the primary stage of God-realization and he clings to the feet of the Lord. Once the devotee tastes the honey in the lotus in the form of the Lord's feet, he never finds pleasure in worldly objects[1]. At the touch of this divine grace new spiritual horizons are widened and he feels real fervour of devotion, nonattachment to worldly affairs and attains genuine serenity and peace of mind[2].

The Bh. P. has given three types of worship—the Vedic, the Tāntric and mixed; the Bh. P. favours the last. The external type of worship is described in details in Bh. P. 11.3. 48-54, 11.27. 19-49 etc. but it prefers the internal type of worship as follows :

"In his own body cleansed by Vāyu and Agni, he (the votary) should contemplate the subtle Paramātman as the summit of *Nāda* i.e. the Supreme being in the lotus of his heart. Having worshipped the Lord in his body, his body is filled with the presence of the Supreme Soul."[3]

Vandana is unqualified submission to him in recognition of his supremacy; its external expression being physical prostration before the image of the Lord.

Dāsya is the sense of belongingness to God. It is the result of the unqualified submission mentioned above—an achievement as well as the means to higher forms of devotion.

Sakhya is a still higher achievement. The sense of servitude to God leads the devotee to win over God as his friend as good wives do in the case of good husbands[4].

Ātmanivedana is the last stage. Out of the highest love and devotion, the devotee surrenders totally to God. As the Bh.P. puts it, "When he dedicates to Me all his works and activities, I choose to make him the best of men; then he attains immortality and becomes fit to be one with Me"[5].

---

1. *kṛṣṇāṅghri-padma-madhu-liḍ na punar visṛṣṭa-māyā-guṇeṣu ramate vṛjināvaheṣu* //—*Bh. P.* 6.3.33.
2. *Ibid.* 10.14.29 and 11.2.43.
3. *Ibid.* 11.27.23-24.
4. *mayi nirbaddha-hṛdayāḥ sādhavaḥ sama-darśanāḥ vaśī-kurvanti māṁ bhaktyā sat-striyaḥ sat-patiṁ yathā. Ibid.* 9.4.66.
5. *Ibid.* 11.29.34.

This is the outline of the hierarchy of the forms of devotion. The Bh.P. emphasizes the special efficacy of God's name. Like fire consuming the fuel, God's name shows its efficacy irrespective of the person taking it. Even if it is uttered to call a member of one's family or in joke or unknowingly the name of Viṣṇu annihilates all sins, whether it is taken in a conscious or semi-conscious stage[1]. The story of Ajāmila is given as an illustration. The story underscores the original good behaviour of Ajāmila, his fall and at the time of his death when his fund of previous deeds (*prārabdha karma*) of this span of life was exhausted, he uttered the name of God and was helped by the angels of Viṣṇu. God's name is not a license for misbehaviour.

(10) *Other Paths*

The Bh. P. many times uses the term *bhakti-yoga*. It is true that the Bh. P. has approved of and adopted the technique i.e. the eightfold path of *Yoga*, but not its philosophy. The *nirbīja samādhi* in the Bh. P. is on a higher plane than the *samprajñāta* and *asamprajñāta samādhi* in *Pātañjala Yoga*. In breath control (*prāṇāyāma*) the Bh. P. prefers *sa-bīja prāṇāyāma* to the *nirbīja*[2] fixing one's gaze at the tip of one's nose. According to Patañjali, the *yamas* and *niyamas* are five each, but the Bh. P. elaborates them in twelve each. The connotations of some terms are different. Thus *aparigraha* is 'acceptance of just what is needed' (Bh. P. 3.28.4), *Śauca* is 'disinterestedness in action.'[3] As to the place of *Jñāna-yoga* vis-a-vis *Bhaktiyoga*, 'the *Jñāna-yoga* of the *Bhāgavata* forges a remarkable compromise between Patañjali and *Upaniṣads* on the one hand and Tantric thoughts on the other. With due representation of willing, knowing and feelings within its structure, the *Jñānayoga* of the *Bhāgavata* takes its rightful place beside the *bhāgavata dharma* or *bhaktiyoga*[4].

1. *Bh. P.* 6.2.14-19.
2. *mano yacchej jita-śvāso brahma-bījam avismaran* / *Bh. P.* 2.1.17.
3. *Ibid.* 11.19.38. *Karmasvasaṅgamaḥ Śaucam* /
4. *PSB*. II. 106.

(11) *Bhāgavata Dharma*

This *Bhāgavata Dharma* comprises of those moral qualities and spiritual practices which purify the mind for receiving the divine grace. The Bh. P. includes under these the ten Yoga virtues of *Yama* and *Niyama*, the 'decorations' of the mind such as universal friendliness (*maitrī*), kindness (*karuṇā*), joyfulness (*muditā*), and indifference (*upekṣā*), the six Vedāntic virtues of serenity (*śama*), self-control (*dama*), tolerance (*titikṣā*), renunciation (*uparati*), concentration and faith, the nine-fold path of devotion and Tantric methods of spiritual worship. They are thirty in all[1], but the singular *bhāgavata dharma* is chanting of the name of Hari[2].

The best follower of the *Bhāgavata dharma* is called *Bhāgavatottama*. 'Tranquil and possessed of unitary vision' he launches crusade against the sorrows of the world'[3]. Said Prahlāda, 'I would not seek Liberation (*Mokṣa*) till a single being remains in bondage'[4]. Such a devotee lives in God and God lives in him[5].

Thus the Bh. P. has blended the *Upaniṣadic* path of knowledge with Yoga technique of Patañjali and the Tantric method of worship and opening of the mystic plexuses (*kamalas*) located in the body, along with the nine-fold path of devotion. The result is the unique doctrine of Divine Love or *Bhāgavata dharma*.

The brief survey of the teaching of the Bh. P. shows how the best elements in Vedic and non-Vedic traditions were blended in a religion that was meant for the masses—Indian and foreign, open to all men and women irrespective of class or community. Full of divine Love and Grace, God waits—nay, invites all with the enchanting music of his divine flute. He expects nothing in return. As Bh. P. expresses in the concluding verse:[6] 'Surrender yourself completely to him. Remember his name. The Supreme Lord annihilates your sins and removes all your suffering; To that Supreme Hari I bow'.

---

1. *PSB*. I. 170.
2. *Bh. P.* 12.3.52.
3. *PSB*. I. 210.
4. *naitān vihāya kṛpaṇān vimumukṣa ekaḥ* /—*Bh. P.* 7.9.44.
5. *Ibid*. 9.4.68.
6. *Ibid*. 12.13.23.

COMMENTATORS ON THE BHĀGAVATA PURĀṆA[1]

(A BRIEF NOTE)

Due to the enormous popularity[2] and extraordinary reputation of the Bh. P. as being the most famous epic in India, eminent commentators belonging to different schools of the Vedānta have tried to show that the Bh. P. supports their particular school of thought. Of these the oldest and the most respectable annotator is Śrīdhara Svāmin (ŚR), the author of the Com., *Bhāvārtha-dīpikā*, who follows the *Advaita* school of Śaṅkara. He assures that, in his Com., he has given the traditional interpretation[3] implying Citsukha's (1220-84 A.D.) Com. on the Bh.P. It is an authoritative commentary, lucid and to the point. They say that next to Vyāsa (the author of the Bh.P.), and Śuka (its exponent to King Parīkṣit), it is ŚR who understood the real import of the Bh.P. in its entirety.[4] Nābhā-dāsa-ji's record of the legend[5] that Lord Bindu-mādhava of Kāśī approved ŚR's Com. as the authoritative interpretation of the Bh. P., is another evidence of ŚR.'s prestige and popularity. ŚR has received complimentary tributes from commentators of other schools of the Vedānta who bodily incorporate his Com. into their own, and some openly admit his authority by urging that their annotations are just to elucidate and supplement ŚR[6]. It may be due to the deep reverence expressed by

---

1. The present translator has utilised the Commentaries published in the Bhāgavata Vidya Peeth Ahmedabad's edition and in the Vrindavana edition of the X Skandha.

2. M. N. Chatterji in the Intro. to the I Vol. of his translation of the the Bh. P. (Calcutta 1895) records 136 commentaries and treatises on the Bh. P. To this a score more new publications can be listed during the last 80 years.

3. *Sampradāyānurodhena paurvāparyānusārataḥ |*
Śrī-Bhāgavata-Bhāvārtha-dīpike'yam Pratanyate || —ŚR Intro. v. 4.

4. *Vyāso vetti, Śuko vetti, Rājā vetti na vetti vā |*
Śrīdharaḥ sakalaṁ vetti, Śrī-Nṛsiṁha-prasādataḥ ||

5. *Bhakta māla—chappaya* 440

6. *Svāmi-pādair na yad vyaktaṁ, yad vyaktaṁ cā'sphuṭam Kvacit |*
tatra tatra ca vijñeyaḥ Sandarbha-Krama-nāmakaḥ || JG. Intro v

Caitanya to ŚR that his followers like JG and VC presented a sort of *apologia* for their commentaries mentioned, above, even though ŚR. finds no Rādhā in the Bh.P. Due to ŚR's reference to Bopadeva (13th cent.) and references of other writers like Viṣṇupurī to him, he is assigned to the middle of the 14th cent. A.D.[1] Rādhā Ramaṇa Gosvāmī (RR) wrote his *Dīpanī* to elucidate ŚR, though he tilts to Gauḍīya Vaiṣṇavism. Beyond the names of his parents (Govardhana Lāla and Kiśorī) and paternal grand-parents (Jīvana Lāla and Śrīkṛṣṇa Kuvara he gives no personal details. His grand father seems to be his spiritual preceptor.[2] Vaṁśīdhara, whose loyalties are with the Rādhā cult[3], has written a learned and elaborate Com. on ŚR. He was a Gauḍa Brahmin of Kauśika *gotra*,[4] a follower of Gauḍīya Vaiṣṇavism and he extensively quotes JC and VC. It is at the request of the scholars at Mathurā that he wrote this encyclopaedic Com.[5] His reverential approach to ŚR is worth noting. "Śrīdhara alone knows the implication of ŚR's Com. After paying obeisance to Nṛsiṁha who conferred His grace on ŚR, I begin the exposition of ŚR through ŚR's favour". VD deserves careful study not only for understanding ŚR but the Bh.P. as well.

Anvitārtha-prakāśikā by Gaṅgā Sahāya is a very useful Com. as it explains practically every word and every important grammatical form. The author wrote this in his old age. He is silent about his personal details.

The Viśiṣṭādvaita school is represented by Sudarśana Sūri and Vīra-rāghava. Sudarśana-Sūri, the celebrated author of Śruta-prakāśikā,[6] a Com. on Rāmānuja's Śrī

1. Baladeva Upādhyāya—*Purāṇa vimarśa*, pp. 572-73.

2. *Pituśca pitaraṁ vande Śrīmaj-jīvana-lālakam |*
mantra-rājo'padeśena yena nistārito'smyaham ||
RR. Intro. vv to xi *Skandha*.

3. Vide his opening salutation to Kṛṣṇa, the Lord of Rādhā
Śrī Kṛṣṇaṁ Rādhikā-nātham āśraye sarva-kāraṇam |

4. *Vaṁśīdharaḥ Kauśika-gotra-Gauḍa-vaṁśyaḥ Kṛtī Śrīdhara-vṛtti-vṛttim| Karomi*—Intro. v

5. *atha Mathurā-vidvajjanapreraṇayā Śrī-Vaṁśīdhara-Śarmā maṅgalaṁ vyākaroti* VD Intro.

6. *Ānanda-tīrtha-Vijaya-tīrthau praṇamya maskari-vara-vandyau*
tayoḥ Kṛtiṁ sphuṭam upajīvya pravacmi Bhāgavataṁ purāṇam
Padaratnāvalī, Intro. v. 11

Bhāṣya, wrote a brief yet learned Com. *Śuka-pakṣīyā*. He is reported to have died in 1367 A.D. when Śrīraṅgam was sacked by the forces of Allauddin Khilaji. VR (Vīrarāghava's *Bhāgavata candrikā*) is 'pleasant like the moon-light'—an excellent textual exposition of the Bh.P. from the Viśiṣṭādvaita point of view. The v.l.s recorded by him and the explanations given are important. He was the son of Śrī Śaila of Vatsa *Gotra* and a pupil of Lakṣmaṇa Muni, his father's disciple. He is supposed to belong to the 14th Cent. A.D.

Vijayadhvaja's *Padaratnāvalī* is an able exposition of the *Dvaita* School. He closely follows Ānanda-tīrtha's *Bhāgavata-tātparya-nirṇaya*, not a Com. but a digest of the Bh.P. The text of the Bh.P. used by VJ records a number of different readings, changes in the number and the order of verses and even in chapters as well. This is especially found in the X Skandha to a considerable extent. He is an intelligent annotator giving unexpected explanations with the help of grammar, lexicon and other *purāṇic* and *smṛti* references. He is supposed to have lived in the 15th Cent. A.D.

Śukadeva's (SD) *Siddhānta-pradīpa* presents Nimbārka's philosophy through the Bh.P. But one of the finest expositions of the Bh.P. is Vallabha's *Subodhinī*. Though it does not cover all the *Skandhas*, and its claim to present seven interpretations of the Bh.P. may be disputed, one must admit its profound scholarship, clarity of thought and felicity of expression. It is a pleasure to read *Subodhinī*. Its author Vallabha (1479-1531 A.D.) is the founder of the Śuddhādvaita school and what is popularly called *Puṣṭimārga*, so popular in Gujarat. But Vallabha was a *Kṛṣṇa-yajurvedī* Brāhmaṇa from Andhra. He wrote his famous Com. *Aṇubhāṣya* on the *Brahma sūtra* and established his *Brahma-Vāda* (*Śuddhādvaita*). Gosvāmī Puruṣottama (1700 A.D.) wrote *Subodhinī-Prakāśa* to elucidate the *Subodhinī*. But Vallabha's descendant Giridhara (later part of 19th Cent.) son of Gopāla, has given us a very lucid exposition of the Bh.P. in his Com. *Bāla-prabodhinī*, very useful even to novices.

Of the Bengal School of Vaiṣṇavism JG and VC are used. Jīva Gosvāmī (16th Cent. AD) the author of *Ṣaṭ-sandarbha* is a great exponent of the Caitanya school. He has written *Krama-Sandarbha* and *Vaiṣṇavatoṣaṇī* (on X Skandha) on the Bh.P. He headed the Caitanya school after his uncles—Rūpa and Sanātana Gosvāmī. It won't be an exaggeration if one credits him to have established *Gauḍīya* Vaiṣṇavism on sound Vedāntic footing. As an ardent devotee of Rādhā-Kṛṣṇa JC is at his best in *Vaiṣṇavatoṣaṇī*, though the usefulness of *Krama-sandarbha* is not denied. As noted above (on ŚR) JC modestly states that his Commentary is merely an elucidation and elaboration of ŚR, though actually it is an independent exposition based on a different philosophy. Viśvanātha Cakravartī (VC) in his *Sārārtha-darśinī*, on the Bh.P. closely follows JC, but his treatment is more detailed and helpful to a common reader.

The translator has used a few more Commentaries like Bhagavat-Prasāda's *Bhakta-manorañjanī* (of Svāmī-nārāyaṇa cult)but the Commentators are generally reticent about themselves.

THE GLORY OF BHĀGAVATA PURĀṆA[1]

CHAPTER ONE

Nārada meets Bhakti (Devotion in a human form)

1. We extol the glory of Lord Kṛṣṇa who is the embodiment of the Truth, Consciousness and Bliss, the Cause of the Creation (Protection and Destruction) of the universe, who annihilates the three types of torments (viz. (1) pertaining to one's body, (2) caused by other beings (3) inflicted by the Providence).

2. I pay my obeisance to that sage (Śuka) who (in the early stage of childhood) renounced all actions even though the ceremony of the investiture of the sacred thread had not taken place. While he set out (as a recluse to enter the fourth stage of life viz. *Sannyāsa*—ŚR) and whom the sage Vyāsa (his father), being grieved at his desertion of home, called back as "Oh Son", (to which) the trees (with which Śuka had identified himself) on account of his (Śuka's) entry (existence) into the hearts of all beings, responded to Vyāsa (Śuka replied through the medium of trees to remove the paternal bond from the heart of Vyāsa—ŚR).

3. In the forest called Naimiṣa, Śaunaka who was a connoisseur in enjoying the sweetness of nectar-like stories (of the Lord), bowed down to Sūta who was comfortably seated, and requested him.

Śaunaka said:

4. Oh Sūta! your knowledge is like the splendour of

---

1. This glorification of the *Bhāgavata Purāṇa* is extracted from the *Padma Purāṇa—Uttara Khaṇḍa*, chs 193-198. In the preamble of ch. 193, goddess Pārvatī requests Lord Śiva to narrate to her the glory of the *Bhāgavata Purāṇa* which is regarded as the greatest among all the *Purāṇas*. Lord Śiva reports to her the dialogue between Sūta and Śaunaka wherein the *Bhāgavata* is glorified by Sūta to Śaunaka. I have followed here the commentary *Ṛju-nāmnī* by Pt. Rāma Pratāpa, son of Vrajalāla, of *Śāṇḍilya gotra*, a resident of 'Vijayapura' in Śekhāvaṭī.

millions of suns capable of totally annihilating the darkness of ignorance. Be pleased to tell me the essence of the stories (of the Lord), serving as an elixir (completely gratifying) my ears.

5. In what way is the power of discrimination, developed through devotion, spiritual knowledge and renunciation, enhanced? How are delusion and infatuation removed by the votaries of Lord Viṣṇu?

6. In this advent of the terrible Kali age, a (normal human) being has become demonic in nature. What is the best remedy for the expiation of such a being who is subjected to (and overcome with) afflictions?

7. Be pleased to explain to us the ever-effective remedy, which is the auspicious-most in the propitious ones and the sacred-most among the sanctifying ones, and which leads to the attainment of Lord Kṛṣṇa.

8. The philosopher's stone[1] may give worldly pleasures, and the Lord of gods (Indra), affluence in the heaven. But if a spiritual preceptor is pleased, he confers (attainment to) Vaikuṇṭha, the region of Viṣṇu which is very difficult to obtain even for *yogins*.

Sūta said:

9. Oh Śaunaka! You entertain love (for Lord Kṛṣṇa) in your heart. Hence after pondering deeply, I shall explain to you the conclusions deduced by all established truths (philosophies) which are capable of destroying the fear of *Saṁsāra* (mundane existence, the chain of births and deaths).

10. Listen to me attentively. I shall now relate to you what will swell the flood of devotion (to God), and bring about the Grace of Lord Kṛṣṇa.

11. It is with a view to remove completely the fear of falling a victim to the jaws of the serpent in the form of Time, that a sacred treatise called *Bhāgavata* was set forth by the sage Śuka in this Kali age.

12. There is not a single other remedy to achieve purification of the mind. One can (however) get the opportunity

1. *Cintāmaṇi*—A fabulous precious stone, supposed to yield to the possessor, all his desires.

of (listening to) the *Bhāgavata*, if there be (balance of) meritorious actions in previous births.

13 When the sage Śuka took his seat in the assembly-hall to narrate the story (of the *Bhāgavata*) to king Parīkṣit, all gods arrived there carrying with them actually the jar full of nectar.

14. Bowing down to Śuka, all the gods, clever as they were to accomplish their purpose, requested, "After receiving first the (jar of) nectar, kindly let us have the nectar in the form of stories of the Lord.

15. If this exchange (of nectar for the stories of Lord Hari) is acceptable, the nectar may be drunk by the King (Parīkṣit), while all of us will drink (listen to) the nectar-like *Śrīmad Bhāgavata*.

16. "Where is the ordinary nectar? Where is the (sanctifying) story of the *Bhāgavata* ? (The nectar can stand no comparison at all with the *Bhāgavata*) just as a very costly jewel can never be compared with a glass bead". Reasoning thus (with himself) Śuka laughed out (the barter proposed by) gods. So goes the traditional report.

17. Knowing thoroughly that they (gods) were not the devotees of the Lord, he refused to narrate to them the nectarine story of the Lord. Hence the story of *Śrīmad-Bhāgavata* is un-obtainable even to gods.

18-19. In those ancient days, even god Brahmā was wonder-struck to see the liberation (from *Saṁsāra*) of King Parīkṣit, that way[1] (through merely listening to the story of the *Bhāgavata*). On his return to Satya-loka (Brahmā's region), he weighed in balance all ways leading to *Mokṣa*. But all others proved to be (comparatively) light, while this (listening to the *Bhāgavata*) proved the heaviest in weight. At that time, all the sages also were astonished.

20. They realized that the sacred text called the *Bhāgavata*, the recitation or hearing of which instantaneously confers the 'fruit' of attaining to the *Vaikuṇṭha*, is verily the Lord Himself (incarnate) in this world.

---

1. According to a *Smṛti* text quoted by the Com., a person dying by serpent-bite does not go to good regions. Hence the wonder of sages when Parīkṣit secured Liberation even after death by a snake-bite.

21. Formerly it was prescribed to Nārada by compassionate sages headed by Sanaka, that listening to the *Bhāgavata* completely within the duration of one week, definitely confers Liberation (from *Saṁsāra*).

22. Although this (*Bhāgavata*) was heard by the heavenly sage Nārada due to his relation with god Brahmā, the procedure of listening to the *Bhāgavata* within the duration of seven days, was explained to him by the boy-sages (Sanaka etc.).

Śaunaka asked:

23. What interest did Nārada have in listening to the procedure (of reciting the *Bhāgavata* within a week) inasmuch as his mission is trouble-shooting in the world, for which he is always on the move? And where did he meet them (sages Sanaka and others).

Sūta replied :

24. I shall now relate to you an incident conducive to the (enhancement of) devotion. It was narrated to me in strict privacy by Śuka who regarded me as his disciple.

25. Once those four absolutely sinless sages (Sanaka, Sanandana etc.) arrived at Badarikāśrama with a view to contact other saints. They saw Nārada there.

The Boy-sages (Sanaka and others) asked :

26. Oh Brāhmaṇa sage! How is it that your appearance is down-cast? What anxiety worries your worship? Where are you proceeding in haste? And whence have you come?

27. You now appear listless like a man who has lost all his wealth and property. This is not proper in the case of a person (like you) who has renounced all attachment. Please let us know the reason.

Nārada explained :

28-29. Knowing that the earth is the best of regions (in the universe), I arrived here and during my wandering (through wander-lust) to different sacred places, I visited Puṣkara, Prayāga, Kāśī, the Godāvarī (some holy place on the bank of that river), Haridvāra, Kurukṣetra, Śrī-raṅgaṁ, Rāmeśvara (site of Ramā's bridge over the sea).

30. But at no place did I get any solace or delight giving satisfaction to the mind. Now the earth is thoroughly in the grip of Kali, the friend of unrighteousness.

31. There is no place for truthfulness, austerities, purity (both physical and mental), compassion and liberality. The wretched beings thereof are solely occupied in filling their belly (for which) they make false statements.

32. The people are stupid and extremely dull-witted. They are luckless and are afflicted (with disease, difficulties etc.). The (so-called) saints are engaged in heretical activities while the recluses) *sannyāsins* (or the renouncers of the worldly life) entertain family and property.

33. Young women (in disregard of older generation) control the household. One's wife's brother becomes a counsellor (his advice prevails). They sell their daughters out of greediness. The husbands and wives quarrel with each other.

34. (Sites of) hermitages (of sages), holy places and sacred rivers are occupied by *yavanas* (foreigners). Here (in India) the sacred shrines (of gods) have been destroyed and polluted by wicked enemies of religion.

35. There is no (real) *yogī*, possessor of mystic powers. There is none who has acquired spiritual knowledge or performs righteous acts. In the forest-conflagration in the form of the Kali age, all spiritual discipline has been reduced to ashes.

36. In this Kali age, the country will be full of people who sell food, Brāhmaṇas, selling the *Vedas* and women living by prostitution.

37. During my course of wandering over the earth, I observed these evils (caused by) the Kali age, and I arrived on the bank of the Yamunā which was (once) the stage of Hari's (Kṛṣṇa's) sports.

38. Listen to me, oh prominent sages, what miraculous phenomenon I noticed there. A young woman with a dejected mind was sitting there.

39. Two old men, with heavy breathing, were lying unconscious beside her. She was nursing them, trying to bring them back to consciousness and shedding tears before them.

40. In all the ten quarters, she was looking for the protector of her person. She was fanned by hundreds of women who were reassuring her.

41. Seeing this from a distance, I approached her out of curiosity. The girl stood up as she saw me. The girl, deeply distressed in mind, spoke to me.

The girl said :

42. Oh saintly person ! Wait for a moment and put an end to my worries. Your very sight itself is a great panacea removing all sins of the world.

43. Most probably my agonies will be pacified by (listening to) your words. It is only when one is highly lucky that persons like you are seen.

Nārada asked :

44. Who are you ? Who are these two (old men) ? And who are these ladies with lotus-like eyes ? Oh good lady ! Tell me in details the cause of your misery.

The girl replied :

45. I am known as *Bhakti* (Devotion). These two who are by name "Spiritual Knowledge" and "Renunciation", are regarded as my sons. These have become aged and worn out due to passage of time.

46. (Pointing to ladies) These are rivers like the Gaṅgā and others who have come to serve me. Waited upon even by gods as I am, I get no felicity or bliss.

47. Oh Sage (whose wealth is penance) ! Anxiously and carefully listen to this story of mine. The story of my life is a long one. But please listen to it, and give me some mental happiness.

48. Such as I am, I was born in the *Draviḍa* land and grew up to maturity in *Karṇāṭaka*. At some places in *Mahārāṣṭra* I was respected, but after coming to Gujarat I became old and decrepit.

49. Owing to the terrible age called Kali, I was crippled in my various parts of the body by the heretics (who singing god's name, dancing before him, worshipping him, were

neglected by the people due to heretical teachings) I was subjected to live in that stage for a long time ; I became weak and sluggish along with my sons.

50. But after reaching *Vṛndāvana* I became rejuvenated, and endowed with enviable beauty. Thus I appear quite young with a lovely form.

51. But these two sons of mine who are suffering great anguish, have slept due to fatigue. I however, propose to go to another place leaving this place.

52. I am pained at the decrepitude of my sons. Though I am their mother, why should I look young and my sons aged.

53. How did this unnatural inversion take place when we three have been staying together? It is natural that the mother should be old and the sons youthful.

54. My mind is overwhelmed with this miraculous change, and hence I am grief-striken. Oh intelligent abode of Yoga! Kindly let me know what can be the cause of this.

Nārada said :

55. Oh sinless lady! I have perceived and understood all your plight through my insight born of spiritual knowledge. You need not be depressed in spirits. Lord Hari will bring bliss in your life.

Sūta said :

56. Grasping within a moment the cause of her misery the great sage spoke as follows :

Nārada said :

Oh young lady! listen to me carefully. The present age is dominated by the terrible Kali.

57. It is due to his influence that righteous conduct, the *yogic* way of life and austerities have been neglected completely. People indulging in fraudulent and wicked deeds are acting like Aghāsura.[1]

1. *Aghāsura* : A demon sent by Kaṁsa to kill Kṛṣṇa. He assumed the form of a boa constrictor and lay with his mouth open. The cowherd boys with Kṛṣṇa entered it, but Kṛṣṇa killed him. —Bh.P. 10.12.

58. In this age, saintly people come to grief and suffer, and unrighteous people feel exultant. Only the person possessing intelligence and fortitude is either wise or learned.

59. Year after year, this earth which deserves not to be touched (by foot in walking) or is not worthy of looking at, is becoming heavier and heavier to *Śeṣa* and there is nothing which is auspicious.

60. At present no body cares to look at you along with your sons. You stand neglected by persons who are blinded with passion, and thus you are overcome with old age.

61. *Vṛndāvana* really deserves praise, as it is due to its contact, that *Bhakti* was rejuvenated as a young woman and where *Bhakti* (gleefully) dances.

62. These two (sons of yours) do not shed off their decrepitude due to absence of people accepting them. Their deep sleep is regarded as a result of the partial satisfaction of their self.

Bhakti asked :

63. Why was this sinful—impious—Kali established by King Parīkṣit? What has become of the essence or fruit of every thing, after the advent of the Kali age ?

64. How is it that Lord Hari who is noted for his grace, tolerates this unrighteousness or this unrighteousness of Kali ? Be pleased to cut (remove) this doubt of mine. I feel happy when I hear your speech.

Nārada said :

65. As I am asked by you with so much affection, be pleased to listen, oh child. I shall explain to you everything and your nervousness (of the mind) will disappear, Oh blessed lady !

66. When the glorious Lord Kṛṣṇa left this earth and retired to his region, since that very day the Kali age which hinders all spiritual efforts, has been commenced.

67. When, during the course of the conquest of the world, (lit. cardinal points) Kali was seen by the king Parīkṣit as resorting to him for protection like an indigent person, the king who, like a black bee sucked (grasped) the essence

of everything, decided, "This (Kali) should not be killed by me".

68. (For) It is only in the Kali age that a person can attain that supreme fruit by chanting the name and glory of Lord Viṣṇu that one can never get through austerities, *yoga* or meditation.

69. Taking into account this unique speciality of the Kali age and regarding it as valuable, though it is lacking in other essential qualities, Parīkṣit established the (presiding deity of that) age for securing the bliss of those who would be born in Kali age.

70. The essence of all substances has now disappeared in every respect due to perpetration of evil deeds. All substances on the earth stay bereft of their essence, like the husk devoid of seed-grains.

71. The importance and efficacy of the story of the *Bhāgavata* have eroded away as the story has been recited in every house and to all persons (irrespective of their devoutness) by Brāhmaṇas out of greed for obtaining food grains.

72. Even the returnees from the *Raurava* hell who perpetrate most terrible and heinous crimes and who are non-believers, have occupied the sacred places and hence the efficacy of holy places has vanished.

73. Even the persons whose minds are full of and distracted with erotic passion, anger, extreme greed and avidity for pleasures, are practising penance. Hence the potency of penance is lost.

74. The power of meditation has disappeared due to non-control of the mind, avarice, hypocrisy, adoption of heresy and absention from the study of sacred texts.

75. Like he-buffalos (regardless of *Śāstric* restrictions) the learned people indulge in sexual intercourse with (their) women, and are very diligent in procreating children, but are indifferent to the means leading to one's salvation.

76. In no place there is devotion to Viṣṇu as traditionally followed in (ancient) sects. Hence the essence and efficacy of everything are completely lost everywhere.

77. This is the very nature of the (Kali) age. Nobody is to be blamed. Hence Lord Viṣṇu (of lotus eyes), though so

close to us (as the Indwelling Lord *antar-yāmin*), forbears this.

Sūta said :

78. Being extremely surprised to hear this speech of Nārada, *Bhakti* again addressed the following words to him. Oh Śaunaka, please listen to them.

Śrī Bhakti said :

79. Oh heavenly sage ! You are certainly blessed (by your saintliness). It is my (sheer) luck that you have come The very sight of righteous persons is highly conducive to the attainment of all things in the world.

80. I bow to that son of Brahmā who is the receptacle (and support) of all auspicious blessings, grasping—understanding whose only one word-construction (viz. taking of the name of god), Prahlāda, the son of Kayādhū, transcended the deluding *māyā* power and through whose grace Dhruva, (the son of Uttānapāda) attained to the eternal abode.

CHAPTER TWO

(*Conversation between Nārada and the Kumaras*)

Nārada resumed :

1. Oh young lady ! You are unnecessarily worrying. Why should you get afflicted with anxieties ? Call upon mentally the lotus-like feet of Lord Kṛṣṇa and gone will be your affliction.

2. Nowhere has gone that Kṛṣṇa who saved Draupadī from the disgrace machinated by Kauravas and who protected Gopa damsels etc. (by killing Śaṅkhacūda and others).

3. Oh Bhakti ! You, on the contrary, have been ever dearer to him than his own life. When earnestly solicited by you, the Lord goes even to the houses of the lowly.

4. In the three epochs beginning with *Satya-yuga* (and

Tretā and *Dvāpara yugas*) spiritual knowledge and renunciation (of the worldly life) were conducive to the Liberation (of the *jīva*), while in the Kali age, *Bhakti* alone brings about the absorption of the soul in the *Brahman*.

5. It is traditionally held that the Lord, the embodiment of spiritual consciousness and the supreme bliss and energy, having come to a decision (mentioned above), created you as a beautiful counterpart of his own, and (you become) beloved of Kṛṣṇa.

6. Once upon a time, with folded palms, you asked him, "What should I do ?" At that time Kṛṣṇa ordered you to look after his votaries.

7. When you complied to undertake that (job), Lord Hari became highly pleased with you and allotted to you *Mukti* (liberation of the soul) as a maid-servant, and these two viz. spiritual knowledge (*jñāna*) and Renunciation (*vairāgya*) as your sons.

8. In the Vaikuṇṭha region, you maintain (and look after the votaries of the Lord) in your own real form. While on the earth you have assumed your reflected image for nourishing (i.e. taking care) of the devotees.

9. You came down to this earth accompanied by Liberation (*mukti*), knowledge (*Jñāna*) and Renunciation (*vairāgya*) and lived very happily from the *Kṛta* age, upto the end of the *Dvāpara age*.

10. In the Kali age, when affected with the disease called heretic doctrines, *Mukti* caught consumption (and went on decaying), and by your order, she immediately returned to Vaikuṇṭha.

11. When mentally recalled by you, *Mukti* comes down even here (on the earth), and goes back to Vaikuṇṭha) again. You regard these two (*Jñāna* and *Vairāgya*) as your sons and have kept them by your side.

12. It is due to their negligences in the Kali age that these two sons of yours have grown dull and aged. You, however, stop worrying. I am thinking about a remedy.

13. Oh beautiful lady ! There is no age like the Kali age and I shall see to it that you are established in every house and in every individual.

14. If I fail to propagate you in this world by eclipsing other faiths and sponsoring the celebration of great festivals (of God), I cease to be a servant of God.

15. Those beings who will be accompanied with you (i.e. be possessed of Devotion) shall go to the abode of Kṛṣṇa and transcend the fear (of *Saṁsāra*), even though they be sinners.

16. Those pure personages in whose heart abides devotion permanently in the form of love for God, never see in their dreams *Yama*, the god of death.

17. To those persons whose mind is full of devotion, none has power to touch him, be it a disembodied spirit, a goblin, a demon or even an *Asura*.

18. Lord Hari is not attainable by austerities or by the study of the *Vedas* or even by the path of philosophical knowledge or that of ritualistic action, for he is realised by devotion as is evidenced by the cowherd women (of Vraja).

19. Love for devotion is engendered in men after thousands of births. I repeatedly emphasise that a devotion alone is paramount in the Kali age and it is by devotion that Lord *Kṛṣṇa* stands manifest before a devotee.

20. Those persons who bear malice towards devotion, stand ruined in the three worlds. Formerly the Sage Durvāsas who found fault with devotion (i.e. Ambarīṣa, the devotee) landed into trouble thereby.[1]

21. Enough of the observance of different vows. Have done with pilgrimage to sacred places. Enough of *yogic* practices and performance of sacrifices. Stop the discussions about the stories of spiritual knowledge. For *Bhakti* alone bestows liberation from Saṁsāra.

Sūta said :

22. Hearing her own glory so conclusively affirmed by Nārada, She became full of nourishment in all her body and spoke to Nārada the following words :

1. For the story of Ambarīṣa vide Bh.P. 9 Chs. 4 & 5.

Bhakti said :

23. Oh Nārada ! You are really very blessed, in that you cherished a firm and unflinching love towards me. I shall never desert you, but will ever reside in your heart.

24. Merciful as you are, you have in no time removed my torments, Oh saintly person! My sons have not returned to consciousness. Please do bring them back to themselves, I urge.

Sūta said :

25. Hearing her speech, Nārada was moved with compassion and massaging them with the tips of his fingers, he began to rouse them to consciousness.

26. Bringing his mouth near their ears, he said loudly, "Oh *Jñāna*, get up quickly. Oh *Vairāgya*, wake up immediately."

27. Being roused by the chanting of the *Vedas* and *Upaniṣadas* and by loud recitations of the *Bhagavad Gītā*, they were slowly and with great efforts, made to wake up.

28. They were so much lethargic that they did not open their eyes to see and went on yawning agape. Their heads were white like cranes, and their emaciated limbs of the body were like pieces of dry wood.

29. Seeing them emaciated with hunger and inclined to relax into drowsiness, the sage became filled with anxiety, "What can be done by me ?"

30. Thinking deeply in his mind how the sleepiness can be removed, and how the formidably intractable agedness be cured, he, in his own mind, appealed to Lord Viṣṇu, Oh Śaunaka.

31. Came a voice from the heaven, "Oh Sage ! Be not so despondent. There is no doubt that your effort will be crowned with success.

32. Oh celestial sage ! Do perform righteous acts for achieving this. And saintly persons who are the ornaments of their order, will guide you about the specific act to be performed.

33. As soon as that act is done, both the stupor and

decrepitude of these both will disappear in a moment. And devotion will (automatically) spread in all directions."

34. The speech from the space above was distinctly heard by them all. Nārada got surprised, saying, "The (import) of this (speech from the heaven) is not comprehensible to me."

35. The means to be adopted to achieve the purpose of these two (viz. regaining of consciousness by *Jñāna* and *Vairāgya*) has been mystically indicated.

36. Where will be the saints (found)? What am I to do now in the matter as required by the voice from the heaven?"

37. Stationing them there (on the bank of the Yamunā), Nārada set out from one sacred place to another, asking great sages on the way (the specific righteous act enjoined by the voice from the heaven).

38. The report was given (patient) hearing by all, but no conclusively positive answer was given by anybody. Some said, 'It (the malady) is incurable', while others said it is undiagnosable'.

39-40. Some persons remained silent, while others dodged the issue by hastily departing. There was a tumultuous roar throughout the three worlds which were astonished to find that the triad of *Bhakti*, *Jñāna* and *Vairāgya* did not come to consciousness in spite of the fact that attempts to awaken them were made by loud chanting of the *Vedas* and *Upaniṣads* and the recitation of the *Bhagavad Gītā*.

41-42. People confided (into the ears) to each other "there cannot be any remedy which is not personally known to Nārada. How is it possible for other human beings like us to suggest?" In this way the congregation of sages who were consulted came to a conclusion and declared that (the remedy) was difficult to be found.

43. Being overwhelmed with anxiety, Nārada came to the Badarikāśrama. He made up his mind, "I shall practice austerities for them here".

44. In the meanwhile, the most pious sage (Nārada) beheld in front of him prominent sages like Sanaka (Sanandana etc.) whose splendour was like that of millions of suns (combined). He asked them :

Nārada asked :

45. It is due to my great fortune that you met me. Kindly be compassionate to me, you (eternally) youthful sages ! and tell me the remedy.

46. All of you are adept in *yoga*, highly intelligent and deeply learned. Though you seem to be five years of age, you were born long before (our) ancestors.

47. You are permanent residents of Vaikuṇṭha and are always deligently engaged in chanting the name, and singing the excellences of Lord Hari. Being (as if) inebriated with the nectarlike juice (in the form) of the sports (of the Lord), you have devoted your life solely to (extolling the) stories of the Lord. (lit. you live upon the stories).

48. 'Hari is our asylum', these words being always in your mouth, old age which is ordered by the Time-spirit, does not affect you.

49. Formerly, it was simply by the contraction of your eyebrows (expressing displeasure) that the two door-keepers (Jaya and Vijaya) of Lord Hari instantly fell down to the earth and were, through your grace, restored (to their former position).

50. Oh! It is a matter of sheer good luck that I could see your honour here. (I urge) May favour be conferred on a miserable person like me, by compassionate (sages like you).

51. Reveal to me the spiritual remedy suggested by the heavenly voice. May you kindly explain to me the details how I should adopt it, (in practice).

52. How can *Bhakti*, *Jñāna* and *Vairāgya* be restored to happiness? In what way can they be established lovingly and with efforts, in all classes of the society ?

Kumāras replied:

53. Oh celestial sage ! Do not feel so anxious and worried. Restore cheerfulness to your mind. For, there has been in existence an easy remedy, since long.

54. Oh Nārada ! You are really blessed. You are the crest-jewel of all persons who have renounced the world. You

are the sun illuminating (the path of) *yoga* and always the foremost among the devotees of Lord Kṛṣṇa.

55. It should not be regarded as surprising that you are moved so much (deeply) for *Bhakti*. The (effort towards) establishment of *Bhakti* is always natural with the devotees of Lord Kṛṣṇa.

56. A number of ways have been revealed in this world by sages. But all of them can be brought in the practice, through extreme exertions, and most of them confer the fruit of residence in the celestial world.

57. The path leading to *Vaikuṇṭha* has still remained secret. It is generally through great luck that one can get a guide directing one to that path.

58. The righteous action that was formerely indicated to you by the heavenly voice, will now be explained to you. Listen to it with concentrated yet cheerful mind.

59. There are sacrificial performances to be carried with materials to be oblated (in fire), sacrifices consisting of performance of various kinds of penances, the sacrifice in the form of *yogic* practices, (e.g. meditation, *samādhi* etc.) studies in Vedic lore—But all these point to the way of ritualistic *Karmas* (leading to the celestial world).

60. The sacrifice in the form of knowledge is really indicated by (the words) "righteous actions", and has been prescribed by the learned and the wise. And that sacrifice is the recitation of *Śrīmad Bhāgavata* which has been extolled by (the sage) Śuka and others.[1]

61. *Bhakti*, *Jñāna* and *Vairāgya* will be greatly invigorated by the sound the recitation (of the *Bhāgavata*). The anguish of both (*Jñāna* and *Vairāgya*) will be mitigated completely and happiness will be restored to Bhakti.

62. For all these evils of Kali age will be completely and definitely annihilated by the sound of the chanting of the *Bhāgavata*, as the wolves do at the roar of a lion.

63. *Bhakti* which leads to the abiding sentiment of love (towards the Lord) when associated with knowledge and

1. Hence the *Devī Bhāgavata* is ruled out here—RN.

Renunciation will play with (i.e.spread in) each hearth and every person.

Nārada asked :

64. The triad of *Bhakti*, *Jñāna* and *Vairāgya* was made to wake up by the (loud) chanting of the *Vedas* and *Upaniṣads* and by the recitation of the *Bhagavad Gītā*, but it did not get up.

65. How can it be roused to consciousness by the narration of the *Bhāgavata*; for the import of the Veda has permeated not only every verse but every word of the stories (of *The Bhāgavata*).

66. Be pleased to resolve this doubt, as the sight of (person like you) is always fruitful (lit. never futile). You are always kind (and affectionate) to all who resort to you for asylum. So please do not defer (the solution of my doubt).

The Kumāras replied :

67. The story of *The Bhāgavata* is composed out of the essence of the *Vedas* and the *Upaniṣads*. But it appears as the best of them of all, because it is independent in existence and stands for its fruit.

68. The sap (vital juice of a tree) is circulating from the roots to the top (of a tree) but it has no (sweet) taste. But when it accumulates separately as a fruit, it is attractive to the world.

69. Just as ghee, though lying latent in the milk, cannot be available for taste as such (in the milk). But when it is separated from the milk, it is fit to be offered to gods and enhances their taste.

70. Just as sugar stands permeated in the sugarcane from its roots, the middle stem and the end, but it is very sweet when separated (and processed) from the sugar-cane. The same is the case with the *Bhāgavata* story.

71. This Purāṇa called the *Bhāgavata*, is equal (in status and efficacy) to the Vedas. It has been made public for establishing *Bhakti* (devotion), spiritual knowledge (*Jñāna*) and renunciation (*Vairāgya*).

72-73. When Vyāsa, even though adept and well-read in the *Vedas* and the *Upaniṣads* and the author of the *Bhagavad*

Gītā, was infatuated in the ocean of ignorance and was greatly agitated (through mental dissatisfaction), it was you who initiated him in the *Bhāgavata* consisting of four verses, hearing which Vyāsa instantaneously became free from torments.

74. What is wonderful here (in the efficiency of the *Bhāgavata*) that your honour has asked this question? (It is our considered opinion that) listening to *Śrīmad Bhāgavata* puts an end to grief and sorrow.

Nārada said :

75. I have resorted to you for an asylum in order that you should enkindle (the divine) love in me—you whose very sight instantaneously dispels completely everything inauspicious (including misery etc.) and enhances the happiness and auspiciousness of beings tormented with the conflagration in the form of saṁsāra, and you who drink nothing else but the story of the *Bhāgavata* as sung by the serpent Śeṣa with all his (thousand) mouths.

76. Verily, when a man gets into the company of saintly persons through great luck, brought about by the accumulation of merits in his past lives, it is only then that true spiritual knowledge arises after completely dispelling the darkness of infatuation and pride caused by ignorance.

CHAPTER THREE

(*Removal of Bhakti's Miseries*)

Nārada said :

1. For the sake of establishing Bhakti, Jñāna, and Vairāgya, I shall perform the sacrifice (for the spreading) of knowledge, exerting myself to the utmost, by reciting the *Bhāgavata* which is the illuminating sacred text introduced by Śuka.

2. May the place where I should perform this sacrifice (*of Bhāgavata*-recitation) be described (by you). And the

importance and glory of this sacred scripture of Śuka be explained by you, the experts in the Vedic lore.

3. May it be elucidated to me after this, in how many days the story of the *Bhāgavata* is to be heard, and the ritualistic procedure to be followed with reference to this (*jñāna-yajña*)?

Kumāras explained :

4. Listen, Oh Nārada ! inasmuch as you are deeply modest and judicious, we shall narrate that to you : In the vicinity of *Gaṅgādvāra* (i.e. Haridvāra) there is a place called *Ānanda* on the bank (of the *Gaṅgā*).

5. It was peopled with hosts of sages and was visited by celestial beings like gods and *siddhas*. It was covered with various kinds of trees and creepers and spread over with soft sand.

6. It was a lovely place far away from crowds, and was beautified with golden lotuses. The feeling of enmity had no place in the hearts of these beings which lived near that place.

7. The *Jñāna-yajña* (viz. recitation of the *Bhāgavata*) should be performed there by you. And without any (extra) exertion on your part, the story (of the *Bhāgavata*) will be full of extraordinary and unprecedented sweetness in that place.

8. Accompanied in the fore-front by the pair (*Jñāna* and *Vairāgya*) which was (formerly) lying before her devoid of strength and with their bodies worn out with old age, *Bhakti* herself will visit that place, in person.

9. Wherever there is the recitation of the story of the *Bhāgavata*, *Bhakti* (*Jñāna* & *Vairāgya*) attend to it. Hearing the words of the story (of the *Bhāgavata*), the triad gets rejuvenated.

Sūta said :

10. Having explained thus, (to Nārada), the *Kumāra*-sages thence hastily accompanied Nārada and arrived at the bank of the Gaṅgā, for making people drink the (nectarine) juice of the (*Bhāgavata*) story.

11. When they reached the bank (of the *Gaṅgā*), there

was a loud uproar on the earth, in the celestial world and in the region of God Brahmā as well.

12. All those who were eager to enjoy the delicious flavour of the story of the *Bhāgavata*) and especially the votaries of Viṣṇu came a-racing to that place, to drink the nectarine juice of *Śrī Bhāgavata*.

13-14. The sages Bhṛgu, Vasiṣṭha, Cyavana, Gautama, Medhātithi, Devala, Devarāta (Yājñavalkya), Paraśurāma, Viśvāmitra (the son of Gādhi), Śākala, Mārkaṇḍeya (the son of Mṛkaṇḍu), Dattātreya (the son of Atri), Pippalāda[1], Vāmadeva, the lord of *yoga*, Vyāsa and Parāśara, the counter part of Śuka[2] (*chāyā-śuka*), all these multitudes of sages of whom Jājali and Jahnu were the leaders, came along with their sons, disciples and wives, as they entertained a deep attachment and longing (to listen to the *Bhāgavata*).

15. There arrived the (presiding deities of) *upaniṣads*, the (four) *vedas*, sacred incantations (like *Sanjīvana* capable of reviving the dead), *tantras* (both *yāmala* and *ḍāmara* types), seventeen *Purāṇas* and six systems of Philosophy, as well.

16. (There came also) sacred rivers (of whom the *Gaṅgā*[3] stands first), lakes (of which Puṣkara is the prominent one), holy places (like Kurukṣetra), the cardinal points and forests (like the Daṇḍaka).

17. Mountains (like Meru and Himālayas), celestial beings like gods and demigods like Gandharvas and Kinnaras (divine musicians) came there. Bhṛgu, due to his position of being the preceptor, advised and brought the remaining persons who failed to come (due to their worldly interests).

18. The Kumāra-sages (Sanat-Kumāra and his brothers) who were already initiated and were thoroughly devoted to Kṛṣṇa, were offered excellent seats by Nārada and were paid homages by all, occupied their seats.

19. The devotees of Lord Viṣṇu, those who renounced

1. The plural is used to indicate the persons born in the *gotra*.
2. *Vyāsa-moha-nirāsāya chāyayā racitaḥ*—RN.
3. As a matter of fact, it should be the Yamunā, as the *Gaṅgā* was already present.

the world, the *Saṁnyāsins* (recluses) and the celibates were seated in the front (of all the listeners), and Nārada (being the convener or chief member of the audience) occupied the first (front-most seat).

20. One side was occupied by the host of sages, the other side by the celestial beings. The *Vedas* and *Upaniṣads* sat on one side; the (presiding deities of) holy places occupied another side, while the ladies were seated in (still) another part.

21. There was a loud hailing with lusty shouts of (words such as) 'Victory' (*Jaya*) and 'Salute' (*namas*), and a fanfare of conchblasting, and a heavy shower of aromatic powder (of camphor, sandals etc.), parched grains of rice, and flowers.

22. Some leaders of gods ascended their aerial cars and profusely showered all the congregation with flowers of wish-yielding (heavenly) trees.

Sūta said :

23. Thus while all were listening with concentrated minds, the Kumāras began to extol, in clear terms, the glory of the *Bhāgavata* to the great-souled Nārada.

Kumāras said :

24. We shall now describe to you the great glory of the *Śuka-Śāstra*[1] (*Śrīmad-Bhāgavata* as enunciated by Śuka), by listening to which Liberation (from *Saṁsāra*) is (secure as if being) just on the palm of one's hands.

25. One should constantly listen to the story of *Śrīmad Bhāgavata* (throughout one's life), for by simply listening to it, Lord Hari occupies one's heart.

26. Listen to the *Bhāgavata Purāṇa* which work consists of 18,000 verses (*Ślokas*) and is divided into 12 *Skandhas*, and forms a dialogue between King Parīkṣit and the sage Śuka.

---

1. A better v.l is :
atha te varṇyate 'smābhir mahimā Śuka-Śāstra-jaḥ /
The great glory derived from the Śuka-Śāstra is being described to you now by us.

27. So long as the story of the scripture enunciated by Śuka, viz. the *Bhāgavata* is not heard even for a moment, a man has to revolve in this rotating wheel of *Saṁsāra* due to his ignorance.

28. Of what use are the many *Śāstras* (scriptures) and *Purāṇas* listening to which causes nothing but confusion? The *Bhāgavata* is the only scripture which loudly announces the granting of Liberation from *Saṁsāra* (by listening to it).

29. The house in which the story of the *Bhāgavata* is recited, is transformed into a sacred place and it annihilates sins of persons who dwell in it.

30. Thousands of Horse-sacrifices and hundreds of Vājapeya sacrifices do not stand in comparison with the one-sixteenth of the efficacy of listening to the story of the *Bhāgavata*. (Śuka's scripture).

31. Oh Sages who regard austerities as your wealth! Sins persist in this body so long as *Śrīmad Bhāgavata* is not properly listened to by men.

32. Neither the Gaṅgā nor the holy place Gayā or Kāśī or the sacred lake Puṣkara or the holy place Prayāga can equal the recitation of the *Bhāgavata* in its efficacy.

33. If you desire to attain the *summum bonum*, you should always read or recite with your own mouth either a half or a quarter of a verse from the *Bhāgavata*.

34-36. Wise persons knowing the truth as it is, do not desire to distinguish between the sacred syllable OM (the ultimate source of the *Vedas*), the Gāyatrī (the mother of the *Vedas*), the *Puruṣa sūkta* (RV 10.90), the three *Vedas* (*ṚK*, *Sāman* and *Yajus*), the *Bhāgavata*, the sacred *mantra* of twelve syllables (viz. *Om Namo Bhagavate Vāsudevāya*), the Sun god who appears to assume twelve forms (one per month of the Hindu calendar), the sacredmost place Prayāga, *Kāla* or the Time spirit represented by one year, Brāhmaṇas, Agnihotra (offering of oblations daily to sacrificial fire—a duty of every householder), Surabhi, the wish-yielding cow, the twelfth day of the dark and bright halves of a lunar month, the Tulasī plant, the season called spring (consisting of months *Caitra*, and *Vaiśākha*) and Lord Viṣṇu, the Supreme-Most person.

37. There is absolutely no doubt that the sin committ-

ed in millions of previous lives of a person is destroyed completely, if that person every day reads the scripture of the *Bhāgavata* understanding its import.

38. A person who always reads at least the half or a quarter of a verse from the *Bhāgavata* attains the combined merits of the *Rājasūya* and *Aśvamedha* sacrifices.

39. Recitation of the *Bhāgavata* every day, the practice of meditating on Hari, watering the Tulasī plant every day, and feeding and service rendered to cows—all these bear equal fruit.

40. To a person who (happens to) hear at least a sentence out of the *Bhāgavata* at the time of death, Lord Viṣṇu, out of love, offers him (a place in) Vaikuṇṭha.

41. It is definitely certain that a person who presents the *Bhāgavata*, placing it on a throne (seat) of gold, to a votary of Viṣṇu attains the *Sāyujya* type of Liberation consisting in absorption in Lord Kṛṣṇa.

42. A wicked person who has not drunk (heard) the story of Śuka's scripture, paying to it at least slight attention, since his birth, has led a futile life like that of a Cāṇḍāla (a person belonging to the lowest caste), or like a donkey, and made his mother a sufferer by causing pangs of his birth to her.

43. He is a perpetrator of sinful deeds who has not at all heard even a sentence from the *Bhāgavata*. He is called a breathing corpse. About him say the leaders of the hosts of gods in heaven, "Fie upon such a man who is comparable to a beast and is nothing but a burden to the earth"

44. The story elucidated in the *Bhāgavata* is certainly very rare (to listen) in this world. It is obtained (heard) as a fruit of the culmination of meritorious actions performed in crores of previous lives.

45. Oh highly intelligent Nārada who are a treasure house of *yoga* ! One should listen to the story of the *Bhāgavata* with a perfect concentration (of mind). There is no restriction of the number of days within which it should be heard. The hearing of the *Bhāgavata* is always commended at all times.

46. It is ordained that while hearing *the Bhāgavata* one should always observe (the vows of) truthfulness and celi-

bacy. But that being impossible in the *Kali* age, specific observances as laid down by Śuka for this should be known.

47. Due to the impossibility of the control of the mental activity, of abiding by the rules (to be prescribed later in Chapter Six), and observance of consecration (known as *Viṣṇu-dīkṣā*), listening to the *Bhāgavata* for a (specific) period of one week is advised.

48. The fruit that one attains by hearing every day the *Bhāgavata*, with faith and devotion, in the month of Māgha (after performing early bath, worship of the Lord etc.), the same is allotted by the sage Śuka to the listening[1] of the *Bhāgavata* within the duration of a week.

49. Listening to the *Bhāgavata* within a week's period is recommended, due to non-subjugation of the mind, (human) susceptibility to disease (and illness), shortness of the life-span of men and the prevalence of plethora of evils in the Kali age.

50. One can easily attain the whole of that fruit by listening (to the entire *Bhāgavata*) in a week, which one cannot obtain even through the performance of penance, through the *yogic* process, and through meditation (and a absorption of the mind in the mind in the Supreme Soul).

51. The Bhāgavata week roars more loudly (i.e. brings more prosperity) than the performence of sacrifices; it leads to higher merits then (the observance of) vows; it brings more excellence than by performing austerities; it is always supremely suprior to sacred places.

52. It is superior to *yoga* (involving control of the mind), to the contemplation (with concentrated mind) and to the spiritual knowledge. How can we describe its excellence? It surpasses (in excellence) everything else.

Śaunaka asked :

53. The incident (of Nārada's meeting and dialogue with the Kumāra sages) as narated by you is really wonderful. How is it that in the present (Kali) age, the *Bhāgavata Purāṇa* set at nought (and excelled) the *Śāstric* knowledge (dis-

---

1. v.l. *Śrāvaṇe*—In the month of *Śrāvaṇa* (as well as in the month of Māgha).

passion, celibacy etc.) and the ordinances prescribed for all classes of people, and became efficacious to lead to the Liberation (from *saṁsāra*, even), the detractors of *yoga* and spiritual knowledge.

Sūta replied :

54. "When Kṛṣṇa became ready to depart from this earth to go to his region (*Vaikuṇṭha*), Uddhava, despite his listening to (the spiritual knowledge imparted in) the Eleventh Skandha (of the *Bhāgavata*) addressed him as follows :

Uddhava said :

55. "Oh Kṛṣṇa ! you, on your part will be going after achieving the work of your devotees. My mind is weighed with a deep anxiety. Please give a hearing to me and bring me happiness.

56. This terrible period of Kali is just impending. Wicked people will reassert themselves again. Even good persons will contract cruelty sheerly through their association with them (the evil people).

57. To whom can this earth overburdened with sinners, resort in the form of a cow? Oh lotus-eyed God ! No other protector except you appears in view.

58. You are affectionate to the devotees ! At least have mercy on the pious people, and do not depart (from this world). Though you are formless, pure consciousness, you have (sportively) assumed a form possessing excellences for the sake of your votaries.

59. How can your devotees continue to live on the earth when bereaved of you? There is a great difficulty in propitiating attributeless God. Hence think over a little."

60. Hearing this appeal from Uddhava, at (the holy place called) Prabhāsa, Hari pondered to himself, "What can be done by me for supporting my devotees".

61. The Lord deposited in the *Bhāgavata* all his spirit and energy. Having disappeared (from the world) he entered and abides in the ocean called *Bhāgavata*.

62. Hence this (*Bhāgavata*) is now the verbal image of

Lord Hari directly. If rendered service to it, heard, recited or (even simply) seen, it annihilates (all) sins.

63. It is due to this reason, that hearing of the *Bhāgavata* in a week, has been regarded as superior to all (other religious practices). In the Kali-age, the Bhāgavata week has been announced to be *the* religion superseding other religious practices.

64. This has been pronounced as the path of righteousness in the Kali age for washing off completely misery, poverty, misfortune and sins and for subduing the passion of lust and anger.

65. Otherwise how can human beings free themselves from the deluding potency of Lord Viṣṇu which is extremely difficult even for gods to overcome? Hence the *Bhāgavata* week (course of listening to the *Bhāgavata* within a week) has been proclaimed (and strongly recommended).

Sūta said :

66. While the glorious merits of the great *dharma* consisting of listening to the *Bhāgavata* in a week's duration, was being proclaimed by the sages, a miracle took place there. Oh Śaunaka, listen to it carefully as it is now being described.

67. *Bhakti* (Devotion), the embodiment of absolute love in God, unexpectedly manifested herself accompanied by her two sons ((*Jñāna* and *Vairāgya*) now fully re-juvenated and repeatedly uttering the names of the Lord, 'Oh Lord ! Oh Kṛṣṇa ! Oh Govinda ! Oh Hari ! Oh Murāri ! (Destroyer of the demon Mura)'

68. The members of the assembly saw her come attired in excellently charming garments, and adorned with ornaments in the form of the teachings of the *Bhāgavata* and began to guess as to how she entered and how she appeared in the midst of the sages.

69. 'It is from the very import of the story (of the *Bhāgavata*) that she has now sprung up', observed the Kumāra-sages. Hearing these words, she along with her sons humbly made the following submission to (the sage) Sanatkumāra.

Bhakti said :

70. "Mutilated and practically dead as I was, due to Kali age, you resuscitated me today by feeding me with the nectar-like story (of the *Bhāgavata*). May you, the sons of God Brahmā, direct me what place I, along with my sons should occupy". They thereupon, spoke the following words to her :

71. "Assuming the excellent form of Govinda, you persistently preserve the divine love among the devotees and cure completely their disease of *Saṁsāra*. Resorting to absolute firmness, you perpetually occupy the minds of the devotees of Viṣṇu.

72. Thereby the evils (like hereticalness) born of the Kali age which are capable of dominating the world, will not dare cast a glance at you". Even as they were instructing her (as guidance), she immediately occupied the hearts of the devotees of Hari as her abode.

73. Blessed are they in the entire world (s) in whose hearts abides unflinching devotion to Hari, the Lord of Śrī (Affluence), even though they may be destitute of wealth. It is hence that Hari, being tied with the bond of devotion, enters (and abides) in their hearts completely giving up his realm of Vaikuṇṭha.

74. What more can we extol now the great glory of this embodiment of the Veda, designated as the *Bhāgavata*, in this world. It is by resorting (i.e. listening) to and by expounding it in details, that both the eloquent preacher as well as the attentive listener attain oneness with Lord Kṛṣṇa. This path is self-sufficient; there is no propriety in following other paths of righteousness.

CHAPTER FOUR

(*Salvation to a Brāhmaṇa—Ātmadeva*)

Sūta said :

1-4. Observing the manifestation of extraordinary devotion in the minds of his votaries, the glorious Lord, the possessor of six excellences, who is so affectionate and compassionate to his devotees, left his own Realm (*Vaikuṇṭha*) and entered (to abide permanently) into the pure, sinless hearts of his devotees. He wore a garland of forest flowers (reaching down to his knees[1]) and was dark-blue in complexion like a cloud. Clad in yellow-coloured (silken) garment, he attracted the hearts of all (by his personal charm). He was ornamented with a girdle tinkling with small bells, a dazzling diadem and resplendent ear-rings. He had three beautiful folds on the belly[2] and was adorned with the beautiful Kaustubha gem. He was endowed with the fascinating beauty of crores of Love-gods (cupids) and was besmeared with celestial sandal paste. With a flute in hand, he was the sweet embodiment of the highest bliss and consciousness.

5. Uddhava and other devotees of Viṣṇu dwelling in the Vaikuṇṭha, attended it in invisible forms with the desire of hearing the story of the *Bhāgavata*.

6. Then (at the appearance of the Lord) there arose an applause and shouts of hailing ("victory to the Lord"), extraordinary super-abundance of joy, shower of scented powder and flowers and a fan-fare of conch blasting.

7. The members of the assembly became oblivious to the existence of their own person, homes and their own selves. Noticing their state of complete absorption, Nārada spoke as follows :

8. "Oh great sages ! This supremely pre-eminent greatness (and efficacy) accruing from (the special sacrifice called) the *Bhāgavata* week has been witnessed by me today. All beings including the irrational and egoists, beasts and birds that are present here—all of them become absolutely cleared of sins.

9. Hence, in the *Kali* age, in this world, there is no other act which purifies the mind as well as destroys the flood of sins, similar to the story of the *Bhāgavata Purāṇa*.

10. Be pleased to tell me what types of sinners are puri-

---

1. ājānu-lambinī mālā sarvartu-Kusumojjvalā /
madhye sthūla-kadambāḍhyā vanamāle'ti kīrtitā //
—Quoted in *ASD*, p. 490

2. Or better : He stood in a beautiful posture with his person slightly bent in three places (the *Tribhaṅgī* pose).

fied by the sacrifice in the form of (the recitation of) the story of the *Bhāgavata.* Taking into consideration the welfare of the world, some indescribable new path has been revealed by you who are so very compassionate.

11. Even those human beings who always indulge in committing sins, take pleasure in depraved conduct (throughout their lives); and have adopted evil ways of life; are consumed by the fire of wrath; are crooked and passionately wish for another man's wife, all such persons get purified in this *Kali* age by performing the sacrifice in the form of the *Bhāgavata*-week (when the Bhāgavata is recited completely).

12. Persons who indulge in lying (lit. are lacking in truthfulness), offend their parents; are overwhelmed with covetousness; have abandoned the duties prescribed for their particular stage of life (*āśrama*); are hypocrites, envious of others and even commit injury to living beings—all such persons become pure and sinless through (their attendance at) the sacrifice in the form of *Bhāgavata* week in the *Kali* age.

13. Persons who have committed five heinous sins[1], who practice roguery and fraudulent tricks, who are ruthless like *piśācas* (demons), have grown rich by exploiting Brāhmaṇas and indulge in adultery—all these get their sins wiped out through the sacrifice called The *Bhāgavata* Week in this *Kali* aeon.

14. The fools persistently and deliberately always commit sins through their body (physical activities), speech and mind (sinful mental activities), and have grown fat (rich) by misappropriating other people's property, are full of evil desires and are wicked at heart—all these become sinless through the sacrifice in the form of the *Bhāgavata*-week in this *Kali* age.

---

1. Manu has enumerated them as follows :

(1) Killing a Brāhmaṇa, (2) Wine-drinking, (3) Stealing, (4) Sexual intercourse with one's preceptor's wife, (5) Contact with the above type of sinners (vide *Manu-Smṛti.* 11.54).

These are elsewhere recorded as follows :

brahmaghnaś caiva goghnaś ca svarṇasteyī ca madyapaḥ /
tat-saṁsargī pañcamaś ca hyugrapāpāḥ prakīrtitāḥ //

This list substitutes 'killing a cow' for 'intercourse with one's teacher's wife' in *Manu Smṛti* 11.54.

15. I shall now narrate to you an ancient historical legend by simply listening to which, (one's) sins are annihilated.

16. In ancient times there was a beautiful town on the bank of the Tuṅgabhadrā, all the inhabitants whereof were diligently abiding by the duties of their respective classes (*varṇas*), spoke the truth, and were exclusively devoted to righteous acts.

17. In that town, there lived Ātmadeva who was adept in the entire Vedic lore, and was well-versed in the righteous acts and rites prescribed in the Vedas and the Smṛtis. He was like another sun in glory.

18. Though he maintained himself on alms, he was wealthy. His beloved wife known as Dhundhulī was born in a respectable family and beautiful in appearance, but she always asserted her own say in all matters.

19. She was deeply interested in rumour-mongering ; was merciless, always garrulous, miserly, given to wrangling though prompt and diligent in her household duties.

20. Though that couple mutually loved and lived in (apparent) happiness, they did not find real pleasure in their house (property etc.) despite their possession of wealth and other desired objects.

21. Ultimately they took to perform righteous acts with the object of getting a child. They began to give cows, land, gold as gift to the distressed and the needy.

22. Even though they spent half of their wealth in giving donation, they begot neither a son nor a daughter. They were extremely weighed down with anxiety.

23. One day, out of his feelings of misery, the Brāhmaṇa left the house and repaired to a forest. At noon he became thirsty and approached a tank.

24. After drinking water, he sat down in a dejected mood. He had become emaciated due to his grief of childlessness. Within a short while (*muhūrta*—about fortyeight minutes) a certain recluse (*sannyāsī*) happened to come to the same place.

25. Seeing that the recluse had drunk water, the Brāhmaṇa approached him. Bowing down to his feet, he stood before the recluse heaving sighs.

The Sannyāsī said :

26. How is it that you are crying, Oh Brahmāṇa? What is the deep anxiety that overwhelms you ? Please tell me immediately the cause of your misery.

The Brāhmaṇa replied :

27. Oh Sage ! How can I explain to you my misery which is due to the sins accumulated during my past lives. My fore-fathers drink my water oblations which have become lukewarm due to their sighs for my childlessness.

28. Gods and Brāhmaṇas do not accept with pleasure whatever I give them as gifts. I have become completely dejected due to my grief of issuelessness. I have come here to give up my life (commit suicide).

29. Cursed is the life of an issueless man. Wretched is home devoid of children. Worthless is the wealth of an issueless person. Fie upon the family which is childless.

30. Whichever cow I keep becomes completely barren. And a tree that is planted by me becomes devoid of flowers and fruits (an index of barrenness).

31. Whatever fruit is sent to my house immediately becomes dry and rotten. What is the propriety of living in the case of a luckless and childless person like me ?

32. Saying these words he, being overpowered with grief, lamented loudly, by the side of the recluse. Then the heart of the *sannyāsin* was deeply moved with compassion for him.

33. The recluse who was well-versed in *yoga* read the series of letters written on the Brāhmaṇa's forehead. Comprehending it fully, he explained that in details to the Brāhmaṇa.

The Sannyāsī said :

34. Please give up this ignorance in the form of the desire for children. Very powerful is the course of destiny. Take recourse to thoughtfulness and free yourself from this desire for *saṁsāra*.

35. Listen to me Oh Brāhmaṇa. I have seen today your destiny controlled by the fruition of past deeds. For seven terms of your existence (or life), you shall never beget a son.

36. In ancient times, King Sagara came to grief through his sons. The same was the case with the king of Aṅga[1]. Therefore, give up all hope and desire for rearing a family. There is absolute happiness in *sannyāsa*.

The Brāhmaṇa said :

37. Of what use is your advice of discrimination (*viveka*). Give me a son (if possible) by the force of your merits. Otherwise I shall swoon with grief in your presence and give up my life.

38. This Saṁnyāsa (life of a recluse), being devoid of the pleasure (derived from the company) of sons (grandsons) etc. is definitely dry and useless, while (the life of) a householder, accompanied as it is with sons and grandsons is sweet and charming in this world.

39. Noticing the insistence of the Brāhmaṇa (to beget a son), the sage (to whom penance was a wealth) spoke out, "In his attempt to wipe out (change) his destiny, king Citraketu[2] had to suffer (heavily).

40. Just as all the efforts of an unlucky person are frustrated, you will not be happy even after begetting a son. Despite this, you are still insistent, what should I call a seeker like you ?"

41. Observing his determined insistence (on begetting a son), the recluse gave him a fruit and instructed, "Make your wife eat this fruit. She will give birth to a son".

42. "Your wife must observe for a period of one year the vows of truthfulness, cleanliness, compassion, almsgiving, and eating one meal per day—thereby she will beget a son of extremely pious nature".

43. Saying these words, the *yogī* went his way. Return-

---

1. This refers to Sagara's grief when his sixty thousand sons were burnt to ashes by Kapila.

It is better to take *Aṅga* as a term of address.

2. King of Śūrasena who was childless even though he had a million wives. To beget a son, he performed a sacrifice with the help of sage Aṅgiras. He got a son who was poisoned by one of his wives through rivalry. For details vide Bh. P. 6.14-16.

ing home, the Brāhmaṇa handed over the fruit to his wife and went away somewhere.

44. His wife, though youthful, was crooked by nature. She lamented before her (female) friend, "Oh I am worried with an anxiety. Hence I shall not eat the fruit.

45. By eating the fruit, I shall become pregnant and pregnancy will greatly increase the size of my belly. I shall have to be moderate in eating, which will lead to weakness. How can I be able to carry on my domestic work ?

46. How will it be possible for a pregnant woman to run in case there is unfortunately a sudden attack of dacoits on the village? In case the foetus stays on in the womb like the sage Śuka[1], how can she deliver it ?

47. If (at the time of the delivery) the foetus comes in a slanting position, I shall surely die. (Even otherwise) how can a lady of delicate health as I am, bear the extreme pangs of delivery ?

48. When I become less active (in advanced pregnancy and confinement after delivery) my husband's sister will take away everything belonging to me. The vows of truth, cleanliness and others appear to be very difficult for me to observe.

49. Even after safe delivery, there is a lot of trouble in rearing up a child. It is my opinion that a barren woman and a widow are the really happy women.

50. With such a fallacious reasoning, the fruit was not eaten by her. When she was asked by her husband whether she ate up the fruit, she replied that she had.

51-52. One day, her sister happend to come to her house, of her own accord. She narrated everything to her and said, "The anxiety(to cover-up the deceitfulness towards her husband) heavily weighs over my mind. I have become weak due to that worry. Oh (younger) sister ! What should I do now ?" She re-assured her, "I am pregnant. I shall give you the child after delivery.

53. Till that time stay comfortably at home pretending to be pregnant. Offer some money to my husband and he will hand over the child to you.

---

1. Śuka stayed for sixteen years in his mother's womb.— RN.

54. People will say that due to (premature) delivery in the sixth month, the child did not survive. I shall feed that child by visiting your house every now and then (for suckling it.)

55. With a view to verify the efficaciousness of the fruit, you give it now to the cow for eating." Due to her feminine nature, she carried out all the instructions of her sister.

56. In due course, the woman gave birth to a child which its father brought secretly and handed over to Dhundhulī.

57. She reported to her husband that she had an easy delivery. People became happy to learn that Ātmadeva begot a child.

58. He performed the requisite ceremony at the birth of a child (*jāta-karma*) and presented gifts to Brāhmaṇas. There was a fanfare of musical instruments and songs before his door and many auspicious rites were performed by the couple.

59. She complained to her husband as follows, "There is no milk in my breasts. I myself being milkless, how can I feed the child with the milk of another (unrelated) woman ?

60. My sister gave birth to a child which has expired. Inviting her, request her to stay in our house, so that she will give suck to your baby."

61. For the protection of his son, he carried out thoroughly whatever was told to him. The mother called her son as 'Dhundhukārī'.

62. Later on, after a period of three months, the cow gave birth to a (human) child which was beautiful and shapely in all the parts of its body, brilliant, clean and pure and resplendent like gold in complexion.

63. On seeing the child, the Brāhmaṇa was so pleased that he personally performed all the ceremonials (like *jāta-karma*) pertaining to the birth of a child. Thinking it (the birth of human child from a cow) as a miracle, all people came to see him.

64. "Look here ! How good luck has now oome to the lot of Ātmadeva ? Certainly it is miraculous that a god-like child is born of a cow."

65. Fortunately nobody came to know the secret (of this wonderful phenomenon). Seeing that the child had its ears like those of a cow, he (the Brāhmaṇa) called him 'Gokarṇa'.

66. In course of time, when the sons attained youth, Gokarṇa became a wise, learned scholar, while Dhundhukārī, a very wicked fellow.

67. He was lacking in (the habit of) taking (regular) bath and (observing the rules of) cleanliness and good behaviour. He used to eat prohibited things and always flared up in rage (if advised). He accepted undesirable gifts[1] and ate food touched by the hand of a dead body.[2]

68. He stole things, hated all people, set fire to other people's houses, and taking young children (apparently) to fondle, he used to throw them into wells immediately.

69. With lethal weapons in hand, he used to kill (living beings). He greatly harassed the blind and distressed people. He delighted in the company of Cāṇḍalas (people of the lowest caste) and always carried a noose in his hands and was accompanied with dogs.

70. He squandered his ancestral property in the company of prostitutes. One day, he belaboured his parents and carried off the utensils (from his house) himself.

71. It is reported that when his miserly father[3] was deprived of wealth, he bewailed loudly, "Childlessness is preferable to a wicked son who is a veritable source of trouble.

72. Where should I stay? Where should I go? Who will relieve me of my miseries? What a calamity has befallen me? I shall commit suicide due to this distress."

73. At that time, the learned Gokarṇa approached his

---

1. RN quotes *Brahmāṇḍa P.* to enumerate such gifts :
tila-dhenur gajo vājī pretānnam ajinaṁ maṇiḥ !
surabhiḥ sūyamānā ca duṣṭāḥ sapta-prati-grahāḥ //

2. RN. explains that this is a custom in certain parts of the country but v.l. *savya-hastena* 'eating with the left hand', is easier.

3. RN. quotes a *nīti*-work and explains that a person who gives food, protects from fear, offers his daughter, imparts instruction and initiates in a sacred formula (*mantra*) — all these are regarded as fathers.

father and elucidating the efficacy of renunciation, he tried to admonish his father.

74. "This *saṁsāra* is certainly unsubstantial, full of miseries and induces infatuation. A man is not the controller of his son and property (lit. whose is the son and whose is the property?). A person attached to them consumes day and night (as if with fire).

75. Indra (the Lord of heaven) does not enjoy the slightest pleasure; nor does so the emperor of the world. There is real pleasure (in the life of) a sage who is dispassionate and leads a secluded life.

76. Give up your ignorance in the form of (attachment to) your progeny, for delusion leads to hell. This body is going to fall (one day). Therefore, discarding everything, repair to the forest."

77. Hearing Gokarṇa's words, his father, being desirous of going to the forest, asked, "Oh child, explain to me in details, what I should do while living in the jungle.

78. I, being ignorant, was bound down by the ties of affection and thus being crippled I was pushed by my past actions into the dark well of *saṁsāra*. A receptacle of compassion as you are, do lift me up."

Gokarṇa said :

79. Discard the notion of your identification with the body which is composed of bones, flesh and blood. Give up completely and forever your idea of mine-ness with regard to your wives, sons etc. Perceiving the ever-momentariness of the world, take interest in sweet renunciation and be thoroughly established in your devotion to the Lord.

80. Giving up worldly duties, always resort unflinchingly to the path of righteousness—Render service to saintly persons. Give up your thirst for worldly pleasures. Immediately cease to brood over the merits and demerits of other persons, and drink to the full the sweet juice of Hari's stories.

81. Leaving his house in response to the admonition of his son, he retreated to a forest with a firm determination, even though he was more than sixty. Being engaged every day

in the worship of Hari, he become one with Kṛṣṇa by readin g regularly the tenth Skandha of the *Bhāgavata Purāṇa*.

CHAPTER FIVE

(*Gokarṇa attains to Go-loka*)

1. After the retirement of his father (to a forest), Dhundhukārī beat his mother soundly (and demanded), "Tell me where money is deposited, else I shall kick you down (to death)."

2. Alarmed at his threat, and being distressed with the harassment meted out (to her) by her son, she flung herself in a well at night, and thereby met with death.

3. Gokarṇa who established himself in *yoga*, set out foı pilgrimage to holy places. He transcended (the duality of) pleasure and pain. He had neither an enemy nor a friend.

4. Surrounded by (i.e. in the company of) five prostitutes, he continued to stay in the house. His mind got confused with (the anxiety of) the maintenance of those prostitutes and he began to commit the most heinous crimes.

5-6. Once those unchaste women expressed their desire to get ornaments from him. He, being blinded with passion and forgetful of his death, went out of the house to get them. Thieving wealth from various places, he returned to his house and gave to them many costly garments and ornaments.

7. Seeing the heap of enormous wealth, the women conspired that very night, "This man is a regular thief. Hence the king will get him apprehended.

8. It is certain that after confiscating wealth he will surely kill him. Hence why should he not be killed by us secretly, for the preservation of his wealth.

9-10. After killing him and distributing his wealth (among ourselves), we shall go wherever we are pleased to go." Determining thus, they bound him with cords while he was asleep and placing the noose round his neck, they strangled him. But he did not die immediately. So they became full of anxiety.

11. They threw a heap of burning coals over his face. Being extremely tormented by the flames of fire, he was overwhelmed with distress and he succumbed to death.

12. They interred that (dead) body into a pit, as women are generally brutal and wreckless. Their clandestine acts cannot be known by any one. So was the case with this as well.

13. When people enquired, they used to tell, "Our dear lord being induced by his greed for wealth, has gone to some distant land, and would return within a year."

14. A wise man should never place his reliance on women even though they be dead. The fool who puts his trust in them, is overwhelmed with calamities.

15. Who is dear to (young) women whose words are full of nectarine sweetness, whetting the feeling of love of the lustful, but whose heart is (sharp and cutting) like a razor-blade ?

16. Those prostitutes with many customer-husbands absconded along with Dhundhukārī's wealth, while he became a hideous, dreadful goblin as a consequence of his evil deeds.

17. In the form of a tempestuous wind and tormented by cold and heat of the sun, and without any food and drink, he ran all the while (hither and thither) in ten directions.

18. Calling upon his fate ('Ah ! misfortune') now and then, he did not find an asylum anywhere. After some time, Gokarṇa learnt from the people about his death.

19. Apprehending the forlorn plight of Dhundhukārī's spirit, he performed the *Śrāddha* ceremony specifically for him at Gayā. And whatever sacred place he (Gokarṇa) visited, he performed a *Śrāddha* for him.

20. In the course of his journey, Gokarṇa came to his native town, and reached the courtyard of his house for sleeping at night, without being noticed by others.

21. Perceiving that his brother had slept there, Dhundhukārī manifested to him his most terrific form at midnight.

22. Once, he assumed the form of a ram; again he

appeared as an elephant; then he revealed himself as a he-buffalo; at one time he appeared as the lord of gods; another time, as the fire-god and then he assumed the human form.

23. Observing this inauspicious perversity, the pious Gokarṇa concluded that this must be some unfortunate hellish being and addressed him thus.

Gokarṇa said :

24. "Who are you assuming extra-terrific forms at night ? As a consequence of what actions, you are reduced to such a stage ? Tell me whether you are a ghost or a fiend or a demon ?"

Sūta said :

25. It is reported that when thus enquired by him, the ghost now and then cried at the top of its voice, and that due to his inability to speak, he made gestures only.

26. Then Gokarṇa took some water in his folded palms and sprinkled it on the ghost. His sins being reduced by the sprinkling (of the sacred) water, the ghost began to speak.

The ghost said :

27. I am your brother Dhundhukārī by name. It is through my own fault that I forfeited my Brāhmaṇa-hood.

28. Innumerable are the misdeeds committed by me due to my being merged in deep ignorance. I, a murderer of people, was tortured to death by women (prostitutes).

29. As a result, I was reduced to the state of a ghost which plight I am suffering now. I live upon the air now, for as per ordinance of destiny, the fruits of my actions are becoming effective now.

30. Oh brother, you are an ocean of compassion! Please redeem instantly your distressed brother." Hearing his speech, Gokarṇa replied as follows :

Gokarṇa said :

31. It is a great wonder to me as to why you have not been redeemed, when I have offered the ball of cooked rice as an oblation for you, as per scriptural injunction at Gayā.

32. If no salvation results as a consequence of a *Śrāddha* at Gayā, no other remedy exists in this world at all. Oh spirit ! Tell me in details, what should be done by me, for you.

The spirit replied :

33. "My redemption will not take effect even if you perform hundreds of *Śrāddhas* at Gayā. Now think about some other remedy."

34. Hearing his words, Gokarṇa was wonder-struck (and said) : "If no redemption is possible through the performance of hundreds of *Śrāddhas* (at Gayā), then your salvation is an impossibility.

35. However, you may fearlessly stay in your own place, Oh spirit, while I shall consider over the matter and do something which will lead you to liberation."

36. As per Gokarṇa's advice, Dhundhukārī retired to his own place. Gokarṇa pondered over the remedy that night but could not find any clue.

37. The next morning, finding that he had arrived, people came to see him, out of friendliness. He narrated to them everything as to what (and how) had taken place the previous night.

38. Learned persons, experts in *Yoga*, specialists in *Śāstric* lores, and Vedāntins referred to their *Śāstric* texts, but did not discover any expedient for the redemption (of Dhundhukārī).

39. Then the decision of the Sun-god regarding the salvation (of Dhundhukārī) came to be regarded as the final by all. They say that Gokarṇa then restrained the velocity of the Sun-god.

40. "Oh witness of the world ! I bow to you. Be pleased to tell me some expedient for redeeming (my brother)". Hearing that, the sun-god replied in a distinctly audible voice, from far above.

41. "Redemption will result from (the reading) of *Śrīmad Bhāgavata*. This religious guidance of the Sun-god was distinctly heard by all.

42. All (unanimously) opined, "It is easy. This should

be done with full efforts." Determining (that this recitation will lead to the ghost's salvation Gokarṇa set out to read the *Bhāgavata*.

43. With the object of listening to it, people from (different parts of) the country and villages, assembled there. It is reported that (physically handicapped persons like) the lame, the blind as well as old persons and mentally retarded ones also came to annihilate their sins.

44-45. The assembly of listeners was so big that even gods were wonder-struck. When Gokarṇa occupied his seat and began to tell the story (of the *Bhāgavata*) the evil spirit (of Dhundhukārī) came there. Looking for a seat here and there, he found a tall bamboo with seven joints, standing there.

46. Entering in a hole at the root of that bamboo, he occupied it with a view to listen (to the *Bhāgavata*). As it was not possible for him to remain stable in his airy form, he got into the bamboo.

47. Regarding a Brāhmaṇa devotee of Viṣṇu as the chief member of the audience, Gokarṇa, the son of a cow, began the story (of the *Bhāgavata*) from the first *Skandha*, in a distinctly loud tone.

48. In the evening when (the exposition was adjourned and) the text (of the *Bhāgavata*) was being kept covered, a marvellous incident took place. While all the pious members of the audience were looking on, one knot (out of the seven joints) of the bamboo cracked loudly.

49. In the evening of the second day, there was the cracking of the second joint. Similarly on the third day, at the time of sun-set, the third joint burst open.

50. In this way the seven joints of the bamboo were burst open; and as a fruit of listening to the twelve *Skandhas* of the *Bhāgavata*, even the evil spirit cast off his fiendish body.

51. He assumed a divine form dark like a cloud in complexion, adorned with wreaths of the *Tulasī* plant, wearing yellow (silken) garments, a diadem on the head, and ear-rings in his ears.

52. He immediately bowed down to his brother Gokarṇa

and said, "Oh brother ! I have been redeemed from the sinful ghost-hood by you, out of kindness.

53. Blessed is the story of the *Bhāgavata* which annihilates all the agonies of an evil spirit. So is blessed the *Bhāgavata-week* which confers Vaikuṇṭha (Kṛṣṇa's realm) as an abode to the listeners.

54. When a person attends the *Bhāgavata-week* all the sins begin to tremble (saying), "Now the story of the *Bhāgavata* will instantaneously and thoroughly eradicate us."

55. Just as the fire burns down sacrificial sticks wet or dry, small or big, so does listening to the *Bhāgavata* reduce to ashes all sinful acts done by word, deed or mind, whether knowingly or unknowingly, committed with respect to beings great or small.

56. "Fruitless is the life of a person who, though born in the Bhārata-varṣa, does not listen to the story of the *Bhāgavata*." This has been declared by the wise in the concourse of Brāhmaṇas (and by Bṛhaspati in the assembly of gods).

57. What is the use of this transitory body protected through deluding affection, well-nourished and strengthened, if the story of the scripture of Śuka (the *Bhāgavata*) be not heard ?

58. Built on the column-like skeleton of bones, bound up with (the tendons of) muscles, plastered with flesh and blood and covered with skin, this body is a stinking receptacle of urine and faeces.

59. It is always afflicted through the effects of age and sorrow, the very home of diseases, sick or injured, never satisfied, difficult to maintain, censurable, defective and momentary.

60. The body is generally described as that which ends in worms (if buried), excretion (if eaten by carnivorous animals) and ashes (if cremated). Why should not one accomplish acts leading to stability with this unstable (instrument).

61. The food that is cooked in the morning gets rotten in the evening. How can the body which is nourished on the liquid (essence) of such food, possess permanence ?

62. By listening to the *Bhāgavata* in the (prescribed)

course of a week, Lord Hari is just near one's self in this world. Hence the above week is the only expedient for removing all blemishes and sins.

63. Those who failed to listen to the *Bhāgavata* story are born only to meet death like bubbles in the water or mosquitoes in living beings.

64. Is there anything miraculous that the knots in the (living) heart are resolved by listening to the *Bhāgavata Kathā* when dead material like a dry bamboo is broken up at the joints.

65. When one listens to the *Bhāgavata* in the *Bhāgavata* week, the knot in the heart gets cut asunder, all the doubts are resolved, and all his vicious actions become extinct.

66. It has been stated (lit. remembered) by the wise that it is liberation itself when the sacred water in the form of the story of the *Bhāgavata* is stored up in one's mind—the story which most effectively deterges the dirty stains caused by the contact of mud (evil acts committed) in *saṁsāra*.

67. It is reported that even as he (the angelised Dhundhukārī) was speaking thus, a celestial car radiant with extremely brilliant halo and carrying residents of Vaikuṇṭha arrived there.

68. Even while all were looking on, Dhundhukārī (the son of Dhundhulī) ascended that aerial car. Seeing the votaries of Viṣṇu in that car, Gokarṇa addressed the following words.

Gokarṇa said :

69. At this very place, there are many sinless members of my audience. Why are not celestial cars brought for them simultaneously ?

70. May the beloved ones of Hari explain why there is inequality in accruing the fruit (of the *Bhāgavata* week) when it is seen that all of them equally participated in listening (to the *Bhāgavata*).

The servants of Hari explained :

71. The variation in getting the reward is caused by the disparity in listening. It has been simply heard by all, but

has not been pondered over with (an equal degree of) devotion.

72. Oh courteous Gokarṇa ! The distinction in receiving the fruit varies according to the (intensity of) adoration. The evil spirit heard the *Bhāgavata* while observing fast for seven days.

73. He has deeply meditated over it with a steady concentrated mind. Spiritual knowledge if not firmly imbibed is not fruitful. The same is the case with inattentive listening.

74. An incantation (*mantra*) not handed down through the tradition of competent spiritual preceptors or an advice received with a doubtful mind is ineffective. Muttering of sacred syllables with distracted mind is useless. Wretched is the country where votaries of Viṣṇu do not live. Wasteful is the *Śrāddha* if the food is offered to an unworthy recipient.

75-76. Gifts donated to a Brāhmaṇa not well-versed in the Vedas are fruitless. The family which is lacking in proper behaviour, is doomed.

Firm faith in the words of the spiritual preceptor, feeling of humility about one's own self ; control of evil mental tendencies, unflinching devotion in listening to the *Bhāgavata*—if such and like conditions are observed, then alone the listening to the *Bhāgavata* becomes efficacious.

77. By the end of the next listening (to the *Bhāgavata*-week), they will certainly (attain to and) reside in the Vaikuṇṭha. Oh Gokarṇa, the Lord Viṣṇu (Govinda) will personally take you to the *Go-loka*.

78. Having explained thus, all those glorifiers of Hari ascended to Vaikuṇṭha. In the (next) month of Śrāvaṇa, Gokarṇa rècited the story (and the exposition) of the *Bhāgavata* again (in a week).

79. For seven nights (i.e. a week) they listened to it again (in accordance with the prescribed conditions). Oh Nārada, now listen to what happend at the conclusion of the story (i.e. the end of the *Bhāgavata* week).

80. Lord Hari manifested himself, accompanied by his votaries and celestial cars. There were loud shouts in chorus,

a continuous loud acclaim of the words *jaya* (victory to) and *namaḥ* (bow to), to express greetings and respect.

81. Out of joy Lord Hari blew his conch Pāñcajanya there and embracing Gokarṇa, Hari gave him a form similar to himself.

82. In a moment, Lord Hari made other members of the audience dark-blue like clouds in complexion, clad in yellow silken garment, wearing diadems on the head and ear-rings in their ears (like himself).

83. All beings, including dogs and *Cāṇḍālas* who were living in that village, were accommodated in the celestial cars through the compassionate favour of Gokarṇa, and were taken to Vaikuṇṭha, the realm of Hari which the *yogīs* attain (at the end of their life).

84. Lord Viṣṇu, the divine cowherd, so kind to his devotees, who was highly pleased by listening to the story (of the *Bhāgavata*) from Gokarṇa, took Gokarṇa with himself to *Go-loka* which is so dear to cowherds.

85. Just as formerly all the residents of Ayodhyā accompanied Rāma, so did Kṛṣṇa take them all to his realm called *Go-loka* which is difficult even for *yogīs* to attain.

86. Due to their (proper) listening to *Śrīmad Bhāgavata* all of them attained to that (highest) realm which is inaccessible to the Sun, the Moon and the *Siddhas*.

87. How is it possible for us to describe to you all the glorious rewards stored in the stories of the *Bhāgavata* narrated during the sacrifice called the *Bhāgavata-week*. Those who have drunk with their ears even a single syllable of the story of the *Bhāgavata* as explained by Gokarṇa do not return to *Saṁsāra* (lit. to the mother's womb in the next birth).

88. People who listen to the recitation (and exposition of the *Bhāgavata*) during the course of the *Bhāgavata*-week attain to the highest realm to which other persons cannot reach even by subsisting on air, water, dry leaves, thus emaciating their bodies, and by performing austere penance extending over a very long period, and through Yogic practices as well.

89. Even the great sage Śāṇḍilya who is submerged in the spiritual bliss of Brahman, reads (regularly) this sanctifying story on the mount Citrakūṭa.

90. If this extremely sacred story (of the *Bhāgavata*) is heard only once, it burns down all the mass of sins. If recited at the time of the performance of the *Śrāddha* ceremony, it brings thorough satisfaction to the forefathers. If it is devoutly read every day, it terminates the *saṁsāra* (the cycle of births and deaths).

CHAPTER SIX

(*The Procedure of Listening to the Bhāgavata*)

1. Now we shall explain to you in details the correct procedure of (properly) listening in the *Bhāgavata*-week. It has been laid down that this procedure is to be accomplished with the help of friends and (expenditure) of wealth.

2. Inviting an astrologer and discussing with him the auspicious time (for the beginning of the recitation of the *Bhāgavata*), one should set aside that much amount (for the *Bhāgavata*-week) as is required for the marriage ceremony (of one's daughter).

3. Bhādrapada, Āśvina, Kārttika, Mārgaśīrṣa, Āṣāḍha and Śrāvaṇa—these months for the beginning of the recitation of the story of the *Bhāgavata*, indicate the final liberation of the member of the audience.

4. Those (objectionable) objects (e.g. vegetables in the month of Śrāvaṇa, curds in the month of Bhādrapada) should be given up during the course of those specific months. One should secure the cooperation of other help-mates who are enthusiastic and industrious.

5. The message that there is going to be the recitation of the *Bhāgavata* story at this place and that they should come alongwith their families, should be sent to different places with special efforts.

6. Those who are away from the listening to the stories of Hari and also from chanting the name of Acyuta (and thus are denied the opportunity), women and persons belonging to

the lowest castes, should receive the knowledge (i.e. news) of the *Bhāgavata*-week.

7. Letters should be directed to various places to persons who have renounced the world and the votaries of Viṣṇu who are eager for chanting his name. The draft of the letter is stated as follows :

8-10. "There is going to be a very rare congregation of pious persons for the period of one week. Here is also going to be the recitation of the *Bhāgavata* story of unprecedented sweetness. Your honours who are addicted to drinking the nectar (of God's name and are deep in love of God should come quickly for drinking the ambrosia in the form of *Śrī Bhāgavata*. If you have no time to spare, you should, however, come atleast for one day, for a moment's attendance here is very difficult to get."

11. In this way, invitations should be courteously sent to them. Lodging arrangements of all (the probable) guests should be made.

12. The arrangements for listening to the exposition of the *Bhāgavata* should be made at a sacred place, or in a forest, or even at home. Where there is an extensive ground, the venue of the exposition of the *Bhāgavata* story should be fixed at that place.

13. The ground should be cleansed, swept, plastered with cowdung and painted with red chalk. The furniture and other things in the house should be placed in the corner of the house.

14. Some five days in advance, one should collect with efforts, carpets etc., to cover the ground. A high pandal decorated with the stems of banana trees, should be erected.

15. It should be decorated with a canopy and (pendents, wreaths etc., of) fruits, flowers and leaves on all sides. Flags should be hoisted on four sides, and thus the pendal should be gorgeously beautified.

16. Ascending series of seven platforms (in the pendal) representing the seven upper worlds (e.g. *bhūr-loka, bhuvar-loka, svar-loka* and others in the universe) should be constructed and Brāhmaṇas and renunciators (of the worldly life) should be requested and seated there.

17. Preceding that, seats should be provided one after another (on those platforms) and an excellent seat (overlooking all) should be prepared for the exponent (of the *Bhāgavata*).

18. If the expositor (of the *Bhāgavata*) faces the north, the audience should face to the east and vice versa. (If the exponent faces the east, the audience should face the north).

19. Experts in the knowledge of time, place etc., have declared their decision that according to *Āgamas* the East is presumed to lie between the worshippers (members of the audience) and the exponent of the *Bhāgavata*.

20. The exponent selected should be a Brāhmaṇa votary of Viṣṇu who has renounced the world, and can explain difficult points in *Vedas* and *Śāstras*, expert in giving appropriate illustrations (in elucidating a matter), an intelligent orator completely free from avarice and cravings.

21. Persons who themselves are confused by different paths of religion, are excessively fond of women, profess heresies, are disqualified for even uttering the text of the *Bhāgavata* (the story of Śuka's scripture), even if they are otherwise learned ones.

22. By the side of and as a help to the exponent (of the *Bhāgavata*), another learned Brāhmaṇa equal in competence to the exponent who is capable of resolving the doubts (of the audience) and diligent in enlightening the people, should be installed.

23. With a view to carry out the sacred vow (of reciting and explaining the *Bhāgavata* in the prescribed week), the (proposed) exponent should get himself shaved on the previous day. At dawn, he should complete his morning duties and take bath.

24. After briefly completing his morning prayers (*sandhyā*), he should with special attention (and efforts) worship the god Gaṇeśa elaborately, for removing the difficulties (if any) in the recitation of the *Bhāgavata*.

25. After the usual oblations of water offered for the satisfaction of his forefathers, he should go through expiatory rites for his personal purification. He should draw the *sarvatobhadra* type of mystical diagram for invoking Hari, and should instal (the representation of) Lord Hari therein.

26. Observing the (sixteen items in the) prescribed course of worship, he should adore Kṛṣṇa muttering the specific *mantras* (incantatious). After circumambulating him, and lying prostrate before him (to show respect), he should recite the (following) prayer:

27. "Oh ocean of compassion ! I, a wretched person, am merged in the ocean of *saṁsāra*, and my body is seized by the crocodile in the form of *Karma*. (Kindly) lift me up from the ocean of the mundane existence."

28. Then, the worship of the book — *Śrīmad Bhāgavata* should be performed with devotional love and enthusiasm, according to the prescribed procedure, lighting before it the lamp and burning incense.

29. Holding a cocoanut fruit in the palm of his hands, he should then pay his respects. He should then offer his prayer (*Śrīmad Bhāgavata*) with a happy mind.

30. "This (Book) is veritably Lord Kṛṣṇa himself under the designation *Śrīmad Bhāgavata*. Oh Lord ! you have been resorted to by me, for liberation from the ocean of Saṁ śāra.

31. Oh Keśava ! I am your servant. My earnest desire (to complete the recitation and exposition of the *Bhāgavata* within this week) without any obstacle or difficulty, may please be fulfilled by you in every respect."

32. After submitting this humble prayer, one should worship the proposed reciter and adoring him with dress and ornaments, should pray him (as follows) at the end of worship:

33. "Oh representative of the sage Śuka ! You are well-versed in all *Śāstras* and expert in elucidating. Be pleased to dispel my ignorance by enlightening me in this story (the *Bhāgavata*)."

34. In his presence, some religious observance should be gladly undertaken for one's spiritual good, and that should be abided by to the best of one's ability for the period of a week.

35. In order to forestall any break in the exposition of the story (the *Bhāgavata*), five Brahmaṇas should be appointed, their duty being continuously uttering in a low voice the twelve-syllabled *Mantra*, viz. *Om namo bhagavate Vāsudevāya*.

36. Having bowed and duly adored Brāhmaṇas, devotees of Viṣṇu and others who are chanting the name of God, one should occupy one's seat with their permission.

37. A listener who, setting aside all anxiety and thoughts pertaining to the world, wealth, property, houses and progeny, concentrates his mind on the exposition of the story (*Bhāgavata*) and is of pure heart, obtains the highest reward.

38. Commencing (the recitation of the *Bhāgavata*), the intelligent reciter should properly read the (*Bhāgavata*) story in a calm and steady voice, upto the end of three and half *praharas* (Ten hours and a half).

39. There should be a break for a period of two *ghaṭikās* (48 minutes) at mid-day. During that interval singing about the glories of Hari and chanting of his name should be continued by votaries of Viṣṇu.

40. Moderate and light diet is conducive to the control of the urge for urination and clearing of bowels. Hence diet consisting of food prescribed for sacrificial oblations should be taken only once, by one who desires to listen (to the *Bhāgavata*).

41. If one has the requisite stamina, one should listen to the *Bhāgavata* without taking any food for seven days (of the *Bhāgavata* week), as one may do so with ease subsisting only on ghee or milk (during that period).

42. The *Bhāgavata* may be listened to while subsisting on fruits or by taking food once a day; whichever vow can be comfortably observed during the period of listening (to the *Bhāgavata*) should be taken.

43. In my opinion, if taking of meals (during the *Bhāgavata* week) is conducive to (attentively) listening to the exposition of the story (*Bhāgavata*), it is preferable to observance of fast if it comes in the way of hearing the *Bhāgavata*, and as such it is not recommended.

44. Oh Nārada! Now listen to the rules of conduct to be observed by persons who have taken the vow of (listening to the recitation during the *Bhāgavata* week). Persons who have not received initiation in Viṣṇu worship are not eligible to hear the *Bhāgavata*-story.

45. The observer of the vow of the *Bhāgavata* week

should (during that period) always remain celibate, sleep on the floor, and after the completion of the exposition of the *Bhāgavata* for that day, should take meals on leaves (stitched together or a big banana leaf).

46. The observer of this vow should abstain from eating pulses, honey, oil (undigestable sweet boiled food or) sweet dishes, food with mentally evil association (fruit with fleshy kernels or blood-red interior) and stale food (during the *Bhāgavata week*).

*47. The observer of this vow should not eat the egg-plant, flesh of birds or of animals killed with a poisoned weapon, burnt food, a kind of pulse called *masūra*, cowach (*niṣpāva* or Śuka-Śimbi)[1] and flesh.

*48. The observer of the vow of the Bhāgavata-week should give up eating onions, garlic, Asafoetida, carrots, a red variety of garlic (gṛñjana),[2] the stalks of lotus, beat-like red-coloured bulbous roots, *Kūṣmāṇḍa*[3] (a kind of pumpkin gourd).

*49. The observers of these vows should abstain from twice-cooked food, impure food (due to child-birth, etc., in the family) fish, meat, goat-milk and water from a pool.

50. The observer of the above-mentioned vow should give up (i.e. control completely) lust, anger, arrogance, conceit, jealousy, greed, hypocrisy, infatuation and hatred.

51. The observer of aforesaid vow should abstain from speaking ill of the Vedas, votaries of Viṣṇu, Brāhmaṇas, preceptors, dedicated servants of cows, women, kings and high souled persons.

52. The above-mentioned observer of vows should not talk with a woman in menstruation period, persons of the lowest castes, Mlecchas (foreigners eating beef), persons outlawed and fallen from their own castes, persons of the higher

* These are additional verses in the Bhagavata Vidya Peetha Ahmedabad edition; vv 47 and 48 in other editions are found as vv 50-51 in the Ahmedabad edition.

1 RN quotes *Śuka-Śimbi*, as the synonym of *niṣpāva*.
Śuka-Śimbi = cowach ASD, p. 560

2. *gṛñjana* ASD, p.190.

3. ASD, p.158

castes whose thread ceremony has not taken place, an enemy of Brāhmaṇas and persons not belonging to Vedic religion.

53. Such an observer of vows should observe truthfulness, purity (physical and mental), compassion, silence, straightforwardness, humility and show broad-mindedness.

54. A poverty-stricken person, one suffering from tuberculosis, a sufferer from disease, a luckless fellow, a sinner, a childless person and one desirous of Final Liberation, all these too should listen to the story of the *Bhāgavata*.

55. A prematurely non-menstruating woman, a woman incapable of conceiving more than one child, a barren woman, a woman whose all children are dead and a woman who miscarries—all such women should make special effort to listen to the *Bhāgavata*-story.

56. If the Bhāgavata-story is heard as per procedure mentioned above, they will reap an imperishable fruit. This most excellent divine story of the *Bhāgavata* is capable of bestowing the fruit of performing ten million sacrifices.

57. Having observed the procedure of this vow (alongwith rules of conduct) of the *Bhāgavata* week one should conclude it with performing the specific rites. Those who are desirous of getting the fruit of this *Bhāgavata* week should perform the concluding rites as are done at the time of concluding the *Janmāṣṭamī* fast (the birth anniversary of Lord Kṛṣṇa.)

58. There is generally no insistence on the performance of concluding rites of the *Bhāgavata* week in case of devotees of the Lord who possess nothing of their own. As the devotees of Viṣṇu are above desires, they are purified by merely listening to the *Bhāgavata*.

59. When the sacrifice in the form of the *Bhāgavata* week is completed, the members of the audience should worship the book (*the Bhāgavata*) and its reciter with utmost devotion.

60. Afterwards remnants of eatables offered to the deity, garlands of the Tulasī plant should be distributed to the members of the audience, and *Kīrtana* (singing of the glories of Hari and chanting his name) accompanied with musical

instruments like drums or tabors (*mṛdaṅga*) and cymbals be commenced.

61. 'Victory (to Hari)', 'Bow (to Hari)' — such shouts in chorus and blasts of conchs should be frequently raised. Money and food should be distributed to Brāhmaṇas, mendicants and beggars.

62. The next day the *Bhagavad Gītā* should be read if the chief listener has renounced the world. In case he be a a householder, oblations should be poured into the sacrificial fire for expiation of sins committed if any, during the course of the *Bhāgavata* week.

63. Reciting each verse of the Tenth Skandha of the *Bhāgavata*, oblations (per verse) of rice boiled in milk and mixed with honey, ghee, sesamum seeds and food-grains should be offered to the sacred fire.

64. Or inasmuch as the supreme (*Bhāgavata*) Purāṇa is essentially identical with *gāyatrī*, similar oblations should be offered while muttering the *gāyatrī mantra*, with concentrated mind.

65-66. In case, one is incapable of performing the *homa* (as described above), a wise man should give materials suitable for offering as oblations[1] for reaping the reward thereof. For plugging various loopholes (e.g. difficulties and defects in the recitations) and for rectifying and neutralising the lapses committed by omitting and adding unwarrantedly the text of the *Bhāgavata* he should recite *Viṣṇu-sahasra-nāma* (A list of thousand names of Viṣṇu).[2] By the recitation of the names of Viṣṇu everything becomes fruitful and there is nothing more powerful than the name of Viṣṇu.

67. (Thereafter) he should serve twelve Brāhmaṇas with meals consisting of sweet dishes and rice boiled in milk and sugar, after which he should offer them gold and a cow for the consummation of the vow.

---

1. RN quotes a Com. on *Āśvalāyana Sūtra* and enumerates the following articles suitable for oblations:
   payo dadhi yavāguśca sarpir odana-taṇḍulāḥ|
   * *somo māṁsaṁ tathā tailam āpo haumyaṁ prakīrtitam|*
   * a better v.l. *tailam āpaśca somaśca vrīhayaś'ca yavās tilāḥ|*
2. This is in the Mbh. and some Purāṇas.

68-71. If he can afford it, he should prepare a lion of gold weighing three *palas*[1]. The book (the *Bhāgavata*) written in a beautiful hand, should be placed on it. Worshipping the book by invoking the presence of the Deity and by performing other formalities (sixteen in all) including the gift of money, he should give it to the self-controlled exponent (of the *Bhāgavata*) after adoring him, by offering clothes, ornaments, sandal-paste etc. Thus the chief-listener becomes free from the bonds of *saṁsāra*. When the chief-listener completes all this procedure (of listening to the recitation of the *Bhāgavata* in the *Bhāgavata*-week) which wards off (and annihilates) all sins, the *Śrīmad Bhāgavata Purāṇa* accords auspicious rewards. There is no doubt that it is the means to attain (the four objectives in human life), viz. religious merits, worldly prosperity, fulfilment of all desires and liberation from *saṁsāra*.

The Kumāra sages said :

72. Thus everything has been narrated to you, what more do you wish to hear ? Enjoyment of worldly prosperity as well as liberation from *saṁsāra* both are on the palm of your hand through the *Śrīmad-Bhāgavata*.

Sūta said :

73-74. After addressing Nārada in this way, the high-souled *Kumāra*-sages recited and elucidated with due formality the sacred story of *Bhāgavata* which wipes out all sins and confers (on the listeners) worldly enjoyment (here) and Emancipation from *Saṁsāra* (here-after) while all living beings, observing self-control, were listening to it for seven days. Thus they glorified the Supreme Person, god Viṣṇu.

75. At the end of that *Bhāgavata*-week, *Jñāna* (knowledge), *Vairāgya* (Renunciation) and *Bhakti* (Devotion) got the highest nourishment and energy and exhibited superabundant youthfulness that enchanted the minds of all beings.

76. Having accomplished his cherished ambition, Nārada was deeply satisfied. He was filled with supreme bliss and his hair stood on their end all over his person.

1. **RN equates it with 192 māṣas.**

77. Having carefully listened to the (*Bhāgavata*) story, Nārada who was dear to the glorious Lord, folded his palms and addressed them in a voice choked with feeling of love.

Nārada said :

78. I am really blessed, since I have been favoured by you who are extremely compassionate. To-day the glorious Lord Hari, the destroyer of all sins, has been attained by me.

79. Oh sages who regard austerities as your wealth ! I think listening (to the *Bhāgavata*) is greater than and preferable to all other righteous paths, for Lord Kṛṣṇa who resides in Vaikuṇṭha is attained by listening to it.

Sūta said :

80. While Nārada, the foremost among Viṣṇu's devotees, was speaking thus, Śuka, the master *yogin* arrived there during the course of his wanderings.

81. At the end of the (recitation of the *Bhāgavata*) story, there came Śuka slowly reciting the *Bhāgavata*[1] with deep love—Śuka, the son of Vyāsa who always appears sixteen years of age, and who is like the Moon (bringing flow-tide) to the ocean of spiritual knowledge and who is perfectly satisfied with (the bliss of) self-realization.

82. As soon as the members of the assembly saw the highly resplendent Śuka, they immediately stood up (to show respect) and offered him the highest seat. The divine sage Nārada (received) him with great love and reverence. When seated comfortably, he spoke out. Listen to his pure, faultless speech.

Śrī Śuka said :

83[1]. This (*Bhāgavata Purāṇa*) is the (ripe) fruit of the wish-yielding tree of the Vedas, that has been dropped down from the mouth of (the sage) Śuka (as from the mouth of a parrot=*Śuka*), that is replete with ambrosial juice (viz. the highest bliss). Oh appreciators of beauty ! The connoisseurs

1. The same as *Bhāgavata Purāṇa* 1-1.3. For other interpretation vide the Foot-notes to that verse.

of its (i.e. of the *Bhāgavata Purāṇa*) peculiar excellences, you do drink constantly this *Bhāgavata*—a fruit which is entirely a sweet juice—here and in the state of Final Beatitude.

84. Here in this celebrated *Bhāgavata* composed by the great sage, is explained the highest path of righteousness, completely free from deceit, viz. interest about this world and even the desire about liberation. Here the thing to be known is the absolute Reality. It gives the highest bliss and destroys the three kinds of miseries. Can the Supreme Lord be realized in the heart immediately by the teaching of other treatises? No. But in this (*Bhāgavata*) he can be so comprehended at once by the meritorious who have a desire tohear (and study) this.[1]

85. *Śrīmad Bhāgavata* is the ornament (the most distinguished) of the *Purāṇas*. It is the (real) wealth of the devotees of Viṣṇu. In it is glorified the supreme, pure knowledge which is the goal of *Paramahaṁsas* (recluses of the highest order). Here is celebrated the cessation of activities coupled with knowledge, renunciation and devotion. By listening to it, reading it carefully and pondering over it, a man attains to Final Beatitude through devotion (*bhakti*).

86. This nectarine juice in the form of the *Bhāgavata* is not available in the heaven, in Satya-loka (god Brahmā's abode), in Kailāsa (the residence of Lord Śiva) and (even) in Vaikuṇṭha (the abode of Lord Viṣṇu). Hence, drink deeply, O fortunate ones. Please do not give up drinking.

Sūta said :

87. While Śuka, the son of Bādarāyaṇa (Vyāsa) was telling in this way, Lord Hari, surrounded by Prahlāda, Bali, Uddhava, Arjuna and other devotees, manifested himself in the midst of the congregation, and the celestial sage Nārada worshipped them all.

88. Noticing that Lord Hari who occupied a great and top-most seat, was in a happy mood, they began to chant his name and glorify his deeds in front of him. God Śiva, god-

1. This verse is the same as Bhāgavata Purāṇa 1.1.2.
For various interpretations vide *infra* Bh.P.1.1.2.

dess Bhavānī (Pārvatī) and God Brahmā (the lotus-seated God) arrived there to attend the *Kīrtana* (chanting the name and glorifying the deeds of the Lord).

89. Prahlāda was beating time with the clapping of hands, while Uddhava, due to his quickness of speed, held the brass cymbals. The celestial sage Nārada played on his *vīṇā* (lute), Arjuna, the expert in tunes, presented sweet vocal music ; Indra played upon the tabor (*mṛdaṅga*), the Kumāra-sages raised in chorus, in melodious voice, the shouts of 'victory to the Lord' at (appropriate) intervals in the *Kīrtana* ; while Śuka, the son of Vyāsa, stood in front of the Lord expressing different emotions in his charming composition.

90. There in the middle of that assembly, danced like dancers, the trio—Bhakti, (Jñāna and Vairāgya) who were in the full bloom of their youthful splendour. Observing this extraordinary transcendental *Kīrtana*, Lord Hari also was highly pleased and addressed them as follows :

91. "Oh my devotees (*Bhāgavatāḥ*) ! I am now highly pleased with the (recitation of the *Bhāgavata*) story and the chanting and glorification of my name (*Kīrtana*). Seek any boon from me". Hearing these words of Hari, they were greatly delighted and their minds being overwhelmed with devotional love, they spoke to Lord Hari :

92. "You should completely satisfy our earnest desire that in all (future) recitations and expositions of the *Bhāgavata*, you should make it a point to be present with all your devotees (without fail)". Assenting to their request (in words "Be it so"), Lord Hari disappeared (instantly).

93. Thereupon Nārada bowed to (i.e. in the direction of) the feet of Hari as well as to Śuka and other ascetics. All the members of the audience who drank the nectar-like story of the *Bhāgavata* became extremely delighted and had all their delusions completly dispelled and left the assembly.

94. Then Bhakti (Devotion) along with her sons (*Jñāna* and *Vairāgya*) was established (for their protection) in his own scripture (the *Bhāgavata*) by Śuka. Hence, Hari definitely enters (and occupies) the hearts of his devotees when they recite the *Bhāgavata*.

95. Verily the Bhāgavata loudly proclaims its power

to secure eternal happiness to persons tormented with the burning fever of poverty and misery, to those who are trampled under the feet by the ogress *Māyā* (the deluding potency of the Lord), and to those thrown in the ocean of this cycle of births and deaths.

Śaunaka asked :

96. Be pleased to resolve my doubt (about the chronological sequence) as to when the *Bhāgavata* was narrated by Śuka to king Parīkṣit, when it was recited again by Gokarṇa and also when it was recounted by Sanatkumāra and other sons of Brahmā to Nārada ?

97. When thirty years of Kali age which started since the passing away of Kṛṣṇa, elapsed, Śuka began to narrate the story of the Bhāgavata from the nineth day in (the bright half of the month) *Bhādrapada*.

98. Two centuries of Kali age, after the completion of Parīkṣit's hearing of the *Bhāgavata*, Gokarṇa began the recitation of the story of the *Bhāgavata* from the nineth day in the bright fortnight of *Āṣāḍha*.

99. When thirty years of Kali age rolled away (after Gokarṇa's exposition of the *Bhāgavata*), the sons of God Brahmā (viz. Sanatkumāra, Sanaka and others) began the (aforesaid) recitation (and elucidation) of the *Bhāgavata* from the nineth day in the bright half of *Kārttika*.

100. In this way whatever has been asked by you to me has been completely explained to you. Oh sinless Śaunaka ! The story of the *Bhāgavata* is a panacea to the ailment of *saṁsāra* in the Kali age.

101. Oh saintly persons ! Drink with deep (devotional) respect this (nectar-like) story (of the *Bhāgavata*) which is so beloved of Kṛṣṇa and which destroys all sins and defects and is the sole means to attain liberation from *Saṁsāra* and which exhibits the beauty of Devotion. What, on earth, are you going to gain by visiting and staying at holy places?

102. It is traditionally reported that noticing his officer ready with a noose in his hand (to take away the life of man on the earth), Yama (the god of Death) whispers in his ear, "Avoid people who are inebriated with the joy in stories of

the Lord, for I am not competent to exercise authority on (the lives of) the devotees of Viṣṇu but have mastery over other persons (only)".

103. Oh people with minds afflicted with attachment to the poison-like worldly pleasures in this unsubstantial world! Please do drink, for at least half a *Kṣaṇa*, the incomparable nectar of the *Bhāgavata* (narration of Śuka) for your spiritual welfare. Oh! Why are you unnecessarily going to the wrong (heretic) path replete with censurable talks? King Parīkṣit will testify to the statement that liberation from *saṁsāra* is attained as soon as the story of the *Bhāgavata* reaches the ear.

104. The story of the *Bhāgavata* was narrated by Śrī-Śuka who was immenred in the flow of the sentiment (of Devotion — *bhakti-rasa*). He who gets his voice associated with (i.e. recites) that story becomes a master of Vaikuṇṭha (by his ultimate merger in Lord Hari).

105. After probing deeply the mass of *Śāstras*, this most sacred esoteric truth known as the reality in all well-established texts has been narrated to you. There is nothing purer than the *Bhāgavata*. Do drink the (nectar-like) essence of the twelve *Skandhas* of the *Bhāgavata* for attaining supreme bliss.

106. He who listens to the (elucidation of the) story of the *Bhāgavata* regularly with devotion and he who narrates (expounds) it in the presence of the pure devotees of Viṣṇu, both of them obtain the real fruit of hearing and reciting the *Bhāgavata* (viz. liberation). For, as a matter of fact there is nothing in this world which is inaccessible to them.

PART I

FIRST SKANDHA

CHAPTER ONE

1. Let us meditate upon the Supreme Spirit who is real; from whom emanate the creation etc. (i.e. creation, preservation and destruction) of this (universe), (as can be inferred from) his presence in all that exists and his absence from all that is non-existent; who is omniscient and self-refulgent; who extended (i.e. revealed) to the first knower (or wise one) viz. god Brahmā, through his heart, the Veda about which even the learned ones are perplexed; in whom (i.e. resting on whom) the creation of the three attributes (viz., *sattva*, *rajas* and *tamas*) appears real like the apparent transmutation of the light, water and earth (for example, appearance of water in the heat and light of the sun as in the mirage etc.); who by his lustre has always dispelled illusion.[1]

---

1. This verse has been differently interpreted by different commentators.

(1) ŚR. (Śrīdhara), the oldest commentator on the Bh.P. (*Bhāgavata Purāṇa*) states that he is recording the traditional interpretation of the Bh.P. in his Com. (commentary), the *Bhāvārtha-dīpikā*.

sampradāyānurodhena paurvāparyānusārataḥ |
Śrī-Bhāgavata-Bhāvārtha-dīpikeyam pratanyate ||

According to ŚR., the Supreme Spirit or Reality is both immanent and transcendent. The universe originates from the Supreme Spirit. is sustained therein and finally dissolves into the same Spirit. During this world process, the Supreme Spirit is eternally established in its original grandeur, the world process being traceable to cosmic illusion.

He interprets the verse as follows:

(i) Let us meditate on the Supreme Lord (who is) real; in whom (i.e. depending on whom) the creation of the three attributes of the Cosmic Illusion (viz. *sattva*, *rajas* and *tamas*)—though unreal—appears to be real, just like the transmutation of Fire, Water and Earth *enter se* (For example, a mirage wherein water, though non-existent, appears to exist in the blazing heat and light of the Sun.). In him, this three-fold creation is unreal. By his own lustre, He has dispelled delusion. (Let us contemplate on) him from whom is the creation (preservation and destruction) of the universe (as can be) inferred by logical concomitance and discontinuation.

OR (ii) the Supreme Being is the cause and the universe the effect. He, being the cause, is in (all) things and is different as the things are effects.

OR (iii) This universe being composed of parts, its creation etc. is due to him as can be deduced from positive and negative proofs, but he should be distinguished from the primordial nature (*prakṛti* or *pradhāna* as he is self-refulgent and omniscient (of his own accord.) Hence neither *prakṛti* nor *jīva* are worth meditating. Nor so is god Brahmā as) he—the Supreme Being—revealed to the first sage (god Brahmā), through his mind, the Vedas which have perplexed the learned ones.

ŚR. concludes that the word *dhīmahi* in this verse shows that this *Purāṇa* deals with the science of the Supreme Being. He quotes other Purāṇas in his support.

ŚR. is obviously a follower of non-dualism (*advaita*) of Śaṅkara.

(2) VR. (Vīra-rāghava), a follower of Rāmānuja explains his ontology succinctly in his com. *Bhāgavata Candrikā.* According to Rāmānuja. Brahman or the Supreme Reality is qualified by sentience and non-sentience (*cidacid-viśiṣṭa*). Brahman enters the world of sentient and non-sentient things which emanate out of him and are sustained by him and enter into him. This relation of Brahman to the sentient and non-sentient creation has been elaborated by Rāmānuja in his concept of *śarīra-śarīri-bhāva* (body-Soul relation), *viśeṣaṇa-viśeṣya-bhāva* (substance-attribute relation), *śeṣa-śeṣi-bhāva* (dependent and—'depended-upon' relation), *aṁś-āṁśibhāva* (part-whole relation), *ādhārādheyabhāva* (supporter-supported relation), *niyantṛ-niyata-bhāva* (ruler-ruled relation) and *rakṣaka-rakṣyabhāva* (redeemer-redeemed relation).

The interpretation of this verse as gathered from VR's exposition is as follows :

Let us meditate on that real Supreme Brahman from whom emanate the creation etc. of this sentient-cum-non-sentient universe, both as the material cause and the efficient cause (as he is different from the Primordial Nature *prakṛti*—and individual Souls—*Jīvātman*) ; him who is omniscient, independent (not controlled by *karmas*), self-resplendent; who by his will-power revealed to God Brahman, the Vedas about which learned sages (like Kapila, Kaṇāda etc.) get perplexed; from whom proceeds the combination of the elements such as Fire, Water and Earth; about whom the three-fold creation (of the attributes *sattva*, *rajas* and *tamas*) is unreal (*guṇa-traya-sṛṣṭaḥ prapañcaḥ... yasmin...mṛṣā, mithyā*); who has dispelled delusion by the light of His infinite knowledge.

(3) VJ. (Vijaya-dhvaja), a follower of Dualistic (*dvaita*) Vedānta of Madhva, in his com. *Pada-ratnāvalī*, construes this verse differently and interprets as follows:

Let us contemplate on that eternally blessed Nārāyaṇa from whom come forth the creation etc. ('etc.' includes sustenance, destruction, control, bondage, liberation) of this existing universe as evidenced by logical positive, and negative proofs (and by *Śruti* and *Smṛti*); who thoroughly comprehends all objects; who is his own Lord (or who manifests himself at his own will) and is not subordinate to anyone else; who, out of affection, extended to the first sage (god Brahmā) the Veda (along with its auxiliaries—*aṅgas*).

About whom (the past, present and future) gods like Brahmā and others have no knowledge. In whom the three-fold creation of Īśvara, individual souls and non-sentient things is of no avail like the combination of Fire, Water and Earth (They are real due to His support), who has dispelled illusion (Viṣṇu does not create the universe as an illusion but as a reality).

(4) The word *dhīmahi* in this verse seems to have led the writers of the *Matsya* and other Purānas to equate this verse with the sacred *Gāyatrī Mantra* (RV. III, 62.10 and occurring in other Vedas). This Vedic verse is in the Gāyatrī metre and is addressed to Savitṛ (the Sun who is the source and inspirer of everything). It literally means 'We contemplate upon that longed-for refulgence of the divine Savitṛ who may inspire our intellects.' (For the sacredness of the *Gāyatrī mantra* see P.V. Kane—*Hist. of Dharmaśāstra* Vol. II, 1.303-304). Commentators of different schools of Vedānta endorse the above view of the Purāṇa-writers. VJ. spells out this equation between the *Gāyatrī Mantra* and this verse (Bh.P.1.1.1) as follows :

Gāyatrī		*Bh.P.* 1.1.1
tat savitur devasya	:	*Jamnādyasya yataḥ*
vareṇyam	:	*param*
bhargaḥ	:	*dhāmnā svena sadā nirasta-kuhakam*
	:	Also *svarāḍ*
dhiyo yo naḥ pracodayāt	:	*tene Brahma hṛdā Ādi-kavaye*
dhīmahi	:	*dhīmahi*

VJ. states that the Bh.P. verse is an 'explanation or elucidation' of the *Gāyatrī Mantra.*

(5) SD. (Śuka-deva) in his *siddhānta-Pradīpa* presents the point of view of the Nimbārka or the dualistic-cum-nondualistic (*Dvaitādvaita*) Vedānta. Here significant differences in the interpretation of the words in this verse (from that of ŚR.) are briefly noted.

janmādyasya—This refutes the schools which deny the existence of Brahman.

satyaṁ dhīmahi—Let us meditate on the Lord who is described by Śruti as being 'Real, Infinite knowledge, Brahma'.

param—cause of the universe.

janmādyasya yato'nvayād itarataḥ—Herein *janmādi*—means creation, preservation, destruction and liberation. The Lord is within all (*sarvātmā*) both by positive and negative proofs (*anvaya* and *vyatireka*).

yo'rtheṣvabhijñaḥ—This refutes the *Sāṁkhya* theory that the primordial Nature (*pradhāna*) is the cause of the world. He knows all objects while they are being created.

muhyanti yat sūrayaḥ—Though He is the cause of the world, Kapila and founders of other schools of philosophy do not know him and are deluded.

tejo-vāri-mṛdāṁ yathā vinimayaḥ—Hereby he refutes Vaiśeṣika theory of the creation of the universe. Just as the effects of Fire, Water and Earth viz. sparks, bubbles and pitcher are created out of some positive—existing—substances, the threefold creation is also real. This refutes the doctrine of the *māyā-vādins* (believers in cosmic illusion) who regard the three-fold creation as illusory.

dhāmnā svena sadā nirasta-kuhakam—Faultlessness of Brahman. Owing to his inherent refulgence, the Supreme Lord is never soiled by the faults due to the three-fold creation.

(6) VB. (Vallabha), the exponent of pure non-dualistic (Śuddhādvaita) Vedānta, declares in his Com. *Subodhinī* that the world is real and is subtly Brahman. The individual souls and the inanimate world are in essence one with Brahman. He admits that individual soul (*jīva*), time (*kāla*), *prakṛti* or *māyā* are eternal existences. Brahman can create the world without any connection with *māyā*. He (Brahman) is not only an agent (*kartā*) but also an enjoyer (*bhoktā*). According to VB., the highest goal is not liberation (*mukti*) but rather eternal service of Kṛṣṇa and participation in his sports in the celestial Vṛndāvana. Non-difference alone is said to be real.

This philosophical stand of VB. is found forcefully maintained in the Commentaries of Puruṣottama, GD. (Giridhara) and Others.

The following are the important differences in explanation from ŚR:

janmādi asya yataḥ—(i) That from which the sky is created. (ii) That of which (sustenance and destruction) creation is the beginning.

asya—One assuming the form of crores of worlds and one who is beyond the capacity of the mind to cognize.

yataḥ—*Brahman*, though the 'seed' (cause) of the universe does not undergo a modification just as the wish-yielding cow, tree or gem remain unchanged when they give the desired object.

anvayād itarataḥ etc.—Brahman is both the material and instrumental cause of the world.

svarāṭ—(i) Due to His self-splendidness (omniscience—GD.) He is not interested in objects of enjoyment etc. (ii) One who is absorbed in the joy of His own Self. has no worldly occupation (*kleśa*).

hṛdā—Along with the Purāṇas—'Purāna is regarded as his heart' (*Purāṇaṁ hṛdayaṁ smṛtam*)

yatra-mṛṣā—The characteristics of non-sentients and individual souls (*jaḍa-jīva-dharmāḥ*) are not found in the Supreme Lord. GD. (Giridhara) in his Com. *Bālaprabodhinī* explains: In the Supreme Lord's person, the creation of three attributes of the primordial nature (*prakṛti*) viz. *sattva*, *rajas* and *tamas*, are false.

dhāmnā svena etc.—(i) Destroyer of the nescience of all by manifesting himself.

kuhaka—Fraud, viz. false identification of the body and sense-organs with the soul.

satyam......dhīmahi—Let us love or meditate on the Supreme Man, who is unaffected by Time and well known in the world and described in the Vedas.

(7) The Bengal School of Vaiṣṇavism with their emphasis on Rādhā and the *Parakīyā Preman* cult shows great reverence to ŚR. who in fact

knows nothing of Rādhā and never advocated *Parakīyā Preman* (love between a man and a woman who is the wife of another person).

Caitanya had to develop this concept to absorb the Buddhist Sahajīyas and their followers in orthodox Hindu fold. JG. (Jīva Gosvāmī), a great exponent of this school, states that his Com. on the Bh.P.—*The Krama Sandarbha*—is complementary to ŚR. elucidating some points omitted or briefly explained by him.

Svāmi-pādair na yaa vyaktaṁ yad vyaktaṁ cāsphuṭam kvacit |
Tatra tatra ca vijñeyaḥ Sandarbha-Krama-nāmakaḥ |

Actually they differ so much from ŚR. They admit of five principles: God, souls, *māyā* or *prakṛti*, the inherent power of God (*svarūpa śakti*) with its elements of *jñāna* (knowledge), *śuddha-tattva* (pure matter) and *kāla* (Time). The ultimate reality is Viṣṇu, the personal God of love and grace, possessing the usual attributes of *sat*, *cit* and *ānanda*. He is both *nirguṇa* and *saguṇa* as he inheres the qualities of omniscience, omnipotence etc.

According to JG., this verse enjoins meditation upon the Supreme Being who is the creator, omnipresent, free from all defects, full of inherent knowledge and the giver of liberation. The Com. of JG. is too big to be summarised here.

GS. (Gaṅgāsahāya) in his Com. *Anvitārtha-prakāśikā* maintains that this verse is pregnant with the contents and meaning etc. of the entire Bh.P. All the 10 characteristics of *Purāṇas* are found herein. Obviously he accepts the Sk. terms of the characteristics mentioned in the Bh.P. II.10. 1., viz. (1) Sarga, (2) visarga, (3) sthāna, (4) *poṣaṇa*, (5) *ūti*, (6) *manvantara*, (7) *īśānukathā*, (8) *nirodha*, (9) *mukti*, (10) *āśraya*.

The characteristics are found in this verse as follows:—

Text of the verse	*Signifies the characteristic*	*In Skandhas*
janmādyasya yataḥ |	*sarga*	III, IV, V
	visarga	
	sthāna	
tene brahma hṛdā	*poṣaṇa*	VI
ya ādi-kavaye |		
muhyanti yat sūrayaḥ |	*ūti*	VII
	manvantara)	VIII
	īśānukathā)	IX
tejo-vāri-mṛdāṁ vinimayaḥ |	*nirodha*	X
dhāmnā svena sadā	*mukti*	XI
nirasta-kuhakam |		
satyaṁ param |	*āśraya*	XII
dhīmahi	The use of 1 p. atm. pada shows 'the rightful claimant' and the meditation suggested in this.	I II

2. Here, in this celebrated *Bhāgavata* composed by the Great Sage[2], is explained the highest Duty (*Dharma*), completely free from deceit, (viz. interest about this world and even the desire about liberation—ŚR). (It is the *Dharma*) of the righteous who are devoid of envy (and hence kindly to all beings—ŚR.). Here the thing to be known is the absolute Reality (*Or* it is the individual soul, when a part of this thing or Reality is meant; it is *māyā* or Cosmic Illusion, when the power of the thing is implied; it is the universe when its effects are understood—the non-difference of these all from the absolute Reality can be easily understood—ŚR.) It gives the highest bliss and destroys the three kinds of misery[3]. Can the Supreme Lord be realized in the heart immediately by the teachings of other (treatises)? No. (But in this (*Bhāgavata*) he can be so comprehended at once by the meritorious who have a desire to hear (and study) this (*Bhāgavata Purāṇa*).[4]

2. The great sage Nārāyaṇa is regarded as the original author of the *Bhāgavata*. The four verses in the-Bh. P. II.9.32-35, narrated by the Supreme Lord to God Brahmā are regarded as the nucleus of this big epic. But VR. takes this sage as Vyāsa.

3. The following is the traditional classification of miseries : (i) *ādhyātmika*—The internal and external pangs and miseries suffered by the body and/or the mind. (ii) *ādhibhautika*—miseries from contact with gross elements and their products, e.g. accidents, tortures etc. (iii) *ādhidaivika*—tortures meted out after death, in the other world, according to one's misdeeds.

GD. (Giridhara) however limits these miseries to life on the earth and classifies : (1) caused by fever, grief etc., (2) caused by evil influence of stars, ghosts etc., (3) caused by heat, cold, tigers, serpents etc.

4. The Sk. commentators, hold that this verse describes the four requisites of the Bh.P., viz. (1) *adhikārin*—Persons qualified to read the Bh.P. (2) *Viṣaya*—The main topic of this work. (3) *Prayojana*—The object or the 'Why' of the treatise. (4) *Sambandha*—The relationship of (2) and (3).

The following are the summaries of the Sk. commentaries of the principal schools of the Vedānta :

(1) VR. explains

The main subject of discussion in this *Purāṇa* is *dharma*. It is twofold : (1) *siddha* (established) viz. the Supreme Soul described herein 'from *Vedya... tāpatrayonmūlanam*'. (ii) *sādhya* (to be achieved) is the 'devotion' described in *nir-matsarāṇāṁ satām*. The objective is two-fold: Direct—The revelation of the presence of God in the heart and, Indirect—destruction of three types of misery.

(i) *sādhya-dharma*—In this Purāṇa the highest Duty of the non-jealous saintly persons is described. It being the 'highest', is above exorcizing or magical practices and fruit-yielding actions prescribed in the Vedas and implies virtues like tranquillity, self-restraint, essential for aspirants to Liberation. Grace and pleasure of the Supreme Lord is its objective and achievement.

(ii) *siddha-dharma*—This Purāṇa is called *Bhāgavata* as it deals with the form, nature, inherent qualities and powers of the Lord. It is composed by Bādarāyaṇa Vyāsa. Herein is described the Thing which is the Reality, giver of the auspicious bliss of Liberation, destroyer of the three types of misery. This Reality is to be comprehended by the good, saintly persons.

Other false scriptures are of no use. People in whom the desire to hear the Bhāgavata arises become blessed immediately and the Lord at once enters their hearts as soon as they listen to this Purāṇa.

(2) According to VJ., this verse describes the main topic of the Bh.P., the means to achieve it, the qualifications of the listener-and the objectives of this Purāna.

Here in the beautiful profound *Bhāgavata* is taught the Path which leads to the attainment of the Supreme Lord (or that which controls the 'falling' man or destroys the sins) and completely absolves one from hypocrisy, i.e. the ego of being the doer of acts, and makes him perform acts without any desire to enjoy their fruits. This path or *Dharma* is the highest due to the doer's offering of all the acts to God (*OR* It destroys the enemy (*para*) viz. the cycle of the transmigration of the soul). Hence this Path is characterised by devotion (*bhakti-yoga-lakṣaṇaḥ*). Persons of pious actions and free from envy are eligible for this. The object of knowledge is the eternally existing flawless Reality imparting the highest bliss and uprooting three types of misery. Here, the relation characterised by the path of devotion (*Bhakti-Yoga*) and its object, i.e. God are expounded. There is no propriety in recounting other paths which may lead to heaven. When this treatise called the *Bhāgavata* composed by the great sage is properly studied by persons with disciplined intellect and adopted in serving the spiritual preceptor and such other great ones and the Lord, God is seen 'fettered' in their heart at once, by the ties of devotion. Persons duly equipped with *sādhanā* can visualize the Lord the very moment they are introduced to the *Bhāgavata*.

(3) JG. states that this verse establishes the superiority of the Bh.P. to other treatises dealing with (religious) acts, knowledge and devotion. The repetition of the word 'here-in' (*atra*) is for emphasizing this speciality of the Bh.P. over other scriptures.

The Bh.P. teaches about the great religion viz. devotion to the Supreme Lord. This devotion is so motiveless that the devotee does not hanker after liberation also. The envylessness of the devotees implies kindly feelings to all beings so that the devotees refrain from animal-sacrifices. The Reality described herein is so powerful that it destroys three types of misery caused by *Māyā* (illusion) and nescience and gives the highest bliss. The adjective 'Śrīmad' in 'Śrīmad Bhāgavata' implies its great potentiality. Its author is the great sage Nārāyaṇa who composed it originally in 4 verses. The greatness of the author establishes the superiority of this work. By following other scriptures men may attain liberation with difficulty but the superiority of the Bh.P. lies in its power to put its listeners in immediate communion with God. Thus this being the science of immediate God-realization, the Bh.P. is the greatest of all scriptures.

(4) SD. explains :

This verse establishes the superiority of the Bh.P. over other scriptures from the point of its *anubandhas* (viz. the main topic, objective, the relation between the two and the qualifications of the listener of the Bh.P.). The Bh.P. is qualified by the adjective 'Śrīmad' as it contains the beautiful description of the person, qualities etc. of the Supreme Lord. This is composed by the great sage Vyāsa (the son of Parāśara), the knower of the Vedas and an incarnation of the Supreme Lord. The greatness of the authorship shows the superiority of this scripture over others. Herein is to be known the great religion of devotion (*Bhakti*) which is selfless (motiveless) and which is adopted by pious person free from jealousy. The Thing (the Reality) the principle called Śrīkṛṣṇa which uproots the three kinds of misery and blesses with liberation, is to be understood here. The Reality consisting of the three principles, viz Brahma, the sentient individual soul and the non-sentient are to be comprehended. Thus this scripture is superior to others due to its authorship, topic of discussion and the qualification of its listeners. The meritorious who have a desire to listen to the Bh.P. at once find Śrīkṛṣṇa 'stabilised' (present) in their heart.

This verse gives the five objectives :

(1) The Thing (Reality, Śrī-kṛṣṇa)—object of devotion.
(2) The Sentient, individual soul, the devotee.
(3) Liberation—the fruit of the grace of the Lord.
(4) The sentiment of devotion (*bhakti-rasa*).
(5) 'Opposition' suggested by the word (*para*).

The other scriptures, their injunctions, the eligibility of their followers etc. are different or opposite to those of the Bh.P.

The envyless devotee is the eligible person (*adhikārī*) and liberation is the objective (*prayojana*).

(5) GD. (Giridhara), a descendant of VB. and an exponent of pure non-dualistic (*Śuddhādvaita*) school of Vedānta lucidly explains as follows:

As there are number of works dealing with paths of Knowledge, Action and Devotion, the superiority of the Bh.P. over all other works and from the points of four *anubandhas* is given. Here in the *Śrīmad Bhāgavata* is taught the best path of Duty, of all those described in other scriptures. It is free from deception and is of the nature of nine-fold devotion. The singular *dharma* is used as all these varieties of devotion result in one—viz. attainment of Liberation. The *adhikārin* of the Bh.P., being jealousy-less, kindly disposed, pious person, it is superior to *Karma-kāṇḍa* which gives scope to jealousy. Reality, the object to be known, is a bestower of the highest bliss and destroyer of three kinds of misery. That this pure principle called Vāsudeva who liberates all, is understood by women and Śūdras (i.e. by persons not eligible for Vedic rites) and by all irrespective of their intellectual equipment, shows the superiority of this treatise to others. The author—Bādarāyaṇa Vyās

3. *This (Bhāgavata Purāṇa) is the (ripe) fruit of the wish-yielding tree[5] of the Vedas, that has been dropped down from the mouth of (the sage) Śuka (as from the mouth of a parrot=Śuka); that is full of (lit. endowed with) ambrosial juice[6] (viz. the highest bliss). Oh appreciators of beauty, the connoisseurs of its (the Bh.P.'s) peculiar excellences[7], you do drink[8] constantly this Bhāgavata—a fruit which is entirely

---

or the Supreme Lord—is also the most authoritative one. This shows the greatness of the Bh.P. among treatises of Jñāna Kāṇḍa.

The desire to listen to the Bh.P. does not arise without meritorious action. Lord Vāsudeva described in the 1st verse gets instantaneously bound in the heart of those who desire to listen to the Bh.P. What of those who are intent on hearing (and studying) it? The repetition of the words showing instantaneousness (viz. *sadyaḥ* and *tatkṣaṇam*) shows how very quickly His presence is established in the heart. This immediate fulfilment of the objective proves that the Bh.P. is superior to other scriptures. Hence its superiority to other treatises dealing with *upāsanā kāṇḍa*.

GD. repeats the four *anubandhas* of the Bh.P. like other Commentators.

*VJ. interprets as follows :

'Oh men of the world who can appreciate excellence ! Till the fall of your material body (*liṅga-Śarīra*) you do drink again and again the delicious juice of the ripened fruit called the *Bhāgavata* which was made to fall by me (Vyāsa) from the wish-yielding tree, viz. the Vedas, the sweetness of which s increased due to its flow from the mouth of Śuka ('the sage') and 'the parrot.' It is wellknown that the parrots eat only the ripe fruit.

5. *nigama-kalpataroḥ*—*Kalpataru* is a mythological wish-yielding heavenly tree. The Vedas are the means of obtaining the objectives of human life (*puruṣārthas*). As the Vedas are thus productive of all desires, they are compared with *kalpataru*—ŚR., VR. As the Bh.P. contains the essence of the Vedas, it is called the 'fruit' of the Veda-Tree—VR.

6. *amṛta-drava-saṁyuta*—*amṛta*—(i) The highest bliss—ŚR. (ii) Liberation—VR., VJ.

(a) mixed with the essence of liberation. Devotion full of the joy of experiencing (the presence of) the Lord—VR.

(b) That which leads to Liberation (*mukti*)—VJ.

(iii) The essence of the sports of Hari—JG.

7. *bhāvukāḥ*—(i) Expert judges of qualities of special kinds of tastes —ŚR.

(ii) Persons devoted to the enquiries about the glorious Lord—VR.

(iii) The abode of the highest auspiciousness (*parama-maṅgalāyana*) —JG.

8. *pibata rasam*—It is not possible 'to drink' a fruit. But the Bh.P is like a fruitwhich is entirely full of juice without any seed.

a sweet juice—here and in the state of the Final Beatitude.[9]

4. In the Naimiśa[10] forest, a sacred place of Viṣṇu, sages whose leader was Śaunaka[11] held a sacrificial session lasting for one thousand years, for attaining the heavenly abode of Viṣṇu.[12]

5. The sages, who had offered the morning oblations[13]

(i) The word *rasa* is used as a correlative of *phala* as juice when fallen down cannot be drunk—ŚR., VR.

(ii) *Pā* (*pib*) means 'to eat' as well—VJ.

9. *ālayam*—(i) upto death—VR. (ii) till the fall of the physical body (*liṅga śarīra*)—VJ. (iii) *laya* or *pralaya* is the 8th *sāttvika* stage. Till one reaches that stage—VC. (Viśvanātha Cakravartī). (iv) Which is the cause of the dissolution of the cycle of births and deaths (*prapañca*)—VB. Or it (The Bh.P.-juice) should be drunk disregarding the desire for liberation

10. ŚR. and VB. record the popular etymology of the word "Naimiśa" as "a place where the felly of the wheel (created by god Brahmā) was broken" : *Brahmaṇā visṛṣṭasya cakrasya nemiḥ śīryate kuṇṭhībhavati yatra* / ŚR. quotes the authority of the Vāyavīya which states that when some sages went to Brahmā for a suitable place for performing penance, he created a wheel and asked the sages to follow it till it came to a standstill. The wheel owing to the breakage of its felly stopped at a place which came to be known as Naimiśa:

The alternative spelling of this word is "Naimiṣa" which according to the quotation of the *Varāha P.* given by ŚR. is derived from Viṣṇu's exploit of destroying an army of Dānavas (demons) within the twinkling of eyelids (*nimiṣa*).

Modern Nimsar, on the bank of the Gomatī in the Sītāpur district of the Uttar Pradesh is regarded as the site of the old sacred place called Naimiṣāraṇya (Vide *Śiva P.*, *P.* 432, F.N.).

11. He belonged to the Bhṛgu clan according to MBH. He was the leader of the sages who performed the great sacrificial session in the Naimiṣa forest and to whom the MBH, and the Purāṇas were recited by the Sūta. (Vide Śiva P. 1, F.N. 1).

12. According to ŚR., *svarga* means the God Viṣṇu, He explains *svargāya lokāya* as follows :

svaḥ svarge gīyata iti Svargāyo Hariḥ, sa eva loko bhaktānāṁ nivāsa-sthānaṃ, tasmai tat-prāptaye /

VJ. slightly differs. He interprets *svarga* as Viṣṇu *Svarato Viṣṇuḥ tena gato loko Vaikuṇṭhākhyaḥ tasmai* /

VB. also disapproves the explanation of ŚR. and explains "Bhagavadānandāṁśa-bhūtah svargaḥ /Lokātmakastu mahān aiśaḥ /Sa hyatra phalam /"

13. In the place of *huta-utāgnayaḥ*, VJ. accepts the reading *huta-hutāśanāḥ* which is better, though we have followed ŚR in the above translation.

(both of the daily routine and the special ones of the sacrificial session), once[14], respectfully asked the Sūta[15] who was hospitably received and (comfortably) seated :

6. Oh sinless one ! Mythological epics (*Purāṇas*)[16] along with history (*Itihāsa* e.g. the *Mahā Bhārata*) and [17] Law-books (like Smṛtis composed by sages, e.g. Manu, Yājñavalkya and others) as well[18], have been not only studied but also expounded by you.

7. Oh Sūta ! Whatever the venerable Bādarāyaṇa[19], greatest among the learned ones, knows and whatever other sages who

---

14. *ekadā* : VB. interprets as "the time of singing or reciting the Kṛṣṇa-legend" (*Hari-Gāthopagāyana-kālaḥ*). It is at this time of the sacrificial session that the Sūtas come. VB. thinks that this Sūta is not a Brahmin and though as per formalities, he was expected to stand in the assembly of those Brahmin sages, he was specifically asked to sit comfortably for narrating Kṛṣṇa's life. (vide *Subodhinī* 1.1.5, page 8).

15. A.D. Pusalkar thinks that this narrator of the Purāṇas is a Brahmin, a view accepted by the editor of the Śiva P. (vide P.1, FN. 2). But I think it is still an open question.

The Sūta who narrated the BH.P. was the son of Romaharṣaṇa, the disciple of Bādarāyaṇa (BH.P. 1.1.6-8).

16. *Purāṇa*—'Ancient legendary history'. Name applied to 18 well-known sacred works containing the whole body of Hindu mythology; supposed to be composed by Vyāsa. Each *Purāṇa* treats of the following topics: The creation, the destruction and renovation of the universe, the genealogy of Gods and ancient heroes, the reigns of Manus and the narratives of their descendants. These are enumerated thus :

Sargaś ca Prati-Sargaś ca Vaṁśo Manvantarāṇi ca |
Vaṁśānucaritaṁ caiva Purāṇam pañca-lakṣaṇam ||

Different lists of the 18 Purāṇas are available. ASD 67 gives the following titles :

1. Brahma, 2. Padma, 3. Viṣṇu, 4. Śiva, 5. Bhāgavata, 6. Nārada, 7. Mārkaṇḍeya, 8. Agni, 9. Bhaviṣya, 10. Brahma-Vaivarta, 11. Liṅga, 12. Varāha, 13. Skanda, 14. Vāmana, 15. Kūrma, 16. Matsya, 17. Garuḍa, 18. Brahmāṇḍa.

For a succinct statement about the epics and Purāṇas vide A.D. Pusalkar's *Studies in the Epics and the Purāṇas*, (Bombay, 1963).

17. Ca, VJ. include *Upa-Purāṇas*, 18 in number, but *Bhāratīya Saṁskṛti Kośa* (Vol.I, P. 667) enumerates 51 titles.

18. *Śāstrāṇi*—VB includes secular sciences like *artha-Śāstra* under this.

19. A name of Veda Vyāsa, the reputed author of the *Brahma Sūtras*. Authorship of all *Purāṇas* and *Upa-Purāṇas* and the *Mahābhārata* is attributed to him.

know the *saguṇa* (possessing attributes) and *nirguna* (attributeless) [aspects of] Brahman[20], know,

8. Oh gentle one ! You know all that (completely and) accurately through his (Bādarāyaṇa's) favour. Teachers disclose even their deepest secrets to an affectionate pupil.

9. Oh long lived one ! You are fit to tell immediately what is entirely for the good of men, as has been properly decided by your honour directly from the (Purāṇic) text.

10. Oh honourable one ! In this Kali age, men are generally short-lived, lazy, of dull intelligence, unfortunate and victims of diseases.

11. Numerous are the religious rites (requiring a number of technical performances) which deserve to be heard in details. Hence, Oh righteous one ! After determining the essentials out of these by your keen intelligence, tell them to us, the reverentials, so that our minds will be thoroughly soothed.

12. Oh Sūta ! God bless you. You know (the objective) why the venerable Lord of the Sātvatas[21] (or the protector of His worshippers—ŚR) was born of Devakī[22] and Vasudeva.

13. Well, Sir ! You will be pleased to describe to us who are desirous of hearing about him who se incarnation is for the good and prosperity of all beings.

---

20. I followed ŚR in interpreting the words *para* and *avara*. The other commentators differ as follows :

VR. The Supreme Soul (*paramātma-tattva*) and the lower self or *prakṛti-puruṣa-tattva*.

VJ. takes these as two aspects of Brahman and as an alternative explanation "One who knows the past and the future"—an explanation endorsed by VB. VB. also thinks that *para* signifies Gods like Brahman while *avara* means men like ourselves. GS. takes *para* as 'Brahman' and *apara* as *prakṛti* etc.

21. *Sātvata*—Name of the Yādava clan. It is also interpreted as 'Worshipper'.

22. *Devakī*—Wife of Vasudeva, mother of Kṛṣṇa and cousin of Kaṁsa; regarded as an incarnation of Aditi and Pṛśni. According to *Padma P.*, in Devaki's marriage a voice from heaven predicted the death of Kaṁsa at the hands of the 8th child of Devakī. As a precautionary measure, Kaṁsa imprisoned both Vasudeva and Devakī and tried to kill all her children. But Kṛṣṇa, the 8th child, was saved. Kṛṣṇa killed Kaṁsa and got his parents honourably released. She stayed with him throughout his life. After Kṛṣṇa's death, she entered fire. (PCK p. 452)

14. A person who, having fallen into this dreadful circuit of worldly existence, becomes utterly helpless and utters his name, is then immediately liberated. Fear itself is afraid of him.

15. Oh Sūta! Sages who have taken resort to His feet and who are the abodes of tranquillity, purify immediately by their presence (when approached); whereas the water of the divine Gaṅgā sanctifies after actual contact, i.e., ablutions (lit. 'by actual service').

16. Or what person desirous of purity of heart, will not listen to the glory of the venerable Lord whose deeds are praised by persons of auspicious fame[23]—the glory that cleanses the sins of the Kali age.

17. Describe to us who are very eager (to hear) his great[24] acts which are eulogised by the learned ones (like Nārada, Vyāsa or Brahmā etc.)— acts of him who sportively assumes[25] different forms.[26]

---

23. It is alternately explained : '......Lord who is of sanctifying fame as well as of praiseworthy deeds.' VJ., VD.

24. 1. great e.g. the creation of the universe—ŚR. SD. 2. removing sins—udgata-doṣa—VJ. 3. creating (lit. giving) highest rapture—JG. 4. giving the desired objects to devotees—VC. 5. awarding the four highest goals in human life (*puruṣārtha*) viz. *dharma, artha, kāma and mokṣa*—G.D.

25. *dadhataḥ*—This present participle signifies the eternal nature of His pastimes—VC.

26. *Kalāḥ*—1. Forms e.g., Brahman, Rudra etc.—ŚR. 2. All incarnations—VJ., VC. 3. Incarnations in the shape of man etc.—JG. 4. Kṛṣṇa was the only complete incarnation (*pūrṇāvatāra*) is implied by this—VR., GD. 5. VD. waxes eloquent in explaining the concept of incarnation (*avatāra*). The incarnations are of three types—(i) *puruṣāvatāra* viz. Saṅkarṣaṇa, Pradyumna and Aniruddha of the Pañcarātra system; (ii) *guṇāvatāra* e.g. Brahman (representing *rajo-guṇa*), Rudra (for *tamoguṇa*) &c. (iii) *līlāvatāra*—All incarnations from Sanaka, Sanandana upto Kalki (described in BH.P.I.3).

VD. gives another fourfold classification of these incarnations in ascending powerfulness, according as they are due to : (1) influence or *āveśa* (e.g. Sanaka, Nārada, Pṛthu etc.); (2) miraculous power or *Prabhāva* (e.g. Mohinī, Vyāsa, Datta etc.); (3) magnificence or *Vaibhava* (e.g. Nara, Nārāyaṇa, Hayagrīva etc.) and (4) of the highest stage or Parāvasthā, which are in ascending hierarchy Narasiṁha, Rāma and Kṛṣṇa.

Thus Kṛṣṇa is regarded as the most complete incarnation. *Kṛṣṇa eva svayaṁ bhagavān, na tato'dhikaḥ Ko'pyasti*—VD.

18. Oh intelligent (Sūta)! Describe to us fully the auspicious narratives of the incarnations of Hari, the Supreme Ruler, who by his mystic power called "Illusion"[27] indulges at will in his pastimes.

19. We, however, do not feel thorough satisfaction in hearing about his glorious[28] prowess which according to listeners who are connoisseurs of tastes is of increasing sweetness[29] every moment.

20. Lord Keśava, (though the Supreme Being is) concealed in human disguise[30], has certainly performed superhuman acts of heroism, along with Balarāma[31].

21. We, apprehending the arrival of the Kali age, have engaged ourselves in a sacrifice of a long duration in this field consecrated by Lord Viṣṇu. Hence, we have sufficient leisure[32] to hear the story of Hari.

---

27. *ātma-Māyā*—(1) His own power called 'miracle' (*āścarya-śakti*).—VR. (2) 'Knowledge' (*saṅkalpa-rūpa jñāna*) (3) 'Will-power', but with the following different implications: (a) *Svarūpa-bhūta-icchā*—VJ. (b) *nijecchārūpa-śaktiḥ*—JG., VD. quote *mahāsaṁhitā* :

Ātma-māyā tad-icchā syād—Guṇa-māyā jaḍātmikā/

(4) 'Mystic power' (*yoga-māyā*)—VC.

28. *Uttama-śloka*—(i) whose glory dispells the darkness in the form of ignorance of the mind or nescience (*avidyā*—SR., GD. (ii) which is praised by the best (persons)—VC., VD. (iii) whose glory is the best—VC. (iv) one who is praised by the liberated who experience the joy of Brahman, VB.

29. *Svādu-svādu*—more tasteful than tasteful things—ŚR. However, VJ. is followed here.

30. *Kapaṭa-mānuṣaḥ*—(a) 'Disguised as man; Having the appearance of man.'—VR., GD. &c. JG. explains: The Supreme Lord has no material body implied by the word 'man'. He is the Supreme being appearing in human shape. (b) 'Mānuṣeṣvapi kaṁ sukham patati prāpnoti / : VJ.

31. *Balarāma*: An incarnation of *Śeṣa*, son of Vasudeva and originally of Devaki but by womb-transfer, was born of Rohiṇī, another wife of Vasudeva. He was fair in complexion and was usually dressed in blue. He was brought up along with Kṛṣṇa by Nanda in Gokula. He is represented as armed with a ploughshare and a pestle-like club. He was a lifelong associate of Kṛṣṇa, sharing with him all vicissitudes of life. He was noted for his great physical power and short temper and addiction to wine and dice. He married Revatī. At the time of the last internecine fight among the Yādavas, he quietly retired and left his human mortal body by yogic process and resumed his form as Śeṣa (Details—Viṣṇu P. ; Harivaṁśa). DHM. 40-41, PI. 2.463-65.

32. *kṣaṇa*—Joy, desire (*utsava*)—VD.

22. By the creator (or Lord Viṣṇu) you have been clearly pointed out as the helmsman (of a ship) to us (who are) desirous of crossing the ocean (in the form of) the Kali Age which is difficult to be crossed over and which deprives (men) of goodness[33] (or 'Strength' as applied to ocean).

23. Tell us to whom righteousness has now resorted for refuge (when) Kṛṣṇa, the master of *Yogic*-mystic powers, wellversed in the Vedas, the protector of religion, has returned to his abode.[34]

CHAPTER TWO

Vyāsa said :

1. Being highly pleased at these courteous questions of the Brāhmaṇas (Sūta, Ugraśravas) the son of Romaharṣaṇa, complimenting their words (enquiry) began to reply in details.

Sūta said :

2. I bow down to that sage (Śuka) whose ceremony of the investiture of the sacred thread had not taken place (i.e. in that early stage of childhood), who had renounced all actions and set out (of home[35]) and whom the sage Vyāsa (Śuka's

---

33. *sattva*—'courage, morale'—VD.

34. *svāṁ kāṣṭhām*—
—His own boundary i.e. His own Self—ŚR.
—His own direction, i.e. Vaikuṇṭha-loka—VR.
—His own attribute, full form (*guṇa-pūrṇa-svarūpam*)—VJ.
—His quarter, i.e. His own eternal abode (*nija-nitya-dhāma*)—JG.
—His boundary, the span of life of 125 years while he was in this world —VC.

35. *pravrajantam*—ŚR. : Set out as a recluse (to enter the 4th stage of life, viz. *Saṁnyāsa*). But VJ. refutes this on the grounds of the ineligibility of Śuka to *Saṁnyāsa* as his thread ceremony had not taken place. Here *pravrajyā* does not mean *saṁnyāsa* but "abruptly going out." VB. explains *pravrajanam* as "leaving out all contacts" and not *saṁnyāsa*.

father Dvaipāyana)[36], being grieved at his separation from him, called back as "Oh Son" (to which) the trees, being like Śuka on account of his (Śuka's) existence (entry) into the hearts of all beings[37] responded (to Vyāsa).

3. I seek refuge in the son of Vyāsa (viz. Śuka, the spiritual master of sages who had, out of compassion for people in the worldly existence desiring to cross over the (ocean of) the blinding darkness (of ignorance), narrated the secret one among the Purāṇas [38] (viz. *the Bhāgavata Purāṇa*), which is the only one lamp of spiritual truth, full of its own (uncommon) glory[39], and is the essence of all the Vedas.

4. After paying obeisance to Nārāyaṇa[40] and also to Nara[41] the best of men[42], and also[43] to the goddess of learning, one should narrate *Jaya* (another name of the *Bhāgavata Purāṇa*. See VR. and SD.).

---

36. *Dvaipāyana*—The name of Vyāsa, the son of Parāśara, so called because of his birth on an island in the Jumna—PCK. p. 479.

evaṁ Dvaipāyano jajñe Satyavatyām Parāśarāt |
Nyasto dvīpe sa yad bālas tasmād Dvaipāyanaḥ smṛtaḥ ||

—MBH. I.63.86

37. *sarva-bhūta-hṛdayaḥ*—ŚR. : Śuka replied through the medium of trees to remove the paternal bond from the heart of Vyāsa.

VB. : One who controls the hearts of all beings; or whose heart is in all beings.

JG. : Upon whom the heart of all beings is placed.

38. *purāṇa-guhyam*—ŚR & JG. interpret as above, but VR. : "The secret Purāṇa", VJ. adds *purāṇasya bhagavataḥ sannidhātuṁ yogyam.*

39. *svānubhāvam*—JG.: This expresses the uncommon glory of the BH.P., but VJ. : He who expounded Brahman (svānubhāvam) and who narrated the BH.P. which is'...etc. (VJ. construes this verse differently as indicated above).

40. *Nārāyaṇa* : Viṣṇu so called because he lay on the waters of the Deluge before the beginning of Creation : *Āpo nārā iti proktā āpo vai nara-sūnavaḥ | Tā yadasyāyanaṁ pūrvaṁ tena Nārāyaṇaḥ smṛtaḥ ||*

41. *Nara* : An incarnation of Viṣṇu; born of Dharma and Mūrti daughter of Dakṣa. A friend and associate of Nārāyaṇa while performing penance at Badarikāśrama. As ŚR. and JG. note Nārāyaṇa and Nara represent Kṛṣṇa and Arjuna.

42. *narottama*—The best of beings. Some treat this as the adjective qualifying Nara.

43. VJ. reads "Vyāsa" for *caiva*. He interprets this verse rather differently :

5. Oh sages ! I have been very nicely asked by your honour about the welfare (or bliss) of the people because (your) relevant question is about Kṛṣṇa, whereby the soul becomes completely soothed.

6. That is certainly the sublime religion[44] for men, (religion) from which is created the devotion to Lord Viṣṇu—devotion which is without any (ulterior) motive, unobstructed (or constant) and by which the soul becomes deeply pacified.

7. Loyal devotion (applied) to Lord Vāsudeva[45] immediately[46] generates non-attachment which leads to causeless[47] knowledge.

8. If that religion, howsoever well-practised, does not create love for the stories of Lord Kṛṣṇa, it is certainly sheer labour.

9. Verily, wealth is not the proper objective of the religion leading to Liberation[48]. The desire (for worldly

---

"After paying homage to Nārāyaṇa (the subject of the *Bhāgavata Śāstra*), Vyāsa (the author of the BH.P.), the goddess Lakṣmī, Vāyu, the greatest of men, the highest teacher, Sarasvatī (the goddess of learning) and Nara, I expound the BH.P. (due to the favour of the above deities)." JG. states : 'Of this Bhāgavata Śāstra, Nara & Nārāyaṇa are the presiding deities (*adhiṣṭhātṛ-devate*), Śrī-Kṛṣṇa is the *Devatā*, Sarasvatī is the *Śakti*, Vyāsa is the Seer (*Ṛṣi*), OM (*praṇava*) is the *Bīja*, and Gāyatrī is the Metre (*Chandas*). As pointed out by Nīlakaṇṭha in his Comm. on the Devī-Bhāgavata, the 1st verse of the BH.P. is not in the Gāyatrī metre (vide Ft. Note on BH.P.I.1.1.)'

44. ŚR.: This verse answers the 1st question (in Bh.P.I.1.9). *para dharma* : Religion is of two kinds—*apara dharma* (i.e. Dh. the object of which is Liberation) and—*para dharma* (which creates devotion to Kṛṣṇa).

45. Vāsudeva—VR. : All pervader, VJ.' One who dwells (pervades) everywhere or One who makes all to dwell in Him. *vasati sarvatra, svasmin sarvaṁ vāsayati*=vasuḥ. *vasuś cāsau devaś ca* /

46. *āśu*—JG. Quickly. As soon as the Bh.P. is heard, the knowledge described therein is created.

47. *ahaituka*—ŚR : Free from unnecessary arguments & JG. : Derived from the Upaniṣads. VD. : The object or cause of which is "*A*" (i.e.) Vāsudeva. VJ. : With no ulterior motive like money etc. VR. : *Bhakti* as an end in itself. SD. That which does not result in anything but devotion. VB. : Knowledge which is not inferrable but is generated directly by realization (*sākṣātkāra*)

48. *āpavargya*—VR., VJ. : "That which leads to Liberation". JG. : Devotion—Unconditional devotion of the individual spirit to the divine spirit. The devotion which does not expect any gain in return but gives oneself up to God.

things) is never enjoined for the attainment of that (kind of) wealth which has religion as its end (object).[49]

10. It is not proper to satisfy the senses (by enjoyment of desired objects but to limit) that much enjoyment of desired objects as is essential for (the sustenance of) life. The aim of life in this world is enquiry about the Truth (or the essential nature of the Supreme Being = *Tattva*) and not (the desire for enjoyment in Heaven) by performing religious rites.

11. Those who possess the knowledge of the Truth (*tattva*) call the knowledge of non-duality[50] as the Truth. It is also variously designated as Brahman, Paramātman or Bhagavān.

12. The sages who have faith in it (Brahman) visualize their own soul in themselves, through devotion which is combined with knowledge and non-attachment and which is developed by listening to the Vedānta.

13. Hence, Oh greatest of the twin-borns! Gratification (grace) of Hari is the consummation of religion practised well by men according to the division of castes and stages of life.

14. Therefore, the Venerable Lord of the Sātvatas (deserves always to be) heard, eulogised, meditated and worshipped with concentrated attention.

15. Who will not love (listen to) His narratives by whose sword-like meditation, the learned ones, becoming one with the

---

49. *dharmaikāntasya*—VJ "That of which Dharma is the only definite fruit". VR. endorses the same when he says : *Dharmaika-prayojanasyārthasya vittasya lābhāya prayojanāya kāmo na smṛtaḥ/Arthasya prayojanaṁ na kāmo bhavati /* It may be noted that by *kāma* he means our needs of life *annapānādi*.

50. *advaya*—ŚR. : Non-duality. Here Bh.P. anticipates the theory of momentariness of the Buddhists. VJ : "Having neither equal nor superior". VR. : "incomparable with It", also *avyaya-bheda-rahita*, or *jātyādi-bheda-rahita*. JG. : Knowledge is nothing but consciousness (*cit*) and has no second (*advaya*) and is of the Supreme Being. Although the Bh.P. uses the word *Tattva* in the sense of Brahman, Paramātman and Bhagavān, one is the Pure knowledge beyond everything, the other is the internal controller having abundance of Māyā—power, while the last is complete within Himself. Verse 12: *ātmani*—ŚR : "In sentient beings", JG. "In the purified hearts of sentient beings"

Supreme Spirit[51] cut asunder the knot-like acts producing bondage.[52]

16. Oh Brāhmaṇas! Love about the narratives of Vāsudeva will be generated in (persons) desirous of hearing (or devoted to service) and full of faith, by performing holy pilgrimages and through the service of the great (holy) people.

17. The reason is that Kṛṣṇa, hearing and glorifying (whose episodes) is meritorious and who is the well-wisher of the good, exists in the hearts of the listeners to His narratives and shakes off all evil.

18. When Evils are all but destroyed by continuous services of the devotees of the Lord[53], firm devotion to the Lord of excellent fame[54], is generated.

19. Then, mind, not being affected by perturbations (qualities or "aspects"[55]) like Passions (*rajas*) and Ignorance (*tamas*) and by desire, avarice and others, and being stabilised in goodness, is quietened (soothed).

20. Thus the knowledge[56] of the reality of the Lord is produced in the person whose mind is pacified and who has freed himself from attachment through the devotion of the Supreme Lord.

21. As soon as the Supreme Lord is seen within oneself, his knot (of ego) in the heart[57] is cut asunder, all doubts are

---

51. *yuktaḥ*—ŚR : With power of self-control, JG : With a subdued mind.

52. *granthi*—ŚR. : Knots i.e. acts producing ego, JG.: Acts producing ego in different bodies.

53. or the study of the *Bhāgavata*.

54. *uttama-śloka*—ŚR.: (1) As in Bh.P. 1.1.19 He whose glory dispels darkness of ignorance in mind. (2) The Lord who is praised by persons whose hearts are absolved from ignorance.

55. *bhāva*—According to Sāṅkhyas, the perturbation of Prakṛti results in the non-balance of its *guṇas* i.e. "attributes or constituents" which Dr. Radhakrishnan prefers to call "aspects". But he prefers to use the original Sk. *guṇa* in *Hist. of Ind. Phil. Vol. II* pp. 262-65. I have however, followed the traditional translation of these terms.

56. JG. thinks that the communion with the Supreme Lord is felt from within without the influence of thinking power.

57. VJ. takes *hṛdaya-granthi* as Mind and not ego. Quoting Vedic scriptures he states that on this point ŚR.'s explanation is against the tenets of the BH.P. (*Bhāgavata-jñānād advaita-niṣedhāc ca* |)

solved and his actions (good or bad, of the previous period which are not exhausted by enjoying the fruits) are annihilated.

22. Hence, verily, wise men always practise with great delight (their) devotion in Lord Vāsudeva which purifies their hearts.[58]

23. *Sattva* (goodness), *rajas* (passion) and *tamas* (ignorance)—These are the attributes or constituents of Nature (*Prakṛti*). The Supreme Being possessing these attributes is one. Here He assumes names like Hari, Viriñci (Brahmadeva), and Hara (Śiva) for the preservation (creation and destruction) of the universe. There (from among them) the good (Final Beatitude) comes from Him whose body is *Sattva* (goodness) itself.

24. To the earthly wood, the smoke issuing from it is superior. To such smoke the Fire is superior as being connected with all sacrificial acts prescribed in the Vedas. (Similarly) the quality of *rajas* is better than that of *tamas*, but *sattva-guṇa* (the quality of goodness) is the best as the Supreme Spirit (*Brahman*) is realized in it.[59]

25. Therefore, formerly sages worshipped Venerable Viṣṇu (who is of purest goodness i.e. *sattva-guṇa* incarnate). Those who follow them here become fit for final beatitude.

26. So also, disregarding the lords of goblins of terrible forms, persons desirous of Liberation (being) quiet and free from malice adore images of Nārāyaṇa.

27. Verily, longing for wealth, power and offspring, persons whose nature (is dominated by) the qualities of *rajas* (passion) and *tamas* (ignorance) and who are of the kindred nature (as lords of manes etc.) adore the Lords of the manes, goblins and created beings and others.

28. Vāsudeva is the highest objective of the Vedas.

58. ŚR. : "Though the Supreme Being assumed three different names for three different functions, the real good of men will result in devotion to Vāsudeva who is full of *Sattva-guṇa*.

59. ŚR. Explains : The quality of *rajas* is more expressive of the Supreme Being than *tamas*. The particle *tu* shows that *rajas* has but little value as compared with *sattva* (Goodness) which fully expresses the nature of the Supreme Being. Thus the superiority of Viṣṇu, the presiding deity of *sattva-guṇa* over the other two presiding deities of *rajas* and *tamas* (viz. Brahmadeva and Śiva is obvious.

(Vedic) sacrifices are intended for Vāsudeva. The Yogic practices (and as a matter of that) all (religious) actions have Vāsudeva as their goal.

29. The object of knowledge is (the comprehension of) Vāsudeva. Religious penance is for the sake of Vāsudeva. Vāsudeva is the goal of Religion. Vāsudeva is the end to be reached in liberation.

30. The Supreme Lord who is without attributes (and) all-pervading by nature, formerly created this (Universe) by His will-power called Illusion (*Māyā*) which consists of (three) qualities (viz. *sattva*, *rajas* and *tamas*) and is of manifested and unmanifested form or "expressive of cause and effect (law of causation).

31. (The Supreme Lord) having manifested Himself by His Knowledge or Intellectual Power[60] and entering into these attributes created by *Māyā* appears as if He has attributes.

32. Just as the same fire placed in wood from which it is created, appears of different forms, (so also) the *Puruṣa*[61]—the Soul of the Univer e appears different in created beings.[62]

33. This (Supreme Lord), by entering into beings created by Himself by the effects full of attributes, of gross and subtle elements, organs of senses and Soul-mind, enjoys their attributes.[63]

---

60. *vijñāna*—ŚR. : Intellectual power, VR. : Soul (*jīva*), SD. : Individual soul (*jīva*) who is a part of the Universal soul and is of the nature of knowledge.

61. *pumān*—ŚR. : The Supreme lord, the Soul of the universe. VR. : The individual soul (jīva). VJ. however, supports the above (our) translation.

62. VC. differs : "Just as the fire consumes the wood in which it is created, the universal soul (*paramātmā*) when realized by devotion etc. removes the limitations (*upādhıs*) due to *māyā*." SD. thinks that this verse shows the driving force of the Lord. The *paramātmā* appears differently as a driving force in all movable and immovable objects but He is one.

63. VR. differs. He takes *asau* as individual soul. The gist of his interpretation: "The individual soul enters the bodies of gods etc. created according to their past actions, and enjoys the objects of senses and does acts resulting into merits or sins". Alternatively he suggests that the Supreme Lord enjoys through individual souls and not directly. VJ. thinks that the Supreme Lord enters these bodies in a detached manner. If he enters an unfortunate body, the Supreme Soul has not to suffer miseries like the individual soul.

34. Certainly, this Creator of the Universe[64], being fond of pastimes[65] like incarnations in gods, non-human being sand men, protects the Universe, by his power.

CHAPTER THREE

Sūta said :

1. At the beginning, with the desire to create the Universe, the Lord assumed the form of Man[66] (*puruṣa*) consisting of sixteen parts[67] created from the *tattvas* (primary substances) of which *Mahat*[68] (the Great or "Intellect") is the first.

---

64. *loka-bhāvanaḥ*—ŚR. "Protector of the Universe". VJ., VR. : "The Creator of the Universe".

65. *anu-rata*—SD. "Ready to protect the religion as needed at a particular period". VJ. thinks that *anu* means The Lord is not bound to but may at His will incarnate as per necessity of the world. He is not bound by the law of Karman to do so.

66. *pauruṣam rūpam*—ŚR. : Though the Supreme Spirit has no such human form, for the convenience of meditation or worship. He is regarded as *Virāṭ* (one residing in or knowing the affairs of sentient beings.)

VJ. explains : The Supreme Being collected and preserved the whole of the universe in its subtle form in his "Belly", at the time of the Deluge and lay covered in the darkness of his *Prakṛti*. At the time of Creation of the Universe, he drank up the Darkness covering him and manifested himself. This is "the assumption of the Puruṣa form". Alternatively "the assumption of forms like Rāma, Kṛṣṇa etc" may be accepted.

VB. : He assumed of his own accord body consisting of pure *sattva* (the constituent power—guṇa—of goodness) which is composed of *tattvas* (principles). It may not be a human form.

JG. : Puruṣa implies 3 forms of Viṣṇu, as (1) the Creator of the principle Mahat (Intelligence), (2) the Being in the Egg, and (3) the Being in all *bhūtas*. The Supreme Lord described as possessing 6 attributes of glory etc. is now described as *Puruṣa*. *Rūpa* according to VR. indicates here the cause of Brahmāṇḍa (*Brahmāṇḍa-kāraṇaṁ samaṣṭi-tattva-jātam*), while with SD. *rūpa* is the effect of *Samaṣṭi* (aggregate which is considered as made up of parts each of which is consubstantially the same with the whole) and the material cause of *vyaṣṭi* (an aggregate viewed as made up of many separated bodies)—*samaṣṭi-kāryātmakaṁ vyaṣṭyupādāna-bhutam*)

67. *ṣoḍaśakalam*—ŚR., SD., VB. : 10 organs of senses+Mind+5 *mahābhūtas* (Elements)=16 parts.

68. *mahadādibhiḥ*—ŚR. : Consisting of the "principles" (*tattvas*) called

2. Brahmā, the Head of the progenitor of the Universe,[69] was born of the lotus of the deep-lake-like navel[70] of the Lord who was lying on the waters (of the post-Deluge ocean) extending his *yogic* meditation-slumber[71].

3. Verily that form of the Lord on the formation of whose limbs is based the extent of the Universe, is very pure, excellent, and full of *sattva* (goodness).

4. They (i.e. yogins) with their vision of vast knowledge[72] visualise this form wonderful (on account of its having) thousands of feet, thighs, arms, mouths, thousands of heads, ears, eyes and noses, shining on account of thousands of crowns, garments and earings.

5. This[73] (original form of the Supreme Being, the *Ādi-Nārāyaṇa*) is the indestructible seed[74] and the receptacle (place of return) of different incarnations and from whose parts and parts of parts[75], beings such as gods, subhuman beings (like animals, birds), men and others, are created.

---

by Sāṅkhyas as *Mahat* (the Great or Intellect), *ahaṁkāra* (ego or self-sense) and 5 *tanmātras* (subtle pure elements corresponding to the 5 organs of sense).

69. *viśva-sṛjām patiḥ*—Brahmā, the Creator of the universe at first created 10 Prajāpatis (Lords or generators of created beings) e.g. Marīci, Atri, Aṅgiras, Pulastya, Pulaha, Kratu etc. In the Vāyupurāṇa we have another list : Kardama, Kaśyapa, Śeṣa, Vikrānta. etc. (For details vide PI. II.404)

VB. remarks that the word *pati* shows that to these generators of created beings, the order of Brahmā was inviolable.

70. *nābhi-hradāmbujaḥ*—VB. explains that the word *nābhi* (Navel) is used to signify the existence of the Universe in the belly of the Lord. ŚR. says that this refers to the Supreme Being's assumption of *Puruṣa* form in the *Padma Kalpa*.

71. *Yoga-nidrā*—ŚR. : "The sleep of *samādhi* (meditation). VB. says that *yoga-nidrā* is a certain kind of power of the Lord. It relieves the agonies of beings and brings them to him. He extends it for the creation of the Universe.

72. *adabhra-cakṣuṣā*—ŚR. : "With their eyes of vast knowledge" VJ.: "Of full knowledge" SD. : "Of great knowledge".

73. *etad*—VR. thinks that this is the *Aniruddha* form, VJ. calls this *Padma-nābha* while JG. "the Being in the egg of Brahman".

74. *bīja*—ŚR. : Place of origin; JG. : Embryo. VR.: The root cause.

75. *aṁśāṁśena*—ŚR. : Nārāyaṇa is the seed of incarnations as well as of all animate things as they are created out of his parts. Brahmā is the

6. At first[76], that very God manifested (Himself) as Youths[77] and (becoming) Brāhmaṇa, practised unbroken celibacy which is difficult to practise.

7. Secondly, also, the Lord of Sacrifices (Nārāyaṇa) with the object of creation, assumed the body of a boar for raising up the Earth which had sunk down to the lower region called Rasatala[78].

8. And thirdly, He, having become the Divine Sage (Nārada[79]) in the Ārṣa Creation (pertaining to sages), expounded the religio-mystical treatise pertaining to the *Sātvatas* (the devotees of Viṣṇu) namely *Pañcarātrāgama* by following which actions become void of their binding force.[80]

9. In the fourth incarnation, having been born of the wife of Dharma (namely Mūrti, daughter of Dakṣa Prajāpati) as the twin sages Nara and Nārāyaṇa[81], He performed severe penance with fully pacified mind.

---

part (*aṁśa*) of Nārāyaṇa and Brahmā's progeny like the *mānasaputras* (Marīci and others) are parts of part (*aṁśāṁśa*). VR. *cidacit tattvaikya-deśena*.

76. *prathamam*—ŚR. : This word is used for numerical reference only and does not indicate superiority or inferiority.

77. *kaumāram*—ŚR. : This is a name of Creation like Ārṣa, Prājāpatya etc. It includes Sanaka, Sanandana, Sanātana, Sanatkumāra. They were mind-born sons of Brahmā, and were Brāhmaṇas. They refused to create progeny and led a celibate life. SD., VR., JG. agree with ŚR.

78. *Rasātala*—One of the seven sub-terranean regions. They are as follows : Atala, Vitala, Sutala, Talātala, Rasātala, Mahātala and Pātāla. These are inhabited by Nāgas, demons etc.

79. *Nārada*: The beloved 10th son of Brahmā; one of the 12 who knew the Dharma ordained by Hari; a celibate; was taught the *Bhāgavata* by his father; he recited it to Vyāsa; author of *Sātvata Tantra*; mentioned many times in the Bh.P.

—PI. II.225

80. *naiskarmyam*—ŚR. : That from which the cause of the binding force of an action becomes null and void. VS. : means leading to Liberation. VR. observes Those who perform *nivṛtti* type of *karma* should not follow *pravṛtti dharma* VJ.: By performing *karmas* as prescribed in the *Sāttvata Tantra*, one attains liberation.

81. These twin sages performed penance at Badarikāśrama. When Indra sent god of Love and heavenly damsels to disturb his contemplation, Nara created a number of beautiful ladies and asked the god of Love to select one for heaven. They took Urvaśī to heaven and reported the superior powers of the sages. Arjuna and Kṛṣṇa are regarded as the incarnations of Nara and Nārāyaṇa respectively.—PI. II.205., 231.

10. The fifth (incarnation) was by name Kapila[82], the chief of Siddhas (who) explained to Āsuri[83] the Sāṅkhya doctrine[84] which determined all the principles, which was lost (formerly) in the course of time.

11. In the sixth (Incarnation) He, being requested by Anasūyā[85] became the child (lit. accepted the child-ship) of Atri[86], taught Metaphysics (ŚR: knowledge of the Soul) to Alarka[87], Prahlāda[88] and others.

---

82. *Kapila* : Born of Kardama and Devahūti; taught knowledge of Brahman to his mother; propounder of the Sāṅkhya philosophy which he taught to Āsuri; one of the twelve who knew the Dharma ordained by Hari; burnt down 60,000 sons of Sagara when they attacked him on suspicion of theft of their sacrificial horse. (PI. I.311). Apart from the mythological account, Kapila seems to be a historical figure—an exponent of a system of philosophy in Pre-Buddhist period.

83. *Āsuri* : N. of the disciple of Kapila; a *siddha* but did not comprehend Hari's Māyā; was invited to Yudhiṣṭhira's Rājasūya sacrifice. PI.I.180.

84. *Sāṅkhya* : The system takes its name from its method of arriving at conclusions by theoretical investigation. The word *Sāṁkhya* is derived by some from *Saṁkhyā* or number and is appropriate to this system which gives an analytical enumeration of the principles of the cosmos. But this tendency to enumeration is common to all Hindu systems of thought...In the early texts, *Sāṁkhya* is used in the sense of philosophical reflection and not numerical reckoning. This particular system, which expounds by careful reflection the nature of *puruṣa* or spirit and the other entities, acquired this significant title. ——S. Radhakrishnan—*Hist. of Ind. Phil. II.* 248-334.

Cf. *Śuddhātma-tattva-vijñānaṁ Sāṅkhyaṁ yadabhidhīyate* |
Śaṅkara—Comm. on *Viṣṇu-sahasranāma.*

85 *Anasūyā* : The wife of the sage Atri and a daughter of Kardama; mother of Datta, Durvāsas and Soma; mother of 5 Ātreyas and a daughter Śruti —PI. I.53.

86. *Atri* : A son of Brahmā; married Anasūyā appointed by Brahmā for the creation of the world. While engaged in meditation on Mount Rkṣa, the Trimūrtis blessed him with 3 sons being their own parts (*aṁśas*). Accordingly Datta (Viṣṇu), Durvāsas (Śiva) and Soma (Brahmā) were born. —PI. I.41.

87. *Alarka* : PCK (p. 76) records different Alarkas, but the one mentioned here seems to be the king of Kāśī; youngest son of Ṛtadhvaja and Madālasā; was expounded the spiritual knowledge by his mother and Dattātreya.

88. *Prahlāda* : Son of Hiraṇyakaśipu and Kayādhū; was initiated in the Bhāgavata Dharma by Nārada. For him Viṣṇu incarnated as Man-lion and killed Hiraṇyakaśipu. Prahlāda became the Lord of Daityas. His

12. Then, in the seventh (incarnation), Yajña[89] was born of Ruci and Ākuti. He along with gods of whom Yama[90] was the first, protected the period assigned to the Manu called Svayambhū.[91]

13. In the eighth (incarnation), Lord Viṣṇu (lit. One with wide steps) was born of King Nābhi and queen Meru Devī, He (as Ṛṣabha)[92] showing to the strong-minded ones the path (of sannyāsa), the most respectable of all the stages of life.

14. Oh Brāhmanas! Having been implored by sages, (He) assumed the ninth body (incarnation) pertaining to (i.e. known as) Pṛthu. From this (earth), he milked (medicinal) plants. Thereby he became the most pleasant.

15. At the time of oceanic deluge in the epoch (Manvantara) called Cākṣuṣa[93] He assumed the form of a fish[94] and protected Vaivasvata Manu[95] by making him board the earth-boat.

---

spiritual preceptor was Dattātreya. It was due to him that Kṛṣṇa spared the life of Bāṇa. Prahlāda lived in Sutala and attained liberation by Satsaṅga.—PI. II.435-36.

89. *Yajña* : An incarnation of Viṣṇu, son of Ruci and Ākutī; reported to have married his twin-sister Dakṣiṇā; was Indra in the period called *Svāyambhuva Manvantara.*

90. *Yama* : Name of the 1st son out of 12 sons born of Yajña and Dakṣiṇā. He was a god in Svāyambhuva Manvantara.

91. *Svāyambhuva Manvantara* : Period relating to Svayambhū. Svayambhū was the first Manu (out of 14 Manus). Śatarūpā was his wife. They had 2 sons—Priyavrata and Uttānapāda and 3 daughters viz. Ākūti, Devahūti and Prasūti who were married to Ruci, Kardama and Dakṣa respectively. As Ākūti was married by *putrikā-dharma*, he took over son Yajña. In the period (Manvantara) of Svayambhū, Marīci, Atri, Aṅgiras, Pulastya, Pulaha, Kratu, and Bhṛgu were the seven mind-born sons of Brahmā, Yajña was the Indra and Dakṣiṇā the Indrāṇī and their sons called Tuṣita were the gods.—BPK. 370.

92. Ṛṣabha—Ādinātha, an incarnation of Viṣṇu. For details see Bh.P. V.3-6.

93. *Cākṣuṣa*—The epoch (Manvantara) of the 2nd Manu Cakṣu. He was the son of Vyuṣṭa and Puṣkariṇī; wife Ākūti, son Manu.—PI. I,574

94. *mātsyaṁ rūpam*—The Fish incarnation. Though this is the 10th incarnation here, it is regarded as the 1st incarnation of Viṣṇu, popularly.

95. *Vaivasvata Manu*—In his former life, V.M. was King Satyavrata of Tamil Nad, who by his obligations on Viṣṇu in his initial stage of Fish-

16. In the eleventh (incarnation) in the form of a tortoise, the omni-present Lord supported the Mandara mountain on his back while gods and demons were churning the ocean.[96]

17. The twelfth (incarnation) is of Dhanvantari[97], and the thirteenth, the female form of Mohinī[98] who after deluding others (i.e. demons) enabled (lit. made) the gods to drink nectar.

18. Assuming the fourteenth Man-lion form[99], he tore up the chest of the powerful king of the Daityas with his claws like a weaver of mats (tearing) the rushes (grass).

19. Proposing to beg three paces (of land) but desirous of recovering (lit. taking back) heaven, he assumed the Pigmy

---

incarnation was blessed with Manu-ship. He is the 7th Manu whose epoch continues at present. In his regime, Vasu, Rudra, Āditya, Viśve Deva, Marudgaṇa, Aśvini-kumāra and Rbhu are the gods. Purandara, the Indra and Kāśyapa, Atri, Vasiṣṭha, Viśvāmitra, Gautama, Jamadagni and Bharadvāja are the 7 sages.—BPK.307, also PI. II.601.

96. This refers to the occasion of churning the ocean for nectar. The gods and demons cooperated in churning the ocean with Mount Mandara as the churning staff, serpent Vāsuki as the string. Fourteen valuable things such as the goddess Lakṣmī, Kaustubha gem etc. were obtained. Nectar (*amṛta*) was one of them. The deadly poison Halāhala was drunk up by god Śiva to save the world.
(For details vide PI. I.87)

97 *Dhanvantari*: An incarnation of Viṣṇu. He appeared with the jar of nectar during the ocean-churning for nectar. Another account shows him to be the son of king Dīrgha-tamas of Kāśī; the originator of Āyur-Veda and the father of Ketumān.—PI. II.156-57

98. *Mohinī* : The 13th incarnation of Viṣṇu to delude the Āsuras from having any share in the nectar and distribute it to Devas (gods).
—PI. II.156-57.

99. *Narasiṁha* : (also Nārasiṁha and Nṛsiṁha) : Viṣṇu came down on the earth to punish Hiraṇyakaśipu for his insolence and cruelty. Hiraṇyakaśipu harassed his son Prahlāda for his devotion to Viṣṇu.—the omni-present. When asked whether Viṣṇu existed in the column of his hall, Prahlāda said "Yes" on which Hiraṇyakaṣipu kicked it, when Viṣṇu appeared before the demon and killed him.

form[100] and arrived at Bali's[101] sacrifice.

20. In the sixteenth incarnation, being angry at the hostility of kings to Brāhmaṇas, he extirpated the warrior class from the earth for twentyone times.[102]

21. In the seventeenth (descent on the earth) he was born of Satyavatī from Parāśara[103]. Seeing people of low intelligence, he divided the tree in the form of Veda into several branches.

22. After this (i.e. after the 18th incarnation), with a desire to help gods (lit. to do the work of gods viz. to kill Rāvaṇa etc.), he assumed kingship and performed acts of valour such as control of the sea (by building a bridge over it.)

23. In the nineteenth and the twentieth (incarnations),

---

100. The origin of this incarnation is "The three strides of Viṣṇu" mentioned in the Ṛg-veda. In the Tretā-yuga (2nd Age), the pious Daitya King Bali acquired the dominance of the three worlds by defeating the gods. To remedy this Viṣṇu was born as a diminutive son of Kaśyapa and Aditi. The dwarf appeared before Bali and begged of him to donate him three paces of land. The generous king agreed. Viṣṇu manifested his original form and covered the heaven and earth in two strides. But respecting his (Bali's) virtues, He made Bali the King of the subterranean region Sutala and assured him of Indra-ship in the 8th Manvantara (Epoch).

101. *Bali* : A son of Virocana and grand-son of Prahlāda; married Vindhyāvalī and Aśanā; had 100 sons of whom Bāṇa was the eldest; defeated gods on the battlefield and performed 100 Horse-sacrifices. In the 100th horse-sacrifice, he was deceived by Viṣṇu in a dwarf form. (for the rest vide the above note).—P.I. 2.469-71.

102. This refers to Paraśurāma incarnation of Viṣṇu, in the Tretā age. He was the son of Jamadagni and Reṇukā (a princess). Haihaya king Kārtavīrya Arjuna forcibly took away Jamadagni's Kāmadhenu (Wish-yielding cow). The scuffle led to Paraśurāma's killing of Kārtavīrya. Jamadagni disapproved of this and ordered Paraśurāma to go on pilgrimage for one year in expiation of this. After the departure of Paraśurāma, the sons of Kārtavīrya killed Jamadagni. In the struggle between Bhārgavas and Haihayas that followed this, Paraśurāma defeated them 21 times, which has been poetically described as "extirpation" of the Kṣatriya class. After this he retired to perform penance on Mahendra mountain. He is regarded as "deathless", was discomfited by Dāśarathi Rāma,; taught Astra-vidyā to Bhīṣma and Karṇa; guided Kṛṣṇa and Balarāma to Gomāntaka.

—PI. II.291.

103. *Parāśara* : Son of Śakti, grandson of Vasiṣṭha; father of Vyāsa.

—PI. II.293-4.

having taken birth in the Vṛṣṇi family as Rāma (Balarāma) and Kṛṣṇa, he lessened the burden of the earth.

24. Then after full advent of the Kali Age, (He) will be born with Buddha as His name, and as a son of Ajana in the Kīkaṭa country.[104]

25. Then in the twilight of the Kali Age, when kings will be as good as robbers, this protector of the world will be born of Viṣṇuyaśas under the name Kalki.

26. Oh twice-born ones! Just as thousands of canals flow forth from inexhaustible lake, similarly innumerable are the incarnations of Hari, the ocean of goodness (the *Sattva-guṇa*).

27. Sages, Manus[105], gods as well as very powerful sons of Manu along with Prajāpatis (gods presiding over creation) are all parts of Hari only.

28. But[106] Lord Kṛṣṇa is the Supreme Being himself and all these, parts and smaller parts of the Supreme Being who give happiness to the world (when it is) troubled by the enemies of Indra (i.e. demons) in every epoch.

29. The man who, exerting himself with devotion, recites in the morning and in the evening this mysterious (account of the) births (incarnations) of the Lord, is completely released from all kinds of misery.

30. This form of the formless Lord whose true constitution is the Spirit itself, has been indeed created in the Soul

---

104. *Kīkaṭa* : Name of the land where Buddha was born; noted for the sacred Gayā, the garden park Rājagṛha and the hermitage of Cyavana. —PI. I.381.

105. *Manu* : Progenitors and sovereigns of the earth for 1/14 part of Brahmā's day (i.e. 4,320,000 human years). The Manus are 14 in number viz. 1. Svāyambhuva, 2. Svārociṣa 3. Auttami, 4. Tāmasa, 5. Raivata, 6. Cākṣuṣa, 7. Vaivasvata, 8. Sāvarṇi, 9. Dakṣa-sāvarṇi, 10. Brahma-sāvarṇi, 11. Dharma sāvarṇi, 12. Rudra sāvarṇi, 13. Deva sāvarṇi, 14. Indra sāvarṇi.

106. JG. explains the difference between Bhagavān and his parts as follows: The Supreme Lord, by His divine will, can manifest His power anywhere without interruption, while the parts (*aṁśas*) or incarnations can manifest these for performing their appointed mission. Though Kṛṣṇa is included in the list of incarnations, He is not merely a part (*aṁśa*) of the Supreme Being but the Supreme Being Himself. The particle *tu* in the above verse is used to distinguish him from other incarnations.

(or Spirit) by the attributes of Illusion such as Intelligence and others.

31. Just as a stream of clouds (is attributed) to the sky or the dust (particles of the earth) is ascribed to the wind (by ignorant persons), similarly the quality of being seen is attributed to the seer by unintelligent ones. (The spirit is wrongly misunderstood as being material body.)

32. From this is created a different body which is made up of unmanifested attributes (or parts of the body like hands, feet etc.) and which is subtle due to the invisibility and inaudibility of its essential nature. It is the *Jīva* (spirit) due to which transmigration (takes place).[107]

33. When these two forms *sat* and *asat* (i.e. two bodies gross and subtle) attributed to the soul through ignorance are negatived by Self-knowledge, it is the visualization of Brahman (i.e. identification of Jīva with Brahman)[108].

34. They know that if this divine (pertaining to the Omniscient Spirit) and resplendent (or sportive)[109] Māyā

---

107. ŚR. says that the hypothesis of a subtle body which is invisible, inaudible and formless, is necessary to account for the repeated births or transmigrations of the Soul.

108. VR. interprets *Brahma* as "the liberated soul" and *darśana* as "the knowledge of the nature of the 'pure' soul devoid of any contamination or contact with *Prakṛti*". So this verse means : "That knowledge by which one realizes that origination (birth) and destruction (death) really belong to the non-Spirit (*acit*) and that they are ascribed to the Soul through ignorance (*avidyā*) and that they are to be denied of the Soul (*Ātman*) by the knowledge of the *ātman*, is the real knowledge of *Brahman*."

But VJ. states: "That knowledge is the knowledge of *Brahman* leading to liberation from *saṁ sāra* (the cycle of births and deaths)—the knowledge which consists in seeing that the forms consisting of the Primordial Nature (*Prakṛti*) and its products are, from the very beginning, different from the Supreme Soul (*Paramātman*) due to His self-knowledge. It is due to Nescience (*Avidyā*) that he mistakes them as belonging to Himself.

109. SR : Sporting in the cycle of creation, preservation and destruction of the universe.

VR : When this cosmic illusion (*Māyā* or *Prakṛti*) becomes capacious with *Mahat* etc. and the consequent pride or belief of thinking the body and the Soul as identical, ceases or disappears, then the individual Soul comes to be worshipped (respected) as having realised his own glory as the liberated with the eight excellent qualities which are manifested on the realization of the Supreme Soul.

(illusion), transforming itself to knowledge ceases itself (automatically), (the Jīva or Spirit) becoming perfect (i.e. identical with Brahman) is glorified in its own greatness).

35. The wise ones describe in this way, the births and deeds of the Birthless and Actionless, the Lord of the hearts (antaryāmin) whose deeds are mystically described in the Vedas[110].

36. Or he whose sports are not ineffective, creates, protects and eats up (destroys) this Universe but is not attached to this.[111] And this Master of six qualities[112] lies concealed in the hearts of all beings and remaining (aloof) independent, he enjoys (as if it is fragrance) the objects of six senses.

37. Just as an ignorant person does not understand the performance of an actor, (similarly) no being of dull intelligence can comprehend by mind, words or skill (in argumentation or Logic)[113] the pastimes of the Supporter (of the universe) who extends greatly[114] his names and forms.

38. He who is attached to the fragrance of his lotus-like feet, without crookedness and obeys him continuously, knows the way to the Pre-eminent Lord, the protector of the universe (who is) of infinite power and the holder of the discus (lit. a part of the chariot).

39. Hence, Oh venerable ones ! Blessed are you in this world ! As you have thus shown complete devotion to Vāsudeva, the Lord of all the people, there is no terrible transmigration again.

40. The venerable sage (Vyāsa) compiled this epic (Purāṇa) called *Bhāgavata*, equal in status to the Vedas, describing the deeds of him of pious reputation.

---

110. VJ. differs : "The wise describe the secrets contained in the Upaniṣads : The births (incarnations) of Him whose birth is not like that of other individual souls, whose acts are not meant for any selfish purpose, who is present in and controls the minds of all.

111. ŚR: The differentia between the *jīva* and God is the unconcernedness of God with the universe.

112. Viz. Jñāna, Śakti, Bala, Aiśvarya, Vīrya and Tejas.

113. *nipuṇena* : VD. By skill in knowledge and *yoga*.

114. *vitanvataḥ*—VR. : He extends the world of forms by his mental resolve or will

VJ. : *manovacobhir nāma-rūpātmakaṁ prapañcaṁ sṛjataḥ* /

41. For the highest good of the people, he (Vyāsa) made his son (Śuka), pre-eminent among those who have realized the Soul, receive this great (*Bhāgavata Purāṇa*) which is the means of securing Bliss[115].

42. He (Śuka) made the great king Parīkṣit hear[116] attentively this (*Bhāgavata*), the choicest essence of all the Vedas and History (Mahābhārata).

43-44. Oh Brāhmaṇas! While he (Parīkṣit) was sitting on the banks of the Ganges fasting himself unto death, and was surrounded by great sages, and Śuka, the Brāhmaṇa sage of great brilliance (splendour) was narrating the *Bhāgavata*, I learnt the *Bhāgavata* while I sat there due to his favour. I shall narrate to you whatever I have learnt to the best of my ability (intelligence).

45. When Kṛṣṇa retired to His abode along with Righteousness, knowledge and other things, this sun in the form of the *Bhāgavata Purāṇa* has now arisen in the Kali Age for persons who have lost their (intellectual) sight.

---

115. *svastyayana* : Lit. averting of evil by recitation of *mantras* or performance of expiatory rites.

116. Parīkṣit : A son of Uttarā and Abhimanyu; a great king of Hastināpura; the foremost of Bhāgavatas; married Irāvatī, daughter of Uttarā; had 4 sons of whom Janamejaya was the eldest; visualised the symbolic advent of the Kali Age. Due to his act of throwing a dead snake round the neck of a meditating sage, he was cursed with death by Takṣaka's bite. Parīkṣit, knowing his doom, sat in *prāyopaveśa*, where Śuka visited him and narrated the Bhāgavata Purāṇa. Afterwards Parīkṣit sat in contemplation in detached spirit, was bitten by Takṣaka and his body was reduced to ashes by the poison.

CHAPTER FOUR

(*Arrival of Nārada*)

Vyāsa said :

1. Śaunaka, the oldest[117] of the sages (who were) performing the sacrifice of long duration, (being) the head of the congregation of sages[118], and conversant with the *Ṛgveda*, highly praised the Sūta who was thus speaking[119] and addressed (him as follows).

Śaunaka said :

2. Oh Sūta ! Oh highly fortunate one ![120] The finest of speakers ! Tell us the sanctifying (holy) narrative pertaining to the Supreme Lord (the holy narrative of the *Bhāgavata*), which[121] was recounted by venerable[122] Śuka.

3. In what age or (in which) place and with what objective was this (narrative) commenced ? By whom[123] was the dark sage[124] (Vyāsa) inspired to compile this text ?

4. His son who is a great Yogin (contemplative saint) and who has visualized the Supreme Spirit (*Brahman*)[125], and

---

117. *vṛddha*—VB. : Advanced in knowledge and not necessarily in age.

118. *kula-pati*—Originally it signified a Brāhmaṇa sage who maintained, fed and taught 10,000 pupils. ŚR. interprets it as above (*gaṇa-mukhya*). VB. explains it as the regulator or controller of the group of sages (*kulasya ṛṣi—kulasya patiḥ niyāmakaḥ*).

119. *bruvāṇa*—VB. : "Śaunaka was so eager that he did not even wait for the completion of the Speech of the Sūta, as is the normal etiquette".

120. *mahābhāga*—VB. : "It was the great luck of the Sūta that he heard the *Bhāgavata* from Śuka".

121. ŚR. and VB. read *yad* while VJ. reads *yam* i.e. the narrative of the Bhāgavata.

122. *bhagavān*—VB. : "possessing all good qualities" (*pūrṇa-guṇaḥ*).

123. *kutaḥ*—VB : What reason impelled him to compile the Bh. P.

124. *Kṛṣṇaḥ*—ŚR. : *Kṛṣṇa Dvaipāyanaḥ*.

125. *sama-dṛk*—ŚR. : *sama=Brahma*; VJ. *Viṣṇu* (*mayā=Śriyā saha vartate iti*/ "One in association with the goddess Lakṣmī") VB. One knowing (Brahman).

who is devoid of any sense of discrimination and distinction,[126] whose mind is concentrated on one thing (viz. the Supreme Spirit),[127] and (who is) wakeful from the sleep (in the form of Illusion or Ignorance)[128] appears as a dullard avoiding society.[129]

5*. The heavenly damsels, seeing the sage (Vyāsa) (who was) following his son, blushed and put on their garments, even though he (the sage) was not naked but (they) did not do so in the presence of his son (Śuka who was naked). Observing this strange (behaviour) the sage enquired of them (about the reason); they said, "In your outlook, there is the discrimination between man and woman,[130] but it does not exist in your son whose outlook is pure.[131]

6. How was he (Śuka) recognised[132] (when he) arrived in the country Kuru-Jāṅgala[133] and (was) wandering in the city called Hastināpura[134] like a mad, dumb and dull-witted (person)?

7. Oh Sir! How did the dialogue wherein[135] this (sacred) Veda-like text[136] pertaining to Lord Viṣṇu (i.e. the

---

126. *nirvikalpakaḥ*—ŚR.: Devoid of any knowledge of distinction from one thing to another (*nirasta-bheda*)

127. *ekānta-matiḥ*—ŚR.: with mind devoted to one thing. VJ.: whose mind always is engrossed in Hari. VB.: free from worldly attachment.

128. *unnidra*—ŚR.: Wakeful from the sleep of illusion (Māyā) VJ.: From whom sleep in the form of ignorance and other defects, is away.

129. *gūḍha*—VB.: avoiding society. Also "unostentatious", also *aprakaṭa*.

*This verse is not noted by VJ.

130. *strī-bhidā*—ŚR.: The power of seeing the difference between man and woman.

131. *vivikta-dṛṣṭi*—ŚR.: of pure outlook *viviktā-pūtā dṛṣṭir yasya* |

132. *alakṣita*—ŚR.: known (*jñāta*).

133. Kuru-Jāṅgala: The kingdom of Parīkṣit.: Visited by Śuka. Its capital was Hastināpura.

134. *Hastināpura*—The ancient capital of the Kurus. Founded by King Hasti. Though a central scene of action in the MBH (*Mahābhārata*), nothing of the Pāṇḍava era is reported to have been excavated so far.

135. *yatra*—ŚR.: From the conversation.

136. *Sātvatī Śrutiḥ*—*Sātvatī* "Pertaining to lord Hari" according to all comm., but Śruti "compilation" (ŚR.) "equal (in sacredness) to the Vedas" (VR.) "Vaiṣṇava Veda" (VB.).

Bhāgavata Purāṇa) take place between the sage (Śuka) and the royal-sage of the Pāṇḍava family ?

8. That illustrious (sage Śuka) really awaits at the houses of the house-holders only for (so short) a period (as required for) milking cows,[137] thereby transforming it (the house) into a holy place.[138]

9. Oh Sūta ! (Parīkṣit) the son of Abhimanyu is reported to be the best among the devotees of the Lord (Viṣṇu). Describe to us his extremely wonderful birth and deeds.

10. For what reason did the emperor (Parīkṣit), the enhancer of the honour of Pāṇḍavas (lit. Pāṇḍu's[139] progeny), disregarding the glory of emperorship, sit on the bank of the Ganges fasting himself unto death ?

11. Oh (Sūta) ! How wonderful it is ! How did the young hero (warrior-king) to whose footstool (near the throne), enemies, for their own good, bring riches (as tribute) and pay their homage, desire to renounce the royal majesty (lit. wealth) which it is very difficult to give up, along with (his) life ?

12. The persons who are devoted to Lord Viṣṇu (lit. He whose renown or glory dispells the darkness of ignorance) live for the happiness,[140] abundance,[141] and prosperity[142] of

---

137. ŚR. states that this verse raises the doubt how the BH. P. could be narrated within a short period as Śuka stayed at the house of a householder for the time required for milking a cow. This period is, according to ŚR., 1/8th of a *muhūrta* i.e. 15 *kalās*.

138. VR. & VJ. : "Sanctifying the house (by his steps)".

139. *Pāṇḍu*—A royal sage born of Vicitravīrya's queen Ambālikā and Vyāsa (Kṛṣṇa Dvaipāyana) ; superseded his elder blind brother Dhṛtarāṣṭra and was installed as king; married Kuntī alias Pṛthā, sister of Vasudeva, and Mādrī; being prevented from sexual intercourse by a curse, got five sons born to his queens by invoking gods by incantations known to Kuntī; dies as a royal sage in the forest and his second queen Mādrī immolated herself with him; his sons are the Pāṇḍavas. (PI. II. 310.)

140. *śivāya*—For "happiness" (ŚR.), "auspiciousness" (VR.), "quite happiness" (VB.).

141. *bhavāya*—For "abundance" (ŚR.), "ever increasing prosperity" (SD.VR.), "attainment of the goal of life viz. Kāma" (GD.), "For retirement from worldly affairs or *saṁsāra*" (VG.).

142. *bhūtaye*—For "affluence or supremacy (ŚR., SD), "wealth" (VR. VC.), "attainment of mystic powers or *siddhis*" (VB.).

others and not for themselves. Why did this (king) becoming completely indifferent to his body which gave shelter to others, give it (body) up ?

13. Tell us in details everything that has been asked here. I regard you as well-versed in all subjects of speech that are other than the Vedas (i.e. the *Purāṇas* VJ).

Sūta said :

14. In the third cycle of ages, when the Dvāpara Age has already commenced, the sage (lit. one expert in Yoga) Vyāsa, a small part of Hari, was born from Parāśara and Vāsavī.[143]

15. Once upon a time, after the disk of the sun had risen, he sat in a solitary place after (bathing and) sipping the (sacred) water of the Sarasvatī[144] from the palm of his hand (as per his routine of morning duties).

16. The sage who knows the past and the future,[145] perceiving the promiscuous mixing up[146] of the courses of conduct suitable to particular ages, in every Age, in this world due to Time of imperceptible velocity[147]

17-18. And (observing) the deterioration of the power of things created from the elements (such as men, etc,) and

---

143. *Vāsavī*—N. of the daughter of King Uparicara Vasu; brought up as Satyavatī in the house of a fisher-man; the mother of the sage Vyāsa. (BPK. 285).

144. *Sarasvatī*—A sacred river famous in the Vedas. The Ghaggar in the Panjab is regarded as its modern name. ŚR. interprets "upaspṛśya" as "having taken bath" etc while VJ. "After the performance of morning duties e.g. sandhyā, etc".

ŚR. suggests that Vyāsa was sitting at this time in Badarikāśrama (which is so far away from the Panjab). VD. explains this by stating that ŚR. does not mean the Badarikāśrama near Mount Gandhamādana but a separate place of the same name in the forest on the bank of the Sarasvatī in Sindh. SD. and JG., note this place as Śamyāprāśa.

145. *parāvarajñaḥ*—VJ. : "Seer of the past, present and the future".

146. *vyatikara*—ŚR. & VJ. : mixing up; VR. "Inverted order" VB. : "Destruction".

147. *a-vyakta-raṁhas* : ŚR. : Whose course cannot be perceived" VJ. : Of unexpressed (unexhibited) velocity.

VB. : Whose velocity lies within Prakṛti. (Prakṛti and others are dependent upon Time (kālādhīna).

(finding that) men have become lacking in religious faith, energy[148], in intellectual capacity and in longevity of life due to that (subtle force of Time) and seeing the unfortunate men, the sage of unerring view,[149] meditated with his divine vision, upon what was beneficial to all classes of people and their stages of life.

19. Observing that the Vedic rites performed by four sacrificial priests[150] purify the people, he (Vyāsa) separated the (single) Veda into four for the continuity of (the institution of) sacrifices.

20. The four Vedas namely the Ṛg., Yajus, Sāman and Atharvan were divided. [51] And History-cum-Mythology (the Mahābhārata and the Purāṇas) is called the fifth Veda.

21. Out of these, Paila[152] was the recepient of the *Ṛg-veda*, the wise sage Jaimini[153] the master of singing the *Sāman*, Vaiśampāyana[154] alone was expert in the *Yajur Veda*.

22. The terrible sage Sumantu[155] (was well-versed) in

---

148. *niḥsattva*—Without courage or constancy (ŚR.) Without energy (VJ.).

149. *amogha-dṛś*—VJ. : Whose knowledge is fruitful (*avandhyajñāna*) VR. Whose wishes are not fruitless (*avitatha-saṅkalpa*)

150. The four sacrificial priests are Hotṛ, Udgātṛ, Adhvaryu and Brahmā and they represent the Ṛg, Sāman, Yajus and Atharvan (Vedas) respectively.

151. *uddhṛtaḥ*—ŚR. : "Separated"; VJ. : "The Vedas are not compiled but simply arranged by Vyāsa. As History-cum-Mythology is meant for the elucidation of the contents of the Vedas, MBH. and Purāṇas are regarded as the 5th Veda. As JG. points out, this classification of ancient literature in 5 Vedas is as old as the *Chāndogya Upaniṣad*.

152. *Paila* : Son of the sage Vasu; disciple of Vyāsa to learn the *Ṛgveda*; he taught it to Indrapramati and to Bāṣkala; was invited to work as *Hotṛ* in the Rājasūya sacrifice of Yudhiṣṭhira; He classified the *Ṛgveda* in two parts and imparted them to his two disciples mentioned above. (PI. II. 391)

153. *Jaimini* : A pupil of Vyāsa in charge of *Sāma-veda*; was invited to Yudhiṣṭhira's Rājasūya, Janmejaya's Sarpa-satra; Sūtras of *Pūrva Mimāṁsā* and *Aśvam edha Parvan* are traditionally regarded as being compiled by him (PI. I. 653, BPK 120).

154 *Vaiśampāyana* : A pupil of Vyāsa in charge of *Yajur Veda*. He was the maternal uncle of Yājñavalkya. (BPK. 303).

155. *Sumantu* : VJ. states Sumantu as the son of Varuṇa (& reads *Vāruṇaḥ* for *dāruṇaḥ*). He was taught the *Atharva-veda* by Vyāsa.

the *Atharva Veda* relating to the Aṅgirasas, and my father, Romaharṣaṇa, in History-cum-Purāṇas.

23. The sages divided their own respective Veda in different parts. Those Vedas were separated into (a number of) branches by (their) disciples, disciples of disciples and their students.

24. The venerable Vyāsa who was compassionate to the helpless, arranged the Vedas in such a way as can be retained in memory even by persons of low intelligence.

25. The three Vedas are not to be heard by women, Śūdras and lowest among the twice-born ones (i.e. unworthy persons of Brāhmaṇa, Kṣatriya, and Vaiśya castes). In order that the welfare of such (persons) ignorant about actions leading to the good (results) may be (achieved) this way here, that the sage (Vyāsa) compiled the narrative called the *Bhārata*.

26. Oh twice-born ones! The mind of (Vyāsa who was) thus always and in all respects trying for the welfare of all beings, was, however, not satisfied thereby—

27. Vyāsa, the knower of the path of duty, whose mind was not much pacified and who was sitting in solitude on the holy bank of the Sarasvatī, conjecturing (about the reasons etc. of his unhappy state of mind), spoke out this:

28. "Being intent (keen) on observing my duties, the Vedas, preceptors and (holy) fires have been sincerely (lit. without any deceit) worshipped and (their) commands have been obeyed by me."

29. "And verily, the (meaning) of the Vedas has been explained by compiling a work of the title *Bhārata* in which (subjects such as) religion and others are known by (under-privileged persons e.g.) women, Śudras and the like."

30. "Alas! In spite of all these, my individual soul (though) the best in those possessing the lustre of Vedic studies[156] and entire in itself[157] (Or "all-pervading") by

---

156. *Brahma-varcasyuttamaḥ*—ŚR.: The best of possessors of the lustre of Brahma (Veda).
VR.: The purest one (*uttamaḥ*) in lustre born of the study of the Vedas (*Kṛtasvādhyāya-nimitte tejasi*).
VJ: *Vṛttyadhyayana-sampannānāṁ madhye śreṣṭhaḥ* /

157. *vibhuḥ*—ŚR.: "Complete in itself" (*paripūrṇaḥ*)
VR.: "Master" or "Controller", VJ. pervading (*vyāpta*).

itself appears to be underdeveloped (not having reached the stage of the Supreme Spirit[158] (or not reached its natural condition)."

31. Or (because) religious systems (religion) pertaining to the Supreme Lord which are liked by the ascetics of the highest order, have not been considered (by me) in details. And those are really liked by the Infallible Lord (Acyuta)

32. In this way, (while Vyāsa was) considering himself deficient and was distressed (at the thought of his deficiency), Nārada approached the hermitage of Kṛṣṇa Dvaipāyana as described above.

33. The sage (Vyāsa), having known the arrival of Nārada who was worshipped by gods, at once, rose from his seat to welcome him and worshipped (received) him with due formalities.

CHAPTER FIVE

(*The Dialogue Between Vyāsa and Nārada*)

Sūta said :

1. The divine sage (Nārada) of great fame,[159] holding a lute in his hand, and being comfortably seated, spoke with a slight smile,[160] to the Brāhmaṇa sage who was sitting near him.[161]

---

158. *asampannaḥ*—ŚR. : Not reached its natural stage. VJ. : One who has not achieved his life's mission. VR. : *a-samṛddha*.

159. *bṛhacchravaḥ*—ŚR. : whose fame is great. GD. : One whose fame for omniscience has spread everywhere.

160. Commentators attribute various reasons for this smile. ŚR. : "Because even a great man is sometimes deluded". VD. : "This great man does not deserve to be thus perplexed". VB., VC. : Nārada smiled as he was unable to conceal his pleasure (about the prospective discussion).

161. *upāsīnam*—VD ; Who received him with due formalities.

Nārada said :

2. Oh highly fortunate son of Parāśara, is your son, associated with (lit. proud of) your body or with your mind,[162] quite satisfied with your body or mind (respectively) ?

3. Have you not thoroughly comprehended[163] whatever you desired to know[164], as you have compiled the great, wonderful[165] *Bhārata* which is full of matters[166] pertaining to the principal goals of human life (viz. *dharma*, *artha*, *kāma*, *mokṣa*) ?

4. The eternal Brahma[167] (Supreme Spirit) (Or the Veda) which has been so much coveted[168] by you (for its knowledge and attainment) has been known and attained by you. (Or in the case of the Veda: "has been studied and considered by you by composing the Vedānta Sūtras").[169] Still, Oh learned (sage)[170], you are worrying yourself as if you have not achieved your goal.

---

162. *śārīra ātmā mānasa eva vā* : *śārīra ātmā* : ŚR., VC : Soul who is proud of the body (*śarīrābhimānī ātmā*). SV. : "Presiding over the body".

mānasa ātmā : ŚR., VC : proud of the mind. SV. : controller of the mind. BP. : Soul which is proud of the gross and subtle bodies.

163. *susampannam*—ŚR. Fully acquainted with. GD. : Properly comprehended with ease.

164. *jijñāsitam*—ŚR. : What was worth knowing e.g. religion etc.

165. *mahadadbhutam*—VR. : Extensive (*vipulam*) and wonderful in its composition and meaning (*śabdataḥ arthataś ca citram*) SV : *śabdārthābhyāṁ vicitram*/

166. *sarvārtha-paribṛṁhitam*—ŚR. : Full of matters concerning the four goals of human life e.g. *dharma*, *artha*, *kāma* and *mokṣa*. SV. & VB. support this as follows : *sarvaiḥ sāṅgopāṅgaiḥ ca dharmabhir arthaiḥ paribṛṁhitaṁ pūrṇam*/

167. *Brahma*—It means both "the Veda" and "the Supreme Spirit" and the verse is to be construed as applying to both. ŚR. takes it in the latter sense.

168. *jijñāsita*—ŚR. : Considered, but GS. adds "Considered by composing the *Brahma Sūtras*." SV. VR. and VB. take "Brahma" as "the Veda" and interpret, "You have studied the Veda word by word and from the point of its meaning and implication have composed the *Mīmāṁsā Sūtras*.

169. *adhīta*—ŚR. : "Attained" (*adhigata*, *prāpta*).

170. *prabho*—VJ. : One of vast learning (*prabhūta-jñānin*).

Vyāsa said:

5. (Although) all that has been described by you, is certainly in me; my soul[171], however, is unsatisfied. I ask the (underlying) latent[172] cause of it to you, as you have unfathomable knowledge[173] and are born from Brahman[174].

6. Verily your honour knows all the secrets[175], as you have adored the Primeval Man (Lord Viṣṇu, who is) the regulator of (everything) high or low[176], and who, without being attached[177] creates, protects and destroys the universe by means of attributes (viz. *sattva*, *rajas* and *tamas*), as soon as He wills it (by His will-power).

7. You who travel in the three worlds (the Heaven, the earth and the subterranean regions) like the Sun (and thereby know the external things), and who, like the breath (wind) moving within, (are) a witness unto the hearts of others[178], explain to me sufficiently clearly the deficiency in me though I have dived deep into the Supreme Spirit by Yogic practices (e.g. meditation etc.)[179] and have mastered the Vedas by religious observances[180].

---

171. *ātmā*—ŚR. : The soul both corporeal (*śārīra*) and mental (*mānasa*).

172. *avyaktam*—ŚR. : Not clear, latent; VB. : not explicit VR.. : Not known to me.

173. *agādha-bodha*—ŚR. : Whose intelligence is unfathomable VR., VJ. : Of unfathomable knowledge. VC., VD. : Omniscient.

174. *Ātma-bhava*—: VB. : Incarnation of the Lord. *ātma-bhūta*—VB. : Self-knower (*ātmavid*).

175. *samasta-guhyam*—VR., BP. : Minds of all beings.

176. *parāvareśaḥ*—ŚR. : Regulator of all cause and effect (*kārya-kāraṇa-n'yantā*).VR. : The Lord to whom gods like Brahmā and others are subordinate; Controller of all.

177. *asaṅgaḥ*—VD., VR. Unattached to attributes (*Guṇa-saṅga-rahitaḥ*)

178. *ātma-sākṣī*—ŚR. : Knowing the intelligence and course of conduct (*buddhi-vṛtti-jña*).

179. *dharmataḥ* ŚR. : *pare Brahmaṇi dharmato yogena niṣṇātaḥ*/ VR. takes *dharmataḥ* as *nivṛtti-dharmaiḥ*.

180. *Parāvare Brahmaṇi*—ŚR. : *avara-brahma* is the Vedas which are mastered by means of "Self-study, observance of religious vows etc." VB. explains *para* as that which has been explained by the Upaniṣads (*Vedānta*), *apara Brahma* is the Veda.

Nārada Said :

8. Your honour has not practically described the pure[181] glory of the Lord. I think that knowledge[182] by which the Supreme Being is not pleased is incomplete.

9. Oh great sage ! You have not really described the glory of Vāsudeva (in the same proportion) as you have extolled in details the goals (of human life) like Religion (*dharma*) and others(viz. *artha*, *kāma* and *mokṣa*) and[183] its cognate subjects.

10. The speech composed of words with rhetorical charm[184] but which seldom describes the world-purifying glory of Hari, is[185] regarded like a place of pleasure worthy of enjoyment for worldly persons where ascetics[186] of pure mind[187], who dwell in (are merged in) the Supreme Spirit (Brahma[188]) never like to stay, like swans from the Mānasa lake, who have beautiful dwelling places, do not find pleasure in the pools that are the pleasure-resorts of crows alone.

181. *omala*—VR. : Cleansing the sins of the speaker and the hearer.

182. *darśana*—ŚR. : "Knowledge", VR. : Visualization of the Lord (*Bhagavaddarśana*). VD., VC. : Science of investigation into the nature of the Supreme Spirit (*Vedānta-darśana*).

183. *ca*—ŚR. : This word shows the inclusion of the different practices of religion.

184. *citra-pada*—In Rhetorics, *citra* is one of the 3 main divisions of *Kāvya* (Poetry). It is of 2 kinds: *śabda-citra* and *artha-citra*, and the poetical charm lies mainly in the use of figures of speech, dependent on the sound or sense of the word. The Bh. P. naturally regards Lord Hari's glory superior to rhetorical beauty. VD. explains this as "Wonderful" (*vismayasya sthānam* : *vismayakāri*)

185. Hari's devotees are likened to swans dwelling in the Mānasa lake. Just as these swans avoid dirty places which are enjoyed by crows, similarly poetry not singing of the glory of the Lord is not liked by the true devotees. ŚR. and VR. interpret *vāyasam tīrtham* as a place of enjoyment of pleasures for persons desirous of worldly things. VD. explains *vāyasa* as "Trade or profession for one's livelihood".

186. *haṁsa*—ŚR. : (1) Swans, (2) Recluse.

187. *mānasaḥ*—(1) Living in the Mānasa lake (2) Of good (*sāttvic* frame of mind). To this VD. adds : (3) Devotees staying in the mind of Hari, (4) Mind-born sons of Brahmā, like Sanaka, etc.

188. *uśikkṣayaḥ* : ŚR., VR. Vj. agree to this but with different etymologies.

11. That outflow of words[189] which though not properly composed[190] in every verse, makes good people (saints) hear, sing and praise the names (which are as if) imprinted[191] with the glory of the Infinite Lord, destroys the sins of the people.

12. Knowledge, (though) actionless[192] and pure[193], (if) devoid of devotion to the Imperishable Lord (Viṣṇu), does not appear sufficiently bright (purificatory).[194] And how can again the action which is always unblissful, even though (performed) without any desire of its fruit appear bright (i.e. will have purificatory effect, if it is not dedicated to God.)?

13. Oh highly fortunate one! (Your Honour) of correct insight[195], of pure (spotless) glory[196], lover of the truth, and observer of religious vows, should recollect (and describe) with concentrated mind[197], the various acts of the Lord with wide steps[198] (i.e, Viṣṇu in Vāmana incarnation) for liberation from all bondages (of this Saṁsāra).

14. Since you were looking for (objects) other than (the Lord's deeds) and were desirous of speaking (i.e. describing) something else (than the pastimes of the Lord), your

---

189. *vāg-visarga* : ŚR. : "Application of words" (*vācaḥ prayogaḥ*) VJ. : Special composition or arrangement of words. VR. : *vāk-sṛṣṭi-rūpaḥ prabandhaḥ*.

190. *abaddhavatī*—ŚR. : Ill-worded Full of corrupt words.

191. *nāmāni*—VB : Not merely names but bearing the imprint of Lord's glory.

192. *naiṣkarmya*—VR. : Knowledge about the correct path of devotion to the Lord. RR. : Means or path of Liberation (*niṣkarman*).

193. *nirañjana*—VR. : Untouched by the collyrium of love and hate. VD. : Free from illusion (*avidyā*). VJ. : Unsoiled by objects of enjoyment.

194. ŚR. : "Does not result in proper "direct" knowledge.

195. *amoghadṛś*—ŚR. : Of true intellect.

196. *śuci-śravas*—ŚR. : of pure renown.

197. *samādhinā*—VD. : out of the 3 ways of speech. *samādhi-bhāṣā* is characterised by objective description (*Darśana-guhyasamādhi-bhedena tridhā bhinnānām bhāṣāṇām madhye yathāsthita-vastu-kathana-lakṣaṇayā samādhi-bhāṣayā anusmara*|)

198. *urukramasya*—SD., VB. and VR. think this a reference to Viṣṇu in the Vāmana incarnation who after getting permission from Bali to get 3 steps of land assumed his *viśva-rūpa* and covered the earth and the sky in 2 steps and pressed down Bali to the subterranean regions with the 3rd step. VJ. interprets this as "Of great exploits."

mind, which has become unstable on account of the words and forms (created by your above-mentioned desire) will not get a stable position anywhere and on any matter, like a boat driven by a gale (lit. "struck by a wind").

15. A gross negligence[199] (has been committed by you) in advising censuarble acts (for the sake) of religion, to persons who by nature are addicted to secular desires. Ordinary people have followed those actions, thinking them to be (real) religion, on account of (Vyāsa's) words.[200] (Ordinary man) does not think of setting aside that (way of life).

16. By abstaining from worldly acts, a very clever person becomes capable of knowing the blissful nature of the All-pervading, Limitless Lord. Therefore, your honour (should please) describe the diversions of the Supreme Lord to (persons) who are devoid of spiritual intellect[201] and who due to qualities viz. *Sattva, Rajas, and Tamas* are engaged in acts (holding out future promises).

17. (If) a person, discarding his own (form of) religion, resorts to the lotus-like feet of Hari, (and happens) to fall while in an immature stage, will evil befall unto him in whatever place or in whichever (circumstances) he may be? Or what benefit has accrued to a non-devotee following his own religion?[202]

---

199. *vyatikrama*—ŚR. : Transgression (improper for Vyāsa) V.J. : Gross injustice.

200. *yad vākyataḥ*—ŚR. and JG. but VR. "For the sake of the good of the beings you (Vyāsa) have acted to the contrary. Due to your description of the 1st three goals of human life (viz. *dharma. artha,* & *kāma*) people do not know that you intended to advise them to set aside these three for the sake of the 4th goal, viz. *mokṣa.* JG. thinks that this verse pinpoints Vyāsa's deficiency. He had done wrong to the world by describing a course of religion devoid of Hari's glorious acts. (In MBH. *Kṛṣṇa* is a secondary figure.)

201. *anātmnaḥ*—ŚR. : Proud of the physical body. JG. : Devoid of spiritual intellect. SD. : Of undetermined intellect.

202. VJ. "No puruṣārtha (goal of human life) is achieved by faultless observation of one's own *pravṛtti-dharma*. I request you to describe the science of *Nivṛtti-dharma*" VC. The daily and occasional religious observances should be abandoned in favour of devotion to Hari.

18. The learned one should specially try for that objective (viz. "the experience of the supreme Spirit" which is not obtained while wandering in higher or lower (types of births). That happiness (i.e. enjoyment of worldly objects) comes to (our) lot unsolicited like misery from other sources (from actions of previous life) everywhere due to (passage of) time which has great velocity.[203]

19. Oh ! A person who is serving Lord Kṛṣṇa will not certainly be entangled into the cycle of transmigration of the soul. There is such an attraction of that sweetest thing[204] that he who remembers the (joy or test of) clasping the feet of Lord Kṛṣṇa, will never desire to let them go.[205]

20. This universe is verily the Supreme Lord Himself but in a way different[206]. As your honour already knows it, (it is) from him that the preservance, destruction and creation of the Universe (take place). Only a spanful has been indicated to you by me.

21. Oh (sage) of unerring view![207] You know it yourself that (though) you are birthless, you are born as a part of

---

203. *gambhīra-rahasā*—VR. Whose velocity is too fast to be observed. VJ. : Whose speed is unmanifested but covers many births (earthly existences)

204. *rasa-grahaḥ*—ŚR. : *rasena rasanīyena gṛhyate vaśī-kriyate* | Or *rase-rasanīye grahaḥ=āgrahaḥ yasya*|.
VB. : *rasena grahaṇaṁ yasya* |

205. According to VR : The devotees of the Lord even though they have not mastered the Bhakti-yoga thoroughly, do not even then return to the cycle of births and deaths (*saṁsāra*) like ignorant persons, or non-devotees (VJ).

206. ŚR. adds one more explanation : This universe is the Supreme Lord. The individual spirit, though apparently separate from the Lord, is also the Supreme Lord. There is nothing animate or inanimate beyond the Supreme Lord who alone is the Truth or Reality. VJ. states the position of the Dualistic School : The Lord is verily like the universe (Not the Universe itself). He is different from it. For it is from the Lord that the creation, preservation and destruction of the Universe proceeds (and He is endowed with all powers of omniscience, omnipotence etc.). The Lord Himself knows this. (Like a pupil exhibiting his little knowledge before the preceptor) I have shown my limited knowledge to you).

207. *amogha-dṛś*—ŚR. : Full of accurate knowledge. VR. : One who sees the whole of reality as it is.

the Supreme Soul (who is) the Greatest Man, for the welfare of the world. Therefore, let the glories[208] of the Lord of great prowess be described in details by you.

22. The act of extolling the qualities of the Lord of excellent renown, has been declared by wise men, as the indestructible fruit[209] of a man's penance, hearing (the scriptures), performance of the best sacrifices, recital of Vedas and of intelligence and charities.

23. Oh sage ! As for myself, formerly (in a former cycle of Ages), in (my) previous birth, I was born of a certain female servant of sages conversant with the Vedas. Even while (I was) a child, I was appointed to wait upon (some) ascetics who wished to stay together (in one place) during (the four months of) the rainy-season.

24. Although the sages[210] had equality of outlook (towards all beings) they began (to show) favour to me whose unsteadiness had completely disappeared, (who was) self-controlled, obedient, and a willing servant of few words.

25. Being allowed by the twice-born (sages) to eat the remanents of the food sticking to their dishes whereby (my) sin had been destroyed, I used to take meal once a day.[211] I was behaving thus and my heart had been well purified. (Thus) a self-interest in their (Bhāgavata) religion also had developed (in me).

26. There, by the favour of the singers, I heard attractive (interesting) narratives of Kṛṣṇa, every day. Oh Vyāsa! (As) I heard every word[212] of those (narratives) with special attention, my devotion in the Lord whose renown is so dear, developed.

27. Oh great sage! Then I developed liking for (the Lord) whose fame is dear (to all). My intellect became un-

---

208. *abhyudaya*—ŚR. : "Prowess"; VR. : viz. Birth, actions, qualities. (*Janma-karma-guṇādī*).

209. *avicyutārthaḥ*—VD., VR : *artha*=purpose ; SD. : *artha*=Fruit (*phalam*).

210. VB. says that these were the 4 sages : Sanaka, Sanandana etc. in their previous birth.

211. VJ. the recluses eat once a day, so did Nārada.

212. v.l. *anusavam*—VR. and VJ. Interpret this as "Three times a day, viz. morning, noon and evening (*tri-sandhyam*)."

deviating[213] from the right course whereby I could see that due to my illusion, this grossness and subtlety[214] had been imagined in me who am (really) higher Brahma (Supreme Spirit).[215]

28. In this way, during the rainy season and the Autumn, I, who heard attentively the spotless glory of Hari extolled thrice a day[216] by the sages of noble souls, had got created in me devotion which removes the *rajas* and *tamas* of the Soul.

29-30. At the time of their departure those sages, who were kind to the poor, taught the most esoterical knowledge[217] which has been conveyed by the Supreme Lord Himself, to me who, as a child was attached to them, and (was) humble, full of reverence, self-controlled and had been serving them (with devotion).

31. On account of which (knowledge) only, I came to comprehend the efficacy of the power called Illusion[218] of Lord Vāsudeva, the Creator of the Universe. (It is) by that knowledge (that) the people attain to His feet (i.e. Liberation).

---

213. *a-skhalita*—ŚR.: "Unobstructed"; SD.: "Steady, firm".

214. *sad-asat*—ŚR. Gross and subtle. While JG. takes it as *vyaṣṭi* (An aggregate viewed as made up of many separate bodies) and *samaṣṭi* (An aggregate considered to be made of parts each of which is consubstantially the same with the whole). To quote JG. *aham etat sadasad vyoṣṭi-samaṣṭyātmakaṁ yaj jagat tad vyaṣṭyaṁśaṁ mayi jīvarūpe sva-viṣayaka-bhagavan-māyayā kalpitam paśye.*

215. According to VJ., "I see that all this universe of cause and effect is the creation by the will of Hari who is in me and that it is maintained and destroyed by him". He strongly objects to the *adhyāsa* theory as false knowledge (*mithyā-jñāna.*)

216. See F.N. 212 above.

217. *guhyatema*—ŚR. and BP. : Knowledge about the practice of religion is *guhya* (secret); pure knowledge derived from the practice of religion is *guhyatara* (secret of a higher degree); Knowledge derived from the above about the Supreme Lord (*Īśvara-jñāna*) is the most secret (*guhyatama*).

218. *māyānubhāvam*—*Māyā* has been variously interpreted by commentators as intellectual capacity (*cicchakti*) of the Lord (JG., VD.), the *prakṛti* consisting of 3 attributes viz, *sattva*, *rajas* and *tamas* (VR.). "anubhāva" is the power or the effect of Māyā.

32. Oh Brāhmaṇa ! (It has been) well-known[219] that action which is dedicated to the Lord, the Supreme Spirit, the Controller of the universe, removes the three types of miseries (viz. those pertaining to the body, caused by Fate and caused by animals etc.—called in Sk. *ādhyātmika*, *ādhidaivika* and *ādhibhautika*).

33. Oh good observer of religious vows! Verily the stuff which causes disease to beings, does not cure it (the disease by itself). But (if) administered after medical Purification[220], it cures[221] (that disease).

34. In the same way, the performances of all[222] actions[223] (which are) the causes of worldly existence[224] (i.e. the transmigration of the soul) are capable of destroying themselves[225] if those (very actions) are dedicated to the Supreme Spirit.

35. In this world, knowledge which is coupled with

---

219. *saṁsūcita*—VD. : "Suggested, not directly spoken". JG. : (Suggested) by persons well-versed in Scriptures. VR. : by Śrutis and Smṛtis; VJ. : Properly suggested to the people, (*Samīcīnaṁ sūcitaṁ lokasya*).

220. *cikitsitam*—ŚR. : is purified by other objects. BP. : If mixed with medicinal quick-silver vermillion, etc.

221. *punāti*—VD. : purifies, removes the dirt (disease) GD: acts as prophylactic. VR. interprets this verse differently : "Oh careful observer of religious vows ! Just as unwholesome food which causes disease does not cure the disease if taken in for remedial purpose." *cikitsitā 'pi vyādhir apathyādinā punaḥ vardhate ityarthaḥ.*

222. *sarve*—VD. VR. : This includes meritorious actions also. GS. : Both usual (*nitya*) and occasional (*naimittika*) actions performed with attachment (*kāmya-karma*).

223. *kriyā-yogaḥ*—BP. VJ. : *kriyā lakṣaṇā yogā upāyāḥ|*

224. *saṃsṛti-hetavaḥ*—VD. : Causes of bondage.

225. *ātma-vināśāya kalpate*—ŚR. : are capable of destroying the effects of actions. He gives the following progressive stages or steps: 1. Service of the great—2. Their favour—3. Faith in religion—4. Hearing the stories of God—5. Love of God—6. Knowledge about (*viveka-jñāna*) the self—7. Firm devotion to God—8. Awareness of the real nature of God.—9. Manifestation of attributes or qualities of Godhead e.g. Omniscience and others in the devotee.

VD. interprets differently : "In this world, knowledge which is accompanied with devotion (e.g. *śravaṇa*, *kīrtana* and others) is definitely pleasing to the Supreme Lord. This knowledge is born of actions which are performed without attachment and dedicated to the Supreme Lord."

devotional contemplation[226], is certainly dependent on actions which are performed for the gratification of the Supreme Spirit.[227]

36*. Where persons always perform actions according to the teaching of the Lord, they extol the qualities and names of Kṛṣṇa and meditate on him.

37. Salutations to you Venerable Vāsudeva. Obeisance to Pradyumna, Aniruddha and Saṅkarṣaṇa[228]. We meditate (on you all).

38. He who thus by taking the names of these (abovementioned four) forms, worships the Sacrificial Man who is formless yet has his body made up of holy incantations, becomes full of correct perception.[229]

---

226. *bhakti-yoga*—JG. : It includes chanting of Hari's name and musing over his deeds.

227. JG. thinks that this verse describes the superiority of actions which are pleasing to the Lord Hari, while VJ. thinks that performance of actions removes the bondage of Karma by generating knowledge.

VR. explains: "Just as actions always done according to the instructions of the Lord, create devotion, similarly they make (the devotee) to meditate upon his attributes and names".

The so-called instructions of Hari mentioned in VR. above are quoted from the Bhagavad Gītā e.g. *yat karoṣi yad aśnāsi* etc. (BG. IX. 27), *mayi sarvāṇi karmāṇi* etc. (BG. III. 30).

According to VJ. this verse explains how knowledge is generated by performance of actions (*karmas*). When they perform sacrifices as ordained by the Lord, at various steps, they remember the glorious qualities of the Lord and sing Lord Kṛṣṇa's name. In this way knowledge develops through performance of actions.

228. Although these are names of Kṛṣṇa, his son, his grandson and his (Kṛṣṇa's) brother, these are technically called the Vyūhas in the Pañcarātra system of philosophy. Its application to the Bhāgavata sect is as follows : The Ist category evolved from Prakrti is *mahat* which contains the germs of the entire universe; it is pure translucent *sattva* (also called *Citta* or *Vāsudeva*). From the category of *Mahat* the threefold *ahaṁkāra* viz. *vaikārika*, *taijasa* and *tāmasa* was produced. This *ahaṁkāra* is called *Saṅkarṣaṇa*. The category of *Manas* is produced from *Vaikārika ahaṅkāra* and it is called *Aniruddha* in the terminology of the *Bhāgavata* cult. *Pradyumna* stands for the desire; desires are but functions of the category of *manas* and not a separate category.

229. *samyag-darśana*—ŚR. : The Being of perfect knowledge.

39. Oh Brāhmaṇa! Keśava (Lord Viṣṇu), knowing that I practised his sacred precept, bestowed on me knowledge pertaining to the Controller of the Universe and devotion unto him.

40. Oh sage with wide knowledge! You also describe the great glory of the All-pervading Lord, which satisfies the desire for enjoyment on the part of the learned ones. Persons who are constantiy afflicted by miseries take resort to (his) glory (as it is not) otherwise pacified (at all).

CHAPTER SIX

(*Dialogue between Vyāsa and Nārada*)

Sūta said : *

1. Oh Brāhmaṇa! Having thus heard about the birth and deeds of the divine sage (Nārada), the venerable Vyāsa, the son of Satyavatī, asked him again.

Vyāsa said :

2. When the religious mendicants (*sannyāsins*) who initiated you in the special spiritual knowledge departed (to a distant country), what did your honour do in that primary stage of life ?

3. Oh son of the self-existent god Brahmā ! In what way did you lead your later life ? How did you give up your body when the time (of your death) arrived ?

4. Oh the best of gods ![230] How is it that (even though) Time is all-destructive[231] it has not shadowed[232] your memory (of matters) pertaining to the previous epoch ?

---

*VR. : Vyāsa was eager to know the sequel of the narration after BH. P.1.5.30 (*anvavocan gamiṣyantaḥ kṛpayā dīna-vatsalāḥ* etc).

230. *surasattama*—VJ: Greatest of the knowers.

231. *nirākṛtiḥ*—ŚR.: "Concealing" (*apalāpa*). VD., VR. : "Destruction". VR. "All destructive".

232. vyavadhāt: ŚR: Broken, erased (*khaṇḍitavān*) VR.: Concealed (*tirohitavān*).

Nārada said :

5. When the recluses who taught me the special spiritual knowledge set out (on their distant journey) I, who was in my primary stage of life, did as follows.

6. My mother, to whom I was the only son, being an ignorant woman—a maid servant—bound me by (her) affection as I was a son who had no other shelter.

7. Although she desired (to provide) for my well-being, she, being not independent, was unable to do so. People are subject to (the Will of) the Almighty like a doll of wood.

8. And I, as a child of five years of age, being ignorant of directions, regions or time, stayed in the Brāhmaṇa's house expecting that (termination of the bond of maternal affection).

9. Once, when my innocent mother went out at night (to milk the cow), a serpent (as if) ordered by the god of death, was touched[233] by her foot on the way, bit her while she was milking (the cow).

10. Then, looking upon it (my mother's death) as the grace of the Lord who is solicitous about the well-being of his devotees, I proceeded to the northern direction.

11. (While going alone) in that direction, I saw prosperous countries and capital towns, villages, habitations of cowherds and mines, villages of cultivators, habitations adjacent to hills and streams, parks, jungles and gardens[234].

12. (I saw) mountains of variegated colours due to the ores of different metals[235], (covered with) trees the branches of which are broken by elephants, lakes of clear water and lotus-pools enjoyed by gods (and) beautified by the droning of the black-bees which are roused by wonderful warblings of the birds (lit. wing-vehicled beings).

13-14. I who traversed alone such a long distance saw a vast, unbearably terrible looking forest* which had cavities form-

---

233. ŚR: "was slightly trod upon".

234. I have followed ŚR. in this interpretation.

235. ŚR. : "Mountains of variegated colours due to metals like gold and silver".

*The 2nd line of verse 13 is constructed with verse 14 and thus inserted herein.

ed by Nala grass, (solid) bamboos, clumps of white reeds and Kuśa grass and clusters of hollow bamboos (whistling with wind) which was (as it were) a play-ground of serpents (wicked elephants) owls and jackals.

15. I, who was physically and mentally exhausted, and was both thirsty and hungry, got relieved from the fatigue by bathing in the deep lake in the river-bed and by drinking (the river-water and by performing the religious sipping of (water (from the cavity of the hand).

16. In that tenantless forest, I, who was seated at the foot of a Pippala tree[236], meditated internally (by my mind or intellect) upon the Supreme Spirit that was (present) within me, as per instructions heard (from the recluses.).

17. While I was meditating upon the lotus-like feet (of Hari) with my mind overwhelmed or subdued with devotion, and my eyes overflowing with tears for longing (to see Hari), Hari manifested himself slowly in my heart.

18. Oh sage! I, whose hair were standing on their ends owing to the rapturous love (for the Supreme Spirit), and who was deeply satisfied and was immersed in the flood of delight, could not see both.[237]

19. When I could not see the beautiful form of the Lord so pleasing to the mind and dispeller of sorrow, I felt dejected and suddenly stood up through bewilderment.[238]

20. Being desirous of seeing it (the form of the Lord) when I again tried to see him by concentrating my mind within itself, I was not able to see him and became anxious like a diseased person.

21. (He) who is unapproachable to speech, addressed in a voice deep yet sweet and grief-assuaging, to me who was thus struggling alone (to see him) in solitude.

---

236. v.1. *āśrita*—VB: Leaning against (the Pippala tree).

237. *ubhayam*—ŚR: "Myself and others"; VR: "Body and Soul" the Individual Spirit and the Supreme Spirit. SD. construes it differently: "Being excessively unsatisfied due to my inability to see him, I became over-eager and with a desire to see him again, I concentrated my mind within me and tried to see him but in vain."

238. From *Apaśyan sahasv* etc. BH.P.I.6.19b to the end of 22 are deleted in some Mss.

22. "Alas ! In this life you are not eligible to see me here. I am difficult to be seen by immature Yogins whose taints (sins) have not been wiped out.

23. On Sinless one ! It was just out of love for you that the Vision (Form) was shown to you once. A saintly person who loves me shakes off all the desires in his heart gradually.

24. Due to the service of the saints for a short while, your mind has become firmly fixed in me. After leaving this inferior world (censurable body as Nārada was lowborn), you will attain the position of my personal attendant (*pārṣada*).

25. This intellect of yours which is stabilised in me, will never be incapaciated. And despite creation or destruction of the world, your memory shall persist due to my grace".

26. That Great Spirit of sky-like form, invisible (yet) controller of all, stopped after speaking this (much). I, who deserved compassion, paid my obeisance with my head to him who was the greatest of the great ;

27. With the sense of bashfulness shed off, reciting the names of the Infinite (Lord), musing over the mystic and auspicious deeds (of the Lord), with a satisfied mind free from desire, pride and jealousy, I wandered over the earth waiting for the time (of my death).

28. Oh Brāhmaṇa ! In this way, with my mind (intellect) fixed in Kṛṣṇa and unattached, and of pure soul, death appeared (suddenly to me) at the proper time like a garland-like lightning.[239]

29. That great spirit of ethereal form (having no material body), invisible (yet) controller of all, stopped after speaking this (much). I who was an object of his grace, paid obeisance with my head to him who was greater than the great.

30. Biding for the time (of my death), I wandered over the earth, reciting the names of the Infinite without any sense

---

239. *vidyut saudāminī yathā* —ŚR.: "Lightning flashed in the vicinity of a mountain of crystal called Sudāman." This alternate explanation has been echoed by VR. who adds, "This example is given to suggest the transitory nature of death." VC. thinks that just as one lightning emerges out of another, the body of Viṣṇu's attendant (pārṣada) was ready after the falling away of Nārada's human body.

of shyness and musing over the mystic and auspicious deeds (of the Lord), with a heart satisfied, free from desire, pride and jealousy.

31. Oh Brāhmaṇa ! In this way, just as lightning flashes in the vicinity of the crystaline mountain *Sudāman*[240] at the proper time, death came, in due course, to me whose mind was pure and fixed on Kṛṣṇa and was unattached (to worldly things).

32. While I was being transferred to that pure body pertaining to the (attendant of the) Lord, (my) gross body composed of the five elements fell off[241], indicating the exhaustion of actions (due to which one gets one's body).

33. I entered along with his breath in god Brahmā who desired to sleep within Lord Nārāyaṇa when at the end of the world he (Nārāyaṇa) sleeps on the waters of the ocean withdrawing this (world) within him.

34. At the end of one thousand ages,[242] he woke up and desired to create the world (when) I, along with sages of whom Marīci was prominent, was born from the breath (or organs of senses) of god Brahmā.

35. I wandered in and out of the three worlds, without the violation of any vows[243] (as) my movements were unhampered by the grace of the great Viṣṇu.

36. Playing on this lute (*Vīṇā*) gifted to me by the Lord and adorned with Brahman in the form of the seven notes of the musical gamut I go about singing the episodes of Hari.

37. When I sing of the exploits of the Lord whose feet are holy and glory lovable, he manifests himself in my heart immediately like an invitee.

---

240. *Saudāminī*—SR. and VR. explain it as above. VR. adds: this example is given to suggest the momentary nature of death.

241. VB. explains that Nārada had not to undergo pains of death. SD. states that Nārada returned to his original divine body after the complete fruition of the Brāhmaṇa's curse whereby he was born as the son of a maid servant.

242. *Yuga*—The group of four ages (viz. Kṛta, Tretā, Dvāpara and Kali)—VD.

243. *askandita-vrataḥ*—(i) Whose vow of celibacy remained unviolated—ŚR., VR. (ii) One whose vow of devotion to the Lord remained unbroken—VD., JG.

38. For, this singing of the deeds of Hari is (regarded) as a boat to cross the ocean of worldly existence for those whose hearts are often afflicted by yearning for enjoying (the pleasures of the world).

39. The mind (lit. Soul) which is frequently afflicted by passions and avarice is not pacified (to that extent) by the paths of *Yoga*[244] consisting of *Yama, niyama* etc., as is directly done by the service of Kṛṣṇa.

40. Oh sinless one! Whatever has been asked by you about the mysteries of my birth and deeds, has been narrated by me to your mind's satisfaction.

Sūta said :

41. After having spoken thus to the son of Vāsavī (Vyāsa), the Venerable Nārada bade good-bye and departed while playing upon his lute; for the sage has no purpose of his own.

42. Oh! How blessed is this divine sage (Nārada) who while singing of the glory of Viṣṇu (lit. god with a bow of horns) is transported with joy and delights this afflicted world by playing upon the lute (Vīṇā).

CHAPTER SEVEN

(*Punishment of Aśvatthāman*)

Śaunaka said :

1. Oh Sūta! After having listened to the suggestion of Nārada, what did the venerable and glorious Bādarāyaṇa do on Nārada's departure?

244. *Yamādibhir yogapathaiḥ*--Patañjali in YS ii. 29 gives the following 'aids' (*aṅgas*) of Yoga: Abstentions (*Yama*), observances (*niyama*), postures (*āsana*), regulations-of-the breath (*prāṇāyāma*), withdrawal-of-the-senses, (*pratyāhāra*), fixed attention, (*dhāraṇā*), contemplation, (*dhyāna*) and concentration (*samādhi*). YS ii. 30 enumerates *yamas* as follows: "Abstinence from injury, falsehood, theft, incontinence and acceptance of gifts." (For details vide J.H. Woods—*The Yoga System of Patañjali*, pp. 177 ff). The path of Yoga was greatly respected and followed by Jainas and Buddhists. The five great vows (*Pañca Mahāvratas* of Jainas correspond

Sūta said :

2. On the western bank of the Sarasvatī, the presiding deity of which is god Brahmā (*Or* which is resorted to by Brāhmaṇas) there is a hermitage called Śamyāprāsa which encourages (lit.extends) the sacrificial sessions of the sages.

3. Sitting in his own hermitage beautified by a cluster of jujube trees, Vyāsa, after 'touching water' (i.e. sipping it from the palm of his hand as is usually performed before any religious act or taking meals), concentrated his mind (as instructed by Nārada).

4. In his mind purified by devotion and thoroughly concentrated, he saw at first the Primeval Being and (his power called) Māyā (Illusion) depending on him.[245]

5. Though the individual soul is beyond the three attributes, he, being deluded by her (Māyā), regards himself as consisting of the three attributes and suffers calamities (e.g. birth, death, three types of misery etc.) caused by the notion.

6. Realizing that the path of devotion to Viṣṇu directly subsides the calamities (of *saṁsāra* mentioned above), the learned Vyāsa composed the *sāttvata saṁhitā* (the *Bhāgavata Purāṇa*) for ignorant people.

7. Verily, by listening to this (the *Bhāgavata Purāṇa*) devotion unto Kṛṣṇa, the Supreme Man, is developed. It (devotion) dispells all grief, infatuation and fears (of man).

8. Having composed and arranged the *Bhāgavata Saṁhitā*, the sage taught it to his son Śuka who was firmly fixed in renunciation.

Śaunaka said :

9. The sage (Śuka) is (known) to be devoid of attachment to the world and is unconcerned everywhere (to every thing). For what purpose did he who was delighted in his Higher Self, learn this big tome ?

---

to *yama*. The Bh. P. has elaborated the five *yamas* and the five *niyamas* of Patañjali into twelve each (vide the Bh. P. 3.28. 2-4, 11.19.33-35.).

245. *Māyāṁ tadapāśrayām*—The binding power called Māyā which involves individual Souls (*jīvas*) in worldly existence and transmigration (*saṁsāra*) but which is subservient to Hari-VJ.

Sūta said :

10. Hari is of such (excellent) attributes that sages who are delighted in the Soul and even those whose knots of worldly bonds are severed, perform motiveless devotion to Viṣṇu (lit. the god with wide strides).

11. The venerable son of Bādarāyaṇa (Śuka) whose mind was fascinated with the (excellent) qualities of Hari and who liked the devotees of Viṣṇu (Or who was loved by the devotees of Viṣṇu) studied this great legendary narrative (the *Bhāgavata Purāṇa*).

12. I shall, henceforth, narrate to you the birth, deeds and death (or liberation) of king Parīkṣit and the great journey (to heaven) of the Pāṇḍavas in such a way as will bear upon the stories of Kṛṣṇa.

13*. When, in the battle of Kauravas and Sṛñjayas, the warriors had gone the way of heroes (i.e. died on the battlefield) and the son of Dhṛtarāṣṭra (Duryodhana) had his thighbone broken by the stroke of the mace hit by Bhīma.

14. The son of Droṇa (Aśvatthāman) thinking that it would be liked by the master (Duryodhana) cut off and presented (to him) the heads of the sons of Draupadī (while they were asleep)—an act disagreeable to Duryodhana[246] and for which people censured him.

15. Then (Draupadī), the mother of the children, having heard of the death of her sons became terribly tormented and wept bitterly with her eyes flowing with tears. Arjuna consoling her said.

16. "Oh blessed lady! I shall have redressed your grief when I shall present to you the head of the wretched Brāhmaṇa

*This introduces the story how Kṛṣṇa protected Parīkṣit (who was in his mother's womb) from the Brahma-missile of Aśvatthāman.

246. VR. thinks that the murder of the children of Draupadī was not liked by Dhṛtarāṣṭra. VC.'s statement that this killing was disagreeable to Duryodhana, has no basis in the *MBh.* According to the MBh. *Sauptika Parvan* 9.54, Duryodhana praises Aśvatthāman as follows : 'What you, Kṛpa and Bhoja achieved for me today, was not done by Bhīṣma, Karṇa or your father. That wretched Dhṛṣṭadyumna was killed along with Śikhaṇḍin. I, therefore, regard myself as equal to Indra today. . . Farewell. May you be blessed. We shall meet again in heaven .

murdered,[247] cut off by arrows discharged from my Gāṇḍīva bow, and when you, whose sons are killed, would set your foot on it (Aśvatthāman's head) and take your bath."

17. Having thus consoled his beloved (wife Draupadī) with various sweet soothing words, Arjuna whose friend and charioteer was Kṛṣṇa, put on his armour, wielded a terrible bow and with monkey banner flying on his chariot rode in it, pursuing the son of his preceptor.

18. Seeing from a distance Arjuna pursuing him (Aśvatthāman), the murderer of (Draupadī's) children, with a trembling heart, fled in his chariot to the best of his capacity on the earth to save his life, as the god Brahmā[248] (v.l. Arka the Sun-god) did through the fear of god Śiva.

19. When the son of Brāhmaṇa (Aśvatthāman) found that his horses were fatigued and he had become helpless, he thought that the use of the missile Brahma-Śiras [249] was his only protection.

20. Then, being in a peril of life, he sipped water from the palm of his hand concentrated his mind and let the missile go, even though he did not know how to withdraw it.

---

247. *ātatāyin*—A person who commits a heinous crime, e.g. a thief, a ravisher, a murderer, incendiary, a felon etc. Śukra Nīti enumerates them as follows :.

Agnido garadaś caiva śastronmatto dhanāpahā |
Kṣetra-dāra-haraś caitān ṣaḍ vidyād ātatāyinaḥ ||

248. ŚR. refers to the episode of god Brahmā's flight when Rudra wanted to punish him for his lust after his daughter. ŚR. notes another v.l. Arka—the Sun-god—and states that this refers to the story in *Vāmana Purāṇa.* Vidyunmāli, a demon, got from Śiva, a heavenly car of gold in which he followed the Sun, dispelling the darkness in the part of the world when the Sun had set. The Sun, finding the disappearance of night from the world, melted down the heavenly car of Vidyunmāli. At this, Śiva got enraged with the Sun and opened his third eye. The Sun, terrified at the terrible fire so released, ran for his life but was scorched by it and fell down at Vārāṇasī where he is known as 'Lolārka'. VJ. reads *ārki*, the son of Arka, i.e. the Saturn and refers to the story in the *Vāyu Purāṇa* in which the Saturn had to flee for his life before the fire emanating from the third eye of Rudra.

249. ŚR. regards Brahma-Śiras and Brahmāstra as the same. But as VD. points out, they are different missiles. He quotes *Skanda Purāṇa* as his authority.

21. Then, seeing the terrific glare of light (of the fierce flame of the missile) manifested in all directions and endangering his life, Arjuna spoke to Kṛṣṇa.

Arjuna said:

22. Oh Kṛṣṇa ! Oh highly fortunate one! The saviour of your devotees from fear! You are the reliever of persons who are being burnt in the fire of worldly life. You are the First, Primeval Man, the direct controller of the universe, higher than the Primordial Nature (Prakṛti). Having dispelled the Cosmic Illusion (Māyā) by your intellectual power (Cicchakti) you stay established in your own pure nature.*

24. You are the same as He (God, described above). By your power, you confer blessings such as Dharma and others (Wealth, Liberation etc.) on all beings whose minds are deluded by Illusion (Māyā).

25. Moreover, this incarnation of yours is both for lessening the burden of the earth as well as for the convenience of

---

*Some more interpretations :

(i) ŚR: 'You are the direct controller (of the universe) as you are the Man beyond the Primordial Nature (*Prakṛti*). You are the First cause who having dispelled Illusion (*Māyā*) by your intellectual Power (*Cicchakti*) are established in the absolutely pure state of your Self.'

(ii) VR. distinguishes between the individual Soul (*Jīva*) and God; the individual soul, due to his limited knowledge, wrongly attaches the attributes of the body to the Soul while God dispels them by His Power of Knowledge (*Cicchakti*), God being within all individual Souls, dispenses the fruit according to the actions of respective individual Souls and acts as their support.

VR. interprets the text of this verse as follows: 'You alone are the veritable Ruler (of the universe). You are the First (cause of the universe), Man (existing in all individuals and controlling them) untouched by the attributes of *Prakṛti* (Primordial nature). By your Power of knowledge you are untouched by *Māyā*. You lie established in your own absolute greatness.'

(iii) VJ: "You are the destroyer of sins (*Puruṣaḥ*), the First (= existing before everyone and everything); the controller incarnate, superior to Intelligent Primordial Nature (*Prakṛti*). By your Power of Knowledge, you, having removed the power of bondage (*Māyā*) stay established with Your Self which is absolute (=beyond the bonds of *Prakṛti*).

constant meditation by your devotees who have set their hearts only on you.

26. Oh God of gods! I do not know the nature and the source of this very terrible fire which is encompassing us from all directions.

The Lord said:

27. Know that this is the *Brahma* missile (*astra*) detonated by the son of Droṇa (Aśvatthāman) under peril of life. He does not know the method of withdrawing it.

28. There is no other missile except this very *astra* (missile) which can curb its power. You are conversant with missiles. By the force of the same (*Brahma*) missile, therefore, destroy the fierce fire of that *astra*.

Sūta said:

29. Hearing the words of the Lord, Arjuna, the vanquisher of valiant foes, touched water (i.e. sippedit as *ācamana*), circumambulated him (Kṛṣṇa) and discharged his Brahmāstra against (Aśvatthāman's) Brahmāstra.

30. The flames emanating from Brahmāstra-charged arrows of both (Arjuna and Aśvatthāman) mingled with each other and surrounded by fiery arrows they covered the earth, heaven and the space-between and increased the conflagration like the fire and the Sun (at the end of the world.)

31. All beings who were scorched (by the Brahmāstras) and saw the terrific fire of (their missiles) burning the three worlds, felt that it was the fire of *Pralaya* (which burns down the world).

32. Seeing the distress of the people and the destruction of the world and noticing the view of Vāsudeva, Arjuna withdrew both the missiles.

33. Then Arjuna, with his eyes reddened with rage, swiftly overtook the terrible Aśvatthāman (lit. the son of Gautamī) and roped him forcibly like a (sacrificial) beast.

34. The Lotus-eyed Lord (Kṛṣṇa) spoke angrily to Arjuna who fastened the enemy with a rope and desired to take him per force to the camp.

35. Oh Pārtha, you should not spare this (fellow). Kill this wretched Brāhmaṇa who has murdered innocent children while they were asleep at night.

36. A person, knowing the restrictions of religion (Law) does not kill an enemy who is intoxicated, inattentive (or unguarded), haunted by a ghost (or insane), asleep, or a child or a woman; (nor does he kill) a dullard (lunatic), a suppliant for protection, (an enemy) with a broken chariot or (feeling) in a frightened condition.

37. He who supports his life by killing others is merciless and wicked. To mete out capital punishment to him is in his interest as he really goes to hell on account of that crime (if not expiated by judicial punishment).

38. It was in my presence (lit. while I was hearing) that you promised to Draupadī: 'I shall bring to you the head of the man who killed your sons.'

39. Oh valiant one! Let, therefore, this sinful desperado, the murderer of your sons, be slain as he is a disgrace to his family and has acted against the interests of his master.

40. Though thus urged by Kṛṣṇa who tested his (Arjuna's) sense of Dharma, the great son of Pṛthā (Arjuna) did not wish to kill his teacher's son (even though he was) the slayer of his children.

41. Having returned to his camp, Arjuna, whose dear charioteer was Kṛṣṇa, presented him (Aśvatthāman) to his beloved who was weeping.

42. Seeing the evildoer, the preceptor's son, produced before her, bound with a rope like a (sacrificial) beast with his head bent low due to his censurable act, the good-natured Draupadī bowed to him out of pity.

43. And the virtuous lady (Draupadī), not tolerating the act of bringing him thus bound (with cords) said, "Let him be released immediately, especially as this Brāhmaṇa is veritably the preceptor.

44. Through his favour Your honour has studied the *Dhanurveda* (the Military Science) along with its secret formulae (incantations or *Mantras*) and a number of missiles along with the technique of discharging and withdrawing them.

45. This (Aśvatthāman) is venerable Droṇa existing in

the form of a son. Kṛpī who is Droṇa's (better) half, is alive; she did not immloate herself after him as she was the mother of a warrior.

46. Therefore, Oh highly fortunate one who know religion, the family of the preceptor which deserves constant respect and worship, should not be subjected to misery by Your honour.

47. Let not his mother Gautamī who regards her husband as a god, weep just as I constantly do, with my face full of tears, due to grief at the death of my children.

48. The Brāhmaṇa race which is provoked by Kṣatriyas of uncontrolled tempers and is subjected to grief, burns down within a short time, that Kṣatriya family with its kith and kin."

Sūta said:

49. Oh Brāhmaṇas, King Yudhiṣṭhira (son of Dharma) approved of the queen's speech of great significance which was consistent with religion and justice and was remarkable for its compassion, sincerity and equitability.

50. Nakula, Sahadeva, Sātyaki, Arjuna, the venerable son of Devakī and other ladies present also expressed their approval (of her speech).

51. There (then) the enraged Bhīma spoke:

'It is desirable (even from the point of Aśvatthāman) that he should be killed as he killed the sleeping children in vain neither in the interest of his master nor his own.'

52. Hearing the words of Bhīma and Draupadī, the four-armed[250] Kṛṣṇa looked at the face of his friend (Arjuna) and spoke smilingly as follows:

Śrī Kṛṣṇa said:

53. "The (two) injunctions that a Brāhmaṇa even though fallen, should not be killed and that a wreckless ruffian deserves capital punishment, have been laid down by me. Carry out the twofold command.

---

250. ŚR. states that Kṛṣṇa manifested his four arms as he used two arms to prevent Bhīma from killing Aśvatthāman and two to ward off Draupadī who suddenly came in the way of Bhīma for warding him off from that act.

54. Carry out what you have promised to your beloved (Draupadī) at the time of consoling her. Do what is agreeable to Bhīma, Pāñcālī and me as well."

Sūta said:

55. Understanding at once the intention of Hari, Arjuna, with his sword, took away the jewel that was in the head of the Brāhmaṇa along with the locks of hair.

56. Releasing him (Aśvatthāman) from the rope (with which he was bound), Arjuna drove him (Aśvatthāman) out of the camp, as he had lost all his lustre due to the murder of children (committed by him) and the loss of the brilliant gem.

57. (For, disgraceful) shaving of the head, confiscation of property as well as expulsion from the place (of residence) is a (veritable) capital punishment to unworthy Brāhmaṇas; there is no other physical punishment prescribed for that caste.

58. All the Pāṇḍavas along with Draupadī, who were afflicted with grief for their sons, performed rites connected with the funeral of their relatives.

CHAPTER EIGHT

(*Kuntī's Eulogy of Kṛṣṇa and Yudhiṣṭhira's Repentance*)

Sūta said *

1. Then, they (Pāṇḍavas) along with Kṛṣṇa and with women (going) in front, proceeded to the Ganges for offering libations of water to their dead kinsmen who desired (such) water.

---

*VJ.'s text gives the following additional verses, the gist of which is as follows :

All the Pāṇḍavas along with Draupadī were deeply grieved at the death of their sons. They performed the prescribed funeral rites of their kinsmen.

Then the Lord showed to Draupadī the various warriors slain, as promised by him formerly when she fell at his feet weeping.

2. Having offered the libations and bewailing bitterly again, all of them bathed in the waters of the river sanctified by the dust of the lotus-like feet of Hari.

3-4. Explaining the irresistability of the (effects of) Time (or Death) on living beings, Mādhava (Kṛṣṇa) along with sages consoled the Lord of Kurus (Yudhiṣṭhira and his younger brothers, Dhṛtarāṣṭra[251], Gāndhārī[252] aggrieved at the loss of her sons, Pṛthā (Kuntī)[253] and Draupadī, who sat there bereaved of their relatives (and hence) given to sorrow ;

5-6. Having made Yudhiṣṭhira[254] regain his kingdom cheated away from him by rogues, and having got killed the wicked whose life was cut short due to touching the hair of the queen (Draupadī) and having enabled (Yudhiṣṭhira) to per-

---

'Oh queen! See the wives of your enemies who with hair dishevelled, are lamenting, embracing their husbands whose thighs or chests are broken with the mace of Bhīma'.

251. Dhṛtarāṣṭra—Eldest son of Vicitravīrya or rather Vyāsa and Ambikā. He married Gāndhārī and had one hundred sons the eldest of whom was Duryodhana. He was blind and hence his younger brother Pāṇḍu superseded him to the throne. The Mahābhārata war was fought between the sons of Dhṛtarāstra and Pāṇḍu. After the war, Dhṛtarāṣṭra, bereaved of his sons, stayed for some time with the Pāṇḍavas and then resorted to forest along with Gāndhārī and Kuntī where they were burnt in a forest conflagration—DHM 91.

252. Gāndhārī—Daughter of Subala, king of Gāndhāra, wife of Dhṛtarāṣṭra.

253. Kuntī (Pṛthā)—Daughter of the Yādava Prince Śūra, sister of Vasudeva; given as a child to Śūra's childless cousin Kuntibhoja. Pleased with her services in her maidenhood, Durvāsas gave her a charm whereby she could invoke any god. She used the incantation to invoke the Sun-God and she gave birth to Karṇa without loss of her virginity. Later, she married Pāṇḍu and bore him three sons—Yudhiṣṭhira, Bhīma and Arjuna who were respectively from the gods Yama-dharma, Vāyu and Indra.

During the forest-dwelling of Pāṇḍavas, she stayed at Hastināpura. After the Bhārata war, she retired into the forest along with Dhṛtarāṣṭra and Gāndhārī and all of them perished in a forest-fire. HDM 171.

2 4. *ajātaśatruḥ*—Normally it means 'One having no enemy;' but VJ and VD interpret *ajāta* as Duryodhana as he was born from a pitcher and not in the normal way. In support of this they quote from Mbh. 1.114 wherein the birth of the sons of Dhṛtarāṣṭra is described. These annotators interpret this as 'one whose enemy is Su (Dur) yodhana'

form thrice the horse-sacrifice with the best method[255], he (Kṛṣṇa) caused his Yudhiṣṭhira's) fame spread in all directions like that of god Indra (the Performer of hundred Sacrifices).

7-8. Oh Brāhmaṇa! And having taken leave of Pāṇḍavas and having exchanged mutual worship with Brāhmaṇas like Dvaipāyana (Vyāsa), Kṛṣṇa, accompanied by Sātyaki and Uddhava got into chariot with the intention of going to Dvārakā when he saw Uttarā[256] running towards him stricken with panick.

Uttarā said:

9. "Protect me, Oh great Yogin, save me, Oh God of gods, Protector of the world. As people are victims of death[257] I do not see safe shelter with any one else but with you.

10. Oh all-pervading Lord! An arrow with a red-hot iron tip rushes towards me. Oh Lord! Le it burn me at will but let not the embryo (in my womb) be fallen."

Sūta said:

11. Having heard her speech, the Lord who loves his devotees, knew that it was the missile of Aśvatthāman discharged to extirpate the race of Pāṇḍavas.

12. Oh great sage, then at that very time, Pāṇḍavas, having noticed five blazing arrows rushing towards them, resorted to their missiles.

---

255. *uttama-kalpakaiḥ*—(i) With faultless detailed formalities of recitation of Mantras, gifts to Brāhmaṇas at the appropriate stages of the sacrifice—VR.

(ii) With the best method of performing religious rites—VJ.

(iii) With the best materials—VB., VD.

(iv) With the best performers of sacrifices like Vyāsa and others—VD.

256. The daughter of Matsya King Virāṭa and queen of Abhimanyu. Mother of Parīkṣit. When Aśvatthāman discharged the Brahmāstra against the child in her womb, she invoked Kṛṣṇa's help who protected her by his Sudarśana discus and saved Parīkṣit—PI. 1.219.

257. *Yatra . . . parasparam*—Where men are the death of one-another ŚR.

13. Having seen the disaster of Pāṇḍavas who were absolutely devoted to him, the mighty Lord ordained their safety by his missile called Sudarśana.

14. Hari, the Lord of yoga, who is the Soul residing within all beings, covered the embryo (in the womb) of the princess of Virāṭa (Uttarā) by (his power called) Māyā (Illusion) for the continuation of the Kuru race.

15. Oh descendant of the Bhṛgu clan (Śaunaka)! Even though the missile called *Brahmaśiras* is irresistible and uncounteractable, it became quiescent when it came into contact with the lustre of Viṣṇu.

16. Do not regard this as a miracle, for Acyuta who though unborn, creates, protects and destroys the world by his refulgent (power) Māyā, is miraculous in every way.

17. The virtuous Pṛthā (Kuntī) in the company of Draupadī, and her sons who were saved from the flames of the missile *Brahma-Śiras* addressed thus to Kṛṣṇa who was about to start.

Kuntī said:

18. I bow to you the First (=the cause of world) Man, the Lord (of the universe), beyond Prakṛti, imperceptible yet pervading all beings from within and without.

19. (I am) ignorant (and hence can simply bow down to) you who are concealed behind the screen of Māyā (Illusion), beyond the ken of sense-perception and immutable. You cannot be realised by the false perception of ignorant person just as an actor in his role in the drama is not recognized by an ignorant spectator.

20.* You cannot be perceived by pure-hearted sages of the highest order. How can we, women, know you in order to follow the path of devotion unto you?

---

*Some more interpretations :

ŚR : How can we, women, know you that are incarnated (on this earth) to teach the *Paramahaṁsas* (recluses of the highest order) the *Bhakti Yoga* (path of devotion) and to attract the minds of the (meditative) sages of devotion and to teach them (how to follow) the path of devotion.

VR : How can we women (ineligible for performing *yoga* and of impure mind) know you ? You reveal yourself to the intense devotion of recluses of the highest order, pure in mind and given to meditation of yourself.

21. Again and again I bow to Kṛṣṇa Vāsudeva, the joy (son) of Devakī, the young child of the Cowherd Nanda, Govinda.[258]

22. Bow to him from whose naval sprouts up the Lotus; salute to the wearer of lotus-garland; respects to the lotus-eyed god; bow to him whose feet are like lotus.

23. Oh Hṛśīkeśa![259] Just as (your) sorrow-stricken (mother) Devakī who was incarcerated for a very long time by Kaṁsa,[260] was released by you, so also I along with my sons, was often saved in a number of difficulties by you alone as my protector.

24. Oh Hari, we have been completely protected by you from poison,[261] from the great fire,[262] from the sight of cannibalistic demons[263], in the assembly of the wicked[264], from the danger of forest-dwelling[265], from the missiles of great warriors in every battle[266] and the missile of the son of Droṇa (Aśvatthāman).

---

258. VJ. gives rather unusual derivations of some of the epithets used here, e.g. *Vāsudeva*—One who shines after pervading the world. *Govinda*—One who is attained to by Vedas. *Nandagopa-Kumāra*—One who cured the leprosy of a king called Nanda.

259. The controller of the sense-organs, i.e. Kṛṣṇa.

260. *Kaṁsa*—A tyrannical king of Mathurā, son of Ugrasena and cousin of Devakī. He married two daughters of Jarāsandha, king of Magadha. He deposed his father. Due to a prediction that the eighth child of Devakī will kill him, he imprisoned both Devakī and Vasudeva. He tried to kill all the children of Devakī but Kṛṣṇa, the eighth child was smuggled away and was kept under the protection of Nanda, the cowherd chief. Kaṁsa became a great persecutor of Kṛṣṇa and tried to kill him but was eventually killed by Kṛṣṇa—DHM 149.

261. *viṣāt*—Refers to administration of poison-food to Bhīma by Duryodhana and throwing him in the Gaṅgā after fastening down with creepers (Mbh. I.127.45-54).

262. *mahāgneḥ*—This refers to Duryodhana's attempt to burn down Kuntī and Pāṇḍavas in the house of *lac* at Vāraṇāvata (Mbh. I.147).

263. This refers to the encounter of Pāṇḍavas with demons like Hidimba (Mbh. I. 153), Baka (Mbh. I. 162 etc).

264. This refers to the assembly of dice-players in which Draupadī was humiliated (Mbh. II. 67-68).

265. Refers to the different hazards which Pāṇḍavas faced during their stay in the forest for twelve years.

266. Refers to the Bhārata war in which Pāṇḍavas had to face a number of enemy missiles.

25*Oh Master of the Universe! May there always be calamity at every step (if in every such calamity we are blest with) your sight which relieves people from the cycle of rebirths.

26. Verily a man puffed up with pride of noble birth, power, learning and wealth never deserves to speak of (i.e. remember) you who are worthy of being known by desireless persons or Paramahaṁsas.

27. Salutations to you, who regard your sincere devotees as your wealth[267] and from whom tendencies towards attributes (*guṇas*) viz. the objectives of *Dharma*, *Artha* and *Kāma* have disappeared; I bow to you who delight in His your Self and devoid of attachment and who is the Lord of (one who can grant the Final Beatitude.

28* I look upon you as Time (or Death), the Controller of the Universe, beginningless and endless. Although quarrels (wars) among beings arise from you (as the efficient cause), you move with equality (and dispense pleasure and pain according to their past actions).

29. Oh Lord! Nobody knows what you intend to do. You appear to behave like men. Nobody is either favourite with you nor any one antagonistic in the least. It is the mind of men which is prejudiced.

---

*VJ. differs :

'Oh Lord of the Universe ! May there be continuous difficulties in our various worldly dealings. In these, however, we should have a sight of you which shows the way to Liberation (*Mokṣa*).

267. *akiñcana-vittāya—akiñcana* is one who wishes to get nothing else but Śrī Kṛṣṇa; hence 'a sincere devotee'. This compound means :

(i) Who are the wealth to his sincere devotees;

(ii) One who loves his sincere devotees.

* Another interpretation :

I regard you as Time-bodied one who control god Brahmā and others and hence who are free from birth and death. Quarrels among beings arise due to Time though you move with equality (the charges of inequality and mercilessness cannot be levelled against you).—VR.

SD: It is due to ignorance that persons bear a prejudiced attitude to you even though you are really devoid of favouritism or antagonism. VB. endorses the same interpretation with his usual details.

30.* Oh soul of the Universe! That you who have no birth and no actions, have incarnations and actions to perform among non-human beings (e.g. the boar-incarnation), human beings (e.g. Rāma, Kṛṣṇa), sages (e.g. Vāmana) and acquatic animals (e.g. the Fish incarnation) is a great imitation (a matter of your will to imitate these).

31. When for a fault committed by you, the cowherdess (Yaśodā) took a rope, the then spectacle of your standing with head bent down, showing expression of fear on your face with eyes full of tears mixed with black collyrium, really enchants me, as even fear is afraid of you.

32. Some (persons) say that you, though unborn, appeared to take birth in the Yadu race for (spreading) the reputation of your dear friend Yudhiṣṭhira of pious fame and that of beloved Yadu, just as the sandal tree (grown on the Malaya) for the (reputation of the) mountain Malaya.

33. Others say that you are the unborn one who, in response to (their) prayer, was born of Vasudeva and Devakī for the good of the world and the destruction of the enemies of gods.

34. Others say that as per prayer of god Brahmā (lit. the self-born god), you were born to lessen the burden of the earth which, like (an overloaded) boat in the sea, suffered from overpressure (of demons and wicked persons).

35. Some others (regard that you are born) for performing deeds worth hearing and remembering by (persons) suffering in this worldly existence on account of nescience,[268] desires and actions (*karmas* done previously).

---

* Another interpretation:

You are the birthless (due to absence of actions leading to birth) and the actionless (due to disinclination to do any action on account of non-existence of actions motivating new actions) soul of the universe. That you should have births in (and indulge in actions suitable to) non-human beings, human beings, sages and acquatic animals is extremely deceptive.

268. *avidyā*—(i) Ignorance about the nature of the highest joy—ŚR.
(ii) Ignorance caused by the confusion between the Soul and the body—VR.
(iii) Absence of the knowledge of the Soul and the non-Soul—SD.

36. Only those persons who constantly hear, sing, glorify, remember and take delight in your likeable deeds, will see before long your lotus-like feet which terminates (dries up) the current of worldly existence.

37. And, Oh Lord (Kṛṣṇa) who fulfill the wishes of your devotees! Do you today abandon us, your friends and dependants, who have brought so much grief to the princely class and have no other refuge than the lotus-like feet of your honour?

38* If Your honour is out of sight, what are we Pāṇḍavas and Yadus but (merely) name and form, just as the senseorgans are worthless (dead) in the absence of the Soul (lit. controller of the sense-organs).

39. Or holder of the mace (Kṛṣṇa)! The land (in our kingdom) will not appear beautiful (after your departure) just as now it appears decorated by your feet imprinting on the ground your special (divine) marks.

40. It is by your (favourable) looks that these lands with well-ripened plants and creepers, with their forests, mountains, rivers and seas, prosper (richly).

41. Therefore, Oh Lord of the Universe! the Universal Soul! All-pervading Lord! Cut asunder my bond of love to my kinsmen—this strong attachment towards Pāṇḍavas and Vṛṣṇis.

42. Oh Lord of Madhus (=Yādavas)! May my mind be constant and firm in devotion to you and be not attached to any other object just as the stream of the Ganges flows into the sea (alone without minding any obstacles).

43. Oh Śrī Kṛṣṇa, friend of Arjuna, the best of the Vṛṣṇis, Fire (destroyer) of the prowess of the kings who harassed the earth, of undiminished power and might, Possessor of the wealth of wish-yielding cows (Govinda), one who incarnates for removing the afflictions of cows, twice-born ones (Brāhmaṇas) and gods, Oh Lord of Yogas, the Preceptor of all, Oh Venerable Lord, I bow to you.

---

* Another interpretation :

(i) When we have visualised you as when the sense-organs find their controller (the Soul), we have become through your grace, Yādavas and Pāṇḍavas—VR.

(ii) The sense-organs function when the controlling agency—the Soul—is with them. The existence of our name and form is due to your presence with us. Otherwise we shall be reduced to nameless and formless category.

Sūta said:

44. Vaikuṇṭha (Kṛṣṇa) whose entire glory was thus eulogized in sweet words by Pṛthā (Kuntī), smiled gently as if enchanting the world by his Māyā.[269]

45. Having blessed her (Kuntī) that her desires would be fulfilled [270] and entering Hastināpura, he took leave of the ladies and was about to leave for his capital when he was detained by the king, out of love.

46. Even though he (Yudhiṣṭhira) was advised with illustrations from historical incidents by Vyāsa and others who did not comprehend the intention of the Lord (that it was Bhīṣma who was to enlighten Yudhiṣṭhira and not they) and by Kṛṣṇa (himself) of miraculous deeds, he (Yudhiṣṭhira) did not understand it (as) he was overcome with grief.

47. Oh Brāhmaṇas, the king Yudhiṣṭhira (son of Yama-dharma) brooding over the death of his friends (and well-wishers) and with his mind becoming defunct in judgment like that of common people, spoke as follows.

48. Alas ! Look at the ignorance grown in the heart of a wicked man like me. For the sake of my body which is for others (for being devoured by carnivorous animals like dogs, jackals etc.) many divisions[271] (of the army) are killed.

49. Even for crores of years there is no hope of my release from hell as I have done wrong to children (like Abhimanyu, Lakṣmaṇa), Brāhmaṇas (like Droṇa), relatives, friends, elders, brothers and preceptors.

50. The precept that killing enemies in a righteous war is not a sin in the case of a king protecting his subjects, cannot convince (enlighten) me (as I was not a ruler of the people).

51. Here the sin accrued to me by the wrong done to women whose relatives were slain for my sake, cannot be expiated by me by (religious) acts prescribed for householders.

---

269. Māyā: (i) ŚR. quotes 'Māyā is the smile (of the world) which maddens the world.

(ii) Divine Love—VC.

270. After accepting Kuntī's prayer (regarding her constancy in devotion etc.)—ŚR.

271. *Akṣauhiṇī*—A division of the army consisting of 21870 chariots, as many elephants. 65610 horses and 109350 foot-soldiers : Total—218700.

52. Just as one cannot purify muddy water by mud or the sin of drinking wine by means of (profuse) wine, similarly one cannot expiate a single act of killing a living being by (performing) a number of sacrifices (involving the deliberate slaughter of animals).

CHAPTER NINE

(*Yudhiṣṭhira's Acquisition of Kingdom*)

Sūta said :

1. Thus, being afraid of disaffection of the subjects Yudhiṣṭhira, with a desire to know religious duties of all (kinds), proceeded to the battlefield[272] (Kurukṣetra) where Devavrata[273] (Bhīṣma) was lying.

---

272. Vinaśana—Although ŚR. and VJ. identify this with Kurukṣetra, SD. identifies it with the spot where Bhīṣma fell from his chariot in the battle ("yatra Devavrato Bhīṣmo rathad apatad Vinaśanam . . . Kurukṣetrāntargataṁ sthānam/" Bh. P. 1.9.1.

273. Devavrata—Lit. an observer of religious vows; an epithet of Bhīṣma, the 8th son of Śantanu and Gaṅgā; and heir to the throne of Hastināpura after his father; to enable his father to marry Saty avatī, he renounced his claim to the throne and vowed not to marry or beget children; he came to be known as Bhīṣma due to this dreadful vow; after his father's death, he installed Satyavatī's son Vicitravīrya on the throne and got him married to two princesses of Kāśirāja; afterwards when Vicitravīrya died childless, he advised Satyavatī to persuade her daughter-inlaws to have issues by *niyoga* and Bhīṣma became the guardian of his nephews and grandsons; in the great Bhārata war, he was the first commander-in-chief of the Kaurava army. On the tenth day of the battle, Arjuna being shielded by Śikhaṇḍin, pierced Bhīṣma with innumerable arrows and Bhīṣma fell down from his chariot only to be upheld from the ground by "the bed of darts". Due to the boon given to him by Śantanu, Bhīṣma could choose the time of his death. He survived 58 days after this. When Yudhiṣṭhira approached him after the war, he delivered to him several didactic discourses on all aspects of religion. At last when the Sun crossed the vernal equinox, he cast off his mortal coil with his mind fixed on God. Bhīṣma was an ideal hero noted for his continence, wisdom, firmness of resolve and devotion to God.

(ASD. 407, DHM. 53-55 and PI. II. 566-67).

2. Then all the brothers riding in chariots decorated with gold and drawn by excellent horses followed him along with Brāhmaṇas like Vyāsa, Dhaumya[274] and others.

3. Oh Brāhmaṇa sage ! The Lord (Kṛṣṇa) accompanied by Arjuna (followed him) in a chariot. With them (in their company) the king appeared (glorious) like Kubera[275] (the God of wealth) surrounded by Guhyakas[276] (his attendants).

4. Seeing Bhīṣma lying on the ground like a god fallen from the Heaven, Pāṇḍavas along with their followers and Kṛṣṇa (lit. the holder of the discus) bowed (to him).

5.* Of greatest saint ! All Brāhmaṇa sages, divine sages and royal sages assembled there to see (Bhīṣma) the prominent one among the Bhārata clan.

6. Parvata[277] Nārada[278], Dhaumya[279], the venerable Bādarāyaṇa (Vyāsa)[280], Bṛhadaśva[281], Bharadvāja[282], and the

---

274. Dhaumya—The family priest of Pāṇḍavas; was invited for Yudhiṣṭhira's Rājasūya sacrifice; accompanied Pāṇḍavas in their exile in the forest; followed Yudhiṣṭhira on a visit to the dying Bhīṣma.

(PI. II. 185)

275. Kubera—The god of riches; the ruler of the city of Alakā in the north; the head of demi-gods like the Yakṣas, Guhyakas and Kinnaras; traditionally he is regarded as a custodian of gold, silver, precious stones and such treasures.

276. Guhyakas—A class of demigods who, like the Yakṣas, wait on Kubera and guard his treasure.

(ASDP. 190).

* VD. distinguishes between the classes of sages as follows : Brāhmaṇa sages emphasize both Work and Knowledge; sages among gods emphasize knowledge and give second priority to Work or actions; sages among kings lay stress on penance and protect their subjects.

277. Parvata—A nephew of Nārada; visited Bhīṣma while he lay on his "dart-bed". Generally mentioned as a heavenly sage along with Nārada.

—(BPK. 179, PI. II, 301, PCK 569-70)

278. Nārada—See note 79.

279. Dhaumya—See note 274.

280. Bādarāyaṇa (Vyāsa)—See note 19.

281. Bṛhadaśva—According to PI. 2. 492, he was the son of Sahadeva and father of Bhānumat; called on the dying Bhīṣma. In the MBH, he is said to have narrated the story of Nala to Yudhiṣṭhira, taught him the technique of gambling by dice. (BPK 213).

282. Bharadvāja—Son of Bṛhaspati; was invited for the Rājasūya of Yudhiṣṭhira; called on the dying Bhīṣma; later he came to see King Parīkṣita when he was practising his Prāyopaveśa. (PI.II.541-42).

son of Reṇuka[283] (Paraśurāma) along with his disciples.

7. Vasiṣṭha[284], Indra-pramada[285], Trita[286], Gṛtsamada[287], Asita[288], Kakṣīvān[289], Gautama[290], Atri[291], Kauśika[292] and then

---

283. Son of Reṇukā—Paraśurāma.

284. Vasiṣṭha—Lit. "the wealthiest". A celebrated Vedic sage to whom many hymns are ascribed. In the Bh. P., he is a mind-born son of god Brahmā in the Svāyambhuva epoch (manvantara). In the present epoch (manvantara), he was again born from god Brahmā; married Arundhatī; had 100 sons who were killed by Viśvāmitra. He tried to commit suicide but the rivers Vipāś and Śatadru did not drown him. He was the family priest of Ikṣvākus. The detail of the struggle between Vasiṣṭha and Viśvāmitra is given in the MBH., the Rāmāyaṇa and the purāṇas. The feud started with Viśvāmitra's futile attempt to carry away Vasiṣṭha's wish-yielding cow Nandinī and ended with his attainment of the status of a Brāhmaṇa sage (Brahmarṣitva) and Vasiṣṭha's recognition of Viśvāmitra as such and Viśvāmitra's paying due honour to his former rival.

(DHM. 339-42, BPK 280)

285. Indra-pramada—A sage who called on Bhīṣma lying on his bed of arrows (BPK. 32).

286. Trita—According to Nirukta a Vedic seer connected with Gṛtsamada family. In the MBH. he is said to have been pushed in a well by his brothers to appropriate his cows, but was saved by gods. He was invited to Yudhiṣṭhira's Rājasūya sacrifice; he called on Bhīṣma in his death-bed.

(PCK. 399-400, PI. 2.43, DHM. 321-22).

287. Gṛtsamada—A sage who called on dying Bhīṣma. His identity with the famous Ṛgvedic seer and other sages of the same name is unconfirmed. For details about other Gṛtsamadas vide PCK. 322-23, DHM. 114, BPK. 94).

288. Asita—A famous sage who called on dying Bhīṣma; was invited for Yudhiṣṭhira's Rājasūya; came to Syamanta-pañcaka to see Kṛṣṇa; accompanied Kṛṣṇa to Mithilā; acted as a sacrificial priest at Kṛṣṇa's sacrifice in Kurukṣetra.

(PI. 1.136, BPK.26, PCK, 88-89).

289. Kakṣīvan—Originally a Vedic sage connected with the worship of Aśvins; an Aṅgiras and seer of mantras; called on Bhīṣma while he was lying on his bed of darts.

(PCK. 181, PI. 1.296, DHM. 139-40).

290. Gautama—PI. mentions 16 sages of this name. This Gautama who came to see dying Bhīṣma, is said to have called on Parīkṣit engaged in Prāyopaveśa (fast unto death).

—PI. 1.556-57.

291. Atri—PI. mentions 7 sages of this name (PI. 1. 41-42). He is regarded as the son of Brahmā and father of Dattātreya; taught ānvīkṣiki to Alarka, Prahlāda and others; visited Bhīṣma in his death-bed; came to see Parīkṣit practising prāyopaveśa.

292. Kauśika—PI. 1. 473-74 enumerates 11 sages of this name while PCK. 286-87 mentions 20 persons of this name. About the sage mentioned in this verse both regard him as a sage who called on dying Bhīṣma.

Sudarśana'[293].

8. Oh Brāhmaṇa ! And other sages like Brahmarata (Śuka)[294] and others like Kaśyapa[295], Aṅgirasas[296] (and others) arrived there along with their disciples.

9. Seeing that those great personages have assembled to visit him, the greatest of Vasus (Bhīṣma) who knew religious duties and understood the proper behaviour suitable to particular time and place* respectfully received them (*by his mind and words due to his physical inability to get up*-Śr.)

10. And (Bhīṣma) who knew the superhuman power of Kṛṣṇa, the Lord of the Universe who has assumed human form by His power called Māyā[297] (Illusion) and who (though)

---

293. Sudarśana—A sage who visited Bhīṣma in his death-bed. Other 10 persons of the same name mentioned in BPK. 349-50 are different.

294. Brahmarata alias Śuka—Son of Vyāsa; a yogin from his birth. He was initiated in spiritual lore by Bahulāśva Janaka of Mithilā; was taught the Bhāgavata Purāṇa by Vyāsa which he narrated to king Parīkṣit while he observed prāyopaveśa (fast unto death).

295. Kaśyapa—Out of the 7 Kaśyapas mentioned in PI. 1. 341-42, the sage mentioned here was a contemporary of Kṛṣṇa; was invited for Yudhiṣṭhira's Rājasūya sacrifice; came to Syamantapañcaka to see Kṛṣṇa; one of the sages who left for Piṇḍāraka; met by Takṣaka on his way to king Parīkṣit.

(PI. 1.342 also BPK 55).

296. Aṅgirasas—A contemporary of Kṛṣṇa; with his pupils visited Bhīṣma lying on his bed of arrows; came to see Kṛṣṇa at Syamantapañcaka; went to Dvārakā to request Kṛṣṇa to return to Vaikuṇṭha; came to see Parīkṣit practising prāyopaveśa.

The remaining 10 persons of the same name given in PI. 1.22-24 are different.

—PI.1.22-23.

297. Māyā—This word is highly ambiguous. Brahma Sūtra iii. 2.3 compares it with dreams but commentators argue that world is not māyā as dreams are. Bhāskara takes it as "artha-pratyaya-Śūnyatva", with Śaṅkara it is "dṛṣṭa-naṣṭa-svarūpatva", with Rāmānuja "as caryātmakatva" and "sarva-bhavana-samartya" with Vallabha. In stead of entering into the disputations of different schools of Vedānta, I have translated as "the power of Brahma called Māyā", though son etimes it is simply translated as "Illusion".

Verse 9: The portions marked with asterisks are the interpretations given by commentators mentioned in the brackets e.g. VJ., ŚR.

occupying the hearts (of all) was sitting (by his side) worshipped him (Kṛṣṇa).

11. With his eyes blinded with tears of affection, he spoke to the sons of Pāṇḍu who sat near him with humility and love.

12. "Oh sons of Dharma! Alas how painful! How much unjust! You who have resorted to Brāhmaṇas, religious duties and Acyuta (Kṛṣṇa) do not deserve to lead such a miserable life!

13. When the unrivalled chariot-fighter Pāṇḍu passed away, with young offspring, my daughter-in-law Pṛthā (Kuntī) whose children were very young, was frequently subjected to great sufferings for your sake[298].

14. And I think whatever unpleasent (has happened to you) is brought about by Time (Fate) under whose influence lies all the world along with its guardians[299] of the quarters (of the world) just as a row of clouds under the control of the wind.

15. (Can there be calamity) where the king is the son of Dharma (Yudhiṣṭhira), Bhīma (wolf-bellied one) with a mace in hand, the dark-coloured hero (Arjuna) the bearer of the Gāṇḍīva bow and the knower of missiles and (having) Kṛṣṇa as a well-wisher?

16. Oh King! No body really could divine the intentions (lit. desire to do certain things) of this (Kṛṣṇa). As a matter of fact, even learned people who try with a desire to fathom it become perplexed.

17. Therefore, concluding (deciding) that all this is in the power of the Providence, Oh King! Lord (of the people) the most excellent Bharata! protect these protectionless subjects in compliance of His orders.

---

298. JG. on verses 12-14 differs: 'It is very distressing to think that although you are the son of Dharma, you consider yourself unworthy of living. Moreover, being the refuge of Brāhmaṇas, it is also distressing to think and improper on your parts to consider that you are not fit to live.

299. Sa-pālaḥ—Along with the guardian deities of the eight cardinal points. They are as follows: Indra of the East, Agni (Fire) of the South-east, Yama of the South, Nirṛti of the South-east, Varuṇa of the West, Vāyu (wind) or Marut of the North-west, Kubera of the North, Īśāna or Śiva of the North-east.

18. This venerable Lord is veritable Nārāyaṇa the Primeval Man who deluding the world with his power called Māyā (illusion) moves incognito among the Vṛṣṇis.

19. Oh King ! Lord Śiva, the divine sage Nārada, the venerable lord Kapila know his (Kṛṣṇa's) secretmost prowess.

20. He whom you regard as maternal-cousin, a dear friend and the best well-wisher and to whom out of good feelings you employed as a counsellor, an emissary and a charioteer, is Nārāyaṇa Himself.

21. There never has been any change in his mind (regarding the dignity or otherwise) for acts performed by him (who is) the Soul of all, who is impartial, without a second, free from ego, and free from all sins.

22. (In spite of Kṛṣṇa's being equal to all), Oh protector of the earth ! Look at his compassion on (his) staunch devotees that Kṛṣṇa himself has appeared before me, when I am giving up life.

23. While concentrating the mind upon whom with devotion, and repeating whose name by words, a *Yogi*, who quits his body, becomes liberated from desires and actions.

24. Let the venerable four-armed God of gods whose lotus-like face is beaming with gracious (pleasing) smile and reddish eyes and who is the object of meditation, wait till I cast off this mortal frame (body)."

Sūta said :

25. On hearing that (speech of Bhīṣma), Yudhiṣṭhira asked (questions on) various (types of religious) duties (to Bhīṣma) who was lying in the bed of arrows (lit. cage of arrows) while the sages were listening.

26. Oh sage ! (Bhīṣma) the philosopher, described to him the religious duties prescribed according to the nature of men and those according to castes and stages of life; duties of two-fold characteristics (viz. those characterised by *Pravṛtti* or active participation in worldly life and those characterised by *Nivṛtti* or abstention from worldly activities) due to attachment (rāga) and non-attachment (vairāgya) as (they, i.e. duties, have been) handed down in the sacred books (Vedas) (āmnāta).

27. [He explained] briefly and in details rules (duties) regarding charities, kingship, (laws pertaining to) the path of liberation, (duties) of women and those pertaining to the Bhāgavata religion.

28. (He described) the four goals of human life, viz. righteousness, attainment of worldly prosperity, Love and Liberation, along with the means to attain them as exemplified in different histories and legends.

29. While he was explaining religious duties, the time of the Summer solstice (as) longed for by Yogis who have the power to die as per their pleasure, also drew near.

30. Then (Bhīṣma), the leader of the thousands (of charioteers) concluded his speech. With his eyes unclosed, he fully concentrated his mind completely free from attachment, on the Primeval Man, the four-armed Kṛṣṇa with shining yellow garments, standing before him.

31. Bhīṣma whose sin was destroyed[300] by his purest concentration of mind[301] and whose pangs of wounds caused by weapons had immediately been removed (subsided) by his (Kṛṣṇa's favourable) glance[302] and the movements of whose sensory organs had stopped and the delusion (regarding the identity of the mind and the body) disappeared and who was (about) to quit this body praised Janārdana, i.e. Kṛṣṇa (as follows):

32. "Thus (at the time of my death) my mind free from thirst (i.e. desire for enjoyment of the fruition of actions) is fixed in the venerable Lord (Kṛṣṇa) the best in the Sātvata (Yādava) clan, who is overfull of abundance (lit. has surpassed

---

300. hatāśubhaḥ—'The Fate that was delaying his union with God'—VR., SD.

301. dhāraṇā—'Fixed attention'—
Patañjali defines it as 'Binding the mind-stuff to a place' (deśabandhas' cittasya dhāraṇā—Yoga Sūtra 3.1).
Vyāsa explains, "Binding of the mind-stuff, only insofar as it is fluctuation to some place" like the heart-lotus or the tip of the nose or to an external object is Dhāraṇā. Viṣṇu Purāṇa and Nāradīya Purāṇa recommend Viṣṇu for such objects of concentration.
Woods—YSP p. 203-04.

302. īkṣayā—'By the mere sight of Kṛṣṇa'—VR.

abundance), and is full of ecstatic happiness that is inherent in Him, and who sometimes with a desire to play, associated himself with Prakṛti[303] or Māyā (illusion), from which starts the stream of worldly existence.

33. Immaculate be my devotion to the friend of Vijaya (Arjuna), i.e. Kṛṣṇa, who has assumed a body most fascinating in three worlds, with *Tamāla* (tree) like complexion, wearing spotless garment yellow like the rays of the morning Sun, and lotus-like face covered with pendent locks of hair.

34. May my mind be (concentrated) in Kṛṣṇa whose face was bedecked with drops of perspiration scattered by his hair flowing in all directions, (appearing) grey with dust (kicked up by the hoofs) of horses in the battle, and with his armour glittering with the dint of my keen-edged arrows piercing his body (lit. skin).

35. May my love be (fixed) on Pārtha's (Arjuna's) friend who, immediately after listening to the words (of request) of his friend, posted his chariot between the two armies, his and his enemy's, (and who as it were) carried away the lives (the life-spans) of the hordes of the enemy by a glance of his eyes.

36. Let my love be upon the feet of the Lord who by his spiritual knowledge (power) removed the wrong knowledge (understanding) [of Arjuna] who at the sight of the head (i.e. the leaders) of the (enemy) army at a distance, became averse to kill his kith and kin, thinking that to be a wrong act.

37. In order to (enable me to) carry out my vow, in supersession of his own (regarding non-participation in the battle with arms), he who was seated in a chariot jumped out, and carrying the wheel of a chariot and shaking the earth and with his upper garment fallen away, attacked me like a lion killing an elephant.

38. May the Lord Mukunda who being pierced by sharpened arrows, was bathed in blood, as his armour shattered;

---

303. Prakṛti—The Sāṁkhyas regarded this as the evolver of the universe and called it Pradhāna. It is translated as Nature or Matter as opposed to Spirit (Puruṣa). Later on, it came to be regarded as the personified will of the Supreme Being and the proto-type of the female sex, identified with Māyā or illusion and the Śakti or the energy of the deity.

ŚR. interprets this as 'Yoga Māyā'. Dowson—HMP. 240.

who in order to kill me, violently attacked me (rushed at me) who was endeavouring to kill him, be my shelter.

39. Let my devotion be in the Lord who treats the chariot of Arjuna as a member of his family, who has taken a whip (in his hand) and held the reins of the horses (in another), whose splendour is worth looking at, while I am lying at the door of death, as those who were killed after having a look at him, attain his resemblance in form.

40. [Let my love be on Kṛṣṇa] by imitating whose actions became verily merged with him, the cowherdesses who have performed the great worship by (their) graceful movements, amorous gestures, sweet smiles, solicitous looks, though (they were thus) blind with fatuation (for him).

41. This (Universal) Soul who, being attractive to look at, was endowed with the place of honour (agra-pūjā) in the assembly crowded with sages and prominent kings at the time of the Rājasūya sacrifice of Yudhiṣṭhira, has manifested himself to me (lit. my sight).

42. I who have shed off differences (dualism—*bheda*) and delusion (*moha*), have attained to him, the unborn (aja), enthroned in (each and every) heart of beings (corporate beings)[304] created by him just as the Sun (though one) appears different to every (individual) onlooker."

Sūta said :

43. In this way, having merged himself with Lord Kṛṣṇa with the functions of his mind, speech, sight, he (Bhīṣma) ceased to breathe within.

44. Knowing that Bhīṣma is being merged with the attributeless Brahman, all kept quiet like birds after sunset.

45. There was a beating of drums by men and gods. The good ones among the kings praised him. Flowers were showered down from heaven (the sky).

46. Oh Bhārgava (Śaunaka of the Bhṛgu clan), Yudhiṣṭhira having got performed the funeral rites etc. of the deceased (Bhīṣma) became mournful awhile.

---

304. JG. observes that this verse should not be explained as having any reference to Brahma, as in V. 30 the reference is clearly to Kṛṣṇa.

47. Then (after the death of Bhīṣma), sages pleased Kṛṣṇa by (reciting) his sacred (guhya) names and with their hearts pleased and devoted to Kṛṣṇa they went back to their hermitages.

48. Then Yudhiṣṭhira along with Kṛṣṇa went to Hastināpura and consoled his uncle (Dhṛtarāṣṭra) and miserable Gāndhārī.

49. Then as per order of the uncle (Dhṛtarāṣṭra) and the consent of Vāsudeva, the powerful Yudhiṣṭhira ruled his ancestral kingdom as per religious precepts.

CHAPTER TEN

(*Kṛṣṇa's Departure to Dvārakā*)

Śaunaka said :

1. How did Yudhiṣṭhira,[305] the greatest among the upholders of religion, who regained his kingdom[306] after killing the heinous criminals, the grabbers of his wealth (kingdom),[307] proceed to rule his kingdom ? What did he do then ?

Sūta said :

2. Hari, the donor of prosperity to His devotees,[308] made the Kuru family which (due to internecine war and the missile Brahmāstra fired at their last scion Parīkṣit, then in womb) was burnt down like the jungle of bamboo-canes in a forest conflagration, sprout forth again (by reviving Parīkṣit). Verily, He

---

305. v.l. *gaviṣṭhira*—One who is firm in his promise.

306. *pratyavaruddha-bhojanaḥ*—

(i) One whose enjoyment is lessened due to grief caused by the killing of his relatives—ŚR.

(ii) One who got enjoyment by the acquisition of kingdom—ŚR.

(iii) One who has regained his kingdom —VR.

307. *sva-riktha-spṛdhaḥ*—Those who fought for acquiring wealth—ŚR.

308. *bhava-bhāvanaḥ*—Makes Lord Śiva to meditate upon his Pastimes—VD.

(Hari) felt profound happiness after installing Yudhiṣṭhira on his own kingdom.

3. He (Yudhiṣṭhira) whose delusion had been dispelled by the dawning of accurate knowledge after listening to the speeches of Bhīṣma and Acyuta (Kṛṣṇa), and whose supporter was the invincible (Kṛṣṇa) and who was surrounded by his younger brothers, ruled over the earth circumscribed by the seas, as Indra, whose supporter was Acyuta (the Lord Viṣṇu) governed the Heaven.

4. It rained at the proper times; the earth (as if) milched out all the desired products; cows with big udders overflowing with milk, gladly drenched even the ground of the cowpens.

5. In every season, rivers, seas, mountains, medicinal plants, trees and creepers—all yielded (lit. fruitioned in) his (Yudhiṣṭhira's) desires.

6. While Yudhiṣṭhira (lit. one having no adversary) was the king, there was no mental anguish, physical pain and miseries caused by superhuman agencies, elements or body, to any being.

7-8. Having stayed in Hastināpura for alleviating the grief of his friend and for the pleasure of his sister, and having requested for and obtained permission to leave, Hari mounted the chariot embracing and saluting Yudhiṣṭhira, himself being embraced and bowed (by his hosts according to their status).

9-10. Subhadrā, Draupadī, Kuntī, the daughter of Virāṭa (Uttarā), Gāndhārī, Dhṛtarāṣṭra, Yuyutsu, the twins (Nakula and Sahadeva), Kṛpa (of the Gautama clan), Bhīma, Dhaumya and ladies like Satyavatī (lit. the fisherman's daughter) and others swooned away (or were bewildered) as they could not bear separation from Kṛṣṇa (lit. the wielder of the Śārṅga bow).

11. A wise man, freed from association with bad persons due to good company, is not enthusiastic about giving it up; (similarly), having once listened to his enlightening glory, a wise man would not bear separation from him.

12. How can the sons of Pṛthā (Pāṇḍavas) who have entrusted (i.e. fixed) their minds on him in their acts of seeing,

feeling, talking (or conversing), sleeping, sitting and eating (with him), endure the (grief of) separation (from him)?

13. Looking at him with unwinking eyes and following him with their minds, all of them verily moved here and there and brought articles of worship etc. as they were deeply attached to him through affection.

14. When the son of Devakī (Kṛṣṇa) moved out of the house, the women-relatives controlled their (oozing) tears of (affectionate) anxiety, lest any evil should befall.

15. (At the time of the departure of Kṛṣṇa) were sounded the tabors, conchs, kettle-drums, lutes, cymbals, horns, *dhundhurī* (a musical instrument), large military drums, bells and large kettle-drums.

16. Ascending the tops of the palaces with a desire to see Kṛṣṇa, ladies of the Kuru clan, with eyes expressive of love, bashfulness and smiles showered flowers on Kṛṣṇa.

17. Arjuna (the Lord of Sleep), the dear one (friend of Kṛṣṇa) held over his dearest friend, a white umbrella decked with pearl-strings and jewelled handle.

18. Uddhava and Sātyaki held very wonderful fans (on both his sides) on the way. The lord of Madhu (Kṛṣṇa) who was being showered with flowers, appeared resplendent.

19. The true blessings uttered by the twice-born (Brāhmaṇas) which were inapplicable to the attributeless but to the soul possessing qualities, were heard (by Kṛṣṇa) at different places (wherever he went).

20. The mutual conversation of the ladies of the capital of the King of Kurus, whose minds were concentrated on Kṛṣṇa (lit. one whose glory dispels the darkness of ignorance) was attractive to the ears (minds) of all.[309]

---

309. *sarva-śruti-manoharaḥ*—In SK. Śruti means 'the Veda' and 'the ear' and hence the commentators have differently interpreted this phrase as follows :

1. Even Upaniṣads incarnate would have complimented that conversation (sañjalpa)—ŚR., VC., SD.
2. Captivating to the ears, i.e. minds of all—VR., VD.
3. The presiding deities of the Vedas wondered how these ladies knew better the Lord—VD.
4. Containing the essence of all Upaniṣads—GD.

21.* This is verily the Primeval Man (spirit) who, without a second, existed in his own nature undifferentiated,[310] without any manifested universe before the disturbance of the equilibrium of the qualities (*guṇaś*) [which results in the creation of the universe] and in the night of the dissolution of universe when the individual souls lie absorbed[311] in the Supreme Spirit, with their powers lying dormant.

22. It is he, the revealer of the Vedas (scriptures) who, again, with a desire to attribute name and form to the nameless and formless spirit, presided over (lit. followed) his nature (*prakṛti*) which being directed by his power (viz. Time) has a desire to procreate, and deludes the individual souls—his own parts.

23. Verily this is he (i.e. Kṛṣṇa) whose feet (or real form), the sages who have subdued their sense-organs and have control over their life-force (by prāṇāyāma etc.) visualize, in this (very) world, with their hearts purified, due to their devotionful longing (to see him)[312]. Certainly[313] this very Kṛṣṇa is capable of completely purifying our intellect[314].

---

*VR. explains—This Kṛṣṇa is the same person who is one and is both the material and efficient cause of the Universe (its creation etc). He alone was during the period called the night of Deluge (when all the three attributes were inactive) when all forces lay dormant, when He Himself, the Soul of the Universe of animates and inanimates, the Controller within, had withdrawn in himself the thought of creation and lay without creating gross products (the earth and other Bhūtas).

310. *aviśeṣa ātmani*—ŚR. explains 'niṣ-prapañce nijasvarūpe'.

311. *nimīlitātman* etc.—ŚR. raises the point about the possibility of merging of the souls (jīvas) as they are themselves Brahman and replies, "When all the powers of the individual souls are dormant, it is as good as destruction—*suptāsu śaktiṣu satīṣu jīvopādhi-bhūta-sattvādi-śakti-layaḥ eva jīva-layaḥ|*

312. GD. emphasizes that it is due to his grace (and not simply by the efforts of the sages) that he can be seen.

313. VJ. prefers the reading *na tu* and explains: He purified the heart thoroughly by devotion and not by action (*karma*).

VC. follows the reading *nanu* and explains : It is certain that this (Kṛṣṇa) alone can purify the intellect thoroughly and not Yogic exercises etc. The sagehood (*sūritva*), mastery over sense organs and control of life-force etc. are due to devotion (to him) alone and not to yogic practices.

314. ŚR. gives an alternative explanation :

24. Oh friend! This is verily he (Kṛṣṇa) whose meritorious episodes are eulogised in the Vedas, mystical scriptures (like Upaniṣads and Āgamas) by persons well-versed in the mysteries (of this literature), and who is the only one Lord, who out of his sportiveness creates, protects and destroys the universe, and is not attached to it.

25. In every age, when evil-minded kings rule (lit. live) irreligiously, this (Lord Kṛṣṇa) certainly assumes forms (incarnations) by his *sāttvic* power[315] and sustains the sovereignty (divine faculties of omnipotence, omnipresence etc.), truth, religious order,[316] grace and glory for the prosperity[317] (of persons who have resorted to his feet).

26. Oh! How wonderful it is that this Superman (lit. Supreme Being), the Lord of the Goddess Lakṣmī, has[318] made the race of Yadu[319], the most praiseworthy of the praiseworthiest by his birth (despite the curse of Yayāti and has rendered the forest of (the demon) Madhu[320] the sacredmost of the most sacred regions by his birth as well as by his wanderings.

When he goes out of sight, he may not please destroy his knowledge from our mind i.e. He would not be unseen although he might journey to a distant place. We should accompany him.

315. v.l. sātvataḥ—'To his devotees like gods etc.' (VJ.).

316. *ṛtaṃ*—(1) Speech which is both sweet yet true—VC., SD.
(2) Religious practice (anuṣṭhīyamāno dharmaḥ) —VB. I preferred this older connotation to
(3) *yathārthopadeśakatva* of ŚR., BP., GD.
(4) pious act (*puṇyaṁ karma*)—VR.

317. bhavāya—stability, preservation—ŚR., SD.; but I followed VJ., VC., VR., GD. and translated it as 'prosperity'.

318. The use of the present tense for this past event is vigorously defended by VC. on the ground that the pastimes of the Lord never end, due to their continuance in the infinite number of the worlds. VD. endorses VC. 's view.

319. *Yadu*—Son of king Yayāti of the Lunar race and founder of the Yādava clan in which Kṛṣṇa was born. He refused to bear the curse of old age passed upon his father by the sage Śukra and in consequence he incurred his father's curse. —DHM. 371.

320. *Madhu-vana*—This forest was the dwelling place of demon Madhu. Śatrughna founded a city—Mathurā—after Madhu's death here. This region includes the city of Mathurā and its surrounding region including Vṛndāvana—VB., GD.

27. Oh! Dvārakā (Kṛṣṇa's capital) surpasses the glory of the Heaven![321] It gives sanctity and glory to the earth as its resident-subjects always see their lord's smiling looks favoured on them in his grace.[322]

28. Oh friend! The ladies whose hands have been clasped by Him (in marriage) must have certainly worshipped the Lord (God) by observances of religious vows, ablutions and oblations to the sacred fire as they frequently drink the nectar of his lower lip for which the women of Vraja (Gokula) whose hearts were yearning for that nectar, entranced with fascination.[323]

29-30. Those ladies like the mothers of Pradumna (i.e. Rukmiṇī), Sāmba (viz. Jāmbavatī), Ambā (i.e. Nagnajitī) who were taken away (by Kṛṣṇa) after paying (their price) of valour, by subduing the powerful kings like Caidya (Śiśupāla)[324] and others at the assembly of suitors convened for the selection of the bridegroom by the bride, and thousands of others abducted ladies after killing the son of the Earth[325] (viz. the

---

321. VB. gives the details of the excellence of Dvārakā over the Heaven as follows :

There are gods in Svarga, in Dvārakā dwells the God of gods. There are heavenly damsels in Svarga while in Dvārakā lives the goddess of Wealth (Lakṣmī). The denizens of Svarga fall down (when their balance of good deeds is exhausted) while the citizens of Dvārakā go up (and are liberated from the worldly existence).

322. v.l. *anugrahoṣitam*—Who made it his place of residence out of his grace—ŚR. Vide VR.

anugraheṇa uṣitam adhivasantam /

VC.—Where his grace is desired—*anugraha eva iṣitaḥ iṣṭaḥ yatra tam* /

323. VC. and VD. explain:—The ladies of Vraja whose hearts were set on testing the nectar of (Kṛṣṇa's) lower lip, frequently fell in ecstatic swoon by remembering the previous night's kisses in the morning (one cannot imagine their condition at the time of actual kissing.)

324. *Caidya* (Śiśupāla)—son of Damaghoṣa and Śruta-śravā (sister of Vasudeva). He was the arch-enemy of Kṛṣṇa, as he (Kṛṣṇa) carried off Rukmiṇī, his proposed wife. At the time of the Rājasūya sacrifice of Yudhiṣṭhira, he was slain by Kṛṣṇa in punishment of opprobrious abuse. —BPK 3118-9, DHM 294.

325. *Bhauma*—The son of the Earth i.e. the Asura Naraka; ruled at Prāgjyotiṣa; carried away 16000 women to his palace, robbed Aditi of her ear-rings and demanded Airāvata from Indra; at Indra's request

Asura Naraka—these, indeed, ennoble womanhood from which tenderness (or freedom) has been taken away and which is bereft of sanctity, since their lotus-eyed husband does not depart from their apartments and touches their hearts by his presents of desired objects (or by his sweet words of address).

31. Greeting with a smiling glance the words of women of the city talking among themselves in this way, Hari went his own way.

32. Yudhiṣṭhira apprehending danger from the enemies due to affection, appointed an army with four divisions (viz. Infantry, Cavalry, chariots and elephants) out of fond solicitude for the protection of the slayer of the Asura Maḍhu.

33. Having prevailed upon the affectionate Kauravas (i.e. King Yudhiṣṭhira and others who belonged to the Kuru clan) who, being distressed at the separation, accompanied him to a long distance, to return, he (Kṛṣṇa) proceeded to his capital with his dear ones.

34-35. Oh Bhārgava! Passing through the region of the Kurus, the Jāṅgalas, the Pāñcālas, the Śūrasenas, along with the Yāmunas, through Brahmāvarta, Kurukṣetra, the kingdom of Matsyas, the Sārasvatas, through deserts and arid regions, the lord with his horses somewhat tired reached the territory of Ānarta which lies beyond Sauvīra and Ābhīra.

36. He was greeted with respectful presents by the people of those (respective) regions through which he travelled. He bent his course westward in the evening when the Sun was sinking into the sea (-water).[326]

---

killed by Kṛṣṇa at Prāgjyotiṣapura; the articles carried away by him were returned to their owners while all the women joined Kṛṣṇa's harem; Bhagadatta who sided with Duryodhana in the Mahābhārata war, was Naraka's son. —PI. 2.206-7, BDP. 163 PCK 1.513-14.

326. SR. alternatively explains :

(1) dismounting on the ground, and repairing to the banks of a river, he performed his evening duties.

(2) he went to the pastures in the guise of a cowherd.

CHAPTER ELEVEN

(*Kṛṣṇa's Entrance into Dvārakā*)

Sūta said:

1. Arriving in the country called Ānarta, his own kingdom, overflowing with prosperity, he blew his excellent conch, allaying thereby their depressed spirits.

2. Just as a white-bellied swan singing loudly in a cluster of red lotuses appears beautiful, so shone brightly the white-wombed conch, reddened by the red lower lip of Kṛṣṇa (lit. one whose steps are wide) and held in the hollow of (his red-) lotus-like palms while it was being blown by him.

3. Hearing that sound (blast) of the conch creating consternation in the heart of the terrors of the world, all subjects desirous of seeing their Lord, advanced to welcome him.

4. There, just as a lamp is offered to the Sun, those reverential subjects presented offerings to Him who is ever delighted and contented in himself, due to self-realization.

5. Like children speaking to their parents, they, with faces blooming with affection, and voice stiffled with joy, addressed their protector, the friend of all:

6. "Oh Lord! We are always submissive to your lotus-like feet adored by Brahmā, his off-spring (Sanaka etc.) and Indra (the lord of gods), the highest resort for the seekers of the supreme beatitude here, a shelter where Time [or death] which dominates everything else, is powerless.

7. Oh creator of the Universe! Be thou for our prosperity.[327] You alone are our mother, friend, husband, father, spiritual preceptor, the supreme deity, by serving whom we consider ourselves as having become blessed.

8. Oh! It is due to you that we have been blessed with a protector. We can behold what the gods can scarcely see, your form beautiful in all respects, your face beaming with affectionate smile and loving looks.

9. Oh lotus-eyed (Lord), when, with a desire to see (your) friends, Your Honour[328] departed to the land of Kurus

---

327. *bhavāya*—our good, consisting of knowledge, devotion etc.—VJ.

328. v.l. *no bhavān*—Your Honour, leaving us in slight —ŚR.

or of the Madhus (Mathurā and region around it, including Vṛndāvana), Oh Acyuta ! to us, who are yours, (even) a moment (of separation from you) appears like a long period of ten million years—even as it happens to the eyes (blind-folded) in the absence of the light of the Sun."

10. Hearing such words spoken by his subjects and spreading out grace by his affectionate glances, Kṛṣṇa who was kind to his devotees, entered the city.

11. (The city which was) guarded by the Madhus[329], Bhojas[330], Daśārhas[331], Arhas[332], Kukuras[333], Andhakas[334] and Vṛṣṇis[335] who were as powerful as himself (i.e. Kṛṣṇa), like Bhogavatī[336] guarded by serpents.

12. Beautified with lotus-pools surrounded by orchards, flower-gardens consisting of sacred trees and creeper-pavilions, (full of) richness of flowers etc. (produced in) every season.

13. With triumphal arches erected in front of the city gates, house-doors and the public roads : the solar rays have been obstructed in the interior by the tops of banners and flags painted (with various designs).

14. With royal roads, streets, market places and quadrangular places swept clean and be-sprinkled with fragrant

329. *Madhus*—A family of the Yādava clan—BPK 233.

330. *Bhojas*—Descendants of king Mahābhoja of the Yādava clan —BPK 228.

331. Daśārha—Son of king Nirvṛti or Vidūratha of the Yādava clan, a founder of the dynasty of the same name. (BPK 137). Here it refers to that clan. They were related to Pāṇḍavas and defended Dvāravatī—PI. 2.79.

332. *Arhas*—a group of people defending Dvārakā and related to Pāṇḍavas—PI. 1.113.

333. *Kukuras*—a son of Andhaka and father of Dhṛṣṭa. Here his descendants, the defenders of Dvārakā. are implied—PI. 1.383.

334. Andhakas—A community of the Yādava tribe defending Dvārakā; at Dvāravatī their overlord was Ugrasena. Relieved by Kaṁsa's death, ended themselves by fighting with their kinsmen. Pl. 1. 67.

335. Vṛṣṇis—The descendants of Vṛṣṇi, the son of Madhu, whose ancestor was the eldest son of Yadu. Kṛṣṇa belonged to this branch of the Lunar race. —DHM 369.

336. Bhogavatī—The subterranean capital of the Nāgas in the Nāgaloka portion of the Pātāla. —DHM 54.

waters and strewn with fruits, flowers, grains of sun-dried rice and tender sprouts.

15. The doors of each house (of which city) were beautified by jars full (of water), curds, dried grains of rice, fruit and sugar canes, religious offerings, incense and lamps.

16-17. On hearing about the approach of the dearest one (Kṛṣṇa), the great-minded Vasudeva[337], Akrūra[338], Ugrasena[339], and Balarāma[340] of marvellous bravery, (17) Pradyumna[341], Cārudeṣṇa[342], Sāmba[343] the son of Jāmbavatī—all having refrain-

---

337. *Vasudeva*—son of Śūra of the Yādava clan; married seven daughters of Devaka, the youngest of them Devakī was the mother of Kṛṣṇa. After the death of Kṛṣṇa and Balarāma, he gave up his life in spiritual meditation and his four queens immolated themselves along with his body. (DHM 342-43, MNK Mahābhārata Nāmānukramaṇī—300-1).

338. *Akrūra*—A Yādava, uncle of Kṛṣṇa; the son of Śvaphalka and Gāndinī; married a daughter of Ugrasena; as per order of Kaṁsa, brought Kṛṣṇa and Balarāma from Vraja to Mathurā for Dhanuryāga; on the way Kṛṣṇa showed to him his real Divine form. He is chiefly noted as being the possessor of the Syamantaka gem; was killed in the internecine fight amongst the Yādavas at Prabhāsa. (PI. 1.3-4, DHM.10).

339. *Ugrasena*—King of Mathurā, father of Kaṁsa and Devaka. He was deposed by Kaṁsa but Kṛṣṇa after killing Kaṁsa, restored Ugrasena to the throne. Later he stayed at Dvārakā. After Kṛṣṇa's death he entered fire.—(PI. 1.210).

340. *Balarāma*—Kṛṣṇa's elder step-brother.

341. *Pradyumna*—the eldest son of Kṛṣṇa by Rukmiṇī; when a child only six days old, he was stolen by the Asura Śambara who tried to kill him. Through sheer providence, he survived all attempts and grew up to manhood under the loving care of Māyāvatī, actually Rati, his (Pradyumna's) wife of his previous birth as Kāma. He killed Śambara, married Māyāvatī and both alighted by air inside Kṛṣṇa's palace. Kṛṣṇa presented the couple to Rukmiṇī. Pradyumna married Kakudmatī, the daughter of Rukmin and had by her a son named Aniruddha. Finally, Pradyumna got killed in the drunken brawl of the Yādavas at Prabhāsa. His wives burnt themselves as Satī.—(DHM 237-38; PI. 2. 416-17).

342. *Cārudeṣṇa*—a son of Jāmbavatī and Kṛṣṇa; a good archer. (PI. 1.598.)

343. Sāmba—A son of Kṛṣṇa by Jāmbavatī; was a noted warrior but led a dissolute life and scoffed at sacred things. When his friends disguised him as a pregnant woman and asked great sages like Viśvāmitra, Durvāsas, Nārada etc. whether she would beget a male child,

ed from sleeping, sitting and eating due to the extreme joyous excitement.

18. And being full of respect, joy and in a hurry out of love (for Kṛṣṇa), they, leading the principal elephant (of state) before them, advanced in chariots (to meet him) in company of Brāhmaṇas (with auspicious articles in their hands) reciting the Vedas, accompanied by the blowing of conches and musical instruments.

19. And hundreds of the best courtisans whose beautiful faces and cheeks were glowing with glittering ear-rings, being eager to see him, advanced to greet him in their conveyances.

20. Actors, dancers, singers, scholars versed in ancient legends, family bards and heralds[344] sang the wonderful deeds of him whose glory dispels ignorance.

21. Approaching near them, the Lord paid suitable respects to all the kinsmen, citizens and retainers, there.

22. Bowing down his head, saluting (orally), embracing, touching by hands, looking with smile, (giving) desired boons and consoling, the supreme Lord paid honours to all (classes of people) up to the outcaste dog-cookers (caṇḍālas).

23. Even he himself, being endowed benedictions by the superiors (or preceptors), Brāhmaṇas with their wives[345], old men, by bards and others, entered the city.

24. Oh Brāhmaṇa ! When Kṛṣṇa proceeded on the royal (main) road, women of the good families in Dvārakā, being

---

the sages told that Sāmba will give birth to an iron pestle (or club) which would destroy the Yādava clan. Though Ugrasena got the iron pestle pounded and cast into the sea, the particles grew into rushes, reeds which turned into weapons at the drunken brawl amongst the Yādavas and killed them all. Sāmba was killed in this fight.—(DHM 276, BPK 341, MNK 379).

344. Though all these are panegyrists, the last is applied to those who are learned among them.

ŚR. quotes the duties of these as follows :

Sūtāḥ paurāṇikāḥ proktā Māgadhā vaṁśa-śaṁsakāḥ/
Bandinas tvamala-prajñāḥ prastāva-sadṛśoktayaḥ //

but VD. states that Bandis are the eulogists of the present kings :

Vartamāna-nṛpāṇāñca stotāro bandinaḥ smṛtāḥ //

345. VB. thinks that this adjective should qualify all the persons in this verse.

greatly delighted at His sight, ascended on the tops of their houses.

25. For, the eyes of the residents of Dvārakā were not thoroughly satisfied, although they were always used to see the Imperishable (Kṛṣṇa), whose person is the home of beauty (and)

26. Whose bosom is the home of the goddess of wealth, whose face is (like) a drinking vessel (of the nectar) to the eyes, whose arms (are the shelter) of the guardians (of the quarters) of the world, and (whose) lotus-like feet are (the refuge) of the Cakravāka birds[346] (in the form of the devotees who sing of Śrī Kṛṣṇa, the essence of the universe).

27. Richly adorned with a white umbrella (lit. sunprotector) and Chouries, bestrewn with flowers showered (on him) on the way, the wearer of the yellow raiment (Kṛṣṇa) shone with the garland of forest flowers[347] just as a cloud would shine with (the shining beauty of) the Sun, the Moon (along with stars), the rainbow and the lightning[348].

28. (When) he entered (his) parents' house, he was embraced by his mothers. With joy, he bowed down with his head to his seven[349] (mothers) of whom Devakī was the chief.

29. Placing the son on the lap, the mothers who with their breasts wet with the milk of motherly affection were beside themselves with joy, sprinkled him with tears (of joy).

---

346. *sāraṅga*—A pun implying—
(1) the Cakravāka birds and
(2) singers of the essence (of the universe, viz. Lord Kṛṣṇa)—sāraṁ Śrī Kṛṣṇaṁ gāyantī ti sāraṅgā bhaktāḥ /—ŚR.

347. *Vanamālā*—A garland prepared out of the flowers of Kunda, Pārijāta, lotus, Mandāra and Tulasī leaves :

Tulasī-Kunda-Mandāra-Pārijātāmbujais tu yā /
Pañcabhir grathitā mālā vanamāleti kīrtyate //

348. In plain words : Kṛṣṇa had a white umbrella on his head and *Chowries* on both sides. Flowers were showered on him on the way. He wore a yellow garment and a garland of forest flowers. On account of these, he appeared like a dark cloud.

349. Vasudeva had eighteen wives. Kṛṣṇa saluted them all, but special respect was shown to Devakī and her sisters. Vide ŚR:

mātṛ-sodaryād ādara-viśeṣa-jñāpanārtham uktam /

30. Then (Kṛṣṇa) entered his own mansion full of all coveted objects and unsurpassed by all other palaces wherein were the edifices of his sixteen thousand and also (one hundred and eight other) wives.

31. Having observed from afar their husband, returned home from a distant journey, the wives of Kṛṣṇa in whose minds rapturous joy was generated, and with eyes and faces full of bashfulness, immediately sprang from their seats (a bodily action) along with their vows[350] (which is a mental action).

32. Oh best of Bhṛgus ! They being of deep dispositions, embraced their husband with (their) hearts, eyes and (as if through) children. Owing to the distressed condition of their mind, the tears in their eyes though restrained, oozed out of the eyes of those bashful ladies.

33. Although he stood by their side in privacy, his pair of feet assumed newness (every moment). Who can desist from his feet which the goddess of prosperity (Lakṣmī) though (notoriously) fickle, never forsakes ?

34. Just as the wind subsides (after burning down a forest of bamboos) by means of fire begotten (of their mutual friction), similarly (Kṛṣṇa) (although) himself unarmed, got repose after creating hostility among the kings whose birth was a load to the earth, and causing them to kill one another, (with their power exhibited by their armies surrounding them).

35. Coming down in this world of mortals by his divine power (Māyā) and revelling among a bevy of beauties, gems of that sex, the very Supreme Lord enjoys himself like ordinary man.

36. Smitten by the pure and charming smile exhibiting their unrestrained nature and bashful looks of women, the adversary of the God of Love (i.e. Śiva) being fascinated abandoned his bow (*Pināka*). (But) women of transcendent beauty

---

350. *vrataiḥ sākam*—ŚR. explains : 'While observing the vows of women whose husbands have gone abroad'. It can also be taken as *sākaṁ vrataiḥ* which means that the rules for such women as prescribed by Yājñavalkya:

> *Krīḍāṁ śarīra-saṁskāraṁ samājotsava-darśanam |*
> *Hāsyam para-gṛhe yānaṁ tyajet proṣita-bhartṛkā ||*

also : rose up along with the other ladies.

not by their cunning (deceits) ruffle the serenity of Kṛṣṇa's mind.

37. Verily people regarding (Lord Kṛṣṇa) just like (themselves), consider Him attached and following like pursuits, although he is really free from worldly feelings and passions. Hence the unwisdom (of the people).

38. This is the superiority of the Almighty that though he is associated with the Primordial Matter, He (Kṛṣṇa) is never affected by its qualities, just as Intellect though resorting to (i.e. in spite of its being in association with) the soul, does not acquire the properties of the soul.[351]

39. They, the ignorant wives (of Śrī Kṛṣṇa) not understanding correctly the greatness of their husband, thought the Lord as their slave abjectly ministering to their humour in private just as people (lit. minds) [think wrongly about God].

---

351. This verse is interpreted differently. For example : "That is the control of the Controller (the Supreme spirit) that he (Kṛṣṇa) is not affected by the qualities of the Nature (Primordial Matter) despite His ever presence in the (working of the) Nature, just as the Intellect, though in intimate association with the eternally existing Soul is affected by the qualities inherent in the Supreme Spirit."

ŚR. explains *ātmasthaiḥ* etc : "as the intellect and happiness in the Soul do not unite with each other, similarly Kṛṣṇa is not affected by the attributes of Nature." He further adds, "It may be said that the intellect joins with the attributes of the Supreme Spirit and the material body with its qualities unites with the intellect and the individual spirit with condition; but the Supreme Spirit does not imbibe the qualities of nature, although He is present in it."

VJ. a follower of the Dualistic School of Vedānta explains : The ruling nature of the Supreme Spirit consists in that, though (he is) abiding in Primordial Nature (Prakṛti), he is not limited by Sattva and other attributes, as also by Śabda etc. which are under his control; just as the (Intellect) of the wise. though abiding in the Primordial Nature (Prakṛti), is not affected by the qualities of the Prakrti, as the Intellect fixed on Kṛṣṇa, is not affected.

JG. follows mainly ŚR. but in explaining the 2nd line of the verse he states, ". . . as the mind of the devotees under the benign care of the Supreme Lord, is in no way affected by, though it may come in contact with Nature".

CHAPTER TWELVE

(*Birth of Parīkṣit*)

Śaunaka said :[352]

1. The foetus in the womb of Uttarā which was killed by the missile Brahmaśiras of immense heat, fired (lit. flung, hurled) by Aśvatthāman, was restored to life by the Lord.

2-3. If you be so pleased[353] to speak, I desire to hear the birth, actions (life), the way he met death and the state after death of that highly intelligent and great-souled Parīkṣit. Narrate to us reverentials (about him whom) Śuka imparted knowledge.

Sūta said :

4. Dharmarāja who, due to his service to the lotus-like feet of Kṛṣṇa, became unattached to all objects of enjoyment, protected the subjects keeping them contented, with paternal care.

5. Riches, sacrifices, subjects,[354] the queen-consort, brothers, the earth and sovereignty over the isle of Jambū,[355] and glory reaching as far as the heaven.

6. Oh Brāhmaṇas! Did those objects of enjoyments covetable even to gods, yield joy to the king whose mind was concentrated on Kṛṣṇa as (objects) other (than food do) to the hungry ? [No].

7-8. Oh son of Bhṛgu ! while being scorched by the flames of the missile (Brahmāstra) in the womb of the mother, the hero (Parīkṣit) saw a certain Being, of the size of a thumb,

---

352. In Bh. P. 1.7.12 Sūta has promised to describe the life and career of Parīkṣit. After describing how Kṛṣṇa returned to Dvārakā after restoring the Pāṇḍavas to their ancestral kingdom, this topic is now taken up.

353. ŚR. states that this expresses prayer or a request and not a command.

354. *Lokāḥ*—attainment of heavens as a result of the sacrifices —ŚR.

355. *Jambūdvīpa*—One of the seven island-continents surrounding Meru. It is so named on account of the abundance of Jambū (Engenia Jambolana) trees. India forms the major part of this island.

pure, wearing a crown of shining gold, of beautiful appearance, dark complexion, with garments (shining) like the lightning and Imperishable—

9. Of beautiful long four arms, (with) ear-rings of bright (heated) gold, (with) eyes red like blood, with a mace in hand, going around him in all directions, waving (around) constantly the meteor-liked bright mace—

10. (Parīkṣit) examined carefully who was this (Being) near him extinguishing the flames of the missile by his mace like the Sun dispersing the mist.

11. Having warded off (the Brahmāstra), the omnipresent Lord, Hari, of infinite nature and the protector of religion,[356] disappeared then and there, while the foetus of ten months was looking on.

12. Then, (at the auspicious time) when the favourable planets were in the ascendance, (indicating progressive) increase of all qualities the scion to the dynasty of Pāṇḍu was born, with the prowess like Pāṇḍu reborn.

13. Having got the ceremonial repetition regarding the auspiciousness of the day[357], the king, with a happy heart, got the ceremony of birth[358] (or astrological calculation of the nativity of a child) performed by Brāhmaṇas like Dhaumya, Kṛpa and others.

14. The king, the knower of the sacred places (and of the proper time, person etc. for donating gifts) gave gold, cows, lands, excellent villages, elephants, horses and sweet food (dishes) to Brāhmaṇas at the auspicious time of the birth of his progeny[359].

---

356. *Dharma-gup* : (1) The protector of religion or righteousness (ŚR.) (2) The protector of kings—the protector of religion (VD.) (3) The Performer of his duty of protecting his devotees (VR.) (4) The observer of religion (VJ.)

357. *Puṇyāha-vācana*—Repetition of the words 'This is an auspicious day' three times at the commencement of most of religious ceremonies. —ASDP (V.S. Apte : the Practical Sanskrit-English Dictionary, 1965).

358. This is technically known as Jātakarman.

359. ŚR. quotes here a smṛti text which states, "gifts given at the time of a male child and at the time called 'Vyatipāt' fruition in eternal good". It further states that gods and Manes (Pitṛs) remain present at the time of the birth of a male child to twice-born, declaring that as an

15-16. Brāhmaṇas, pleased (as they were) with the modest king, spoke, "Oh chief among the descendants of Puru ! When this pure scion of the Puru race was nearly brought to death by the unavoidable Fate, he was given to you by the mighty Viṣṇu out of his grace."

17. He, therefore, will be widely known in the world as 'Viṣṇurāta'. (There is) no doubt that he will be the most famous and the greatest devotee".

Yudhiṣṭhira said :

18. Oh, the best amongst the venerable ones ! Will he emulate his great-souled forefathers of holy reputation, the royal sages, in fame and good will (lit. expression of approbation)?

Brāhmaṇas said :

19. Oh son of Pṛthā (Yudhiṣṭhira), this (Viṣṇurāta alias Parīkṣit) will be the protector of subjects like Ikṣvāku, the son of Manu incarnate, friendly to Brāhmaṇas and true of word like Rāma, the son of Daśaratha.

20. This (Parīkṣit) will be munificent and protector (of the seekers of shelter) like Śibi[360], the king of Uśīnara, and a contributer to the glory of his relatives, the performers of sacrifices like Bharata[361], the son of Duṣyanta.

21. This (Visṇurāta will be) the foremost among the archers like both the Arjunas (viz. Arjuna, the Pāṇḍava and Arjuna son of Kṛtavīrya of Haihaya dynasty), unassailable like fire, unsurpassable (of unfathomable mind) like the sea.

22. He will be brave like the lion (lit. king of beasts),

---

auspicious day (*puṇyāha*). ŚR. quotes another text which explains that there is no impurity on account of the birth of a child until the umbilical cord is cut. VD. endorses the above views by quoting from the *Viṣṇudharma* and *Varāha*. VB., GD. and others follow ŚR.

360. Śibi—He is said to have saved Agni (the god of fire) in the form of a dove from Indra in the form of a hawk, by offering his own flesh equal to the weight of the dove to be so released. When the dove went on increasing weight in the balance, Śibi offered his own body completely.

361. *Bharata*—a son of Duṣyanta and Śakuntalā; brought up in his childhood by Kaṇva; became a *cakravarti* after his father; performed 55 horse sacrifices on the banks of the Gaṅgā and the Yamunā; he subjugated Kirātas, Hūṇas, Yavanas, Andhras and all other Mlecchas. He was such a reputed emperor that India was named after him.

worthy of taking shelter just as the Himālayas (are worth inhabiting), forbearing like the earth[362] and tolerant like parents.

23. (He would be) like the God Brahmā (or his grandfather Yudhiṣṭhira) in impartiality (or absence of hatred), like lord Śiva (the Lord of the Mountains) in graciousness, like the god Viṣṇu (the shelter of the goddess of wealth) in being the refuge of all beings.

24. This (Prince would be) equal to lord Kṛṣṇa in the eminence of virtues, generous like Rantideva[363] and righteous like Yayāti.[364]

25. (He will be) like Bali[365] in courage; of (sincere) devotion like Prahlāda, performer of (many) horse-sacrifices, a worshipper of scholars[366].

26. This (prince will be) the father of royal sages, the dispenser of punishment to persons going astray (taking to the

---

362. VC. adds that Parīkṣit was more forbearing than the earth, as the earth has not to suffer sharp, scathing words of the enemies, as he would have to do.

363. *Rantideva*—A pious and benevolent king of the Lunar race, sixth in descent from Bharata. He was enormously rich, very religious, charitable and performer of grand sacrifices. So many animals were sacrificed at his sacrifices and in his kitchen that a river of blood had issued from hides and was afterwards appropriately called Carmaṇvatī (Chambal in Malwa region). (DHM 263, ASDP. 795.)

364. *Yayāti*—Son of Nahuṣa of the Lunar race; had two wives, Devayānī, the daughter of Śukra the preceptor of the Asuras, and Śarmiṣṭhā, the Asura Princess daughter of Vṛṣaparva. From Devayānī was born Yadu and he founded the Yādava dynasty. Puru was his son from Śarmiṣṭhā. He bore the curse of Śukra and exchanged his youth to his father's decrepitude. Yayātī afterwards felt ashamed, returned the youth to Puru; made him a king and retired to forest. Puru was the founder of the Paurava dynasty. (DHM 376-77.)

365. *Bali*—A good and virtuous Daitya king, son of Virocana and grandson of Prahlāda. Through his devotion and penance, he defeated gods and extended his authority over three worlds. Viṣṇu had to incarnate as a dwarf and beg from Balī a piece of land measuring three steps. When the boon was granted, Viṣṇu manifested his real form and stepped over heaven and earth in two strides. Bali was made to live in Pātāla, the lowest region of the world. (DHM 43.)

366. vṛddbānāṁ jñāna-vṛddhānām paryupāsakaḥ sevakaḥ. The usual meaning is 'servant of the old people'.

wrong path), the controller of Kali for the (preservation of) religion on the earth.

27. Having heard of his (prospective) death from Takṣaka commissioned by (the curse of) the sage's son, (Śṛṅgin, the son of Śamīka), he, freeing himself from worldly attachments, will resort to the feet of Hari (in the holy assembly on the bank of the Ganges).[367]

28. This (prince) who after having enquired (and subsequently realized) the true nature of the Soul[368] from the sage (Śuka), the son of Vyāsa, will certainly attain to the place, free from fear from any quarter (i.e. liberation).

29. After predicting to the king (the details of Parīkṣit's future life), all the Brāhmaṇas, expert in astrological calculations of nativity, getting (their due) worship (and offerings), returned to their respective homes.

---

367. *Hareḥ padam*—Gaṅgā- tīra - sat - sabhām, tatra hi bhagavat-padam abhivyaktam/VB.

GD. endorses the same in different words.

368. jijñāsita-ātma-yāthātmya—

To understand the different interpretations of the commentators it is important to note that different schools of Vedānta hold different views regarding the relations between individual Soul (jīva) and God. Thus Madhva regards *jīvas* as parts of God but they are distinct from him, and the identity of the Brahman and the *jīvas* is only in a remote sense. According to Nimbārka, individual Souls (*jīvas*) are different from God and yet are similar to him : He regards *jīvas* as God's parts, but emphasizes the distinctness of the *jīvas* as well as their similarity to him. Rāmānuja thinks that God holds the *jīvas* within himself and by his will dominates all their functions, by expanding or contracting the nature of *jīva's* knowledge. Vallabha holds that the *jīvas*, being parts of God, are one with Him. They appear as *jīvas* through his function as *āvirbhāva* and *tirobhāva*, by which certain powers and qualities that exist in God are obscured or manifested in the *jīva*.

Like ŚR. given above, VC states :

jijñāsitaṁ vicāritam ātmano yāthārthyam vāstavaṁ tattvam yena /

(ii) who has enquired of and got the decisive (accurate) knowledge about the real nature of the individual Soul and the Supreme Soul—VR.

(iii) One who has enquired of and got a clear decision by 'This-thus-ness' (*idamitthatayā*) of the real nature of the identity of the individual Spirit (jiva) and God—VB.

30. As the king, meditating him (supreme lord) whom he saw in the embryo, (will) examine (look for him) (for discovering him) in the men here, he will come to be known as Parīkṣit in this world.

31. The (well-known) prince who was daily being fed by his grand-fathers (on 64 objects of enjoyment) quickly thrived like the moon which grows in size by its digits, during the bright half of the month.

32. The king, wishing to expiate the sin for injury to (and killing of his) relatives, by performing a horse-sacrifice, and being short of funds for the same, pondered over the ways (to procure money) by means other than levying (new tax and inflicting fines).

33. Guessing his (Yudhiṣṭhira's) desire, and being directed by Lord Kṛṣṇa, the four brothers brought immense riches left (buried) in the northern quarters[369].

34. Having procured the requirements of sacrifice, Yudhiṣṭhira, the son of Dharma, afraid of sin, worshipped Hari by performing three horse-sacrifices.

35. The Lord who was invited by the king (Yudhiṣṭhira) made him (the king) to perform the sacrifice by the Brāhmaṇas and stayed for some months with a desire to render services to his friends.

36. Oh Brāhmaṇa (Śaunaka), then, after taking leave of king (Yudhiṣṭhira), his brothers and Draupadī (Kṛṣṇā), surrounded by Yādavas and accompanied by Arjuna went to Dvāravatī (Dvārakā).

---

369. This refers to the treasures of king Marutta left over by him after performing his sacrifices. This Marutta was the son of Āvikṣit and father of Dama. His sacrifices were of high order. He was a great friend of Indra. (PI. I. 649)

CHAPTER THIRTEEN

(Discourse of Nārada)

1. Having learnt the knowledge of the Soul[370] from Maitreya[371] during the course of his (Vidura's) pilgrimage, Vidura[372] returned to Hastināpura as his desire for knowledge was satisfied.

2. While Vidura (Kṣattā) asked a number of questions to Maitreya (Kauṣārava), he certainly[373] desisted from them when complete, whole-minded devotion for Govinda (Kṛṣṇa) was generated in him.

3. Oh Brāhmaṇa ! finding his relative arrive, Yudhiṣṭhira along with his younger brothers, Dhṛtarāṣṭra, Yuyutsu[374], Sañjaya, Kṛpa, Kuntī,

---

370. *ātmanogatim*—(i) The Lord Hari, (who is the highest goal of achievement)—ŚR.
(ii) Knowledge about the real nature of Śrī Kṛṣṇa—VD.
(iii) Devotion to Hari—JG., VD.
(iv) Knowledge about the Supreme Spirit—VR., VJ.
(v) Knowledge about heaven, hell etc. to which the individual soul goes (after death)—VJ.
(vi) The diversions or the workings of the Lord (Kṛṣṇa), the (Supreme) Soul—VB.

371. *Maitreya*—Also Kauṣārava, a *siddha* who under instructions from Kṛṣṇa explained the science of the Supreme Soul (*ātmavidyā*) to Vidura. The conversation between Vidura and Maitreya is given in BH. P. Skandha III and IV. (P.I. 2. 739-40.)

372. *Vidura*—A son of Vyāsa by a maid-servant. She was sent by Ambikā, the widowed queen of Vicitravīrya, to Vyāsa when she (the queen) was pressed by her mother-in-law Satyavatī to submit to Vyāsa. Vidura is called a *kṣattṛ* (vide the next verse) which is normally applied to a child born of a Śūdra man and Kṣatriya woman (ASDP. 384). He was however treated as a step-brother of Dhṛtarāṣṭra. He was well disposed to Pāṇḍavas and warned them of the evil designs of Duryodhana. According to MBH., Vidura left Hastināpura finally along with Dhṛtarāṣṭra and Gāndhārī for penance. He then went away to perform austere penance alone in the forest. When Yudhiṣṭhira contacted him in a lonely place, Vidura, by his Yogic power, gave up his body and entered the person of Yudhiṣṭhira (MBH. Āśrama 26.20.33). —MNK. 309-12.

373. *ha*—This particle shows 'complete satisfaction'—VJ.

374. *Yuyutsu*—Dhṛtarāṣṭra's son from of a Vaiśya woman. He was a partisan of Pāṇḍavas.

4. Gāndhārī, Draupadī, Subhadrā, Uttarā, Kṛpī[375], women of Pāṇḍu's clan and other women, along with their children,

5. advanced to receive him with great joy, like the body animated by the re-entry of life in it. Having formally received him by duly embracing and saluting Vidura,

6. they who were distressed with anxious sorrow caused by separation from him, shed tears of affection. The king paid respects to Vidura when he occupied his seat.

7. When Vidura enjoyed his food, was relieved of fatigue and was seated comfortably in his seat, the king bowed him respectfully and asked him in the presence of his relatives who were listening.

Yudhiṣṭhira said:

8. "Do you remember us who grew up under the shadow of your wings (i.e. protection due to your partiality to us), who were saved along with our mother from a number of calamities like (the administration of) poison, (setting on) fire (the house of *lac*) and others.

9. In what way was your maintenance[376] (livelihood) carried on while you were travelling over the globe? What places of pilgrimage and important sacred places on this earth[377] were visited (lit. served) by you?

10. Oh self-controlled one (Vidura)! Devotees of the Lord (Viṣṇu) like you are themselves *tīrthas* (sacred places) incarnate. With the Holder of the Mace (God Viṣṇu) residing in the hearts, they sanctify the places of pilgrimage (and restore their original holiness by removing the sins of other persons accumulated in them).

---

375. *Kṛpī*—Droṇa's wife, sister of Kṛpa, Aśvatthāman's mother.

376. VB. explains that here the genitive case (*vaḥ*) is used, as Vidura was unattached and actively disinterested in his life. Hence the instrumental case is not used. VJ. states that Yudhiṣṭhira wanted to know whether Vidura observed vows like eating once a day etc. during his pilgrimage.

377. The distinction between *Tīrtha* and *Kṣetra* is as follows: *Tīrthas* are generally connected with water like sanctified rivers as the Ganges, lakes, like Puṣkara, Mānasa etc. *Kṣetra* is originally a limited sacred tract of land e.g. Kurukṣetra, Jagannātha Purī. Later on, they came to mean 'holy places' in general.

11. Oh father (uncle), have you visited our well-wishers and relatives whose god is Kṛṣṇa? Or have you heard that the Yādavas are living happily in their own city (Dvārakā)?"

12. Vidura, who was thus addressed by Dharmarāja (Yudhiṣṭhira), described fully everything that was experienced by him, in a serial order except the destruction of the Yadu-clan.

13. The compassionate (Vidura being) unable to see distressed persons, did not, of course, report the disagreeable (destruction of the Yādava clan) which (though) took place of itself, was very unbearable to men.

14. Then being received like a god, (Vidura) teaching philosophy (lit. giving instructions on truth) to his elder brother, and securing the love of all, stayed happily for some time, in the city of Hastināpura.

15. While Yama bore the curse[378] of (living) the life of a Śūdra for a hundred years, Aryaman (the 2nd Sun out of the twelve Suns) dispensed punishment to the sinners according to their (respective) sins.

16. With kingdom restored to him and with great royal splendour, Yudhiṣṭhira, having seen his grandson, the maintainer of his family, was happy with his brothers (who were) like the guardians of the quarters (of the world).

17. In this way, unendurable Time of the negligent (blundering people[379]) attached to households (domestic

---

378. The sage Māṇḍavya was wrongly sentenced to be impaled as he was mistakenly arrested along with the thieves. When the king came to know of the truth, he went to the sage Māṇḍavya, got him down from the stake of impalement and sincerely apologised. Māṇḍavya went to Yama and demanded of him the reason of impalement despite his innocence. Yama explained to him that it was due to his transfixment of an insect during his childhood. He cursed Yama to be born as a Śūdra for giving him such a disproportionately heavy retributory punishment for a comparatively light offence committed during infancy, due to ignorance.

379. JG., VC., VD. exempt Pāṇḍavas from this category, as according to BH. P. 1.12.6 Yudhiṣṭhira (and others) were unattached to enjoyment due to their devotion to Kṛṣṇa. JG. specifically states that Vidura gave the advice only to Yudhiṣṭhira and not to Pāṇḍavas. VR. states that the time or period ordained for worldly enjoyment of Pāṇḍavas had passed.

affairs) passed away inperceptibly, due to their desire (of enjoyment) of such pleasures.

18. Noticing the indications of the Time, Vidura spoke to Dhṛtarāṣṭra, "Oh king! look at the fear (-ful period); let your departure be quick.

19. Oh king, the mighty Time against which no defence can ever be made from any quarter in this world, has now arrived for us all.

20. And overpowered by whom, these people are instantly deprived of their dearest life—what of other things like wealth etc.

21. Your father (i.e. uncle Bhīṣma), brothers, friends and sons are killed. Youth has departed. Your body is overpowered by old age. Still you take shelter in the house of the enemy.

22. Oh! How wonderfully strong is the desire of a living being, for life, on account of which Your Honour accepts like a domestic dog, a lump of food scornfully given to you by Bhīma.

23. What value is to that life spared by them (Pāṇḍavas) who were put to fire, were administered poison and whose wife was insulted by you and whose lands, wealth and kingdom were also taken away (deprived by) you.

24. This body of a miserly man like you who wishes to live, becomes old by old age even though you do not wish it, like (the withering away of) your under and upper garments.[380]

25.* Certainly that person is called wise who being free from attachment to worldly objects and released from the bondage (of pride or ego) and departing in a mysterious way, leaves this body, free from (the desire of) glory etc.

---

380. VJ., VC. and VD. explain that the upper and inner garments signify gross and subtle bodies. Wrinkles, baldness mark the oldness of the gross body and blindness, deafness etc. of the subtle body.

*VR. interprets as follows :

A person who being desireless (about his body etc.), free from the worldly bondages (of merits and sins), whose passing away is not known (to his relatives), quits this body from which objectives of worldly life (*puruṣārthas*) are expected, is called a *Yogin*.

VJ. gives a different interpretation, which may be summarised as follows :

26. He is the best of men in whom indifference to the world (worldly objects) is generated either from within or due to the advice of others and who has subdued his mind and who, with Hari in his heart[381], goes out of home as a recluse.

27. Let Your Honour proceed to the northern direction without the knowledge of your relatives. Mostly the coming period is destructive to the qualities of men.

28. In this way, the king of the Ajamīḍha[382] family, whose intellect was his sight (i.e. who was physically blind) and who was thus enlightened by his younger brother Vidura, firmly cut as under his bond of affection to his relatives and proceeded as per way directed by his brother.

29. The virtuous daughter of Subala[383] ever devoted to her husband, followed him to the Himālayas, (which is) a great delight of the recluses just as fighting (lit. hard blows in fight) is (enjoyable) to warriors[384].

30. When Yudhiṣṭhira (lit. the adversaryless king, enemy of none) after performing *Sandhyā* (prayer to the Sun) and offering oblations to fire, and having bowed to Brāhmaṇas by giving sesame seeds, cows, land and gold, entered the house (palace of Dhṛtarāṣṭra) for paying respects to the elders, he did not find his uncles and Gāndhārī (the daughter of Subala).

A person, free from the (pride of his) body, the object of which is the achievement of happiness here and hereafter and thereby liberated from the bonds (of love for one's wife and others) and whose movements (i.e. departure to forest etc.) are not known, is called wise and should by penance make his body fulfil its objective (viz. liberation).

381. VB. is strongly against even spiritual suicide. One should know the Lord, concentrate on him in his heart, give up the idea of quitting his body. He should continue to recite mentally the most valuable name of God and leave his house as it would come in his way of spiritual progress.

382. *Ajamīḍha*—A son of Hastin. Had three queens of Kuru line. One branch of his descendants, e.g. Priyamedha and others became Brāhmaṇas while another branch, e.g. Bṛhadiṣu and others, was Kṣattriya —BPK 6, PI. 1.30.

383. *Subala*—King of Gāndhāra; father of Gāndhārī, Dhṛtarāṣṭra's queen.

384. v.l. *sat-samprahāram* : Just as a severe battle in which hard blows are given, is liked by the brave, the Himālayas though cold and full of hardships (due to its mountaneous nature) are liked by ascetics.

31. Agitated in mind, he asked Sañjaya who was sitting there, "Oh son of Gavalgaṇa[385], (Sañjaya) where is our father (uncle) who is stricken with age and blind in eyes?

32. Oh friend! Where has Mother (Gāndhārī) distressed due to the killing of her sons, gone (along with) friendly uncle (Vidura)? Has he (Dhṛtarāṣṭra), being aggrieved at the killing of his relatives and afraid of me (as) the guilty ignorant (person),[386] thrown himself in the Gaṅgā along with his wife?

33. Where have uncles who have protected all of us from dangers (difficulties) after the demise of our father Pāṇḍu, gone from this place?

Sūta said:

34. Not finding his master (Dhṛtarāṣṭra), the Sūta (Sañjaya) who, out of compassion and bewilderment due to his affection (for Dhṛtarāṣṭra). grew extremely distressed and emaciated, did not reply (for some time).

35. Wiping out tears by (his) hands and mustering courage (within himself), and remembering the feet of his master, he replied to Yudhiṣṭhira.

Sañjaya said:

36. 'Oh, son of a high family! I do not know the decisions (regarding the course of actions) of your uncles or that of Gāndhārī. Oh long-armed one, I am bereaved of the great-souled ones.'

---

385. *Gavalgaṇa*—A sage like learned Sūta, father of the famous Sūta Sañjaya of Dhṛtarāṣṭra.

386. *āśaṁsamānaḥ śamalam*—Various conjectures are given by the commentators in explaining these words. For example:

(1) Yudhiṣṭhira has not spared a single son. What is the propriety of living now?—VC.

(2) Yudhiṣṭhira has killed his brothers, usurped their kingdom and expelled me. Has he not become so evil-minded?—VJ.

(3) 'Let the sin of my death also be visited on his head'. With this desire Dhṛtarāṣṭra threw himself in the Ganges.—JG.

It can also be translated: "apprehensive of an offence from me, a dull-witted person."

37. At that time (there) arrived the great sage Nārada along with Tumburu[387]. He (Yudhiṣṭhira) along with his younger brothers, rose up, saluted them, received them in a way, and asked.

Yudhiṣṭhira said:

38. "Oh revered (sage), I do not know the movements of my uncles. Where have they gone from here? Or where has the poor mother afflicted with the killing of her sons, gone?

39. Oh illustrious one, you are like a helmsman who shows the coast beyond, in this boundless ocean (of worldly existence)."

Thereupon the great Nārada, the best of the sages, replied.

40. "Oh king, do not grieve for anybody as the whole world is under the control of the Almighty, the Controller (of the universe) whom all worlds along with their guardian deities worship, and who unites or separates the beings.

41. Just as bullocks with noses bored through with strings are bound in a row to a rope (carry the load of the master[388], persons bound by different designations[389] to the big cord in the from of the Veda, carry out the orders of (or perform the worship of) the controller of the universe.

42. Just as assembling and removal of articles of game are done according to the sweet will of the player, so is the union and separation of human beings (brought about) by the will of the Almighty.

43. Even if you consider the world as eternal or non-eternal or both, or neither (eternal and non-eternal) it does not behove you at all to lament for them (relatives) unless it be out of affection, a manifestation of delusion.

---

387. *Tumburu*—A Gandharva disciple of Nārada, expert in divine music; accompanied Nārada at the time of this visit to Yudhiṣṭhira and returned with him to heaven. Sang the praise of Kṛṣṇa when he held the Govardhana. His two daughters Manovatī and Sukeśā reside in the Sun's chariot in the months of Caitra and Madhu. —PI. 2.29

388. Though no words in the text of this verse support this these words are added in this translation on the authority of eminent commentators like ŚR., VJ., SD., GD.

389. Designations such as Brāhmaṇa, Kṣatriya or of stages in life, e.g. Brahmacārin, Gṛhastha.

44. Therefore, dear sir, give up this grief caused by ignorance of your mind, (thinking) 'How will they who are without protection and in a miserable condition, live without my protection ?'

45. This body is composed of five elements and is subject to the (influence of) Time and (effects of) actions and attributes. How can (a person) save another, like one being swallowed by a serpent (is unable to save) others ?

46. The handless (animals) are the means of sustenance (of life) to the beings possessed of hands (viz. human beings); the footless (i.e. grass) (is so) to the quadrupeds; the inferior are (the food) of the superior; (thus all less powerful) beings are the means of sustaining life to (all other more powerful) beings.

47. Oh king, this (universe) is, therefore, the self manifesting glorious Lord (himself). He is one, the soul of Souls. He shines (manifests) internally and externally (both as enjoyer and the objects of enjoyment). Look, He is manifold (in form) due to Māyā.[390]

48. Oh great king, the Supreme Lord, the creator of beings, has today come down on this earth as the Destroyer for exterminating the enemies of Gods.

49. The work to be done for Gods is (practically) completed, (only some) balance is expected to be completed. You wait for some time, till the God (Lord Kṛṣṇa) is here (on this earth).

50. Dhṛtarāṣṭra, accompanied by his consort Gāndhārī and (his) brother (Vidura) has gone to the hermitage of sages, by the southern side of the Himālayas.

51. (The hermitage) is called *Saptasrota* (the shrine of seven streams) as verily the divine Ganges with her seven currents branches itself off into seven separate streams for the satisfaction of the seven sages.[391]

52. Taking bath three times a day (as per twilights),

---

390. I have mainly followed ŚR. in this literal interpretation, though as usual commentators of non-Śaṅkara Schools stress their viewpoints as 'tātparyārtha'.

391. The usual list of seven sages is Marīci, Atri, Aṅgiras, Pulastya, Pulaha, Kratu and Vasiṣṭha.

and offering libations to the fire according to the prescribed religious rules, he who lives on water only, stays with a quiet Soul, free from earthly desires.

53. With mastery over (*Yogic*) posture and control over breath and restraint of six organs [five sense organs+mind, the internal organ], he (Dhṛtarāṣṭra) has washed off (lit. shattered) the dirt of the three attributes (viz. *sattva*, *rajas* and *tamas*) by his concentration on Hari (Lord Kṛṣṇa).

54. Having withdrawn mind (ātman associated with Ego-ahaṁkāra —) from the gross body and merged it with intelligence (*buddhi* or *Vijñānātmā*) and that with Soul (*kṣetrajña*) and the Soul with Brahman, the basis of all, just as the Vacuum (space) within a jar merges in the bigger Space.

55. One who has destroyed the resultant of the attributes of the Illusion (*māyā*) and restrained mind (the essence i.e. controller of the mind) and one who has abstained from eating altogether, he (Dhṛtarāṣṭra) sits motionless like a pillar. You should not become an obstacle to him who has given up all actions.

56. He will verily give up his own mortal frame on the fifth day from today and it will be reduced to ashes.

57. When the body of the husband (Dhṛtarāṣṭra) will be burnt by fires along with the hut (hermitage), the virtuous wife (Gāndhārī) standing outside will enter that very fire.

58. Oh son of the Kuru family, having seen that miracle, Vidura with a mixed feeling of joy (at Dhṛtarāṣṭra's liberation) and sorrow (for his brother's demise) will go on a pilgrimage to sacred places."

59. Having told this, Nārada, along with Tumburu, ascended to heaven. Yudhiṣṭhira, bearing his words in mind, gave up sorrow.

CHAPTER FOURTEEN

(*Conjectures of Yudhiṣṭhira*)

Sūta said :

1-2. When Arjuna (lit. the victorious) left for Dvārakā to see the relatives and to know the actions (and intentions) of Kṛṣṇa of holy reputation, several months elapsed, but Arjuna did not return. Then Yudhiṣṭhira (the foremost of the Kurus) saw omens of terrific nature.

3-5. (He observed):

The terrible state of Time in which the nature of the seasons was reversed, more sinful behaviour of people full of wrath, avarice, falsehood, crooked ways of the world, friendship mixed with dishonesty (fraud), quarrels among father, mother, friends, brothers and between husband and wife, advent of evil time, extremely dreadful unlucky portents, nature of the people characterised by avarice, (so) the king spoke to his younger brother (Bhīma).

Yudhiṣṭhira said :

6. Arjuna (the Victorious) has been sent to Dvārakā with a desire to see our kinsmen and to know the deeds of Kṛṣṇa of auspicious glory.

7. Oh Bhīmasena, seven months are now over, but your younger brother (Arjuna) has not returned, nor do I really understand its reason.

8. Has the period predicted by the divine sage (Nārada) arrived now when the Lord desires to quit his body, which is his instrument to play his part as man[392].

9. From whom (i.e. through the grace of Kṛṣṇa we got) wealth, kingdom, wife, life, family and subjects. Due to whose (Kṛṣṇa's) favour we (achieved) victory over the enemies and the world.

---

392. *ātmano... ut-sisṛkṣati*—

(i) When he desires to leave the earth (which is his body), the arena of his sports—VJ.

(ii) When he wishes to return his portion of Divinity to Vaikuṇṭha i.e. give up his mortal frame—VC.

10. Oh tiger-like man (Bhīma), look at the terribly ominous portents pertaining to the heaven, the earth and my body forboding calamity befalling (deluding) our intellect in near future.

11. Oh Bhīma, my (left) thigh, eye and arm are now and then throbbing. And tremblings in the heart portend evil happenings in near future. [These evil omens will bring evil unto me in near future.]

12. This female jackal vomitting fire, howls (wailingly) at the rising sun. Oh Bhīma, this dog wails at me without any fear.

13. Auspicious beasts go by my left, while others (like donkeys etc.) pass me by the right side. Oh tiger among men (Bhīma), I perceive that my horses are weeping.

14. This pigeon is the messenger of death. The owl which causes my mind to tremble and the crow, both sleepless (throughout the night) desire (as it were) to annihilate (the universe) by their ominous cries.

15. The quarters (of the world are) foggy; misty halos appear round the moon and the Sun[393], the earth along with the mountains is quaking; there fell a bolt from the blue along with the thundering of the clouds.

16. The rough wind blows darkening (the world) with the dust; the clouds are showering nauseating blood all around.

17. Look, the Sun is dim (lit. bereft of its splendour); there is a mutual clash of the planets in the sky. The heaven and the earth are as if ablaze with crowds of evil spirits[394].

18. Rivers, big and small, lakes and minds as well are agitated. The fire does not burn with ghee. (I cannot comprehend) what (calamity) this period would bring.

19. The babies (or calves) are not sucking (their mothers') breasts (or udders of cows—in the case of calves). The mothers are not yielding milk. In the cow sheds the cows weep with tearful faces and the bulls are not joyous.

---

393. I followed ASDP on *paridhayaḥ* but ŚR. differs. He explains, "As the halo of light encircles the fire, the misty quarters have covered the world."

394. 'The followers of Rudra mixed with other beings'—ŚR.

20. Idols of Gods are as if weeping, perspiring and moving. What calamity to these charmless, cheerless countries, towns, villages, gardens, mines and hermitages indicates to us?

21. On account of these portentous phenomena boding great calamities, I guess that the earth, being deprived of the Lord's feat the beauty of which is unique (lit. not found in any other person), has become luckless (now)."

22. In this way, Oh Brāhmaṇa, while the king was thinking with his mind which anticipated the befalling calamities, Arjuna (lit. the warrior with the monkey at the banner of his chariot) returned from Dvārakā (the capital city of the Yadus).

23-24. Seeing Arjuna, pale, feeble, shedding tears from his lotus-like eyes, with his head hung down, lying prostrate at his feet in an unusual manner, the king remembering the words of Nārada in the presence of his friends, spoke with a distressed heart.

Yudhiṣṭhira said :

25. Are our kinsmen Madhu, Bhoja, Daśārha, Arha, Sātvata, Andhaka and Vṛṣṇi living happily in Dvārakā (Ānartapurī)?

26. Or is our venerable maternal grandfather—Śūrasena hale and hearty? Is the maternal uncle Ānaka-dundubhi[395] (Vasudeva) along with his younger brothers, well?

27. Are his wives, our aunts, the seven sisters of whom Devakī is the chief, happy themselves, along with their sons and daughters-in-law?

28-29. Is the son-less (or whose son Kaṁsa was wicked) king Āhuka (Ugrasena) and his younger brother (Devaka) alive? Are Hṛdīka along with his son (Kṛtavarman), Akrura, Jayanta, Gada and Sāraṇa (brothers of Kṛṣṇa) and others like Śatrujit doing well? Is Lord Balarāma, the head of the Sātvata clan in happiness?

30-31. Is Pradyumna, a great warrior[396] among the

395. Vasu deva is so called as Gods beat the drums at the time of his birth as Lord Viṣṇu was to be incarnated as a son to him.

396. *mahāratha* is thus defined :
eko daśa-sāhasrāṇi yodhayed yastu dhanvinām / Śastra-śāstra-pravīṇaś ca vijñeyaḥ sa mahārathaḥ /

Vṛṣṇis, well ? Are glorious Aniruddha, of terrific speed (in fighting), Suṣeṇa (Kṛṣṇa's son), Cārudeṣṇa, Sāmba, the son of Jāmbavatī, and other prominent sons of Kṛṣṇa like Vṛṣabha along with their sons going on well (lit. living happily) ?

32. Similarly, are Kṛṣṇa's followers such as Śrutadeva, Uddhava and others, and other prominent Yādavas like Sunanda, Nanda, Śīrṣaṇya,

33. and all (others) depending on the power of arms of Balarāma and Kṛṣṇa hale and hearty ? Do the Yādavas our firm allies and friends, think of our well-being ?

34. Is lord Govinda (Kṛṣṇa) who is the friend and well-wisher of the Brāhmaṇas and affectionate to his devotees, at ease in the company of his friends in his assembly-hall called Sudharmā[397] in the city (of Dvārakā) ?

35. The Primeval Man, the friend of Ananta (Balarāma) lives in the ocean of the Yadu clan for the welfare, protection and prosperity of the people.

36. In their own city (Dvārakā), protected by whose (Kṛṣṇa's) arms, the Yādavas (who are) honoured (by the citizens) sport in delight (or pass their time in great happiness) like the followers of Viṣṇu[398] (the Lord of Vaikuṇṭha).

37. By defeating gods in a battle by their pre-eminent act of serving whose (Kṛṣṇa's) feet, sixteen thousand ladies of whom Satyabhāmā was the first, took away (for their enjoyment) blessed objects (e.g. the *Pārijāta tree*) worthy of Indrāṇī.

38. Yādavas, the great warriors, dependent on the success of whose (Kṛṣṇa's) arms and free from fear from any quarter, often tread on (and occupy seats in) the assembly-hall called Sudharmā, proper for the greatest among the gods, which (i.e. the assembly hall) they (the Yādavas) brought down (on the earth) by force.[399]

A warrior skilled in the use of arm and the military science, who can engage ten thousand warriors simultaneously is called *Mahāratha*.

397. *Sudharmā* : The assembly-hall of Indra in heaven. At Kṛṣṇa's behest, Indra sent it to Ugrasena for the use of Yādavas. After Kṛṣṇa's death, it returned to Indra's heaven.—DHM 306.

398. *Mahā-pauruṣikāḥ* : (i) followers of Viṣṇu—(ŚR, VC, SD, GD).
(ii) Yakṣas (a tribe of demigods, followers of Kubera)—VR., VJ.
(iii) Possessed of great manly vigour—(VB.)

399. According to ŚR verses 34 to 38 form one group.

39. Dear brother[400], you appear to me pale (lit. one who has lost his lustre). Are you hale and hearty? Or did you, who stayed there over-long, not receive due respect and were insulted ?

40. (I presume that) you were not hit at (treated) with harsh, bitter (lit. affection-less) words etc. Or have you not kept your word to suppliants after promising them (and thus creating hopes in them) ?

41. Have you, the giver of protection, abandoned (i. e. refused to extend protection to) a Brāhmaṇa, a child, a cow, an old man, a diseased person, a woman or other being who sought your shelter ?

42. Have you visited (i.e had an illicit intercourse with) a woman not deserving to be approached or a woman worth going but dressed in dirty clothes (i.e during her menses) ? Or were you discomfited on the way by your equals (lit. non-superiors) or inferiors ?

43. Have you taken your meals leaving behind (hungry) children and old men deserving to be fed? Have you committed some censurable act unworthy of you ?

44. Are you always brooding ; "I am now a nonentity[401] (as I am) permanently bereaved of the most beloved, intimate friend and personal relative (Kṛṣṇa)?" Otherwise there is no explanation of your (mental) affliction.

---

400. *tāta* A term of affection, endearment or pity, applied to any person, but usually to inferiors, juniors, pupils, children etc.—ASDP 471 (1965 Edn.)

401. Śūnya— (1) Void—ŚR.
(2) Dejected, void of joy—VR., SD.
(3) Inauspicious, unlucky—VJ.
(4) Life-less (GD).

CHAPTER FIFTEEN

(*Ascent of the Pāṇḍavas to Heaven*)

Sūta said:

1-2. In this way Arjuna, the friend of Kṛṣṇa, emaciated due to separation from Kṛṣṇa, and whose form became the ground for different suspicions and conjectures by his brother, the king (Yudhiṣṭhira) [and] whose lotus-like face and heart were dried up due to affliction, and who had lost his complexion, was not able to reply as he was brooding over the same powerful (Kṛṣṇa),

3. Controlling (his tears of grief) with great difficulty and wiping out his eyes by his hands, and being nervous on account of increased affection and eagerness due to his (Kṛṣṇa's) disappearance,

4. Remembering companionship, obligations and friendliness in Kṛṣṇa's charioteership, Arjuna spoke to his elder brother, the king, in a voice suffocated with tears.

Arjuna said:

5. Oh great king, I have been deceived by Hari who assumed the form of my kinsman and deprived me of my great lustre, the wonder of gods.

6. I have been undone (now) by that Supreme Man. By separation from whom[402] (him), even for a moment, the world becomes unpleasant (ugly) to look at, just as this (father etc)[403] is spoken of as 'dead' when it is bereaved of the vital spirit;

7. By whose (Kṛṣṇa's) power the prowess of kings who, being infatuated with passion, assembled for *svayaṁvara* (self-election of a husband by the bride) at the palace of Drupada, was surpassed by me (by merely taking up the bow) and the fish was hit (by me) with the equipped bow and won Draupadī.[404]

---

402. Verses 6-13 form one group and the word *yasya* (whose) is connected with *tenāhamadya muṣitaḥ* in verse 13.—ŚR.

403. eṣaḥ—The body (VJ.)

404. This refers to *Draupadī - svayaṁvara* in which Arjuna fulfilled the condition precedent for winning Draupadī as bride.

8. Ah ! In whose (Kṛṣṇa's) presence I quickly defeated Indra along with gods [405] and donated the Khāṇḍava forest to the Fire-god; and got constructed by Maya the assembly-hall, an illusive marvel of architecture, (lit. the illusion in the form of wonderful architecture) and kings from (distant) quarters offered tributes at the time of your (Rājasūya) sacrifice.

9. By whose prowess (my) elder (and) your younger brother possessing the power and energy of ten thousand elephants[406] killed for the (performance of the Rājasūya) sacrifice (Jarāsandha) who had placed his foot on the heads of kings. As the kings who were captured (by Jarāsandha) for the sacrifice to the lord of goblins (*Mahābhairava*) were liberated by him (Bhīma), they brought tributes for your (Rājasūya) sacrifice[407].

10. Who, by killing their husbands, made the wives of those deceitful gamblers to loosen their hair—the gamblers (by whom) in the assembly-hall, were scattered and seized the beautiful braided hair of your wife which were the most praiseworthy due to the great consecration at the (Rājasūya) sacrifice and from whose (your wife's) face fell tears on the feet when she bowed (to Kṛṣṇa who appeared there in that assembly hall of the gamblers).[408]

11. Who, by coming to the forest and eating the remnant (crumb) of a vegetable preparation, protected us from an unsurmountable calamity (viz. the curse of the sage Durvāsas) engineered by the enemy (Duryodhana) through Durvāsas who wanted to dine at the head of ten thousand (disciples), but whereby (i.e. due to Kṛṣṇa's eating the vegetable) the whole group of sages who were immersed in water, felt the three

For details MBH.I.Chs. 187, 188, 189.

405. Vide MBH. 1. 226.

406. VJ. reads *gadāyudha-sattva-vīryaḥ* and explains as 'one possessing the mace as a weapon and mental and physical power' *gadākhyam āyudhaṁ ca . . . sattvam mānasa-balaṁ ca vīryaṁ kāyabalaṁ ca vā yasya sa gadāyudha-sattva-vīryaḥ*.

407. This refers to the incident described in MBH. II. Chs. 22, 23, 24.

408. Vide MBH. 11. Ch.67.

worlds as satiated[409] (and did not feel hungry).

12. By whose prowess, Lord Śiva along with Pārvatī was made to surprise in the fight (I put with him) and gave me his missile (Pāśupata). Others (viz. guardians of the quarters of the world) also did the same. And I, in this very physical body, reached the palace of the great Indra (at Amarāvatī in heaven) and shared half the seat of the great (god)*.

13. While I was staying there, for the destruction of the enemies, the gods along with Indra took shelter of the pair of my arms characterised by the Gāṇḍīva bow. Oh descendant of Ajamīḍha, the exploits were performed (by me by his prowess)[410].

14. By whose friendship I succeeded with my chariot, in crossing over the limitless ocean in the form of the Kuru army consisting of (warriors gifted with) irresistible power. I have captured the wealth of the enemies and snatched away the highly effulgent jewelled diadems from their heads.

15. Oh Lord, he moved ahead of me (as a charioteer) in the armies of Bhīṣma, Karṇa, the preceptor (Droṇa) and Śalya, which were adorned with multitudes of chariots of powerful, great Kṣatriyas, (he), by the glance of his eyes deprived the generals of their duration of life, minds (i.e. powers like energy etc.), strength and skills in firing missiles.

---

409. This refers to MBH. Vana. 263 in which it is described how Duryodhana sent Durvāsas with his ten thousand disciples to Yudhiṣṭhira in the forest at an odd hour. But Kṛṣṇa appeared at the hermitage of Pāṇḍavas and asked them to give him something to eat. He ate a small remanent of vegetable and identifying himself with three worlds expressed appeasement of hunger of all beings in the universe. The sages automatically felt satisfied and left the place refusing the invitation of Yudhiṣṭhira.

*Vide MBH. Vana. 39. 32-64, Vana. Chs. 40, 41, 42, 43.

410. The clause : "I am today robbed (undone) by the Supreme Man", is to be connected with the next three verses (14, 15, 16) as well. The word *bhūmnā* is interpreted differently as follows :

(1) Who is present in His own greatness (*nijamahimā-avasthānena* —ŚR.).
(2) Supreme Man (*parama-puruṣa* —VR.)
(3) The greatest of all (*sarva-mahattamena*—JG.)
(4) The superman whose form consists of limitless joy—VJ.
(5) VC. treats it adverbially as 'I am *thoroughly* or extremely cheated.'
(6) *paripūrṇatamena puruṣeṇa*—GD.

16. Just as the missiles of Asuras hurled at Prahlāda did not hurt (him, similarly), the missiles aimed at me by the preceptor (Droṇa), Bhīṣma, Karṇa, Aśvatthāman (the son of Droṇa), Suśarmā[411], Śalya, Jayadratha[412] (the king of Sindhu), Bālhika[413] and others did not injure me (as I was) dependant on the (power of) his (Kṛṣṇa's) arms.

17. The controller (of the universe), the giver of strength[414] was employed as a charioteer by me, a vicious-minded fellow (though) His lotus-like feet are resorted to by the excellent persons for Liberation (from the cycle of births and deaths), and (overpowered) by whose prowess, (my) enemies, seated in chariots became vacant-minded and did not assail me while I was standing on the ground due to the exhaustion of the horses of my chariot, on the day of killing of Jayadratha[415]

18. Oh king, Mādhava's jokes graced with his dignified sweet smile and his heart-touching words such as 'Oh son of Pṛthā', 'Oh Arjuna', 'Oh friend', 'Oh descendant of the Kuru family', break[416] my heart when recollected.

19. Due to my association with him in all activities such as sleeping, sitting, wandering, prattling (or boasting)

---

411. Suśarmā, son of Vṛddhakṣema, the king of Trigarta (identified with Jalandhar Doab and Kangra by General Cunningham) was a sworn enemy of Pāṇḍavas; accompanied Dūryodhana in his attempts to carry away Virāṭa's cattle; he along with his brothers collectively known as *Saṁśaptaka* joined the side of Kauravas in the Bhārata war and was killed by Arjuna—MN, p. 393; PCK 398-99.

412. *Jayadratha*—King of Sindhu - Sauvīras; married Duryodhana's sister Duḥśīlā; attempted to carry away Draupadī; was killed by Arjuna on the 14th day of the Bhārata war. —CHM 136.

413. *Bālhika*—Son of Pratīpa, younger brother of Śantanu. He was the king of Bālhikas now identified as the people of Balkh.

414. *ātmada*—(i) the giver of strength (*balada*)—VR, VJ, VD.
(ii) One who offers Himself to His devotees —GD.

415. This refers to the episode when Arjuna who wanted to fulfill his vow of killing Jayadratha before the sunset, found his horses fatigued, got down from the chariot, created a pond of water by shooting an arrow on the ground, and fought single-handed with the enemies, while Kṛṣṇa took care of the wounded, tired steeds. —For details vide MBH. Droṇa.99. 35-63.

416. *luṭhanti*—as it were rolling in the heart, do not go out of my heart—VJ.

and eating, he was taunted by me, 'Oh friend, you are really a speaker of the truth'. He tolerated all my faults (like this), just as a friend forgives the comments of a friend or the father, or (the prattling of) the child.

20. Oh great king! I, being vacant-minded due to the bereavement of my dear friend, the Supreme Man, was defeated like a woman by the wretched cowherds on the way while I was protecting the wives of Kṛṣṇa[417].

21. The same was the bow; the arrows; the chariot and the steeds were the same; I am the same warrior to whom kings pay every respect. But when devoid of the Lord (Lord's power), in a moment, everything became unreal like oblation offered to ashes (instead of to the fire), gifts of a juggler (or 'donations given to an undeserving Brāhmaṇa'), or seed sown in barren ground.

22-23. Oh king, in our friend's capital (Dvārakā) (out of) our friends about whom you have enquired, only four or five have remained alive—our friends who, being overwhelmed by the curse of Brāhmaṇas and with minds excited with intoxication by drinking the wine (prepared from the wild rice), slew each other with clenched fists (full of *erakā* grass)[418] as if (they were) unacquainted with each other.

24. It is definitely due to the design of the great Providence that creatures protect (procreate) or destroy each other.

25-26. Oh king, just as, in water, big acquatic animals swallow smaller ones, the powerful (creatures) devour the weak ones, and those which are big and powerful eat each other, similarly, by making the mightiest and greatest Yadus kill others, and by making Yadus to destroy each other mutually, the Omni-

---

417. After the internecine fight among the Yādavas and Kṛṣṇa's passing away, Arjuna escorted the wives of Kṛṣṇa and other Yādavas to Indraprastha. On his way the Ābhīras attacked him and carried away the Yādava women. For details—MBH. Mausala 7. 51-72.

418. According to MBH. *Mausala* 3.36 ff., this grass turned into clubs in the hands of the drunk Yādavas who cudgeled each other to death with it. It is explained that grass grew out of the particles of iron pestle which, according to the curse of sages, was to annihilate the Yādava clan and which the Yādavas tried to destroy by reducing it to powder.

present Lord (Kṛṣṇa) lessened the burden of the earth[419].

27. The words uttered by Kṛṣṇa pregnant with significance for the occasion and the place, and alleviating the pangs of heart, captivate my mind when recalled.

Sūta said:

28. In this way, the mind (intellect) of Arjuna who was meditating over the lotus-like feet of Kṛṣṇa, with very deep affection, became quiet (blissful) and pure (unattached).

29-30. The mighty Arjuna from whose intellect were completely wiped out all[420] the passions etc. due to devotion the speed (i.e. intensity) of which had been accelerated by continuous meditation of the feet of Vāsudeva, again recollected the knowledge which was sung (explained) to him by the Lord at the head of the battle, but which remained suppressed due to (effects of) time, actions and attachment to pleasure.[421]

31.* Arjuna who, by attainment of (i.e. realization of

---

419. ŚR. interprets : "In this way, having killed Duryodhana, Jarāsandha and others by the most powerful great Pāṇḍavas and finishing with Śālva and others by Yadus, and by making Yadus destroy each other, the Lord lessened the burden of the earth."

VJ., being more faithful to the wording of the text, is accepted above.

420. According to VJ., this does not imply the annihilation of each and every act but of those only which deserved to be so destroyed by the great divine grace of the Lord :

Ato'tra aśeṣa-śabdo nirmathana-yogya eṣa prārabdha-viṣaya iti bhāvaḥ !"

421. JG. differs. He regards time (*Kāla*) and acts (*Karma*) as Kṛṣṇa's sports and *tamas* as mind's lack of meditation of Kṛṣṇa due to absorption in his sports. Arjuna realised the fulfilment of Kṛṣṇa's promise of absorption in him given at the time of the Kuru-war (viz. *mām eṣyasi* in the BG. 18.65).

To quote JG. *Kālo= bhagavallīlecchā-mayaḥ* /

Karma= tallīlā /

Tamas= tallīlāveśena tad-ananusandhānam /

adhyagamat= tan-mahāvicchedasya tasyānte'pi tathā. . . . punar mām evaiṣyasī'ti etad vākyaṁ yathārthatvena 'nubhūtavān /

* I have followed ŚR. in the above translation. But the terms in this verse have been variously interpreted as follows :

his identity with) Brahman[422] (leading to) attributelessness due to the disappearance of nescience and the absence of the subtle body (which is the indestructible origin of the gross or visible body) became free from (the recurrence of) the gross body (i.e. the cycle of births) and his doubt about duality[423] having been (thus) dispelled, became free from affliction.

32. Having heard of the way followed by the Lord and the annihilation of the Yadu clan, the firm-minded Yudhiṣṭhira decided to proceed to heaven.

---

422. *Brahma-sampatyā*—(i) By the knowledge of the identity of oneself with Brahman obtained by listening to Vedānta—ŚR.

(ii) By the knowledge of Brahman—VR.

(iii) By the direct apprehension of Brahman (*Brahmāparokṣa-jñānena*) —VJ.

(iv) By the perception of the Supreme Brahman in human form (Kṛṣṇa)—JG.

(v) By the realisation of the identity of one's individual self and everything else with Brahman.

Sarvaṁ khalvidam Brahma, ahaṁ Brahmāsmi iti Brahmātma-jñānena—GD.

423. *Saṁcchinna-dvaita-saṁśayaḥ*—

(1) Whose doubts about the separateness of gods etc. and the duality about one's self are dispelled—VR.

(2) Whose misapprehension and doubt about the distinctness of the individual Soul and the Brahman is removed.

VJ. interprets *dvaita* as 'wrong knowledge' *dve itam dvitaṁ, dvidhā gataṁ jñānaṁ* tasya bhāvaḥ dvaitam anyathā jñānam while *saṁśaya* is 'the oscillation between two entities'. (For details about "Illusion and Doubt" in Madhva system of which VJ. is a follower see S.N. Dasgupta Hist.Ind. Philosophy, Vol.IV, pp.173-78).

(3) JG. takes *saṁśaya* as the doubt that there is a universe quite distinct from the Supreme Being who resides in the heart.

(4) VC. thinks that the doubt is 'Whether I am in any way related to my body'. He adds : When Kṛṣṇa was in this world, though Arjuna and Kṛṣṇa were two persons, their one-ness was due to friendship. After His disappearance, Arjuna doubted whether Kṛṣṇa would absorb him into the bliss of oneness of friendship. This doubt was dispelled.

These different meanings of the above words lead to different interpretations of the above verse. Thus, for example, the gist of VR's interpretation is as follows: "Due to the knowledge of Brahman, he becomes entirely free from misapprehension regarding the Soul as gods, men etc.—a distinction which depends upon the body feeling himself separate from the gross and subtle body, also from the subtle *Prakṛti* and the three attributes (*guṇas*). Thus there being no occasion for rebirth, he becomes free.

33.* Having heard of the destruction of Yadus and of the passing away of the Lord[424] as reported by Dhanañjaya[425] (Arjuna), Kuntī, who, by single-minded devotion concentrated herself on the Lord Adhokṣaja (Kṛṣṇa—lit. one who is beyond the ken of sense-organ) detached herself from the worldly existence[426].

34.* Just as a thorn is removed with another thorn (and both are thrown away), similarly the Unborn[427] Being (Lord Kṛṣṇa), gave up that body with which He removed (the burden of the earth, (because) to the Lord both (the bodies which became burdens and His own mortal body) are equal.

35.* Like an actor, just as he assumed various forms (bodies) like those of fish and others and gave them up, he abandoned the body through (the instrumentality of) which he removed the load on the earth.

36. When Lord Kṛṣṇa whose meritorious legends (stories) are worth hearing, left this earth with his body, on that very day, the Kali (age) which is the cause of irreligious actions in thoughtless (lit. unawakened) minds, followed.

37. Finding the spread of a number of irreligious tendencies such as avarice, untruthfulness, crookedness, violence in houses, towns, the nation, and in his own self, the wise Yudhi-

---

424. Commentators like ŚR., JG., VC., GD. quote BH. P. 11.31.9 and maintain that Kṛṣṇa's death was not a fact but it appeared to be so to mankind. VJ. omits this and the next 2 verses. Vide Bh. P. XI. 31.6 also.

425. According to VD., 'Dhanañjaya' means Nārada as he got over (*jaya*) thoughtlessness (*dhana—dhaṁ dhairyaṁ nāśayatī' ti dhanam avivekaḥ*). Kunti heard from Nārada the prediction about the annihilation of Yadu clan and death of Kṛṣṇa before she proceeded to Himālayas.

It is to be noted that JG. and other commentators hold that the annihilation of Yadus was only apparent.

426. (1) became liberated while alive (Jīvan-mukta)—ŚR.

(2) Quitted her body—ŚR.

(3) Ceased to be born again; became liberated—JG.

VJ. omits these.

427. Brahman exists. No birth is possible in its case. Hence it is unborn. ASDP (p. 21) quotes on *aja* :

na hi jāto na jāye'haṁ na janiṣye kadācana /
Kṣetrajñaḥ sarva-bhūtānāṁ tasmādaham ajaḥ smṛtaḥ //

ṣṭhira decided[428] to go away from the worldly life.

38. In the city of Hastināpura, the emperor (Yudhiṣṭhira) installed on the throne his grandson who was self-restrained and equal to him in virtues, as the ruler of the land engirdled by waters (seas).

39. Then the monarch (Yudhiṣṭhira enthroned at Mathurā) Vajra (the son of Kṛṣṇa's grandson Aniruddha) as the king of (the country called) Śūrasena. Having performed the sacrifice dedicated to Prajāpati, he 'drank up' (i.e. established within himself by *yogic* process) the fires (viz. *Dakṣiṇāgni*, *Gārhapatya* and *Āhavanīya*).[429]

40-41. Having given up then and there all his silken garments and gold ornaments like bracelets, and becoming free from all possession, pride and having severed all ties, he sacrificed his speech organ (or offered all sense organs as an oblation to the mind) into the mind, the mind (was merged) into the life-breath, and the life-breath (Prāṇa) into another (viz. *apāna*). (He then merged) this respiratory vital air (apāna) into (the presiding goddess of) Death and verily the Death unto[430] the aggregation of five elements (body).

---

428. *paryadhāt*—Put on dress (suitable for the life of a recluse)—ŚR., VC., SD.

429. As a householder (*gṛhastha*) one has to maintain these sacred fires, viz. Āhavanīya, Gārhapatya and Dakṣiṇāgni for performing the daily *homa* (P.V. Kane—*Hist. of Dharmaśāstra*, Vol. II. i. 675-685). Before renouncing one's house the *iṣṭi* (sacrifice) called *prājāpatya* is performed in which all one's possessions are to be distributed and the three fires—maintained by him are to be 'drunk up, to be presumed to have been established within one's self—by reciting certain hymns.

Prājāpatyā bhaved iṣṭis sarvasvaṁ yatra dakṣiṇā /
Parivrajyā' pakrame sā vihitā pūrvasūribhiḥ //
Prājāpatyā nirūpyeṣṭim sarva-vedasa-dakṣiṇām /
Ātmanyagniṁ samāropya Brāhmaṇaḥ pravrajed gṛhāt //

VD. says that as per Devala Smṛti even a Kṣatriya can follow the procedure prescribed for Brāhmaṇas.

430. As ŚR.. VD. and other commentators explain, this is a figurative description of Yudhiṣṭhira's dissociating his self from all externalities. Yudhiṣṭhira finally thought of himself to be different from his body which is to be quitted unto death. "taṁ mṛtyuṁ pañcatve pañca-bhūtānām aikyaṁ dehe, dehasyaiva mṛtyur nātmanā iti bhāvitavān" /
This process of figurative sacrifice is described in later verses also.

42. Then the silent sage (Yudhiṣṭhira) offered the aggregate of five (elements) into the triad (of the attributes, viz. *sattva*, *rajas* and *tamas*) of *Prakṛti* or *avidyā* and sacrificed these three attributes into Nescience (*avidyā*). (He then) merged everything into the Soul and the (individual) Soul in the immutable Universal Soul (called *Brahman*).

43-44. Clad in tree-barks, abstemious in food, desisting from speech, with dishevelled hair, showing himself like a dullard, madman or a goblin, expecting nothing (or without waiting for anyone) he went out (of the palace and the capital) like a deaf incapable of hearing (anything). Meditating about the Supreme Spirit (*Brahman*) in (his) heart, he entered the northern direction to which other great Souls of the past have proceeded and whence no one returns.

45. Having seen that subjects all over the world were influenced by Kali, the associate of irreligion, all the (Pāṇḍava) brothers, fully resolved, followed him.

46. Knowing in their mind that the lotus-like feet of Kṛṣṇa is the ultimate refuge, they who have well achieved the goals of human life (called *puruṣārthas*) concentrated their minds on the same.

47-48. They whose intellect has been specially purified by devotion increased by meditating upon him, and whose minds are concentrated on that Supreme Man called Nārāyaṇa, attained that position which is very difficult to reach by the non-saints who are attached to objects of sensual pleasures, and being free from sins, attain his abode with their souls free from *rajas* and *tamas*.

49. Having quitted his mortal frame in Prabhāsa, even the self-possessed (or self-knower) Vidura whose mind being possessed by Kṛṣṇa, was one with him rejoined his post[431] (as Yamadharma) along with the Manes.

50. Then, having known the loss of interest (expectation) of her husbands in her, Draupadī concentrated her mind on Lord Vāsudeva and attained to him.

---

431. Yama, the god of death and the dispenser of rewards and punishments according to the acts of individuals, wrongly punished the sage Māṇḍavya for which Māṇḍavya cursed him to be born as a Śūdra on the earth. When the period of the curse was over, Yama who incarnated as Vidura, the Śūdra, rejoined his post as before.

51. He who thus faithfully listens to the beneficial and holy (account) of departure of Pāṇḍu's sons, the beloved ones of the Lord, frequently gets devotion unto Hari (engendered in him) and attains liberation.

CHAPTER SIXTEEN

(Dialogue between the Earth and Dharma)

Sūta said :

1. Oh Brāhmaṇa (Śaunaka)! Then Parīkṣit the great devotee of Kṛṣṇa verily ruled the earth according to the education given to him by great Brāhmaṇas (e.g. Kṛpa). He exhibited the same great qualities as predicted by the experts in astrology on the day of his (Parīkṣit's) birth.

2. He married Irāvatī, the daughter of Uttara.[432] He brought forth from her four sons, the first of whom was Janmejaya.

3. Appointing Kṛpa (son of Śaradvat) as the family-priest, he performed, on the bank of the Gaṅgā, three horse-sacrifices with plenty of gifts (to Brāhmaṇas after their completion) wherein sacrifices (deities of the sacrifices) attended in visible form.

4. During the course of his conquest of directions (i.e. the complete earth), at one place, he, by his might, captured Kali, a Śūdra, assuming the insignia of royalty, (while Kali was) kicking a pair of a cow and a bull.

Śaunaka said :

5. For what reason did the king (simply) arrest Kali (and not kill him[433]) as the wretched Śūdra assuming the royal insignia, kicked the cow?

---

432. The son of king Virāṭa and brother-in-law of Abhimanyu. Uttara was killed by Śalya in the Kuru war. His daughter Irāvatī married Parīkṣit. —P.I.1.217 DHM 329.

433. What were his (Kali's) special qualities due to which he was spared —SD.

6. Oh greatly fortunate one ! Please tell it (the above query) if it is related to the stories of Kṛṣṇa or concerns the saints who are enjoying (lit. licking) the honey in the lotus in the form of his feet.

7. What is the propriety of speaking on other evil topics which is a worthless waste of life of people with a short span of life but desiring final beatitude.

8. The god of Death (the deity called 'death') has been invited here for killing the beasts for this sacrifice. Therefore no one can die so long as the god of death is here.

9. Your honour has been invited by the great sages in order that words of nectar in the form of sports of Hari should be drunk to the fill in this world.

10. Verily, the lives of the idle, the dull-witted and short-lived persons are taken away by sleep at night and by the useless acts (committed) during the day.

Sūta said :

11. When Parīkṣit heard the not-very pleasant[434] news (report) of Kali's aggression in Kuru-jāṅgala[435] lying within his jurisdiction (he who was) an expert in warfare[436] took up the bow.

12. Surrounded by his army consisting of chariots, cavalry, elephants and infantry, he started from his capital, in his beautifully decorated chariot yoked with dark-coloured horses and flying a banner with the emblem of a lion, for the conquest of the directions (the whole of the earth).

13. Having conquered Bhadrāśva, Ketumāla, Bhārata, Northern Kurus and big regions such as Kimpuruṣa and

---

VJ. opines that this is not a question but an objection (for failure in duty) against Parīkṣit.

VR. takes the 2nd line as a separate sentence as follows : 'Who was that Śūdra wearing emblems of a king who kicked the cow ?'

434. (i) He was a bit pleased as he got a scope to show his bravery. —VC

(ii) very unpleasant—VR.

435. According to PSK (*Prācīna Sthala Koṣa*) this dry part of the Kuru country corresponds to modern Rohtak-Hissar region (p.539). But Bh.P. 1.10.34 shows it to be on the road from Indraprastha to Dvārakā.

436. v.l. *Saṁyuga-Śauri*—who was like Kṛṣṇa in fighting.

others,[437] he received tributes.

14. Hearing everywhere the extolling of glories of his great-souled ancestors, (which were) expressive of Kṛṣṇa's greatness,

15. And about his own protection from the fire of Aśvatthāman's missiles, of the friendship between the Yādavas and the sons of Pṛthā (i.e. Pāṇḍavas) and their devotion to Kṛṣṇa,

16. Being extremely pleased, the greatminded (Parīkṣit) whose eyes were expanded with affection gave them (the songsters of glory) very costly clothes and necklaces.

17. Hearing that Kṛṣṇa to whom the world bows, served (his) favourites—Pāṇḍavas—in the capacity of a charioteer, a President of the assembly, an attendant, a friend, an envoy, a sentinel, a follower, praising and saluting (them), the ruler of men (Parīkṣit) became devoted to (his) lotus-like feet.

18. Hear from me a wonderful event which occurred soon, while he was thus every day following the conduct of life of his ancestors.

19. (While himself) walking on one leg, Dharma (in the form of a bull) finding the (earth in the form of a) cow

---

437. In the V Skandha of the Bh.P., the ancient geographical ideas are given. The earth consists of seven islands. The first of these islands Jambu-dvīpa consists of nine *Varṣas* (continents) : (1) Ilāvṛta, (2) Bhadrāśva, (3) Hari, (4) Ketumāla, (5) Ramyaka, (6) Hiraṇyamaya, (7) Uttara-Kuru, (8) Kimpuruṣa, (9) Bhārata. India is a part of (9). The mountain Meru stands in the centre of the Jambudvīpa. The following table reproduced from Baladeva Upadhyaya's *Purāṇa Vimarśa* will give some idea of the distribution of these *Varṣas* :

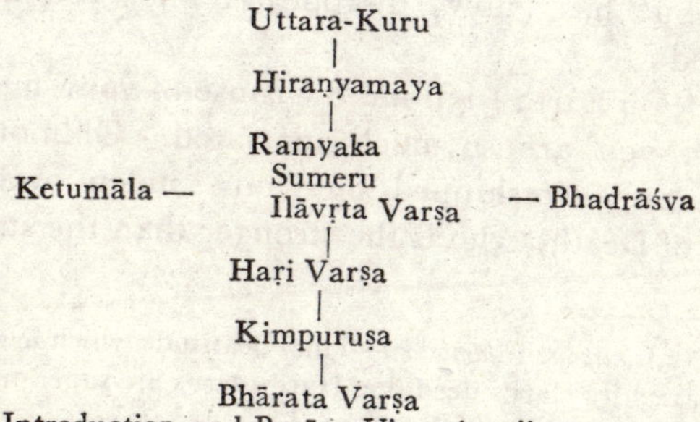

Uttara-Kuru
|
Hiraṇyamaya
|
Ramyaka
Ketumāla — Sumeru Ilāvṛta Varṣa — Bhadrāśva
|
Hari Varṣa
|
Kimpuruṣa
|
Bhārata Varṣa

Vide—PSK—Introduction and Purāṇa Vimarśa, vii.5. 317-350 for details.

devoid of (her) lustre and face full of tears like a mother who has lost her young one, asked her.

Dharma said :

20. Oh blessed (one), are you well (free from diseases)? By your melancholy countenance, you appear pale. Oh mother, I find you full of mental agony. About what distant relative are you lamenting?

21. Are you aggrieved to find me with one leg and deprived of (the other three) legs? or about yourself apprehending your being enjoyed by the Śūdras (in near future) or (over) Gods and others whose portion (of the offerings) of sacrifices is lost (due to non-performance of sacrifices) or (over) subjects due to Indra's refusal to pour rain?

22. Oh earth! Are you grieved for women who are not protected (by their husbands) or for children who are not only uncared for but are also oppressed by their fathers (cruel) like man-eaters; or for the goddess of Speech or Learning (who has been) living in the family of vicious Brāhmaṇas or (feel sorry for) those born in the best families('Brāhmaṇas') serving the kings who are not favourable to Brāhmaṇas.

23. Are you sorry for the mean Kṣatriyas who are possessed by Kali or the countries abandoned(or ruined) by them, or for the mankind indulging in eating, drinking, wearing (fancy) clothes, (enjoying) baths and sexual intercourse everywhere (lit. here and there)?

24. Or, Oh mother Earth, (are you lamenting) remembering the deeds on which depends the Liberation[438],—(deeds) of Hari who assumed incarnation for lessening your heavy burden, but has (now) disappeared and (you find yourself) abandoned?

25. Oh Earth! tell me the cause of your mental agony by which you are so much emaciated. Oh mother, is your good fortune so worshipped by Gods, stolen away by Time (the god of Death) who is the stronger than the strong.

---

438. v.l. *nirvāṇa-viḍambitāni*—Final Beatitude which has been ridiculed or surpassed by Hari's deed, i.e. Hari's deeds are superior to the Liberation—ŚR. and JG.

The Earth said :

26. Oh Dharma, you know verily all about which you have asked me. Due to Kṛṣṇa you were possessing four legs which were conducive to the happiness of mankind.

27.* In whom (Kṛṣṇa) truthfulness, purity, compassion, patience, generosity, contentment, straightforwardness, steadiness of the mind, self-restraint, (control of the organs of senses), austerities, equality, endurance, unconcernedness (even to one's benefits), mastery over learning,

28.* Knowledge, non-attachment, capacity to exercise authority, heroism (courage on the battlefield), strength, judgement or perception of what is proper to do, independence, dexterity, beautiful complexion (personal charm), fortitude softhearedness.

29.* Extreme splendour, humility, good behaviour, skilled activities of the organs of senses, receptacle of enjoyment, mental poise (non-perturbation of the mind), faith, fame, adorability, freedom from pride,

30. Oh Lord, these and[439] other eternal, great qualities (which are) prayed and desired for by a person anxious for greatness, perpetually exist (in him) without decay (lit. never get annihilated).

31. I grieve for the people who are affected by the sight of the evil-minded Kali, (as they are) now bereft of Kṛṣṇa who is the receptacle of all qualities.

32. I feel grief for my own self and about you who are the best of gods. Similarly (I feel grief for) the gods, the

---

*** In verses 27, 28, 29, the interpretation of ŚR. is mainly followed though other commentators emphasize slightly different shades of meaning of the qualities enumerated herein.**

439. *ca*—In addition to the 39 qualities enumerated above, SD. adds the following eternal great attributes : "beauty, sweetness, tenderness, affection, calmness, protectiveness and others".

JG. has listed 63 attributes while commenting on verses 27-29 and adds 5 more as understood under *ca*—and 17 more as *anye*—which are impossible for a *jiva* (individual soul) to attain. This long list is omitted as it is not directly related to the interpretation of these verses and no other commentator even in the Bhāgavata Vidyā Peeṭh edition subscribes to it.

manes, sages, good persons, all strata of the society (castes) and all stages of life (*āśramas*).

33. Being enamoured of the beauty of (his) feet, the Goddess of Wealth for whose favourable side-glance gods like Brahmā and others performed penance for a long time and (thus) was resorted to by the best, adores those (Kṛṣṇa's) feet leaving her own residence in the lotus-garden.

34. I, whose body was adorned with the Venerable Lord's footprints with the marks of the lotus, the thunderbolt, the goad (to control elephants) and flag, possessed the prosperity from him and surpassed the three worlds in beauty. But subsequently at the time of the annihilation of that prosperity he abandoned me who became arrogant.

35. Verily, the self-reliant Being removed the heavy burden of one hundred *akṣauhiṇīs*[440] (a big division of the army) of the kings of the Asura race, and assuming a beautiful form in the Yādava clan restored to you (who were) distressed by incompleteness in legs, your pristine state (of four-leggedness) by his manliness.

36. What lady can endure the separation from that Supreme Man who by his amorous looks, enchanting smile and sweet conversation, stole away the steadiness of mind along with pride of women of Madhu clan like Satyabhāmā and others? Being adorned with whose footprints there was (thrill and hence) hair-erection in the form of crops of foodgrains etc. due to the happiness felt by me.

37. In this way, while the goddess of the Earth and Dharma were conversing, the royal sage called Parīkṣit arrived there where the Sarasvatī flows to the east.

---

440. *akṣauhiṇī*—a division of the army consisting of 21870 chariots, 21870 elephants, 65610 horse and 109350 foot—PASK, p.8

CHAPTER SEVENTEEN

(*Punishment and Control of Kali*)

Sūta said :

1. There (on the eastern turn of the Sarasvatī in (Kurukṣetra) the king (Parīkṣit) saw the pair of the cow and the bull being beaten like protectionless beings and also the Śūdra wearing the insignia of royalty, with a rod in his hand.

2. (He saw that) the bull, white like the lotus-fibre, as if passing urine through fear, (and thus losing strength every moment), trembling on one leg, sinking down under the beating by the Śūdra.

3. (And) the cow also yielding (milk the products of which, as oblations to sacrifices, are useful for) religion, distressed, (being) heavily kicked by the Śūdra, calf-less, with face full of tears, weak and desiring to eat grass[441].

4. Riding his gold-plated[442] chariot and holding bow equipped (with arrow) he asked in a voice deep like (thunder of a) cloud.

5. "Who are you who, a mighty person, are hurting the weak ones by force in this world under my protection? Like an actor you are dressed as a king but are a Śūdra in your actions.

6. Who are you who after the departure of Kṛṣṇa and Arjuna (lit. the master of the Gāṇḍīva bow) to a distant place (the other world) are striking the innocent ones in solitary places? You are the culprit deserving to be killed.

7. (Address to the bull). Who are you white like lotus-fibre, (who) being defective in three legs, walk on one leg only? Are you some God who in the form of such a bull make us sorrowful?

8. With the exception of your tears of sorrow, tears of grief of other animals do not fall on the surface of this earth

---

441. SR. clarifies : The earth became lean due to non-performance of sacrifices which led to droughts and failure of crops and that she desired to have her share in sacrifices.

442. *Kārtasvara-paricchadam*—SD. and VB. take this as referring to Kali and interpret as 'wearing gold crown, ear-rings etc.' which Kali as a Śūdra is not qualified to wear.

which is embraced (i.e. protected) by the mighty arms of the best kings in the Paurava dynasty.

9. Oh Son of surabhī, do not feel aggrieved. Let thy fear from the Śūdra pass away. (Address to the cow). Oh mother, do not weep. Good betide thee while I am alive to punish the wicked.

10. Oh pious one, the arrogant king in whose kingdom all the subjects are intimidated by the wicked, destroys his reputation, span of life, good fortune and prospects in the next world.

11. It is the highest duty of kings to remove the trouble of the distressed. Hence I shall slay this wicked-most oppressor of beings.

12. Oh four-legged son of Surabhī, who cut down your three legs? Let there be none (distressed) like you in the jurisdiction of the kings who follow Śrī Kṛṣṇa.

13. Oh bull, good betide you righteous people who never commit sins. Report to me who deformed you and (thereby) spoilt the glory of the Pāṇḍavas.

14. Perpetrators of crimes against the innocents and their accomplices as well have fear from me from all sides.[443] When the wicked are punished, it contributes to the good of the virtuous.

15. I shall pull off the arms along with the bracelets[444] even of the immortal himself if he, being uncontrolled, commits an offence (crime) against the innocent persons.

16. The greatest duty of a king who punishes, as per religious codes, persons going astray in normal times, is to protect in this world persons abiding by their own religion.

Dharma said :

17. This your speech which dispels fear (from the minds) of the distressed, is worthy of the descendants of the Pāṇḍavas due to whose (collection of) good qualities Lord Kṛṣṇa undertook to work as envoy etc.

---

443. *sarvato bhayam*—Fear not only from me but from all such as Yama (the god of death) and others—SD.

444. right from the shoulder—ŚR.

18.* Oh great man, we who are extremely puzzled by discordant doctrines (advocated by different theorists),[445] do not know the Being (who is) the cause of misery[446] (of animated beings).

19. Some (i.e. followers of the *Yoga* school) who cover up the differences (between the individual and Universal Souls) call the Individual Spirit as the Master (i.e. dispenser of Pleasure and Pain)[447]; others[448] (Fatalists), regard the fate (i.e. the presiding deities of planets) to possess such power; others (the followers of the Mīmāṁsā) regard actions (such as performance of sacrifices as having this power); while (some)

---

*(1) JG. interprets differently : We (the theists) as well as those who are puzzled by the different statements (of *śāstras*) do not know the Being who is beyond the reach of all persons.

(2) VC. explains : We do not know the being from whom 'seeds' of misery are produced. This man Kalı who is troubling me is visible. But the very fact that he troubles me only (and not others) shows that there must be some special reason—'seed'—of this trouble. We do not know the Being who is the source of the "seeds" of distress.

445. *vākya-bheda vimohitaḥ*—Confused by a number of Vedic quotations explaining the causes of misery—VJ.

446. *kleśa-bīja* : Sins; faults committed against the Lord—VB.

447. *kecid vikalpa-vasanā* etc.—

(i) Or, the atheists who are covered (possessed) by false logic regard themselves as the Masters (of pleasure or pain) as, according to them Gods have no power to ordain happiness and misery as they (Gods) themselves are slaves of their actions; actions being inanimate—*jaḍa*—cannot dispense pleasure or pain—ŚR.

(ii) Those of uncertain (dubious) speech regard themselves as the source of their troubles (or the Sāṁkhyas regard the mind—*antaḥkaraṇa*—as the cause of one's miseries)—VJ.

(iii) The *advaita* Vedāntins who cover up, i.e. do not recognise the difference between individual Soul and God, hold that there is nobody to dispense pleasure or pain as the duality such as pleasure-pain, is born of the ignorance of the Soul —VC.

(iv) SD. puts forth a similar explanation :

vikalpaṁ nānā-kāraṇa-vādaṁ vasate ācchādayanti ye vedāntās tadvido vā, te ātmanas tvampadārthasya ātmānaṁ tat-padārtham prabhuṁ sukha-duḥkha-pradam āhuḥ /

448. Others (i.e. persons with correct knowledge) regard Hari, the Supreme among the gods, the cause of misery :

eke samyak jñāninaḥ daivaṁ sarva-deva-pradhānaṁ Hariṁ Kleśa-bījam āhuḥ—VJ.

others[449] (the materialists) presume nature (as the ordainer of weal and woe).

20. Some have determined that this (happiness, misery) is from (God who is) incomprehensible by logic and indescribable by words. Oh sage-like king, ponder over this by your intellect[450].

Sūta said :

21. Oh great Brāhmaṇa (lit. the best among the Brāhmaṇas) while Dharma was speaking thus, the king-emperor with his delusion dispersed, spoke with tranquil mind.[451]

The king said :

22. Oh knower of *Dharma* (righteousness)! (By not disclosing the name of Kali who is maltreating you) you are expounding religion (which ordains) that the place of the perpetrator of an irreligious act is the same as that of the reporter of the act (i.e. the person who commits a sin and the informer of that sin go to the same place, viz. hell).

23. Or it is certain that course of the *Māyā*—power[452] of God—is beyond the reach of the mind and speech of (living) beings.

24. In the *Kṛta* age, austerity, purity, compassion and truthfulness were the four legs (of Dharma). Three of them were broken by (forms of) unrighteousness, viz. pride, contact (with women) and intoxication (from liquor).

25. Oh Dharma, now-a-days (in this Age) your (remaining) leg, viz. truthfulness on which you subsist,[453] exists (but)

---

449. *apare*—Followers of the Sāṅkhya School—JG.

450. VJ. differs : "Some conclude that the stream of misery springs from *Prakṛti* which is beyond the range of comprehension or from some positive form of ignorance (or rather Nescience) whose nature (as being existent or non-existent) cannot be decided. Oh great king, consider which of these are supported by the Vedas and Smṛtis, and judge accordingly.

451. *samāhitena manasā*—(The king who considered Dharma's speech) with close attention.

452. *deva-Māyā*—The will of the Almighty (VJ., VR.). The *Prakṛti* of Lord Viṣṇu —SD.

453. *nivarttayet* etc. : Whereby the world will achieve you.

this non-righteousness in the form of Kali who is brought up on falsehood (untruthfulness) wishes to deprive you of that (leg) also.

26. And this earth (in the form of cow) whose great burden has been unloaded by the Lord (Kṛṣṇa) has been made auspicious on all sides by his splendid foot-prints.

27. Being renounced by him, unfortunate and pious as she (the Earth) is, she is shedding tears (being apprehensive) that Śūdras in the guise of Kings and inimical to Brāhmaṇas will enjoy her.

28. In this way having consoled Dharma and the Earth, the great warrior took up (drew out) his sharpened sword against Kali the cause of inequities.

29. Knowing him (Parīkṣit) determined to kill him, he (Kali) being overwhelmed with fear, abandoned the emblems of royalty and bowed down his head at his (Parīkṣit's) feet.

30. The heroic (Parīkṣit) who was kind to the poor, fit for refuge and worthy to be praised, did not, out of compassion, kill him (Kali) who was lying prostrate at his feet and addressed him thus, with a smile.

The King said :

31. Verily there is absolutely no danger to you (who are a supplicant for mercy) with folded hands from (us) the upholders of the glory of Arjuna. But you are the friend of the unrighteous. You should not, under any circumstances, live in any part of my kingdom.

32. Whilst you were existing in the body of kings, a number of inequities (such as) avarice, untruthfulness, theft, vulgarity, renunciation of religion, misfortune, fraud, quarrel and pride have followed (commenced to spread their influence).

33. Oh friend of the iniquitous, you should not therefore stay in Brahmāvarta where persons expert in the performance of sacrifices adore the Lord of the sacrifices therewith (by sacrifices) and (which) is habitable by *dharma* (righteousness) and truth.

34. You should not live in that place where the glorious Hari in the form of Sacrifices, being adored, spreads over (confers upon) the performers of sacrifices happiness and

objects of desire certainly. This (Supreme) Soul is present like air, both inside and outside the mobile and the immobile beings.

Sūta said :

35. Thus being ordered by Parīkṣit, Kali who was trembling, spoke to him who has raised his sword like the God of death (Holder of the rod).

Kali said :

36. "Oh Imperial Majesty, wherever I shall stay by your order, I visualize you ready with a bow and arrows.

37. Oh best of the righteous, it becomes you to appoint a place for me where I may dwell with a steady mind obeying your commands."

Sūta said :

38. (Thus) solicited (by Kali), the King then gave Kali the following places used for gambling, drinking, bad women and slaughtering where four kinds of iniquities thrive.

39. When (Kali) supplicated again, the Lord gave him gold (to live in). Then (he gave Kali) five abodes viz. untruth, pride, passion, ignorance and the fifth—enmity.

40. As pointed out by him, Kali, the cause of unrighteousness, lived in these five places allotted to him by the son of Uttarā (Parīkṣit).

41. Hence these should not be resorted to by persons who are anxious to be good—especially by the r ghteous king who is the preceptor and lord of men.

42. He joined the bull's three legs—austerities, purity and compassion (which had been) maimed. And consoling the Earth (restored to her) the prosperity.

43. Now he occupies the throne worthy of kings only, and bequeathed to him by his grandfather (Yudhiṣṭhira who was) desirous of retiring to the forest.

44. Shining with the goddess of prosperity of the Kaurava Kings, the sage-like king (who is a) great fortunate (person), the Supreme authority and whose fame is extensive, is now ruling in Hastināpura.

45. In this way, this king, the son of Abhimanyu whose prowess is such, is (thus) ruling over the earth when you have engaged yourself for the performance of sacrifices.

CHAPTER EIGHTEEN

(Curse of the Brāhmaṇa)

Sūta said :

1. He (Parīkṣit) who due to the grace of Lord Kṛṣṇa of miraculous deeds, did not die in the womb of his mother though he was severely burnt by the missile fired by Aśvatthāman (the son of Droṇa),

2. Who, having offered his heart to the Lord, was not disturbed in his mind by the great peril of death from Takṣaka due to the wrath of the Brāhmaṇa.

3. Who, having abandoned attachment to all matters, comprehended thoroughly the real nature of God (the invincible) and became a disciple of Śuka (the son of Vyāsa), gave up his mortal coil in the Ganges.

4. Even at the time of death, there is no fear or infatuation in the case of persons, acquainted with the life of Kṛṣṇa (lit. one of excellent reputation), and drinking his nectarlike episodes (as) they remember his lotus-like feet.

5. As long as the great king, the son of Abhimanyu (Parīkṣit), was the sole ruler of this earth, Kali could not prevail anywhere (even in places assigned to him) despite his advent here.

6. On the very day, and at the very moment the Lord left the earth, on that very day this Kali, the source of irreligiousness, (in this world), entered here.

7. The emperor did not hate Kali (till his—Parīkṣit's death). He enjoys the essence like the black-bee (which enjoys fragrance without destroying the flower). (For during the Kali age) good actions (even when merely intended) bear fruit quickly while other actions (sins) do not fructify till they are committed.

8. What (harm can be done) by Kali who is brave among the boys, (or powerful among foolish people) and a coward before the valiant and who like a wolf[454] stays among the careless men ?

9. What (you) have asked (me about) this sacred narrative of Parīkṣit connected with the episode of Vāsudeva, has been related to you by me.

10. Whatever anecdotes about the qualities and deeds of the Lord whose great acts are worth narrating, (are there, they) deserve to be listened to by men who are anxious to be good[455].

The sages said :

11. Oh gentle-natured Sūta, may you live for a pretty long years—you who extol to us mortals the brilliant glory of Kṛṣṇa which is like nectar.

12. In this act (of long-term sacrifice) the fruit of which is uncertain, your honour is giving to drink the sweet[456] honey of the lotus-like feet of Govinda to us whose bodies have changed colour due to the smoke of sacrifices[457].

13. We cannot compare the heaven and the Liberation (from the cycle of births) with the slightest period of time (spent) in the company of (devotees who are) associates of the Supreme Lord. What to say of the blessings (i.e. the desired objects like kingdom etc.) of ordinary mortals ?

14. What man capable of appreciating the beauty or excellence will get satiated with the stories of him who is the absolute resort of the best men amongst the great people! The

---

454. *vṛka*—That which covers or destroys righteousness, knowledge etc.—VJ.

455. *bubhūṣubhiḥ*—desirous of attaining Liberation—VJ.

456. *madhu*—intoxicating (making one forget the experience of pleasure and pain)—VC.

GD. explains 'āsava' as 'the wine making one forget the unhappiness of the worldly existence, and 'madhu' as 'sweet'.

457. *dhūma-dhūmrātmanām*—(i) Or whose minds are covered with (full of) ignorance (and are blindly following the *karmas*)—VR.

(ii) VJ. rather differs : In this series of sacrificial acts (performed for getting the knowledge of Hari), there being no breathing space (*anāśvāse*) for attachment to other things (and hence leisure for listening to Hari's stories) you make us—whose bodies are sanctified by sacrificial smoke—drink the sweet honey of Hari's lotus-like feet.

Lords of Yoga among whom Śiva and god Brahmā are prominent, did not reach the ends of the qualities of the Attributeless.

15. Therefore, Oh learned one, your honour who is the chief of the devotees of the Almighty, describe in details to us who are desirous of hearing the pure excellent life of Hari who is absolutely the refuge of the best among the great.

16. By means of the knowledge imparted to him by Śuka (the son of Vyāsa) verily, the great devotee of the Lord (Kṛṣṇa), Parīkṣit, of no mean intellect, resorted to the feet of Viṣṇu (lit. God having Garuḍa—the lord of birds—as the emblem on his flag) which is (also) called Final Beatitude.

17. Therefore narrate to us in plain language that extremely holy account told to Parīkṣit (viz. the *Bhāgavata Purāṇa*) leading to firm adherence to the most wonderful (*bhakti*—devotion) Yoga and containing the stories about the Eternal (Kṛṣṇa) (which are) liked by persons devoted to the Supreme Lord.

Sūta said:

18. Oh, what a happy surprise—that we who are born in a (lower) mixed caste, by our service of the seniors (in age and knowledge e.g. of Śuka), have achieved our object in life. The association,even in conversation with the greatest, removes the agony (inferiority complex) of being born in a lower family.

19. What to say again[458] about the person who chants the name of the Eternal Lord Kṛṣṇa, that sole resort of the greatest, possessor of infinite powers and who is called Ananta, as the excellent attributes of the great souls are his own.

20. He is so much unequalled and unsurpassed in qualities by others[459] that it is really enough if it is suggested that the Goddess of Wealth, discarding other suppliants, serves the dust of His feet who does not seek her favour.

---

458. *kutaḥ punaḥ*—The act of reciting the name of the Infinite removes the contamination of being low born; or where is the impurity of being born in a lower caste in the man who recites the name of the Supreme Lord—ŚR.

459. *asāmyānatiśāyanasya*—There is no necessity to describe the attributes of the great Being who has no equal in quality or who does not excel any one in this respect—JG.

21. Moreover, the water (which has been) flowing from the nail of his toe and (which has been) used for worship by god Brahmā, sanctifies the world along with the god Śiva. What entity other than Lord Kṛṣṇa can be called *bhagavat* in this world ?

22. [460]Being attached to whom (Kṛṣṇa) wise men, having immediately shed off their rooted attachment to their bodies etc., attain the final stage of the sacred order of recluse (called *Parama-haṁsa*) in which non-violence, quietness[461] form the religious duty.

23. Oh Sun-like Brāhmaṇas (or Oh Vedas incarnate)[462], I who have been asked by your honour, shall describe to you in details (his glories) to the best of my abilities. Just as birds[463] soar up in the sky to the extent of their might, similarly the learned ones (the god Brahmā and others) impart the knowledge of Viṣṇu[464] to the extent of their capacity.

24. Once upon a time, (king Parīkṣit) with his bow strung, went a-hunting to the jungle and (while) pursuing a deer, became exhausted and was extremely hungry and thirsty.

25. Not seeing any source of water, he entered that (famous) hermitage (of Aṅgiras) and saw a sage seated in tranquillity, with his eyes closed.

26-27. Parīkṣit whose palate was completely dried up, asked water from the sage who had thus controlled his sense-or-

---

460. Or Persons who are steadfast and attached to the lord having given up rooted attachment fixed on (their) body and other (objects), reach Brahman called (Kṛṣṇa) attainable by the highest ascetic order called *Paramahaṁsa* wherein non-violence and tranquillity are the chief characteristics.—VJ.

461. VJ. reads *uparama* and interprets 'Attachment to Viṣṇu' (*upa* Viṣṇuḥ *sarvādhikas tasmin Harau ramo ramaṇaṁ ratir* viṣaya-nivṛtir vā/VJ).

462. *aryamaṇaḥ*—(i) That which dispels (*minoti*) the darkness (*aryam*) i.e. the sun.

(ii) That by which pure religion (*aryaṁ*-śuddha-dharmam) is comprehended (*mīyate*) i.e. the Vedas—VD. etc.

463. *patatriṇaḥ*—Also: Just as arrows cross the sky to the extent of their latent force (and can never cover the unending sky).

464. *Viṣṇugati*—(i) The deeds or pastimes of Viṣṇu—ŚR., VC., SD., VB.

(ii) The greatness of Lord Viṣṇu—VR.

gans, life-breath, mind and intellect (completely) and (had his heart) detached (from external objects), who had attained (the fourth stage) beyond the three stages (of wakefulness, dream and sleep) and was merged in Brahman[465], in perfect serenity[466]. (He was) covered with the dishevelled locks of his matted hair and had put on the hide of a Ruru-deer.

28. Being unoffered (a mat of) grass or even (a place on) the ground (to sit on) and not getting (usual) respectful offerings and courteous words, he (Parīkṣit) felt himself disregarded and grew angry.

29. Oh Brāhmaṇa (Śaunaka), there arose suddenly in the mind of the king who was distressed by hunger and thirst, an unprecedented hostility and wrath against that Brāhmana sage.

30. While coming out (of the hermitage) in anger, he placed round the neck of the Brāhmaṇa sage a dead serpent with the fore-end of his bow and repaired to his capital.

31. (The king wanted to ascertain) whether he (the sage) had controlled all his sense organs and (consequently closed his eyes (in real meditation) or whether he had pretended meditation (thinking) that he had nothing to do with vile Kṣatriyas.

32. Having heard that his father was subjected to ill-treatment, his (the sage's) son (by name Śṛṅgī) who was young (but) very brilliant and was playing with children, spoke there as follows.

33. Ah what unrighteousness it is on the part of rulers grown fat like crows (lit. eaters of offerings).[467] For this mis-

---

465. *Brahma-bhūtam*—Contemplating about Brahman—*Brahma-viṣayaka-bhāvanayā 'nvitam*/VR.
(ii) Realising the presence of Brahman without any effort—VJ.
(iii) Becoming one with Brahman through its realization—VB., GD.

466. *avikriyam*—(i) Devoid of perturbation due to pairs of contradictory feelings such as pleasure-pain.—VR., VB.
(ii) motionless like a lamp in a windless place or without an activity prejudicial to the deep meditation—VJ.

467. Or How these servants misbehave towards their masters, these dogs that feed upon the offerings and (should) watch the gate.

demeanour perpetrated by door-keeping slaves, is like an evil act by dogs guarding the door ?

34. For the mean Kṣatriyas have been assigned the duty of door-keepers by Brāhmaṇas. How can a door-keeper be fit to partake (food etc.) in the same vessel in that house. ?

35. When Lord Kṛṣṇa, the controller of those who go astray, has departed, I shall today punish the transgressors (of the path of righteousness). Behold my power.

36. Having spoken thus to his companions, the son of that sage with his eye red with anger, sipped (as *ācamana*) the water of the Kauśikī[468] river, and discharged his thunderbolt-like word, i.e. curse.

37. "Takṣaka, urged by me, shall on the seventh day (from today) bite this transgressor of limits (of religion), the fire-brand (destroyer) of his (own) family, who has troubled my father."

38. Then, having approached his hermitage and seeing his father with the dead body of the serpent around his neck, the boy was overwhelmed with grief and wept aloud.

39. Oh Brāhmaṇa, the decsendant of the family of Aṅgiras (viz. Śamika), having heard the loud lament of his son, and having slowly opened his eyes, saw the dead serpent on his shoulders.

40. After throwing away (the dead serpent), he asked his son, "Oh child, why are you crying ? Who has done you any harm ?" When so enquired, the son reported (the details).

41. Having heard that the king was cursed undeservedly, the Brāhmaṇa did not give compliment to his son, (He said) "Alas ! Oh ignorant child ! What a great sin you have committed in inflicting heavy punishment for a minor fault.

42. Oh (child of) immature intellect, you should not equate (judge) the King (lit. God amongst men), known as

468. Modern Kosi; rises in the eastern ranges of the Himālayas in Nepal. Its confluence with the Ganges is at Manhari, Purnea district, Bihar. It was visited by Balarāma. Jamadagni's mother Satyavatī became converted into this river; sacred to Manes (*Pitṛs*)—PSK 637-39, PI.1.475.

It is surprising how a king of Hastinapura strayed a-hunting to such a long distance. Moreover, this contradicts verse 25 above which speaks of non-existence of water nearby. VJ. is probably correct when he explains, "holding Kuśa grass in his hand and performing *Ācamana*".

Para (Viṣṇu) with ordinary men, as the subjects, being protected by his irresistible power, obtain (their) good without fear from any quarter.

43. Oh (child), with the disappearance of god Viṣṇu (the wielder of the discus) designated as king (god amongst men), the world, instantaneously being protectionless and infested with thieves, will be ruined like a flock of sheep.[469]

44. Today the sin committed by robbers of wealth (of people who are) protectorless will be visited upon us (though we are) not concerned[470] with it, for men, most of whom are robbers, kill and curse each other and rob one another of cattles, women and money.

45. Then (in the absence of the ruler), the noble and righteous[471] path of life which consists of the code of conduct for different classes of society and stages of life, prescribed by the three Vedas[472], disappears and there takes place promiscuous mixture of all classes of people as their minds are fixed on (acquisition of) wealth and gratification of the senses as amongst the dogs and the monkeys.

46. But that lord of men who was protector of righteousness, an emperor of great renown, manifestly a great votary of the Supreme Lord, a sage amongst Kings (and) a performer of the horse-sacrifice, being overwhelmed with hunger, thirst and exhaustion was helpless. Certainly, he did not in the least deserve our curse.

47. May the Supreme Lord who resides in all[473], please

---

469. *avivarūthavat*—Like an army without a leader.

470. *ananvayam*—(i) That which will annihilate our progeny completely—VR., VJ.

(ii) Unnecessarily; without any reason—VB.

VB. explains : 'Although we have not directly committed robbery etc., the sin has taken place due to our act (of cursing the king to death and rendering the world protectionless). Hence our responsibility for the sin.'

471. *ārya-dharmaḥ*—Religious duties as expounded by noble ones like Manu and other law-givers—SD.

472. *trayī-mayaḥ*—That which has come down from the three Vedas (viz. *Ṛg*, *Sāman* and *Yajus*)—VR., GD.

473. Both the curser and the cursed—VR.

pardon this boy of immature intellect for the sin committed by him against His sinless servant (devotee).

48. His devotees, even though powerful, do not retaliate even if (they are) reproached, cheated, cursed, insulted or struck."

49. The great sage, though himself maltreated by the king, did not regard it as (the king's) fault at all, but was distressed by the offence committed by his son (in cursing the king).

50. In this world, generally, good persons are subjected to the pairs such as pleasure and pain but they are neither distressed nor delighted as the Soul is not affected by the attributes[474] such as happiness, misery etc.

CHAPTER NINETEEN

(Arrival of Śuka)

1. Thereupon, the Lord of the Earth, pondering over the iniquitous act committed by himself was deeply distressed in mind (and said to himself): 'Alas ! what a heinous offence has been perpetrated by me like a vile person, against an innocent Brāhmaṇa of hidden power.

2. Therefore it is certain that due to the insult of god (-like sage), an unsurmountable calamity is going to befall me in near future. Let that (misfortune) come in full force directly on me (and not on my sons etc.) for the expiation of sin so that I may never commit such act again.

3. Let the fire of the Brāhmaṇa race incensed (by my provocative act) consume[475] even today the kingdom, army and

---

474. *aguṇāśrayaḥ*—(i) Their mind is rooted in virtue —VR.
(ii) Their mind does not harbour the pairs such as love, hatred, which are the effects of *guṇas* (attributes)—VB.
(iii) *Jīva* (the individual Soul) is the abode of vices and virtues or merits and demerits.—VG

475. JG. gives a better interpretation : "Even today, the kingdom etc. go away from me like a thing burnt" (*Rājyādikam adyaiva me mattaḥ sakāśād dagdha-vad apayātvityarthaḥ|*) i.e. I may be bereft of kingdom etc. and not that the kingdom should be reduced to ashes. Otherwise Brāhmaṇas who are residing in the kingdom may get burnt.

rich treasury belonging to me—a wicked fellow[476], so that my intellect may not entertain an evil disposition to Brāhmaṇas, gods and cows.

4. While he was thinking thus, he heard of (the cause of his) death named (i.e. which was to meet him in the shape of) Takṣaka impelled by (the curse of) the sage's son. He regarded the fire (of the poison) of Takṣaka as a blessing, as it was the immediate cause of renunciation on the part of a person attached (to worldly objects).

5. Then having renounced this world and the next (the world of gods) which he had already decided as worth rejecting, he who thought the service of the feet of Kṛṣṇa as higher than all objectives in life, sat on the bank of the Ganges (the river of the immortals) with a vow to abstain from food till death.

6. What man about to die will not resort to the river (Ganges) which carries the waters highly sanctified by the dust of Kṛṣṇa's feet mingled with the pollen of the *Tulasī*[477] of refulgent beauty and which purifies here and hereafter the worlds along with the protectors of the quarters of the world including Īśa.

7. In this way, having decided to sit on the bank of the Ganges, abstaining from food (till death), the descendant of Pāṇḍu (i.e. Parīkṣit) with single-minded devotion to the feet of Lord Kṛṣṇa took the vows of sage's way of life and freed himself from all attachments.

8. There arrived the great sages along with their disciples purifying the world. Verily, under the guise of going on a pilgrimage, the saints themselves purify the holy places.

9. Afterwards (then came) Atri, Vasiṣṭha, Cyavana, Śaradvana, Ariṣṭanemi, Bhṛgu, Aṅgirasas, Parāśara, the son of Gādhi, (i.e. Viśvāmitra), Paraśurāma, Utathya, Indra-Pramada and Idhma-vāha.

---

476. *abhadrasya*—(i) of one devoid of light or
(ii) ignorant.
(iii) sleepy—VJ.

477. Tulasi—the holy basil held sacred by Vaiṣṇavites. VJ. derives it as follows:
(i) That which is comparable to knowledge about Brahman.
(ii) That which decorates Viṣṇu.

10. Medhātithi, Devala, Ārṣṭiṣeṇa, Bhāradvāja, Gautama, Pippalāda, Maitreya, Aurva, Kavaṣa, Agastya (the sage born in water jar), Dvaipāyana and the glorious Nārada.*

11. Also others (such as) prominent divine sages and Brāhmaṇa sages, eminent royal-sages and others like Aruṇa (who initiated rites and formed a distinct class by themselves).

Having worshipped the sages belonging to various patronymic groups who assembled there, the king made obeisance to them by bending his head.

12. When they were comfortably seated, the king, with his pure heart, having saluted them again with his hands folded, stood before them and explained to them what he intended to do (with a desire to elicit their opinion regarding the desirability of such a course).

King said:

13. Ah ! We whose behaviour is worthy of the favour of the greatest ones (like you)[478] are the blessed-most among the kings. Alas! the race of kings whose job (acts necessary) while governing, (e.g. inflicting punishment etc.) is blameworthy, is relegated to a position beyond a place where the water used for washing the feet of Brāhmaṇas goes.[479]

14.** The Supreme Lord has assumed the form of the Brāhmaṇa's curse (which became) the root-cause of complete

---

*VB classifies : (i) Rāma to Pippalāda—propagators of religion.
(ii) Maitreya to Nārada—propagators of the path of devotion.

478. *anugrahaṇīya-śīlāḥ*—Also VR. : whose good character or behaviour is due to the grace of the greatest.

(ii) We, of Pāṇḍu's race, being like Svāyambhuva Manu and others who strive to attain grace from you who are the best of great persons—JG.

479. How regrettable is the lot of the race of kings who, due to the censurable nature of their actions, are deprived of the (holy) water with which feet of Brāhmaṇas are washed—VJ.

**Other interpretations :

(i) May this (punishment in the form of) Brāhmaṇa's curse (adversely) affecting my worldly life be the effective (lit. sufficient) cause of renunciation (of worldly objects) in my case whose mind is devoutly attached to the Supreme Lord. For a person attached to worldly objects (like houses etc.) has the danger of worldly existence while he who is attached to god attains fearlessness or liberation—VJ.

indifference (to worldly objects) in the case of a sinner like me whose mind was firmly attached to houses (wealth etc.); for persons, deeply attached (to worldly affairs) immediately got terrified when so cursed.

15. May (all) Brāhmaṇas and the Gaṅgā know[480] me as the seeker of refuge with the Lord and as one whose mind is fixed on him. Let the cunning Takṣaka deputed by the Brāhmaṇa bite me to his satisfaction. Please sing the songs of Viṣṇu.[481]

16. In whatever birth (form of existence) I may be born again, may I be attached to the Eternal Lord and be associated with those great persons who resort to him for shelter. Let my friendship[482] be with all (like you). I bow to Brāhmaṇas.*

17. The brave king, who had thus made up his mind and placed the responsibility of governing the kingdom on his son, sat on the southern bank of the Gaṅgā[483] on a seat of Kuśa grass the ends of which were towards the eastern direction, himself facing the north.

18. When the king of kings took his seat with the determination of fasting unto death, assemblies of gods in heaven,

---

(ii) In my case who am born in the family favoured by the Lord but am deeply attached to worldly objects (e.g. houses, wealth) and who have committed a sin (by insulting that Brāhmana Śamika), the Supreme Lord, taking into account my birth in the family blessed with his grace, has assumed the form of the Brāhmaṇa's curse, the cause of non-attachment, but by attachment to whom one immediately become free from fear (by attaining his lotus-like feet)—JG.

480. *Pratiyantu*—accept me. May the heavenly river Gaṅgā accept (receive) me as a person whose mind is fixed on God—JG.

481. (i) Extol to me the deeds of Viṣṇu or sing of his glories.—VR.
(ii) (Setting to musical tunes) sing of the songs of Viṣṇu till my death.—VJ.

482. *maitrī*—Let my outlook be of equality.—JG.

*This verse expresses the following last 4 desires of Parīkṣit:
(i) Devotion to the Lord in every birth.
(ii) Close association with the devotee of the Lord.
(iii) Friendship to all beings.
(iv) Respect to Brāhmaṇas.

483. VJ. states that Parīkṣit sat in a mansion on the bank of the Ganges as mentioned in the Mbh. (Obviously he refers to the Mbh. I.42. 29-32).

praising him, showered flowers on the earth with joy and kettle-drums were sounded again and again.

19. Having praised and approved (of the king's vow of fast-unto-death) as 'well done', the great sages who assembled there and who had the nature and ability to bestow favours on subjects spoke to him what was beautiful due to the attributes of Hari[484].

20. Oh the best of royal sages, amongst you (kings of Pāṇḍu's race) who are the followers of Kṛṣṇa, it is no wonder that when you desire to attain vicinity to the Supreme Lord, you instantaneously vacate the imperial throne served by tributary princes wearing crowns.

21. We shall all stay on here now till this foremost devotee of the Supreme Lord,[485] casting off this (mortal) body, goes to the highest world[486] free from illusion[487] and affliction (grief).

22. Hearing the speech of the congregation of sages which was true, impartial, dripping with nectar, pregnant with meaning, Parīkṣit, complimenting the sages of composed mind, addressed them with a desire to hear the deeds of Viṣṇu.

23. Just as the Vedas appear in bodily forms (in the Satyaloka) above these three worlds, all of you have assembled here from all quarters. Being by nature disposed to do good to others, you have no other objective in this or the next world.

24. Oh Brāhmaṇas, with full faith in you, I specifically enquire about this worth-considering problem as to what one should do in all (types of) circumstances. Oh learned ones, carefully consider (and advise me) what (course of) action is sinless (and hence recommended) for persons about to die.

---

484. VR. takes *uttama...rūpam* as qualifying the king and interprets; "The great sages...praised the king charming on account of his qualities worth-praising by the great", while VJ. connects it with the sages' speech : 'which was agreeable (conducive) to the description of the glories of Hari.'

485. *bhāgavata-pradhānaḥ*—who feels that votaries should always be served—VR.

486. Will go to Hari who is beyond the three attributes (*guṇas*), perfect and eternally devoid of misery—VJ.

487. *virajaska*—Full of pure *Sattva*-attribute—VR.

25. By lucky chance, there came wandering over the earth venerable (Śuka), the son of Vyāsa, (who was) devoid of all desires, and (who) did not bear any external mark (indicating his caste or stage of life) and was satisfied with the realisation of the self, appearing like one discarded by the society and surrounded by children (and women).

26-28. Those sages recognised him (Śuka) by his special marks though his powers were latent, and rose from their seats to receive him. He appeared sixteen years of age with tender feet, hands, thighs, arms, shoulders, cheeks and body; his face (appeared attractive) with wide beautiful eyes, prominent nose, symmetrical ears and beautiful eye-brows; his neck (was) shapely like a conch, collar-bones covered (with flesh); his chest was broad and elevated; his navel was like an eddy and belly beautified by folds; his clothing (were) the (four) quarters of the world (i.e. he was nude); his curly hair were dishevelled and arms were long upto the knee; he was beautiful like Hari (the best of immortals); he was of dark complexion and captivating to women by the splendour of the permanent youthfulness of his person and enchanting smile.

29. Then Viṣṇurāta (king Parīkṣit) also bowing down his head offered worship to the guest (Śuka) who had just arrived. Ignorant people, women and children then retired. Thus worshipped he (Śuka) occupied a high seat (offered to him).

30.* Surrounded by multitudes of Brāhmaṇa sages, royal sages and divine sages, the venerable (Śuka), the greatest among the great, appeared there extremely brilliant like the glorious moon in the midst of planets, constellations and stars.

31. Approaching that (comfortably) seated sage of serene mind and keen intellect, the devout, attentive king, with folded hands and head bowed down, paid respects (to him) and asked him in sweet words.

Parīkṣit said:

32. Oh Brahman! What a luck that we mean Kṣatriyas

---

*According to VJ. this verse describes Parīkṣit and not Śuka.

have become today worthy of being served by the good[488], as we are sanctified[489] by venerable persons (like you) by being our guest, out of grace.

33. By remembering whom (holy persons like you) houses of people get immediately purified. What then (of the effect) of seeing you, touching (your feet) and (rendering service to you by acts) like washing your feet and offering you a seat, etc.

34. Oh great Yogin! Verily even the vilest sins of people are instantly annihilated in your presence as the enemies of gods are smashed in Viṣṇu's presence.

35. Most probably Lord Kṛṣṇa to whom Pāṇḍavas were dear and who for the happiness of the sons of his paternal aunt (i.e. Pāṇḍavas) is disposed to be friendly to their family-descendants, is gracious to me.

36. Otherwise how is it possible for us—men especially those who are about to die, to obtain ample sight of yours whose movements are unmanifest to worldly persons and who have attained final beatitude and are the most solicitous (to bestow your favour)[490].

37. Hence I ask of you who are an eminent preceptor of *Yogins*, what a man about to die, definitely should do (which will lead to) Final Beatitude.

38. Oh Lord, kindly tell me what should be heard, muttered, done, contemplated and adored by (such a person like) me and what should be avoided.

---

488. *sat-sevya*—(i) Deserving to serve saintly persons—VR.
(ii) Worthy of being favoured by good men—VR.
(iii) Whose duty is to serve the great souls—VC.

489. *tīrthakāḥ kṛtāḥ*—(i) made worthy—ŚR.
(ii) Transformed into a highly sacred place—VJ.
(iii) When saints visit even a bad place, it becomes a holy place; similarly though we are vile (due to sins committed by us), we become sanctified by visits of saintly guests like you—VC.

490. *vanīyasaḥ*—(i) On account of his magnanimity of heart, Śuka expected Parīkṣit to ask him for something—ŚR.
(ii) Spending most of his life in forests in comparison with other sages—VR.

39. Oh Brahman, (you are unavailable) as the stay of your glorious self at (the doors of) the homes of house-holders is hardly for (such a short period as is required for) milking a cow.

Sūta said:

40. Thus addressed and requested in gentle (persuasive) words by the king, the glorious son of Bādarāyaṇa who comprehended religion, spoke to Parīkṣit in reply.

SECOND SKANDHA

CHAPTER ONE

(The Discourse of Śuka—Description of the Cosmic Form of the Lord)

Śrī Śuka said :

1. Oh king! Out of the topics which deserve to be (carefully) heard (studied etc.) by people, the excellent[491] question posed by you, is very important[492] as it is conducive to the good (final beatitude) of the people, and is acceptable to those who have realized the Soul[493].

2. Oh best of kings, there are thousands of topics[494] which deserve to be heard (studied etc.) by persons who have not visualized the soul, and who are attached to the householder's life (involving five types of sins[495] related to that life).

3. Oh king! life is taken away at night by sleep, in sexual enjoyment, (and evil desires); and by day, for earning money or for maintaining one's family.

---

491. *para*—(i) Within the range of senses (of hearing etc.)—VR.
(ii) The Supreme Soul—VJ.
(iii) Pertaining to Śrī-Kṛṣṇa *or* by hearing which the highest goal in life is achieved—JG.

492. *varīyān*—(i) Worth undertaking (discussion)—VJ.
(ii) Very great as compared with topics related to other incarnations—JG.

493. *ātmavit-sammataḥ*—(i) approved of mainly by self-knowers like god Brahmā and others—VJ.
(ii) Not that you (Parīkṣit) have not realized the soul, but you, who have known the soul, have asked this question for the benefit of the world—SD.

494. VR. states : Persons in worldly life wish to hear thousands of topics, but a man desirous of liberation wishes to listen to (and concentrate) on the Brahman only.

495. In a householder's life, there are generally five articles in the house, whereby living beings are hurt or destroyed. SD. enumerates them as follows : a fire place, a grind-stone (for milling food-grains), a broom, a mortar and a water pot. These prevent a householder from going to heaven. Also vide ASD p. 560. SD. quotes the following verse :

Kaṇḍanī, peṣaṇī, cullī, udakumbhī ca mārjanī /
Pañca-sūnā gṛhasthasya tābhiḥ svargaṁ na gacchati //

4. Being attached to his body, children, wife and other attendants, dependents etc., even though they are unreal, he does not discern their destruction, though he actually sees them die.

5. Oh descendant of Bharata! Therefore, the glorious Hari (reliever of bondage, of *saṁsāra*) the Supreme Lord, the all-pervading soul, should be heard about, eulogised and remembered by a person desiring a state, completely free from fear (i.e. the Final Beatitude or *mokṣa*).

6. *Nārāyaṇa* is remembered at the end of life (time of death), is the highest achievement of human life. This (may be) due to *Sāṅ-khya*[496]-Yoga[497], and through knowledge and performance of one's duties.

7. Oh king! It is well-known (*sma*[498]) that generally, sages[499] who have turned away (abstained) from abiding by religious injunctions and prohibitions[500], and are established (absorbed) in the attributeless (*nirguṇa*) Brahman[501] take delight in discoursing upon the qualities of Hari.

---

496. *Sāṅkhya*—(i) Accurate comprehension of the Soul and the non-Soul—ŚR.
(ii) The path of knowledge (*Jñāna yoga*)—VR.
(iii) Metaphysics etc. of Sāṅkhyas—VJ.

497. *Yoga* (i) The eight-fold path of *Yoga* and *practice*—ŚR.
(ii) The path of action (*Karma-yoga*) without any desire for the fruit of action—VR.
(iii) Worship of the Lord etc. as prescribed in the *Yoga-Śāstra* (authoritative scriptures on *Yoga*)—VJ.

498. According to GD.

499. *Munayaḥ*—Those who are completely devoted to the meditation of Hari—SD.

500. *nivṛtta-vidhi-ṣedhataḥ*—(i) Not observing Vedic injunctions and prohibitions (to perform rites, with a desire to obtain some particular object or fruit, and to abstain from some actions)—VR.
(ii) Free from contamination of the merit or sin arising from the Vedic prescriptions—GD.

501. *nairguṇyasthāḥ*—(i) Who meditate upon Brahman of pure *sattva* attribute, unalloyed by *rajas* and *tamas*—VR.
(ii) Liberated (*muktāḥ*) as *nairguṇya*=the Liberation granted by the Supreme attributeless Lord (Hari)—JG.
(iii) Established in their own soul who is above the three attributes—VB.

8. At the end[502] of the Dvāpara Age, I learnt this Purāṇa called the *Bhāgavata* ('narrated by the Supreme Lord') which is comparable to the Vedas (or, which succinctly describes the Brahman), from my father Vyāsa.

9. Oh king-sage! Though I was firmly established in (the meditation of) the attributeless (*nirguṇa*) Brahman, I studied this (legendary) work, as my mind was fascinated with the sports of the Supreme Lord.

10. I shall narrate that (Purāṇa) to you, as you are a great devotee of the glorious god Viṣṇu. By entertaining faith in this (scripture), pure motiveless devotion to Mukunda is immediately created (in the faithful listeners).

11. Oh King! This chanting of the name of Hari (and meditating upon him etc.) has been prescribed as the sure means of attaining liberation for those deserving emancipation[503], and wishing freedom from the fear (of the cycle of rebirths), and for yogins[504].

12. What is the use of a number of years to a careless man, if they are wasted in ignorance? In this world, it is better to have a short duration of life, (*muhūrta* or a period of 48 minutes), if one utilizes it for trying for final beatitude.

13. Having known the balance of life-period due to him in this world, the famous king-sage Khaṭvāṅga[505] renounced everything in a short time (*muhūrta*), and resorted to Hari, the liberator from the fear (of the cycle of rebirths).

14. While in your case, Oh descendant of the Kuru family, the duration of life is seven days (from now). Utilise all that time for what will help the attainment of the next

---

502. In the transitional period of which Dvāpara was the beginning, i.e. the end of Dvāpara. Vyāsa was a contemporary of Śantanu—ŚR.

503. *nirvidyamānānām*—disgusted with the worldly miseries —VR. & VJ.

504. *Yoginām*—Persons who follow the path of action—*Karmayoga* without any attachment for the accruing fruit—VR.

505. *Khaṭvāṅga* a son of Viśvasaha and a *Cakravartin*. Fought for Devas and defeated the demons in battle. Knowing that he had only a *muhūrta* to live, he returned to the earth, renounced everything, and devoted himself to Nārāyaṇa in a detached spirit, and attained Liberation—PI. 1. 495. vide Infra IX. 9. 41-49.

world.[506]

15. At the end of life, a man, becoming devoid of the fear of death, should sever, with the weapon of disassociation, his attachment for pleasure, for his body, and for whatever (e.g. wife and children) is connected with it.

16. Having renounced (his) home, (such) a person of firm resolve,[507] bathed in holy waters at a sacred place,[508] (should) sit on a seat, prepared as per *Śāstric* rules,[509] in a pure secluded place.

17.* He should repeat, in his mind, the great, sacred—syllable consisting of the three letters—a, u, m—symbolizing the Brahman; without forgetting the 'seed' of the Brahman (viz. the syllable OM), he should control his breath and subdue his mind.

18. He, whose intelligence has been his guide (lit. charioteer), should restrain his sense-organ from (being attracted to) objects of enjoyment. If his mind is distracted with actions, he should fix it on the auspicious object (viz. the Lord Kṛṣṇa).

19. With undivided mind, he should meditate upon only one limb (such as feet or face of the Lord Hari). Having restrained the mind, free from external objects, he should not think of anything else. That is the highest abode of Viṣṇu (reaching which) the mind becomes pacified.

20. By fixation of attention, the wise (and courageous) man should bring under control his mind, which is distracted by

---

506. *sāmparāyika*—Pertaining to the future, i.e. the time for liberation (*mukti-kāla*). Or listen to the *Bhāgavata* which will enable you to remember (muse over) Hari's feet—VJ.

507. This indicates the Ist 'aid' (*aṅga*), viz. *Yama* or 'abstinence' in Yoga. It includes 'abstinence from injury, and from falsehood, and from theft and from incontinence and from acceptance of gifts'. YSP (*The Yoga System of Patañjali*—J.H. Woods HOS 1966), p. 178-80.

508. This stands for the 2nd 'aid' viz. *niyama* or 'observances' in Yoga. They are : cleanliness, contentment, self-castigation, study and devotion to Īśvara or God. YSP—ii. 32, pp. 181-83.

509. This is the 3rd 'aid' viz. *āsana*. See YSP ii-46, pp. 191-92 for details.

*Verses 17-20 explain the remaining 'aids' (*aṅgas*) of Yoga viz. breath-control (*prāṇāyāma*), withdrawal of the senses (*pratyāhāra*), contemplation (*dhāraṇā*) and concentration (*samādhi*) Vide YSP, pp. 195-200.

rajas and confused by *tamas*, and destroy the sin (impurity) created by them.

21. While it (*dhāraṇā*) is being practised, contemplating on (lit. visualizing) the auspicious refuge (of the world i.e. Lord Viṣṇu), *Yoga* characterised by devotion (*bhakti*) is quickly developed in such a *yogin.*

The King said:

22. Oh Brahman! How is the *dhāraṇā* practised? In what way is it approved? What type of dhāraṇā will quickly remove the impurities of man's mind?

Śrī Śuka said:

23. One who has mastered steadiness of seat, and acquired control over one's breath, and mind and senses, should, with determined intellect, fix one's mind on the Virāṭ (gross or great) Form of the Supreme Lord.

24. This special body of the Lord is the biggest among the big. In this (body) is seen the past, present and future universe of gross effects.

25. That Supreme Lord, who is the cosmic Man (*Vairājaḥ Puruṣaḥ*) in this body of the universe, which is like an egg, and is covered with seven sheaths,[510] is the object of contemplation (*dhāraṇā*).

26.* They describe that *pātāla* is verily the sole of his feet, *rasātala* is His heels and the toes *mahātala* forms the ankles of the Creator of the Universe, while *talātala* are the shanks (part of the leg from the ankle to the knee) of this Cosmic Man.

27. *Sutala* is (regarded as) the two knees, and *vitala* and *atala* are the two thighs of this Cosmic Man. Oh King, they

---

510. ŚR. and other Comm. state that the 'sheaths' are those of the five elements, viz. the earth, water, fire, air and the sky and of *ahaṁkāra* (the ego) and *mahat*, the first evolute of *Prakṛti* according to the Sāṁkhyas.

* Verses 26 to 37 describe the details of the Cosmic Man who is to be contemplated. VR. explains that these are to be meditated as that particular part of his body, e.g. *Pātāla* is to be contemplated as the sole of his feet etc. but VJ. specifically points out that *Pātāla* etc. are *Not* identical with the actual parts of his body which is characterised by bliss, energy etc. *Pātāla* etc. are the parts of the universe which are created from and are supported by his limbs.

(authoritatively) state that the Earth (lit. the surface of the earth forms his hips, and the (vault of the) sky his lake-like (deep) navel.

28. They considered that of this Primeval Man, the host of stars form his (broad) chest, the *maharloka*, his neck; the *jana-loka*, his mouth; the *tapo-loka*, his forehead; and the satya-loka, the heads of this Man of a thousand heads.

29. They described Indra and other gods of shining bodies as his arms; the cardinal points as his ears; the sound as his auditory sense; (the two aśvini-kumāras) Nāsatya and Dasra, as the nostrils of the Supreme Lord; fragrance is his sense of smelling and the burning fire, his mouth.

30. The sky forms his eyes, (and) the Sun, the sense of seeing, and the day and night are eyelids of the All-pervading God (viz. Viṣṇu). His eyelashes are the Brahma-loka; water is his palate, (while) taste is his tongue.

31. They describe the Vedas[511] as the head (i.e. the *brahmarandhra*— the aperture in the skull for the passage of the Soul) of the Infinite Lord; Yama (the god of death) as his large teeth[512] (tusks); Traces of feelings of affection (?) as his teeth; Cosmic Illusion (*Māyā*) which maddens the people is his laugh; and the unending creation of the world, his side-glance.

32. Modesty (bashfulness) is his upper lip, (while) greed is his lower lip. The path of righteousness is his chest, while the unrighteous path is his back. Prajāpati (the god of creation) is his penis, while Mitra and Varuṇa are his scrotum (the testicles). The oceans are his belly, and the mountains are his bone-system.

33. Oh king of kings! the rivers are his arteries; the trees are the hair of the God whose body is the Universe; the wind of infinite force, is his breath; Time is his movement (act of moving); the stream of the three attributes (*sattva*, *rajas* and *tamas*) i.e. the worldly existence of beings is his action.

34. Oh Chief (excellent) of the Kuru family, (the wise ones) know that the hair of the Supreme Ruler are the clouds;

---

511. *Chandāṁsi*—Vedic meters like Gāyatrī and others—VJ.

512. The Sun and the Moon are his two tusks (while) stars are his teeth—VJ.

the twilight is the garment of the all-pervading Supreme Lord. They say that the unmanifest (*avyakta*) i.e. the *Pradhāna* ('primordial nature' of the Sāṁkhyas) is his heart, and the moon is his mind, which is the store of all changes (and passions).

35. It is traditionally known that the *mahat* (the Sāṁkhya principle of intelligence) is his intellectual power, and that Śiva is the internal organ (made up of *manas*, *citta*, *ahaṁkāra* and *buddhi*) of the Lord who dwells in the hearts of all; the horses, mules, donkeys and elephants are his nails; all beasts and deer are at his hips.

36. The various kinds of birds[513] are the wonderful expressions (of his skill in arts); (*Svāyambhuva*) Manu is his power of comprehension (understanding); the human race is his dwelling place; Gandharvas, Vidyādharas, Cāraṇas and Apsaras are his *svaras* (musical notes or gamut) and *smṛtis*; and the armies of *asuras* are his strength.[514].

37. The Cosmic Man[515] has the Brāhmaṇa[516] as his mouth, the Kṣatriya as his arms, the Vaiśya as his thighs, the dark-complexioned Śūdra as his feet. He is made up of the substance which is of groups of gods of various names; the performance of sacrifices is his essential work.[517]

38. Such is the extent and configuration (formation) of the body of the Supreme Lord described to you, by me. One

---

513. VJ. reads *vacāṁsi* i.e. Vedic and popular expressions.

514. VR. and SD. read *asurānīka-varyyaḥ*—The Supreme Person among the Asura hosts, i.e. Prahlāda.

515. *mahātmā*=Vairājaḥ (Cosmic Man)—VR., SD.

516. VB. explicitely states that these words do not denote a caste but certain qualities: *Brahma-bhāvaḥ kaściddharmaḥ . . . Brāhmaṇyaṁ na jātiḥ*/ The whole exposition is interesting. Cf RV. (Ṛgveda) 10.90.12, AV. (Atharvaveda) 19.6.6

517. *nānābhidha . . . vitāna-yogaḥ*—

The performance of sacrifice is the act for propitiating him. It is to be done with offerings meant for propitiating groups of gods with various names and are so worshipped—VR.

VJ. interprets differently: The Great Soul has his mouth from which Brāhmaṇa-caste is born . . . He possesses the power to create *svāhā* and *svadhā* which are to be used for gods and manes. His middle part of the body is the Soul creating Havya (things worthy of being sacrificed). He possesses the means to help all sacrifices like *agniṣṭoma*, etc.

should concentrate one's mind on this very huge body of the Cosmic Man, by one's own intellect (intellectual efforts), as there is nothing beyond this (or there is nothing greater).

39. Just as one sees all one's relatives in a dream, he, the Soul, experiences everything directly by his power of intelligence. One should resort (develop oneself) to him who is the real, and a reservoir of bliss. He should not be attached to anything else, otherwise there will be a fall of the Soul.

CHAPTER TWO

(Liberation by the Yogic Path: Instantaneous and Gradual Liberation)

Śrī Śuka said :

1. By the grace of Hari who was pleased with the contemplation (*dhāraṇā*) as described in the previous Chapter, god Brahmā (the self-born)[518] regained his memory[519] which was lost at the time of the deluge[520] (*pralaya*). Determined to create[521] (the world again), he (god Brahmā), with unerring insight, created the world again as (it was) before the deluge.

2*. Such is the path of verbal Brahman (the Vedas) that (as a result of the fruits of *karmas* promised therein) the

---

518. *ātma-yoniḥ*—One born from the Supreme Soul—JG.

519. VR. raises the objection that the occupant of the post of Brahmā is changed after the period of a *Kalpa*. The word 'memory' (*smṛti*) should be interpreted here as 'the knowledge of the procedure of creation (*sarga-viṣayaka-jñānamātra-paraḥ*). VR. endorses this interpretation. VR. explains that god Brahmā, by his penance, could see things in their formative stage and could thus create them again, in this world.

520. *purā* : (i) At the time of the previous deluge — VR.
(ii) At the time of initial creation — VJ.
(iii) After the periodic deluge —VB.

521. *vyavasāya-buddhiḥ*—
(i) Possessing resolute (conclusive) understanding—SR.
(ii) Having the knowledge of the nature of the definite object of memory—VR.

* Other commentators agree in general about the substance of this verse. They, however, interpret some words differently. For example, SD:

mind (wishfully) contemplates over the unmeaningful words (lit. names like heaven—*svarga*—etc.). Like a person who sees (empty) dreams (of pleasure) due to the impressions (left in the sub-conscience or deep mind), he, believing that there is happiness in the path of Māyā (Illusion), wanders (in various *lokas*—heavens etc. without getting real happiness) but does not realize his objectives, viz. unalloyed bliss (of Liberation).

3. [He explains away the doubt or difficulty that the absolute renunciation of the fruits of *karmas* would lead to instantaneous death].

Hence a thoughtful person[521a] should accept that much quantity of objects of enjoyment as is essential for his purpose (of sustaining his life). He should not be attached (even to those objects so accepted) and be convinced (that there is no real happiness in them). When his object is otherwise achieved, he should see (understand) the (wasteful) labour (for attaining them) and should not make attempt for them.

4. When the earth is there, what is the propriety of efforts for bed? There is no necessity of pillows when (one is naturally) equipped with arms. When the hollow of folded hands is available, various kinds of vessels for food are super-

---

"The intellect or mind of the follower of *karma-path* longingly broods over names and forms (viz. wife, children etc.) unconnected with (liberation, the highest) goal of life, wanders in this ordinary world of Māyā and gets his objects in life (pleasures of the world according to his *karmas*) but not the *yogic* attainment (Liberation)."

The substance of VJ.'s explanation is as follows :

The main subject of voluminously worded Veda is (the description etc.) of Hari. The individual Soul who, due to the result of his acts (*karmas*), wanders through this transmigration of births and deaths (in this *saṁsāra* which is the creation of God's will), contemplates in mind on unmeaningful words like Indra. These names are meaningless as they do not have the unlimited power etc. connoted by them. Hence one does not get the objects coveted in life by adoring them. Due to the study etc. (of the *karma-kāṇḍa* in the Vedas) the mind is filled with empty names like heaven (*svarga*) etc. But such a person is attached to the world which is created by Māyā and does not achieve the real *Puruṣārtha*, i.e. *mokṣa* or liberation.

521a. *Kaviḥ* (i) Omniscient—VJ.

(ii) One who judges what is to be accepted or rejected —SD., GD.

fluous. The silken cloths are unnecessary when the directions (cardinal points), bark-garments etc. are there.

5. Are there no tattered cloths(lying) on the way ? Do not trees which support others (with their fruits etc.) give alms ? Are the rivers dried up (devoid of water) ? Are caves (in mountains) closed ? Does not the unconquered Lord (Hari) protect those who seek his refuge ? Why should the wise serve persons blinded with the pride of their wealth ?

6. In this way, having fully realized the truth, and become full of bliss, one should meditate on the Soul (*ātman*) who is automatically existent in the heart, and who (being one's own) is lovable and real and who is the eternal (deathless) glorious Lord. Herein lies the end of nescience which is the cause of the transmigration of the Soul (*saṁsāra*) and (leads to blissful liberation.)

7. When one sees people fallen in the river Vaitaraṇī[522] (of *saṁsāra*—worldly existence) and undergoing different types of sufferings as consequences of their past deeds, who else but the beast (the most dullard person) will neglect concentration on the Supreme Soul and indulge in evil concentration of worldly objects.

8. After concentration, some meditate upon the (Supreme) Man, spanful in height, dwelling in the inner space of the heart in the interior of their own body, and who has four arms holding (in each) a lotus, a disc, a conch and a mace.

9. As long as the mind remains steady in concentration, one should gaze fixedly on this Supreme Lord who manifests himself in meditation.

---

* VJ.'s interpretation :

When (by means of the previously described Path) the mind becomes controlled and quiet by the grace of Hari, the self-dependent Lord, one (the devotee) should realize that the Supreme Soul is far more lovable than one's own body, kinsmen and other things and should resort to him so intensely that one's hair would stand on their ends. This leads not only to the end of Nescience, the cause of Saṁsāra but also to the blissful stage of mokṣa (liberation).

522. *Vaitaraṇī* : The river of hell which must be crossed before entering the infernal regions. It is supposed to be full of blood and all kinds of filth and to run with great impetuosity —DHM 332.

9. The Lord of gracious looks[523], whose eyes are large like a lotus, whose garments are tawnish like the filaments of the *kadamba* flowers, who wears gold bracelets shining with precious jewels and whose diadem and ear-rings are set with radiant precious stones.

10. The Lord whose sprout-like (tender) feet are installed by great *yogins* in the receptacle, at the centre of the full-blown lotus in the form of their heart[524], who bears the special mark of the Goddess of Wealth (called *Śrīvatsa,* on his left breast) and who wears the jewel called *Kaustubha* in his neck and who is beautified by garland of forest flowers (*vanamālā*) of unfading charm.

11. (The Lord) who is adorned with very costly anklets, bracelets, girdle, rings and such other ornaments (studded with precious jewels and whose countenance is lovely on account of glossy, clean bluish ringlets of hair, is beaming with captivating smile.

12. (The Lord) who suggests his unlimited grace (to his devotees) by the free, sportive smile, and by the movement of his eyebrows in casting glances askance.*

13. Step by step one should concentrate by his decisive intellect, the parts of the body of Lord Kṛṣṇa (lit. the wielder of the mace), from his feet to his smiling countenance. As one's intellect gets purified, he should proceed from the part of his body realized in meditation (lit. conquered), and concentrate on the part of His body above it, the previous part.

14. So long as intense devotion (characterised by love for the Lord) is not generated in the Lord of the Universe, to whom gods are inferior, one should devoutly concentrate on the huge form of the han, after the completion of his daily religious routine.

15. Oh beloved king, when the recluse (i.e. the follower of the Path of Bhakti) desires to leave this world, he should

---

523. *prasanna-vaktraṃ* : Ever ready to favour the devotee with grace —VR., VB.

524. Probably the *yogic anāhata cakra* in the cardiac plexus. This is specially useful for meditation in the case of the followers of *bhakti* Path —PYP (*Pātañjala Yoga Pradīpa*), Gita Press, p.252, 5th Edn.

* The 2nd line is translated at the beginning of this group.

adopt steady, comfortable posture and having controlled his breath (vital airs) he should not be attached, (i.e. take into account) time or period (such as summer solstice *Uttarāyaṇa*) or place (e.g. a holy place on the bank of the Ganges etc.).

16. Having controlled one's mind by purified intellect, one should absorb it into *kṣetrajña* and merge it (kṣetrajña) into the Soul and having merged one's Soul into the Supreme Soul or Brahman, the wise person should cease from all activity, and should stay in tranquillity or peace.

17. For, Time, which dominates gods, is powerless there (in the highest stage), much less are gods who control the world, are dominant there. There is absence of the attributes, viz. *sattva*, *rajas* and *tamas* (from which the world is created). There is neither self-sense (*ahaṁkāra*) nor the principal called *mahat* nor *prakṛti* (the primordial substance).

18.* They, who, realizing that whatever is different from it (Supreme Soul), is not really existent, are desirous of abandoning it, and who, avoiding the misconcept of the identification of the Soul with the body etc., hug closely every moment to the feet of venerable Lord, by their heart, and their affection to nobody else but to him, regard that the abode of Viṣṇu is the ultimate one (to be achieved).

19. The meditative sage who is convinced (of his complete identity with Brahman) and who has burnt up all his attachments, by the power of the insight derived from the knowledge of *Śāstras*, passes away thus. He should press his anus

* According to SD. : One should cease from all activity, embracing closely by heart the feet, i.e. the form of the venerable Viṣṇu every moment, and set aside the myth of one's independent existence apart from Brahman. For the Vedāntas, (i.e. the *Upaniṣads*) which deal with nothing else but Brahman, and which exhort that whatever is not Brahman is unreal, and should be abandoned, regard the form of Viṣṇu as the most sublime.

According to VJ : That excellent world is the most exalted place of Viṣṇu on whom devotees seeking liberation from the worldly existence, (i.e. the cycle of births and deaths) meditate and know him to be different from the elements (e.g. the earth, the ether) etc., or the subtle causes of these elements or their presiding deities. Thus they free themselves from worldly miseries and are fixed in firm devotion unto him. They embrace Lord Viṣṇu in their heart every moment and finally attain to him.

and lift up his vital air from that to the six places (*cakras*) described in *Yoga-Śāstra*, and rise above fatigue.

20. He should carry up the vital air residing in the navel (the *maṇipūra cakra* indicated thereby) and take it to the heart (i.e. the *anāhata cakra*). Then by the course of *udāna* (the vital air which rises up the throat and enters into the head), he should take it to the *viśuddha cakra* (located a little below the throat). The mind controlling yogin, with great concentration and restraint, should slowly take it (vital air) to the root of his palate.

21. From that place (*cakra*), he should lift up the vital air to the *ājñā cakra* located between the two eyebrows, and with the seven outlets of the breath (viz. 2 ears, 2 eyes, 2 nostrils and mouth) closed down, and being free from all desires, he should stay for half of a *muhūrta* (about 24 minutes) or so. With a fixed gaze, he should penetrate through the crown of the head (called *brahma-randhra*) and give up the body and merge with Brahman.

22. Oh king! If he desires to go to the place of god Brahmā, or to the sporting grounds or places of enjoyment of the heavenly beings, or for the mastery of the eight superhuman faculties[525], or anywhere in the universe, he should go along with his mind and subtle organs of senses.[526]

23. They say that the masters of *yoga* who have placed their subtle body (*liṅga-śarīra*) into *vāyu* (or mind), possess the power of going anywhere inside and outside the three worlds. Persons (who follow the path of *karma*) do not attain by their *karmas* to that power which is attained by those who are engaged in devotion, penance, yoga and meditation.

24. By passing through the sky, he first goes to the place

---

525. These superhuman faculties are eight in number. They are enumerated as follows : atomization (*yogin* becoming atomsized) ; levitation (*yogin* becoming light); magnification, extension (the *yogin* can touch the moon with his finger), efficacy (non-obstruction of desire of the *yogin*); mastery over the elements; sovereignty over the working of the elements and their products; capacity of determining things according to desire—Vide for details YSP iii. 45, pp. 278-280.

526. VJ. states that he goes to *satya-loka* as well. He increases his knowledge and attains the eight powers.

of the divine fire (*vaiśvānara*).[527] By the path of *suṣumṇā* [this tubular path is extended beyond human body, according to ŚR.], he goes by the shining path of Brahman and becomes completely free from impurity or attachment. Above that is the asterial *cakra* pertaining to Hari. Oh king! the *yogin* then proceeds to that *cakra* called *śaiśumāra* [which will be described in detail in the V *Skandha*].

25. Having crossed the place of Visṇu called *śaiśumāra cakra* which is like the navel of the universe (supporting stars etc.), he proceeds alone with very pure atomic body (subtle *liṅga-śarīra*) to a place where persons who know Brahman stay, and where having the longevity of one *kalpa*, these wise men enjoy themselves.

26. Then (at the end of the *kalpa*), seeing the universe being burnt down by the fire proceeding out of the mouth of the serpent Śeṣa, he (i. e. *yogin*) proceeds to the abode of *parameṣṭhin* where the great *siddhas* stay in their celestial vehicles for a period of two *parārdhas*[528].

27. There is neither sorrow nor old age nor death nor affliction or fear except their mental trouble, out of compassion, at the sight of the endless series of births and unending misery of those who do not know this (path of devotion).

28.* Then fearlessly the *yogin* steadily unites his *liṅga-śarīra* with the elements—the subtle *pṛthvī*, and then the subtle element

---

527. This form of fire is supposed to cover in a way the universe. It is present in living beings in the form of digestion. In the universe, it gives heat and light, and thirdly he is the medium whereby the sages go to the abodes of gods, manes and Brahman.

It is supposed that the sage who leaves this mortal body by the *piṅgalā* passage in the right side of the body goes to heaven and the Path is called *devayāna*. Those who depart through the *iḍā* passage in the left side of the body, go to the abode of the manes, and the yogins who give up the body by the *suṣumṇā* passage, reach the Brahman. (Abridged from VJ.)

528. Parārdha=100,000,000,000,000,000.

*According to ŚR., this verse describes what is technically known as the procedure of 'breaking through the Universe or *Brahmāṇḍa*'. The creation of the universe has taken place as follows : God→prakṛti→mahat →ahaṁkāra—the subtle form of the sound→the element ether→the *tanmātrās* (subtle elements) of touch→Vāyu element→subtle 'form'→the element fire→the subtle taste→the element water→subtle smell→the element earth. This is the *virāṭ* body. This is enveloped by seven 'covers' : the

of water, and assuming the resplendent form of fire, without any haste, he reaches Vāyu and assumes the Vāyu form; then he becomes one with Ākāśa, the prominent symbol of the Perfect Soul.

29. Having reached smell by the sense of smell, taste by the sense of taste, colour by the visual organ, and touch by the sense of touch, sound, the special property of the sky, by the sense of hearing, the yogin reaches the activities of sense organs by means of the vital air (called *prāṇa*).

30. At first, having reached the self-sense (*ahaṁkāra*)—called *vikārya*, because its functions are different, he thus reaches where the subtle elements (*bhūtas*) and (subtle) organs of senses are withdrawn, and which is the cause of the mental (*rājasa-manomaya*) effects as well as of the presiding deities of the organs of senses—the *sāttvic self-sense* (*ahaṁkāra*), the Yogi proceeds to the principle called *mahat* (or *vijñāna*) along with *ahaṁkāra* and to *pradhāna* or *prakṛti* (primordial matter) into which all the three attributes are merged.

31. Oh beloved King! Ultimately the yogin who is serene, in perfect bliss and free from (limiting) conditions, reaches the changeless Paramātman who is bliss incarnate. He who has achieved this glorious divine goal, does not have any attachment to the world again.

32. Oh King! These two paths (viz. of instantaneous Liberation and gradual Liberation) which are described in the Vedas and about which you enquired, are eternal. These were taught by the venerable Lord Viṣṇu to god Brahmā when, in ancient days, he worshipped and delighted the Lord, and asked him about those paths.

33. To the entrant in the worldly existence (*saṁsāra*), there is no other blessed path than this, by practising which, intense devotion unto the Supreme Lord Vāsudeva is created.

34. Lord Brahmā, having thrice studied the entire Veda with concentration, conclusively decided the course whereby intense love to the soul (Hari) is (definitely) generated.

---

covers of the five elements (e.g. earth, water etc.) and that of *ahaṁkāra* and *mahat*. So the process of breaking these envelopes is the reverse of creation, viz. the earth—the water etc. up to *mahat*.

35. In all beings (or the creation consisting of elements) the Lord Hari is seen (as the inner dweller—controller—*antaryāmin*) by intellect and other organs of senses (which by themselves are inert and cannot function without the light of the self-luminous soul or Hari), and which are merely characteristics or useful, as tools of inference.

36. Hence, Oh King, in all places and at all times, Lord Kṛṣṇa is the only object worthy of being studied, sung and remembered by men, with all their heart.

37. Those who drink this nectar, i. e. the account of glorious Hari, the Lord of the pious people, with vessels, in the form of ears, get their minds purified of the contamination of the worldly objects, and attain to his lotus-like feet.

CHAPTER THREE

(*Devotion to Hari—the only path of Liberation*)

Śrī Śuka said:

1. In this way, I have described to you this course (of study etc. about Hari, as prescribed in the Śāstras)—the course about which your honour asked me for the sake of wise and thoughtful persons among men, especially for those who are about to die.

2. One desirous of the glory of Vedic studies should worship the god Brahmā. He who desires to have power and skill of his sense-organs should worship Indra. He who wishes to have progeny should worship Prajāpatis (like Dakṣa).

3. He who longs to have prosperity should propitiate the goddess Māyā (Durgā). One who desires to have personal brilliance should worship the fire-god. One wishing for wealth should worship the eight Vasus. A vigorous person desiring for more strength should propitiate the Rudras.

4. He who wishes to have ample food and eatables should worship Aditi, while he who desires to attain heaven (*svarga*), should propitiate the sons of Aditi, viz. the twelve Ādityas. One desiring to possess a kingdom, should worship the Viśvedevas. One aspiring to control his subjects, should worship the Sādhyas.

5. One desiring a long life, should propitiate the Aśvin gods (both the Aśvinikumāras). He who desires to have increase in physical strength should worship the earth. A man desiring permanent firmness in his acquired position, should worship the Sky and the Earth, the parents of this world.

6. One who desires to have beautiful form, should worship the Gandharvas. One desiring to have beautiful women should worship the heavenly damsel Ūrvaśī. One who desires overlordship on all people, should worship god Brahmā (Parameṣṭhin).

7. One who seeks reputation or success, should worship Yajña, i.e. Viṣṇu. One aspiring after treasures should worship god Varuṇa. One wishing to have learning, should worship god Śiva, and for conjugal love, one should propitiate goddess Pārvatī (chastity incarnate).

8. For the sake of righteousness, one should worship Viṣṇu (the god whose glory is excellent). For the continuity of one's race, one should propitiate the manes (*pitṛs*). One desiring protection from danger, should worship the Yakṣaṣ. One desiring to have strength, should worship the gods called Maruts.

9. One who aspires after kingship or sovereignty, should propitiate Manus, the presiding deities of the eras (*manvantaras*). He who longs for the destruction of the enemies, should worship Nirṛti (*rākṣasas*). One desiring all kinds of enjoyments, should worship god Soma. (But) he who desires freedom from attachment or desires, should devote himself unto the Perfect or the Supreme Man.

10. He who wishes to have no desire at all, or aspiring after all kinds of enjoyments or longing to have Liberation due to the exaltedness of his intelligence, should intensely propitiate, by the path of devotion, the Perfect Man beyond limitations.

11. The attainment of the highest good is this much, in the case of the worshippers (of Indra etc.) in this world, but it is in the association of the devotees of the Supreme Lord that unswerving devotion unto the Lord is generated (that leads to Final Beatitude).

12. Is there anybody who, having got the blissful satis-

faction (of listening to the stories of Hari which is unavailable elsewhere), would not love those episodes, from which arises the knowledge, which completely subsides all whirling waves of passions (like love, hatred etc.), and creates tranquillity of mind and non-attachment to the objects of senses, leading ultimately to the path of devotion which is regarded as the state of liberation itself here and hereafter.

Śaunaka said :

13. After carefully listening to what has been explained to him thus, what other query was again made by the king, the prominent among the Bharata race, to the son of Vyāsa (Śuka) who was a seer of *parabrahman* and well versed in the Vedic lore ?

14. Oh learned Sūta ! You should narrate that to us who are desirous of hearing, for, discourses in the assembly of the devotees of Lord Kṛṣṇa, must definitely lead to the episodes of Hari.

15. Verily, that great warrior king of the Pāṇḍava family, was a great devotee of Kṛṣṇa, as he used to worship Kṛṣṇa as a play, while playing with his toys in the childhood (Or he used to imitate the sports of Kṛṣṇa as a child, in his own childhood).

16. The venerable son of Vyāsa was an ardent devotee of Vāsudeva. When there is a meeting of the pious devotees of Kṛṣṇa, there must be (the discussion about) the great episodes or excellent virtues of Hari (lit. the god who is greatly praised in the Vedas).

17. This rising and the setting sun verily takes away the life of men, except that period used in discussion etc. about Kṛṣṇa, (the god whose reputation lifts the devotee from darkness or *tamas*).

18. Do not the trees live ? Or do not the bellows breathe ? Do not the domestic or other beasts eat and have sexual enjoyment ?

19. The man, to whose ears the name of Kṛṣṇa (the elder brother of Gada) has not reached, is described as similar to (despicable animals like) dogs, swine, camels and donkeys.

20. The ears of the man, which do not hear the exploits

of Kṛṣṇa, are verily like empty holes. Oh Sūta ! the tongue which does not sing of Lord Kṛṣṇa, is evil like that of a frog's.

21. The head (though the best part of the body), even if adorned with turban or a crown, is a great burden, if it does not bow to Mukunda. Or hands, which are adorned with bright gold bangles, are like the hands of a dead body, if they do not worship Hari.

22. The eyes of men, which do not carefully see the images of Viṣṇu, are like the eyes (i.e. the big bright spots on the feathers) of peacocks. The feet of men which do not go on pilgrimage to the sacred places of Viṣṇu, are mere vegetations like trees.

23. A mortal, who does not get the dust of the feet of the devotees of the Lord, is as good as a carcass even though alive. The man who has not smelt the fragrance of the Tulasī leaves placed at the feet of Lord Viṣṇu, is only a breathing corpse.

24. The heart, which at the time of taking different names of Hari, is not moved, and the change in it is not indicated by tears in the eyes, and bristling of the hair on the body through excessive joy, is verily the hardest granite.

25. Oh beloved Sūta ! whatever you speak is dear to our hearts. Please narrate to us what did the great Bhāgavata, the son of Vyāsa, who was well-versed in the knowledge of the Soul and who was well questioned, say to the king ?

CHAPTER FOUR

(*Creation of the Universe*)

Prayers to Hari

Sūta said :

1. Having heard Śuka's speech, which led to the definite understanding of the real nature of the Soul, Parīkṣit (the son of Uttarā) set his virtuous and steady mind on Kṛṣṇa.

2. He renounced attachment which was always sticking (to his mind), to his body, wife, sons, palace, cattle, wealth, kinsmen and kingdom well equipped with the seven constituent elements of the state (enumerated in works on politics).

3. He, a man ofnoble mind and intense faith in listening to the great deeds of Kṛṣṇa, asked him (Śuka) the same topic which you, the greatest among good persons, ask me.

4. Having understood the approach of death and having renounced duties pertaining to the three Purusārthas, viz. *dharma*, *artha* and *kāma*, he with great love or devotion for the Lord, solely devoted himself to self-realization in Lord Vāsudeva.

5. Oh sinless Brāhmaṇa ! The words of an omniscient person (like you) are quite good (correct). While you tell me the episodes of Hari, the darkness of my ignorance is dispelled.

6. I again wish to know how the Lord has created this universe by His Cosmic Power (*Māyā*)—the universe which is beyond the comprehension of great gods (such as Brahmā).

7. Also I wish to know by resorting to what powers the Supreme Man of infinite power, creates, protects and destroys (this universe again) and how he sports himself directly and indirectly (through Brahmā and other gods).

8. Oh Brāhmaṇa ! Really the actions of Hari of mysterious and wonderful deeds, appear incomprehensible even to very wise people (what of a person like me !).

9. Whether it is simultaneously or one after another in succession, that he assumes the different attributes of *Prakṛti*, in order to do his work through many incarnations.

10. As your honour is verily well-versed in the Vedic lore and in the knowledge of Parabrahman, Your Worship may kindly explain this doubt to me.

Sūta said :

11. Śuka, who was thus solicited by the king, to describe the attributes of Hari, meditated on Kṛṣṇa and began to address.

Śrī Śuka said :

12. Salute to the Perfect Man of infinite power, who by his sport of creating, sustaining and distroying this world, has assumed three powers, viz. Rajas (Brahmā) etc. [or 'will, wisdom and action which are eternally in him'].

13. I offer my salutations again and again to him who removes the afflictions of the good, who curbs down the growth of the irreligious, who orders all gods of *Sāttvic* body[529] to bestow fruits (upon the devotees, and who confers the knowledge of the self upon those who have established themselves in the order of *Parama Haṁsas*.

14. I bow again and again to the protector of the *Sāttvatas* (or his devotees) who is beyond the reach of devotionless persons. Salutations to him, who being by nature unequalled and insurmountable, enjoys himself in his natural condition.

15. Salutation to him of auspicious fame; (as) to praise him, to remember him, to look at him, to bow to him, to hear about him and to adore him, immediately purifies sins of men.

16. I bow again and again to him of auspicious glory, by resorting to whose feet, the wise men shed off their heart's attachment here and hereafter, and without any trouble, attain to the state of Brahman.

17. I salute again and again to him, without offering whom (the fruit of one's actions), none can attain happiness (or peace), even though they perform penance, or are very charitable or have attained (high) reputation, or practised Yoga, or are knower of very auspicious *mantras*, or are of pure conduct.

18*. The Kirātas, the Hūṇas, the Āndhras, Pulindas, Pulkasas, Ābhīras, Kakas (Śakas), Yavanas, Khasas and other

529. *akhila-sattva-mūrtaye* : One who is the embodiment of perfect goodness—VJ.

*For the role of Bhāgavatism in the social absorption of foreigners *vide* R.K. Mukerjee's *Hist. of Ind. Civilisation* Vol. I., pp. 230-249.

This shows the attempts of proselytisation on the part of the Vaiṣṇavas. The following is the information in brief about tribes mentioned here, *Kirātas*—a Himalayan tribe in the eastern region.

(sinful) tribes and other sinners are purged of their sins even by taking refuge in those who depend on him. To that Almighty Lord, we offer our greetings.

19*. May the Divine Lord be propitious unto me—the Lord who is (to be meditated as) the Soul, by the knowers of the Soul,[530] as the Supreme God, by the devotees, as the three Vedas incarnate[531] by the followers of *Karma kāṇḍa*, as the veritable *dharma*[532] by the followers of *dharma* (religion), as

---

Hūṇas—The famous invading tribes from central Asia who established their dynasties in India.

Āndhras—According to the *Aitareya Brāhmaṇa*, a non-Aryan tribe living on the southern fringe of Āryāvarta. Formerly they were in the Vindhya region. Their settlement to the south in the present Andhra Pradesh is a later development.

Pulindas—An aboriginal tribe mentioned along with the Āndhras in the *Aitareya Brāhmaṇa*. They inhabited the Vindhya region upto 600 A.D.

Pulkasas or Pukkasa in Manu—An outcaste people.

Ābhīras—A foreign people who entered India at about the Śaka invasion and went on migrating from the Punjab till they settled in north-west Deccan. They are reported to have defeated Arjuna and carried away Yādava women.

Kaṅkas—Śakas. The original home of these people was in the valley of the Oxus and Jaxartes.

Yavanas—The Indo-Greeks who ruled in the north-western part of India.

Khasas—Identified with modern Khakkas who live in Kashmir.

*VJ. interprets : May the Supreme Soul be gracious unto me—Soul who is the Supreme Lord to those who have directly realized Brahman (and have attained liberation), as the Lord is favourable to the followers of the Veda, *dharma* (path of duties prescribed by scripture) and penance and whose characteristics (e.g. creation of the world etc.) have been inferred by sincere devotees like Brahmā, Śiva etc.

530. *ātmavatām*—(i) Steadfast in pure Yoga—VR.

(ii) Those who have directly realized Brahman or attained liberation—VJ.

(iii) Those who have realized the non-difference from Brahman—GD.

531. *trayī-mayaḥ*—(i) follower of the householder's duties, e.g. *agnihotra* prescribed in the Vedas—SD.

(ii) the students of Veda to worship it in the form of three Vedas—GD.

532. *dharma-mayaḥ*—(propitiated) by followers of the duties of celibates—SD.

the goal (to be achieved), by performers of penance,[533] the Lord, whose form is observed with great amazement by sincere worshippers like gods Brahmā, Śaṅkara etc.

20. May the Lord—protector of the good, be gracious unto me—the Lord, who is the master of the goddess of Wealth, the Lord of Sacrifices of all beings, the controller of mental or intellectual faculties, the protector of the worlds, the Lord of the earth, the Lord and protector of Andhaka, Vṛṣṇi and Śāttvata clans.

21. May Lord Mukunda (Kṛṣṇa) be propitious unto me by constant meditation of whose [Kṛṣṇa's] feet, the wise purify their intellect and realize the true nature of the soul, and whom the wise describe as attributeful or attributeless (according to their taste or capacity).

22. May the most Excellent Sage be gracious to me—the sage who formerly (at the beginning of the creation) extended, i.e. awakened, the memory regarding the (procedure of) creation (of the universe) in the heart of Brahmā, and who directed the goddess Sarasvatī (the verbal form of the Veda) along with its characteristic supplements (e.g. śikṣā, vyākaraṇa etc.) to issue from the mouth of Brahmā.

23. May the venerable Lord grace (beautify) my words—the Omnipresent Lord, having created these bodies with five gross elements (or with *mahat* and other elements) lies (dwells) within them as *antaryāmin* and becomes (even etymologically) the real *Puruṣa*—one who lies in a town, i.e. body). He illumines and protects the sixteen qualities (i.e. the constituents) of the body (viz. 11 sense organs and 5 elements), by inspiring with life these sixteen.[534]

(ii) performers of sacrifices should worship him as *dharma*—GD.

533. *tapo-mayaḥ*—(worshipped) by the followers of *vānaprastha* and *sannyāsa āśramas*—SD.

Performers of penance should propitiate him as *Tapas*.

534. *bhuṅkte......ṣoḍaśātmakaḥ*—VR. explains that the Lord possessing the sixteen constituents, viz. eleven sense organs and five elements, enjoys the sixteen 'qualities' viz. five objects of senses, e.g. sound, touch etc., five functions of organs, e.g. speech etc., five functions of Prāṇas or vital breaths and mind.

24. I bow to the venerable Vyāsa,[535] the learned author of the Mahābhārata etc., from whose lotus-like mouth his gentle disciples drank the honey in the form of knowledge.

25. Oh King, the Self-born God (Brahmā), the source of the Vedas, explained this to the enquiring Nārada, which was directly narrated to him (Brahmā) by Hari.

CHAPTER FIVE

(Creation of the Universe)
Dialogue between Nārada and Brahmadeva

Nārada said :

1. Oh God of gods ! Oh Creator of all creatures ! Oh the ancestor of all beings [one who is born before all] ! I bow to you. Please explain to me in detail the knowledge which leads to the thorough realization of the true nature of the Soul (*ātman*).

2. Oh Lord ! Please tell me factually what it is that manifests itself in this form of the world. What is the support of it all ? From what is it created ? Into what is it merged or withdrawn ? In whose power does it lie ? Of what does it consist (whether of itself or as an effect of some cause) ?

3. Verily Your Honour knows everything about this, as you are the master (lord) of the past, the present and the future). The whole universe is definitely and correctly known to you

VB. gives in detail how the Lord divides himself in different 'enjoyer-enjoyed' pairs (e.g. man—woman) and sports himself in the enjoyment of the world.

535. Here the reading in the Nirnaya Sagara edition (Bombay 1905) is followed. The text before VJ. reads...... *Vāsudevāya vedhase*—VJ. interprets this differently :

(1) Salute to the Lord Vāsudeva from whose lotus-like mouth Brahmā and others, who deserved to drink the Soma-juice of knowledge, drank the honey of knowledge.

Thus taking *saumya* as (1) *Uddhava* and others, (ii) Nārada and others (iii) Vyāsa and others, (iv) Vaiśampāyana and others, the salutes are offered to Kṛṣṇa, god Brahmā, Nārada and Vyāsa respectively.

like the *āmalaka* (*Emblic myrobalan*) fruit on the palm of your hand.

4. What is the source of your special knowledge ? What is your support (who supports you)? In whose power are you ? What is your real nature ? I think you alone create all these beings, with the elements, by your divine power (*māyā*).

5. You protect those (beings) depending on you, and there is no transformation in you, even though, without any fatigue you create (these beings) by your power, like a spider producing the fibre.

6. Oh Lord ! I do now know anything else, whether it is of superior, equal or inferior status which is created with names (such as men etc.), with form (such as bipeds etc.), or with attributes (such as whiteness etc.), or whether it is gross or subtle—which has a source in anybody else but you.

7. But you (as described above) performed austere penance with perfect concentration. You, thereby, create a suspicion in us if there is any God superior to you.

9. Oh Omniscient Master of all ! Please explain to me who am asking you this, so that I may understand the truth as explained by you.

Brahmā said :

9. Oh child ! Your query is really praiseworthy. You are compassionate (to all beings). Oh gentle child ! You have therefore made me describe in detail the glory of the Lord.

10. Oh child ! What you (think and) say about me is not untrue as you do not know the Power higher than I, from which (I receive) this much power (as described by you).

11. I shed light on (i.e. manifest) the universe which has already been lightened by him by his lustre, just as the Sun, the fire, the Moon, constellations, planets and stars shine due to his splendour.

12. Salutations to the venerable Vāsudeva. We meditate on him deluded by whose invincible power—*Māyā*—people call me the cause of the universe.

13. Persons being beguiled by her (*Māyā*) who fights shy of standing in the range of his sight, get their knowledge

covered by Nescience, and boast that "this is mine and I" (i.e. I am an independent agent).

14. Oh Brahman, whether it is substance (e.g. five elements, the material cause of this world,) deed or *karman* (the cause of *saṁsāra*), Time, Nature, or individual Soul—there is nothing distinct and apart from Vāsudeva.

15. All the Vedas ultimately speak of Nārāyaṇa[536] (implying the omniscience etc. mentioned in *Śāstrayonitva* of the *Brahma-sūtra*). Gods are born out of Nārāyaṇa's body (and hence inferior to him). The words such as heaven or *svarga* are Nārāyaṇa (or all beings regard Nārāyaṇa as supreme). All sacrificial acts are for the propitiation of Nārāyaṇa.

16*. Yoga (breath control, contemplation etc.) is meant for the realization of Nārāyaṇa. All penance is for the attainment of Nārāyaṇa. Nārāyaṇa is the highest object of knowledge. The final beatitude depends on Nārāyaṇa. (Or Nārāyaṇa is the highest goal).

17. Being directed by the glance of the Almighty who is the soul of all, (who is the *Antaryāmin*), the Seer, the Controller, the Changeless one, I who am created by him, create this universe which is his creative activity or creation.

18. Though he is attributeless, he, through his Māyā, has assumed the three attributes, namely, *sattva*, *rajas* and *tamas*, for the maintenance, creation and dissolution (of the universe).

19. These attributes which are at the basis of the five elements (i.e. *mahābhūtas*), knowledge (i.e. the gods) and activity (the senses and organs) always bind the individual Soul in effects, cause and agency (known as *adhibhūta*, *adhyātma*, *adhidaivata* respectively. Though he is really free, he is enveloped by Māyā.[537]

---

536. *Nārāyaṇa-para*—Nārāyaṇa is the ultimate cause of the Vedas—VR. (ii) Vedas propound or declare that Nārāyaṇa is the Supreme Being—VR. (iii) Vedas say that out of the topics described by them, Nārāyana is the highest and the best—VJ.

*Cf. Bh.P. I.2.28-29, where *Vāsudeva* is used for *Nārāyaṇa*.

537. VJ. explains : Dravya (matter) is the body produced by *tāmasa ahaṁkāra*. jñāna (knowledge) is the mind and other organs of senses

20. Oh Brahman! This is the glorious Lord Viṣṇu (adhoksaja) whose movements are incomprehensible[538] through these three attributes (viz. *sattva, rajas* and *tamas*). He is my lord as well as that of all others.

21. The lord of Māyā desiring to be many (i.e. assuming different forms) accepted as cause, time, action (the fate of *jīva*) and the innate disposition which accidentally (through his will) appeared in him through his *Māyā*.

22. It is due to the presence or direction of God that Time became the cause of the imbalance in the three attributes (*guṇas*), innate nature the cause of modifications or transformations, and *karma* as the cause of *mahat*.[539]

23. *Mahat* which is magnified by or charged with rajas and sattva, undergoes modifications and evolves a thing in which tamas is dominant, and the thing is constituted of substance or gross elements, organs of senses and deities presiding over the organs.

24. That evolute is known as *ahaṁkāra* (I-ness), which undergoing modifications, becomes of three kinds—(1) *vaikārika* (*sāttvika*), (2) taijasa (*rājasa*), (3) tāmasa. It constitutes the power in substance or gross elements, power in activity, i.e. organs of senses and power in the presiding deities of the senses.

25. From the tāmasa *ahaṁkāra*, known as the source of elements (*Bhūtādi*) which underwent modifications, was evolved the ether (the sky). Its subtle form and special characteristic is sound (*śabda*) which leads to the knowledge of the seer and the seen.

---

created by *Vaikārika ahaṁkāra. Kriyā* (activity) is the speech and other functions of senses. These are produced by *taijasa ahaṁkāra*.

538. *sva-lakṣita-gatiḥ*—(i) Whose cause is comprehensible to his devotees only—ŚR., VJ.

(ii) Whose cause is perceptible to the liberated ones.—SD.

539. According to VJ. this describes the creation of *mahat* from the primeval *Prakṛti*. When Viṣṇu desired to create the universe, at that time the balance of the *guṇas* became disturbed, and by the favourable condition of the *adṛṣṭa* (*karma*) of Hiraṇyagarbha, and by the transformable nature of *mūla prakṛti*, and being presided over by Viṣṇu, the principle *mahat* was produced.

26. Out of the ether undergoing transformation emerged *Vāyu* (air), the characteristic quality of which was Touch. Being an evolute of the other, i.e. the sky, it possesses the quality Sound, and it is the cause of life, vigorousness of senses, mind and the body.[540]

27. Due to (the pressure or force of) Time, Karma (the unseen i.e. *adṛṣṭa*) and innate disposition, Vāyu, i.e. air, underwent modifications, and *tejas* (fire or heat), possessing colour and form (and inheriting the characteristics of the previous elements, viz.) touch and sound, was evolved.

28. From *tejas* undergoing change, was produced water with taste as its special characteristic. Through inheritance from the previous elements, water possessed the characteristics viz., form, colour, touch and sound.

29. Out of water undergoing transformation came forth the earth or the *viśeṣa*, with smell as its special attribute, and inheriting from its previous causes, the attributes of taste, touch, sound and form or colour.

30. From the *vaikārika* or *sāttvic ahaṁkāra* (sāttvic ego) were born the Mind (and its presiding deity the Moon) and the ten gods, five presiding over the five sense organs, viz. *Diś* (deity of cardinal points), Vāyu, Sūrya, Varuṇa and Aśvins (presiding over the sense organs—ears, skin, eyes, tongue, nose) and the other five, viz. Vahni (fire-god), Indra, Upendra, Mitra (the sun) and Ka (i.e. Prajāpati) presiding over the conative organs (viz. speech, hands, feet, the anus and the organ of generation).

31. From the *taijasa* (*rājasa*) ahaṁkāra, undergoing change, were evolved the ten organs (five cognitive and five conative sense organs detailed above) viz. the ear (audition), the skin (touch), the nose (smell), the eye (seeing), the tongue (taste), speech, hands, feet, penis and anus. Intelligence or the power of cognition or knowledge and Prāṇa, the power of conation, were evolved out of the *taijasa ahaṁkāra*.

32. Oh knower of Brahman or Vedas! So long as these, viz. *bhūtas* (the elements), *indriyas* (sense-organs), the mind

540. Prāṇa etc.—vitality of which energy, speed and capacity to hold or strength, are the characteristics—VR.

and the *guṇas* were unamalgamated, they were not able to create the body.

33. Then directed by the will of God, they came together and were assimilated with one another as the main and the subsidiary (or the manifest and the unmanifested) constituents, and brought forth this (body of gross and subtle constituents or collective and distributive aggregates).

34. At the end of thousands of years (during the Deluge), with the help of *kāla* (time), *karma* (action and destiny) and *svabhāva* (innate disposition) the Supreme Soul (who enlivened these and hence was called *jīva*) brought life into the egg (of the universe) of unmanifested life.

35. This very Supreme Man possessing thousands of thighs, feet, arms, eyes and thousands of mouths and heads[541] came out bursting open the egg (*brahmāṇḍa*).

36. The wise locate the different worlds in the body of the Supreme Man, as seven worlds below his loins and seven worlds above, commencing from his hip upwards.*

---

541. Cf. RV. X. 90.1.

*The 'creation' or rather evolution of the universe may be briefly represented as follows :

God's will to be many—Influence on *kāla*, *karma* and *svabhāva* by God's Power Māyā—

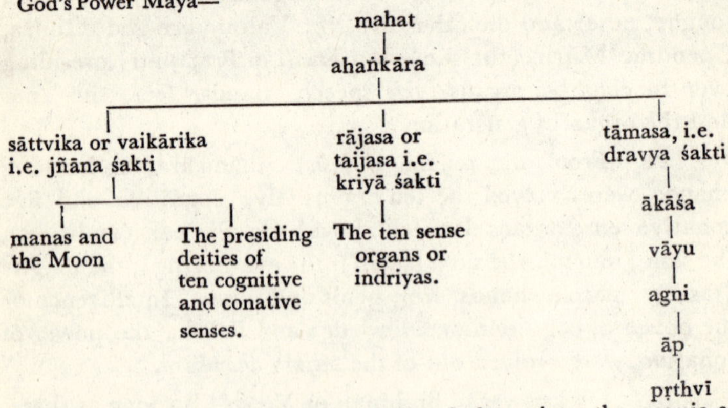

The Lord, by his Power, assimilated them into the cosmic egg (brahmāṇḍa) and later infused life into it. The virāṭ puruṣa with thousands of heads, feet etc. and with seven upper and seven lower regions located in his body came out and the creation, preservation and destruction of the universe followed.

37. The Brāhmaṇa class is the mouth of this Man. Kṣatriyas are his arms. From the thighs of the lord was created the Vaiśya class and the Śūdra came forth from his feet.[542]

38. The *Bhūr-loka* was created from his feet, the *Bhuvar-loka* from his navel. From the heart of the Great Being was produced the *Svar-loka*, and from his chest, the *Mahar-loka*.

39. On his neck is based the *Jana-loka*, and the *Tapo-loka** came from his lips. The *Satya-loka* is created from the heads. *Brahma-loka* is eternal (and therefore not created).

40. The nether region *Atala* is located in his loins. *Vitala** depends on the thighs of the lord. On his knees rests the holy *Sutala* (holy due to the residence of the devotees of the Lord) and *Talātala* is based on his shanks.

41. His ankles support *Mahātala*, and the forepart of his feet, the *Rasātala*. The *Pātāla* is created from the soles. In this way the body of the Supreme Man consists of all the worlds.

42. Or this arrangement of worlds (is differently given): the *Bhūr-loka* has been created from his feet and the *Bhuvar-loka* from his navel and the *Svar-loka* from his head.

CHAPTER SIX**

(*Description of the Virāṭ Puruṣa—exposition of the Puruṣa Sūkta —ṚV.* 10.90)

1. The mouth of the Cosmic Man (*Virāṭ Puruṣa*) is the place, i. e. the source of the speech organs and its presiding deity the Fire. The seven essential ingredients (*dhātu*) such as saliva, blood, flesh, fat, bones and others of his body are the

542. Cf. RV. X. 90.12.

*ŚR. alternatively interprets : *Tapo-loka* was created from his breasts. He adds that for contemplation there is no difficulty if the breasts which are downwards in position from the neck, are taken as the source of the *Tapo-loka*).

** This chapter presents the epic concept of the Cosmic Man which was first elaborated in RV. 10-90 (the *Puruṣa-Sūkta*). This is not exactly a commentary on the *Puruṣa-Sūkta* but it is an elaboration of the Vedic concept of the Cosmic Man. Naturally, as pointed out by B. Bhattacarya in the *Philo. of the Śrīmad-Bhāgavata*, Vol. 1, 130-38, 305-306 etc., this epic concept is philosophically much more advanced than the Vedic concept.

bases of the seven Vedic metres, (viz., *Gāyatrī*, *Uṣṇik*, *Anuṣṭubh*, *Bṛhatī*, *Paṅkti*, *Triṣṭubh* and *Jagatī*). His tongue is the source of food, viz., *Havya* (the food oblated to gods), *Kavya* (the food given to the manes—*Pitṛs*), *Amṛta* (the food remaining after having offered to gods and manes), and all flavours (viz. sweet, sour, pungent, bitter, saline and astringent)—and Varuṇa, their presiding deity.

2. His nostrils are the best places or abodes of all vital airs and of (their presiding deity) Vāyu. His organ of smell is the abode of the two Aśvini-kumāras (the physicians of gods), medicinal herbs and plants, general and special smells.

3. His cognitive sense of sight is the sourse of forms, colours and lights manifesting them, while the sky and the sun are produced in the pupils of his eyes. His ears are the bases of directions and holy places, while his sense of hearing is the source of the ether (the sky) and (its *guṇa*) sound (*śabda*).

4. His body is the base of the essences of all things and their beauty. His skin or organ of touch is the source of touch, Vāyu and all kinds of sacrifices.

5. His hair (on the body) are at the root of all the trees, herbs and plants, supplying the material for sacrifices, while his hair, beard and nails produce rocks, iron, clouds and lightning.

6. His arms are the support of the presiding deities of the cardinal points whose duty is to protect the world. His paces—footsteps—are the support of the three worlds—*Bhūr*, *Bhuvaḥ*, *Svar* and of security (protection of the possession) and refuge (protection from danger).

7-8. The feet of Hari are the abode of the seekers of all desired objects. His penis is the source of waters, seminal fluid, creation, rain and Prajāpati. His organ of generation is the source of the gratification (satisfaction) culminating in the joy of the offspring. His anus is the base of Yama, of Mitra (the Sun) and the act of discharging (the faeces), oh Nārada.

9. His rectum is stated to be the source of violence or harm, goddess of misfortune (Alakṣmī), of death and hell. His back-side is the source of defeat, irreligion and *Tamas* (ignorance).

10-11. His arteries and veins (blood vessels) are the source of rivers, big and small. And his skeleton of bones, that of mountains and hills. His belly is known to be the source or place of the unmanifested primordial matter (*pradhāna*), the essence in food, oceans and the destruction of all beings. His heart is the source of the mind, i. e. of the subtle body (*Liṅga Śarīra*). The *ātman*, i. e. *citta* (reason) of the Supreme Man is the ultimate source of religion, of myself, of yourself, of the four boy-(celibate) sages (Sanaka, Sanandana etc.), Śiva, of knowledge and of *Sattva* (the quality of goodness).

12-17.* Myself, yourself, Rudra, the elders (Sanaka, Sanandana etc.) and sages (e.g. Marīci and others), Gods, demons, men, Nāgas (elephants), birds, deer and reptiles, demigods like Gandharvas, Yakṣas, Apsaras (celestial damsels), Rākṣasas, goblins, serpents, beasts, manes (Pitṛs), Siddhas, Vidyādharas, Cāraṇas and trees and other various kinds of beings living in water, on land and in the air, planets, stars, comets, lightning and thundering, clouds—all are nothing but the manifestation of this Supreme Man. The universe of the past, present and future has been enveloped (encompassed) by him, and he still stands in the span-ful portion in the heart, Just as Prāṇa, i. e. Āditya, the Sun-god, illuminates his own sphere as well as outside (the world beyond it.) so the Supreme Man enlightens (the inside and outside of) the universe (the *Virāṭ Śarīra*). He is the ruler of Lord of mokṣa—liberation or immortality which is free from fear, and hence he renounced (i. e. he is above) the mortal (and hence momentary) enjoyment of the fruits of action. He is not only within all but is a lord of immortality and his own bliss.

18.*-19.* Oh Brahman ! The greatness and power of the Cosmic Man are boundless. They (the knowers) understand that all beings are abiding in the three worlds—*Bhūḥ, Bhuvaḥ, Svar*—which are the feet, i.e. the feet-like *aṁśas* of the Cosmic Man who is (hence called) *sthiti-pād*. He has placed *amṛta* (deathlessness), *kṣema* (absence of troubles) and *abhaya*[543]

VV. 17*, 18*, 19*, 20*. The SK. text is an echo of RV. X. 90. 2-4.

543. VJ. explains *amṛta* as *anantāsana* (the seat formed by Śeṣa), *Kṣema* (that which annihilates the trouble of death, i.e., *Vaikuṇṭha*) while *abhaya* is Cosmic Waters of Nārāyaṇa, i.e. Nārāyaṇa himself or Śvetadvīpa. Hari has supported these regions on his three heads. He (VJ) offers another

(state of freedom from fear, mokṣa) respectively in the three worlds, viz. *Jana*, *Tapas* and *Satya* which are situated above the *Maharloka*. The three *āśramas* (states of life) which do not procreate children, i. e. *Brahmacarya*, *Vānaprastha* and *Sannyāsa* are his three feet which are outside the three worlds (viz. *Bhūḥ*, *Bhuvaḥ*, *Svar*), while the other state of life, viz. that of householders who do not observe strict celebacy are within the three worlds (viz. Bhūḥ, etc.).

20. The Supreme Man as *kṣetrajña* (individual Soul) crossed both the paths, viz. the one characterised by *avidyā* or ignorance and *karma* leading to worldly enjoyments, and the other, by *vidyā* or knowledge and its means, viz., *upāsanā* (religious meditation). But the Cosmic Man is the support of both the paths.

21*. God is transcendental to the matter from which the Cosmic egg (*Brahmāṇḍa*) and the *Virāṭ* consisting of *bhūtas* (gross elements like the earth etc. or created beings), *indriyas* (sense organs) and *guṇas* (objects of sense organs) are born, just as the Sun, which warms and illumines the universe, is distinct from it.

22. When I was born out of the lotus in the navel of this Supreme Man, I did not know the materials needed for performing the sacrifices except the limbs of this Man.

23-26. These materials for the sacrifice were collected by me as they were procured from his limbs : sacrificial animals along with the trees required for sacrificial posts, the *kuśa* grass, specific piece of land for sacrifice, the most auspicious time (e.g. the Spring), things (utensils, spoons, etc. required for sacrifice), herbs and other vegetable products (e.g. rice), ghee, honey and other sweet liquids, metals such as gold etc., (differ-

---

explanation :' Brahmā, Viṣṇu and Maheśvara are His three heads which support the regions called Satya, Vaikuṇṭha and Kailāsa wherein are placed *amṛta* etc. These are outside the three worlds, viz. the earth (*bhū*) and others and are abodes of god Brahmā who has not begotten any son. VR. however briefly sums up that the three outer regions (feet) are for the liberated ones who are beyond the jurisdiction of Prakṛti, while the fourth foot is inside the three worlds and is meant for householders.

* According to VJ., Hari originally created the Cosmic Egg, from which *Virāṭ*, viz. Brahmā, was born. He was the support of *bhūtas*, *indriyas* and *guṇas*.

ent kinds of) earths, water, the texts of the *Ṛgveda*, the *Yajurveda* and the *Sāmaveda*, Vedic ceremony called *cāturhotra*, names of sacrifices like the Jyotiṣṭoma, the Mantras from *Ṛgveda* etc. (followed by *svāhā*), *dakṣiṇā* (gifts to Brāhmaṇas at the end of sacrifice), *vratas* (special observances), the specific order and special invocation of deities, *kalpa* (procedure of performing sacrificial acts), *saṅkalpa* (the formal statement of undertaking the sacrifice etc.) and the technique of performing sacrifice, movements such as Viṣṇukrama at the end of sacrifice, contemplations of deities, expiatory ceremony for mistakes of omission and commission, and offering everything to God as his own.

27-28. In this way, I who collected materials for sacrifice, from the limbs of the Puruṣa, worshipped the great God, a personification of Yajña, by performing sacrifice to propitiate him. Then your brothers, these nine progenitors of subjects (*prajāpatis*) worshipped, with perfect concentration of mind, the Puruṣa, (though himself unmanifested, but) manifested as Indra etc.

29. Then Manus and other sages, manes (*Pitṛs*), gods, demons, and men, in their own times, propitiated the Omnipresent God, by performing sacrifices.

30. This universe is placed, i.e. rested on the glorious Nārāyaṇa who, though attributeless, assumes by his *Māyā* qualities at the beginning of the creation.

31. Under his direction, I create (the universe); Hara or Śiva who is under his power, dissolves it, and he, in the form of Puruṣa i.e. Viṣṇu, protects it by means of his *Māyā*.

32. Oh child ! In this way, I have narrated to you whatever you have asked me. In creation, which is of a causal nature (or which is manifest and unmanifest) there is nothing wherein he does not exist.

33. As I have meditated upon the lord with intensely devoted heart, my speech is never observed to be untrue, nor my mind goes to paths other than the truth, nor my sense organs leave the proper path (go to the path of untruth).

34. Though I am regarded as Veda incarnate (full of Vedic knowledge), and full of penance (*tapas*), and I am greatly respected as the chief of Prajāpatis, and though follow-

ing *yogic* practice, I am perfect in meditation, I have not understood from whom I am born.

35. I bow to his feet which destroy the *saṁsāra* of those who resort to them (feet)—the feet which bring happiness and are very auspicious. He has not thoroughly comprehended the power or capacity of his own Māyā, just as the sky does not know its end. How can others comprehend?

36. Neither I, nor you, nor God Śiva or Vāmadeva could understand his real nature. How can other celestial beings know it? We, whose intellects are stupefied by his Māyā, think that we comprehend the universe created (by Māyā) according to our capacity of knowledge.

37. I bow to the glorious lord whose incarnations and deeds we and others sing, but we do not know his essential or real nature.

38.* This is the first Puruṣa, the unborn, who in every *Kalpa* creates himself with himself as the substratum, and the instrument (lit. he creates *ātman* within the receptacle of himself through himself) and protects it and destroys it.

39.** His real nature is absolute, real knowledge which is pure (unrelated to *viṣaya* or object), underlying the interior of all, accurate (and hence above doubt), changeless and attributeless. Being the Truth, it is perfect, full, beginningless and endless (with no changes like birth, death, increase, decrease etc.), eternal and alone (without a second).

40. Oh sage! Sages realize him, when their minds, senses and reason become serene and pure. But the Truth disappears from their sight when it is attacked by the reasoning of non-believers.

41-43. Puruṣa (the inspirer of Prakṛti, described as 'thousand-headed etc. in the *Puruṣa Sūkta*) is the first incarnation of the Supreme Spirit.

* According to VJ., it is this same Puruṣa who is *ātman*, i.e. Nārāyaṇa, the first of all and has no birth like other beings. According to his own will, he incarnates as *Matsya*, *Kūrma* from age to age. He protects gods and men devoted to him on his own support and he destroys the *daityas*.

** VJ. explains : The knowledge is pure (defectless), absolute (not depending upon others), within all and facing all, well-established, i.e. above doubts, eternally blissful, perfect from the point of space, time and attributes, beginningless and endless, free from *sattva* and other qualities, eternal (hence devoid of change) and non-dual.

*Time, nature, (*Prakṛti's* form) of causal relation, the mind (*mahat*), self-sense (*ahaṁkāra*), attributes, the body, five gross elements, movables and immovables, Myself, Śiva, Viṣṇu, the progenitors (*Prajāpatis*) like Dakṣa and others, yourself and others, the rulers of the heaven (*Svarloka*), and the protectors of the world of birds, Garuḍa and others, the rulers of the human world and those of the subterranean regions, Rulers of demigods like Gandharvas, Vidyādharas, Cāraṇas and those of Yakṣas, Rākṣasas and Uragas (reptiles) and Nāgas, the leaders of Sages, Manes (*Pitṛs*), Daityas, Siddhas and Dānavas and others, who rule over ghosts, Piśācas, Kūṣmāṇḍas, acquatic animals, beasts and birds.

44. In this world whatever is endowed with great authority (or six powers of *Bhagavān*), energy, mental power and capacity of senses, dexterity and strength, endurance, personal charm, modesty, prosperity, intellectual faculty, fascinating colour (or complexion), whether with form or without form, (all are nothing but God, the ultimate reality).[544]

45. Oh sage! Give ear unto my narration of the blessed incarnations of the Great Puruṣa (especially of) those which are regarded as his chief incarnation-sports (*līlāvatāras*). As I narrate to you these in a series, let these fascinating accounts which are like nectar and which remove the defects of (i.e. sins committed by) ears, be drunk by you.

---

*ŚR. says that though the list of *avatāras* is indiscriminately arranged, it can be thus classified : (1) From time to mind (mahat) etc. are the effects (ii) Brahmā and others are the *guṇāvatāras* and (iii) Dakṣa and others are *Vibhūtis*.

544. Cf. BG. (*Bhagavad-Gītā*) X. 41.

CHAPTER SEVEN

(*Some Līlāvatāras and their work**)

Brahmā said :

1.** When the Infinite God assumed the Boar-form which was completely composed of sacrifices (*yajñas*), he determined to lift up the earth (which was sinking in the ocean). He, like Indra breaking down the mountains, tore down by his tusk the first demon (*daitya Hiraṇyākṣa*) who came upon him at the bottom of the sea.

2. Then he was born as a son of Ruci and Ākūti (and was) named Suyajña. He procreated from Dakṣiṇā, gods called Suyama. As he removed the troubles of the three worlds, he was called Hari (the remover) by (his maternal grandfather) Svāyambhuva Manu.

3.*** Oh Brāhmaṇa ! And, along with nine sisters, he was born in the family of Prajāpati Kardama from him and (his wife) Devahūti. He explained to his mother the knowledge of *Ātman* (*Brahman*) whereby she, in this very birth, washed off her impurities caused by the mud of association with *Guṇas* and reached liberation—the goal preached by Kapila or Sāṁkhya Philosophy.

4. To Atri who solicited an offspring (son), the glorious lord, being pleased, said, "I have offered myself (as a son) to you" and hence he was called *Datta* (one who is given). It is by the dust of his lotus-like feet that Yadus, Haihayas and others got their bodies (themselves) purified and attained excellence in Yoga, leading to prosperity here and hereafter.[545]

5. In the beginning (of the creation) when I performed penance with a desire to create various worlds and beings, He incarnated as the four sages whose names begin with *Sana*

---

* Vide Supra—Skandha 1.3.6-26 1** Vide infra III. chs 13-19.

***Infra III. chs. 24-33.

545. *ubhayīm*—Leading to enjoyments in this world and liberation hereafter.

VB. explains that the two-fold yogic accomplishment is (1) gradual liberation by possessing *Siddhis* (supernatural powers) like *Aṇimā* (power of atomization) etc. and (2) instantaneous liberation.

VB. derives Atri as "sonless" or "one who desires three sons."

(*Sanatkumāra, Sanaka, Sanandana, Sanātana*), by my offering of my penance. He accurately explained the real nature of *ātman* or *Brahma* which was lost in the deluge of the previous Kalpa. Sages instantaneously realized the soul (*Ātman*) as soon as it (his explanation of the nature of the soul) was heard by them.

6. From Dharma and Mūrtī the daughter of Dakṣa, he incarnated as Nārāyaṇa and Nara. He was distinguished for his penance. The celestial damsels, the army of *Kāma*, the god of Love, having seen Ūrvaśī and other lovelier beauties created by him, were unable to disturb his austerities.

7. The great gods verily burn down *Kāma*, the god of Love, by their angry looks. But they cannot burn down the unbearable anger which consumes them. Such anger is afraid of even entering his pure heart. How can *Kāma* dare to enter his mind again ?

8. The young Dhruva wounded by the arrow-like words uttered by his step-mother in the presence of (his father) King Uttānapāda, took to forest, for performing penance, even as a child. He, who was gracious unto him who praised him, gave an immovable place (*dhruva sthāna*) to him—a situation which is praised by celestial sages who stay above and below him. [ŚR. explains that 'sages in heaven' implies the Great Bear or Bhṛgu and other sages].[546]

9. He, on being praised, saved king Vena who had gone astray and whose might and fortunes were destroyed by the thunderlike curses of Brāhmaṇas and who was falling in the hell. He became his son. In this incarnation he milked the earth of all kinds of wealth.[547]

10. He was born from king Nābhi and Sudevī (another name—Merudevī). He visualised Brahman everywhere and was unperturbed in self-realization with his mind and senses serene and controlled. Being free from attachment, he practised Yoga of undisturbed meditation (and so he appeared as inanimate object)--a state called by sages as the state of a *paramahaṁsa*.

11. That glorious lord incarnated in my sacrifice as Hayagrīva (horse-necked God), of complexion like gold. He is the *Yajña Puruṣa* (presiding deity of all sacrifices). He is the

546. For details vide infra IV. Chs. 8 and 9.

547. ,, ,, ,, infra IV. Chs. 15-23.

main object of worship in the Vedas (or Veda incarnate), the sacrifice incarnate (or for whose grace sacrifices are performed) and who is the soul of all the deities. From the breath of his nostrils beautiful words (i.e. Vedic hymns) came forth.

12. At the end of a Yuga, he was found by Vaivasvata Manu as a Fish who was the support of the earth (or who held the earth which was like a boat), and hence a refuge of all kinds of living beings. He collected the Vedas which fell down from my mouth in the waters, and joyfully sported in the terrible waters (of the deluge).

13. The first divinity in the form of Tortoise supported on his back, the mount Mandara which was the churning-rod, when the Gods and Demons (*daityas*) churned Kṣīrasāgara (the sea of milk). The movements of the mountain while churning were like scratching to him, in consequence of which he enjoyed a pleasant nap.[548]

14. He who removes the great terror of Gods[549], assumed the form of a Man-Lion of terrific appearance with rolling eyebrows and gnashing tusks. He seized and placed on his lap and tore down, in a moment, with his claws, the king of Daityas (Hiraṇyakaśipu) who with rage attacked him with a mace.[550]

15. The king o elephants which became distressed by his leg being caught by an extremely powerful crocodile, in a lake, held out a lotus in its trunk (to offer to the Lord), appealed to him thus : "Oh Primeval Man (the cause of the universe), the lord of all the worlds and beings, one of holy fame, whose name is very auspicious to the ears".

16. Hari of incomprehensible nature, hearing the appeal, took his weapon, viz. the disc *Sudarśana*, mounted on the shoulder of Garuḍa (the lord of birds), cut asunder the jaw of the crocodile by the disc, and holding the elephant by his trunk dragged him out, by his grace.[551]

17. Although the youngest born son of Aditi, he (Viṣṇu) was the eldest (superior to them) in virtues and lord of Sacri-

548. v.l. *nidrekṣaṇo*—whose eyes were half-closed with drowsiness.

549. *traiviṣṭa*—whose laughter strikes terror in the hearts of gods.

550. For details vide infra VII. Chs 8 and 9.

551. For details vide infra VIII. Chs 2-4.

fices. He covered the three worlds in his (three) strides, and in the form of Vāmana (a dwarf), he took over the earth under the pretext of requesting a land three feet in measure (because) kings who are going by the path of righteousness, are not to be removed except (under the pretext of) begging.

18. Bali, who sprinkled his head with the pure water of washing the feet of Vāmana, had no aspiration for sovereignty over gods. Oh beloved Nārada ! He did not desire to do anything else but to fulfil his promise to the Lord and he offered himself by his head to Hari.[552]

19. Oh Nārada ! The Lord, being pleased with your intense devotion, expounded to you the complete details of (*bhakti*) yoga and Bhāgavata which is the means to the knowledge (of *ātman*) which is like a lamp (light) to the truth about soul, which devotees who take refuge to Vāsudeva understand with ease.

20. At the time of the changes of Manvantaras (period of Manu) for maintaining the continuity of Manu's race, he maintains his unchallenged rule in ten quarters like the unobstructed Sudarśana Cakra. He brings discipline among wicked kings and by his deeds his enchanting fame reaches Satya-loka which is above the three worlds.

21. And the venerable Lord incarnated as Dhanvantari who is glory itself. By means of uttering his name (i.e. by the incantation of his *nāma-mantra—Oṁ Śrī Dhanvantaraye namaḥ* —he immediately cures diseases of persons afflicted with many ailments. He, who blesses (his devotees) with immortality, recovered his share in sacrifices which was denied to him (by Daityas). Having come down in this world, he taught it the science of medicine (*Āyurveda*—the Science of life).

22.* The great-souled one of terrific valour (Paraśurāma) twentyone times massacred with his axe of long sharp edge, the Kṣatriya-class which was like a thorn unto the world, and the destruction of which was ordained by fate and which (as if) being desirous of suffering pain in the hell, had left the Vedic way (of life), and hated Brāhmaṇas.

---

552. For details vide infra VIII. Chs. 18-23.

* Vide infra IX. Chs. 15 & 16.

23. The Lord of Māyā who is favourably disposed to us, incarnated in the race of Ikṣvākus along with his parts (*aṁśas* like Bharata etc.). Abiding by his father's order, he, along with his wife and younger brother, entered (stayed) in the forest where the ten-headed (Rāvaṇa) opposing him came to grief (met his death).

24. To him, who like Śiva, wanted to burn down the city of the enemy, the sea whose limbs of the body were trembling with fear, immediately gave passage (to cross it) when Rāma, by his fiery eyes reddened with rage, exploded on account of his distant sweet-heart, scorched the entire world of acquatic animals like crocodiles, serpents etc.*

25. While prominently moving between the two armies (his and Rāvaṇa's), he (Rāma) will[553] quickly end the life and the boastful laughter of Rāvaṇa[554], the abductor of his wife, and who governed various nations in all directions which were resplendent as the tusks of Indra's elephant (Airāvata) which were broken (and were stuck in Rāvaṇa's chest, when he dashed against his chest).**

26. In order to remove the distress of the earth which was pounded by the armies of Daityas, he, of white and black hair[555], will be born (as Balarāma and Kṛṣṇa) by his own

---

* Vide infra IX. Chs 10 & 11.

553. The epic-writer presumes that this dialogue between Brahmadeva and Nārada took place before the incarnation of Rāma, hence the use of future tense.

554. ŚR. gives the v.l. *kakubjuṣaūḍhahāsam*—It means : the boastful laugh of Rāvaṇa, who ruled over various countries in various directions which appeared brilliant with the pieces of tusks of Indra's elephant, which had been scattered in all directions, when Indra's elephant dashed against Rāvaṇa's chest. Rāvaṇa, boastfully laughed and remarked whether the tusks so scattered have imitated his (white) glory of the conquest of directions.

** For details vide infra III. Chs 2 & 3 and Skandhas X & XI.

555. That God Viṣṇu sent His two hairs down to the earth as the incarnation of Kṛṣṇa and Balarāma is repeated in the M. Bh. I. 196. 32-33, and VP. (*Viṣṇu Purāṇa*) 5.1.59.

ŚR. explains that the white hair of the lord is not due to his old age as he is immutable. They show his personal charm only. Quoting M. Bh. (given above), he states that the white hair was born as Balarāma and

aṁśa (part or portion). He whose ways are incomprehensible to men, will perform deeds which will establish his greatness, i.e. supreme nature.

27. That as a child he sucked away the life of Pūtanā (Ulūkikā), and as a child of three months he upturned (and pounded to pieces) the cart (Śakaṭāsura) by his kick, and that while crawling on his knees between two Arjuna trees which were scraping the skies, he uprooted them— this would not have been possible on any other presumption (except that the child was the Almighty).

28. In Gokula, He will bring back to life the cattle of the Vraja and their cowherds who have drunk water mixed with poison, by showering gracious looks at them. He will sport in the river Yamunā for its purification and will drive out the serpent whose tongue always rolls about on account of the power of fierce poison.

29. It must be a miraculous deed, indeed, when in the forest of Muñja grass (on the night of Kāliyādamana) the summer-dry forest caught fire on all sides by forest-conflagration at night. He, of incomprehensible power will, along with Balarāma, save the whole Vraja which remained awake[556] expecting total annihilation, by calling upon them all to shut their eyes.

30. Whatever length of rope or material of binding him will be taken by his mother, it will not be sufficient to bind Him. Yaśodā, the cowherdess, would be astounded to see fourteen worlds in his yawning mouth and (thus) awakened to or made aware of his greatness.

---

the dark hair as Kṛṣṇa. These symbolic hair indicate the fair and dark complexions of the two brothers. The hair do not undervalue this incarnation as Kṛṣṇa is the perfect incarnation *Kṛṣṇastu Bhagavān svayam* BH.P. 1.3.28. Viṣṇu wanted to show that the task of removing the distress of the earth by destroying the demonic forces is as easy as could be done by his hair.

VJ. explains that hari was born by his *aṁśa* called *Sita-Kṛṣṇa-Keśa* (white-black-hair). In *Nṛsiṁha Purāṇa* these are stated to be the two powers of the Lord (VD.)

556. *niḥśayāna* : VR. explains that Vraja was fast asleep at night and they awoke after their rescue. This is not supported by Bh.p. X.19.7-12, where the cowherds are stated to have appealed to Kṛṣṇa for saving them from the fire.

31. He will rescue Nanda from the fear of Varuṇa's noose. He will bring back the cowherds which were concealed in caves by Vyomāsura, the son of Maya. He will take to his world, viz. Vaikuṇṭha, the whole of Gokula, which spends the day in their daily work and which sleeps at night through utter exhaustion, (thus can spare no time for penance etc.).

32. When the cowherds will obstruct the sacrifice (dedicated to Indra) and when in order to drown the whole of Vraja, God Indra will pour down (torrential) rains, he, out of grace, with a desire to save the cattle, will sportively hold mount Govardhana for seven days, on his single hand, without any fatigue, as if it were some mushroom—even though he was a child of seven.

33. While playing in the forest at night which was bright on account of the rays of the moon, and while he is about to start the *Rāsa* dance, he will cut off the head of Śaṅkhacūḍa, the servant of Kubera who wanted to carry away the young damsel of Vraja in whom passion of love for Kṛṣṇa was aroused by songs with long drawn out musical notes, expressing sweet words.

34-35. And other evil persons such as Pralamba, Khara Dhenuka, Dardura, Keśi, Ariṣṭa, the *mallas* (athletes) like Cāṇūra, the elephant Kuvalayāpīḍa, Kaṁsa, Kālayavana, Narakāsura and Pauṇḍraka (a pretender of Vāsudeva) and others of whom Śālva, Kapi, Balvala, Dantavaktra and the Daityas in the form of seven bulls (of Nagnajit), Śambarāsura, Vidūratha, Rukmi and those kings who boastfully take up bows on the battlefield such as Kāmboja, Matsya, Kuru, Kaikaya, Sṛñjaya and others, would be killed by Hari in the form and names of Balarāma, Arjuna and Bhīma, and will go to his holy abode (Vaikuṇṭha), which is beyond the sight of men.

36. Considering that the Veda produced by him cannot be studied completely (from the beginning to the end) by men who, in course of time, will become of limited intellectual capacity, and of short span of life, he will take birth from Satyavatī, and will divide the tree in the form of Veda into different branches, in every age (yuga).

37. Seeing that asuras (enemies of gods) who follow the path of Veda, will harass the world, travelling in cities moving

with invisible velocity constructed by Māyā, he will assume the disguise of heretics, deluding the mind and attracting the hearts of asuras, he will extensively explain to them heretic doctrines.

38. At the end of the *yuga*, the Lord will incarnate and punish Kali when there will be no discussion about the deeds of Hari in the houses of the good ones, and when persons of the Brāhmaṇa, Kṣatriya and Vaiśya classes will be heretics, and Śūdras will be kings, and the words 'Svāhā', 'Svadhā' and 'Vaṣaṭ' will not be uttered at all (when Vedic rituals will not be performed).

39. At the beginning of creation, *Tapas* (penance), myself, sages and nine Prajāpatis; at the time of maintenance (of the universe), Dharma, sacrifice, Manu, gods and kings; at the time of destruction *adharma* (non-righteousness), Śiva, serpents characterised by wrath and vengeance and powerful asuras—these are the forms assumed by God of infinite powers, by his Māyā.

40*. Can any wise or learned man who might have calculated all the particles of dust in the world, count the glorious or heroic deeds of Viṣṇu who stabilised with his support, the terribly tottering Satyaloka, on account of the irresistible velocity (while raising his leg in his Trivikrama incarnation) which shook the universe to its outermost envelop of *Pradhāna* where there is equilibrium of the *guṇas* (sattva, rajas, and tamas.)

41. Neither I nor these sages (like Marīci etc.) and your elder brothers (like Sanatkumāra etc.) know the extent of the power and the greatness of the Māyā of the Supreme Man. How can other people do? The first god Śeṣa, of one thousand mouths (and two thousand tongues) has not yet reached the ends of his excellent qualities of which he has been singing (from times immemorial).

42. Only those can go beyond and understand the real nature of God's *māyā*—power which is very difficult to cross, if the infinite Lord is gracious unto them, and these devotees, with all their heart and soul, sincerely resort to his feet. Such

* The first two lines : Who can recount the great achievements of the wise Viṣṇu who covered in his strides the earth and heavens (Cf. ṚV. 1.154.1).

persons are free from the idea or notion of "I and mine" (even in respect of their bodies), which are the eatables or food of dogs and jackals.

(Many persons, despite the absence of inner knowledge, know Māyā through Hari's grace. For example).

43. Oh child, (through his grace) I know (the nature etc. of) the *Yoga-māyā* of the Supreme Lord. So do you (Sanaka, Sanandana etc.), God Śiva and Prahlāda, the chief of the Daityas, Svāyambhuva Manu and his wife Śatarūpā and their children, viz., Priyavrata, Uttānapāda and three daughters, Prācīnabarhis,[557] Ṛbhu,[558] and Dhruva.

44. Ikṣvāku,[559] Aila,[560] Mucukunda,[561] Videha (king Janaka), Gādhi,[562] Raghu,[563] Ambarīṣa,[564] Sagara,[565] Gaya,[566]

---

557. Prācīnabarhis—Son of Harivardhana and Dhiṣaṇā: a Prajāpati : married Sāmudrī (Savarṇā); had ten sons named Prācetasas. He knew the power of Viṣṇu's Yoga—PI.2.438.

558. Ṛbhu—A son of Brahmā : a Siddha who knows Hari; a resident of Tapoloka; initiated *nidāgha* in the mysteries of *advaita*—PI.1.268.

559. Ikṣvāku—Son of Vaivasvata Manu; founder of Solar race of kings; reigned at Ayodhyā. Max Müller thinks this to be the name of a people in the ṚV.—DHM.123.

560. Aila—Surname of Purūravas; got six sons from Ūrvaśī—PI. 1.282.

561. Mucukunda—Son of Māndhātṛ; helped gods against Asuras and got a boon of long uninterrupted sleep. Kālayavana who was lured into his cave by Kṛṣṇa, woke the sleeper who burnt him down by his fiery glance. Kṛṣṇa gave Mucukunda the power to go anywhere for enjoyment, but he went to Gandhamādana for penance. DHM. 210.

562. Gādhi—A king of the Kuśika race and father of Viśvāmitra —DHM. 103.

563. Raghu—a king of the Solar race; reigned at Ayodhyā; a famous ancestor of Dāśarathi Rāma—DHM. 252.

564. Ambarīṣa—The son of Nābhāga; a devotee of Hari; The curse of Durvāsas proved ineffective; though Lord of seven continents, he devoted himself to the service of Hari and knew the power of his yoga—PI. 1.88-89.

565. Sagara—a king of Ayodhyā of the Solar race; the horse let loose by him for *Aśvamedha* was carried off to Pātāla; his sixty thousand sons dug their way to Pātāla where they found the horse grazing near the sage Kapila who was engaged in meditation; thinking him to be the thief, they disturbed his meditation and were reduced to ashes by his fiery glance; he was noted for his generosity and the chasm dug by his sons and filled by the waters of the Ganges is called Sāgara (sea) after him.—DHM. 271-72.

566. Gaya—A sage who knew the power of Viṣṇu's yoga; PI. 1,514.

Yayāti[567] and others; Māndhātṛ,[568] Alarka,[569] Śatadhanvan,[570] Anu,[571] Rantideva,[572] Devavrata (Bhīṣma), Bali, Amūrtaraya,[573] and Dilīpa;[574]

45. Saubhari,[575] Uttaṅka,[576] Śibi,[577] Devala,[578] Pippalāda,[579] great men Sārasvata,[580] Uddhava, Parāśara,

---

567. Yayāti—the fifth king of the Lunar Race, Son of Nahuṣa; married Devayānī and Śarmiṣṭhā; from the former was born Yadu, the founder of the Yādava clan, and from the latter Puru; the founder of the Paurava race. He became prematurely old by Śukra's curse; he borrowed the youth from his son Puru, but later repenting, returned it to Puru and retired to forest for penance—DHM. 376-77.

568. Māndhātṛ—A king, son of Yuvanāśva, of the Ikṣvāku race; father of Mucukunda, Ambarīṣa and Purukutsa (sons) and fifty daughters. He gave them all to the sage Saubhari. He was killed while fighting with Lavaṇāsura—BPK. 244.

569. Alarka—A pupil of Dattātreya; a sage who realised the force of Hari's *māyā*.—PI. 1.115

570. Śatadhanvan.—A royal sage devoted to Viṣṇu—BPK 306.

571. Anu—A son of Svāyambhuva Manu; knew the power of the yoga of Hari—PI. 1-56.

572. Rantideva—A pious and benevolent king of the Lunar race; sixth in descent from Bharata; he was enormously rich, very religious, charitable and profuse in his sacrifices—DHM. 263.

573. Amūrtaraya—A sage who had transcended the force of *māyā*—PI. 1-85.

574. Dilīpa—Son of Aṁśumat and father of Bhagīratha; ancestor of Rāma; by serving the Nandinī cow at the cost of his life, he was freed from the curse of Surabhi and a son, Raghu, was born to him—DHM. 92.

575. Saubhari—A devout sage; married 50 daughters of king Māndhātṛ and had 150 sons; finding the vanity of *saṁsāra* he retired with his wives to the forest for penance—DHM. 289-90.

576. Uttaṅka—A Brahmarṣi residing on the Meru slope; at his request king Bṛhadaśva of Ikṣvāku line vanquished the demon Dhundhu—PI. 1.215.

577. Śibi—A king famous for the offering of his own body to a hawk to save the life of a dove which had come to his refuge—ASD. 918.

578. Devala—A sage who visited Parīkṣit at the time of the latter's fast unto death.

579. Pippalāda—a pupil of Devadarśa; the sage who communicated the *Aṅgāra-vrata to* Yudhiṣṭhira; came to see Parīkṣit practising *prāyopaveśa*; knew the *yoga*-power of Viṣṇu. PI. 2.333.

580. Sārasvata—a sage represented to be the son of the river Sarasvatī; he protected the Vedas during a great famine. He taught the Vedas to sixty thousand Brahmins who approached him for instruction—DHM. 283-84.

Bhūriṣeṇa;[581] and many others viz. Vibhīṣaṇa, Hanūmān, Śuka, Arjuna, Ārṣṭiṣeṇa,[582] Vidura, Śrutadeva and others;

46. Verily they comprehend and cross over the *māyā* of God. And women, Śūdras, Hūṇas, Śabaras and even sinful souls (*jīvas*) like non-human beings, if they have got the training with regard to the virtuous character of the devotees of Hari of wonderful strides (in covering each world in a step as Trivikrama), can understand and go beyond the *māyā*. What to say about those (i.e. Brāhmaṇas and others eligible to study the Vedas) who can concentrate their minds on the form of the Lord (described) in the Vedas[583]?

47-48. That indeed is the essential form (nature) of the glorious Supreme Man which the learned ones call Brahman, which is eternally blissful and untouched by sorrow. It is eternal, serene, free from fear, of the nature of pure knowledge, untouched by impurities, *sama* (i.e. one without a second), beyond the pale of *sat* and *asat* (i.e. not related to the objects of senses and non-senses), which is the real principle of the Supreme Soul, beyond the reach of the words, i.e. the *Vedas*, wherein causative circumstances produce no fruit, and in whose presence *māyā* comes back (vanishes as if) blushed. Recluses, having concentrated their minds on him, give up their tools (means) of destroying their idea of difference, just as Indra, the god of rains, would ignore a spade for digging a well[584] (i.e. Indra himself being a god of rains, has no need of a spade for digging a well. Similarly those who visualise the Brahman in medita-

---

581. Bhūriṣeṇa—A sage who knew the Yoga power of Hari; son of Brahmasāvarni PI. 2.578.

582. Ārṣṭiṣeṇa—A chief Gandharva who sings Rāma's glory in Kimpuruṣa; came to see Parīkṣit practising *prāyopaveśa*; knew the Yoga-power of Hari.

583. *Śruta-dhāraṇaḥ* (1) Who can contemplate on the described object (Hari)—VR.
(2) Men who can immediately concentrate upon the name and form learnt from the preceptor—VC.
(3) Those who can concentrate their minds upon the reality of the Soul as heard from the spiritual preceptor.
—SD.

584. *svarāḍ...Indraḥ*—ŚR.'s alternative explanation :
Just as a poverty-stricken person, after becoming a rich man, does not care for the spade (with which he formerly earned his livelihood).

tion, automatically rise above the notion of difference, and have no need to resort to other means to wipe out that notion).

49. He is the all-pervading lord who is a dispenser of all blessings on men. It is from him that the results of good actions which are done with the natural qualifications or duties (like *śama, dama*) of Brāhmaṇas and others accrue. (Or, from him comes forth the whole world—the effect produced by transformations which are the natural and specific characteristics of *mahat* and other principles, i.e. he is the dispenser of heaven etc). When the constituents of the body are disintegrated, the body is shattered, but not the internal element the ether. Similarly individual soul in the body is also not destroyed, for he has no birth nor death.

50. In this way, oh child, the glorious lord, the creator has been described to you in brief. Whatever is *Sat* or *Asat* (i.e. cause and effect or the manifest and the unmanifest) is not something different from Hari (everything proceeds from Hari)

51. This Bhāgavata which is narrated to me by the lord is only an epitome of the powers and glorious deeds of the lord. You extol them in details (to others).

52. After determining in your mind to make men devoted to the glorious Lord Hari who is the *antaryāmin*, (soul residing in all) and the support of all, describe Hari and his glories (with special emphasis on Hari's sports).

53. The mind (Soul) of the person who describes the *māyā* of the Almighty or who gives his approbation to this or who always devoutly listens to this, is not bewildered by the *māyā*.

CHAPTER EIGHT

(Queries regarding the relation between the body, Soul and God, etc.)

The king said :

1-2. Oh Brahman ! Nārada of godly vision[585] (or who makes his followers to visualise God) who was directed

585. *Deva-darśana*—One who shows the Supreme Soul (to his followers).

by Brahmadeva, to describe in detail the qualities of the Lord, who is free from Sattva and other attributes, expounded to various persons, the real nature of God. Oh prominent one among the knowers of Veda. I would like to know (what is the truth). The episodes of Hari of miraculous powers, are very auspicious to people.

3. Expound to me (those discourses) in such a way that I shall, after fixing my unattached mind on Kṛṣṇa, the *antaryāmin* (the Soul within all), give up my body.

4. The lord enters the heart, within a short time, of those who always hear with faith his deeds and extol the same.

5. Kṛṣṇa who enters the lotus of his devotee's heart by way of the ear, cleanses all the sins, just as the season called Śarad (autumnal season) does unto waters (of rivers etc.).

6. A person whose sins are washed away and who becomes free from all troubles (resulting from love, hatred etc.), does not leave the feet of Kṛṣṇa, just as a traveller (who has returned home after a long sojourn) does not leave his home.

7.* Oh Brahman ! You know really whether it is causeless or with a cause like Karma that the soul, which is not constituted of elements, (still) comes to possess a body made up of elements. Please explain to me the truth about it.

8. He, (God) from whose navel sprouted forth the lotus which represented the configuration of the worlds, is described as possessing the same form and the same number of limbs as a human being, with the difference that He has limbs of separate and of his own dimensions. (If that be the case) what is the difference between the two (God and his miniature (man) ?

9. The unborn god Brahmā creates beings and controls them through his grace. It is due to his favour that Brahmā (though) born from the lotus (grown) out of his navel could get a glimpse of his form.[586]

---

* Whether it is due only to the will of God or any other cause like Karman, there happens at the beginning the possession of the body consisting of *dhātus* (elements), its material cause, the produce of the Prakṛti, in the case of the Soul which is essentially unrelated to *dhātus* like *Prakṛti*—VJ.

586. VJ. explains verses 8 and 9 : At the beginning, during the great deluge (Mahā-pralaya), when Nārāyaṇa wished to create the

10. In what place does the Supreme Man who dwells in the hearts of all,[587] who creates, protects and destroys the universe, and who is the Lord of *māyā*, stay when he lays aside[588] his *māyā* ?

11. We heard (from you) that the worlds with their protecting deities were created first from the limbs of the Man, and that with these worlds and their presiding deities, the limbs of his body are formed. Please explain this.

12. What is the duration of Kalpa (Brahma-kalpa) ? What is the extent of Vikalpa (*Manvādi-kalpa*) ? How is Time measured ? What is the significance of the past, present and the future ? What is the span of life of men, manes (*pitṛs*), gods etc. ?

13. What is the nature of Time which, though very long, appears to be very short ? What are the places where Karma leads to beings ? Of what nature are they, oh the best of Brāhmaṇas ?

14.* Please tell me about the individual Souls (lit. possessors of attributes) who wish to become gods etc. as a result of the modifications or changes in the attributes, like sattva, rajas etc. ? In what stage does the cumulative effect of good and bad actions take place ? By what combinations of actions

---

universe, he became the Supreme Man (Parama-puruṣa) and created the Cosmic Egg. He, along with the principles (which led to the creation of the universe) entered the watery portion of the Egg and lay on the bed of Śeṣa. From His navel sprang up the lotus containing fourteen worlds. He came to be called *Vairāja* within that Egg. *ayam puruṣa* (this Man) in verse 8 signifies this Cosmic Egg (*aṇḍakośa*) and is called *puruṣa* (man) due to God's presence in the *puruṣa* form. This Vairāja called Viṣṇu is different from the Egg. But it is due to his presence in the Egg, that the parts of the Egg are represented as his limbs.

587. v.l. *sarva-guṇāśrayaḥ*—VR : Possessing six excellent qualities fully. VJ. : The support of God Brahmā etc. representing *Guṇas* in the beginning of creation, Or, possessing all excellent qualities such as knowledge, bliss etc.

588. *ātma-māyām muktvā* VR. : transcending *prakṛti*; VJ. : Suspending the binding force of *prakṛti* under his control.

* Explain to me the place where the effect of Karma takes place. Through what agency (of gods etc.) and of what nature is it ? Tell us in detail the modifications taking place in attributes and individual Souls and the cause of their attaining the bodies of Gods etc.

and by what procedure of doing them is one qualified to get Godhood and such other status.

15. What is the origin of the earth, the nether-world (*pātāla*), directions, the sky, the planets, the constellations of stars, mountains, rivers, seas and islands ? What is the origin of the inhabitants thereof ?

16. What are the dimensions of the Cosmic Egg, separately from within and without ? What are the lives and deeds of the great in them ? Please tell me definite knowledge about the classes of society and the stages of life (*varṇa* and *āśrama*).

17. What are (the different) Yugas, and what is the extent of each Yuga (age) ? What is (the nature of) religion in each Yuga ? What are the most miraculous incarnations of Hari and his deeds ?

18. What is the course of duties common to men ? What are the special duties of guilds of workers and the royal sages ? What is the course of conduct to men, who have to live under emergency (*āpad-dharma*) ?

19. What is the number of *tattvas* or fundamental principles ? What is their characteristic ? What is their nature for distinguishing them from their effects ? What is the method of worshipping the Supreme Man ? And what is the method of practising Yoga consisting of eight stages ?

20. What is the way (like *arcir-mārga*) of the past masters of Yoga possessing eight miraculous powers ? How is the *liṅga-śarīra* (the subtle body) destroyed ? What is the nature of the Vedas (like Ṛgveda, Yajurveda etc.) Upavedas (like Āyurveda, Gandharva-Veda etc.), Dharma (course of conduct) for different classes of society, different stages of life etc., Itihāsa like Mahābhārata) and Purāṇas (18 Mahāpurāṇas and 18 Upapurāṇas) ?

21. What is the nature of the interim deluge or the creation, sustenance and destruction of all the beings ? What is the correct method of performing *Iṣṭa* (maintenance of sacrificial fire, penance, *vaiśvadeva* etc.) and *pūrta* (such as construction of temples, lakes etc.) and attaining the triad. viz., *dharma*, *artha* and *kāma* ?

22. How are the *jīvas* (individual souls) who fall from heaven etc., along with the balance of their karmas, born in

this world ? How did the heretic doctrine come into existence ? What is the nature of the so-called bondage and liberation of the Soul ? How does the Soul attain to his real essential nature ?

23. How does the self-dependent lord sport with the help of *māyā* ? How does the all-pervading lord, at the time of the deluge, cast off the *māyā* and remain aloof as a witness ?

24. Oh venerable great sage ? You should kindly explain to me who suppliantly approached you for knowledge, the reality about all these (and other points as well) in the serial order of inquiring.

25. Oh revered one ! You are the authority on these just like the great God Brahmā, born of the Supreme Spirit, for other people in this world (blindly) follow what was done by the forefathers of their forefathers.

26. Oh Brāhmaṇa! My life (vital airs) will not depart by fasting so long as I drink the nectar (in the form of the stories) of Acyuta, though they may pass away soon due to the wrath of Brāhmaṇa (i.e. the bite by Takṣaka due to the curse).

27. Brahmarāta (i.e. Śuka) was highly pleased, when in that assembly, Viṣṇurāta (i.e. Parīkṣit) respectfully requested him, to narrate the episodes of Hari, the Lord of the good (or god Brahmadeva etc.).

28. He expounded him the *purāṇa* called *Bhāgavata* which is equivalent to Veda, and which was narrated to god Brahmā by the Lord, at the advent of Brahma-kalpa.

29. Whatever Parīkṣit, the foremost in the Pāṇḍava race, asked, (Śuka) began to narrate in all, in the order of questions.

CHAPTER NINE

(*Śuka's discourse—Catuḥślokī Bhāgavata*)

Śrī Śuka said :

1* Oh king ! No relation is logically (correctly) possible between perceptible object (e.g. the body) and the Soul whose essential nature is knowledge (and hence different from that of the body), except through his own māyā, as (it is not possible) in the case of one who sees visions in a dream.

2. In association with māyā which assumes various forms, he appears to have many forms (viz. that of a child or youth or a god or a man etc.). Amusing himself in her qualities (like the body etc.), he (seeing thus conditioned) thinks (supposes) '(This is) mine, (This is) I.'

3** Only when he will enjoy himself in his own glory which is beyond Time and māyā (or Puruṣa and Prakṛti), and being free from delusion, he gives up both of them, and the false notion 'I and mine' and stands out in his full form unconcerned (with anything).

4. The Supreme Lord who was propitiated by sincere devotion (penance), revealed his own real form to *Brahmā*, spoke to him in order to enlighten him on the truth about Supreme Soul (as distinct from the *jīva*—individual Soul).

5. That first and foremost of gods, the supreme preceptor of the worlds (*Brahmā*) seated himself in his lotus and with a desire to create, began to look (consider) the procedure of creating the world. But he could not get the insight (the vision) into the faultless method of world-creation.

6. Once upon a time, while thinking over the methodology of world-creation the great god Brahmā heard twice a word of two syllables (*Tapa*) uttered near him from under the

* With VR., as usual, māyā is the prakṛti controlled by the Supreme Soul. With VJ. it is Hari's will which controls the prakṛti characterised by the attributes like sattva etc. God's will is fundamental. Nothing can take place without it.

**According to VR. it is in the stage of liberation (mukti) that the individual Soul (Jīva) becomes free from illusions, and realises his own innate nature and finds delight in the glorious nature of the lord which is beyond influence of Time and Prakṛti.

water. It consisted of the sixteenth (*ta-*) and twentyfirst (*pa*—) letters of the five classes of consonants. Oh king ! that word is the wealth of those who have renounced (material) wealth.

7. On hearing the word (*tapa*) and eager to see the speaker, he looked in all directions. Seeing nobody anywhere, there, he resumed his seat and coming to the conclusion (considering) that (penance) is for his good, he determined to perform penance, as if he was advised by some preceptor.

8. Brahmā whose insight (in grasping the significance of the uttered syllables) was correct, and who is the greatest of the performers of penance (sage of the sages), controlled his breath and mind, and restrained his both types (cognitive and conative) of sense-organs, and in undisturbed meditation, performed for a period of one thousand celestial years penance which threw light on (the procedure of creation etc. of) the worlds.

9. The Lord, who was (thus) propitiated by penance, showed to him (god Brahmā) his region, i.e. Vaikuṇṭha, where afflictions, delusion and fear do not exist, and which is eulogised by gods and men of abundant merits (or men who have realised the Self), and to which there is no higher place.

10. Where (i.e. in the Vaikuṇṭha) there is neither *rajas* and *tamas* nor *sattva* attribute which is mixed up with them. (There is only the pure *sattva* attribute). The Time has no power there. Nor does māyā exist there. What of others ! There attendants (devotees) of Hari are worshipped by gods and *asuras* (demons).

11. In complexion these attendants are like shining emeralds. They have eyes like a lotus of hundred petals, and have put on yellowish garments (*pītāmbaras*) They are excellent in personal charm, and of very soft delicate bodies. All of them have four arms and wear ornaments of gold, studded with brilliant precious stones. They are of extremely brilliant splendour. Their complexions are varied like the coral, the *lapis lazuli* and the lotus-stalk, and they wear shining earrings, crowns and garlands.

12. Just as the sky appears when the clouds therein are illumined by lightning, the Vaikuṇṭha region appears shining by the greatly beautiful and effulgent aerial cars of the great-souled ones surrounded by young women of lustrous complexion.

13. There the goddess of wealth incarnate pays respects to the feet of the highly praised Hari, in various ways, and with various forms of magnificence (or splendour) seating herself on a swing and singing the deeds of her beloved lord, herself being praised in songs by bees, the followers of the spring.

14. There he (Brahmadeva) saw the Lord of the goddess of wealth (Śrī), the Protector of His devotees, the presiding deity of sacrifices—the all-pervading Lord who is waited upon by his chief attendants, viz. Sunanda, Nanda, Prabala, Arhaṇa and others.

15. He saw God who was eager to bless his devotees (servants) whose looks were (like nectar) gladdening the heart of his devotees, whose face was beaming with gracious smiles and brilliant reddish eyes, who had four arms, and who wore crown and ear-ring, and had put on yellow-garment (*pitāmbara*) and had got a distinguishing mark called Śrīvatsa on his chest.

16. (He saw) God seated on an invaluable throne surrounded by the four (*Prakṛti*, *Puruṣa*, *Mahat* and *Ahaṁkāra*), the sixteen (mind, the ten cognitive and conative sense-organs and five elements) and five (i.e. *tanmātras*) [in all 25 tattvas or powers] as part of his nature. Supernatural powers which are temporary elsewhere (in yogins) were inherent in him. He was the Master as he was enjoying his own powers and bliss.

17. The creator of the Universe (God Brahmā) whose heart was overflowing with joy at his sight, which can be attained by the path of knowledge (followed by great recluses-*Paramahaṁsas*), whose hair stood erect (with rapture), and whose eyes were full of tears of intense love to him, bowed to his lotus-like feet.

18. The Lord, the beloved of all, was pleased with his dear (Brahmadeva) who loved him intensely, and was standing near him. He touched with his hand Brahmā who deserved his guidance (orders) in the creation of the worlds. Then he spoke to him with words brilliant by his gentle smile.

The venerable lord said :

19. Oh Brahman (in whom all the Vedas exist) I who am impossible to be pleased by hypocritical yogins, am delighted by your long penance performed with the desire of creating the universe.

20. Oh Brahman ! Prosperity to you (good betide you). I can confer any boon. Ask me whatever is desired by you. My vision is the culmination of all human efforts.

21. It is due to my desire (to show you) that you had a view of my region (Vaikuṇṭha). You have performed excellent penance in solitude, after hearing my utterance (containing the instruction to perform penance).

22. Oh sinless one ! When you were at a loss to know what to do, I guided you (to perform penance). As *Tapas* (penance) is my heart, and I am the Soul of *tapas* (penance) [I am *tapas* itself].

23. It is by penance that I create the universe. I eat it up (keep it within me) by penance. I maintain it by means of penance. My strength lies in austere penance which is difficult to perform.

Brahmā said :

24. Oh lord ! You are the ruler of all created beings. You, who dwell in the heart (lit. cave) of all beings, know by your unimpeded unlimited knowledge what one desires to do.

25. Oh Lord ! grant to me, a seeker, however, what I pray, so that I can know the subtle as well as the gross[589] forms of yours who are really formless.

26-27. Oh Mādhava (Lord of Lakṣmī)! Just as a spider weaves a web round itself, so you, of efficacious will-power, indulge of your own accord in your sports, by assuming with the help of your *māyā* various forms (such as Brahmā etc.) for creating, preserving and destroying the universe which is developed with various powers. Please develop (lit. put) in me the intelligence (necessary) to understand this.

28. I shall really carry out the instructions of the lord without any slackness or idleness on my part. It is through your grace that I, who desire to procreate the world, will not be subjected to the bondage of *karma*.

29. Oh lord ! (by your friendly action of touching me with hand etc.) I have been done (treated) by you like a friend.

589. According to VJ. *para* is the Vairāja Puruṣa (the Cosmic Man embracing fourteen worlds) and *apara* is the Cosmic Egg with its nine sheaths.

Still I shall stick to carry out your service of creating the worlds untiringly. May there be no pride in me of thinking myself to be unborn, while I am creating the world with all its differences.

The lord said :

30. Receive from me the knowledge (as detailed in the Śāstras) coupled with experience and along with its mystic doctrine (esoteric teaching), with all the accessories to it, as explained by me, though it is a topmost secret.

31. By my grace, may you have a thorough comprehension of the reality as to my dimensions, my real nature, my attributes and actions as actually they are.

32* In the beginning, before the creation, I alone was in existence. There was nothing else—neither the subtle nor the gross (creation) nor their cause Pradhāna or Prakṛti (the primordial nature)[590] [These were then completely absorbed in me—only I simply existed then]. After the creation of the universe what exists, is I. I am the universe. What remains after the Pralaya is myself.

33. That should be known as my māyā[591] on account of which there appears existence, despite the non-existence of the

---

* The four verses beginning from this are said to contain the essence of the Philosophy of the Bhāgavata Purāṇa and are hence known as *Catuḥślokī Bhāgavata.*

590. *sadasatparam*—Reality which is distinct from the sentient (spirit or *jīva*) and non-sentient (*jaḍa* matter)—VR.

JG. and VC. have given sermons on the basis of this verse.

591. According to VJ., *māyā* is chiefly the power of Viṣṇu (*mukhyato Viṣṇu-śaktirhi Māyā-śabdena bhaṇyate*). It is also applied to Jīva and Prakṛti. It is not an unreality like magic tricks (*indrajāla*). To briefly state VJ. : Whatever is recognised or known from the Vedas and other means of knowledge, (though of no use or value to God who has all his wishes fulfilled) and whatever is not contradictory (*bādhaka*) to God, such things, i.e. Jīvas and Prakṛti are to be regarded as the māyā of the Supreme Soul.

In a long commentary on this verse JG. explains his concept of *māyā*. Briefly stated : Māyā is that which appears outside Brahman (the ultimate reality), and ceases to appear with the realization of Brahman. Without the support of Brahman, it cannot manifest itself. It is associated with Brahman in two forms, viz., *Jīva-māyā* and *Guṇa-māyā*. The analogy of *ābhāsa* is the reflection of the solar light from outside

basic reality, as in the case of false appearance (of two moons even though the other moon. has no existence), and there appears the non-existence of the really existents, as in the case of the planet Rāhu (which is never perceived in spite of its existence in the planetary system)—the Soul is the object of such misapprehension.

34. Just as the great elements (the earth, water etc.) which may be said to have entered into created things, great or small, may (also) be said not to have entered into them (due to their pre-existence as the material cause of the universe), similarly, I am in the elements as well as the creation from the elements, and also not in them[592] (as I existed before them and created them all).

35. This much should be understood by him who desires to know the reality about the Soul (*ātman*), the existence of which everywhere and at all times is proved by logical concomitance and discontinuance [i.e. ātman exists at all times, everywhere, as the cause of the effected things, and being different from them in the causal state (*kāraṇāvasthā*), as being a witness, in the states of wakefulness, dreaming and sleep, and as detached or unconnected from everything in the state of *Samādhi* etc.].

36. Correctly follow this doctrine with perfect concentration. Your goodself will never be infatuated and become proud of being a creator in the different creations of the Kalpas.

Śrī Śuka said :

37. Having thus instructed Brahmā who occupies the

---

the solar orb. The solar light cannot exist unless it is supported by the Sun's orb, yet the solar light can have an independent function outside the orb. It may dazzle the eye and blind men to its real nature, or it may manifest itself in various colours. JG. interprets *Tamas* as "darkness" and not Rāhu. Though darkness cannot exist where there is light, it cannot itself be perceived without the light of the eyes. In short, the Prakṛti and its development are appearances brought into being outside the Brahman by *māyā*. But the movement of *māyā* is possible due to the essential power of God. Thus *māyā* and its appearances derive their essence from God and hence cannot affect in any way God or His essential power.

592. *na teṣvaham* : I am both outside and inside them but being unattached, I am not touched by their defects—VR.

highest place in all created beings, the unborn God Viṣṇu withdrew that visible form even while Brahmā was looking on.

38. (God Brahmā) who embodies all creation (by being its head), and who has folded his hands to Hari whose visible form has disappeared, created this universe as it was before (in the previous *Kalpa*).

39. Once Brahmā, the Lord of the created beings and the protector of righteousness, practised the prescribed *yamas* and *niyamas* for attaining the good of the creation which was as if his own objective as well.

40-41. Nārada who was the most beloved of his inheritors (sons), was devoted to his father, and rendered service to him. Oh king, the great sage, being a great devotee of the lord, desired to know from him the Māyā-power of Viṣṇu, the Lord of Māyā, and so pleased his father by his praiseworthy character, modesty and self-control.

42. Finding that his father, the grandfather of all the worlds, was pleased with him, the celestial sage (Nārada) respectfully asked him the very thing you enquire of me.

43. Brahmā, being pleased with him, expounded to him this Bhāgavata Purāṇa of ten characteristics[593], as it was revealed to him by the lord.

44. Nārada narrated it to Vyāsa of immeasurable brilliance, while he was meditating on the Supreme Brahman, on the bank of the Sarasvatī.

45. In recounting the same to you, I shall be satisfying your queries as to how all this world came to be produced from the *Virāṭ Puruṣa* and all other questions.

---

593. Vide Bh. P. II.10. 1-7.

CHAPTER TEN

(*The Ten Characteristics of the Bhāgavata Purāṇa*)

Śrī Śuka said :

1.* Here (in the Bhāgavata Purāṇa) the (constituent) topics detailed are : (1) Subtle creation (*sarga*), (2) gross creation (*visarga*), (3) law and order (ensured by God) (*sthāna*), (4) protection—welfare of all (*poṣaṇa*), (5) material lust from Karmas (*ūti*), (6) the period of Manu and history thereof (*manvantara*), (7) accounts of God's deeds (*īśānukathā*), (8) physical annihilation (*nirodha*), (9) liberation (*mukti*) and (10) the last resort of the universe, the ultimate Reality (āśraya).

2. For arriving at the accurate and real knowledge of the tenth characteristic (viz. the last resort of the universe or ultimate Reality) the great-souled persons describe the first nine topics by direct expression[594] (from the Vedas in eulogies etc.) and by way of purport (by episodes containing it).

3. Due to the disturbance in the equilibrium of attributes, the production of the five elements (*bhūtas*), the objects of senses, the sense-organs and the intelligence (i.e. *mahat*, *ahaṁkāra*) is called the subtle creation. The gross creation produced by the Virāṭ Puruṣa is called *Visarga*.

---

* The Sūta literature which, in the sacrificial milieu of the Brāhmaṇa period, became encyclopaedic, was classified under five topics which were later regarded as the characteristics of the compilations called the Purāṇas. Every Purāṇa thus consists of the following topics :

(1) Creation (sarga), (2) recreation after dissolution (*prati-sarga*), (3) Genealogy of Gods and sages (*Vaṁśa*), (4) History of dynasties (*vaṁśānucarita*), (5) Manu-periods of time (Manvantara). Purāṇas themselves, acknowledged these topics as forming their essential characteristics. Vide *Agni* P.1.14, *Garuḍa* P.1.2.27, *Kūrma* P.I, 1,12, *Matsya* P. 5.3.64, *Śiva* P.—*Vāyavīya Saṁhitā* 1.41, *Vāyu* P.—*Prakriyā Pāda* 4.10.11; *Viṣṇu* P. 3.6.25. Under the influence of Vaiṣṇava theologies, these five topics were elaborated into ten topics enumerated in the above verses and later Bh.P. 12.7.9-22 with a slight change in the nomenclature. As Baladeva Upādhyāya (*Purāṇa-Vimarśa* IV, pp. 125-139) shows there is not much difference between the contents of the five characteristics of Purāṇas in general and ten characteristics of the Bh. P.

594. *śrutenārthena*—VR. combines these words and explains 'as actually described in authoritative books or Vedas'.

4. *Sthiti* is the triumph of the Lord in the maintenance of (the divine) law and order (in everything), while the protection and welfare of all by his grace is *Poṣaṇa*. *Manvantara* consists of the account of the righteous path followed by Manu who observes his duty of protecting his subjects, while *ūti* is the desire for action (directed by) tendencies resulting from Karma.

5. *Īśānukathā* is the description of the incarnations of Hari, and stories of the lives of his devotees with detailed stories.

6. *Nirodha* is the withdrawal of the Jīva, along with all his powers and limitation in Hari when he enters his Yogic sleep. *Mokṣa* or liberation consists of abandoning the unreal form, and to stay in the essential nature of Brahman.

7. That from which creation and destruction are definitely known to emerge, is the resort which is called the Supreme Brahma, Supreme Soul, etc.

8.* He who regards organs of senses, such as eyes etc., as referring to himself is the seer or witness, the *ādhyātmika Jīva*. He is the same in the form of presiding deities of the sense-organs and is the *ādhidaivika Jīva*. He is the *ādhibhautika* (presiding over physical body) Jīva who is conditioned to see a distinction between the above two. (After the formation of the physical body, the two, viz. *ādhyātmika* and *ādhidaivika*, are separated.)

9. As we do not find (know) one in the absence of the other (i.e. if anyone of the three, viz. *ādhyātmika*, e.g. the eye and other organs, *ādhidaivika* (the presiding deity of the organ, e.g. the Sun or light), and the *ādhibhautika*, the physical sense organ, is absent, we cannot get any knowledge. These are thus

---

*VJ. : Viṣṇu is the man who directs the organs of senses pertaining to the body (*ādhyātmika*). He is present also in the presiding deities of the sense organ (such as the Sun, the deity of perception or seeing). He is present in physical objects of perception, e.g. the jar etc. and the determiner between the *ādhyātmika* and *ādhidaivika* (e.g. the eye and the light seen by it). [This Viṣṇu is the *āśraya* (shelter) and controller of Jīvas.]

According to SD. *ādhyātmika* is the set of cognitive and conative sense organs. *Ādhidaivika* is the group of presiding deities of the above organs. Physical body which is different from the above two is the *ādhibhautika Puruṣa*.

interdependent), he who knows all these three is the Soul who is not dependent on others, but is the support (shelter) of all.

10.* When this Virāṭ Puruṣa (Brahmā), bursting open the Cosmic Egg, came out and stood apart from the Brahmāṇḍa, he pondered over a place for himself. He himself being pure, created pure water (called *garbhodaka*).

11. On those waters created by Him, he lay for a period of a thousand years. Waters were created by the Man (*nara*) [and hence came to be called nārā] He is called Nārāyaṇa (as *nārā* or waters were his *ayana* 'place of abode').

12.* It is by His grace that Matter, Action, Time, Innate nature and individual Soul (Jīva) function. They cease to do so when he becomes indifferent to them.

13. Getting up from his yogic bed of meditation, he desired to be many. Through his Māyā power, he divided his golden power (lit. gold-semen) in three parts—*adhyātma adhidaiva* and *adhibhūta.*

14. Listen how the Lord differentiated one and the same energy (semen) of the (Cosmic) Man in three parts as *adhidaiva, adhyātma* and *adhibhūta.*

15. From the ether (*ākāśa*) within the body of the *Puruṣa* who was making movements, were produced the powers of the senses, the mind and the body, and from these was produced (the subtle power of *Prāṇa* called *Sūtra* the chief Prāṇa (vital Power) of all.[595]

16. All the organs of senses in living beings make movements when the chief Prāṇa is active. They stop their activities when he ceases to do so, like servants of a king following him.

---

* VJ : Having created principles (*tattvas*), the Puruṣa entered the Cosmic Egg along with them. Having broken it open, he manifested himself as the same Puruṣa. He wished to have place for sleeping on the bed of Śeṣa (another transformation of his Self). Being himself eternally pure, he created pure water suitable to be a material worthy of use in his worship.

* cf. supra II. 5.14 and 22.

595. VR. thinks that from the Prāṇa (vital energy) of god Brahmā, the Prāṇas of all beings were produced while VJ. states that it is from Hari who was active within the interior cavity of the Virāṭ Puruṣa (or Brahmā) that the powers of Hari were produced, and these were the real source of the chief vital energy (Prāṇa), the possessor of the Powers called—*sahas, ojas* and *bala.*

17. By the activities of Prāṇa, hunger and thirst were aroused in the Lord (Virāṭ Puruṣa), When He desired to eat and drink, the mouth (face) first became separate (was formed) as a distinct organ of the body.

18.* From the mouth, the palate became a separate member, and the tongue also was produced then. Then different kinds of tastes which are obtained (appreciated) by the tongue were produced.

19. From the mouth of this great Being who desired to speak, were created the Fire (God agni, the presiding deity), the organ of speech and the speech which is under the control of the two (viz. the organ of speech and the presiding deity). Certainly, his breath was controlled in water for a long time (which led to the creation of nose for breathing).

20. The two nostrils were formed, when the vital air began to move forcibly. When he (the Virāṭ Puruṣa) wished to have smell, the sense of smell was produced with Vāyu, the bearer of smell, as the presiding deity.

21. Being desirous of seeing himself in the darkness within the body of the *Virāṭ Puruṣa* a pair of eyes was created along with light (*tejas*) and the organ of seeing, and the power of seeing (the light, forms, colours).

22. When the Soul wished to hear the eulogies of the sages, two ears as well as the cardinal points (as presiding deities) and the auditory sense-organ were created. Hence the power of audition.

23. When he wished to feel softness, hardness, lightness, heaviness, warmth and coldness (of things), the sense of touch (*tvac*) was created On it grow the hairs (the sense-organ) and trees (the presiding deities). The vital air having obtained the quality of touch by means of the skin, covers it internally and externally.

24. Through his desire to do various activities, hands

---

* In this description of the members of the body of the Cosmic Man (*Virāṭ Puruṣa*), the group of four, viz. the place, (*adhiṣṭhāna*), the sense-organ, the object of the sense and the presiding deity, though not stated, are to be understood in these verses. For example, this verse indicates that the palate is the position or place, the tongue is the sense organ, different tastes are the objects of the sense, and Varuṇa is the presiding deity of this organ.

grew to him, i.e. he developed hands). In them, the power (to work) as sense, and Indra (as the presiding deity) were produced. The action of receiving depends on them both.

25. When he wished to go to a desired destination, two legs (feet) grew out (from his body). Along with them, Viṣṇu the sacrifice incarnate became the presiding deity. The collection of materials for sacrifice was made by men by the action of going [The organ of motion whereby men can go for collection of sacrificial material was produced].

26. When he wanted progeny, pleasure and heaven (or immortality by one's continuation of race through offspring), the place of generative organ[596], the organ of generation (alongwith Prajāpati as the presiding deity) appeared. Sexual pleasure depends on them both (the deity and the sense-organ).

27. When he wanted to discharge the impurities of the food etc. (eaten by him), the anus appeared along with the organ discharging excrement, and with Mitra as the presiding deity. On these two depends the function of discharging the the excrement.

28. When he desired to move out (completely) from one body to another, the outlet—the navel—was formed with *apāna* (as the sense organ) and *mṛtyu* (the goddess of death as the presiding deity) was formed. On these two depends the separation (departing) from the body.

29. To him who became desirous for the intake of food and drink, stomach, intestines and veins (blood vessels) appeared with rivers and seas (as presiding deities). The satisfaction and the nourishment (of body) depend on them both (the organs and the deities).

30. When he wished to meditate on the Māyā of the Soul (*ātman*), the heart was produced. Then the mind (as the inner sense organ), the Moon (as the deity) and the functions of thinking and desiring (were produced).[597]

---

596. *śiṣna* here stands for both male and female organs.

597. This is obviously based on the *Aitareya Upaniṣad* : *Khaṇḍas* 1 and 2. The mutual relations of the physical member of the sense organ, the organ of the sense, and the presiding deity as given in the Ait. Up. are tabulated below, which may be compared with the above description in the Bh.P.

31. The seven essential ingredients of the body[598] are the inner skin and the outer skin, flesh, blood, fat, marrow and bones which were created respectively from the earth, water, fire, prāṇa, ether, water and the air.

32. The organs of the senses have for their soul (i. e. are essentially related to) their objects (such as sound, touch etc.). *Guṇas* proceed from *ahaṁkāra* (ego). The mind consists of all *vikāras* (emotions, perturbations etc.). And Intelligence is characterised by the knowledge of the things as they are[599].

33. I have expounded to you the gross form of the Lord. It is covered from outside, with eight sheaths, of which the earth is the first.[600]

34.* Beyond this (gross—Virāṭ form of the Lord) is the subtlest, unmanifest, attributeless, (form) which has no beginning, middle or end (i. e. not subject to creation, subsistence and destruction). It is eternal and beyond the reach of words and mind.

No.	The member of the body the Physical Part.	Sense-organ.	Presiding Deity
1	Mouth—face	Speech	Agni (Fire)
2	Nose—nostrils	Prāṇa	Vāyu
3	Eyes	Sight	The Sun
4	Ears	audition or hearing	Cardinal Points
5	Skin	Hair	The Lord of herbs (Oṣadhis)
6	Heart	Mind	The Moon
7	Navel	Apāna	Mṛtyu (Goddess of death)
8	Organ of generation	Semen	Water

598. *dhātu*—The usual list is *rasāsṛṅ-māṁsa-medo'sthimajjā-śukrāṇi dhātavaḥ*/—ASD 524.

But here in Bh.P. *rasa* and *śukra* are omitted and the cognitive organ *tvac* (and *carman*) are substituted for them.

599. Intelligence is a form of *mahat-tattva*—VR.

600. The remaining are of water, fire, air, ether, Mahat, *ahaṁkāra* and *Prakṛti*.

According to ŚR., here ends the description of the gross body (*Virāṭ Śarīra*) of the Lord.

* According to ŚR., SD. and VB. this is description of the subtle body (*samaṣṭi-liṅga śarīra*) of God, but VR. interprets this as referring to *mukta-jīvas*, i.e. the individual souls in liberated condition, while VJ. takes it as applying to the transcendental form of the Supreme Lord Hari.

35. I have described to you these two forms of the Lord. But sages[601] (learned men) do not take (accept) either of them as they are created by Māyā.

36. The Lord assumes the form of Brahmā and takes names, forms and actions, himself being both the things designated and the word denoting it. He is both the doer of actions, (through Māyā, but really) non-doer[602]. He is different and beyond the both.

37-39. He assumes (the names, forms and actions of) Prajāpatis, Manus, gods, sages, manes (*Pitṛs*), siddhas, semidivine beings like Cāraṇas, Gandharvas, Vidyādharas; Asuras, Yakṣas, Kinnaras, celestial damsels, Nāgas, serpents, Kimpuruṣas (the same as Kinnaras), men, Mātṛs (such as Brāhmī, Māheśvarī etc.), evil beings like demons, Pretas,[603] Piśācas, Bhūtas (goblins), Vināyakas, imps like Kūṣmāṇḍa, Unmāda (like Kālakarṇa), Vetāla, Yātudhāna (a kind of demon), planets, birds, deer, beasts, trees, mountains and reptiles.

40. He creates all beings which fall into two categories (moving and stationary), and those divided into four classes according to their process of birth (viz. born out of the egg, the womb, sweat and seeds): and those classified in three as per their habitat (viz. those which live on the land, in the water and in the air). These are the fruits of the actions—merit, demerit and a mixture of the two.[604]

41. The consequences of the actions are three according to the three attributes, *sattva*, *rajas* and *tamas*, and (according to the predominance of the attribute) beings become residents in the heaven, this world and the hell. Oh king, when one out of these attributes is dominated by the other two, each of these courses are then subdivided in three varieties.

---

601. VJ. reads *a-vipaścitaḥ*, i.e. people who are weak in knowledge. Such persons cannot understand the above described two forms which are created by God's will and *Prakṛti*.

602. *akarmakaḥ*—As God's will works (not he), he is not bound by the actions—VR.

603. VD. applies the term *preta* to those who met an accidental death.

604. This is a reply to Parīkṣit's query *yāvatyaḥ karmag atayo yādṛśīr dvija-sattama* (Bh.P. II.8.136).

42*. This very glorious Lord who created the universe, takes the form of Dharma (upholder of the order) and protects and nourishes the universe, by taking incarnations in beasts, men, gods.

43. Then in due course, he, assuming the form of the Time of the world-destruction, the world-consuming Fire and Rudra[605], like a wind dispersing a host of clouds, destroys the world that is created by him.

44.** The divine lord of unimaginable power, glory etc. has been thus described (in his capacity of creator, protector and destroyer). But wise men should not think him to be of this much description.

45. Para Brahman is not a doer in the activity pertaining to creation (protection or destruction of the universe). It is for the sake of refuting his relation as agent that the description is given. It is imposed on him by Māyā.

46.*** Oh king! this kalpa-period of god Brahmā along with its subdivisions (*vikalpas*) has been described to you. In this kalpa, (subtle) creations from *prakṛti* or *mahat* called *Prākṛtikas* and (gross) creations known as *Vaikṛtika* take place. Such types of creations are common to all *kalpas*[606].

47. I shall fully explain to you later the measure of time (both gross and subtle), the definition of *kalpa* and its division. Listen now to Pādma Kalpa.

Śaunaka said :

48. Oh Sūta ! you told us that Vidura, the best of the devotees of the Lord, travelled to the holy places on the earth

---

* Having described creation of the universe in the capacity of Brahman, the author describes the protection aspect in the capacity of Viṣṇu in this verse, and destructive aspect of Rudra in the next verse.

605. GD. *Dīpanī*—Radharaman Gosvami.

** The venerable lord (Viṣṇu) is superior to other great gods (like Brahmā and Rudra). He has been described as quite different from others, and free from all defects (despite his actions of creation, destruction etc.). Wise men should look upon him as distinct from others (and not identical with others)—VJ.

*** This is the reply to the question '*yāvān kalpo vikalpo vā* etc. in Bh.P. 2.8.12.

606. *Kalpa*—a day of Brahmā or 1000 *yugas* or 432 million years of mortal beings. JG. quotes from the *Skanda Purāṇa* (*Prabhāsa Khaṇḍa*) the list of 30 Kalpas. The present is the Śveta-Vārāha Kalpa.

after leaving his relatives who are abandoned with great difficulty.

49. At what place did his discussion with Maitreya (Kauṣārava) on topics pertaining to the Soul take place ? What did the revered Vidura ask him ? What was his (Maitreya's) discourse (in reply) ?

50. Oh gentle Sūta ! Please tell us all about it, and about Vidura's activities, the cause of his leaving his brother and his return as well.

Sūta said : Please listen.

51. I shall narrate to you in the order of questions put to the great sage by Parīkṣit and what discourses he gave on these questions.

SKANDHA THIRD

CHAPTER ONE

(Meeting of Vidura and Uddhava)

Śrī Śuka said :

* 1-2.

It is reported that formerly, venerable Maitreya[607] was asked this very question, in the same manner by Vidura who took to forest, after leaving his affluent house—the house, wherein Lord Kṛṣṇa, the ruler of all, (but as) the ambassador (of Pāṇḍavas) entered (and stayed) as if it were his own, after leaving the palace of the Paurava King (Duryodhana).

The King said :

3. Oh Lord ! Tell us in details, at what place did the meeting of Vidura with venerable Maitreya take place ? and when (or what topic) did they discuss ?

4. For, the question posed by Vidura, of pure Soul, to the great (sage) cannot be of less importance –especially so when it was praised as a good question by Maitreya (himself).

Sūta said :

5. When the great sage, master (lit. knower) of different branches of learning, was thus asked by king Parīkṣit, he, being very pleased, replied, "Listen (I shall narrate to you)."

---

* VR. interprets : Formerly the venerable Vidura who was the advisor of Pāṇḍavas and was an *aṁśa* of Yamadharma, the controller of all beings, left the house of Dhṛtarāṣṭra which he considered as his own and took to forest. It is reported that when Vidura left his own magnificent house and went to the jungle, he asked the venerable sage Maitreya the same question, in the same way.

VR. adds that leaving his own house as well as that of the Paurava King shows the physical and mental renunciation of Vidura.

607. *Maitreya* or *Kauśārava* A son of Kuśārava and Mitrā and disciple of Parāśara; met Kṛṣṇa on the eve of his departure to Heaven and was ordered to be the preceptor of Vidura.—DHM. 195, PI. 2.739-40.

6. When the blind king Dhṛtarāṣṭra supported in an unrighteous manner, his wicked sons, and deceitfully made the relative-less (fatherless) children of his younger brother, to live (lit. enter) the house of lac and set it on fire.

7. When king Dhṛtarāṣṭra did not prevent his son from censurable act of dragging (lit. touching) the hair of the queen of Kuru king (Yudhiṣṭhira), his daughter-in-law, whose tears washed away the saffron on her breasts [Or, which was the cause of subsequent washing away of the saffron on breasts of the wives of the enemies.]

8. As he succumbed to infatuation (or thoughtlessness, or serving his son), he did not return, as per terms of agreement, his due patrimony to the pious Yudhiṣṭhira who always followed the path of truth, and was fraudulently defeated in gambling, though he (Yudhiṣṭhira) respectfully requested for it (his share), after his return from the forest.

9. When the king whose (remaining small) portion of merit was spent up, did not regard as important the speeches of Kṛṣṇa, the Master of the world, (when) deputed by Pāṇḍavas,—speeches delivered in the (royal) assembly, and which were as if nectar-oozing to men (like Bhīṣma).

10. When Vidura was invited by his elder brother for consultation, he went to the palace. What he (Vidura), prominent amongst counsellors, proffered as an advice came later to be called 'Vidura's Advice' (*Vidura-Nīti*) by (political) advisors.

(*Vidura advised*)

11. "Return the hereditary share (of kingdom) to Yudhiṣṭhira who has suffered unbearable wrongs from you. It is against these that the serpent in the form of Bhīma of whom you are so much afraid, is hissing in rage along with his brothers.

12. The God, Lord Kṛṣṇa, along with Brāhmaṇas and gods, has taken (the side of) Pāṇḍavas. The Lord of the Yadus who has subdued all kings of kings, stays in his own city.

13. You, who have lost prosperity due to your aversion to Kṛṣṇa, are nourishing Duryodhana with the idea that he is your child. But he, the hater of the Supreme Man, is an evil incarnate which has entered your house and is staying. For

the good of the family (at least) remove that inauspicious person."

14. (When) Vidura whose character was praiseworthy to the righteous, spoke thus in that assembly, he was insulted by Suyodhana whose lower lip was throbbing through great rage, and also by Karṇa, his younger brother (Duḥśāsana) and Śakuni.

15. (Duryodhana said): "Who asked this crooked slave-born to be here? He is treacherous to his master with whose food he grew fat, and espouses the cause of the enemy. Let him be immediately driven out of the town alive[608] (confiscating his property.)"

16. Though, in the very presence of his brother Dhṛtarāṣṭra, he (Vidura) was cut to the quick by such sharp words which pierced the ears like arrows, he was unafflicted, as he well understood (and respected) the power of māyā (as the cause of this insult). Of his own accord, he left the assembly hall, leaving his bow at the door (indicating his neutrality in the ensuing struggle).

17. He, whom Kauravas got by their good luck, departed from Hastināpura (along with good fortunes of the Kauravas). With a desire to accumulate merit, he visited, one after another, holy places sanctified by the sacred feet of Hari—holy places where God has manifested himself in thousand forms (like Śiva, Brahmā etc.).

18. Unaccompanied by anyone, he travelled to towns, holy groves, mountains, bowers, rivers and lakes of translucent waters, and holy places and temples which were richly adorned with the symbols of the Infinite Lord.

19. While wandering over the earth, he practised observances (vows) pleasing to Hari. He lived on pure consecrated food, performing ablutions in every sacred place, sleeping on the bare ground. Wearing bark garments, he was careless about his person, and became unrecognizable to his friends and relatives.

20. In this way, while wandering in the Bhārata-varṣa, he went to Prabhāsa in due course. At that time, with the help

---

608. v.l. *Śmaśānaḥ*—(i) inauspicious like a funeral place—ŚR.
(ii) So evil that he will bring misfortune wherever he goes.

of Kṛṣṇa, Yudhiṣṭhira, the son of Pṛthā, was ruling over the whole earth which was (controlled) by the army of one king only (i.e. of Yudhiṣṭhira), and was under (the protection of) one royal umbrella.

21. Then, at that place, he heard (the report of) the annihilation of his friends (relatives) who were burnt down like a forest of dry bamboos consumed by conflagration. Then being deeply grieved, he returned to the Sarasvatī.

22. In the Sarasvatī, he resorted to places sacred to Trita, Uśanas, Manu, Pṛthu, Agni, Asita, Vāyu, Sudās, cows, Guha and Śrāddhadeva.

23. In this region, he visited various temples of Viṣṇu constructed by sages and gods—temples which were especially distinguished by the most important of Viṣṇu's weapons, viz., the disc Sudarśana (carved in the gold tops of the temples) the sight of which reminds people of Kṛṣṇa.

24. Passing through the rich countries of the Surāṣṭras, the Sauvīras, the Matsyas, the Kurujāṅgalas, he reached the Yamunā where he met Uddhava, the great devotee of the lord Kṛṣṇa.

25. With great affection, he closely embraced Uddhava that famous follower of Vāsudeva and a former pupil of Bṛhaspati (in politics), and who was perfectly serene in mind. He enquired of him about the welfare of his relatives who were under the protection of the Supreme Lord Kṛṣṇa.

26. "Are the two ancient Puruṣas (Kṛṣṇa and Balarāma) well in the house of Śūrasena—the Puruṣas who incarnated on the earth due to the request of Brahmā born from the lotus in his (Viṣṇu's) navel and who have enjoyed the joy of achieving the welfare of the world.

27. Is the intimate friend of the Kurus, the respected Vasudeva, happy ?—The liberal Vasudeva who like a father, gives sumptuous gifts to his sisters, in addition to the rich gifts given to the satisfaction of their husbands.

28. Dear friend ! Is Pradyumna, the brave commander-in-chief of the Yādava forces, hale and hearty? By propitiating Brāhmaṇas, Rukmiṇī, begot him (Pradyumna), the God of Love in his previous birth, as a son from Lord Kṛṣṇa.

29. Is Ugrasena, the king of Sāttvatas, Vṛṣṇis, Bhojas

and Dāśārhas happy ?—Ugrasena whom the lotus-eyed (Kṛṣṇa) installed as a king when he (through fear of his life) gave up the hopes about kingship.

30. Oh gentle Uddhava ! Is Sāmba, the son of Kṛṣṇa, and similar to him, the chief of warriors who ride chariots in battles, happy ? Is the god Kārttikeya whom Pārvatī bore in the former birth and whom Jāmbavatī gave birth (as a son) after performing many severe observances, happy?

31. Is Sātyaki who learnt the secret technique of archery from Arjuna happy ?—Sātyaki who by his intensely devoted service of Lord Kṛṣṇa attained the path leading to the Lord immediately,—a path which is difficult even for recluses to attain.

32. Is the wise, pious (sinless) Akrūra (the son of Śvaphalka) always devoted to the glorious Lord, happy ?—Akrūra, who lost himself due to his love (for God) and rolled himself in the dust on the road which was adorned with the foot-prints of Kṛṣṇa.

33. Is Devakī, the princess of Devaka of Bhoja clan, happy ?—Devakī, who like the mother of gods (Aditi) of whom Viṣṇu was born, verily bore the Lord in her womb like the Veda triad (*Ṛg*, *Yajus* and *Sāma Vedas*) which contains the meaning which expands into a sacrifice.

34. Is the revered Aniruddha happy ?—(Aniruddha) who fulfills the desires of the *sāttvatas* and who is regarded as the source of Śāstras by the Vedas, as the director of the mind, for he is the fourth principle presiding over *sattva* or *antaḥ-karaṇa* (the inner organ)[609].

35. Oh gentle Uddhava ! Are also Hṛdika, Sātyaki, Cārudeṣṇa, Gada and others, well?—those who in their absolute devotion to Kṛṣṇa worship him as the Lord of their Soul which is different from their bodies (etc.)

36. Is Dharma (Yudhiṣṭhira), with two arms, viz. Arjuna and Kṛṣṇa, protecting according to the duties of kings the

609. SR. explains : *citta* (reason), *ahaṁkāra* (self-sense or ego), *buddhi* (intelligence) and *manas* (mind) are four aspects of *antaḥ-karaṇa* (the inner organ) and Vāsudeva, Saṅkarṣaṇa, Pradyumna and Aniruddha are their respective presiding deities. Hence Aniruddha is called here 'director of the mind' and the fourth principle (deity) governing *antaḥkaraṇa* (the internal organ).

established (socio-religious) institutions ?—(Yudhiṣṭhira) in whose assembly, Duryodhana boiled (with rage and jealousy) at the sight of Arjuna's services and the imperial fortune gained (by him) through victories.

37. Or has Bhīma who is highly intolerant with the wrongdoers and nurtured rage (revenge) like a serpent, given it up (or visited it on the offenders—Kauravas) ?—(Bhīma) whose (heavy) steps the earth could not bear, while he moved about in various ways, brandishing his mace (*gadā*).

38. Is Arjuna, the celebrated warrior among the leaders of armies of chariots, the wielder of the Gāṇḍīva bow, enemy-less (after destroying them all) ? —(Arjuna) with whom was pleased god Śiva who assumed the form of a Kirāta, at his (Arjuna) covering him thickly with volleys of arrows[610]

39. Are the twins (who were brought up as) sons of Pṛthā (Kuntī), who are protected (lit. surrounded) by Kuntī's sons like eyes by the eyelids, enjoying themselves after wresting their share of ancestral kingdom from the enemies in the war, like Garuḍa taking (the share of) nectar from the army of gods?[611]

40. How wonderful, that though bereaved of a great royal sage (like Pāṇḍu), a matchless warrior, who seated in his chariot with only his bow as a helpmate, conquered all the four cardinal points, Kuntī stayed alive for the sake of children!

41. Oh mild-natured Uddhava ! I feel sorry for the downfalling Dhṛtarāṣṭra who showed enmity to his departed brother (Pāṇḍu). I (his living brother and), a friend and well-wisher was expelled from his capital by him who followed his sons.

42. (Though thus maltreated), I felt no wonder as I could see the greatness of Hari who confuses the working of the human mind by his assumption of human form; and, being in disguise, I could leisurely perform pilgrimage on the earth.

43. Though the venerable Lord is powerful enough to

---

610. This refers to the test of Arjuna's heroism taken by god Śiva before granting him the Pāśupata missile (Vide MBH., II.39.32-64.)

611. *vajri-vaktra*—From the mouth of Indra (ŚR., VR., VJ.) But VD. objects that a thing taken from the mouth of another is unacceptable. Hence he dissolves the compound : *Vajrī vaktram (pradhānaṁ) yasya* / 'That of which Indra is the leader !

remove the miseries of his devotees, by destroying the kings who were proud of their triple superiority (viz. in learning, riches and heredity), and who constantly made the earth tremble by their armies, he was indifferent to the sinful conduct of the Kauravas.

44. The incarnation of the unborn god is for the destruction of those who go astray. Though unconcerned with actions, his deeds are reclaiming the errants to the proper path. If (that be) not (the case) who, (being) above *guṇas*, would verily like the assumption of the body and the course of activities.

45. Oh friend ! Extol to me the news (episodes) of the unborn Lord of Holy Fame, who was born in the Yadu race for the good of the kings of the world who have submitted themselves to him (his protection) and for the welfare of those who abide by his orders.

CHAPTER TWO

(*The Dialogue between Uddhava and Vidura*)

Śrī Śuka said:

1. The great devotee of the Lord (Uddhava) who was thus asked by Vidura about the welfare pertaining to the dear one (i. e. of Lord Kṛṣṇa), could not reply as he was painfully reminded of the Lord and was overcome with sorrow at his bereavement.

2-3. How could he (Uddhava) who, as a child of five years, when invited by his mother for breakfast, did not wish to partake of it while worshipping Kṛṣṇa as a part of his sports in childhood, break the news in reply, when he had spent the whole lifetime in his service, and attained old age, and was reminded (sorrowfully) of the feet of the master.

4. For the period of a *muhūrta* he remained silent (in meditation) highly satisfied by the nectar-like feet of Kṛṣṇa and deeply immersed in intense devotion of the Lord.

5. He, on whose body hair was standing on ends, and who was shedding tears from his closed eyes, and who was

drowned in the flood of love for Kṛṣṇa, was seen (as if) his highest purpose was achieved.

6. Gradually, he returned from the abode of the Lord to the world of men. He wiped out his eyes. Uddhava who was wonderstruck (with the deeds of the Lord) replied to Vidura.

Uddhava said:

7. What good news can I give to you when the Sun in the form of Kṛṣṇa has set, and our homes, bereft of splendour, have been swallowed up by the boa-constriction (of Time)?

8. Alas! it is the misfortune of this world, and especially of the Yādavas who lived with him intimately and yet did not know him, just as the fish (living in the sea along with the moon before the churning of the sea) did not recognize the Moon (as such but regarded him as an acquatic animal).

9*. All the Sāttvatas, though capable of knowing intentions of others, and possessing deep understanding, and of singleness of devotion, regarded the Lord of all created beings[612] as the leader of the Sāttvatas only.

10. Those who have sown (i. e. completely fixed) their intellect in Hari, are not deluded by the words of those who are haunted by the Māyā of the Almighty (e. g. the Yādavas) or by those who entertained evil intention to him (like Śiśupāla and others).

11. He had exhibited his form to men who had not performed proper penance and who had not seen it to their satisfaction. He disappeared from the world taking with him his splendid form which was the centre (of attraction) to the eyes of the world.

12. It was a form which was useful for activities in imitation of human beings which he assumed, showing the power of his *Yoga-māyā*. It was the highest peak of perfect beauty

*According to SD. this verse praises the Yādavas and Pauravas who knew the real Lord. "The leaders of the Puru-clan (like Yudhiṣṭhira) and Sāttvatas (like Vasudeva) realised the chief of Sāttvatas, namely, Śrī Kṛṣṇa as being the Brahman, the support of all created beings (*bhūtas*) and resting completely on the Lord, were happy thereby."

612. *bhūtāvāsam* : i) A *jīva*, resident in a physical and inner (*kāraṇa*) body—VB.

ii) A leader of a few men—VJ.

and sublimity, parts of which beautified even the ornaments and a wonder to him also.

13. Seeing his form which gave great delight to the three worlds in the Rājasūya sacrifice of Yudhiṣṭhira, they (people of the three worlds) thought that in creating beautiful human form, the whole of creator's skill is exhausted today.

14. The women of Vraja who got the honour of his smiles overflowing with love, sportive dances and longing looks, followed him with their eyes and minds, leaving their work unfinished.

15. The Lord of all, [Brahman with attributes and beyond attributes] with compassion for his own gentle forms being troubled by other (wicked) ones, and accompanied with *Prakṛti* of which *Mahat* is but a fraction, (or with Balarāma as his great part), though unborn, took birth like fire (which though ever present in the wood, sparks out after friction).

16. The apparent birth of the birthless Lord in the house of Vasudeva, (his) stay in a settlement of cowherds (*Vraja*) as if out of fear of the enemy (*Kaṁsa*), and the flight of the Lord of infinite power, from his own city—this (behaviour like ordinary human beings) distresses me.

17. It pains my heart to remember how he, bowing down to the feet of his parents, beseeched, "Oh father, mother kindly be gracious unto us who being in great fear of Kaṁsa, could not render you any service."

18. What man who having smelt (experienced the great joy in) even a particle of pollen in the lotus-like feet of the Lord, can forget him—the Lord, who with the movement of his creeper-like eyebrow, a veritable god of destruction, removed the load (of the wicked) from the earth.

19. Verily, you have witnessed how, during the Rājasūya Sacrifice, Śiśupāla, the arch-enemy of Kṛṣṇa, attained Liberation after which even *yogins* aspire by observing carefully *yogic* practices. How can one endure separation from (such a gracious Lord like) him ?

20. Similarly, other warriors who, on the field of battle, drank with their eyes the beautiful lotus-like face of Kṛṣṇa, and attained to his feet after purification (death) from the missiles of Arjuna.

21-22. The Lord, who himself is unsurpassed in excellence (lit. without an equal or superior), and is a ruler of the three (worlds or attributes—*guṇas*), and who due to his intrinsic highest blissfulness, is in enjoyment of all (types of) happiness, whose foot-stool is (as if) eulogised by (the sound on the foot-stool made by) the crests of the crowns of the eternal guardians of the world who bring tributes to him—Such a Lord should stand before Ugrasena who is occupying a high seat (on the throne), and should request him, "Your Majesty, kindly pay attention (to us)." Oh Vidura, the servantlike behaviour of the Lord greatly troubles us, his servants.

23. What mercifulness! The wicked Pūtanā who with a desire to kill him, made him suck her breast smeared with deadly poison, (and for this she) attained the place worthy for his nurse (Yaśodā). Is there any other god so merciful like this, to whom we should resort (for salvation or protection ?

24. I regard asuras as the devotees of the Supreme Lord as their minds are fixed on the Lord of the three worlds, through anger and who on the battlefield visualized him armed with the Sudarśana disc and seated on the shoulder of Garuḍa, attacking them.

25. The Lord took birth from Vasudeva and Devakī, in the prison of Kaṁsa, the chief of the Bhojas, as he was so requested by god Brahmā and desired to restore happiness to the earth.

26. Then, by his father who was afraid of Kaṁsa, he was taken to the settlement of cowherds headed by Nanda. He stayed there with Balarāma with his power unmanifested, for eleven years.

27. Surrounded by cowboys and himself tending the calves, the All-pervading Lord sported on the (banks of the) Yamunā in parks, dense with trees full of warbling birds.

28. He who looked like an innocent young one of a lion, displayed his boyish pranks of (apparent) laughing and crying, to the residents of Vraja.

29. The same Lord tended their wealth in the from of cattle with white bulls (prominent in them) and which was

(as if), the abode of the goddess of wealth. He entertained the cowherds accompanying him, by playing upon the flute.

30. Like a boy breaking down his toys, he sportively killed those wiley conjuring demons who could assume any form at will and who were deputed by Kaṁsa (to kill him).

31. He brought back to life the cowherds and cows who died of poisonous water of the Yamunā. Subduing (and expelling) Kāliya, the king of serpents, he made them drink the water again which was restored to its original condition of purity.

32. The omnipresent Lord made the chief of cowherds (Nanda) to perform a sacrifice in honour of cows (in which cows were worshipped) with the help of the best of Brāhmaṇas, as he wished to spend the great wealth in a good way. (In this way, he subdued the pride of Indra).

33. Oh Vidura! When Indra, incensed at the discontinuation of his own (traditional) worship, showered heavily, the settlement of the cowherds which became extremely distressed (by the downpour of rain), was protected (by the Lord) with the umbrella in the form of the hill (*Govardhana*) which he sportively wielded and showed thereby his grace.

34. Respecting (as it were) the evenings bright with autumnal moon, he enjoyed himself singing sweet songs and became an ornament of the circle of ladies (performing Rāsa dance).

CHAPTER THREE

(*The Dialogue between Vidura and Uddhava*)
—*Glorious deeds of Kṛṣṇa*

Uddhava said:

1. Then, with a desire to make his parents happy, he (Kṛṣṇa) accompanied by Balarāma came to the city (Mathurā) and forcibly pulled down Kaṁsa, the head of the enemy-force, from his royal seat, and after killing him, dragged him along the ground (though dead).

2. He learnt from Sāndīpani[613] the Veda with all its details (the six accessories of the Veda) which was recited to him but once. He restored his dead son to him (Sāndīpani) from the belly of Pañcajana[614].

3. Just as Garuḍa snatched away his share (of nectar), Kṛṣṇa, in the very presence of kings invited[615] on behalf of the Princess of Bhīṣmaka, carried away Rukmiṇī—his own share (as she was an incarnation of Lakṣmī)—with a view to marry her by the Gāndharva form of marriage,[616] thus setting his foot on the heads of the kings[617].

4. In another *svayaṁvara*, he tamed the bulls whose noses had not been bored and married the Princess (Satyabhāmā) of Nagnajit. He discomfited the foolish kings who, despite their humiliation (by Kṛṣṇa's fulfilment of the marriage condition) still entertained a desire for her and came to fight him with their weapons, though he could not be injured by them.

5. Like an ordinary man (under the thumb of his wife) the Lord took away the celestial tree Pārijāta to grant the desire of his beloved (Satyabhāmā). At this, Indra (who was incited by Śacī) like a pet deer of women, got blind with rage and pursued him with his army (of gods)[618].

6. Seeing her son (Naraka) who was (as if) swallowing the sky with his body, cut down by the *Sudarśana* disc, he

---

613. *Sāndīpani*—Teacher of Kṛṣṇa and *Balarāma* (DHM 279).

614. *Pañcajana*—Name of a demon who assumed the form of a conch-shell and was slain by Kṛṣṇa to recover Sāndīpani's son. But as he was not found in Pañcajana's belly, Kṛṣṇa brought him back from Yama. For details—infra X Ch. 45.

615. ŚR accepts the v.l. *samāhṛta* i.e. who were attracted by her (Rukmiṇī's) beauty etc.

616. Modern 'love-marriage'. So called due to its supposed prevalence among the Gandharvas. ASD 398 is wrong when it states that it is performed 'without ceremonies'. *Smṛti Candrikā* and other digests state that *homa* and *saptapadī* are necessary. For details Kane *Hist. of Dharma Śāstra* Vol. II—i. Ch. IX. P. 521-24.

617. Kings who were invited by her brother Rukmi whose name had two syllables common with the name 'Rukmiṇī'—(ŚR).

618. Indra's ingratitude is obvious, as it was he who invited Kṛṣṇa to get back the earrings of his mother Aditi from Bhaumāsura. Kṛṣṇa went to Svarga with Satyabhāmā and restored the ear-rings (Vide infra X. Ch. 59).

(Kṛṣṇa) was prayed by the goddess of the Earth (Naraka's mother). Having given the remaining (unannexed) kingdom to Naraka's son, Kṛṣṇa entered the harem.[619]

7. Seeing Hari, the friend of the afflicted person, the princesses who were abducted by Naraka, immediately rose to receive him with their glances full of rapture, bashfulness and love.

8. Assuming suitable forms by his *māyā* powers, he simultaneously married them all, with proper formalities, in different apartments.

9. With a desire to expand his *prakṛti* (or to become many for the sake of *prakṛti*), he got from each of them ten children equal to him in all respects.

10. He commissioned his great prowess and glory in his men (devotees like Mucukunda, Bhīma), and through them he got killed Kālayavana, Jarāsandha, Śālva and others who, with their armies, laid siege to his town.

11. He caused the death of some like Śambara[620], Dvivida[621], Bāṇa[622], Mura[623] and Balvala[624] (through others), while he killed others like Dantavaktra[625] (personally).

12. He then caused the destruction of kings who espoused the cause of your brothers' sons (Kauravas and Pāṇḍavas).

---

619. For details vide infra X. 59.

620. *Śambara*: A demon who stole away Kṛṣṇa's son Pradyumna soon after his birth, and threw him into the sea. Providentially Pradyumna was saved and he killed Śambara—BPK 197.

621. *Dvivida*—A monkey friend of Naraka; to avenge Naraka's death he went on destroying the towns in Kṛṣṇa's kingdom. At Raivata hill, he offended Balarāma insulting his fair companions. In the ensuing fight Balarāma killed him—PI. 2.150.

622. *Bāṇa*—Eldest son of Bali; a devotee of Śiva; arrested Kṛṣṇa's grandson Aniruddha who courted his daughter Uṣā. In the battle that followed for the rescue of Aniruddha, god Śiva and Skanda assisted Bāṇa but were finally overpowered by Kṛṣṇa. At Śiva's request Kṛṣṇa spared Baṇa's life and returned with Uṣā and Aniruddha—DHM. 42.

623. *Mura*—A demon ally of Naraka; defended Naraka's capital Prāg-jyotiṣa with his seven thousand sons. But he along with his sons was killed by Kṛṣṇa with his disc Sudarśana—DHM. 212.

624. *Balvala*—A demon who ruined the sacrifices at Naimiṣa; was killed by Balarāma at the request of the sages.

625. *Danta-vaktra*—King of Karuṣa; took side against Kṛṣṇa on behalf of Jarāsandha, Śālva and was killed by Kṛṣṇa—DHM. 80.

By the marching of their armies to Kurukṣetra, the earth was as if made to tremble.

13. He was not satisfied when he saw Suyodhana, along with his followers, lying prostrate on the ground with thighs broken and with his royal splendour and life cut short by the evil advice tendered by Karṇa, Duḥśāsana and Śakuni.

14. (He thought to himself): What an insignificant portion of the heavy burden of the earth is relieved, though an army of eighteen Akṣauhiṇīs is annihilated through (the medium of) Bhīṣma, Droṇa, Arjuna and Bhīma! For there exists an irresistible army of Yādavas headed by (Pradyumna and others who are) my parts[626] (*aṁśas*).

15. There is no other strategem to kill them (Yādavas) except when there will be a quarrel among themselves, with their eyes reddish with intoxication. When I prepare to leave this world, they will automatically disappear.

16. After planning thus, the Lord, establishing the son of Dharma (Yudhiṣṭhira) in his own kingdom, gave delight to his friends and showed thereby the path of the righteous people.

17. The continuity of the Puru family, which was properly secured by Abhimanyu in Uttarā, but which was verily destroyed by the missiles of Aśvatthāman, was again restored and protected by the Lord.

18. The Omnipresent Lord caused the son of Dharma (Yudhiṣṭhira) to perform the horse-sacrifice thrice. He (Yudhiṣṭhira) who was devoted to Kṛṣṇa, enjoyed himself protecting the earth with the help of his younger brothers.

19. The glorious Lord also, the Soul of the universe and a follower of the path prescribed in Śrutis and Smṛtis enjoyed all worldly pleasures at Dvārakā. But as he was firmly fixed in the Sāṅkhya Philosophy, he remained non-attached (due to his realization of the distinction between Prakṛti and Puruṣa).

20-21. With his lovely smiling looks and words sweet as nectar, with spotless character and with his body as an abode of Śrī (Goddess Lakṣmī) he gave delight to this world as well as to the next, especially so to the Yadus. At night, he showed momentary friendship to women who obtained the pleasure of his companionship.

626. VJ. construes it with Bhīṣma, Droṇa etc.

22. While he was enjoying himself thus for pretty long years, He became unattached to the householder's life and the pleasures therein.

23*. The objects of enjoyment are in the power of the Fate. Man himself is at the mercy of the Fate. What person devoted to the Lord of Yoga (Kṛṣṇa) by yogic process, will put faith in these (objects etc.) ?

24. Once upon a time, in the city of Dvārakā (some) sages were offended by Yādava and Bhoja lads while at play. The sages who knew the intention of the Lord, cursed them.

25. Then after some months, Vṛṣṇis, Bhojas, Andhakas and others, being deluded by God, rode in their chariots to Prabhāsa, in great delight.

26. Thereafter, performing ablutions and offering libations to Manes, gods and sages they, with that water, gave cows of many good qualities, to Brāhmaṇas.

27-28. They donated to Brāhmaṇas gold and silver, clothes and beds, skins and woollen blankets, horses and chariots, elephants, girls and land sufficient for maintenance, sumptuous food with a view to pleasing the Lord. Those brave warriors whose life was dedicated to the service of cows and Brāhmaṇas bowed to them (Brāhmaṇas) with their heads touching the ground.

CHAPTER FOUR

(The Dialogue between Vidura and Uddhava)
—Destruction of the Yādavas and
Kṛṣṇa's Message.

Uddhava said :-

1. Then, having been permitted by them (Brāhmaṇas), they (Yādavas etc.) drank (the flour-made) liquor. They lost

*ŚR differs : When the Lord himself who had everything in his power, felt non-attachment, who would love or entertain faith in things in the power of the fate? A person devoted to Lord Kṛṣṇa would never do so.

their knowledge (sobriety), and cut each other to the quick by bitter words.

2. When their minds became unbalanced and vehement by the evil effect of the wine, the destruction (as a result of fight) among them, after sunset, was like that of bamboos (friction between which creates forest conflagration consuming the forest of bamboos).

3. Seeing that course of events brought about by his māyā, the Lord sipped water of the Sarasvatī, and sat down at the foot of a tree.

4. And (while we were already at Dvārakā), I was asked to go to Badarī by the Lord who removes afflictions of his devotees, (but) who desired to destroy his own clan.

5. Oh conquerer of the enemies ! Though I understood his intention, I followed him, as I could not bear the separation from the feet of the Master.

6. Searching for the most beloved Master (who protects by granting the knowledge of the Soul), I found him, the abode of the goddess Lakṣmī, sitting alone on the bank of the Sarasvatī, without any shelter (as he is the shelter of all).

7. (I saw the Lord) of beautiful blue complexion, composed of pure *sattva*, with calm, reddish eyes, recognisable by his four arms and by yellow silken garments.

8. He was sitting with his lotus-like right foot on the left thigh, leaning against a young Aśvattha tree, with all pleasures of the senses renounced, (yet) in perfect bliss.

9. In the course of his wandering over the world, there came by chance a *siddha* (Maitreya), the great devotee of the Lord, and a friend and well wisher of Dvaipāyana (Vyāsa).

10. While the devoted sage, with his neck (head) bending with joy and devotion, was listening, Mukunda (Kṛṣṇa) removing my fatigue with a long smiling look full of love (compassion), said to me :

The Lord said:

11. Being an *antaryāmin* (dweller in the hearts of all) I know what you wish. What I give to you is difficult for others to obtain; (for) in days gone by, in the long sacrificial session performed by Prajāpatis and Vasus, Oh (former) Vasu, you performed the sacrifice with a desire to attaining me.

12. Oh virtuous one ! This is the last of your births, as my grace has been secured by you in the present birth. How glad I am ! that you have come with singleminded devotion to see me when I am about to leave this mortal world (to go to Vaikuṇṭha), in this solitary place.

13. Formerly (in Pādma Kalpa), at the beginning of creation, the highest knowledge throwing light on my greatness (majesty)—which the learned ones designated as the *Bhāgavata*—was imparted by me to the unborn god (Brahmā) seated in the lotus sprouting forth from my navel.

14. I, who was thus respectfully addressed, and who was the recipient of the favour of a long look of the Supreme Man, with my hair standing on their ends due to my affection (to him), with flowing tears, and bowing with folded hands, addressed to him in faltering words.

15. "Oh Lord ! Out of the four goals of life (viz. *dharma*, *artha*, *kāma* and *Mokṣa*), which goal is difficult to be achieved by those who resort to your lotus-like feet ? But, Oh Almighty, I do not request you for any one of them, as I am eager to serve your lotus-like feet.

16. That you performed actions, though you are devoid of actions and desire to do them, that you have taken a birth though you are birthless, that you resorted to a castle or fled away through the fear of the enemy, even though the god of Death is your form[627], that you married with ten thousand young women despite your enjoyment of your self-blissfulness—by these the intellect of the learned ones gets confused and fatigued.

17. Or, Oh Almighty Lord ! It throws our mind in confusion that you, whose power of self-knowledge is unobstructed and continuous, should invite me for consultations like an ignorant person, though you are never ignorant or careless.

18. You have completely disclosed to Brahmā, the supreme knowledge throwing light on your own (essential) mysterious nature. Oh Lord, if it be within our capacity to receive it, explain it, to us so that we may easily cross the misery (of the worldly existence)."

19. To me who have thus expressed the cherished desire

---

627. *kālātmanaḥ*—You are the destroyer of all—VJ.

of my heart, the Supreme Lord of lotus-like eyes instructed me (gave me insight) into his Supreme Nature.

20. I, who have thus learnt the path of the special knowledge of the real Soul from Lord Kṛṣṇa, whose holy feet have been worshipped by me, bowed to his feet, circumambulated the Lord and have come here with my heart afflicted with separation (from him).

21-22. I, who am full of delight at the sight of the Lord, and distressed at my separation from him, shall go to the site of the Badarī—hermitage which was liked by him, and where Lord Nārāyaṇa and venerable sage Nara, both of whom confer blessings on the world, perform a mild (non-troubling) but severe penance for a long period (up to the end of Kalpa).

Śrī Śuka said:

23. Having thus heard from Uddhava, the unbearable (report of the) death of his friends and relatives, the learned Vidura controlled the explosion of grief by his knowledge.

24. The prominent Kaurava (Vidura), due to his confidence in (Uddhava), the great devotee of Lord Kṛṣṇa, prominent among Kṛṣṇa's circle of friends and kinsmen, spoke thus to him while he was about to depart.

Vidura said :

25. Your honour deserves to convey to me the supreme knowledge shedding light on the mysterious nature ofthe Lord—the knowledge which the Lord of Yoga, the ruler (of the universe) imparted to you. For, the servants of Viṣṇu move about to serve the needs of their devotees.

Uddhava said :

26. The sage Maitreya is to be propitiated by you for this knowledge, as it was in my presence that the Lord himself directed him to do so (i.e. to instruct you) at the time of his departure from the world of mortals.

Śrī Śuka said:

27. In this way, in the company of Vidura, Uddhava got his anguish (at the separation of Hari) subsided by the

nectarlike conversation about the excellent qualities of the Omnipresent Lord, and spent like a moment the night, on the bank of the Yamunā, and then left (for Badarikāśrama).

The King said:

28. How did Uddhava remain (safe from the Brāhmaṇa's curse) when Hari who was the chief of the Vṛṣṇis and Bhojas, leaders of the commanders of warriors joined the majority, and who (Hari) was the Lord of the three (gods, e. g. Brahmā and others) gave up his mortal coil ?

Śrī Śuka said:

29-30. The Lord whose will is always supreme (lit. never futile), began to think when he annihilated his own race by the Time (god of death) in the form of a Brāhmaṇa's curse, and was about to cast off his body.
"Now when I am no more in this world, only Uddhava, the best among those who have realised the soul, deserves to receive the knowledge that is within me (or which relates to me).

31. Uddhava is not a jot inferior to me. He is the master (of himself) unpurturbed by worldly objects (*guṇas*). Hence let him remain (after the annihilation of the Yādavas) to make people receive knowledge about me.

32. Thus directed by the lord of the three worlds, the source of the Vedas, (Uddhava) went to the Badarī hermitage and worshipped Hari by deep meditation.

33-35. Having heard from Uddhava praiseworthy acts of Kṛṣṇa, the Supreme Soul, who out of sport assumed the human body, and of his laying down the body (death) which increased the courage of the wise, and which is more difficult to understand on the part of beasts (beastlike persons) of unsteady minds and of his being seen mentally by Kṛṣṇa, Oh great Kuru, Vidura meditated upon him, but after the departure of Uddhava, became overcome with feelings of love and wept.

36. From the bank of the Yamunā, Vidura, the Siddha, reached the heavenly river (the Gaṅgā) after some (several days, where Maitreya (the son of Mitrā) was met by him.

CHAPTER FIVE

(Dialogue between Vidura and Maitreya)
Tattvas and their Deities.

Śrī Śuka said :

1. At Haridvāra, Vidura, the most excellent among the Kurus, purified due to his devotion to Acyuta (Kṛṣṇa), fully satisfied[628] with Maitreya's straightforwardness, humility and compassion, approached Maitreya of unfathomable knowledge, who was seated there (unoccupied with any work) and asked him.

Vidura said :

2. May your Honour please explain to us what is proper to be done (i.e. the proper course of conduct) in this world, as (we find that) people do some (prescribed) acts for the sake of happiness, but they do neither get happiness nor the pacification or cessation of the other thing (i.e. misery) and are, on the contrary, subjected to misery again and again.

3. It is a fact that really auspicious devotees of Lord Kṛṣṇa (like you) move about in this world with a view to be gracious to people who by their misfortune have become averse to Kṛṣṇa, and (consequently) unrighteous and extremely miserable.

4. Hence, Oh great saint, please advise us the course (of conduct leading) to happiness whereby the glorious Lord, installed in the hearts of men purified by devotion, imparts the ancient lore (based on the authority of the eternal Vedas) leading to the direct realisation of the true nature of the Soul.

5-9. Oh best among Brāhmaṇas ! Please describe (explain) to us : What deeds the Lord, the controller of the māyā consisting of three *guṇas* (or the Lord of the three worlds the self-dependent, performs after taking incarnation; how he, though devoid of activity (or free from desires) created this (universe) in the beginning; how he, having stabilised it (in its existence) arranges for its maintenance; how he abstains

---

628. v.l. *sauśīlya-guṇābhitṛptam*—Adj. qualifying Maitreya : Maitreya was satisfied with humility and other qualities of Vidura.

from worldly activities by withdrawing it (the universe) into the vacuum(*ākāśa*)in his bosom and sleeps in the cave, viz., his *yoga-māyā*; how this Lord of Yoga, of unimaginable powers, though he is one, entered this (universe) and became many (in the form of Brahmā and others); the actions he does for the well-being of Brāhmaṇas, cows and gods as part of his sports in different incarnations; for in spite of hearing the nectarlike (sweet) deeds of the Lord, who is at the head of persons of auspicious fame, (persons whose name is auspicious to utter); (Describe to me) with what first principles (*Tattvas* like *mahat* etc.) the master of the protectors of this world (like Indra etc.), created and regulated the different regions along with their guardians, and those regions beyond the Lokāloka mountains[629]—regions in which all the different classes of beings are distinguished from each other (as god, man etc.) according to the function of their *Karmas*. (Explain to me) how Nārāyaṇa, the self-created creator of the universe, created differences among beings, according to their inborn nature, deeds (*karma*), form and name.

10. Oh respected sage ! I have often heard from Vyāsa, duties prescribed for the twice-born (higher) castes and lower castes. But with the exception of the ambrosial flood of the episodes of Kṛṣṇa, we are satiated with hearing matters which result in insignificant pleasure.

11. Who would feel fed up with the (description of the) episodes of Kṛṣṇa of holy feet—episodes which are glorified by learned persons (like Nārada) in your assemblies. For as soon as he (Kṛṣṇa) enters a man's ears (i.e. Kṛṣṇa's stories are (heard), he cuts asunder (man's) attachment to the house (worldly life) which involves him in mundane existence.

12. Even your friend, the venerable dark sage (Vyāsa) composed the *Bhārata* (the *Mahābhārata*) with a desire to describe the excellences of the Lord. In it (the *Mahābhārata*), the mind of men is certainly attracted to the stories of Hari through repetition of the lower types of pleasures.

13. The ever-increasing inclination to listen (to the sto-

629. *Lokāloka*—'A mythical belt of mountains bounding the outermost of seven seas encircling the world and separating this world from the regions of darkness' DHM/80; —ASK. 820

ries of Kṛṣṇa) engenders (a sense of) aversion to other objects of pleasure, in the faithful. It quickly destroys all the miseries of a man who finds happiness in constantly meditating over the feet of Hari.

14. I feel pity for those ignorant people (who do not understand the teaching of the *Mahābhārata*) who due to their sins, feel aversion to the stories of Hari and (hence) are the pitiable of the pitiables. The vigilant (blinkless) god Time diminishes (destroys) the life of those who waste their time in wasteful verbal, physical and mental activities.[630]

15. Oh Kauṣārava ! Just as the essence (honey) is picked up from flowers, so you extract (the select) narratives from the stories of Hari who bestows happiness. Oh friend of the afflicted! Please recite to us, for our good, the story of Hari of hallowed fame.

16. Please describe to me the superhuman acts performed by the Almighty who, with the power of Māyā under his control, for the creation, sustenance and destruction of the universe, has taken (different) incarnations.

Śrī Śuka said :

17. The revered sage Kauṣārava who was thus requested by Vidura for the final beatitude of men, replied to him with great respect.

Maitreya said :

18. Oh virtuous one ! For rendering great favour to people, you have made an excellent query. You, whose heart is set on Hari, will hereby spread your fame in the world.

19. Oh Vidura ! There is nothing surprising in this about you who are born of Vyāsa, you who have resorted to Lord Hari with devotion, fixed on him only.

20. You are god Yama, the controller of all subjects who, due to the curse of Māṇḍavya, were born from Vyāsa of the female servant who served as his brother's (Vicitravīrya's) wife.

630. The winkless god Time condemns as useless their advocacy etc. for the establishment of their particular philosophical stance (*sva-sva-mata-sthāpana*)—VC.

21. Your honour was always esteemed (loved) by the Lord (Kṛṣṇa) and his followers. When he was about to depart (from this world), he instructed me to impart knowledge to you.

22. Now I shall describe to you in serial order the sportive actions of the Lord which were exhibited by his *Yoga-māyā*, and which comprise within them the preservation, origination and destruction of the universe.

23. The Lord, the supreme soul of all the souls (*jīvas*)[631] and their master, was all alone before (the creation of) this (universe). When the will of the Supreme Lord viz. Māyā disappears[632] (or when he wills to be alone), existent as he is as a cause, he is not perceived separately as a seer or anything to be seen, (though) he was comprehended by various conjectures[633] (while the gross creation existed).

24. Verily (though) he was then this (only) Seer and the only illuminator* he saw nothing (due to non-existence of the universe). He whose powers (such as Māyā etc.) are asleep (unmanifested)[634] but whose sight was wakeful (not asleep) regarded himself as if he were not-existent.

25.** Oh highly virtuous (Vidura)! That is verily the

---

631. *ātmanām ātmā*—The Master who enters into individual souls to sustain them—VR. (ii) He who is like the orb of the Sun to the individual souls who are like the solar rays (emanating from the orb)—JG.

632. *ātmecchānugatam*—(i) When there was the manifestation of his Will to create the universe—VR. (ii) When he willed to create the universe.—VJ.

633. *nānā-matyupalakṣitaḥ*—(i) He is implied by the ideas like Vaikuṇṭha (Viṣṇu's region)—JG. (ii) He is cognised by various thoughts about actions (effects) and objects—SD.

* *eka-rāṭ*—(i) Of uninterrupted uniform light—VR.

(ii) The Almighty possessing all powers—JG.

634. *supta-śaktiḥ*—(i) Whose power in the form of sentience and non-sentience is in a subtle state—VR. According to VJ., this power is *Māyā*. (ii) Whose powers like Prakṛti and others lie dormant—SD.

**Of the Lord, the Seer of entities possessing existence, Māyā is the power (*śakti*), as it is an attribute of the Lord (not distinct from him). It is Prakṛti having the nature of both sentience and non-sentience (*cetanā—cetanātmikā*). It existed in a subtle form in his person. It is by this power (as the cause) that he created this sentient and non-sentient universe as the effect and remained untouched by the deficiencies of the world—VR. For the convenience of translation the terms *cit* and *acit*

potency of this Seer (God) which is of the nature of both cause and effect (or which is essentially the very soul of the visible and invisible). It is called Māyā (the principle of phenomenality). It is by this power, that the all-pervading Lord created the universe.

26. (When) the commotion of *Guṇas* (attributes) is caused into *Māyā* through the power or effect of Time[635], Viṣṇu, the possessor of perfect intellectual power, inseminates into her his own image or the individual soul through Puruṣa who is his own part (*aṁśa*) controlling prakṛti[636].

27. Then under the impelling force of Time, the *mahat-tattva* was generated from *avyakta* (i.e. Māyā).[637] It is of the nature of *vijñāna* which dispels the darkness of ignorance and manifests the universe lying within the body of the self.

28. And it (the *mahat-tattva*) being under the power of his *aṁśa* or (the resemblance of the Supreme Spirit as the efficient cause) the three attributes (*guṇas* as the material cause) and Time (as the driving force) and within the range of sight of the Lord, manifested itself into another form (called 'Ahaṁkāra'—self-sense or ego-hood) with a desire to create this universe.

---

are rendered as 'sentient' and 'non-sentient'. In Rāmānuja's philosophy *acit* as *miśratattva* and *sattvaśūnya* is inert (*jaḍa*) while as *śuddha sattva* it is *ajaḍa* (non-inert, immaterial) but is different from the Soul and God who are also *ajaḍas* (For details vide A. Senagupta—*Philosophy of Rāmānuja*, pp. 78 ff.

635. *kālavṛttyā*—The fate (adṛṣṭa) of individual souls necessary for the fruition of their *karams*—VJ.

636. As usual VJ. puts forth his usual theory of creation that Viṣṇu in the form of Puruṣa, manifested out of his (Viṣṇu's) original form (*mūla-rūpa*), impregnated both the kinds of *māyās* making the intelligent *māyā* to guide the creation while the non-intelligent *māyā* to change in form.

637. VJ. explains : From *māyā* (a synonym of *avyakta*) which was infused with power by the Lord, was produced *Mahattattva* (viz. the body of the four-faced Brahmā). Being impelled by Time (*Kāla*)—the Puruṣa who knows the destiny of every being and who urges on the creation of the universe—Brahmā who is the *vijñānātmā* who (through the grace of Nārāyaṇa) dispels the darkness of ignorance and exhibits the universe in the body of Soul and thinks that it is his body.

29. From the *mahat-tattva* undergoing modifications was born *ahaṁkāra* (ego-hood) which is the substratum of the effect (viz. *adhibhūta*), the cause (viz. *adhyātma*) and the doer (viz. adhidaiva)[638], and which consists of the elements (*bhūtas*) sense-organs (*indriyas*) and the mind (*manas*) which also implies gods.

30. The ego-hood (*ahaṁkāra*) is of three types—*Vaikārika* (characterised primarily by the *guṇa*, *sattva*), *taijasa* characterised by the *guṇa*, *rajas*) and *tāmasa* (characterised by the *guṇa*, *tamas*). From the principle of ego-hood undergoing modifications, the mind was produced from the *vaikārika* type of I-ness (*ahaṁkāra*). Deities (presiding over sense-organs) are the products of the *sāttvika* type of ego-hood. The perception of the objects of senses is due to these (deities)*

31. The cognitive and conative sense organs are the products of the *taijasa* type of ego-hood[639]. From the *tāmasa* ego-hood was evolved the subtle element (*tanmātrā*) viz. sound wherefrom was produced the sky (*ākāśa*) which is the body of the *ātman* (or the means of knowing Ātman).

32.** When due to its union with Time (*Kāla*), the Māyā-

---

638. 1. 29.b: (*Ahaṁkāra*) which is the cause of the effect (viz. the body,) the cause (viz. the organs of senses) and *kartātmā* (the doer of the above two), and these result in the form of elements (*bhūta*), organs of senses etc.—VR.

* The term *deva* literally means 'that which reveals'. They reveal the objects of senses; therefore they are called *devas*. The Bh.P. adopted the Vedic doctrine of spiritism and extended Godhood to cover all principles of creation from *mahat* to the subtle elements (*tanāmtrās*). So there were as many gods as there were principles of creation. Vide below 3.5.38—For details Bhattacharya PSB I.290-93.

639. VR. states that *taijasa* ego-hood does not produce anything *per se* unless it is in union with the *sāttvika* or *tāmasa* ego-hood. VB. explains that knowledge is predominantly *Sāttvika* and action is *tāmasa*. Hence both types of organs are produced by *rājasa* ego-hood with their help. VB. adds *buddhi* and *prāṇa* to the list of sense organs, stating this to be implied by *ca* the last word in 31.a

** The Bh.P. has adopted the doctrine of causation (*at-kāryavāda*) to explain evolutionary process. Accordingly, the effect can have no quality which is not already in existence in the material cause. Hence it presupposes a subtle form of each element with a potential quality serving as the intermediary of the causal relation between one element and another. This subtle element is technically called *tanmātrā* (unit-potential). For details—B. Bhattacharya PSB. I. 295-97.

power and his part (or intelligent image—*aṁśa*), *Ākāśa* (space) was viewed by the Lord, the subtle element (*tanmātrā*) of touch was produced from the space (*ākāśa*). It (touch) underwent modifications and produced Air (*vāyu*).

33. Vāyu though possessing great force, underwent modifications in combination with space (*ākāśa*) and created the subtle element of *rūpa* (wherefrom was produced) light, the eye (illuminator) of the world.

34. When viewed by the Lord, the light, in conjunction with *Vāyu* and due to the influence of Time, Māyā and *Aṁśa* (his part or intelligent form) created water with taste (as its main characteristic).

35. And water in combination with light was seen by Brahmā and underwent modification and through the influence of *kāla*, *māyā* and *aṁśa* developed into the earth with smell as its characteristic.

36. Oh excellent one (Vidura)! They (the learned ones) know that among the elements (*bhūtas*) beginning with space (*ākāśa*), every later evolute possesses the attributes of the previous ones according to its rank (in the evolutionary process), due to its connection with previous *bhūtas*.[640]

37.* These gods (presiding over *mahat* and other principles) who show the indexes of *time*, *māyā* and *aṁśa*[641] and who

---

640. Thus *Vāyu* possesses the attribute sound of *Ākāśa* as well as its own special attribute Touch. The Earth (*Pṛthvī*) possesses its own attribute smell, as well as the special attributes of its previous evolutes, viz. sound (of *ākāśa*), touch (of Vāyu), etc.

* VJ. explains: Brahmā and other gods presiding over *Mahat* and other principles, were created by Viṣṇu. They possess their bodies due to *Kāla*, *Māyā* and *Aṁśa* and were parts (*kalā* or *aṁśa*) of Viṣṇu, and were in a way distinct from him. Due to their mutual unrelatedness, they could not lay the egg of the universe. (Hence) with their hands folded (to their heads) they prayed the Lord.

SD. explains: (The presiding deities of the principles called) *mahat* and others, (though) parts (*kalā*) of Viṣṇu and conditioned by the agitator Time (creating commotion by its influence), Māyā as the material cause, *aṁśa* (the individual soul) and form, were unable on their own to create the universe due to their unrelatedness. Hence they (deities) praised the Lord.

641. According to ŚR, capacity of transformation (*vikṛti*), fickleness (*vikṣepa*) and sentience (*cetanā*) are the marks of *Kāla*, *Māyā* and *Aṁśa*.

are but parts (kalās = *aṁśas*) of Viṣṇu were unable to create (the universe) due to separateness (unrelatedness), they with folded hands, spoke to the Omnipresent Lord.

Gods said:

38. Oh Lord! We bow to your lotus-like feet which are like an umbrella cooling down the heat of those who resort to it. Recluses, taking shelter under them, instantly ward off the great misery of this worldly existence (*saṁsāra*) even from a distance.

39. Oh Supreme Lord! The Creator[642] and controller of the universe! In this worldly existence, beings, affected by three types of miseries, do not get happiness. Hence, Oh Supreme Soul! we are resorting to the shade of your feet which impart knowledge.

40. We take shelter of your sanctifying feet which are the source of the (Gaṅgā) holiest of all the rivers, the waters of which remove sins—the feet which the sages in their detached minds, seek with the help of birds in the form of the Vedas whose nests (dwelling places) are in your lotus-like face.

41. We come for shelter to the place (lit. foot-stool) of your lotus-like feet, concentrating on them in our hearts purified by faith and devotion (with unattached *karma-yoga* and become self-controlled by knowledge which is reinforced by non-attachment.

42. Oh Lord! You have taken re-incarnation for the creation, sustenance and destruction of the universe. All of us have come to resort to your lotus- like feet, the contemplation of which gives Liberation (state of fearlessness) to your men (devotees).

43. Oh Supreme Lord ! We adore your lotus-like feet which in spite of your residence in their bodies (as *antar-yāmin*), are far distant (and hence not accessible) to those men who have a foolishly obstinate attachment to the contemptible body as 'I', and to their houses and property as 'mine'.[643]

---

642. v.l. *ṛte*—No happiness is possible without resorting to your feet (ŚR).

643. *yatsānu . . . . gehe*—Relatives like wife, sons etc. and property or belongings are the ties of the body and house etc. which are the product or effects of the inert matter—VR.

44. Oh Lord of Lords who are praised by the greatest! It is well-known that those whose minds are carried away by sense-organs which are attracted by external objects[644], do not therefore, see those devotees who have taken resort to the glory of your gracious foot-steps.[645]

45. Oh God! Those whose minds are purified by deep devotion generated by drinking the nectar of your stories, get knowledge, the strength of which lies in non-attachment (to the world) and easily attain to *Vaikuṇṭha*.

46. So also other wise persons, having conquered the most powerful *Prakṛti* by their power of *Samādhi-Yoga* (*Yoga* in which mind is to be concentrated on the soul—*ātman*) enter into you—the *Puruṣa*. Theirs is (a path of) hardships. But there is no (such) (harsh) exertion in your service.

47. Therefore, Oh Primitive Being, all of us who have been created serially by you, for the creation of the world, and who possess the three separate *guṇas* (viz. *sattva*, *rajas* and *tamas*) as our characteristic, are not able (to coordinate our activities) to present to you your instrument of sports, viz. the universe.[646]

48. Oh unborn Lord! (Manage thus) that we may offer you your entire oblations at the proper time, and we shall be able to eat our food (i.e. enjoyments as our enjoyment is really your enjoyment) and that these beings (worlds) staying in their own places, may present offerings to us both, and may certainly enjoy their own food without difficulty.

49. Oh God! You are the primary cause of (us) gods along with our descendants (or along with effects); you are the changeless, primeval Puruṣa presiding over all. You who are unborn, have deposited your semen, viz. the all-knowing[647] principle called *mahat*, in your beginningless power called

644. *asat*—false. vain—SD.

645. ŚR explains the better reading *patho .... lakṣyān*, as follows: Those (whose minds are carried by sense organs) do not see the paths shown by your graceful footsteps viz. the path of the good or the nine-fold path of devotion such as *śravaṇa* etc.

646. *sva-vihāra-tantram*—Executing the work assigned to us—(VR).

647. *Kavim*—(i) Brahmā, the *Samaṣṭi-Puruṣa*—VR.

(ii) The individual soul as *samaṣṭi*.

(iii) The Omniscient God knowing the past and future—VJ.

Māyā which is the source of attributes (like *sattva*, *rajas*) and actions (like birth etc.)[648]

50. Oh Supreme Soul! What should we, *mahat* and others, do for you to achieve the object for which we are born? Oh God! For the execution of work assigned to us, grant unto us, who are dependant on your grace, your own eye (the power of knowledge) along with your power (of action).

CHAPTER SIX

(Cosmology : *Creation of the Universe*)

The Sage said :

1-2. Having seen the state of his existing potencies that they were disparate and that their power of creating the universe lay dormant, the Supreme Lord of miraculous deeds bearing with him his divine power called time[649] (which has no separate existence from him) entered simultaneously the group of twenty-three principles (viz. *mahat*+egohood+5 subtle elements+5 gross elements+10 organs of senses both conative and cognitive+mind).

3. The Lord who entered the group (of 23 principles) made the separate principles to work together by his power of action (*kriyā-śakti*) rousing up their dormant working capacity.[650]

4. The group of twenty-three principles, the potency of which to work is thus roused by the Lord, and which were thus impelled by him, created the Virāṭ Puruṣa by contributing their individual parts.

648. You have deposited your power of creating the universe and god Brahmā, (the *samaṣṭi-Puruṣa*) in Prakṛti, which is your own power (an attribute with no separate existence outside God)—the Power which is the cause of the organs of senses, both conative and cognitive—VR.

649. *kāla-saṁjñam* : (i) The divine power which creates commotion to produce the effects; or *Prakṛti* roused to action by Time—ŚR.

(ii) (Lord Viṣṇu entered along with) Lakṣmī, the intelligent *prakṛti*, designated as Kāla.

650. Karma—The actions or fate in store (*adṛṣṭa*) of *jīvas*.

5. The group of the creative principles of the universe, due to the entry of only a part (*aṁśa*) of the Supreme Lord in them, became assimilated with each other and were in commotion leading to the creation (of the Virāṭ Puruṣa) in which are the movables and immovables.

6. That Virāṭ Puruṣa of gold (of the complexion of gold) containing all the beings (in invisible forms) stayed in the egg (called *Brahmāṇḍa*) on cosmic waters for one thousand years[651].

7. Verily he (the *Virāṭ Puruṣa*), the offspring (the product) of the principles of the universe, the possessor of the divine potency of knowledge, action and spirit,[652] divided[653] himself as one (in the form of the spirit residing in the heart), as ten (in the from of the vital airs — *Prāṇas* — viz. *Prāṇa, apāna, vyāna, udāna, samāna, nāga, kūrma, kṛkala, devadatta* and *dhanañjaya*), and as three (viz. forms related to *adhibhūta, adhidaiva* and *adhyātma*).

8. This[654] (*Virāṭ puruṣā*) is the individual soul within all beings. He himself is a part of the Supreme Soul (*paramātman*). He is the first incarnation (*avatāra*) in whom is supported the multitude of all beings.[655]

9. The Virāṭ Puruṣa (God Brahma) has three forms, viz. those related with *adhyātma, adhidaiva* and *adhibhūta*[656], ten forms

651. Cf. Bh.P. 2.5.34; 2.10.11.

652. *deva-karmātma-śaktimān*—According to VR. these powers are : *Jīva śakti* or *avidyā*, the *karma* of *jīvas* and the spirit or intelligent power (*cit śakti*) useful in the creation of the body and other conditions of *jīva*. VJ. reads 'daiva-' for 'deva' and interpreting *garbha* as the Inner controller (*antaryāmin*) of the principles e.g. *mahat* and others, enumerates the potencies as (1) Power superior to gods like Brahmā, (2) the fate (*adṛṣṭa*) of *jīvas* and (3) *Prakṛti* the medium of enjoying pleasure, pain etc.

653. This division is clarified in verse 9 below.

654. *eṣaḥ*—VR. thinks that this refers to god Brahmā who is the support of all individual beings, and who is an incarnation (*avatāra*) of the 'possession' (*āveśa*) type. VJ. states that word *eṣa* refers to Hari in the Puruṣa incarnation. On the support of the Puruṣa depends the creation and preservation of all beings.

655. It is in the body of the *Virāṭ* (*Puruṣa*) that the whole of the universe consisting of mobiles and immobiles is seen—GD.

656. According to VR. *sādhyātma*=with *jīva* (indweller of the body). Sādhidaiva=with the senses in the *samaṣṭi* stage as in the Sun etc. Sādhibhūta=with sounds etc. which are the characteristics of elements (*bhūtas*).

viz. the ten vital airs (*prāṇas*) and one form, viz. that connected with the heart.

10*. Lord Viṣṇu (*adhokṣaja*), remembering the prayer (vide supra 3.5.48) of (the presiding deities of) the Principles of creating the universe, planned (the person of) the *Virāṭ* (or *Hiraṇyagarbha*) by his power of knowledge (or spiritual light), for enabling them to perform their functions.

11. Now, hear from me, how many places of residence of gods (Presiding deities of sense-organs) were created in the body of *Virāṭ* by his penance, viz. the power of his knowledge.

12** (When) his mouth was differentiated, (formed) Fire, the protector of the world, entered it along with his power called speech. Hence *jīvas* (people) get the power of speech.

13. Palate was evolved in Hari (the *Virāṭ Puruṣa*). The protector of the world, called Varuṇa, entered it along with part (*aṁśa*) called tongue (the conative sense-organ of taste) whereby the *jīva* attains the power of taste.

14. (When) the nostrils of Viṣṇu (the *Virāṭ Puruṣa*) were formed, the two Aśvinikumāras occupied (entered) them by their power, viz. the sense of smell, whereby the *jīva* attained the capacity to smell.

15. (Then) the two eyes (of the *Virāṭ Puruṣa*) were formed. The Sun, a protector of the world, entered them with his power, viz., the sense of sight. Hence the *jīvas* get the perception of forms and colours by the eyes.

16. (Then the *Virāṭ Puruṣa* had) his skins developed. The protector of the world called Vāyu entered it along with his power of breath (Prāṇa) whereby the *jīva* gets the sense of touch.

17. (When) his two ears were evolved, the (presiding deities of) quarters along with their power of audition, entered them as their place, whereby he (the *jīva*) can hear the sound.

---

* Lord Viṣṇu entered the person of Virāṭ (God Brahmā) as an *antaryāmin* (controller from within). He enlarged the body of Virāj (god Brahmā) to provide accommodation to the deities (such as Fire etc.) —VJ.

** Cf. supra II.10. 17-30.

18*. (When) the skin was evolved (of the *Virāṭ Puruṣa*), the presiding deities of herbs (and plants) occupied it as their place, by their parts called hair, whereby the *jīva* can feel the itching-sensation.

19. Then his penis was evolved. God Ka (i.e. Prajāpati) along with his power—semen—entered it as his residence. (It is) by this (organ) that the *jīva* (or the world) gets (sexual) pleasure.

20. Then the anus of the Virāṭ Puruṣa was evolved. Mitra, the controller (protector) of the world, along with his part (known as) *Pāyu* (anus), entered it. (It is) by this that the *jīva* has the organ of excretion.

21. His hands were (then) developed. Indra, the lord of the Heaven (*Svarga*), along with his power of making sales and purchases, entered them, whereby a man can earn his livelihood.

22. Then his feet were evolved. Viṣṇu, the Lord of the world, entered them along with his power of locomotion, by which man can reach his desired place.

23. And intellect was evolved in him. God Brahmā, with his power of accurate perception, entered it as his place. (It is) by this faculty that the object of knowledge is comprehended.

24. And his heart was evolved. The moon, along with his faculty called mind, entered it as his abode. Hence the *jīva* (or the world) understands changes (in the state of mind, thoughts etc.).

25.** God Rudra (*abhimāna*) along with his capacity of action (or principle of activity) entered as his place, the evolved egohood (*ātman*) of *Virāṭ Puruṣa*. It is by this (ego-hood) that *jīva* executes his work (as his own).

---

* ŚR. is conscious of the duplication of *tvac* and *carman* (in verses 16 and 18) and explains it as the difference of place and difference in functions, viz. touch and itch. VD. explains that the outer part of the skin is *carman* and *tvac* is related both to its inside and outside.

** VJ. follows a different text as shown by his interpretation : Then the special *nāḍī* called *ātmanāḍī* was evolved. Bṛhaspati with his faculty of intelligence entered it. Hereby god Brahmā arrives at correct conclusion.

26. And his *sattva*[657] (mind and intellect was evolved). *Mahat* (god Brahmā) occupied this abode along with *citta* whereby he (the *jīva*) arrives at comprehension (understanding).[658]

27. From his (Virāṭ Puruṣa's) head was produced the *svar-loka*. The earth came forth from his feet, and the sky from his navel. The products (effects) of *guṇas* (like *sattva*) such as gods and others are seen in these (regions).[659]

28. Gods attained the Heaven by their excellence of *sattva* attribute. Due to their nature predominated by *sattva*, *Paṇis* (i.e. men who deal with gods by performance of sacrifices) and their belongings (like cows etc.) remained on the earth.

29. Due to their nature characterised by the third (*guṇa* viz. *tamas*), the mass of the followers of Rudra resorted to the Lord's navel, viz. the space between the two regions mentioned above.

30* Oh leader of Kurus! From the mouth of the Puruṣa came forth Brahman (the Veda) and the Brāhmaṇa class like syllables coming out from the mouth (head). Hence the Brāhmaṇa Varṇa became the foremost among the Varṇas.

31. From his arms emanated the power of protection and the Kṣatriya class who follows that vow, viz. the duty of protecting the world. This class born from Puruṣa (Lord Viṣṇu) protects the classes of people from wounds (i.e. injuries or troubles) caused by thorns (in the form of miscreants).

32. From the thighs of that All-pervading Lord were born the vocations like agriculture which maintain the livelihood of the public. The Vaiśya class, born from the same part of the

---

657. *Sattva*—The nāḍī called *sattva*—VJ.
The inner organ called *Buddhi* and *citta*—VR.

658. *Vijñānam*—Correct understanding of what should be done —VR.

659. Gods, men etc. possessing the *guṇas* like *sattva*, *rajas* and *tamas* are seen (i.e. created) in these regions—VR.

(ii) Beings in whom the states of happiness, activity etc. which are the characteristics of *guṇas* (like *sattva* etc.) are found in these regions.—VJ.

* VR. explains that as the Vedas (Brahma) which is the subsistence of the Brāhmaṇa class, came forth from the mouth (or head), the Brāhmaṇa Varṇa became the chief (head) class (Varṇa) of all.

body, carries out trades and agriculture for the maintenance of people.

33. From the feet of the Lord was born service for the achievement of religion. Formerly the Śūdra class was born for the sake of service, whereby Hari is pleased.

34. These classes (Brāhmaṇas etc.) who are born along with their means of livelihood (and duties) from Hari, worship with faith their creator and master Hari for self-purification, by following the path of their duties.

35. Oh Vidura! Who can even dare to wish (confidently) to describe fully in details this (universe) which has been created by the *yoga-māyā* of the Almighty Lord who assumes the forms of *kāla* (time), *karma* (action) and *svabhāva* (nature).

36. It is for purifying my tongue of the impurities caused by uttering things unrelated with Hari that I, however, describe the glory of Hari to the best of my intellect, according as I have heard of it.

37. They say that the description of the excellent qualities of him who is the best amongst personages of holy fame, brings the highest benefit to the power of speech of men, and listening to the nectarlike stories (of Hari) as described by the learned is the greatest benefit of the power of hearing.

38. Oh child! Was the greatness of Lord Hari thoroughly comprehended by the First Sage (Brahmā) with his intelligence matured by *yoga* after (performing penance for) one thousand years ?

39. The *Māyā* of the Lord deludes even the possessor of *Māyā* so much that the Lord himself does not know the course of his Māyā. What of others ?

40. Salutations to the Almighty Lord without reaching whom (without realizing whose glory) the Vedas (or the powers of speech), mind (though purified by *yoga*), Rudra (ego-hood) and other deities presiding over organs of senses, have returned.

CHAPTER SEVEN

(*Vidura's Queries*)

Śrī Śuka said :

1. To Maitreya who was speaking thus, Vidura, the learned son of Vyāsa, addressed (the following), as if to please him with his request.

Vidura said :

2. Oh Brahman ! How is it possible that attributes (like *sattva, rajas*) and activity can be predicated of the Supreme Lord who is pure consciousness, devoid of attributes and changeless, even by way of sport (the *līlā*-theory) ?

3. It is the desire in the case of a child which propels it to play, and that desire to play comes from something else (e.g. a toy or invitation to play), but how (is it applicable to God) who is self-satisfied and who is ever without a second.

4-5. (It is argued that) the Supreme Lord created the universe by his Māyā consisting of *guṇas* and (which deludes the Soul to feel that he is the doer and enjoyer). It is by *Māyā* that he protects it and withdraws it. The Soul is essentially of the nature of knowledge or consciousness and unaffected by place, time or condition either internally (through himself) or externally (through other agency). How can such Soul be united with the unborn (*Māyā*) ?

6. Only this Supreme Lord alone is present in all bodies. How can he be subjected to misfortune or pain by *karmas* ? (i.e. *saṁsāra* does not exist in the case of *jīva* as he is the same as Brahman).

7. Oh learned one ! My mind feels depressed in this calamity of ignorance. Oh Lord ! Please remove this great mental delusion from our mind.

Śrī Śuka said :

8. The sage who was thus prompted by Vidura who was desirous of knowing the truth, smilingly replied, with his mind concentrated on the Lord, and free from pride.

9. It is the *Māyā* of the Almighty Lord that is against all logic (supra-logical). Hence (the experience of) affliction

and bondage to (the soul who is essentially) free from bondage (and misery)[660]

10. Just as a man witnessing a dream gets an inconsistent experience of being beheaded etc., though it is not a reality.[661]

11. Just as trembling and other disturbances caused by the water appear to be the attribute of the moon (reflected) in the water, even though it is not attributable to the (real) Moon (in the sky), similarly attributes of the non-Soul (the physical body etc.) seem to belong to the Soul (*jīva*), a seer (who identifies himself with the body).[662]

12. Verily it is by the path of *nivṛtti* (abstinence from work—by giving up desire for its fruit), through the grace of Vāsudeva, and by devotion to the Almighty Lord, that this (mistaken identification of the Soul with the body) slowly disappears here.

13. Now, when the organs of the senses (instead of pursuing outer objects) become steadfast on Hari, the Seer, the internal controller (*antaryāmin*), the Supreme Lord, all the afflictions completely subside (disappear) as in the case of a man who is fast asleep.

14. Repetition (of the description of) and listening to

---

660. JG. in his long com. raises the point why the Soul (*jīva*) who is a form of God suffers the bondage of affliction, and explains that it is due to the supra-logical nature of the *māyā-śakti* of God. The power of God is both internal (*antaraṅga*) and external (*bahiraṅga*). Hence what happens in the region of the external of God cannot affect his own internal nature. Thus though God in the form of *jīvas* may experience bondage or suffering, he is internally unaffected. It is this supra-logical conception which explains how God can be within the power of the *Māyā* as well as its controller.

661. Just as in the case of *jīva*, in the stage when he has not realised the Soul (*ātman*), he wrongly identifies himself with the body which is in reality different from him, and experiences beheading etc. But after self-realization, knowing his separateness from the body, and his being a part of God, he is not thus affected.—VR.

662. VR. points to the distinction between the Soul (ātmā) or *jīva* and Supreme Soul (*paramātmā*). Sorrow, delusion etc. are caused, as *jīva* mistakenly thinks himself to be the body. The Supreme Soul who is not influenced (lit. covered) by *Avidyā* and who is the controller of *Prakṛti* and *Puruṣa* is unaffected by the effects or working of *avidyā*.

the attributes of Hari, cause the complete subsidence (disappearance) of miseries. What again (need be spoken of the effect of) the love felt in the heart, for worshipping the pollen-dust of His lotus-like feet.

Vidura said:

15. Oh Lord ! my doubt has been cut off by the sword of your happy exposition. My mind can properly grasp both the absolute independence of the Supreme Lord and the dependence of *jīva* on him[663].

16.* Oh learned one, you have well explained that all these unreal, rootless, miseries appear due to the basis of the *ātma-māyā* (*māyā* deluding the Soul or *jīva*). The root-cause of the universe is not outside (the *māyā*).

17. Only those two, viz. one who is the stupidmost (and attached to physical body etc.) and one who has reached beyond *Buddhi* (i. e. *Prakṛti* and realized God live happily in the world. But the person who is between these (extremes), undergoes sufferings (as he desires to leave the worldly life but cannot do so, for want of experience of the inner bliss.

---

663. *ubhayatra...sampradhāvati* : (1) Or : My mind can grasp the concepts of bondage and liberation—ŚR.

(2) My mind is attracted both to the listening and repetition of his attributes as well as to the service of his feet—VR.

(3) By 'both' VJ. takes (i) attachment to the body and its belonging and (ii) God, Hari.

(4) JG. understands (i) the Supreme Lord and (ii) jīva or (i) knowledge and (ii) devotion which is a means to it.

(5) VB. follows ŚR above.

* VR. differs : You have explained it well that *ātman* (individual Soul) and *māyā* (prakṛti) are Hari's place of residence. The source of the universe (i.e. Brahman) is outside it and has not created it. Therefore the universe being rootless appears purposeless, a delusion.

(ii) VJ. explains. Oh possessor of the proper knowledge for realization of Brahman, your explanation that all this is due to Hari's own power called *māyā* is convincing enough to clear up all doubts. The idea of delusion in the *māyā* concept is dispelled. But all this appears to me purposeless and baseless except on the presumption of *adṛṣṭa*.

18. Having determined the unreality of the world despite its apparent existence, I shall dispel even that sense by serving your feet.

19. It is by service (of persons like you) that ardent intensity of love for the feet of the changeless Lord Hari (the enemy of the demon Madhu), is created leading to the destruction of miseries (*saṁsāra*).

20. The service of those who are on the pathway to Vaikuṇṭha,[664] and amongst whom the deeds of Janārdana, the God of gods are always eulogised, is very difficult to be obtained (for rendering) by people (who have little penance to their credit).

21. (You said that) having created in the beginning, the principles like *mahat* and others with their modifications in due course, and having raised the *Virāj* (the Egg of the universe) out of them, the All-pervading Lord entered into it.

22. (The *Virāj*) who is called the First Man (*ādya Puruṣa*) possessing thousands) of feet, thighs and arms, and in whom all the worlds along with their modifications are accommodated.

23. As explained by you, in him are the vital-airs (*prāṇas*) of ten kinds, and also in the three forms viz. the sense-organs, the objects and the presiding deities of the sense-organs (also called *indriyas*—sense-organs—here), and the castes (*varṇas*) came forth (were formed) from him. Please describe to us his powers.

24. (*Virāṭ*) wherein lived beings of different forms, with their sons, grandsons, daughter's sons and other descendants of their *gotra* (clan) who have filled the world.

25. Who were the lords of the created beings (*prajāpatis*) created by lord of Prajāpatis (Brahmadeva)? What are (god Brahmā's) creations, subcreations? Who were the Manus and kings in the *manvantaras* (periods of Manus) created by him?

26. Oh Maitreya, describe to me their dynasties, and the deeds of those born in their families; and the situation and the area, dimensions of this world and of the worlds that are above and below this.

27. Tell us about the creation and classification of beasts,

664. Or : who can guide to the path of Vaikuṇṭha—VR.

human beings, gods, reptiles and birds and those born of womb, sweat, eggs (or twice-born) and vegetables.

28. Expound to us the great exploits of Viṣṇu, the creator, the support of the (process of) creation, sustenance and destruction of the world through his *guṇāvatāras* (incarnations characterised by *guṇas*, viz. *sattva*, *rajas* and *tamas*, such as Brahmā etc.)

29-30. Oh Lord (Maitreya), explain the classification of *Varṇas* (castes) and stages of life (*āśramas*) according to their external characteristics, courses of conduct and nature, the births and deeds of sages, the division of the Vedas, the details of sacrifices, the paths of Yoga, Sāṅkhya characterised by renunciation of the fruit of Karmas, and the *Tantra* as enjoined by the Supreme Lord.

31. Oh sinless one, explain to me in details :

The crookedness of the path of the non-believers in Veda, the place etc. of the progeny of the reverse (*pratiloma*) type of marriages, and the several courses of *jīva* as a result of their attributes (*guṇas*) and deeds (karmas).

32. The ways of accomplishing the *puruṣārthas* (objects of life such as *dharma*, *artha*, *kāma* and *mokṣa*) without mutual conflict, the different methods of commerce and agriculture, the duties of kings (or politics), and the courses of study.

33. The prescribed way of performing *śrāddha*, the creation of the manes (*pitṛs*) and the arrangement of planets, constellations and stars in the division of Time.

34. The fruits of charitable gifts, of penance, of meritorious acts (such as performance of sacrifices, constructions of amenities like tanks etc.), the religious duties of men on travel, and of men in adverse circumstances.

35. The course (of action) whereby Janārdana, the source of Dharma will be propitiated, and favours one with his grace.

36. Oh best among the twice-born persons ! Teachers who are kindly disposed to the distressed, explain to obedient disciples and sons, even without being enquired about it.

37. Oh revered one ! In how many ways is the withdrawal (destruction) of the principles takes effect ? At that time

who will resort to him and who will follow him in his *yogic* sleep ?

38. (Tell us) what the real nature of *jīva* is, and the essential state of the Supreme Soul and the knowledge pertaining to *Upaniṣads*, and the purpose of the pupil-teacher relationship.

39. Oh sinless Maitreya, explain the means prescribed by the wise ones, for the acquisition of that knowledge here. Otherwise how can that knowledge, devotion or non-attachment develop in men automatically (if there be no grace of the spiritual guide)?

40. As a friend, please tell me who am making these queries with a desire to know the deeds of Hari, and who am ignorant due to the loss of the vision of knowledge through (the influence of) *māyā*.

41. Oh sinless, one all Vedas, sacrifices, penances and charitable donations will not amount even to a fraction of the act of offering shelter to a Soul (by imparting the knowledge of the Truth).

Śrī Śuka said :

42. The prominent sage who was thus asked by a prominent person among the Kurus, about matters explained in the Purāṇas was overjoyed at being urged to narrate the episodes of the Lord, and spoke to him smilingly.

CHAPTER EIGHT

(Creation of Brahmā—His Vision of Nārāyana)

Maitreya said :

1. The lineage of Pūru is really worthy of being served by the good, as you, who (as an incarnation of Yama) are one of the Protectors of the world, and who regard the Lord as the chief object, are born in it. At every step and at every moment, you bring freshness to the garland of the glory of the invincible Lord (Hari).

2. It is for removing the great misery of people who get into it for the sake of petty pleasures, that I commence the *Bhāgavata Purāṇa* which the venerable Lord narrated to sages.

3. With a desire to know the real nature of the God, higher than Lord Saṅkarṣaṇa, sages, of whom (Sanat-) Kumāra was prominent, asked the respectable Saṅkarṣaṇa, the first of gods, whose ken of knowledge was unobstructed, and who was seated on the ground.

4. (Saṅkarṣaṇa) who was highly worshipful of his support whom (they) call Vāsudeva, and who had turned unto himself his eyes which were closed like a lotus-bud (while in meditation), and who slightly opened them for favouring wise sages (like Sanaka and others).

5. Sages (like Sanatkumāra) touched with their matted hair dripping with the sacred waters of the heavenly Ganges (Mandākinī) the lotus-foot stool of Saṅkarṣaṇa—the foot-stool which the daughters of the king of Snakes worship by offering various gifts with love for getting (good) husbands.

6. (The sages) who knew Saṅkarṣaṇa and (hence) constantly eulogised his deeds in words pronounced falteringly due to intenselove, (asked) Saṅkarṣaṇa whose thousand raised hoods were brightened by excellent precious stones studded in a thousand crowns.

7. It is traditionally reported that the most venerable Saṅkarṣaṇa taught this to Sanatkumāra who was devoted to the duties of the path of renunciation; and that he (Sanatkumāra), when requested, taught it to Sāṅkhyāyana,[665] the observer of vows.

8. With a desire to extol the powers and glories of the Lord, Sāṅkhyāyana, the foremost among the Parama-haṁsas, narrated it first to his disciple and our preceptor Parāśara and then to Bṛhaspati.

9. The merciful sage, blessed by Pulastya[666], expounded

665. *Sāṅkhyāyana*—A sage of the Vasiṣṭha family, probably the same as the author of the Sāṁkhyāyana Brāhmaṇa of the Ṛgveda and other *Śrautasūtras* known by his name BPK 341, DHM 280.

666. ŚR. records a traditional story: When Parāśara's father was eaten up by a Rākṣasa, Parāśara wanted to destroy the Rākṣasa race. But Vasiṣṭha dissuaded him. Pulastya finding that his progeny was thus spared, blessed Parāśara that he would be a narrator of Purāṇas.

to me the first (i.e. the most important) Purāṇa (viz. the Bhāgavata). Oh child (Vidura), I narrate this to you who are faithful, and always devoted (to the Lord).[667]

10. When Viṣṇu delighted in the blissful stage of his own self, inactive and alone, lay on the bed of the king of Snakes (Śeṣa) and closed his eyes in sleep without any interruption of his vision (power of intelligence), this whole universe was immersed in water.

11. Having conserved the subtle elements within his body, and arousing his power called Time, he stayed in the water which was his abode, just like the fire which resides in the wood, without exhibiting his power (of burning).

12. Sleeping over the waters for a period of one thousand aggregates of four *yugas*, he who had obtained the whole system of doing actions through his power called Time, which was vigilant, visualized all the worlds lying dormant in his own body.

13. Then the (aggregate of) subtle elements lying within him which he viewed intently, got agitated by the attribute called *rajas*, (which was) impelled by Time. It sprouted forth from the region of his navel, in the process of evolution.

14. By (the propelling force of) Time which awakens the *adṛṣṭa* (fate) of beings, the Self-born lotus-bred sprouted forth suddenly, illuminating like the Sun, the vast expanse of water with its splendour.

15. Oh Vidura, that very Viṣṇu entered (as an *antaryāmin*) the world-lotus which shows all the *guṇas* (objects) essential for the enjoyment of *jīvas*. Within the lotus was born the creator of the world, the Veda incarnate, whom they call self-born (*svayambhu*).

16. Occupying the stalk of that lotus, and not seeing the worlds, the self-born god Brahmā cast his glances on all sides in the sky, and thus got four faces corresponding to the four directions (of world).

17. The first god Brahmā, seated upon the lotus which sprang up from the unending high billows of waters, tossed heavily by world-annihilating stormy winds, did not under-

667. This tradition of the Bhāgavata is different from that given in the previous *Skandhas* (vide supra I.4, II.9).

stand with certainty, the real nature of the lotus which contained the world, and even of his own self.

18. "Who am I seated on this lotus? Whence has this solitary lotus grown on the waters ? There must be something beneath on which this lotus rests supported. That must be surely some positive existence."

19. Thinking thus, the unborn god (Brahmā) entered through the hollow passage in the stalk of the lotus, into the waters. Going deep down in search of the support of the rough stalk of that lotus, he did not reach it.

20. Oh Vidura ! A very long time with three tyres (divisions, viz. the past, the present, the future) elapsed while he (Brahmadeva) was searching the source of the lotus (the cause of his creation) in the fathomless darkness—Time which is a weapon in God's hand which creates terror in beings and reduces (their) life.

21. Then the God (Brahmā) who did not achieve his objective, returned thence. Having resumed his seat, he gradually restrained his mind by controlling his breath, and sat down resorting to *samādhi-yoga* (the path of deep meditation).

22. The unborn God (Brahmā) in whom knowledge arose by the practice of *yoga* for a period of man's life-span (100 years), visualized that unforeseen Brahman manifested of its own accord in his heart.

23. He saw a Man (Puruṣa) lying on the bed of the spacious body of Śeṣa white like lotus fibres, on the waters of the deluge, the darkness of which was dispelled by the lustre of gems on the myriad heads of the umbrella-like hoods (of Śeṣa).

24. Who excelled in beauty a mountain of emeralds, with (golden) evening clouds overhanging its slopes like garments (which is surpassed by his *Pītāmbara*—yellow silken garment), with a number of gold peaks (which are outdone in their splendour by his crown), with its Vanamālā—garland of forest flowers—abounding in precious stones, springs, herbs and flowers (excelled in beauty by his Vanamālā), and with bamboos resembling its arms, and trees as its feet (surpassed his arms and feet).

25. Who, by the dimensions of his beautiful and uncomparable body, accommodated the three worlds (viz. *Svarga*,

Mṛtyu and *Pātāla*), and who (with his body) decorated by a variety of heavenly ornaments and silken garments beautified the ornaments and garments themselves, by his beautiful person.

26. To men who, for attaining their desired objects, worship him in the pure ways, prescribed in the Vedas, he shows, out of grace, his lotus-like feet with toes beautiful like petals and shining in the rays of his moon-like nails.

27. Who (reciprocally) honours his devotees by his face with a smile that removes the afflictions of the world, (with ears) beautified by resplendent earrings, (face) appearing reddish on account of his lower lip like *bimba* fruit, and shapely with its beautiful nose and eyebrows.

28. Oh child (Vidura), (he saw the Puruṣa) who appeared beautiful and adorned with a garment, golden in colour, like the pollen of the Kadamba flowers, and with a girdle round his waist, and his chest adorned with an invaluable necklace, and with (his) favourite decoration called Śrīvatsa.

29. Who was (like) a great tree of the universe with thousand branches in the forms of arms resplendent with priceless precious stones, and the armlets (*keyūra*), with its root invisible (in Brahman), and whose arms are coiled round by the body of great snake (or Śeṣa).

30. Who was like a great mountain, the support of the movables and immovables, a dear friend of the best of snakes (Śeṣa), who is surrounded by waters, whose thousand crowns are like golden peaks, and the gem Kaustubha (adorning) his chest (was like a mine of precious stones).

31. (Brahmā saw) Hari who wore a Vanamālā (garland of Tulasī leaves, etc.) in the form of his glory, (Vanamālā) which beautified by the Veda singing sweetly his glory like humming bees and who is unapproachable to (gods like) the Sun, the Moon, the Wind and the Fire, and who is unassailable due to the weapons with range throughout the three worlds, circling round him.

32. At that very instant (when Brahmā saw Hari), he obtained the knowledge necessary for the creation of the world. He saw the lotus sprouting out of the (Lord's) pond-like navel, himself, the (cosmic) waters, the Wind (blowing

tempestuously during the deluge) and the sky. He saw nothing more (than these).

33. When he (Brahmā), being associated with the attribute *rajas*, became desirous of creating beings, and having seen only these (the abovementioned five objects such as the lotus, the cosmic water, the wind, etc.) as the causes of the world, fixed his heart on God and, began to praise the Lord who deserved it.

CHAPTER NINE

(*Brahmā's Prayer and Viṣṇu's Boon*)

Brahmā said :

1. Oh Lord ! It is after a penance for a very long time that you have been (luckily) realized by me today. It is indeed the defect of beings conditioned by body that your real essential nature is not understood by them. Nothing other than you, exists. (Anything else that appears to be) is not pure (is false) because it is you who appear to be many due to the intermixture of the *guṇas* of Māyā.[668]

---

668. According to VR. : This verse expresses the self satisfaction of Brahmā's God-realization, viz. the whole of this universe consisting of *cit* and *acit* is the body of God, and it explains that there is nothing which is outside Brahman.

Oh Lord! Really it is after the acquisition (accumulation) of penance for a pretty long period that you have been now seen by me in your real form. The *Kṣetrajñas* (individual Souls) conditioned by physical body as a result of their *karmas*, do not know your real nature which fully possesses the six attributes of Bhagavān. Oh Lord, there is no such thing as is other than you. (You are its soul When you are realised everything is realized). Gods and other things which appear independent of (other than) you are not the objects of correct perception, due to the effect of the attribute of Māyā or Prakṛti. Though you are one, you shine (manifest yourself) as many.

nanu . . . avadyam etc.—VJ. explains : That the real nature of the Lord is not realized by beings is erroneous, as the Lord, though invisible in form, is realized by devotion. It is due to sin

2. This is your form from which, due to eternal manifestation of the power of intelligence, ignorance or *tamas* disappears,—form which, from the beginning, you have assumed for conferring (your) grace on the good; and which is the seed (source) of hundreds of incarnations. And from His region of the navel-lotus, I came into existence (lit. was manifested).

3. Most excellent Lord ! I do not see any form of yours other than this beautiful one of manifest light, beyond (i.e. destitute of) differences, and full of bliss. Hence I resort to this one form of yours which creates the world but itself is different from it, and which is the source of the *bhūtas* (elements) and sense-organs[669].

4. Oh auspiciousness incarnate (i.e. God who is auspicious to the universe), you have really manifested this very (form) to your devotees in their meditation for their good (or prosperity), we offer obeisance to you (a gracious) Lord who is spurned by the atheists (like Mīmāṁsakas, Sāṅkhyas etc.) and believers in false logic and who therefore deserve (stay in) Hell.

5. Oh Lord, you do not go away from the lotus-like hearts of your men (devotees) who enjoy by the passage of their ears the fragrance of your lotus-bud-like feet which is carried (to them) by wind (in the form) of the Vedas and who clasped your feet with intense (and unswerving) devotion.

6. So long as the people do not resort to your feet which offer freedom from fear of *saṁsāra*, they face the fear

---

that God is not realized by beings. Not that there is non-existence of things other than the Lord, but they do not exist independently, but owe their existence to him. But things other than you are impure, and you are absolutely pure. You are present by your incarnations in *mahat* and other principles. It is due to the *guṇas* of *Prakṛti* that things other than you are defective.

JG. : Though you are pure in your internal capacity of infinite glory, you appear many in the form of the world as a result of the intermixture of the attributes of your external power called Māyā.

669. Oh Supreme One, I do not see your essential form other than this form which is full of bliss (dispelling all miseries), devoid of the differences of *jātis* and *guṇas*, whose knowledge (or will—*saṅkalpas*) is unobstructed; which is different from the universe, yet it is the cause consisting of *bhūtas* and sense organs. I take shelter of this form—VR.

pertaining to wealth, house and friends (and caused by) sorrow, desire, dishonour, covetousness and false sense of attachment to possessions (lit. 'this is mine') which is the cause of sorrow.

7. Those are verily deprived of their senses by their fate, whose senses (minds) are averse to (listening and eulogising) your deeds which remove all inauspiciousness (misery etc.). Those wretched ones, with minds overpowered with avarice, continuously perform misdeeds for a very slight pleasure for gratifying their low desires.

8. Oh Acyuta, Lord of wide strides (as Trivikrama), my heart is deeply pained to see these (people) constantly afflicted by hunger, thirst and the disturbance of three bodily humours (viz. *kapha*, *pitta* and *vāta*), by heat and cold, by wind and rain and by other (*ādhibhautika*) factors and by unbearable fire of desires and anger.

9. Oh Lord, while (so long as) people will see (regard) this body (and other things) as different from the Soul (or God), due to the dominant influence of the Lord's Māyā, appearing as the organs of senses and their objects, this worldly existence (*saṁsāra*), unreal as it is, will not disappear, but will bring a host of troubles (and miseries) as a result of *karmas*.

10. Oh God, even sages revolve in the course of worldly existence (*saṁsāra*) in this world, if they are averse to eulogizing your deeds (and such forms of devotion). They who by day, have their senses absorbed in doing actions (for getting worldly objects), and go to sleep with minds full of different desires, get their sleep disturbed every moment, and their endeavours after their objects are frustrated by Fate.

11. Oh Lord, you, path to whom is perceived by the (type of devotion called) *śravaṇa* (listening to the glories of the Lord)[670], really dwell in the lotus-like hearts of men (devotees)

---

670. VR. takes *śruta* as 'knowledge derived from *Śāstras* and *īkṣita* as 'knowledge derived from deep thought about what is permanent and what is perishable'.

VJ. takes *īkṣita* as 'knowledge derived from meditation' and interprets, 'Those to whom the path of devotion to Viṣṇu is shown by study of *śāstras* under a pious and devout preceptor.'

purified by *Bhakti-yoga.* Oh Lord of unbounded glory, in order to confer your grace on the devotees, you manifest yourself in whatever form they meditate upon you.

12*. The Lords dwells in all things. He is the only friend and ruler from within. He becomes extremely pleased by compassion to all beings which is impossible to be found in non-devotees. He is not so much pleased even though he is propitiated with rich articles of worship, (even) by gods who cherish some desires in their hearts. (God is easily attainable only to desireless devotees).

13. The righteous acts which are offered to you never perish. Hence your propitiation, Oh Lord, is the best fruit of all religious acts, such as various righteous deeds, performance of sacrifices, religious gifts, austere penance and observance of religious vows.

14. Salutations to (you) the Supreme Lord, who are eternally free from the illusion of difference,[671] by your own essential light of intelligence, and whose *vidyā-śakti* is know-

---

VC. : The path which was first heard (learnt) from the preceptor, and then realized by meditation.

* VR. : You are not so much pleased (so as to favour the bliss of Liberation) with your devotees (*suragaṇaiḥ*) who cherish desire into their hearts and propitiate you with various articles (etc.) of worship, as you are pleased by that type of unselfish compassion, which is based on the knowledge that ill feeling towards any being is ill feeling against you—a compassion impossible to be found in people who identify body with the Soul (*asad-alabhyaya*). Though present within all, you are not affected by their defects, as you support and control them as an *antarātmā*.

GD. : Just as God becomes extremely pleased by compassion to all beings (without any ulterior selfish motive), he is not pleased by the rich worship even of gods who cherish some desire in their hearts, i.e. though the Lord grants the desired objects to his *sakāma* devotees, he does not bless them with *self-realization*. The Lord being present in all, the ill feeling of *sakāma* devotees against some persons is an ill feeling against the Lord whom they try to propitiate. Hence he is not much pleased with them as with desireless devotees.

671. *bheda-moha* : VD. enumerates these misapprehensions—

(1) the notion of the Lord being imperfect: (2) Some other deity, other than Viṣṇu being the Supreme Ruler; (3) the distinctions (between the levels of) *avatāras*; (4) The notion that the individual Soul is the Supreme Being. (5) That the Supreme Soul is not the individual Soul. (6) That both the Supreme Soul and the individual Soulare distinct.

ledge itself[672]. We offer our homage to you, the controller (of the universe), whose sports and diversion are the Māyā, the cause of the origin, sustenance and destruction of the universe.

15. I resort to that unborn Being by uttering whose names signifying his incarnations (e.g. *Devakī-nandana*—'Devaki's son'), his attributes (e.g. *sarvajña* 'Omniscient'), deeds (e g. *kaṁsāri* 'Enemy or killer of Kaṁsa) (even) in an unconscious stage, at the time of death, people at once become free from the sins of many births, and attain to Brahman uncovered by (the veil of) Māyā.

16. Salutations to the Lord who is the universe-Tree which is the only one, but has three feet (branches) viz. Brahmā, I (Viṣṇu) and Śiva, each of which has numerous branches (e.g. the seven sages etc.)—the tree which has its roots in the Supreme Soul and has differentiated itself by three attributes (*guṇas* under the names of Brahmā, Viṣṇu and Rudra) who are the cause of the creation, sustenance and destruction of the universe.

17. Salutation to the all-powerful, ever-vigilant (unwinking god in the form of) Time who instantaneously cuts asunder the hope of life of this world as long as the people shirk[673] the performance of your worship which is conducive to their own good, and which has been directly ordained by you, and are engaged in the prohibited path of *Karma*.

18. Even though I have occupied a place (viz. Brahmāhood in Satya-loka) which lasts for a period of two *parārdha* years and which is bowed down by all the worlds, I

VR. takes *bheda* as the difference in the categories of *jīva*, e.g. man, God and *moha* as the ignorance caused by the misapprehension of the identity of the Soul and the body.

672. VC. (i) Whose enjoyment (*rasa*) is the sportive looking at Māyā the cause of the origination etc. of the universe.

VC. : (ii) Oh cause of the creation etc. of the universe, whose sport is the special dance with *gopīs* known as *rāsa*.

673. VR. reads an *avagraha* (i.e. *a*-) before *vikarma-nirataḥ* and *pramattaḥ* and explains : Time severs shortly the attachment to *saṁsāra* of a man who is very careful in the performance of auspicious and sacred duties of propitiating God according to his caste (*varṇa*) and stage of life (*āśrama*)—duties prescribed by you in the Vedas—and who does not indulge in impious deed.

am afraid of him (your form called Time). Hence with a desire to attain you, I practised penance for many years and performed many sacrifices. My salutations to you, the Almighty Lord of sacrifices.[674]

19. Salutations to Lord Puruṣottama who, with a view to observing the laws ordained by him, assumed of his own accord the bodies (*avatāras* or incarnations) in the various forms of living beings, such as sub-human beings (e.g. birds, beasts), human beings, gods etc. and enjoyed himself, though he is (absolutely) unattached to worldly pleasures.

20. Though he is never affected by the five varieties of Avidyā[675], he, who has conserved the universe in his belly with a view to increasing the pleasure of rest (for people who are exhausted by their activities in the previous *kalpa*—period), assumed on the waters, tossed with terrible waves, *yogic* sleep, for which the touch of the body of the Serpent Śeṣa was favourable.

21. Oh Praiseworthy Lord, I, who came into being in the lotus-mansion of your navel, and who became, through your favour, an instrument for the creation of the three worlds, bow to you in whose stomach lies the whole world, and who has opened his lotus-like eyes at the completion of your *yogic* sleep.

22. May the Lord furnish my intelligence with that knowledge and omnipotence with which he gladdens the world, so

---

674. SD. construes differently : I bow to the presiding deity of sacrifices of whom I am afraid, though I occupy the post (Bahmāhood) lasting for two *parārdha* years. With a desire to attain Vaikuṇṭha (your residence) which is honoured (bowed to) by all people, I performed penance for many long years.

675. Bh. P. III. 12.2 enumerates the following *vṛttis* (powers) of Avidyā : viz. *mahā-moha*, *moha*, *tāmisra*, *andha-tāmisra* and *tamas*. As PYP (*Pātañjala-Yoga-Pradipa*) points out, the hindrances (*kleśas*) in YS. II.3, viz. *avidyā* (=tamas), *asmitā* (=*moha*) *rāga* (=*mahā moha*), *dveṣa* (=*tāmisra*) and *abhiniveśa* (=*andha tāmisra*) are known in the Sāṅkhya system by the names given in the brackets above (*Classical Sāṁkhya*, p. 295).

Īśvara Kṛṣṇa further classifies them as follows : "There are eight varieties of obscurity (*tamas*) and delusion (*moha*); ten kinds of extreme delusion (*mahā-moha*); both gloom (*tāmisra*) and utter darkness (*andha-tāmisra*) are 18 fold. G.J. Larson's *Classical Sāṁkhya*, p. 275.

that I may be able to create this (universe) as it was in the previous *kalpa*—the Lord who is the friend of all the worlds, and dwells within them as the *antaryāmin*, is gracious (dear) to his devotees.

23. This (Lord) grants boons to those (devotees) who resort to him. He takes incarnations retaining (his original) qualities (like omnipotence, omniscience), along with his own (or soul-) power called Lakṣmī (and not his Māyā power). May he direct my mind to whatever he does while I create, by his order, this universe which is also his own glory, so that I can renounce my attachment to actions, and the consequent sin.

24. I am born here as the *vijñāna-śakti*[676] (the presiding deity over *citta* or the principle called *mahat*) from the deep lake-like navel of the Man of infinite powers, lying on the (cosmic) waters. May there be no loss of the utterance[677] of the Vedas, while I am detailing the wonderful form of this Man viz. the universe.

25. May this Lord, the most Primitive Man, of infinite grace, get up, opening his lotus-like eyes, and with profusely affectionate smiles. May he remove our dejection by his sweet words for the successful creation of the universe.

Maitreya said:

26. Thus having seen his own creator by his power of penance, knowledge and meditation, and having praised him to the best of the abilities of his mind and speech, the god Brahmā remained silent as if exhausted.

---

676. *vijñāna-śakti*—(i) The competence to utter the Veda—(VD.) (ii) my knowledge-form—(VR.) (iii) my knowledge of Vedas—(VJ.) (iv) myself being the *vijñāna*; my being the presiding deity of the principle of intelligence (VC.).

677. *visarga*—(i) Contact of teaching and studying (the Vedas) —VD.

(ii) *utterance*—ŚR., VR., ŚR. explains that as per the famous adage "The plough is the end of Vedic lore", Brahmā was afraid that he would be out of touch with the Vedas while engaged in creation. Hence this prayer to retain his Vedic lore.

(iii) The definite conclusion (viz. Viṣṇu is the most supreme) —VJ

27-28. Then noting the difficulty of Brahmā who got nervous at (the lack of) his knowledge regarding (prospective) construction of the universe, and whose mind was dejected at the sight of the tumultuous deluvian waters, Madhusūdana (Viṣṇu) spoke to him in deep emphatic voice, as if to remove his dejection (lit. sin).

The Lord said :

29. Oh Vedagarbha (i.e. Brahmin), do not get lax (due to despair). Exert yourself for the creation (of the universe). What you pray of me, has been already obtained for you.

30. Oh Brahman, perform penance again and practise the (*yogic*) lore of concentrating on me. You will find in your heart, the unfolding of (the plan of the creation of) the worlds, by both of these (*tapas* and *samādhi*).

31. Oh Brahman, when you are full of devotion and properly poised in meditation, you will see me pervading you and the world, and yourself and the world reposing in me.

32. When the people will realize me as dwelling within all beings like fire dormant in the wood, they will immediately shed off sins or misery.

33. When a person sees that his Self is free from *bhūtas* (elements), *indriyas* (sense-organs), *guṇas* (attributes) and *antaḥkaraṇa* (the mind), and is essentially one with me, he attains identification with Brahman.

34. It is my great blessing that your mind will never get despaired of this creation of the universe, while you desire to create innumerable subjects with various details of actions.

35. As your mind is firmly fixed on me, the evil attribute of *rajas* shall not bind you, the first-born sage, even while you indulge in procreating the beings.

36. Inasmuch as you realize me as unconnected with *bhūtas*, sense-organs, attributes and egohood (*ahaṁkāra*), I have been known by you today, though I am very difficult to be known by corporate beings (or beings attached to body).

37. When through the lotus-stalk you tried to find out the root of the lotus under water, and when a doubt as to my

existence arose in your mind, my true self was revealed to you within you.

38. It was indeed my grace that you made the prayer composed of my glorious deeds, or that you had firm adherence to penance.

39. I am pleased with you. May you be prosperous, as you, desiring success (in the creation) of worlds, have praised my describing me as attributeless (though I appear to be full of attributes.

40. I, who am the Supreme God, the bestower of all desired boons, will immediately be pleased with a person who will always worship me, and pray to me with this prayer (which you have composed).

41. It is the considered opinion of the knowers of the Reality, that my grace is the *summum bonum* to be achieved by *pūrta* (acts for public welfare), penance, sacrifices, gifts and *yogic* meditation.

42. Oh Brahmā, I am the (Supreme) Soul of all beings, the most beloved of all the beloved objects. Hence one should concentrate his love in me, as body and its other belongings are loved for my sake.

43. By means of yourself who is the Veda incarnate, and is created by me, you create again as before (in the previous *kalpa*) the beings that are lying within me.

Maitreya said :

44. Having explained this (the process of creating the universe) to the creator of the world (Brahmā), the Controller of Prakṛti and Puruṣa, with lotus-like navel disappeared in his own form (as Nārāyaṇa).

CHAPTER TEN

(*Brahmā's Penance and Ten-fold Creation*)

Vidura said :

1. How many types of beings did Brahmā, the grandfather of the world and master of his senses procreate, both from his body and his mind, after the disappearance of the Lord Almighty ?

2. Oh Lord, the foremost among the learned, please explain to me, one by one, whatever points I asked you, and solve all our doubts.

Sūta said :

3. Oh Bhārgava (Śaunaka), the sage Kauṣārava, being thus urged by Vidura, was pleased with him, and began to reply those questions which were raised in Vidura's mind.

Maitreya said :

4. Concentrating his mind on the Supreme Soul (Nārāyaṇa) as desired by the unborn Lord, Brahmā accordingly performed penance for period of hundred divine years.

5. God Brahmā, born of the lotus, found that both the lotus occupied by him, and the cosmic waters, were rocked by Wind due to the force acquired by it during the period of the deluge.

6. As his knowledge and power were specially developed by his increasing penance and knowledge pertaining to the Supreme Soul, he swallowed the Wind along with the waters.

7. Having seen that the lotus, which was his seat, pervaded the whole of the space, he thought he should, by this lotus, create again the worlds which were formerly (at the time of the deluge) withdrawn.

8. Being prompted by the Almighty to perform (the act of creation to be done by him), Brahmā entered the calyx of the lotus, and divided the one (lotus) into three divisions though it could have been broken into fourteen (worlds), and many more parts.

9. Thus is explained the arrangement of the world of living beings. The region of god Brahmā is the result of religious duties performed, without desiring their fruit.

Vidura said:

10. Oh Brahman, you have described the form called Time of Hari who has many forms and whose actions are miraculous. Please describe to me that form as it is (actually).

Maitreya said:*

11.** Time is that which has for its form the modification of *guṇas* (like *sattva* etc.). Of itself, it has no special property, but is beginningless and endless. Puruṣa (God) sportively procreated himself in the form of the universe by using Time, as the instrumental cause.

---

* Maitreya here discusses the concept of Time. According to the Bh.P., Time as the power of motivation, does not simply break the equilibrium of tri-partite matter (*guṇamayī ātma-māyā*), but pursues the creative process at every stage. If God is the agent-cause of creation, Time is the efficient cause. Through the operation of Time, ten kinds of creation consisting in material (*prākṛta*), elemental (*vaikṛta*) and mixed (*prākṛta-vaikṛta*) were brought into existence as represented below :

Creation

Material (*Prākṛta*)	Elemental (*Vaikṛta*)	Mixed (prākṛta-vaikṛta)
(1) mahat	(1) vegetation	
(2) ahamkāra	(2) animals	divinely human
(3) tanmātras	(3) human beings.	souls,
(4) external sense-organs.		e.g. Sanatkumāra etc.
(5) presiding deities of senses and the mind.		
(6) avidyā (with its five knots)		

For details on the concept of Time vide B.Bhattacharya —*Philo. of the Bh.P.* I.11. 247-59.

** VR. explains : Time has for its form *Pradhāna* which is a result of (the disturbance of the equilibrium of) the *guṇas*. It is devoid of special characteristics like the Earth (and other elements). He is not dependent on another cause i.e. he exists of his own accord. Hence he is endless. The Supreme Man, with *Pradhāna* as the efficient cause, created himself in the form of the world.

GD. explains : The form of Time is known by the perturbation of the equality in the balance of *guṇas*. It is the cause of this inequality in *guṇas*. It is to be known from its effects. It is not characterised by any peculiarity, and hence it is beginningless and endless. With Time as the instrumental cause, God sportively re-created himself in the form of the universe.

12* Verily this universe is the subtle Brahman which was covered (withdrawn) by Viṣṇu's Māyā. It is manifested by God with the help of Time, of invisible form.

13. Just as it (Time) was now, so it was in the past and shall remain so in the future. His creation is nine-fold (both material and elemental) due to *Prakrti* and *vikṛti***. (The tenth creation is *prākṛta-vaikṛta*).

14. The destruction of the universe is of three types—(1) brought about by Time, (*nitya*), (ii) done by substance viz. Saṅkarṣaṇāgni (*naimittika*), (iii) due to *guṇas* (*prākṛtika*). The production of mahat is the first creation, which is caused by God (ātman) by disturbing the equilibrium of the *guṇas*.

15. The second is the creation of *ahaṅkāra* wherein rises the knowledge of substance and action. The third is that of *tanmātras* (subtle elements) which possess the potential for the creation of gross elements (*bhūtas*).

16. The fourth creation is that of organs of senses, both of knowledge and of action. The fifth is that of gods (presiding over organs of senses) from *vaikārika ahaṅkāra* whence is evolved the mind.

17. Oh Vidura, the sixth is that of ignorance (*tamas*)

---

* VR. explains : The universe is the effect—a gross form of Brahman with the attributes of *cit* and *acit* developed. Time is regarded as possessing controlling capacity as the creation or destruction of the universe takes place through Time which is an invisible form of God. The existent universe during *pralaya*, returns to its subtle form of Brahman along with its attributes of *cit* and *acit*.

VJ. : For the sake of creation etc. of the universe, the *Puruṣa* assumed three forms : Brahmā, Viṣṇu and Iśvara. Creating Brahmā and entering into him as four-faced god Brahmā, he created the world. Similarly he protects the world as Viṣṇu. He created Rudra called Kāla who was of invisible form, entered into it, and destroyed universe. But it is his power of destruction as Iśvara.

VB. : The gross universe is the effect, the subtle Brahman is the cause. Brahmā is the subtle and earlier stage of the universe. The universe subsists or meets destructions by the Māyā of God (Viṣṇu). Time (Kāla) which is endowed with controlling capacity of God and is formless, helps to bring about this process.

**VJ. explains that all creation outside the Egg of the universe is called *prākṛta* and includes in it all the principles from *avyakta* to Pṛthivī. And creation within the Egg is *Vaikṛta*.

whereby rises *abuddhi*[678] (which obscures the correct understanding of *Jīva* and deludes him from the correct perception of God). These six creations pertain to *Prakṛti*. Now listen to those arising from *Vikṛti* (*vaikārika ahaṅkāra*).

18. This (creation) is the sport of the Lord Viṣṇu who assumes the *rajo-guṇa* (the attribute *rajas*), and meditation (lit. retentive memory) about whom liberates from *Saṁsāra*.[679] The seventh is the prominent creation of six types of immovables.

19. *Vanaspatis* (Trees like the holy fig tree which bear fruit without blossom), *Oṣadhis* (plants which die immediately after fruit-bearing), *latās* (creepers), *tvaksāra* (trees of strong bark, e.g. bamboos), *Virudhs* (strong creepers like canes not requiring support for them), *drumas* (trees bearing fruits after blossoming)—all these draw up their nourishment from below, are full of *tamas* (of unmanifested feelings), have an internal sense of touch, and many other peculiarities.

20. The eighth creation is of animals and birds. It is said to have twentyeight varieties. (They are) devoid of knowledge (of tomorrow etc.), full of ignorance (except the knowledge of gratifying their appetite). They know by scent only and are of minds incapable of retaining knowledge for long.

21. Oh extremely pious Vidura, the cloven-hoofed beasts are the cow, the goat, the buffalo, the black-antelope, the pig, the bison, the *ruru* (a kind of deer), the sheep, the camel.

22. Oh Vidura, the one (uncloven)-hoofed beasts are: the donkey, the horse, the mule, the *guara* (a cross of a horse and a female mule), the *śarabha* (a fictitious eight-legged animal who can kill lions) and the *camara* (from whose hair *chowries* are made). Please listen to beasts with five nails.

23. (They are) the dog, the jackal, the tiger, the cat,

---

678. *abuddhi*: Concentration or knowledge about Viṣṇu (a= Viṣṇu)—VJ.

679. *Hari-medhasaḥ* etc.—Alternatively: This creation is of Lord Hiraṇyagarbha (Brahmā) who is characterised by *rajas* and whose thoughts are concentrated on Hari (VD.)

the hare, the hedge-hog, the lion, the monkey, the elephant, the tortoise, the alligator, the shark and others.

24. The birds are : the heron, the vulture, the bat, the hawk, the *bhāsa* (a vulture, a cock), the *bhallūka* (a kind of owl or bear), the peacock, the swan, the crane (*baka*), the ruddy goose, the crow, the owl and others.

25. Oh Vidura, the nineth creation which takes its nutriment from above down the body, is of one type, viz. that of men. They have in them *rajo-guṇa* dominant, are full of activities and take pleasure in things leading to miseries.

26. Oh foremost among the saintly persons, these three creations are *vaikārika*. The creation of gods also, comes under the *vaikārika* category. But the creation of *Sanatkumāra* (Sanaka etc.) comes under both (*prākṛta-cum-vaikārika* category).

27-28. The creation of gods is of eight categories : Gods proper, Manes (*pitṛs*), asuras, gandharvas and apsarās (the divine musicians and dancing girls), Yakṣas and Rākṣasas, Siddhas and Cāraṇas, Bhūtas (goblins) Pretas and Piśācas; Vidyādharas, the Kinnaras (and Kimpuruṣa, a horse-faced tribe etc.). Oh Vidura, I have described to you these ten categories created by Brahmā.

29. After this I shall describe to you the dynasties, *manvantaras* (epochs of different Manus). In this way, at the beginning of every *kalpa*, the self-born Viṣṇu becomes the creator due to the dominance of *rajo-guṇa*. The Supreme Soul of unfailing will-power creates himself out of himself at will*.

30. As there are modifications of *guṇas* in the creation, they (the learned ones) do not expect a particular serial order, just as in a whirlpool in a river (no part of a whirlpool can be considered to be the first). This is due to the Māyā power of the Supreme Lord.

31. Oh Vidura ! Whatever gods, Asuras and others of this *kalpa*, have been described to you by name and form, had the same name and form in the last period of Manu.

*These two verses are probably interpolations in the post-Śrīdhara period for they are neither recorded by the Bengal School of Vaiṣṇavism i.e. JG., VC., nor by the followers of Nimbārka i.e. SD. nor by VB., GD. etc.).

CHAPTER ELEVEN

(*The concept of time: manvantaras and life-spans of men and gods.*)

Maitreya said :

1. The ultimate irreducible particle of the parts of a gross effect (substance), which is ever separate (i.e. has not reached the stage of being an effect), and which is not combined with another in an aggregate, is called an atom (*paramāṇu*)[680]. It is from the aggregation of atoms that men get the illusion of whole substance.

2. When the idea of peculiarity or of differences is separated (not considered), the entire substance in its essence which remains unaltered (with no change of dimensions) is called *parama mahān* (maximum dimension)[681].

3. Oh Vidura, Time is also inferred as subtle, (medium), and the longest according as it pervades the atomic, medium, and the grossest (*parama mahān*) matter. It is God's power which itself remains unmanifest, but occupies and encompasses the manifested substance and is competent to manage creation etc. of the universe.

4. That much period of time which is required to occupy an atom is the atomic period. That which is required to enjoy the matter in its entirety, is called *parama mahān* (the largest general—required to cross the totality of twelve *Rāśis* or *Bhuvanakośa* i.e. a period of a year and a period up to two *parārdhas* by the recurrence of the years.

5-8* Two *paramāṇus* make one *aṇu*. Three *aṇus* make one *trasareṇu*. It is the smallest particle which is visible and is noticed to be going up in the ray of the Sun coming through a window. The time which is required to occupy by three

680. It may be noted that the Bh. P. and the Vedānta (vide *Brahma Sūtra* II. 2.12-17) do not subscribe to the atomic theory of the Vaiśeṣikas.

681. Having the duration of two *parārdhas*—JG.

*These verses contain the following measures of time :—

2 *paramāṇus*= 1 *aṇu*; 3 *aṇus*= 1 *trasareṇu*; 3 *trasareṇus*= 1 *truṭi*; 100 *truṭis* = 1 *vedha*; 3 *vedhas*= 1 *lava*; 3 *lavas*= 1 *nimiṣa*; 3 *nimiṣas*= 1 *kṣaṇa*; 5 *kṣaṇas*= 1 *kāṣṭhā*; 15 *kāṣṭhās*= 1 *laghu*; 15 *laghus*= 1 *nāḍikā*; 2 *nāḍikās*= 1 *muhūrta*; 6/7 *nāḍikās*= 1 *yāma* or *prahara*.

trasareṇus is called a *truṭi*. Hundred *truṭis* make up one *vedha*. Three *vedhas* is regarded as a *lava*. A *nimiṣa* is known to consist of three *lavas*. Three *nimiṣas* make up a *kṣaṇa*. Five *kṣaṇas* are said to form one *kāṣṭhā*. Fifteen *kāṣṭhās* make one *laghu*. Fifteen *laghus* are said to constitute one *nāḍikā* (or *ghaṭikā*). Two *nāḍikās* make one *muhūrta*. Six or seven *nāḍikās* make one *prahara* of men. It is also called *yāma*.

9. A copper vessel of six *palas* in weight and with sides sixteen *aṅgulas* in height, and with a capacity to contain a *prastha* of water, and with a hole (of the dimension) of a gold wire four *aṅgulas* in length and four māṣas (=1/3rd Tola) in weight—the time required to submerge (in water) such a vessel is called *nāḍikā* (*ghaṭikā*).

10. Oh respectful Vidura! Four and four *yāmas* make a day and a night of human beings. Fifteen days make one *pakṣa*. It is bright and dark.

11. The aggregate of two *pakṣas* makes one month which is a day and a night of the *pitṛs* (departed forefathers). Two months make a *ṛtu* (season). Six months make one *ayana*. It is northern (when the Sun apparently moves to the north) and the southern (when the Sun appears to move to the south of the equator).

12. The *ayanas* are called the day and the night of the *Svarga*. A year is made up of twelve months. One hundred years is said to be the maximum life of human beings.*

13. The ever-vigilant controlling god (the Sun) occupies the sphere consisting of the planets, the *nakṣatras* (e.g. Aśvinī, Bharaṇī and other constellations) and other stars and revolves round the world beginning with atomic division of time and ending with one year (the period required to cross the *bhuvana-kośa*).

14. Oh Vidura, the period of a year is thus called *saṁvatsara* (the Solar year), *parivatsara* (related to Jupiter) *Iḍāvatsara* (of 360 days—*savana*) *anuvatsara* (the lunar year) and *vatsara* (related to *nakṣatras*).

15.** Offer your worship to the God Sun who made the

---

*VR. adds that the maximum life of *Pitṛs* and gods is one hundred years according to their respective measures of time.

**VJ. takes this verse as applicable to god Viṣṇu: Perform your sacrifices to Hari the *antaryāmin*, of the five kinds of the year, etc.

five kinds of the year and who by his own power (in the form of *kāla*) urges the powers of things to develop into effects (gross forms) in different ways, and who is a part of the element called *tejas*. He runs through the sky for removing the delusion of men (as if by dissuading them from waste of life in pleasures) and extending the fruits of *guṇas* by performance of sacrifices.

Vidura said:

16. The maximum span of life of the *pitṛs* (manes), gods and men has been stated, (as hundred years according to the measure of time of these). Please tell me the state (life-span) of those learned ones who stay beyond the three worlds.

17. Verily, you the revered one know the course of Time which is capable of destroying everything. The wise ones can visualize the universe by their *yogic* vision.

Maitreya said:

18. It is said that the cycle of four *yugas*, viz. *kṛta, tretā, dvāpara* and *kali* along with their *sandhis* (transitional periods at the beginning of a *yuga*) and *aṁśas* (the transitional period at the end of a *yuga*), consist of twelve thousand years of gods.

19-20* The period of *yugas* respectively (of *kṛta* etc.) is four thousand, three thousand, two thousand and one thousand (divine) years. The *sandhyā* period at the beginning and the *aṁśa* period at the end (of each *yuga*) is respectively eight hundred, six hundred, four hundred and two hundred years (of gods). The learned ones designate the period between *sandhyā* and *aṁśa* as *yuga*, and the (special) laws of conduct (*dharma*) have been ordained with reference to the (particular) *yuga*.

---

*The classification of the *Yugas* in terms of divine (gods') years is as follows:

	kṛta	*tretā*	*dvāpara*	*kali*	Total Divine years
sandhyā	400	300	200	100=	1000
yuga	4000	3000	2000	1000=	10,000
sandhyāṁśa	400	300	200	100=	1000
	4800	3600	2400	1200=	12,000

21. In the *kṛta* age, *dharma* accompanied men on (all his) four legs (viz. penance, purity, compassion and truth). With the increase of irreligion (*adharma*), religion became diminished by one leg, in each of the other *yugas*.

22. Oh Vidura, beyond the three worlds (from *mahar loka*) to *Brahma loka*, a day consists of one thousand cycles of four *yugas*. The night is also of the same duration when the Creator of the universe goes to sleep.

23. At the end of the night, the creation of the world starts and proceeds so long as it is god Brahma's day which covers the period of fourteen Manus.

24. Every Manu rules during his own period which is somewhat longer than seventyone *catur-yugas* (cycles of four yugas[682]) In the eras of Manus, kings in the lineage of the Manu are born in succession. Hermits, gods, king of gods and his attendants are born simultaneously.

25. This is Brahmā's daily creation whereby the three worlds are made to function and in which the birds, beasts, men, *pitṛs* and gods are born according to their *karmas*.

26. In the Manu-eras, the Supreme Lord retains his *sattvaguṇa* and protects the universe by incarnating as Manus and manifesting himself in other human forms.

27. At the end of (Brahmā's) day, assuming a bit of the *tamo-guṇa*, he restrains his prowess, and with everything else withdrawn in him due to the force of *kāla*, he keeps quiet.

28. When it is the nightfall without any moon or the sun (in existence), the three worlds *bhūḥ*, *bhuvaḥ*, *suvaḥ* lie concealed in him.

29. When the three worlds get consumed by the fire from the mouth of Saṅkarṣaṇa (Śeṣa) who is his power, Bhṛgu and others, being distressed by the heat go to *Jana-loka* from *Maharloka*.

30. In the meanwhile, due to *Pralaya* (world-end),

682. This line indicating the vagueness implied in 'longer than' (*sādhikā*) is repeated in other Purāṇas also (e.g. *Viṣṇu P.* 1.3.18). Baldev Upadhyaya on the strength of *Vāyu P.* (57.35) suggests that it should be emended as 'sandhikā' (vide *Purāṇa Vimarśa*, pp. 291-93). The Bh. P. seems to have adopted the reading from the *Viṣṇu P.* which is generally accepted as earlier than the *Bh. P.* vide *Purāṇa Vimarśa*, pp. 542-45.

oceans, with huge billows whipped up by extremely terrible and powerful, winds, overflow and inundate the three worlds.

31. On that water, on the bed of the serpent Śeṣa, lies Hari with his eyes closed in *yogic* sleep, while sages in the Janaloka sing his praise.

32. In due course of time, with such types of days and nights as described above, even the long span of life of hundred years of this (god Brahmā), comes to an end.

33. Half of the life (of god Brahmā) is called parārdha. The first parārdha (of his life) has passed. Now the other half is running.

34. At the beginning of the previous *parārdha*, there was the great *kalpa* called *Brahma kalpa*, as Brahmā was then born. They knew him as *Śabda-Brahma*.

35. At the end of that *kalpa*, there was another *kalpa* called *Padma kalpa*, as there sprouted up the world-lotus from the lake-like navel of Hari.

36. Oh Vidura, the present *kalpa* of the second *parārdha* is known as Varāha (pertaining to the boar), as Hari assumed the boar-form in this (*kalpa*).

37. The period called *dvi-parārdha* is regarded as (a negligible period like) a wink of the unmanifested, infinite beginningless Soul of the Universe.

38. This *kāla* beginning from *paramāṇu* (its lowest unit) upto the end *dvi-parārdha* (duration of Brahmadeva's life) can control those who have attachment to house etc. He has no power over the Almighty God, the *bhūman*.

39. This egg of the universe consisting of sixteen *vikāras*[683] (modifications) and eight *prakṛtis*[684] which is covered from outside by the (seven) sheaths of the earth etc., is fifty crores (of *yojanas*) in breadth.

683. viz., mind, ten organs of knowledge and action and five elements (*mahābhūtas*).

684. viz., *Prakṛti, mahat, ahaṅkāra* and five characteristics of elements (e.g. sound, touch etc.).

40-41. Each of these sheaths (covering the universe) is ten times greater (than its previous one). This universe appears as an atom when merged (in him). Crores of such universes lie in him. That is the highest essential form of Viṣṇu, the great *Puruṣa*. It is called the imperishable Brahman, the cause of all causes.

CHAPTER TWELVE

(Creation of Rudra, the mind-born Sons and of Manu and Śatarūpā)

Maitreya said :

1. Oh Vidura, the greatness of the Kāla-form of the Supreme Lord is thus described to you. Now know from me how *Vedagarbha* (god Brahmā) proceeded with the creation.

2. The creator, at first, created the varieties of ignorance (or *avidyā*) viz. *mahāmoha*, *moha*, *tāmisra*, *andha-tāmisra* and *moha*[685].

3. Seeing the sinful creation, Brahmā did not think highly of himself. With his mind purified by meditation on the Lord, he brought forth another creation.

4. The self-born god (Brahmā) then created the sages Sanaka, Sananda, Sanātana and Sanatkumāra who were not interested in actions (for *dharma*, *artha* or *kāma*) and lived in perpetual celibacy[686].

5. The self-born god spoke to them, "Oh sons, procreate children". But they being absolutely devoted to Vāsudeva and followers of the path of liberation, were not so inclined (to create).

---

685. For details vide supra 3.10. 11 and onwards the *Sāṅkhya* influence is evident. This list is repeated in LP. 2.9.30 and 34-35. This is the tāmasa creation.

686. ŚR. adds: These Kumāras are not created in every *Kalpa* but only in the *Brāhma Kalpa*. This is the description of the *Brāhma Kalpa*, hence the mention of their creation.

6. He was thus disobeyed by his sons who refused to comply with his order. He tried to control his unbearable rage aroused (due to this defiance).

7. Though he tried to control the rage by his mental power, the rage was immediately born as a son of dark-blue complexion from the middle of the brows of Brahmā.

8. The illustrious god Bhava who was born before (other) gods verily cried out, "Oh creator, the father of the world, give me names and fix (some) places for me".

9. The lotus-born god (Brahmā), with a view to granting his request, spoke with sweet words, "Please do not cry, I shall give it to you.

10. Oh great god, as you cried like an excited child, people will call you by the name 'Rudra'.

11. Your places have been already arranged by me as follows : The mind, the sense-organs, the vital breath, the Sky, the Wind, the Fire, the Water, the Earth, the Sun, the Moon and the penance.

12. (The following are your names) : Manyu, Manu, Mahinasa, Mahān, Śiva, Ṛtudhvaja, Ugra-retas, Bhava, Kāla, Vāmadeva and Dhṛtavrata.

13. Oh Rudra, you will have the following wives, namely: Dhī, Vṛtti, Uśanā, Umā, Niyutsarpi, Ilā, Ambikā, Irāvatī, Sudhā, Dīkṣā, Rudrāṇī.

14. As you are a Prajāpati accept these names, places along with these wives, and procreate abundant progeny."

15. Being thus ordered by his father, Lord Nīla-lohita (Rudra) brought forth children who were like him in prowess, form, (complexion) and nature.

16. Seeing the innumerable hordes of Rudras created by (the original) Rudra, devouring the world on all side, god Brahmā got afraid.

17. (He said to Rudra) : "Oh great god, enough of the creation of all such beings who with their terrible eyes are burning all the directions along with me.

18. Perform penance which is conducive to the happiness of all beings. May you be blest. It is by penance that you (lit. Your honour) will create again this universe as it was before.

19. It is only by (performance of) penance that a man can easily attain to the Lord Adhokṣaja, the Supreme light, dwelling in the hearts of all beings."

Maitreya said:

20. Being thus ordered by the self-born god (Brahmā), (Rudra) circumambulated from left to right the Lord of Speech (Brahmā). Complying with his request, he bade goodbye to him and entered the forest for penance.

21. Then while he was musing over the problem of creation and became possessed of the power of the Lord (for creation), ten sons who became the progenitors of the population of the world, were born to him.

22.* (They were): Marīci, Atri, Aṅgiras, Pulastya, Pulaha, Kratu, Bhṛgu, Vasiṣṭha, Dakṣa and the tenth (son) was Nārada.*

23-24. Nārada was born from Brahmā's lap; Dakṣa from his thumb; Vasiṣṭha from his vital breath, Bhṛgu from the skin and Kratu from his hand; Pulaha was born from his navel, the sage Pulastya from his ears, Aṅgiras from his mouth, Atri from his eyes, and Marīci, was created from (Brahmā's) mind.

25. Dharma was born from his right breast wherein abides Nārāyaṇa himself. From his back (was born) *Adharma* which begets the Death, a terror to the world.

26. Desire (*Kāma*) was born in his heart; Anger (*krodha*) from his brow; Avarice (*Lobha*) from his lower lip; Speech was born from (his) mouth; the rivers from his penis and Nirṛti, the shelter of all sins, from his anus.

27. (The powerful sage) Kardama, the husband of Devahūti, was born from his shadow; this (whole) world was created from the mind and the body of the creator of the universe.

28. Oh Vidura, it is reported to us that self-born god became passionate and desired his own beautiful daughter, the goddess of Speech who, though herself above passions, captivated his mind.[687]

---

*For the symbolism of the ten mind-born sons as *Virāj* vide V.S. Agrawal—*MP.—A Study*, p. 38.

687. Cf. The 'marriage' of Brahmā and Śatarūpā in MP. and the explanation of this symbolism vide V.S. Agrawal—*MP.—A Study*, pp. 47-50.

29. His sons, the sages, of whom Marīci was the foremost, saw that their father had set his heart on unrighteousness. Out of familiar confidence, they pleaded with (lit. awakened) him.

30. "That you do not control your passion despite your capacity to do so, and that you are bent on approaching your daughter, has never been done by the ancestors nor will it be done by others after you in future.

31. Oh father of the world, this is not glorifying (creditable) even to the possessors of divine lustre (power). By following this (course of conduct) the people shall never attain any good."

32. (Finding Brahmā bent on the heinous act the sages prayed to God) "We bow to the glorious Lord who manifested this world that was within him. He alone is capable of protecting righteousness."

33. Then the father of the Prajāpatis, seeing his sons, the Prajāpatis speaking this in his presence, became ashamed and gave up his body.

34. The cardinal points accepted that terrible body. The wise people know it as mist or darkness. While he was meditating how he should create the well-planned worlds as before, the Vedas came out from the four mouths of the creator.

35. The duties of the four sacrificial priests[688] (*hotā*, *adhvaryu*, *udgātā*, *brahmā*) along with the *upavedas* and the disciplines of Logic etc., the extensive course of sacrificial sessions, the four legs of Dharma and the duties of the four *Āśramas* were also produced thence."

Vidura said :

36. "Oh sage (lit. one who regards penance as his wealth) you told that the Lord of the progenitors of the world produced Vedas etc. from his mouths. Please tell me by what particular (organ) he produced the specific things."

VJ. however maintains that *vāc* is 'the deity presiding over human speech' and not Sarasvatī who is the natural consort of Brahmā, the Veda incarnate.

688. These Priests are the experts in the Rg and other Vedas serially.

Maitreya said :

37. "From his mouths facing the east (the west etc.), he produced the Vedas—Ṛg, Yajus, Sāman and Atharvan and *Śastra* (simple recitation of *mantras* in praise of gods entrusted to *ṛtvij*), *ijyā* (oblations, worship etc. to be done by *adhvaryu*), *stutistoma* (singing of the *mantras* in praise of gods, the duty of *udgātā*) and *Prāyaścitta* (expiatory rites in case of some lapses in sacrifices to be performed by *brahmā*).

38. Again through the same faces, and in the same serial order, he produced *Āyurveda* (the science of medicine), *Dhanurveda* (science of Warfare), *Gandharva Veda* (the science of Music) and Sthāpatya Veda (the science of Architecture, Sculpture etc.).

39. The Omniscient Lord produced the fifth Veda, viz. Itihāsa and Purāṇas from all his mouths.

40. From his mouth facing the east (came forth the sacrificial acts viz.) *Ṣoḍaṣī* and *Uktha* (and serially from other mouths) *Purīṣī* and *Agniṣṭut*, *Āptoryāma* and *Atirātra*, *Vājapeya* along with Gosava.

41. He created the four feet of Dharma viz. *Vidyā* (knowledge and purity), *dāna* (donations), *tapas* (penance) and *satya* (Truth). He also produced the (four) *āśramas* (stages in life) along with their types of duties.

42. (*Brahmacarya āśrama*)—celibate stage—the 1st stage in life—is of four types viz.) *Sāvitra* (observance of celibacy and study of *Sāvitrī* for three nights from the *upanayana* (thread-bearing) ceremony), *Prājāpatya* (observance of celibacy for one year), *brāhma* (observance of celibacy till the completion of the study of Vedas) and *bṛhat* (celibacy throughout life). (The 2nd stage in life) The *gṛhastha āśrama*—the married stage—is of four kinds according to the way of maintenance of family[689]: *Vārtā* (earning livelihood by agriculture and such other non-prohibited vocations), *Sañcaya* (maintenance of money earned by performing sacrifices), *Śālīna* (to live on whatever one gets

---

689. Vaikhānasa Gṛhya Sūtra classifies *gṛhasthas* as (1) *Vārtā vṛtti* (maintaining on agriculture, trade), (2) *Śālīna vṛtti* (stay in houses performing sacrifices etc.)., (3) *Yāyāvara* (performing *ṣaṭkarmas*) (4) *Ghora cārika*—corresponding to Śiloñccha. For details vide Kane—HDS, Vol. II. I. pp. 641-43.

without requesting or begging), *Śiloñccha*—(maintenance by gleaning grains, grain-gathering).

43. In (the third stage of life called) the *vānaprastha āśrama*, (there are four categories viz.) *Vaikhānasas* (who live upon food-grains which grow naturally without agricultural efforts), *Vālakhilyas* (who subsist on fresh food, giving away hoarded food), *Audumbaras* (who eat fruits etc. gathered from the direction to which they happen to look at first in the morning) and *Phenapa* (who live on fruits, leaves etc. automatically dropped from trees). In (the last stage of life) the *Saṁnyāsa āśrama*, (the four kinds are :) *Kuṭīcaka* (who chiefly abide by all the duties prescribed for the *āśrama*), *Bahvoda* (who perform the most essential duties of this *āśrama* but emphasize on the path of knowledge), *Haṁsa* (who concentrate on knowledge), *Niṣkriya* (who have realized the Soul).[690]

---

690. VJ. and VD. differ: (1) *Vaikhānasas*—Those who subsist on roots. (ii) *Vālakhilyas*—Who eat everything. (iii) *Udumbaras*—Who live upon fruits. (iv) *Phena-pas*—Who subsist on the milk-foam falling out from the mouth of calves while sucking.

This classification is supported by *Bṛhat Parāśara Smṛti* XII. 158 for Vānaprasthas and XII. 164 for Saṁnyāsins.

Kinds of Saṁnyāsins :—

Kuṭīcaka : (i) The Ascetic who lives in his own house and is satisfied on whatever food is given to him—VJ.

(ii) The ascetic who due to weakness etc. does not wander from one holy place to another but stays at one holy place in a hut and lives upon begging after practising *japa* of 12000 Praṇavas—VD.

Bahvoda : (i) He who, in addition to his three baths per day, performs ablution in every new *tīrtha* he sees and has three *daṇḍas*—VJ.

(ii) Who wanders from one holy place to another not living beyond a prescribed period at each place (e.g. 1 night at a village, 3 nights in a city etc.)

Haṁsa : (i) Who carries one *daṇḍa* and the sacred thread—*Yajñopavīta*—VJ. (ii) Who is nude, beyond *dvandvas*, lost in deep meditation of Brahman—VD.

Niṣkriya or *Parama-haṁsa*—(i) Who has abandoned all acts, completely observing *ahiṁsā*.

(ii) One who is absorbed in the meditation of the Brahman, careless about his body etc. and has crossed the seven stages of knowledge (*Sapta-Jñāna-Bhūmikās*).

44. (So also were serially produced) the science of the knowledge of Soul and non-Soul[691], the three Vedas, the science of agriculture and the science of politics (leading to the attainment of *Mokṣa*, *dharma*, *kāma* and *artha*) and also the *vyāhṛtis* (mystic words following *Om* or *praṇava*) viz. *bhūḥ*, *bhuvaḥ*, *suvaḥ* and *bhūr-bhuvaḥ-suvaḥ* (or *mahas*). From his heart came forth *Om*.

45-46. (The Vedic metres) *Uṣṇik*, *Gāyatrī*, *Triṣṭubh*, *Anuṣṭubh* and *Jagatī*, *Paṅkti* and *Bṛhatī* were produced respectively from the hair, skin, flesh, muscles and bones, marrow and *prāṇa* or vital airs of the all-pervading Prajāpati (Brahmā). His life (*jīva*) is said to consist of the occlusives or the consonants of five classes (e.g. velar, palatal etc.) from *k* to *m*, and his body, of vowels (a, i, u etc.)[692].

47. The sibilants (*ūṣma varṇas* like *ś*, *ṣ*, *s*) are called the sense organs of the Soul, i.e. Brahmā, and the semi-vowels (*y*, *r*, *l*, *v*) his strength. And the gamut of music (viz. Ṣaḍja, Ṛṣabha, Gandhāra, Madhyama, Pañcama, Dhaivata and Niṣāda) are created out of the sport of Prajāpati.

48*. Brahmā whose body is *śabda-brahman* is of both manifest (as *vaikharī*) and unmanifest (as *Omkāra*) forms. As unmanifest the Supreme Spirit clearly appears to him as the highest omnipresent Brahman. As a manifest form, it appears as Indra and other forms possessing different powers.

49-52. Then assuming another (body), he set his mind on creation (of the world). Finding the limited creation (of

---

VR. and VC. follow ŚR. VD. claims his acceptance of ŚR's interpretation.

691. *ānvīkṣikī*—The Tantrism in consonance with the Vedas—VJ.

692. VJ. states: The occlusives from *k* to *m* were produced from his *jīva* and the vowels from his body.

*Though I have followed ŚR., this verse is differently interpreted. Thus VR. emphasizes the literary or *śabda* aspect of Brahmā, and explains the different *śaktis* as functions of words, such as *abhidhā*, *lakṣaṇā*. I may add one more interpretation.

God Brahmā is of the form of *śabda-brahma*. He is manifest as the spoken word (*Vaikharī*) and unmanifest as *Praṇava*. But the real Supreme Spirit that is beyond him appears to be all-pervading and possessed of various powers.

progeny) even by sages possessing great power, he again began to ponder, Oh Kaurava (Vidura).

"Oh ! It is really strange that although I am all the while engaged in creating (the world) the beings do not multiply. In this, the Fate must be obstructing."

Thus while Brahmā was doing his duties properly and thinking over the Providence, his body was split into two and it was called *Kāya*. And from the bifurcated forms of the body was produced a pair of a male and a female.

53. There the male part was the emperor Svāyambhuva Manu and that the female part was called Śatarūpā and was the queen of the great person.

54. Indeed, the subjects (created beings) began to multiply in their relationship as husband and wife. He brought forth five children from Śatarūpā.

55. Oh Vidura, (They were) Priyavrata, Uttānapāda and three daughters, Ākūti, Devahūti and Prasūti.

56. He gave Ākūti (in marriage) to Ruci, the middle-daughter (Devahūti) to Kardama and Prasūti to Dakṣa. From these the world was filled (with population).

CHAPTER THIRTEEN

(*The Boar* (*Varāha*) *Incarnation*)

Śrī Śuka said :

1. Oh king, hearing the holiest discourse of the sage, Vidura (a descendant of Kuru) who cherished high respects for narratives of Hari, again asked (Maitreya).

Vidura said :

2. The emperor Svāyambhuva was verily the favourite son of god Brahmā. Oh sage, what did he do after obtaining a loving wife ?

3. Oh foremost among the good, narrate to me, who am full of faith, the life of the king-sage, the first ruler of the world, because he also resorted to Vāsudeva (Viṣvaksena).

4*. (The act of) listening to the virtuous deeds of those who cherish in their hearts the lotus-like feet of Mukunda, is eulogised by the wise, as the main fruit (result) of men's study of the *śāstras* with long efforts.

5. The sage (Maitreya) who was thus urged to narrate the episodes of the Lord had his hair standing on ends (due to intense devotion), and narrated to Vidura who was modest and was (as if) a pillow to the feet of Śrī Kṛṣṇa[693] (lit. the thousand-headed god) requested him (Maitreya) thus.

Maitreya said :

6. When Svāyambhuva Manu was born along with his wife, he folded his hands and bowing to Brahmā (Vedagarbha) he said :

7. "You are the sole progenitor and nourisher and protector of all beings. But how (in what way) are we, your creatures, to render you service ?

8. Oh praiseworthy one, I bow to you. Tell me what action, out of those within our capacity, I should do whereby my fame will spread everywhere (here) and lead to Heaven hereafter."

Brahmā said :

9. "Oh child, I am pleased with you. Oh king, blessed be you both. You have offered yourself to me with a guileless (sincere) heart for guidance.

10. Oh warrior, this much worship should be rendered by children to their father that they should abide by his order respectfully, to the best of their capacity without jealousy or negligence.

11. Have from her children who are like you in qualities. Protect the earth according to law. Worship the Puruṣa (the Supreme Man) with sacrifices.

12. Oh king, the highest service (rendered) to me will

---

* VB. Even though the virtuous deeds of the Lord are heard with great exertions, they are not properly fixed in the heart and hence do not bear fruit. They are properly fixed by listening to the deeds of those who are his devotees. Hence the propriety of listening to Manu's life.

693. As Śrī Kṛṣṇa used to rest his feet on Vidura's laps—ŚR.

be the protection of the subjects. Lord Hṛṣīkeśa (Viṣṇu) will be ever pleased with you for your being the protector of the subjects.

13. Fruitless are the efforts of those with whom Lord Kṛṣṇa (Janārdana) whose form is sacrifice, is not pleased; for, thereby, the Soul (ātman) itself is disrespected."

Manu said :

14. "Oh destroyer of sins, I shall abide by the order of your lordship. But fix up a place for me and for my progeny here.

15. The earth which is the place for all beings is submerged in the great ocean. Oh god, make some efforts to lift up this goddess (earth) (from the ocean)"[694].

Maitreya said:

16. Seeing that the earth is submerged that way in waters, god Brahmā pondered over for a long time, "How can I lift her (the earth) up?[695]

17. While I was engaged in creation, the earth was engulfed by waters and it sank down to Rasātala. What can we, who are entrusted with the duty of creation, do now here? Let the Lord from whose heart I came into existence, do it for me."

18. Oh sinless one, while he was reflecting thus, a thumb-size small boar suddenly dropped down from his nostril.

19. Oh Vidura (of Bharata clan), while he (Brahmā) was looking on, a great miracle took place: The small boar in the sky shot up to the size of an elephant in a moment.

20. Along with Brāhmaṇas with Marīci as their chief, with Kumāras (Sanaka, Sanandana etc.) and with Manu, he saw the boar form and began to think in various ways.

21. "Is it the transcendental Being appearing in the form of a boar ? What a miracle that it should come out of my nose!

694. JG. This indicates that this is the introduction to the Varāha incarnation at the beginning of the present *Kalpa*.

695. ŚR. explains : At the beginning of creation Brahmā drank up the ocean and restored the earth to its place. He did not understand how suddenly it was immersed in water again.

22. It appeared like the tip of a thumb and in a moment it became as big as a great boulder. Can this be the Divine Sacrifice (i.e. Lord Viṣṇu) himself who is trying my mind to exhaustion (by concealing his real form)?"

23. While Brahmā was deeply thinking over it along with his sons, the glorious Supreme Sacrifice-Man (Yajña-Puruṣa) who was like a mountain thundered forth.

24. The all-pervading Hari thrilled with rapture, god Brahmā and the excellent Brahmins, by his roar which reverberated the directions.

25. Having heard the grief-removing roar of the (Being who had assumed the) Boar form by his Māyā, the sages who were residents of the same Tapas and Satya lokas (worlds) praised him with the holy trinity (of the Vedas).

26. Knowing that it is the Veda extolling his attributes that is chanted by the great (god Brahmā and the sages), he whose personality is described in the Vedas[696] again roared and for the prosperity of gods, rushed into the water like a big sporting elephant.

27. He moved through the sky with his tail held aloft. With his shaking mane and kicking hoofs he dispersed the clouds. His body was hard with tough hide bristled with sharp, erect hair. The Lord, the saviour of the earth, appeared brilliant with his white tusk and shining eyes.

28. Though he was sacrifice itself in person, He assumed the form of a boar and was scenting the track of the earth. Though his tusks were sharp, he gently looked at the Brāhmaṇas who were praising him and dashed into water.

29. The roaring ocean whose side was shattered by the velocity of the falling of his body which was like a mountain of adamantine peaks, spread out his arms in the form of swelling surges and as if out of affliction, yelled out, 'Oh Lord of Sacrifices, protect me'.

30. Then cutting down the unfathomable waters to the bottom with his sharp arrow-like hoofs, the Lord who was sacrifice incarnate (lit. who had three joints in the form of *savanas* or sacrificial acts), saw the earth in *rasātala* where at the time

696. *Veda-vitāna-mūrtiḥ*— (i) One whose body is sacrifice (VR.)
(ii) Whose form was entire Veda itself (VC.)

of Deluge (*Pralaya*) he desired to sleep, placing the earth along with the beings, in his stomach.

31-32. He appeared extremely resplendent when he rose up pulling out by his tusks the submerged earth from the *rasātala*. Even there (in the sea), he whose intensified rage was like the Sudarśana *Cakra*[697], saw a demon (Daitya) of irresistible prowess attacking him with a mace and (thus) obstructing him. He killed him easily as a lion kills an elephant. With his cheeks red with the (mudlike) clotted blood of the demon, he appeared like a big elephant who had turned up (red chalk from) the earth.

33.* Oh Vidura, (sages and gods) of whom Brahmā was the leader recognised the Lord (Varāha) of *tamāla* like blue complexion, who was sportively lifting up the earth by the tip of his tusks like an elephant. They folded their hands and prayed him with words like Vedic *sūktas*.

Sages said:

34. "Victory to you, Oh unconquerable Lord! Oh creator of sacrifices![698] We bow to you who are shaking your body composed of three Vedas. We salute to you who have assumed this boar form (to lift up the earth), in the pores of whose hair sacrifices lie hidden.

35.** Oh Lord, the sacrificial form of your body is really very difficult to look at by the sinful people. The Vedic

697. 'Whose rage was intensified by Sudarśana'—VB.
VB. explains : When the mace and weapons of Viṣṇu proved ineffective to kill the demon, the Sudarśana disc had to remind Viṣṇu of the misdeeds of the demon and intensified his anger to finish with the demon.

* VC. and VD. quoting *Bhāgavatāmṛta kārikā* maintain that Maitreya has mixed up two Boar incarnations—the white one in Svāyambhuva Age and the blue one in the Cākṣuṣa *Manvantara*.

698. *yajña-bhāvana* : (i) Who is invoked by sacrifices—ŚR. (ii) The creator or cause of all sacrifices—VD., VR, VC. VB. (iii) Who manifests himself by sacrifices—RR. (iv) Who is worshipped as Yajña with its different parts—VR. (v) Who is propitiated by sacrifices—GD.

** The conception of Yajña-Varāha was formulated first in Va P. 6.16.23. It was adopted later by MP. 248.67-73, VP. 1.4. 32-33, BRP. 213.33.7, PP. Sṛṣṭi-kāṇḍa 16.55.61, *Hari-Vaṁśa* P. 1.41.29-33. The concept was so popular that in addition to literary reference in *Viṣṇu Smṛti*

metres are found in your skin, the *kuśa* grass in your hair, the sacred clarified butter in your eyes, and the fourfold duties of the sacrificial priests in your feet.

36. Oh Lord, *sruk* is in your mouth, *sruvas* are in your nostrils, *Iḍā* in your stomach, and *camasas* in your ears; *prāśitra* (the vessel for Brahmā's share) in your mouth, *grahas* (a kind of cup for *soma*) in your throat. Agnihotra in your chewing.

37. Your frequency of incarnation is the *iṣṭi* (sacrificial act) called *dīkṣā*. The three *iṣṭis* called *upasads* form your neck. *Prāyaṇīya* (*iṣṭi* after *dīkṣā*) and *udayanīya* (*iṣṭi* after completion of sacrifice) are your two tusks. The *Pravargya* Mahāvīra* ceremony preliminary to *Soma* sacrifice) is your tongue. The two fires *sabhya* and *āvasathya* form your head. You are the sacrifice. The arrangement of bricks for sacrifice is your vital breath.

38. Your semen is the *soma* juice. The three *savanas* (morning, noon and evening) form your seat. The seven sacrifices (*Agni-Ṣṭoma*, *Atyagniṣṭoma*, *Ukthya*, *Ṣoḍaṣī*, *Vājapeya*, *Atirātra* and *Āptoryāma*) are your *dhātus* (constituents of the body). All kinds of *satras* (sacrificial sessions) are the joints of your body. You are both *kratus* (sacrifices in which *soma* juice was extracted) and *yajñas* (sacrifices without the extraction of *soma* juice). *Iṣṭis* in sacrifices are your tendons.

39. We bow again and again to you who are all the *mantras*, deities, sacrificial materials, sacrificial acts and the performance of all acts. We repeatedly salute to you who are knowledge realised by nonattachment, devotion and self-control, and who are the preceptor of that knowledge.

40. Oh Supreme Lord, the support of the earth, the earth along with the mountains which you have borne upon the tip of your tusk, appears beautiful like a lotus plant with leaves resting on the tusk of a big elephant.

1.3-9, *Viṣṇudharmottara* 1.2.3-8 we have Yajña-Varāha images (e.g. that at Vihāra in N. Gujarat). The two aspects of this concept viz. (1) its significance as the symbol of Vedic cosmogony and (ii) the correspondence between the elements of sacrifices and the parts of Varāha's body are discussed by V.S. Agrawala *MP—A Study*, pp.313ff.

* Apte's PSD 668. *Mahāvīra* is a sacrificial vessel. When it is red hot, ghee and milk is to be put in it (VD). This is performed before every *upasad* (ŚR).

41. This your boar form consisting of three Vedas, with the sphere of the earth supported by your tusk, appears shining like a great enchantingly beautiful *Kula Parvata*[699] with a cloud resting on its peak.

42. Establish firmly your consort, this earth, the mother of the world of the movables and immovables, for the residence of the people; for you are the father or the Protector. We offer our salutations to her along with you. You have deposited your vital power in her as the Fire is dormant in *araṇi*—(a piece of Śami wood used for creating sacrificial fire by friction with another piece).

43. Oh Supreme ruler, who else can aspire or determine to lift up the earth which sank down to the nethermost region (*rasātala*)? In your case, this is not a miracle as you have created this extremely wonderful world by your Māyā power.

44. Oh Almighty, we, the residents of the Jana, Tapas and Satya regions have been thoroughly purified by the sanctifying drops of water sprayed from the ends of your bristle like hair while you shake your body which is composed of the Vedas.

45. He who aspires to reach to the end of (i.e. to know thoroughly) all your deeds which are endless, must really have lost his senses. The whole universe is deluded by the association of the attributes of your *yoga māyā*. Oh Supreme Lord, bless (us) with happiness."

Maitreya said:

46. While the Protector (Varāha) was thus praised by the sages, the knowers of Brahman, he stabilised the waters by his hoofs and placed the earth on them.

47. The Supreme Lord Hari, the Viṣvaksena and the protector of the world, placed on waters the earth which he easily lifted up from *rasātala* and disappeared (lit. departed).

48. Janārdana (Hari) will be immediately pleased in his heart on him who will thus devotedly hear or make others hear this extremely auspicious and enchanting tale of Hari

---

699. *Kulācala* : A class of seven mountains which are supposed to exist in each division of the continent. Their names are : Mahendra, Malaya, Sahya, Śuktimān, Ṛkṣa-Parvata, Vindhya and Pāriyātra.

whose miraculous deeds are worth describing and knowledge about whom destroys all miseries.

49. What is there difficult to be achieved when the Lord of all blessings is pleased ? Enough with those (pleasures) of insignificant value. The Supreme Lord, the Dweller in the hearts of all, of his own accord, confers *summum bonum* on those who are devoted to him without any ulterior motive.

50. Out of the stories of yore, the nectar-like narratives of the Lord put an end to *Saṁsāra.* Having drunk these through the ears (comparable to the cavity of folded hands) what person who has understood the essential purpose of life, can get satiated (with them). (If such there be), he must be other than a human being.

CHAPTER FOURTEEN

(*Diti's Conception*)

Śrī Śuka said:

1. Having listened to the story of Hari in his Boar-incarnation (for the purpose of the lift-up of the earth) as narrated by Maitreya, Vidura who had taken the vow (of hearing the episodes of Hari) was not much satisfied. Folding up his hands (in bowing), he asked again.

Vidura said:

2. "Oh great sage, we have heard it reported that the first *daitya* (demon) Hiraṇyākṣa was killed by the same Hari who (in the boar-form) was the embodiment of sacrifice (*Yajña*).

3. Oh Brahman, for what purpose was there a confrontation between the demon-king (Hiraṇyākṣa) and him (Hari) who was lifting the earth up with the tip of his tusk."

Maitreya said:

4. Oh warrior (Vidura), yours is a good query as the story about Hari's incarnation that you ask, cuts asunder the noose of death in the case of mortal beings.

5. By (hearing) which (story) as sung by the sage (Nārada), the male child of Uttānapāda (Dhruva) set his foot on the head of the god of Death and ascended to the place of Hari.

6. Even in this case (of the fight with Hiraṇyākṣa) I have heard this account related in ancient times by Brahmadeva, the god of gods, to the gods who enquired him (about it).

7-8. Oh Vidura, Diti, the daughter of Dakṣa, was desirous of a child and with her heart overcome with passion on one evening, desired (the company of) her husband Kaśyapa, the son of Marīci, who was seated in meditation in his fire-worship hall after offering oblations of milk to the Supreme Man, the protector of sacrifices, in the evening.

Diti said:

9. "Oh learned, this god of love with a bow in his hand torments me, a poor thing, for your sake just as an elephant attacking a plantain tree crushes it.

10. May you be prosperous ! Please confer your favour on me who am burning at the (sight of the) prosperity of my co-wives who are blest with children.

11. The fame of women who are greatly respected by husbands, spreads over the world, and of those to whom the husband like you, is really born as a son.

12. Formerly our father, venerable Dakṣa, who was affectionate to us his daughters, asked us separately, "Oh daughters, whom do you select as your husband ?"

13. Having understood the inclination of us, his daughters, he, the progenitor of the race, gave you thirteen daughters who liked your nature.

14. Oh lotus-eyed auspicious sage, now satisfy my desire. Oh plentiful one, an entreaty of the distressed to the great ones is never fruitless."

15. Oh valiant one, Kaśyapa replied in consolatory words

to her who, being over-whelmed with passion, has become pitiable and was persuading him with many arguments (words).

16. "Oh timid one, here I am ready to comply with whatever you desire. Who would not fulfil the desire of her who helps accomplishment of the three *puruṣārthas* (goals) in life?

17. Just as the people cross the sea in ships, a married person giving shelter to persons of other *āśramas*, crosses the sea of misery.

18. Oh proud lady, they (the learned ones) call her (the wife) as the equal partner (lit. half the part) of the man who aspires after happiness. After entrusting the responsibility of his work to her, man can move about free from the fever of anxiety.

19. Depending on whom (the wife), we easily overcome the enemies in the form of senses which are difficult to be conquered by men of other (non-*gṛhastha*) āśramas, just as the lord of a fort (subdues) the enemies (due to his fortified position).

20. Oh mistress of the house, it is not possible for us to become so completely (obliging) like you, even (if we try) throughout our life (and in the next birth as well). Nor others who appreciate (your) virtues (can do so).

21. I shall, however, try to comply with your request (desire) for offspring. But please wait for a *muhūrta* so that they (the people) will not reproach me.

22. This is the most terrible of times when everything looks awful, as at this time goblins, the followers of Rudra wander about.

23. Oh pious lady it is in the evening that Lord Śiva, the creator of beings and the king of ghosts, moves about riding his bull and surrounded by his goblin-attendants.

24. Your brother-in-law[700] god Rudra whose shining mass of hair (on head) became scattered and tawny by the dust raised by the whirl-wind in *śmaśāna* (the crematory ground) and whose pure gold-like body is smeared with ashes, witnesses (everything) with his three eyes (viz. the Sun, the Moon and the fire.) Hence there is no secrecy anywhere.

---

700. Kaśyapa's wife Diti and Śiva's wife Satī were the daughters of Dakṣa. Hence Kaśyapa and Śiva were brothers-in-law, and Śiva was also Diti's brother-in-law.

25. In this world there is no one who is his relative or non-relative. Nobody is specially respectable or censurable to him. By performance of various vows, we desire to have the (prosperity and greatness of) Māyā which he has enjoyed and spurned (lit. kicked).

26. Thoughtful people who wish to tear off the veil of Māyā[701] praise his life which is spotless or unattached (to sensual pleasures). He has none equal or superior to him. He is the ultimate goal of the saintly people; yet he himself followed the vow of *piśāca* type of life.[702]

27. The unfortunate sinners decorate with garments, garlands, ornaments and pigments their body, (which is nothing but) the food of dogs, as if it (the body) were their Soul. They do not understand the motive behind his (Rudra's) behaviour and laugh at him who is absorbed in (the meditation of) the Soul[703].

28. God Brahmā and others obey the limits (laws) set by him. He is the cause of this universe. Māyā is his obedient servant. His behaviour is like a Piśāca. Oh (how) incomprehensible are the ways of the Almighty[704].

Maitreya said :

29. Though she was thus admonished by the husband, she whose senses were thoroughly overwhelmed with passion, caught hold of the garment of the Brāhmaṇa Sage like a shameless prostitute.

---

701. *avidyā paṭala* : nescience, the film or coating over the eye (of knowledge)—VJ., VD.

702. Those who have realized the Brahman behave like an innocent child (bāla), a mad person (*unmatta*) or like a goblin *piśāca*. God Śiva adopted the third type of life. Or 'lives in the company of goblins (*piśācas*)' —VD. Vj's interpretation, "Under the order of Hari who has neither equal nor superior, Rudra followed the *piśāca* type of life" is far-fetched as we have to supply words : *yaś ca Hariḥ ......tasya Harer ājñayā*, to the text of this verse.

703. VC. construes differently : without understanding the purpose of Rudra who is absorbed in Hari, that the garments etc. are to be offered to Lord Hari and hence I do not enjoy them.

704. VJ. interprets the verse as the glorification of Hari and not Rudra. Thus Rudra's behaviour as *piśāca* is in obedience to Hari's command. Incomprehensible are the ways of Hari the Perfect Being who makes gods like Rudra, the objects of worship by the world, obey him.

30. Knowing his wife's importunity to that prohibited act, he then bowed down to the dictates (of the providence) and sat down with her in a secluded place.

31. He then took bath, controlled his breath and meditating silently over the pure, eternal Light, repeated internally the Gāyatrī (or the syllable Om).

32. Oh Vidura, even Diti, feeling ashamed of that sinful act, approached the Brāhmaṇa-Sage and with her face cast down, addressed him.

Diti said :

33. 'Oh Brahman ! May not the Lord of goblins (*bhūtas*) kill the child in my womb. I have committed a fault against Rudra, the Lord of *bhūtas* (beings).

34. Obeisance to the great god Śiva who is the remover of miseries (Rudra), who is irresistible, giver of blessings (to those who cherish desire and the highest bliss to the desireless devotees). He, though weaponless, takes up arms against the wicked, and is anger incarnate (at the time of destruction or *pralaya*).

35. May the Lord of Satī, my sister's husband, the great god with abundance of grace, be gracious unto us women who are treated as worthy of compassion even by ruthless hunters.

Maitreya said :

36. Prajāpati (Kaśyapa) who has completed his evening rituals spoke to his wife who was trembling (greatly with fear) and who was desirous of securing the good of her progeny both here and hereafter.

Kaśyapa said :

37-38. On account of your impure mind, inauspiciousness of the (evening) time, disobedience to my order and complete disrespect for gods (attending Śiva), Oh evil woman, you will beget two wicked sons the worst ever born from wombs. Oh wrathful woman, they will frequently make the worlds and the protectors of the worlds, cry out (by their atrocious acts).

39-40. When the poor and innocent beings will be massacred and women are seized per force and the great souled ones are incensed, the venerable Lord of the universe, the creator of the world, will be enraged. He will come down as an incarnation and will kill them as Indra (the wielder of the Vajra) destroyed the mountains.

Diti said :

41. Oh Lord, I desire that both of my sons should meet death directly at the hands of the glorious Lord whose noble arms appear splendid by the disc (*sudarśana*). May not they be a victim of Brāhmaṇa wrath.

42. Not even the denizens of hell show favour to a person burnt by Brahma-daṇḍa (curse of a Brāhmaṇa) and the tormentor of beings, in whatever class of creatures he be born.

Kaśyapa said :

43-44. On account of the sorrow and repentance for your misdeed, and your present consideration of what is proper and improper, and due to your great respect to Lord Viṣṇu and regard for Śiva and myself one son out of your son's son will be respected by saintly persons. They will sing of his pure fame which would be comparable to the glory of the venerable Lord.

45. In order to emulate his pious nature, good persons will purify their hearts (by imbibing virtues) like non-enmity (friendliness to all) and others, just as they purify gold of inferior carat by purificatory processes.

46. By his intellect (or devotion) not directed to anyone else except the Lord, the venerable self-perceiving Lord by whose grace this universe becomes propitious, and who is the indweller of the universe, will be pleased with him.

47. Verily, he would be the greatest devotee of unlimited vision and of great prowess and the greatest of the great. For, by his deep devotion, he will establish Lord Viṣṇu in his heart, purified by devotion, and give up the ego about his body etc.

48. He will be devoid of desire for worldly pleasures, of good nature, a mine of excellent qualities, delighted at the prosperity of others and pained at the sufferings of the afflicted. With no enemy in the world, he will relieve the sorrows of the world, just as the Moon removes the summer heat.

49. Your grandson will see both in his mind and outside before him, Hari of excellent virtues, of lotus-like eyes,

who assumes the form according to the desire of his votaries, and who is a grace to his consort Lakṣmī and his face adorned with refulgent ear-rings."

Maitreya said :

50. Hearing that her grandson would be a votary of the Lord, Diti was greatly delighted. Knowing that both of her sons would meet death at the hands of Kṛṣṇa, her heart was elated.

CHAPTER FIFTEEN

(*Sanaka and Others curse Jaya and Vijaya*)

Maitreya said :

1. Being afraid of the destruction of her sons by Hari[705] Diti bore (in her womb) the luster (semen) of Prajāpati Kaśyapa for a hundred years—the lustre that subdued the lustre of others.

2. When by the power of the foetus, the world became void of light (due to the diminished light of the Sun etc.) and the gods in charge of protection of quarters were devoid of their power, they reported to Brahmā (the creator of the universe, the trouble due to) the spread of darkness in all directions.

Gods said :

3. Oh Lord, you know this darkness whereby we have been deeply agitated, because there is nothing unmanifested to you whose path (range of knowledge) is unaffected by Time.

4. Oh God of gods, the creator of the world, the crest-jewel of the protectors of the world, you know the mind of beings both superior and inferior to us.[706]

---

705 *Surārdanāt*: (i) The distress that would be caused to gods by her (prospective) sons—ŚR.
(ii) Being anxious lest Indra and gods should harm her sons—VR.

706. *pareṣām* etc. : Beings of the past and the future—VR., VD.

5*. We salute to you whose power is his special knowledge and who has assumed the body (as Brahmā) through Māyā and accepted *rajas* as a special attribute. We bow to you, the cause of the manifest-world (whose cause—the Supreme Soul—is unmanifested).

6-7. There is no defeat from anyone to those whose *yoga* is quite perfect (ripe) and who have conquered their breath, sense-organs and the mind and have been favoured by your grace and who, with unswerving devotion meditate upon you, the highest (God), the creator of all beings, whose form is composed of the causal relation, i.e. of cause and effect, and in whom the world is woven.

8. We bow to you the chief controller (or the chief vital breath) to whom all beings offer worship. Just as cows are bound down by cords, they (people) are restricted by his (your) word (i.e. Vedic injunctions).

9. Oh mighty one you who are of this nature, bring about good to us whose (routine) performance of activities is stopped due to darkness. You should look with extreme mercy upon us who are distressed.

10. Oh god, this is the semen of Kāśyapa which is deposited in Diti's womb as embryo which grows enveloping all directions in darkness, like fire consuming fuel.

Maitreya said :

11. Oh long-armed Vidura, the venerable son of the Supreme Soul (Brahmā) who was the object of the words of entreaty by gods, laughed loudly and replied to gods in sweet words.

Brahmā said :

12. Sanaka and others, my mind-born sons before your creation are free from all worldly desires and they wander over the worlds through the sky.

---

* We pay obeisance to you whose knowledge is uninterrupted, who know the whole of this universe by Māyā (the power of intelligence bestowed as a favour on you by Nārāyaṇa) and who have assumed *rajo-guṇa* (the attribute *rajas*) by Nārāyaṇa's command (and still it does not come in the way of your knowledge), who are the cause of the manifest (universe) but whose cause, viz., the Brahman is unmanifest)—VJ.

13. Once upon a time, they went to Vaikuṇṭha, the region of Lord Viṣṇu of pure Soul, Vaikuṇṭha which is respected by all.

14. All persons who dwell there have the form like Viṣṇu. They propitiate Hari by the righteous path without any ulterior motive to accomplish.

15. There dwells the venerable First Puruṣa who can be known only through word (i.e. Vedānta). He assumes pure Sāttvic form. The foremost one showers his grace on us, his devotees, to make us happy.

16. There is a park called the Final Beatitude which by its wish-yielding trees and by its beautiful blossoms of flowers etc. throughout all seasons, shines like veritable Mokṣa (Final Liberation) itself.

17. Where (in the Vaikuṇṭha region) devotees of Viṣṇu along with their beautiful wives in the aerial cars, disregard the fragrant wind even though their minds are distracted by the fragrance of the blossoming, honey-dripping flowers of creepers in the spring near water and sing of the deeds of the Lord which purify the sins of the world.

18. There the loud confusing cries of birds like pigeons, cuckoos, cranes, *cakravāka*, (the ruddy goose), *cātakas*, swans, parrots, *tittiris* and peacocks stop for a while when the chief black-bee (in Viṣṇu's *vanamālā*) hums loudly as if singing the story of Hari.[707]

19. There when the fragrance of Tulasī is appreciated by Viṣṇu by wearing (as an ornament) the garland of Tulasī, even flowering plants like the Mandara, the Kunda, the Kurava, the night-lotus, the Arṇa, the Punnāga, the Nāgakesara, the Bakula, the lotus and the Pārijāta, in their goodness of heart, paid respects to the penance of Tulasī.

20. It (the Vaikuṇṭha) is crowded with aerial cars (made) of (jewels like) *Vaidūrya* (*Lapis lazuli*), emerald (and of) gold which can be seen only by those that bow to Hari's feet. Here, damsels of big hips and beautifully smiling faces cannot,

---

707. VD. explains that the chief bee's humming which sounds like 'Hari, Hari' is regarded as 'Hari Kathā'. This verse emphasizes that even birds in Vaikuṇṭha-Park are also Viṣṇu's devotees.

with their beguiling smiles and other allurements, excite passion in those devotees whose minds are fixed on Kṛṣṇa.

21. The goddess of Wealth (Lakṣmī) of beautiful form, for whose favour others are striving, stays (permanently) in Hari's residence giving up her noxious quality (of fickleness). With her lotuslike feet jingling with anklets and arms freely dangling with a lotus in hand in a sportive manner, she (i.e. her reflection) in the crystal walls chased with gold, appears as if dusting (the house with lotus).

22. Oh gods, where (in Vaikuṇṭha), in her own garden, the goddess Lakṣmī attended upon by her maid-servants, was worshipping the Lord with Tulasī petals, saw her face with beautiful locks of hair and prominent nose reflected in the ponds of pure nectarlike waters and with sloping bank (*ghāṭs*) of corals, felt that it was kissed by her Supreme Lord.

23. To which (Vaikuṇṭha) do not reach those who listen to the mind-spoiling evil stories pertaining to topics other than the deeds of creation etc. of Hari, the destroyer of sins. Alas ! These stories (on subjects concerning *Artha* and *Kāma*) when heard by unfortunate people, deprive (the hearers) of all good merits and throw them in dark hells from which there is no relief.

24. Birth in the human species is aspired after even by us (as) it is possible to gain the knowledge (i.e. realization of Brahman or the Truth along with the performance of Dharma, in it. Those who (having thus got birth as a man) do not propitiate the venerable Lord, are alas, deluded by your Māyā of very wide expanse.

25. There (to Vaikuṇṭha, above our region) go these (men) who by the service of the greatest among gods, have kept off Yama, the god of death, (or who are above the discipline of *Yama*, *Niyama* etc.)[708] and who being of enviable character are (spiritually) above us. While mutually discussing about the supremely glorious Lord, their mind, being overwhelmed with intense love and devotion, the hair stand on end on their bodies and tears flow from their eyes.

26. The sages were greatly overjoyed when, by their power of eightfold Yoga, they reached Vaikuṇṭha which they

708. v.l. *dūre'ham*—who have subdued their ego. (VD.).

had not seen before, and which, being presided over by the Lord of the universe, was adorable to all the worlds, and which was shining with the lustre of various heavenly cars of great gods.

27. Having crossed the six enclosures without being prevented or attracted by the wonderful sights thereof, the sages saw, at the seventh, a pair of gods of the same age, each armed with a mace gorgeously dressed and wearing extremely valuable armlets, ear-rings and diadems.[709]

28. Each of them wore around his neck and between their four bluish arms, a garland of forest-flowers (*Vanamālā*) about which swarmed the intoxicated bees, and whose face with best brows, wide nostrils and red eyes, appeared excited (angry).

29. While these two were looking on, the sages entered without asking for permission, the (seventh) gate as (they did) through the (previous) gates the panels of which were made of diamonds chased with gold. They go everywhere without any obstruction as they are free from fear due to their equality of outlook to all (or due to their sight being fixed on the Soul or the Lord).

30. The two (gods) whose nature was contrary to that of the Lord, looked at those four nude boy-sages who, despite their age, looked five years old and had realized the real nature of the Soul. Laughing (disrespectfully) at their prowess, they prevented (the sages) both by their cane (and command) even though the sages should not have been treated so.

31. When the most venerable sages were disallowed by Hari's door-keepers, while the gods were looking on, they (sages) whose eyes were suddenly overwhelmed with some anger due to their disappointment of seeing their most beloved God, spoke (as follows):

---

709. This poetic description is an amalgamation of all earlier *pada* concepts of the RV. 1.12.20; 10.90.3 and those of Brāhmaṇa and Upaniṣadic concepts regarding the 'highest place'. For the evolution of this Vaikuṇṭha concept see B.Bhattacharya—*Philosophy of Bh. P.*, Vol.1, pp. 154-164.

The sages said:

32. "What a partial nature of you both who dwell here among persons who attain to this region by rendering the highest service to God and who possess the same qualities (e.g. impartiality) as of the Lord! Is there any suspicious character here resembling you in crookedness of mind (and hence worth apprehending) by you, when the Supreme Man is so very tranquil and free from all hostilities.

33.* For learned men do not see any difference here in the Lord (Viṣṇu) in whose belly lies the whole (universe). They see the (individual) Soul in the Supreme Soul like the space (in a pot) in (the bigger space of) the sky. You possess the characteristics of gods.[710] What (cause) has arisen which makes you suspect such a stomach-tearing fear to Hari ?

34. So we consider what can be done for the great welfare of you two stupid servants of the Supreme Lord of Vaikuṇṭha for this impropriety of making differences and discriminations even here. You go from this place (Vaikuṇṭha) to those sinful worlds where the three enemies (Lust, Anger and Avarice) dominate."

35. Having understood the terrible (implication of their) utterance and realizing the impossibility of protection from the Brāhmaṇa's punishment with the help of missiles, the two servants of Hari immediately prostrated themselves before them touching their feet as (they knew that even) Hari entertains great awe for them (Brāhmaṇas).

36. "May the punishment inflicted upon us, sinners, by your Venerable Selves be implemented. It will absolve us completely of our violence of even God's order. But we pray by the slight repentance awakened in us by your favour, may not the delusion erasing the memory of the Lord affect us who may go down to lower births for this offence."

---

* VR. explains : The Lord contains the whole universe in his belly and difference regarding credentials of anyone entering it does not exist. Have you checked the universe from entry into the Lord's stomach? The *yogins* see the Individual Soul in (i.e. inseparably dependent on) the Supreme Soul as the space (*ākāśa*) in a pot (*ghaṭa*) is inseparably connected with the limitless space (or the sky).

710. *sura-liṅginoḥ*—You are really *daityas*, though your outward appearance is like gods.

37. At that time, knowing the offence given to the saints this way by his servants, Lord Padmanābha (Viṣṇu), the delight of the noble ones, along with Lakṣmī went there on foot which are sought after by Paramahaṁsas and great sages.

38. They saw him who was the ultimate object—the Brahman—to be realized in meditation, coming within the range of their sight. His men (attendants) promptly brought to him the usual articles (e.g. the umbrella, Chowries, at the time of going). From the pearl-fringes of his moonlike white umbrella were dripping drops of water as they (the hanging pearl-laces) were gently moving in the enjoyable breeze caused by the two *Chowries* (*cāmaras*) which were beautiful like swans.

39. (They saw him) whose extremely beautiful face was showing grace to all (the sages and the door-keepers); who is the home of (all) desirable qualities; who was (as if) touching the interior of hearts by his affectionate glances and who with the resplendent Lakṣmī on his blue broad chest was heightening the beauty of his abode (Vaikuṇṭha) situated above the heavens like a crest-jewel.

40. (They saw him) wearing a shining girdle round the yellow garment covering his big hips, and with his Vanamālā (hovered round) by humming black-bees, and who wore beautiful bracelets on his wrists, and who rested one hand on Garuḍa's shoulder and who was sportively waving a lotus with another hand.

41. (They saw him) whose face was beautiful due to his prominent nose, and cheeks suitable to grace the ear-rings shaped like *Makaras*, surpassing the lightning in brilliance; whose diadem was set with jewels and who was wearing round his neck the Kaustubha jewel and an attractive and precious necklace hanging between his big arms.

42. His devotees, with their intelligence, judged that the pride of Lakṣmī about her being possessed of the highest beauty was subdued in the presence of the Lord. Having seen the Supreme Lord assuming bodily form for me, Śiva and you (Sanatkumāras), they bowed to him with their heads but their eyes were never satisfied by gazing at him.

43. When they breathed, the air fragrant with the Tul-

asī and the filaments of the lotus of the feet of the lotus-eyed Lord entered through their nostrils, and caused excitement in the minds and bodies of the sages who have experienced the permanent—everlasting—bliss (of Brahman).

44. Seeing his face charming like the interior of a blue lotus and his *Kunda*-flower-like smile on his very beautiful lips, they felt that their desires were fulfilled. Again, when they saw his pair of feet with ruby-like nails, they meditated upon him.

45. They eulogised Viṣṇu who is the object of meditation for men who seek liberation by the Yoga-process in this world, and who showed the most venerable *Puruṣa*-form giving delight to the eyes and who is possessed of his inherent eight siddhis which are not accessible to others.

Kumāras said :

46. Oh Infinite One, you, though present in hearts of the sinners (non-devotees), are unmanifested to them, but not so to us. But it is just today that you are visible to our eyes. You entered our hearts by the way of the ears when your mystery was explained to us by our father who is born of you.

47. Oh venerable Lord, we recognize you to be that Supreme Paramātman who every moment generate (inspire) love in these devotees by means of the attribute Sattva—Paramātman whom passionless sages, whose knot of I-ness (ahaṁkāra) is severed, know in their hearts by intense Bhakti-*yoga* (and who are) understood by them through your grace.

48. Oh Lord ! Those blessed ones who have resorted to your feet and have tasted the flavour of episodes about you whose glory is highly praiseworthy and purifying, do not count (attach much value to) Mokṣa, your maximum grace. Will they attach any value to other attainments (such as Indrahood) which are affected with terror at the bent of your brows?

49. May we at will be born even in hells by our sins, if our hearts sincerely rejoice at your feet like black bees (in lotus), and if our words, like Tulasī, get their charm (beauty) from your feet, and if our ears (passage in the ear) is filled with (the description) of your (host of innumerable) attributes.

50. Oh Lord of immense glory ! Our eyes have to our best satisfaction obtained the bliss of looking at this form which

you manifested. You who are never visible to persons with uncontrolled senses have appeared to us this way. Oh glorious Lord, we pay obeisance to you (who are of this nature.)

CHAPTER SIXTEEN

(*The Fall of Jaya and Vijaya*)

Brahmā said :

1. While the sages who were by nature Bhakti-yogis were singing his eulogy, the All-powerful Lord whose abode was in Vaikuṇṭha, received them cheerfully and spoke as follows :

The Lord said :

2-3. Oh sages, as these two servants of mine, Jaya and Vijaya, disregarding me, have gravely insulted you and slighted you who perform penance for me.

gods, I have approved of the punishment meted out to them by

4. I, therefore, apologize to you today, for Brāhmaṇa is my highest deity. I regard that the offence given to you by my servants is as good as done by me.

5. When a servant has committed an offence, the world takes the name of the master. That blame spoils the reputation of the master as white leprosy dispigments the skin.

6. I am that Vaikuṇṭha by hearing whose nectarlike, pure glory, the world down to Cāṇḍāla is instantly sanctified. I who have obtained such excellent purifying reputation from honourable persons like you, would sever even my own arms if they be of a hostile nature to you.

7. By serving whom (Brāhmaṇas) I have got even the dust on my lotus-like feet so sanctifying as to purge the whole world of all impurities and have got such a good nature established in me that the goddess Lakṣmī, for the favour of whose passing glance others (i.e. gods like Brahmā etc.) observe rules (of penance), does not leave me even though I am not attached to her.

8. I do not enjoy with that much relish the sacrificial oblations offered by a performer of sacrifice as I do the ghee-dripping food through the mouth of a Brāhmaṇa who has offered all the fruits of his actions to me and who eats every morsel of that food with satisfaction.

9*. Who will not tolerate the Brāhmaṇas the dust of whose holy feet I bear on my crowns (in all my incarnations) though I am endowed with the power of the infinite and unrestrained *yoga-māyā* and though the water used for washing my feet in worship instantly sanctifies the world including god Śiva (who bears the Moon as an ornament on the forehead).

10. Brāhmaṇas, milk-yielding cows and protection-less beings are my own person (body). Those who look upon them as different from me, get themselves torn with rage by the bills of vulture-like servants of Yama who is appointed for dispensation of punishment—servants whose anger is like serpents.

11. I am won over by them who, looking upon even harsh-speaking Brāhmaṇas as *me* (Hari) address and honour them with a joyous heart, and with their lotus-like faces beaming over (lit. sprinkled) with nectar-like (sweet) smiles, praise them in affectionate terms like a (loving) son unto (his angry) father (or an affectionate father to his excited son) or as I have done (to Bhṛgu or to you).

12. It will be a favour to me if these two servants who did not understand the intention of their Lord (*me*) should again return to my presence after immediately undergoing the lower stage for insulting you. May the banishement of the servants terminate before long.[711]

---

*VC. construes differently : 'It is due to my bearing the dust of the holy feet of Brāhmaṇas that I became possessed of the excellence of the Yoga-māyā, etc.

711. *Yat . . . vivāsaḥ* : (i) May their special residence with me (as master and servant) be restored soon—ŚR., VC.

(ii) VR. : It is my grace due to which these servants, undergoing the punishment for their misdemeanour will return to me within a short period.

(iii) Had it not been my grace, they would never escape the Asura-yoni due to Brahmanical curse. Their early return after completion of their term in Asura-life is due to my favour. The word *hi* denotes the consent of Sanaka and other sages for this way out of the curse.

Brahmā said :

13. At that time, the mind of those sages which was over-whelmed with (the poisonous snake bite in the from of) rage was not satisfied even though they tasted (i.e. heard the sweetness of) the Lord's attractive and brilliant speech composed of a stream of Mantras—speech similar to river Sarasvatī which is lovely, heavenly, suitable to the assembly of sages.

14. Giving ear with close attention to the true but beautiful speech which was brief yet difficult to comprehend due to its weighty import, unfathomable intention and deep significance, they did not understand what he wished to do, despite their consideration.

15. The highly delighted Brāhmaṇas with hair standing on their ends (on their skin) folded their hands and addressed to him who had manifested the highest glory of his supreme authority by his *yoga-māyā*.

The sages said :

16. Oh god, we do not understand your implication when you, the Supreme Lord say (to us), 'You have done me a fovour! (lit. favour has been done to me by you)'.

17. It is reported that to you, the protector of Brāhmaṇas, Brāhmaṇas are the supreme deity. But you, the supreme Lord, are both the soul and the God unto the Brāhmaṇas who are adorable to gods.

18. You are the source of eternal Dharma. It is protected ed by your forms. You are regarded as the highest fruit (of Dharma and hence) deserve to be kept secret (—a fruit not perishable like the attainment of heaven) and you are changeless and imperishable.

19. How is it conceivable that Your honour is to be favoured by others—Your Honour by whose grace the *Yogins* become unattached (to the world) and easily transgress (the *saṁsāra*—cycle of birth and) death.

20* The Goddess Lakṣmī, the dust on whose feet is applied to their heads by others desirous of attaining different *Puruṣārthas*, appears to crave for the place of the black-bee chief whose dwelling is in fresh Tulasī garland offered (in

*This refers to supra III, 16.7.

worship) to your feet by the blessed ones. Hence verily she serves you everv now and then.

21. You who are highly attached to your great devotees, do not show much regard to goddess Lakṣmī who waits upon you by her pious acts of worship (which nobody else can perform. You are the receptacle of all excellences[711]a. Such as you are, are you purified by the dust on the road sanctified by the feet of the Brāhmaṇas and by the mark of Śrī Vatsa ? Do these add to your adornments ?

22. Oh Triyuga![712] It is really for the sake of Brāhmaṇas and gods that you, the Supreme Lord, Dharma incarnate, have protected this world of movables and immovables by your three feet (viz. *Tapas*—penance, *Śauca*—purity, and *Dayā*—mercy). By means of Sattva, your body which favours us with blessings,[713] you have done away with the attributes *rajas* and *tamas* which obstruct Dharma.

23. Oh God, if you do not protect by sweet words and proper honour, the race of the best of Brāhmaṇas who deserve specially your protection, then your own auspicious path (of Vedas) will be lost. For people will regard that behaviour of the most excellent (person like you) as the standard (to follow).

24. That (loss of Vedic path) is not at all desired by you. You are an ocean of the attribute of Sattva. You who have destroyed your adversaries by your powers, desire to achieve the good of the world. You are the ruler of the three worlds and protector of the universe. By such bowing (to the Brāhmaṇas) your splendour does not diminish. It is for the guidance of the world.

25. Oh Supreme Lord, we shall sincerely approve of

---

711 a. You are absolutely pure as you are the receptacle of all attributes worth possessing. Do the dust on streets traversed by Brāhmaṇas and the Śrī Vatsa mark (left by the kick of Bhṛgu) sanctify you ? Or do you regard them as ornaments?—ŚR.

712. *tri-yuga*—(i) He who manifests himself as *avatāra* in three-*yuga* period.

(ii) One who possesses six excellences viz., knowledge, power etc. —the characteristics of *bhagavān*—ŚR., VR., VC., etc.

713. *varadayā*—By your body (*avatāra*) called Kapila—VJ.

whatever punishment or respectful treatment your honour will mete out to both of these. Or you may inflict suitable punishment on us who have pronounced the curse on those innocent door-keepers.

The Lord said :

26. "Oh Brāhmaṇas, please note that this curse of yours was ordained by me. These two will immediately take birth as non-heavenly beings (Daityas). Having developed their *yoga* by concentration intensified by wrath, both these will soon return to me."

Brahmā said:

27-28. "Then the sages, having seen Viṣṇu, the receptacle of delight to the eyes, and his abode, the self-illuminating Vaikuṇṭha, circumambulated the Lord, bowed down to him. Taking leave of him, they returned, full of joy, praising the glory of Viṣṇu.

29. Lord Viṣṇu said to his servants, "You go (now). Do not be afraid. May you be happy. Though I am competent to do so, I do not wish to counteract the power of Brāhmaṇas, as it is my will.

30. Formerly this has been ordained by enraged Laksmī whom you prevented at the door from entering as I was then absorbed in Yogic sleep.

31. Within a short period of time, you will return to my presence after undergoing the curse of Brahmanical insult by means of your concentration in me due to anger."

32. Having ordered the door-keepers thus, Lord Viṣṇu entered into his abode which appeared beautiful by a row of heavenly cars and which was endowed with splendour excelling all[714].

33. Those two prominent gods (Jaya and Vijaya) whose glory and pride deserted them due to the irrevocable Brahmanical curse, fell down from Vaikuṇṭha (Hari's abode).

---

714. Which surpassed everything else in beauty as it was meant for goddess Lakṣmī—VB.

Or, He entered his mansion along with Lakṣmī who excelled all—VR.

34. Oh children (Gods), while they were thus falling down from the region of Vaikuṇṭha, there was a loud cry expressing grief (Alas! Alas!) from great persons in heavenly cars.

35. And those very prominent attendants of Hari have now entered the powerful lustre (semen) of Kāśyapa deposited in the womb of Diti.

36. It is by the lustre of the twin-Asuras that your glory has been eclipsed. And Lord Viṣṇu himself wills it.

37. The Lord (Viṣṇu), the supreme ruler of the three worlds, the First Being, the cause of the creation, maintenance and destruction of the universe, whose *Yoga-māyā* cannot be transgressed by masters of Yoga, will do what is good to us. Of what use (effect) is our thought (brooding) in that matter ?

CHAPTER SEVENTEEN

(The Birth of Hiraṇyākṣa and Hiraṇyakaśipu—Hiraṇyākṣa's Victories)

Maitreya said:

1. Having heard the cause as explained by the Self-born god (Brahmā), all the gods, with their fear dispelled, returned to Svarga.

2. On account of her husband's prediction, Diti was apprehensive of the troubles (to be caused) by her progeny[715]. At the end of hundred years she gave birth to male-twins.

3. At the time of their birth, there were many evil portents boding terrible calamities to the world, appearing in the heavens, on the earth, and in the sky.

4. The earth, along with mountains, quaked violently everywhere. All the directions were ablaze. Meteors and thunders showered down. Comets foreboding distress appeared (in the sky).

---

715. *apatya-pariśaṅkinī*—Afraid of harm to her children by Hari—VJ.

5. An extremely biting stormy wind frequently roaring (through the sky) blew with its army of whirlwinds, uprooting big trees, and raising its banner of dust (aloft).

6. When stars (and luminaries) in the sky disappeared, being covered by dark clouds roaring with laughter in the form of lightnings, not a single spot could be seen, due to surging darkness.

7. The ocean with its tidal waves and its interior agitated (by acquatic animals), roared as if depressed in spirits. Rivers as well as wells and tanks with lotuses withering there-in, were perturbed.

8. There were frequent misty halos round the Sun and the Moon eclipsed by Rāhu. There were roars of thunders without clouds—deep sound like rattling of chariots came out from the mountain caves.

9. In villages female jackals vomited terrible fire from their mouths, and howled out ominously, along with cries of he-jackals and hooting of owls.

10. Here and there dogs gave out different types of barking sounds with their neck raised, as if in singing or crying.

11. Oh Vidura, herds of maddened donkeys ran about kicking the surface of the earth with their hard hoofs and brayings vehemently.

12. Birds being terrified by the donkeys, screamed out and flew out of their nests. Beasts which were in the jungle and in their pens, excreted dung and urine.

13. Cows were frightened and blood issued from their udders. The clouds showered pus. The idols of gods shed tears. Trees were uprooted though there was no wind.

14. Evil planets (like the Mars) crossed and passed over auspicious planets, and the constellations or stars, and reverting in a crooked course, they fought with each other.

15. Seeing such other terrible omens, people, with the exception of Brahmā's sons (like Sanat Kumāra), being ignorant of the real implication of these portents, were terrified, and thought that the (time of the) destruction of the universe had come.

16. Those two primitive Daityas, with their bodies hard

as rock, grew up fast like big mountains, exhibiting their in-born prowess.

17. They stood touching the heavens with the crest of their gold crowns, embracing all the directions by their arms adorned with brilliant armlets, shaking the earth at every step, surpassing the Sun's lustre by the brilliance of the girdle round their waist.

18. The Prajāpati (Kāśyapa) gave them names. Of the twins who was first born of his body was known as Hiraṇyakaśipu and people call (the other) Hiraṇyākṣa, whom she (Diti) gave birth first*.

19. Hiraṇyakaśipu had no fear of death by the boon of Brahmā. He became arrogant. He subdued by the power of his arms, the worlds along with their protectors.

20. He loved his younger brother Hiraṇyākṣa who wished to please him (Hiraṇyakaśipu). Spoiling for fight every day, he took a mace in his hand, and went to heaven seeking war.

21-22. When gods saw him advancing with irresistible speed, making the tinkling sound of his gold anklets, and wearing the Vaijayantī garland[716], shouldering his big mace, proudly confident of his physical and mental powers, and of the boons (conferred by Brahmā), unconfrontable and undeterred, they concealed themselves like serpents afraid of Garuḍa.

23. When the king of Daityas saw that Indra along with all the gods had verily hid himself at the sight of his terrible might, and was not excited[717], he roared loudly.

24. Returning thence (from Svarga) and with a desire to sport, (Hiraṇyākṣa) of immense might, dived into the unfathomable, terribly roaring ocean, like an intoxicated elephant.

25. When he entered the ocean, the soldiers of Varuṇa, viz. all the acquatic animals, lost their morale. Though they

---

* When twins are born, the first child that is born is regarded as the younger, for the elder child gets a position behind it in the womb. This concept underlies the above verse.

716. *Vaijayantī*—(i) A long necklace or garland of eight kinds of pearls—VD.
(ii) A four-fold garland of flowers—VJ.

717. v.l. *klībān*—the effeminate Indra and the gods etc.

were not (physically) struck down (by him), they got terrified, and overwhelmed by his splendour, they ran away to a long distance.

26. Oh child, for many years he (Hiraṇyākṣa) of monstrous strength, wandered through the ocean often beating down with his mace of black iron[718], huge waves which were frequently swelled by his heavy breath. (Finally) he arrived at Vibhāvarī, the capital of Varuṇa.

27. Seeing there Varuṇa, the protector of the Asura region, and the lord of acquatic animals, he smiled, and ridiculing him with a bow like a mean person, he spoke, 'Your imperial majesty, be pleased to give me a fight'.

28. 'Oh Lord, you are the protector of the world, a great sovereign of wide reputation. You are the subduer of the valour of warriors who consider themselves haughty and valiant. You have formerly performed the Rājasūya sacrifice after conquering all the Daityas and Dānavas in the world.'

29. The glorious lord of waters who was thus bitterly derided by the enemy who was puffed up with excessive arrogance, controlled, by force of his reason, his anger which was thus provoked. He spoke out, 'Oh (valiant warrior), we have now grown tranquil.

30. Oh leader of Asuras, I do not see any other person except the Primeval Man who can satisfy in fight a pastmaster in the science of war like you. Go to him whom high-minded warriors like you eulogize.

31. He takes incarnations for putting down wicked persons like you, and for favouring the good, with his grace. You approach that warrior. You will (then) be rid of your pride and will lie (slain) in the bed of warriors (battlefield) surrounded by dogs."

---

718. **Or the mace which was firmly tied down with the rope of *mūrvā* grass—ŚR.**

CHAPTER EIGHTEEN

(*Hiraṇyākṣa's Fight with Varāha*)

Maitreya said:

1. Having thus heard the speech of the Lord of Waters (Varuṇa), the haughty and ferocious (Hiraṇyāksa) just ignored it. Having learnt from Nārada the arrival of Hari, Oh Vidura, he hurriedly rushed into Rasātala.[719]

2. He saw there Hari (conqueror of all) who was holding the earth, and was lifting it up with the tip of his tusks, and surpassing his (Hiraṇyākṣa's) splendour by his reddish eyes. He laughed out saying, "Oh this is an amphibious beast."[720]

3. He spoke to him, "Come here, Oh fool; leave the earth. This has been given to us, the dwellers of Rasātala by the creator of the universe (otherwise it would not have come down to us). Oh you meanest of gods who have assumed the form of a boar, you cannot get away with the earth safely in my presence.[721]

4. Are you employed by our enemies for destroying us? You kill Asuras by Māyā and thus conquer them by fraudulent means. Oh dunce, I shall wipe out the sorrows of my friends by killing you, whose strength lies in *yoga-māyā*, but have little personal bravery.[722]

---

719. *saṁviviśe*—dived forth for Rasātala with his eyes closed—VJ.

720. ŚR. states that this apparently provocative speech is the praise of Nārāyaṇa as Hiraṇyākṣa was his attendant in his previous birth. Hence *Vana . . . . mṛgaḥ*. He is the Nārāyaṇa who sleeps on waters, and who is sought after by Yogis or who hunts after the wicked for killing—ŚR.

721. Eulogistic interpretation : Oh omniscient one (*ajña*) to whom all gods are inferior, while I am witnessing you setting me at naught, carry away the earth. There is no doubt that you will acquire our prosperous kingdom. But as a favour to us, kindly leave it. You have assumed this boar form as a pastime (*līlā*)—ŚR., VR.

722. Eulogistic interpretation : (i) For the sake of Liberation, you are resorted to by our halfbrothers (gods and sages). By your Māyā—power you kill the Asuras and thus kill them from afar (yourself standing aloof). You are the maintainer of the ignorant. You are so powerful by your *yoga-māyā* that the prowess of others is insignificant before you. I shall establish you in my heart (like a *Yogin*) and put an end to the miseries of my friends.—ŚR.

5. When you lie dead with your head shattered by the mace (*gadā*) hurled by my arms, the gods and sages who worship you with offerings, being uprooted, will be no more.[723]

6. Though afflicted by the Tomara—(a javelin) like piercing (sharp) words of the enemy, he put up with that (mental) torment,[724] when he found that the earth on the tip of his tusk was frightened, and he came out of water like a big he-elephant along with the she-elephant when it is attacked by a crocodile.

7. Just as a crocodile pursues an elephant getting out of water, the Demon with hair of gold, of terrible tusks and of thundering voice, followed him who was rising out of water and roared, "Is there anything reproachful to the shameless wicked ?"[725]

8. He (Varāha) placed the earth on the water within the range of perception, and infused in it his power of supporting (mountains etc.). Despite the watching of the enemy (Hiraṇyākṣa), he was praised by Brahmā and was showered over with flowers by gods.[726]

(ii) Are you resorted to by our enemies, viz. Sanaka etc. and gods for Mokṣa (as one attains Mokṣa by worshipping the Lord in this world) ? No. They cannot, as they are inimical to us, your devotees. I am not your enemy. That you kill Asuras is just to deceive the people. As a matter of fact you give them *sāyujya Mukti*, for Asura means Yogin. You kill only the sensual ones. You indirectly vanquish the Asuras. I shall establish you in my heart—you who give knowledge to the ignorant. And by concentrating on you, I along with my family will get liberated–VB.

723. When you will be standing at ease with your head unhurt even by the mace struck by our arms, your new devotees who will worship you with offerings and your old devotees, viz. gods and sages, will not be without roots, i.e. will stay firmly established—ŚR.

724. (i) Seeing the torment caused to Brahmā and others who put a superficial interpretation on the speech of Hiraṇyākṣa—ŚR.

(ii) He tolerated the apparent hatred in the sharp words piercing like a Tomara (a javelin) as he appreciated Hiraṇyākṣa's inner devotion. —VJ.

725. (i) Out of compassion for the frightened earth some flight is not reproachful.—ŚR.

(ii) Fie on us (wicked ones) who pursue the Varāha who lifts the earth for the good of the world. What shameful act would shamelessly selfish persons like me not do ?—ŚR.

726. v.l. *viśvasṛjāmprasūnaiḥ*—(i) He was praised by gods and sons of Brahmā—ŚR. (ii) He was eulogised by gods who were the flower-like progeny of Brahmā—VD.

9. He (the Varāha), feigning extreme wrathfulness, and with a (derisive) laughter, spoke to him (the demon) who was pursuing him with a big mace, and had put on gold ornaments and a wonderful armour of gold, and was constantly wounding him to the quick with harsh words.

The Lord said :

10. Oh Hiraṇyākṣa, it is true that we are wild beasts in the jungle. I am in search of domestic lions (dogs) like you. Oh evil fellow, warriors do not care for the bragging of yours who are bound down by the cords (noose) of death.

11*. Here we are, the usurpers of the deposit of the denizens of Rasātala. We are shameless and are made to run away by your mace. (Though unable), we have to take a stand with great difficulty on the battlefield, as stay we must. Where can we go after provoking enmity with the powerful ?

12. You are verily the chief of the leaders of foot-soldiers. Quickly and without hesitation try to defeat us. Wipe out the tears of your relatives by defeating us. He who does not fulfill his vow is not fit for society.

Maitreya said :

13. He who was thus censured and ridiculed by the Lord in anger, grew extremely angry like a big serpent forced to play.

14. Being enraged, breathing heavily and with senses agitating in wrath, the Daitya rushing vehemently at Hari, struck him with his mace.

15. Just as a Yogin evades the god of death, the Lord, moving aside, parried the blow of the mace aimed at his chest by the enemy.

---

* VR. takes these statements as interrogatives implying negative replies : We take away the earth on which you place your foot (i.e. is your support). But is it the property of the dwellers of Rasātala ? (No, it is not their personal property). Are we the shameless who are put to flight by you with a mace ? (No. We shall make you flee). etc.

VB. interprets differently : We take away the deposit (the earth), as masters do not steal it away like thieves. Those who fly away without putting up a fight and simply boast are shameless. But a person with a sense of shame will not fight with a servant (like you in previous birth) | etc.

16. Being enraged, Hari rushed at him who had taken his mace again and was brandishing it, constantly biting his lower lip in anger.

17. Oh gentle Vidura, the Lord then struck the enemy on his right brow with his mace. But he, a pastmaster in mace fight, returned the blow.

18. In this way, the extremely enraged Hari and Hiraṇyākṣa began to strike each other with their heavy maces for defeating the other.

19. When the combatants competed with each other, exchanging heavy blows with their massive maces, and their rage went ablazing at the smell of the blood flowing from their bodies, and began to move in wonderful ways with an ambition for victory, their fight appeared like that of two powerful bulls fighting for a cow, on the earth.

20. Oh Vidura, Brahmā surrounded by sages arrived there to see the fight of the combatants aspiring for the earth-combat of the Daitya (Hiraṇyākṣa) and the great (Supreme) Soul who by his Māyā assumed the boar form, the limbs of which are sacrifices.

21. Seeing that the Daitya who had possessed valour and pride and had lost all fear, offered resistance, and was of irresistible prowess, Lord Brahmā, the leader of thousands of sages, spoke to the Primitive Boar, Nārāyaṇa.

Brahmā said :

22-23. Oh God, this is (the demon) who does wrong, inspires fear and does evil to gods, Brāhmaṇas, *Kāmadhenus* (wish-yielding cows), and innocent beings who resort to your feet. This Asura has obtained boons from me. He is in search of a competent fighter but has found none. He roams over the world troubling the people.

24. Oh God, do not play with him as a child does with an enraged serpent—him who is master of *Māyā*, haughty, uncontrolled and the wicked-most.

25. Oh Acyuta, so long as this terrible (Hiraṇyākṣa) does not grow terrible and unconquerable by resorting to his (Āsurī) Māyā at his favourable time, kill him.

26. Oh Lord, this most terrible even-tide (evening-time)

which is destructive of the world, is approaching. Oh the Soul of all, bring victory to gods before that time.

27. Now this auspicious period, called *Abhijit*, which lasts for two *muhūrtas* has arrived. At least for the good of your friends, the gods, quickly finish with this unconquerable Daitya.

28. Fortunately this (Hiraṇyākṣa), of his own accord has come to meet death ordained for him. Heroically kill him in the battle, and place (establish) the people in happiness.

CHAPTER NINETEEN

(*Varāha kills Hiraṇyākṣa*)

Maitreya said:

1. Having heard Brahmadeva's sincere and nectarlike speech, and having laughed (at Brahmā's naivete to advise astrologically favourable moment to the Lord himself whose form is time, he accepted his (prayer) with a side-glance implying affection.

2. Then that Ādi-Varāha who was born from Brahmā's nostrils, jumped at the enemy who was fearlessly moving in front of him, and struck the Asura on his chin by his mace.

3. A miracle happened. That (Lord's) mace struck down by his (Asura's) mace fell down rolling from the Lord's hand and the Asura's valour appeared splendid.

4. Then although he (the Asura) got an opportunity, he did not strike the Lord who was weaponless. He respected the prescribed code of conduct, in the battle enraging Hari.

5. When there was a loud uproar at that snatching away of the mace, the All-pervading Lord appreciated the (Asura's) righteous conduct, and remembered (mentally commissioned) his *Sudarśana*-disc (*cakra*).

6. 'May you be prosperous', 'kill him'. Such were the various shouts (utterances) all around in the sky from the celestial beings who were ignorant of his prowess, when he with

his eager Sudarśana was attacked in close quarters by his chief attendant (now born as) the vile son of Diti.

7. Observing the lotus-eyed Lord standing before him with the Sudarśana-disc (ready for discharge) in his hand, he (the Asura) with his senses throbbing with rage, and breathing heavily, bit his lip in rage.

8. He (the Asura) of fearful tusks, stared at him with glaring eyes as if to burn him down, and springing upon him, assaulted him with his mace, shouting, 'You are killed'.

9. Oh pious Vidura! while the enemy was just looking agape, the Lord, as the sacrifice in the Boar form, easily kicked with his left foot the mace which came with the velocity of a stormy wind.

10. And (the Varāha) said, "Take up the weapon. As you wish to conquer, try (again)". When addressed thus, he (the Asura) struck again, and roared lustily.

11. Seeing the mace coming towards him, the Lord stood firm and easily caught hold of the weapon like Garuḍa catching a female serpent.

12. When his personal valour failed, the great Asura, being humiliated, and splendourless, did not wish to take the mace (though) offered by Hari.

13. He took up a trident spear, eager to envelop (eat up) everything like a flaming fire, and aimed it at the chest of Viṣṇu who had assumed the form of sacrifice like the use of black magic against a pious Brāhmaṇa.

14. Just as Indra cut down the feather thrown out by Garuḍa[727], he (Varāha), with his disc of sharp edge cut asunder the trident, forcibly hurled by the great Daitya warrior—the trident of extreme refulgence which shone through the sky (as it darted towards Hari).

---

727. The comparison is between the shining Triśūla darting through the sky and the refulgent feather of Garuḍa falling through the sky illumining it on its way down. This refers to the incident when Garuḍa was carrying away Amṛta (nectar), Indra came in the way and hurled his *Vajra* (thunderbolt) at him. To respect the bones of the sage Dadhīca of which Vajra was made, Garuḍa dropped a feather and told Indra that he was not affected by the impact of Vajra but he dropped the feather out of respect for sage Dadhīca—MBH.I-33. 18-23.

15. When his trident was shattered to pieces by Hari's disc (*Sudarśana-cakra*), the Asura got extremely enraged. Shouting lustily he confronted Hari and dealt a punch with his hard fist on his broad magnificent[728] chest and disappeared.

16. Oh Vidura, Lord Ādi-Varāha who was thus struck, did not move even slightly like an elephant struck by a garland.

17. Then he created and used different forms of his black magic against Hari, the Lord of *Yoga Māyā*. Seeing it (Asura's *māyā*) all creatures got panicky and thought that the end of the world (*pralaya*) was imminent.

18. Terrible stormy winds began to blow and spread darkness of dust. Volleys of stones as if discharged from slings, fell from all quarters.

19. The sky, being covered with clouds accompanied by lightning-flashes and thundering and pouring frequently pus, hair, blood, excretion, urine and bones, seemed devoid of luminaries.

20. Oh sinless Vidura, the mountains appeared to shower various weapons[729] and naked female Rākṣasas with their hair let loose, appeared with spears.

21. Very harsh and murderous cries (such as 'cut down, break down, etc.) were shouted out by a host of blood-thirsty Yakṣas, Rākṣasas, foot-soldiers, (riders on) horses, chariots and elephants.

22. Lord (Varāha) of three feet[730] discharged his favourite missile Sudarśana destroying the Asura type of black magic manifested (there).

23. Simultaneously there was a sudden trembling in the heart of Diti who remembered her husband's words and blood oozed out of her breast.

---

728. *vibhūtimat*—the abode of Lakṣmī (VR.)

729. VC. takes this as qualifying Rākṣasa women—'Naked Rākṣasa women discharging various kinds of weapon',

730. This is the incarnation of *Yajña-Varāha* or Boar which was sacrifice incarnate. The three *savanas* are regarded as the three feet of *Yajña*. Hence this attribute is applied to Viṣṇu as Varāha.—ŚR., VB.

VJ. states : 'Amṛta, Kṣema and Abhaya' are the three feet of Lord. In Puruṣasūkta Puruṣa is *tripād*.

24. When his magical forces were totally destroyed, he again approached Keśava (Viṣṇu), and tried angrily to crush him in the clasp of his arms, but found him outside his clasp.

25. While he was dealing blows with his adamant-like (hard) fists to Viṣṇu, he hit the Asura at the root of his ear by his hand (i.e. foreleg) as Indra, Lord of Maruts, did to Vṛtra.

26. By the casual blow of the conqueror of the universe (Viṣṇu), the Asura fell like a giant tree uprooted by a stormy wind. His body was rolling about. His eye-balls fell out. His arms, feet and hair lay shattered.

27. Brahmā and others (sages) who came there saw the Asura of terrific tusks and lips bitten, lying on the ground, but with undiminished lustre. They exclaimed in praise, 'Oh who could attain to such (type of) death !'

28. This wicked Daitya kicked by Viṣṇu's fore-leg, gave up his body while looking at the face of Viṣṇu on whom the *yogins* meditate by *samādhi-yoga* in solitude with a desire to get liberation from this *Liṅga-śarīra*,[731] enveloping the Soul.

29. These two Viṣṇu's attendants who have come down to evil births due to a curse, will again be reinstated to their (former) status, after some births in this world.

Gods said :

30. "Oh Lord, we bow to you again and again. You who are the cause of extension of Yajña[732] assumed the form of pure *Sattva* attribute for the maintenance (and protection) of the world. It is a matter of joy that this Daitya who was a scourge (lit. afflictor) of the world is killed. We are quite happy in the devotion of your feet."

Maitreya said :

31. In this way, having killed Hiraṇyākṣa of irresistible valour, Hari, the Primitive Boar, being praised by Brahmā

---

731. In Vedānta philosophy this subtle body is regarded as the indestructible original of the gross or visible body. ASD 816.

732. *yajña-tantave* : (i) the source or promoter of *yajña* (sacrifice) —VR., VC,

(ii) who are yourself the institution of *yajña* (incarnate)—VB.

and other gods, retired to his region (Vaikuṇṭha) of uninterrupted bliss.

32. Oh good friend, Hiraṇyākṣa of great valour was disposed of (killed) like a toy in a big battle. This exploit of Hari who assumed the boar incarnation has been narrated to yuo by me as described to me by my teacher.

Sūta said:

33. Oh Brāhmaṇa (Śaunaka), on hearing this episode of the Lord from Maitreya, Vidura, the great devotee of the Lord was highly delighted.

34. How much more shall we be delighted to hear the deeds of Lord Viṣṇu when we feel such a joy at hearing the deeds of the pious persons of sanctifying reputation and highly glorious fame?

35. He (Viṣṇu) instantaneously rescued from danger the big elephant which being caught by a crocodile, meditated of his lotuslike feet while the she-elephants (his companions) were trumpeting.

36. What grateful person will not serve him who is easily propitiated by straightforward persons completely depending on him but difficult for propitiation to the wicked.

37. Oh Brāhmaṇas, a person becomes free from the sin of killing a Brāhmaṇa, if he (the sinner) hears, sings or takes delight in the episode of his miraculous action of killing Hiraṇyākṣa—a sport of Hari who assumed the boar form for the purpose (of lifting up the earth).

38. This (episode of Hari) is highly meritorious, extremely sanctifying, conferring wealth, fame, longevity, blessings; in battles it protects life and organs of senses and inspires heroic spirit. The listeners of this ultimately attain to Nārāyaṇa as the final resort.

CHAPTER TWENTY

(*Various Creations of Brahmā*)

Śaunaka said:

1. Oh son of Sūta Romaharṣaṇa, having established himself on the earth, what did Svāyambhuva Manu do to create openings (ways) for the creation of beings of later birth (as they were absorbed within God)?

2. The great devotee (of Kṛṣṇa) viz., Vidura, was absolutely devoted to Kṛṣṇa.[733] He abandoned his elder brother (Dhṛtarāṣṭra) along with his sons, as he was wicked to Kṛṣṇa.

3. Vidura who was born of Dvaipāyana, was in no way inferior to him in greatness. He was devoted to Kṛṣṇa with all his heart.[734] He was also attached to the devotees (of the Lord).

4. Vidura cleansed his sins by resorting to sacred places. What did he ask of Maitreya who was the foremost one among the knowers of the truth after approaching him while he was sitting at Kuśāvarta ?

5. Oh Sūta, while they were conversing, sacred stories relating to the lotuslike feet of Hari, must have issued—stories which were sanctifying like the waters of the Gaṅgā which resorts to his lotuslike feet.

6. Please extol to us the deeds (of Hari) which are sublime and worth describing. God may bless you. But what man of taste will feel satiated while drinking the nectar in the form of Hari's *līlās*?

7. Ugraśravas who was thus asked by the sages dwelling in the Naimiṣa forest fixed his mind on the Lord and spoke to them, 'Please hear'.

Sūta said:

8. Having heard the lifting up of the earth from the *Rasātala* by Hari assuming the body of a boar through his Māyā,

---

733. *aikāntikaḥ suhṛt* : One who is convinced about Hari being the only supreme being.—VJ.

734. *sarvātmanā* : (i) Thinking him to be his every relation such as father, mother etc.—VR.

and Hari's *līlā* of easily slaying Hiraṇyākṣa, Vidura felt rejoiced and asked the sage (Maitreya).

Vidura said:

9. Oh Brāhmaṇa, God Brahmā knows the course of the unmanifested Lord.[735] What did the Lord of Prajāpatis begin to do for the creation of beings after procreating Prajāpatis (progenitors like Marīci etc.)?

10. How did Brāhmaṇas like Marīci and Svāyambhuva Manu create this world at the behest of Brahmā?

11. Did they create this world with their wives? Or did they do so independently (without wives?) Or was this world produced jointly by them all?

Maitreya said:

12. The principle called *Mahat* was evolved out of *Prakṛti* composed of three *guṇas* (viz. *Sattva*, *Rajas and Tamas*) which got agitated by (the will of) the unperturbable Lord due to the incomprehensible destiny (*adṛṣṭa*) of *jīvas*, by the will power of the Supreme Being (the controller of *Prakṛti*) and through the force of unwinking (ever alert) Time.[736]

13. *Ahaṁkāra* (*bhūtādi*) was created out of *Mahat* which was predominently full of *rajas*. It (*ahaṁkāra*) was of three forms (namely *Vaikārika*, *Rājasa* and *Tāmasa*) and it was urged by *adṛṣṭa* (destiny of *jīvas*). It (*ahaṁkāra*) created the groups of five each : of subtle elements (*tanmātrās*), five gross elements

---

735. *avyakta-mārga-vit* : ŚR. takes it to qualify Maitreya and interprets: "who knows the reality which is not within the range of our senses."

736. As usual, commentators impose their views of creation on this verse. For example, VJ. : Due to the impelling of Lord Viṣṇu who lay on his bed along with Lakṣmī, on the waters of the deluvian ocean, there was disturbance in the balance of *guṇas* leading to the creation of Mahat and its presiding deity Brahmā. This agitation in *guṇas* was due to God who gave effect to the destiny (*adṛṣṭa*) of *jīvas* and the Time of creation.

VB. states that *Mahat* did not evolve out of *Prakṛti*, but was due to the disturbance in the attributes of Brahman. The three attributes of Brahman are : (1) *Daiva* (Lord's will, or desire to create), (2) *Para* i.e. *Puruṣa* or *akṣara*. This is *Rājasa*; (3) *Kāla* (the ever alert Time. This is Tāmasa). *Daiva* or Lord's will being indescribable is called incomprehensible. The agitation of the three attributes (*g uṇas*) o the Lord led to the evolution of *Mahat*.

such as the sky etc., five conative organs of senses and five cognitive organs of senses and their presiding deities.

14. The above things as separate ones were unable to create this *Brahmāṇḍa* of five *bhūtas*. When they came together by the inscrutable power of the Lord, they created the golden Egg.

15. That Egg being devoid of *Ātman* or Intelligent Being to preside over it, lay for one thousand years in the waters of the ocean. (At the end of that period) *Īśvara* (the controlling Almighty) entered into it.

16. From his navel sprouted forth a lotus with the great splendour of one thousand sons. It was the abode of all living beings. Therein was manifested God Brahmā.

17. God Brahmā who was guided by the Supreme Being who was lying on the ocean, created the well-arranged universe as before, with its own arrangement of names and forms.

18. Out of his ignorance or *Tamoguṇa*, Brahmā created *avidyā* of five forms, viz., *tāmisra*, *andha-tāmisra*, *tamas*, *moha*, and *mahātamas*.[737]

19. Not being pleased with his body which was composed of *tamas*, he cast it off. *Yakṣas* and *Rākṣasas* accepted that body which was in the form of night and which was the cause of hunger and thirst.

20. Being overcome with hunger and thirst, they ran at him to eat him up. Being afflicted with hunger and thirst they cried out, "Don't protect him, devour him".

21. God Brahmā being frightened, requested them, "Oh don't devour me, protect me. You *Yakṣas* and *Rākṣasas* are born of me".

22. Shining with brilliant light he chiefly produced these deities who playing with the light, i.e. day time, thus shed by him, claimed the day as theirs.

23. God Brahmā created sexually over-passionate Asuras from the lower part of his body. Out of lust, they approached him for copulation.

24. Thereupon god Brahmā laughed. But when he was pursued by the shameless Asuras, he got enraged, afraid and fled away in great haste.

737. For these *avidyās* vide supra III.10,17; III.12.2.

25. He approached Hari who removes the distress of the afflicted and confers boons on them, and who with a view to bestowing his grace, manifests himself to his devotees in the form desired by them.

26. (Brahmā prayed): 'Oh Supreme Soul, protect me. It is at your command that I created (these) beings. Oh Lord, these wicked beings fall upon me to satiate their lust.

27. You are the only one who can certainly remove the distress of the afflicted persons. You are the only one who can give trouble to those who do not resort to your feet'.

28. (Hari) who vividly reads the minds of others understood Brahmā's pitiable condition and told him, "Give up your terrible body". Being thus commanded, Brahmā abandoned it.[738]

29*-31. Oh Vidura, all the Asuras thought (the evening to be a woman) and were foolishly infatuated of her—a woman whose lotuslike feet were jingling with anklets, whose eyes were overcome with intoxication, whose loins (middle) were covered with shining silken *sāri* (fixed up) with a girdle of small tinkling bells, whose big high breasts closely brushing each other left no space on her bosom (i.e. completely occupied it), whose nose was shapely, rows of teeth beautiful, smiles fascinating and glances sportive. The mass of hair (on whose head) were dark blue. She (as it were) concealed herself (from their glances) out of shyness.

32. (The Asuras appreciated in wonder): "Oh what a beautiful form! What boldness! What a fascinating prime of youth! Without a touch of passion she moves amongst us who are full of lust."

33. Entertaining different ideas about the Evening in the form of a young woman, the wicked-minded Asuras, out of lust, asked her courteously:

---

738. ŚR. explains that all such references to abandon the body mean eschewing the particular state of mind and assumption of body implies assumption of a particular state of mind.

*ŚR. and VR. state that the body thus given up by Brahmā became the evening time when sexual passions are normally aroused. This explanation introduces the following description of the evening as a beautiful lady.

34. "Oh lady of beautiful thighs, who are you ? Whose daughter are you? Oh beautiful girl, what is your object here? Why do you torment us, the unfortunate ones by exhibiting the invaluable commodity of your beauty ?

35. You may be anybody. But we have the good fortune of having a look at you. You agitate the hearts of the onlookers by your play with the ball.

36. Oh beautiful lady, while you are frequently beating down the falling ball with the palm of your hand, your lotus-like feet are not steady at any place. Your middle (waist) being afraid of the heavy burden of your big breasts, feels fatigued. Your clear eyes appear serene[739] and the braided hair beautiful."

37. In this way, the dull-witted Asuras, thinking the evening time to be a woman as it appeared to them as such, and attracted their hearts, accepted her.

38. With a laugh of deep erotic significance god Brahmā created the tribes called Gandharvas (heavenly musicians) and Apsarās (celestial damsels) by his self-appreciating personal charm.

39. He verily gave up that splendid lovable body of moonlight which Gandharvas headed by Viśvāvasu accepted with joy.

40. Creating ghosts and goblins out of his lassitude, he closed his eyes when he saw their nudity and dishevelled hair.

41. They took over god Brahmā's body called 'yawning'[740] which was abandoned by him. By that body is created that complete sluggishness of senses called 'sleep' among living beings. They (goblins) possess the impure beings in that stage (of relaxation). It is called madness (*unmāda*).

42. Feeling himself possessing procreative power, venerable Brahmā created the class of celestial beings called Sādhyas and *Pitṛs* (manes) while he kept himself invisible.

43. *Pitṛs* took possession of the body from which they were created and on account of that, experts in *Karma-path* give to Sādhyas and manes (the offerings called *havya* and *kavya* due to them).

---

739. v.l. *acala*—steady.

740. The bodies of bhūtas are fourfold : (1) Tandrā (lassitude), (2) Jṛmbhā (yawning), (3) Nidrā (sleep), (4) Unmāda (madness) ŚR.

44. By his power of remaining invisible, he created Siddhas and Vidyādharas (demigods) and passed on to them his miraculous body called *antardhāna* (disappearance).

45. Decorating his body (with sandle-paste, flowers etc.) and appreciating his reflection (in the mirror) Brahmā created from his image Kinnaras and Kiṁpuruṣas.

46. They accepted the form (characterised by Narcissism) abandoned by Brahmā. Hence they get together with their wives at dawn and sing in praise of his deeds.

47. Lying with the extremities of his body fully extended and full of deep anxiety at the insufficient growth of the creation, he angrily cast off that body (which became characterised by anger, extension etc.).

48. Oh Vidura, the hair dropped from that body became serpents. From the body which was moving here and there were born cruel cobras with big hoods and broad necks.

49. When the self-born god (Brahmā) felt that he had achieved his purpose, he created from his mind Manus, progenitors of prolific population on the world.

50. The self-possessed Brahmā gave up his body in human form to the Manus. Seeing the Manus, Beings who were previously created highly praised the Lord of Prajās (Brahmā).

51. "Oh creator of the world, what you have done is verily well-done. In this (Manu-creation) all the religious courses are well-established. (Herein) all of us eat food together."

52. The sage Brahmā who possesses (the power of) penance, knowledge, devotion, Yoga along with the power of profound meditation and perfect control over sense-organs, created the sage-world (*ṛṣi-sarga*) so dear to him.

53. To each one of the sages, god Brahmā gave a portion of his body characterised by complete meditation, *yoga*, miraculous powers, penance, knowledge and non-attachment.

CHAPTER TWENTY-FIRST

(*Kardama's Penance—Viṣṇu's Boon*)

Vidura said :

1. Oh venerable sage, (I pray you) to please describe to me the greatly respected dynasty of Svāyambhuva Manu in which descendants multiplied in marital relations.

2. Svāyambhuva Manu had two sons, Priyavrata and Uttānapāda, who protected the earth consisting of seven insular-continents[741] according to religion.

3. He had a daughter well known as Devahūti. Oh sinless one, you told that she was the wife of Prajāpati Kardama.

4. Please tell me who am desirous of hearing, how many children had the great Yogī Kardama got from her who possessed *śama*, *dama* and other qualities of Yoga.

5. How did respectable Ruci or Dakṣa, the sons of God Brahmā get the daughters of Manu as wives (Ruci marrying Ākūti and Dakṣa marrying Prasūti) and procreated children, Oh Brahmaṇa ?

Maitreya said :

6. When the venerable sage Kardama was commanded by God Brahmā to create beings, he performed penance for ten thousand years on the bank of the Sarasvatī.

---

741. According to Purāṇic geography the earth consists of seven insular continents, viz., Jambū, Plakṣa, Śālmali, Kuśa, Krauñca, Śāka and Puṣkara (N.L. De—*GDAMI* p. 178). V.S. Agrawala and D.C. Sircar point out that the Purāṇic concept of seven concentric island-continents is a later development. The original concept was of *caturdvīpā Vasumatī*, i.e. the earth was like a lotus with Mt. Meru as its *Karṇikā* (pericarp) and the following island-continents as its petals in the four directions of Meru : (1) Kuru or Uttara Kuru in the north, (2) Jambū or Bhārata in the south, (3) Bhadrāśva in the east and (4) Ketumāla in the west. These have been tentatively identified with (1) northern portion of Asia, north of the Altai mountain, (2) India, (3) China and east Asia and (4) the valley of the Oxus and west Asia. Ancient Buddhist texts support the concept of *caturdvīpā Vasumatī*. —For details see V.S. Agrawala—*MP—A Study*, pp.184-188. Sircar—SGAMI, pp. 17-26. Baldeva Upadhyaya *Purāṇa Vimarsha*, pp.317-330.

7. Then Kardama with great devotion, intense meditation and worship[742], rendered service to Hari who gives boons to those who resort to him.

8. Then the lotus-eyed God Viṣṇu became pleased with him. Oh Vidura, in the Kṛta age, he manifested himself in an auspicious form, though he is known (to the world) by the verbal description in the Vedas[743].

9-11. In the sky, he saw the Lord who was free from all impurities and was resplendent like the Sun. He wore a garland of white lotuses that blossom by day and night. His lotus-like face was beautiful with smooth blue-black locks of hair. He was clad in pure silk garment. The Lord wore a crown and ear-rings and held in his hands a conch, a disc, a mace and a white lotus for sport. His captivating smiles and looks delighted the heart. His lotus-like feet were placed on the shoulders of Garuḍa. He had Lakṣmī (Śrī-Vatsa) on his bosom and the Kaustubha gem round His neck.

12. Overjoyed at the fulfilment of his desired object, Kardama prostrated himself on the ground. He, who was intensely devoted by nature, folded his hands and praised the Lord (in the following words).

The sage said :

13. Oh praiseworthy Lord, what a joy it is ! Real usefulness of our eyes has been achieved today by visualising you whose entire personality consists of perfectly pure *Sattva*[744]—a sight coveted by Yogins who have been developing their Yoga through many progressively pious births.

14. Your lotus-like feet are like a boat to cross the ocean of *Saṁsāra*. But those whose intelligence is deadened by your

---

742. *kriyā-yoga*—(i) Following the prescribed religious duties according to his *varṇa* and *āśrama* without selfish motive. —VR.

(ii) Service of the Lord who manifests himself while in meditation. —VB.

(iii) Acts of worship prescribed in the Vedas and the Tantras.—VJ.

743. *śābdaṁ braahma*— (i) Form known only from the description in the five Upaniṣads and possessing all excellences—VR. (ii) Full of all excellent attributes to be known from Vedic texts.—VJ. (iii) Manifesting form full of *sat*, *cit* and *ānanda*—VC.

744. *sattva-rāśiḥ*—Reservoir of all that is good and powerful—ŚR.

Māyā, resort to them for petty pleasures which are available even in hell. But, Oh Lord, you fulfil even those trivial desires.

15. I am of such a nature (as described above). I wish to marry a girl similar to me in disposition and useful like a cow to a householder's life (in yielding three objectives in life, namely, *dharma*, *artha* and *kāma*). With this unbecoming motive, I approached your feet which are like a wish-yielding tree and which are the source of all (four *puruṣārthas*).

16. Oh Supreme Lord, this world[745] is overwhelmed with desire. It is really bound down by the cord in the form of words (Vedic injunctions) expressed by you[746], the lord of *Prajās*. Oh embodiment of pure[747] Dharma, I am verily a follower of the world. I carry offerings to you (i.e. abide by your order of performing the prescribed *kārmic* duties for repaying the three traditional debts (*ṛṇa*) of man for which wife is essential)—you are the soul of Time.

17. Having abandoned worldly men and their followers like beasts[748], (your devotees) resort to the umbrella in the form of your feet. They forget the conditions, i.e. the needs of their bodies (such as hunger, thirst, etc.) in the discussion of Your attributes—a discussion which is intoxicating like wine (making them forget their worldly ties) and sweet like nectar.

18. Your wheel of Time which is based on three supports and which attracts and affects the world and has terrific speed, does not erode the life of your devotee while it moves on—This wheel of Time rotates round the axis of eternal Brahman. It has thirteen spokes (twelve months plus one additional i.e. *adhika* month). It has three hundred and sixty joints (number

---

745. *loka*—Marīci and others—VC.

746. *te*—(i) It is at your behest that Marīci and others procreate. It is not their fault—VC.

(ii) Your son Brahmā, the creator—VB.

747. *śukla*—(i) One who destroys the misery of *Saṁsāra* and bestows higher bliss—VJ.

(ii) This adjective suggests that there will not be any misery from *Saṁsāra*—VB.

748. VC. regards that both the learned ones in śāstras and their followers, being devoid of devotion (*bhakti*) are like beasts. Hence no sin in committed in abandoning them.

of days in the year). It has six tyres (i.e. seasons), innumerable blades (such as small units of time like *kṣaṇa*, *nimiṣa* etc.), three supports, namely, three periods of four months—*caturmāsa* each.

19. Oh Lord, you are only one, i.e. there is none other except you. With the desire of creating the world and by the powers such as *Sattva* etc., assumed by you through your Yoga-Māyā, you create, protect and destroy this world like a spider (doing with his web).

20. Oh Supreme Lord, although you extend (offer) by means of your Māyā, worldly pleasures in the form of objects of senses to us, your devotees, this is not really your desired object. Still, let it be offered out of your grace towards us; for you have manifested yourself as a person decorated with resplendent Tulasī (and hence have Time-Space limitation) through Māyā. (This manifestation will lead to worldly pleasures here and Liberation hereafter)[749].

21. I bow to you again and again. By your Supreme knowledge, you are free from the experience of the fruit of *Karmas*. You manage the working of the universe by your Māyā. Hence your lotus-like feet are worthy of being bowed (by devotees, whether they cherish desire or not). You shower desired objects upon a devotee who is motivated (even) by trivial desires.

The sage said :

22. Being thus praised sincerely, Lord Viṣṇu, the God with a lotus in His navel, who appeared lustrous (in his seat)

---

749. Most of the commentators follow ŚR. A few different interpretations are noted below :

(i) Oh Lord, by your Māyā you create *ahaṁkāra*, subtle elements and their special characteristics. Or you create ego whereby we cease to aspire after your place (*pada*). But I feel that despite my nonliking for your place, you will bless me with it out of your grace. As you have manifested yourself in your miraculous person with Tulasī garland, I believe it is for the grace of attaining your place. — VR.

(ii) Oh Lord, you have adopted the Brahmāṇḍa or Bhūtasūkṣma by your own will (Māyā) without being impelled by any one else. But this is not your essential form described in the *Upaniṣads*. The Lord is visualised by me as decorated with Tulasī garland, ear-rings etc. This is for showing grace to the devotees.—VJ.

above the wings of Garuḍa and whose eyebrows moved gracefully by his gracious looks and his affectionate smile, spoke to Kardama in nectarlike sweet words.

The Lord said :

23. Having known your intention, I have already arranged for that very object for which I have been properly worshipped by you, with self-imposed religious observations.

24. Oh Kardama (Lord of *Prajās*)! My worship performed by persons with their minds concentrated in me is never futile. In case of persons like you, it is not all fruitless.

25. Manu, king of kings, the son of Prajāpati (Brahmā) is well known for his prosperity and righteous conduct. He lives in Brahmāvarta, but rules the whole earth surrounded by seven oceans*.

26. The sage-king who is well-versed in Dharma will come here day after tomorrow, along with Queen Śatarūpā with the object of seeing you.

27. Oh Kardama, he will offer to you as a worthy bridegroom his daughter of dark eyes, of proper age, character and qualities and of marriageable age.

28. Oh Brāhmaṇa, that princess, of herself, will willingly resort to you (as your wife) in this place where you have spent years in meditation occupied with the desire of having a suitable wife.

29. From you, she will give birth to nine children (lit. she will ninetimes give birth to your semen borne by her) and sages will soon beget children from your daughters.

30. Having carried out properly my command (for pro-

---

* *Saptārṇava*—N.C. De identifies the seven oceans surrounding the earth as follows : (1) Lavaṇa (—the Indian ocean surrounding India—Jambū-dvīpa), (2) Kṣira (Kṣīra is a hyper Sanskritisation of 'Shirwan', i.e. the Caspian sea to the north of *Śāka dvīpa*), (3) *Surā* (Sanskritisation of the sea of Sarain, i.e. the Caspian sea forming the Southern or South-eastern boundary of *Kuśadvīpa*), (4) Ghṛta—the Erythraean sea or the Persian gulf, (5) Ikṣu—another name of the river Oxus—the big river taken as a sea, (6) Dadhi—a Sanskritisation of Dahae—the Scythic tribe living on the shore of the sea of Aral. Name of the people transferred to the sea, (7) Svādu—Sanskritisation of *Tchadun*, a river in Mongolia flowing through *Plakṣa-dvīpa*.—N.L. De—*GDAMI*, p. 179.

creation) you, of pure mind, will offer upto me all the fruits of your action and finally attain unto me.

31. Having conferred mercy (on the needy, in the householder's stage of life) and having offered protection from fear (as a *saṁnyāsin*—recluse) and being self-controlled, you will realize yourself and the world in me and myself in yourself.

32. Oh great sage, a portion of mine will be born of you as a son from your wife Devahūti. I shall compose a treatise of ultimate truths (the *Sāṁkhya Śāstra*).

Maitreya said :

33. Having addressed thus, the Lord who manifests himself to senses which are turned inwards, then departed from Bindusaras surrounded by Sarasvatī.

34. While Kardama was looking on, he (Viṣṇu) who had been praised by all prominent Siddhas and was sought after by (all) Siddhas[750] went away, hearing the collection of *Stoma* hymns sung in Sāma notes, as a result of (the flutterings of) Garuḍa's wings.

35. On the departure of the pure lustrous God Viṣṇu, the venerable sage Kardama stayed at Bindusaras waiting for the time (of Manu's arrival).

36. Manu got into his chariot decorated with plates of gold. Along with his wife and daughter he drove over the world.

37. Oh good archer Vidura, on the day which was appointed by Lord Viṣṇu, he arrived at the hermitage of the sage who had completed the vow of celibacy.

38-39. The place where drops of tears fell from the eyes of the Supreme Lord who was overcome with compassion for Kardama who sought him so intensely, that is verily the Bindusara[751] surrounded by the Sarasvatī whose waters are sanctifying, pure, sweet as nectar and resorted to by multitudes of great sages.

---

750. *Siddha-mārga*—Alternatively : the path to Vaikuṇṭha—ŚR. RR. doubts whether *Siddha* means *Vaikuṇṭha*. VR., VB. derive it : Path that is self-established. SD. : The path of knowledge and devotion that has been established.

751. N.L. De identifies this near Sitpur (Siddhapura in Gujrat) about 64 miles to the north-west of Ahmedabad—*GDAMI*, pp. 38 and 158.

40. It is surrounded by holy trees and mass of creepers. It is inhabited by sacred animals and sweetly singing birds. It is beautified by a charming forest rich in fruits and flowers of all seasons.

41. It is vocal with warbling of crowds of joyous birds; is roamed about by (intoxicated) black-bees. It is full of noise by the dancing (and crying) of proud peacocks and the cooing of the joyful cuckoos.

42. It is beautified with trees such as Kadamba, Campaka, Aśoka, Karañja, Bakula, Asana, Kunda, Mandāra, Kuṭaja and young Mango trees.

43. It is resounded with the sweet notes (warblings) of waterbirds like Karaṇḍava, Plava, swans, Kurara, waterfowls, cranes, ruddy-goose and Cakras.

44. It is visited by deer, boars, wild dogs, elephants, monkeys called *Gopucchas* and other species and musk deer.

45. The ancient king entered the sacred place along with his daughter. He saw the sage sitting after completion of the worship of fire.

46. The sage appeared brilliant as his body had undergone austere penance, but was not ostensibly emaciated (weak) on account of the affectionate glances of the Lord at him and due to hearing the nectarlike lunar rays in the form of Viṣṇu's words.

47. The sage was tall. His eyes were wide like the petals of a lotus. He had matted hair. He wore bark-garments. He appeared untidy like an unpolished precious stone.

48. Thereupon, the sage, being pleased with the king, who had approached his hermitage paid obeisance to him, greeted him with courteous benedictions and gave him befitting reception.

49. The sage, remembering Lord Viṣṇu's command spoke these pleasant words in soft and pleasant tones to the king who had accepted the reception, and took his seat modestly.

50. "Your Majesty, you are the protective power of Hari. Your tour is really for the protection of the righteous and the destruction of the wicked.

51. I bow down to you who are (the representative) of Pure Lord Viṣṇu. At appropriate time and place, you discharge the functions of the Sun, the Moon, the Fire, Indra, Vāyu, Yama, Dharma and Varuṇa.

52-54. When you who wield your fierce bow of terrific twang, frightening the enemies, do not go about in your victorious chariot, decked with precious stones making the whole earth quake by the trampling (march) of your army and when (if) you do not move about like the Sun leading a massive army, all the limits, i.e. rules and regulations pertaining to *Varṇas* and *Āśramas* which are laid down by Lord Viṣṇu, will be violated by the villains.

55. When you sleep (are slack), unrighteousness will be spread by men who are given to pleasures and are uncontrolled (by principles), and this world will be at the mercy of the miscreants and will meet destruction.

56. Oh Warrior, may I however ask you why you have come here? We shall sincerely be happy to comply with your wishes."

CHAPTER TWENTY-TWO

(*Marriage of Kardama and Devahūti*)

Maitreya said :

1. The emperor (Manu) whose all excellent attributes and deeds were thus eulogised, spoke rather bashfully (due to his modesty at hearing his own praise or the fear of the rejection of the marriage proposal) to the sage full of quietism (and dissociation with worldly acts).

*Manu said** :

2. With a desire to preserve himself, Brahmā who is the Veda incarnate, created from his mouth you Brāhmaṇas who

* Verses 2 and 3 are the echo of the *Puruṣa-sūkta*.

are full of *tapas*, learning, yoga and are free from lust.[752]

3. The thousand-legged God (Brahmā) created us from his thousand arms for their (Brāhmaṇas') protection. It is said that Brāhmaṇas form his heart and Kṣatriyas his body (limbs).

4. Hence Brāhmaṇas and Kṣatriyas protect each other. The immutable, disinterested God who is the Soul (*antaryāmin*) of all[753] thus protects all.

5. All my doubts have been resolved by your very sight as Your worship himself has explained to me, out of favour, the duty (*dharma*) of one who desires to protect (the world).

6. It is my good luck that I could see your revered self who are difficult to be met by those who have not controlled their minds. I am happy that I could touch the holy dust of your honour's feet with my head.

7. It is a great fortune that I have been advised (taught) by you. A great favour has been done to me. Your sweet words have been luckily received by my open ears (i.e. I could eagerly hear etc).

8. Oh sage, your worship should kindly listen to the request of a distressed person like me whose mind is tormented by affection for his own daughter.

9. This daughter of mine is the sister of Priyavrata and Uttānapāda. She desires to marry a husband who is suitable to her in age, character, excellences and other attributes.

10. When this (daughter) had heard from Nārada Your honour's excellent character, learning, beauty, youth and qualities, she has firmly decided to marry you.

11. Oh eminent Brāhmaṇa, therefore accept this (daughter) who has been respectfully offered by me. She is in all respects suitable to you in carrying out sacrificial and other duties as a householder.

---

752. *Tapo-vidyā. . . yuktān* : (i) Possessed *karma upāsanā* (devotion) and *jñāna* (knowledge)—VR. (ii) Full of *tapas*, knowledge of *śāstras* and devotion (*bhakti*)—VJ.

753. *sadasadātmakaḥ* : (i) Whose nature is of causal relation, lit. who is of the form of cause and effect—VR.

(ii) Who is comprised of cause and effect.

12. It is not commendable even for a person who has given up attachment, to reject a desired object when it offers itself. What need be said in the case of a person who is attached to worldly objects?

13. A person who, having disrespected an offer (of a desired object) begs the same of a miser, gets (finds) his widespread fame diminished and his self-respect ruined by disrespect (from others).

14. Oh learned one, I have heard that you are ready to get yourself married. As you are to terminate your period of celebacy, you please accept (my daughter) offered to you.

The Sage said :

15. I definitely wish to marry. Your daughter is also not proposed to any other person. This first (or important) union in marriage of ours is suitable.

16. Oh King, may the desire (of procreation) expressed in the *mantras* of Vedic marriage-ceremony be fulfilled by my marriage with your daughter. Who will not feel respect for your daughter who surpasses ornaments by her complexion?

17. (Who would not like to marry your daughter) on seeing whom playing (with a ball) on the terrace of your palace and looking with a perturbed glance at the ball and her feet beautified by tinkling anklets, (Gandharva) Viśvāvasu got his mind bewildered by infatuation (made love for her) and fell down from his aerial car.

18. When Manu's daughter and Uttānapāda's sister who is the ornament of beautiful women, and who cannot be even seen by persons who have not served the feet of Lakṣmī, approaches with a request for marriage, what wise man will not give his consent?

19. Hence I will accept this pious (daughter of yours) on condition of staying with her till she bears a child to me. Thereafter I shall think more of the duties as taught by Viṣṇu (such as *śama*, *dama*) essential for attaining knowledge and which are characterised by *ahiṁsā*.

20. That infinite Eternal Lord, the Lord of all Prajāpatis is the highest authority to me—the Lord from whom was

evolved this wonderful diversified universe, in whom it is sustained and in whom it will get dissolved.

Maitreya said :

21. Oh Vidura (wielder of a terrible bow), having spoken this much, the sage became silent quietly meditating over Lord Viṣṇu from whose navel has sprouted forth a lotus. But the heart of Devahūti was captivated by his smiling face (or he enticed Devahūti's heart by his smiling countenance).

22. Having learnt the firm resolution of the queen and his daughter, he was overjoyed and gave in marriage to the sage who was endowed with excellent qualities, his daughter who was equal to him.

23. Empress Śatarūpā, out of affection bestowed upon the couple very costly marriage gifts such as ornaments, garments and articles of household use.

24. The King felt free from anxiety at the marriage of his daughter with a suitable bridegroom. He whose heart was greatly agitated by sorrow (due to the prospective departure of his daughter) took her in his arms.

25. Being unable to bear separation from her, he constantly shed tears. Calling her 'Oh dear, Oh child', he drenched the hair of his daughter with his tears.

26. He took leave of the eminent sage. Being permitted by him, he got into the chariot with his wife and set out to his capital along with his retinue.

27. (On way) he saw the beautiful hermitages of tranquil-minded sages on both the beautiful banks of the sacred river Sarasvatī.

28. Hearing that the king was returning, his subjects from Brahmāvarta became delighted, and came forward to greet him by songs, eulogies and playing on musical instruments.

29. (The place) where the hair of the Yajña Varāha fell while he shook his body, there arose the town called Barhiṣmatī endowed with all kinds of riches and prosperity.

30. Those hair became the ever-green *kuśa* and *kāsa* with which the sages defeated the trouble-makers of sacrifices and performed sacrifice, (worshipped Yajña-Viṣṇu).

31. Having spread out a layer (= seat) of Kuśa and Kāśa grass, revered Manu performed sacrifice for Viṣṇu (*Yajñapuruṣa*) and the earth as his place of residence from him.

32. The king went into (his capital) Barhiṣmatī wherein he lived. Therein he entered his palace which (is free from) the three types of afflictions (viz. *ādhibhautika*, *ādhyātmika*, *ādhidaivika*).

33. With his wife and along with his subjects, he enjoyed pleasures without conflicting other *puruṣārthas* (viz. *dharma*, *artha* and *mokṣa*). His glorious fame was being sung by heavenly musicians along with their wives. Every day, at dawn, he heard the stories of Hari with a devoted heart

34. Pleasures could not swerve the sage Svāyambhuva Manu (from the path of *dharma*) to the slightest degree as he was a past-master in *yoga-māyā* (and hence could create his desired objects), and was intensely devoted to Viṣṇu.

35. As he was (always busy in) listening to, meditating over, composing and describing the stories of Viṣṇu, (even) the small units of time during the period allotted to him (called Manvantara) were not spent unfruitfully.

36. In this way, he passed his prescribed period (called *Manvantara*) consisting of seventy-one Yugas. He overpowered (counteracted) the influence of three *gatis* (viz. weals or woes of the *ādhyātmika*, *ādhibhautika* and *ādhidaivika* types), by his devotion to Vāsudeva.

37. Oh Vidura, how can afflictions of a physical and psychological nature or sufferings due to heavenly or human cause affect one who has resorted to Hari?

38. He was always obliging to all beings. When consulted by the sages, he explained to them the various auspicious paths of duties prescribed for men belonging to all Varṇas (classes of people) and Āśramas (stages in life.).

39. This wonderful life of the ancient (first) praiseworthy king Manu has been described to you. Now listen to the great fortune of his daughter (Devahūti).

CHAPTER TWENTY-THREE

(*Married Life of Kardama and Devahūti*)

1. When the parents of Devahūti departed, the pious lady who was expert in reading the inward thoughts of her husband, always attended upon him affectionately as the goddess Pārvatī did for Śiva, the Lord of the world.

2-3. Having given up passion, fraud, hatred, avarice, objectionable behaviour and pride, she who was very alert and was always ready (to serve Kardama), gave satisfaction to her brilliant husband by her confidence (in him), her physical and mental purity, respectfulness, self-control, service, sincere affection and sweet speech.

4-5. The eminent divine sage was verily overwhelmed with affection (favour) for that daughter of Manu and spoke in words choked with intense love to Devahūti—Devahūti who was devoutly attached to him and was expecting great blessings from her husband whom she considered more powerful than destiny (or a deity). She was greatly emaciated and weak by rigid observance of the vow (of serving her husband) for a long period.

Kardama said :

6. "Oh daughter of Manu, I am today highly pleased by your respectful, excellent service and intense devotion. To every being possessing a body, one's own person is extremely dear and worthy of being cared for. You, however, have not spared it (your body) as you wasted it over for me (in my service).

7. Just have a look at the blessings of the Almighty Lord secured by me who have been thoroughly devoted to my path of righteousness—blessings secured by the dint of my penance, meditation, Vidyā, and concentration of mind. These blessings which transcend fear and sorrow, have been achieved by you by your service to me. I give you the divine insight.

8. Of what merit are other pleasures, the desires (expectations) about which are foiled by the (slightest frowning) bend of the eyebrow of Lord Viṣṇu of immense powers ? You have achieved your object. Enjoy the rich heavenly pleasures

which accrue to you by your observance of the path of virtue —pleasures unattainable even to kings who covet for them."[754]

9. Realising that Kardama who spoke thus was proficient in all yoga-māyā and Vidyās, the lady (Devahūti) became free from anxieties. With her face beaming with smiles and slightly bashful looks, she spoke in words faltering with love and modesty.

Devahūti said:

10. "Oh eminent Brāhmaṇa, I am happy to know that all this (described by you) is within your powers—you who are the master of the unfailing powers of Yoga-māyā, my lord. (I request) that there should be at least one contact with your person which has been promised by you, oh Lord. To beget a child from a great husband (like you) is a blessing to virtuous women.

11. Oh Lord, for that purpose (be pleased to) arrange for the necessary materials as per prescription (in the *Kāma-Śāstra*). My body which has been tormented by (sexual) passion provoked by you and which has been emaciated with excessive desire for sexual enjoyment, will thereby become fit for it. Therefore think of a suitable mansion."

Maitreya said :

12. Kardama resorted to meditation for fulfilling the desired object of his beloved. He created an aerial mansion capable of going as per the occupant's will, oh Vidura.

13. It was a heavenly structure yielding all desired objects, decked with all (nine kinds of) costly jewels. (In it) all kinds of riches and prosperity were ever-increasing. It was beautified by columns of precious stones.

14. (It was) furnished with heavenly articles (like furniture and utensils). It was pleasant in all seasons. It was decorated with various kinds of silken buntings and flags.

15. (It was beautified) with garlands of flowers of varie-

754. *nṛpa-vikriyābhiḥ*: (i) Men with the perverted notions of themselves being kings.—ŚR.

(ii) By kings who perform Aśvamedha and other sacrifices specially prescribed for them—VD.

gated colours with swarms of sweetly humming bees hovering around them, and with fine cotton and silken clothes.

16. (It appeared beautiful as) it was furnished with separate beds, cots, fans and seats in each of the storeys constructed one above the other.

17. It appeared very attractive on account of the various works of art arranged and exhibited at different places and with its emerald floors and daises of coral.

18. It shone with its doors of red coral, thresholds and panels of diamonds. On its tops of blue sapphires were set gold pitchers.

19. The excellent rubies set in its walls of diamonds appeared like eyes of the aerial car. It was also furnished with wonderful canopies of variegated colours and costly arches of gold.

20. At various places it was filled with the warbling and cooing of swans and pigeons which mistook artificial birds as real ones like themselves and flew to them.

21. It was provided with play-grounds, sleeping apartments, places for enjoyment, quadrangles and outer yards constructed for enjoyment at will, so much so that it appeared wonderful to (Kardama) its maker.

22. Kardama who knew the inner thoughts of all beings spoke of his own accord to Devahūti who was not much pleased at heart to look at that type of mansion.

23. "Oh timid lady, take bath in this pool of water and get in this heavenly mansion. This sacred pool which is created by Viṣṇu, blesses men with all desired boons (objects)."

24-25. In compliance of the order of her husband the lotus-eyed lady who wore a dirty garment and had the hair on head tangled and her body covered with dust and discoloured breasts, entered the sacred waters of the pool in the Sarasvatī (wherein lived auspicious acquatic animals).

26. (When she took a plunge) under the waters of the pool she saw in a house a thousand maids, all of youthful age and fragrant like lotus.

27. Seeing her, those girls at once stood up and respectfully folding their hands said, "We are your servants. Please order us what we should do for you."

28. With costly materials necessary for bath, the respectful damsels made her take bath and gave her two new clean silken garments to wear.

29. (They gave her) very valuable brilliant ornaments according to her liking; they served her food of all excellent qualities and nectar-like (sweet and) stimulant drink.

30. In the mirror she saw herself wearing a garland of flowers, dressed in fine garments, her body very clean and decorated with auspicious marks and greatly respected by the girl attendants.

31. (She saw herself) bathed and washed from head (to foot), beautified with all kinds of ornaments, wearing gold pendants round her necks and gold bangles (on her hands) and with tinkling gold ornaments.

32. (She put on) gold girdle studded with many jewels around her hips, and with very costly necklace of pearls and was decorated with auspicious (marks and designs drawn in) saffron etc.

33. Devahūti whose face looked very beautiful by her excellent rows of teeth, well-shaped eyebrows, with her beautiful affectionate side glances of eyes which rivalled with lotus (in beauty) and with her dark blue hair (dangling on her forehead).

34. When she remembered her beloved husband, the foremost among the sages, she found herself there with a thousand girls where Prajāpati Kardama was sitting.

35. Seeing that she was in front of her husband and surrounded by thousand maids, and seeing the power of his Yoga, she was confused with wonder (doubted what it all meant).

36-37. Oh Vidura, the sage in whom love for Devahūti was aroused made her ascend in the aerial car (*Vimāna*)—Devahūti who washed herself clean in the bath and became resplendent as a new person and appeared in her original pre-marriage beauty with her attractive breasts covered (and hence concealed from view)[755].

38. In that aerial mansion, he whose greatness (or freedom) was not diminished and who was loved by his wife and whose person was attended upon by Vidyādhara damsels,

---

755. v.l.—stanam—adj. qualifying *rūpam* : 'beauty of the charming breasts which were covered etc.

shone like the extremely beautiful moon surrounded by stars and with full blown night lotuses around him in the sky[756].

39. With that aerial car, Kardama who was praised by Siddhas and was accompanied by a bevy of jewel-like (extremely beautiful) damsels, enjoyed like Kubera for a long time in the valleys of mount Meru, the foremost amongst the *Kulaparvatas*[757] which are the places of enjoyment for the eight protectors of the world (*lokapāla*). The valleys of mount Meru were enjoyable on account of gentle breeze, a friend of the god of Love. They were full of the echoes of the cataracts of the heavenly river.

40. He enjoyed himself with his beautiful wife in celestial gardens like Vaiśrambhaka, Surasana, Nandana, Puṣpabhadraka, Caitrarathya and in the Mānasa lake.

41. With his spacious, resplendant aerial car which could move anywhere according to the occupants' will, he travelled freely all over worlds like a wind, surpassing other gods.

42. What is difficult to attain for men of boundless mental powers who have resorted to the sacred feet of Hari who destroys the calamity of Saṁsāra.

43. Having shown to his wife the sphere of the earth full of wonders on account of all the arrangement of continents etc. the great *Yogin* returned to his hermitage.

44. Dividing himself into nine[758], the sage enjoyed the beautiful daughter of Manu who was eager for sexual happiness. He enjoyed with her for a number of years as if it was but a short period.

45. In the aerial car, lying with her beautiful husband on the excellent bed which increased her love and pleasure, she was not aware of the time passed.

46. A hundred years rolled away like a moment while the

---

756. ŚR. brings out full comparison as follows: Sage Kardama = the full moon; Spacious aerial mansion = the sky; beautiful maids around him the stars; fully bloomed night-lotus = the lotus-like eyes of the maids.

utkaca...gaṇavān—surrounded by a bevy of maids of beautiful hair: who gave pleasure—VB. VJ. gives a more erotic explanation.

757. Principal mountains viz., Mahendra, Malaya, Sahya, Śuktimān, Ṛkṣa, Vindhya and Pāriyātra—ASD 364.

758. Intending to beget nine children.—VR.

couple who were passionately eager for sexual pleasure were thus enjoying themselves by the force of their Yogic powers.

47. Due to his intense love (for her) he regarded her as his half. He who could read inner wishes of all (and hence knew her desire to have many children) was competent to satisfy them. The sage who realised his own Self[759], divided himself into nine parts and deposited his semen in her.

48. Hence Devahūti gave birth to female children immediately on the same day. All of them were beautiful in all their limbs in every respect and they gave out the fragrance of red lotus.

49-50. At that time the beautiful[760] virtuous wife anticipated that her husband was about to renounce the householder's life (and to become a Saṁnyāsin). Though she was overcome with fear and pain, she smiled outwardly. She was scratching the ground with her foot beautiful with gem-like nails. With her head hung down (in modesty) she spoke soft winning words, controlling frequently her tears.

Devahūti said:

51. Your worship has fulfilled every promise that you gave to me. You however should give me protection[761] (against fear from misery of Saṁsāra) as I have resorted to you.

52. Oh Brāhmaṇa, your daughters will themselves have to find out suitable husbands. When you proceed to the forest as a recluse, there should be someone (a son) to relieve me of my sorrow[762].

53. Oh Lord, I have given up (every thought about) the supreme self. It is enough that I have spent this much time (life) in satisfying the cravings of my senses.

---

759. VC. and VD. explain that due to his knowledge of the Supreme Self, Kardama was not so much attached to Devahūti as she was to him so intensely. Consequently Devahūti's contribution was the greater at the time of conception. This resulted in the birth of all female children.

760. *uśatī*—Desirous of having a son (VJ., VD.).

761. *abhayam*—(i) a son to protect me (VJ.).

(ii) Forgiveness for the request I am making again (JG.).

762. *viśokāya*—To advise and guide me in real knowledge as begetting daughters does not amount to repaying the debt of forefathers, stay till a son is born—ŚR.

54. I who am attached to the objects of senses, have associated myself with you (for that satisfaction) without realizing your higher (and real) Self. However let this association lead to my protection (i. e. liberation from Saṁsāra).

55. The Association with the wicked formed through ignorance is the cause of the *Saṁsāra*. That very association if formed with the good ones, leads to non-attachment to *Saṁsāra*.

56. A person whose action does not contribute to the righteous path (*dharma*) or to non-attachment or to the service (worship) of the sacred feet of Hari, is meant as good as dead though physically alive.

57. As a matter of fact, I am completely deceived by the Māyā of the Lord, for, though I have (by marriage) obtained you who can give me liberation, I did not cherish any desire for it (liberation).

CHAPTER TWENTY-FOUR

(*Kapila-Incarnation*)

Maitreya said:

1. When the praiseworthy daughter of Manu spoke despondently, the merciful sage, remembering the words of Viṣṇu (of white complexion) addressed her thus:

The sage said:

2. Oh blameless princess, do not thus torment yourself (and me as well). The imperishable and immutable[763] Lord will soon enter your womb.

3. You have been observing vows. God bless you. Be devoted to the Lord with faith, self-control (*dama*), *niyama*

763. *akṣara*—(i) Immutable. Hence unrelated to the chromosomes of the parents—VJ.

(ii) Knowledge incarnate; the Inner Controller—*antaryāmin*—VB.

(iii) Not assuming ordinary body (due to its independence of the semen etc. of the parents)—VD.

(observance of the ten prescribed restraints), penance and charitable donation of wealth.

4. Viṣṇu, so propitiated by you will be born to you as a son and spread my fame. He will instruct you about Brahman[764] and thus He will cut the knot (of *ahaṁkāra*) in your heart.

Maitreya said:

5. With great respect Devahūti trusted the advice of the Lord of Prajās (Kardama). She devoted herself to the immovable, unchangeable Supreme Soul, the preceptor[765] (of the Vedas).

6. After a lapse of long period, Lord Viṣṇu (Madhusūdana) was born of her by Kardama's seed just as the fire does in a piece of wood.

7. At that time, showering clouds appeared. Gods sounded the heavenly musical instruments in the sky. The celestial singers (Gandharvas) began to sing and the heavenly damsels (*apsarās*) danced in joy.

8. Heavenly flowers showered by gods (who move through the sky fell (on the earth). All directions became clear, waters translucent and minds tranquil.

9. God Brahmā accompanied by Marīci and other sages came to the hermitage of Kardama surrounded by the Sarasvatī.

10. God Brahmā who has inborn perfect knowledge knew that the Supreme Lord had taken birth through his Sattva attribute for the promulgation of the true knowledge of the Principles (*Sāṁkhya Śāstra*), Oh Vidura (destroyer of enemies)!

11. With a pure heart, Brahmā expressed his respects for what he intended to do (viz. propagation of *Sāṁkhya Śāstra*). With his spirits (senses) ebullient with joy, he spoke to Kardama (and Devahūti) as follows :

Brahmā said :

12. Oh child, you have sincerely offered me worship in

764. *Brahma-bhāvanaḥ*—The creator of God Brahmā—VJ.
765. *guru*—(i) One who dispels ignorance (VR., SD.).
(ii) Propounder of knowledge about Brahman (VJ.)

obeying respectfully my words. (In this way) you honour others.

13. This much service should be rendered by children to their father, viz. the words of the father should respectfully and willingly be complied with.

14. Oh courteous child, these beautiful daughters of yours will multiply manifold and increase the creation of the world with their progeny.

15. Today, therefore, you give your daughters to the chief sages with proper regard to their tastes and character.

16. Oh sage, I know that the First Puruṣa (i.e. Viṣṇu) has incarnated through his Māyā and assumed the person (body) called Kapila who is a treasure (of blessings) to all beings.

17-18. Oh daughter of Manu, this (Puruṣa) of golden locks of hair, of lotuslike eyes and of lotuslike feet marked with lotuses has entered your womb, for uprooting all *karmas* by means of the *śāstric* knowledge, Direct Perception or knowledge (*vijñāna*) and *yoga*. This enemy (killer) of Kaiṭabha will cut the knot of Nescience and doubt, and wander over the earth.

19. He is the chief of the category of Siddhas (who have obtained Perfect Knowledge). He will be deeply respected by the Masters of the Sāṁkhya Śāstra.[766] He will be known as Kapila in the world. He will increase your fame.

Maitreya said :

20. Cheering up the couple (Kardama-Devahūti) Brahmā, the creator of the world, with four Kumāras (Sanaka etc.) and Nārada mounted his swan-vehicle and went back to Satyaloka, the uppermost region above Svarga, the third world.

21. Oh Vidura, when god Brahmā departed, Kardama as per Brahmā's instruction gave, as per Vedic rituals, his daughters to the procreators of the universe.

22. He gave (in marriage) Kalā to Marīci, Anasūyā to Atri, Śraddhā to Aṅgirasas and married Havirbhū to Pulastya.

766. On the strength of *Padma P.* VJ., JG., VC., RR and VD record that Kapila the founder of the atheistic Sāṁkhya is different from this eacher of the Theistic Sāṁkhya.

23. He gave Yuktā to Pulaha, the virtuous Kriyā to Kratu, Khyāti to Bhṛgu and Arundhatī to Vasiṣṭha.

24. To Atharvan he gave Śānti who is the presiding deity of a Yajña (lit. who extends Yajña in the world). He satisfied the prominent Brāhmaṇas who were thus married and their wives as well.

25. Oh Vidura, then the sages, after the completion of marriages, took their leave of him (Kardama). They set out with great joy to their respective hermitages.

26. Having learnt that Viṣṇu, the great God, had taken incarnation, Kardama approached him while alone (privately), bowed to him and spoke :

27. "Oh ! It is really after a very long time that gods are kindly disposed here to souls who are being roasted in the hell (-like Saṁsāra) by their own sins.

28. Ascetics (who have renounced the world) try to visualize the Lord's feet, in secluded places, by following correct course of concentration in the *Bhakti-yoga* (path of devotion) which has been properly developed by them through many (previous) births.

29. That Supreme Lord who supports the cause of his devotees, is born today in the house of lowly (rustic) persons (like us), disregarding the humiliation therein.

30. You have taken incarnation in my house for the purpose of proving true to your word, as well as for propagating the knowledg of the Sāṁkhya doctrine. (Thus) you increase the veneration for your devotees.

31.* Oh Lord, although you are devoid of forms[767], whatever forms (e.g. four-armed god, etc.) are liked by your devotees, are the proper forms for you.

---

* Oh Lord, you are devoid of ordinary or vulgar forms. Your superhuman forms (e.g. that of four-armed god etc.) are proper for you. (But) whatever form (e.g. that of a human being) is liked by your devotees is (also) liked by you.—ŚR.

767. *arūpiṇaḥ*—(i) Devoid of vulgar forms—ŚR.

(ii) Having no form of god or man (etc.) which one gets due to *karmas*—VR. GD.

(iii) The forms liked by your devotees are not your real forms. All your forms are due to Māyā. This is what ŚR. means by *Prākṛtarūpa-rahitaḥ*,—VC

32. I take shelter in you whose foot-stool is always worthy of paying obeisance by the learned ones who wish to perceive the Truth directly (as) you are perfect in the divine faculties (of omnipotence, omnipresence etc.), non-attachment, glory, knowledge, prowess (or strength) and majesty (or splendour).

33. I resort to Kapila[768] who is the Supreme God. All the powers are within his control. He is in the form of Prakṛti, Puruṣa (who presides over Prakṛti), Mahat, Kāla (Time—the agitator), Ahaṁkāra[769] (of three types as per three *guṇas*), the protector of the world. By his power of intelligence, he has absorbed the whole of the universe within himself. He is omniscient (*mūla Brahma* : a witness to the evolution and devolution of all principles like Prakṛti etc.).

34. You are the Lord of all creation. Hence I would like to ask something of you today. By you (being born as a son to me) I have repaid all the three debts (pertaining to gods, sages and forefathers). All of my desires have been really satisfied. Having taken to the path of *Saṁnyāsa* (recluse) I shall now wander meditating on you in my heart, free from all sorrow.

The Lord said :

35. Oh Sage, whatever I state about Vedic and worldly *karmas*[770] is authoritative to the world. It is for validating what I told (promised) to you that I am born (as your son).

36. In this world, this incarnation of mine is for the exposition of the true knowledge of principles (like Prakṛti, Puruṣa etc.) leading to self-realization to those who seek liberation from the *Liṅga śarīra* (subtle body).

---

768. One who protects *ka* (Brahmā) and *pi* (Pinakin—Śiva). Hence Viṣṇu—VJ.

769. *tri-vṛt*—(i) One who is covered (described) by three Vedas —VJ.

(ii) Of the form of *jīva* in whom development of three *guṇas* takes place—VR.

770. *Satya-laukika* : (i) Path leading to *dharma*, *artha* and *kāma* and *mokṣa*—VD.

(ii) Brahman and the means of realizing it—VR.

(iii) Means leading to Liberation (*mukti*) and enjoyment (*bhukti*)—SD.

37. This subtle course of realization of the Soul (*ātman*) is lost for a long period. Please note that it is for the reinstitution of that path that I have assumed this body.

38. You have my permission. You may go at will. Dedicate all *karmas* to me. Having thereby conquered Death (i.e. *saṁsāra*) which is difficult to achieve, you resort to me for Liberation (*Mokṣa*);

39. By your mind realize within yourself Me, the Supreme Soul, the self-illuminating Light within the (cave of) hearts of all beings. (Thereby) being free from sorrow you will attain to Liberation.

40. I shall enunciate to my mother this spiritual lore which annihilates all *karmas*. She will thereby transgress *Saṁsāra* (cause of fear) and attain to the Highest bliss.

Maitreya said :

41. Prajāpati Kardama who was thus addressed by Kapila, was pleased. He circumambulated Kapila and went to the forest.

42. The Sage took the vow (e.g. *ahiṁsā* etc.) of the recluse's way of life. He took resort only in the Supreme Soul. Free from attachment and renouncing fire-worship and home, he wandered all over the world.

43-45. He concentrated his mind on the Brahman which is different from cause and effect, which (though) devoid of attributes—(*guṇas*)—manifests the three *guṇas* and which is experienced only by complete unswerving devotion. Kardama became free from *ahaṁkāra* (ego), attachment. He transcended the pairs of opposites (e.g. pleasure-pain; heat-cold). He looked upon all equally and concentrated himself on self-realization only. His mental capacities turned inward (to Brahman) and became calm (and serene). Full of wisdom, he was (quiet) like a calm ocean unperturbed by waves. With highest devotion to Lord Vāsudeva, the Omniscient, the inner controller (*antaryāmin*) of all beings, he realized his Supreme Soul and became free from bondage (of ignorance).

46. He saw his Supreme Soul abiding in all beings and realized all beings within God and within his own Self (Ātman) as well.

47. He became free from desires and hatred (likes and dislikes). He looked upon all as equals. With highest devotion to the Lord, he attained Liberation (place where all *bhāgavatas* reach).

CHAPTER TWENTY-FIVE

(Dialogue between Kapila and Devahūti : Importance of the Bhakti-yoga)

Śaunaka said :

1. Kapila, the expounder of the *Tattvas*[771] (fundamental principles) i.e. of *Sāṅkhya Śāstra* is himself devoid of birth.[772] But for the exposition of the true nature of the Self (*ātman*) to men, he directly manifested himself of his own accord through his own Māyā.[773]

2. I have heard many times about the Lord[774] (Kapila). But really my senses are not fully satisfied by hearing his glory. Kapila is the seniormost (best) among all persons and the greatest among the *Yogins*.

3. I am full of faith (in him). Narrate to me the praiseworthy deeds of the Lord who, though of absolutely in-

---

771. *tattva-saṅkhyāta*—(i) Expounder of the correct knowledge of *avyakta* and other *tattvas*—VJ.
(ii) Exponent of the Sāṅkhya system of philosophy —VC., GD.

772. *ajaḥ*—(i) Devoid of birth as a result of previous *karmas* —VR., GD.
(ii) Śrī Nārāyaṇa himself and not an *āveśa*—VJ.
(iii) Whose *līlā* of taking birth is superhuman—not the ordinary one—VC.

773. *ātma-māyayā*—(i) Out of his compassion for devotees—VD.
(ii) Of his own free will—VJ., GD.
(iii) By his incomprehensible power called Māyā—VC.
(iv) By his power of creating everything —VB.

774. *Śruta-devasya*—also is taken to qualify Kapila and means 'Whose glory is described in the Vedas'—VB.

'Who becomes manifest in the heart of the audience by listening to Śāstras'—SD.

dependent mind, assumes body through his own Māyā power for (the fulfilment of) the wishes of his devotees.

Sūta said :

4. (Just as you now ask me), venerable Maitreya, the friend of Dvaipāyana was also urged (by Vidura) to explain the Science of Soul. Being pleased, he expounded this (doctrine) to Vidura.

Maitreya said :

5. When his father (Kardama) left for the forest, (they say that) praiseworthy Lord Kapila stayed in the Bindusaras with a desire to do good to his mother.

6. Devahūti who remembered the words of the creator (Brahmā), spoke the following words to her son who was sitting quietly (actionless), and who guided through, to the end of the Path of Knowledge (or *Sāṅkhya Śāstra*).

Devahūti said :

7. Oh All-pervading Lord, I am extremely disgusted with the thirst for enjoying the objects of wicked senses. By catering to the (urge of the) senses, I find myself lost in the darkness of ignorance.

8. Today, at the end of many births, and by your grace, I have secured you as a good vision (insight) which leads to the end of this blinding darkness of ignorance which is very difficult to cross.

9. Your Honour is verily the first glorious Lord, the controller of all human beings. Just like the rising Sun (enabling people to see) you are an eye to the world which is blinded with the darkness of ignorance.

10. Hence, Oh Lord, you should dispel my delusion—the delusion viz. strong attachment to my body and my belongings (as 'me and mine') which has been created by you (in us).

11. With a desire to know (the real nature) of *Prakṛti* and *Puruṣa*, I have come for shelter to you who are worth resorting to for protection. I bow to you who are like an axe (to cut

down and put an end) to the tree of Saṁsāra of your devotees and are the greatest among the knowers of true *dharma*.[775]

Maitreya said :

12. Having heard his mother's laudable (lit. non-objectionable) desire which would create in men liking for the Liberation (*mokṣa*),[776] Kapila was rejoiced at heart. He who was the ultimate goal [777] of self-controlled saintly people[778] spoke with his face beautified by gentle smile[779].

The Lord said :

13. The *yoga*, which leads to the realization of the Self[780] (*ātman*), is for men the path to Liberation (*mokṣa*). Herein is the complete cessation of pain as well as pleasure.

14. Oh sinless one, I shall explain to you the *Yoga* complete in all respects[781] which in ancient times, I expounded to sages desirous of hearing.

---

775. *saddharma* : (i) *nivṛtti dharma*—VR.
(ii) *Śama* and other *brahma-dharmas*—VB.
(iii) The way to *Mokṣa*—GD.
(iv) Path of Bhakti—VC.

776. *apa-varga-vardhanam*—VC. and VD. treat this as a pun and explain : That which eliminates the three *puruṣārthas*.

777. *gati*—The means of Liberation (*mokṣa*)—VR.
The fruit ; the ultimate result—GD.

778. *ātmavatāṁ satāṁ*—The saintly persons who mediate on the Soul. —GD.
Those who realised Lord Kṛṣṇa. Self-control is their external index—VB.
The devotees to whom the Self (*ātmā*) i.e. Kapila is the object of worship—VC.

779. VC., VD. state : Kapila smiled because he was amused at the anxiety and fear of his (God's) mother of Saṁsāra. He, however, wants to explain the *Sāṅkhya-Śāstra* to her for the sake of others.

JG. : "Mokṣa is for other people. I shall give her the highest bliss of *Bhakta-hood*".

780. *ādhyātmikaḥ* : (i) Pertaining to unswerving devotion to the Self (*ātman*)—ŚR., VC. (ii) Leading to the knowledge of the real *ātman* as distinguished from Prakṛti—VR. (iii) The path of unswerving (fixed) concentration on the Supreme Soul. (iv) Yogas are of three types—(i) *ādhidaivika* useful in the realization of the Lord. (ii) *ādhyātmika* leading to the realization of the Supreme Soul—(iii) *ādhibhautika*—leading to the attainment of *siddhis*—VB.

781. *sarvāṅga-naipuṇam*—efficacious by *Śama*, *dama* and other complementary observances—VR.

15. The mind is certainly regarded as (the cause of) bondage and liberation of the Soul[782]. When attached to the objects of senses, it causes bondage. But when attached to the Supreme Man, it leads to liberation.

16. When the mind is cleansed of impurities like lust, avarice etc. born of *ahaṁkāra* (ego) about one's self and one's belongings, it becomes pure, free from (non-responsive to) pleasure and pain, and is perfectly tranquil and in balanced state.

17-18. Then the man with his mind filled with knowledge, non-attachment (to the world) and devotion, realizes[783] his Self (*ātman*) to be absolute, distinct from and beyond *Prakṛti*, immutable, self-luminous, atomic, indivisible, passive (non-participant) and (finds) *Prakṛti* to be powerless[784].

19. In order to attain Brahman, for Yogins, there is no other auspicious way comparable to devotion directed to the Lord who is the Soul of all (as *sarvāntaryāmin*).

20. The wise know that attachment (to objects of senses) is the unbreakable chain that fetters down the Soul (*ātman*) in the *Saṁsāra*. But that very attachment, if applied to the good (saintly persons) is the open gate-way to Liberation (*Mokṣa*).

21. The Saints (i.e. those who follow the path described in *Śāstras*) are forbearing (tolerant), compassionate, friendly to all beings. They have no enemies[785]. They are quiet[786], good[787] and regard good character as their ornament[788].

22. With their hearts fixed on me only, they practise

---

782. Cf. *mana eva manuṣyāṇāṁ kāraṇaṁ bandha-mokṣayoḥ*/ Maitrī 6.34 VP.

783. VJ. : Then the man (or *jīva*) realizes his Self to be the *bimba* of Hari.

784. *hatamojasam*—Prakṛti which has lost its binding power.

785. *ajāta-śatravaḥ*—VJ. dissolves this as *aja+ata+śatravaḥ* and explains : Who are the enemies of passions like *kāma*, *lobha* (avarice) etc.

786. *śāntaḥ* : (i) possessed of *śama*, *dama*—VR. JG.
(ii) steadfastly devoted to Nārāyaṇa—VJ.

787. *Sādhavaḥ*—(i) Who help others in achieving their objects—VR.
(ii) straightforward—VC.

788. *sādhubhūṣaṇāḥ* : (i) To whom devotion to God is an ornament —VJ, (ii) Though themselves saintly, they regard other saints highly (like ornaments)—JG. (iii) To whom *Sādhus* are dear as ornaments —VC. (iv) Who regard *ūrdhva-puṇḍra* and other marks as ornaments—SD.

firm devotion to me. For my sake, they have abandoned all other activities and their friends and relatives.

23. Taking refuge in me, they listen and narrate sweet stories (about me). As their minds are fixed on me, various kinds of troubles do not affect them*.

24. Oh pious Lady, there are the saints who have dissociated themselves from all attachments. Hence association with such deserves to be sought by you. (You should associate yourself with them) as they remove the evil of attachment (to worldly objects).

25. In association with saints, there are (discussions about my) stories which give proper and complete knowledge about my power and which are pleasant to the ears and the heart. By serving (listening to) them, there will soon develop intense faith in, love for and devotion to Hari—which is the path that leads to Liberation.

26. Due to devotion generated by contemplation of my sportive work (viz. the creation, maintenance and destruction of the universe), a man gets disgusted with the pleasures of senses and to the objects seen (in this world) and to those reported (available in the world beyond)[789]. Being alert, and by practising Yoga, he tries to control his mind by easy and straight courses of *bhakti* Yoga.

27. By not enjoying the *guṇas* of Prakṛti[790] and by his knowledge reinforced by *Vairāgya* (non-attachment) and by Yoga and devotion concentrated on me, he attains to me, who reside in all beings, in this very human body[791].

Devahūti said :

28. What type of devotion is proper for you ? Of what

---

* VB. enumerates sixteen characteristics of the saints. Of these three are *bhautika* (pertaining to *bhūtas*), four *ādhyātmikas* and seven *ādhidaivikas*. The comm. being very lengthy is not summarised here.

789. *dṛṣṭa-śrutāt* : Seen by persons of higher (spiritual) status and heard by those belonging to the lower status—VJ.

790. *guṇānām asevayā*—Not enjoying articles of food (drink &c) prohibited by Śāstras and polluted or desecrated by the outcastes. This emphasizes proper discrimination in enjoyment—VR.

791. VR. strongly objects to the concept of 'Liberation—while alive'. *Jīvan-mukti*—This means while in meditation, a man visualizes or experiences Brahman.

description is it ? So that thereby I can quickly and easily attain to your place namely Liberation (*Mokṣa*).

29. Oh embodiment of Liberation (*nirvāṇa*)[792], what is the nature of the *yoga* spoken of by you as reaching the Supreme Lord directly like a shaft (hitting its target) ? How many parts (*aṅgas* or auxiliaries) has it whereby one gets the comprehension of the reality.

30. Oh Hari ! As I am a woman of slow understanding, please explain this to me so that I shall easily understand this difficult *yoga* by your favour.

Maitreya said :

31. Having thus understood the object of his mother, Kapila felt affection for her from whom he was born (lit. got a body for manifesting himself). He explained to her the enumeration of *tattvas* or Fundamental Principles which they call *Sāṁkhya śāstra* and also the extensive course of Bhakti-yoga (Path of devotion).

The Lord said :

32-33. In the case of man whose mind is one, i.e. unswerving the natural, effortless, abiding disposition (devotion) of the presiding deities of the cognitive sense organs (lit. sense organs which cognise objects) and of the conative senses (which perform the acts prescribed in the Vedas) to Hari, the embodiment of Sattva is Bhakti. This unselfish (free from worldly desires) devotion to the Venerable Lord is superior to Liberation (*Mokṣa*) as it makes the vesture or sheath of the *Liṅga Śarīra* (subtle body) dissolve just as the fire in the stomach digests the food that is swallowed (eaten).

34. Some do not desire to get one-ness with myself (i.e. Sāyujya Mukti).[793] They are delighted in serving (worshipping) my feet and are happily engaged in activities for my

---

792. *nirrāṇātman*— (i) unexcelled bliss incarnate—VR., GD. (ii) Embodiment of highest joy.—VJ. VC. and SD. read : *nirvāṇārthaḥ*—The cause or means of Liberation.

793. *ekātmatām* : (i) The state of being similar in attributes like me—VR.
(ii) Liberation which I confer on them—VJ.
(iii) One-ness with Brahman—VC.

sake[794]. With deep interest and affection, the devotees of the Supreme Lord enjoy in describing to one another my exploits.

35. Oh mother, these saints see my splendid heavenly forms with beautiful kindly face and reddish eyes—forms which bestow blessings on them. They speak with them in affectionate terms.

36. Even though the devotees do not covet for it, Bhakti takes to the subtle state (Mokṣa)[795] the devotees, with their minds enchanted by and with their sense organs attached to those beautiful limbs of mine; my dignified movements, smiles, glances and sweet speeches.

37. After (the disappearance of Avidyā) they do not aspire after the magnificent enjoyments and prosperity (in Satyaloka and other places) of mine, the Lord of Māya. Nor do they wish for the eight super-human powers (*siddhis*) which naturally flow form Bhakti. Nor do they long for the auspicious wealth of the Supreme Lord in Vaikuṇṭha. But they do enjoy it in my region, the Vaikuṇṭha.

38. Oh Mother of perfectly serene mind, in Vaikuṇṭha, my devotees are never ruined. My weapon, the Winkless Time, does not affect them as I am their beloved Soul, (and am like) a son, friend, preceptor, relative and their beloved God.

39-40. I take them beyond Death (i.e. *saṁsāra*)—those who abandon this world as well as the next and their Self which wanders in both these worlds along with their *Liṅga Śarīra* (subtle body) and who give up their wealth, cattle, houses and such other belongings and resort with devotion to me who am Omnipresent (or have faces on all sides).

41. The terrible fear (of *Saṁsāra*) cannot be removed by anyone else except me, the Supreme Lord, the controller of Prakṛti and Puruṣa and the in-dwelling Soul of all beings.

---

794. *madīhāḥ*—They entertain a strong desire to enjoy my beauty, sweetness etc.—VC.

795. *aṇvīṁ gatim*—Commentators express their differences of opinion about this final stage called Mokṣa as per the tenets of their schools. Thus with VR. it is 'The subtle path called *archir-mārga* leading to Mukti. It is subtle as it is traversed by few'. With VJ. it is *sāyujya-lakṣaṇā mukti* wherein the *jīva* has similarity in attributes with God. To JG. and VC. it is subtle as it is beyond Prakṛti and hence difficult to grasp and giving "attendantship" (*pārṣadatva*) of God. To GD., it is the very resplendent subtle body of the residents of Vaikuṇṭha.

42. It is through my fear that the wind blows, the Sun shines, Indra showers rain, the fire burns and the Death does its duty.

43. By means of Bhakti-yoga strengthened by knowledge and renunciation, *yogins* resort to my feet, the (seat of) Mokṣa for eternal blessings.

44. If mind is firmly set on me by intense Bhakti-yoga, it becomes quiescent and steady. This is the only way for attaining the highest bliss in this world.

CHAPTER TWENTY-SIX

(*Kapila's description of Creation* (*Sāṁkhya Cosmology*) *

The Lord said:

1. Now I shall explain to you separately the characteristics of the fundamental principles. By knowing these, man is liberated from the ties (*guṇas*) of *Prakṛti*.

2. I shall explain to you that knowledge which, as the wise say, cuts the knot of *ahaṁkāra* (egoism) in the heart, and

*Although the Sāṁkhya theory is described previously (vide supra II.5, III.5, III.7 and implied in I.1.1) this chapter and the next give a more systematic exposition of the same. This account differs materially from the classical Sāṁkhya which is tacitly atheistic in its earliest available text ĪSK. (Īśvarakṛṣṇa's *Sāṁkhya-Kārikās*) and expressly so in later works like Sāṁkhya aphorisms attributed to Kapila. As Dasgupta points out, the theistic Sāṁkhya in the Bh. P. is 'quite different and distinct' from 'the theistic Sāṁkhya of Patañjali and Vyāsa-bhāṣya.' (*Hist. of Ind. Philo.* IV. 36). Most of the *Purāṇas* of the Viṣṇu group and some of the important Pañcarātra *āgamas* (e.g. the *Ahirbudhnya-Saṁhitā*) follow the Sāṁkhya theory as expounded in the Bh. P. If the table of contents of the *Ṣaṣṭi-tantra* as given in the *Ahirbudhnya-Saṁhitā* be that of the original work (as Dasgupta believes), the Sāṁkhya system might be originally theistic. But all discussions regarding the problem of the authorship and contents of the *Ṣaṣṭitantra* are mere speculations and inconclusive, despite the contributions of great scholars like Schrader, Keith, Garbe, Dasgupta and others. Hence the emphasis on ĪSK—the earliest representative of classical Sāṁkhya here.

leads man to self-realization, and ultimately to the summum bonum (*Mokṣa*).

3.* *Puruṣa* is the beginningless (eternal) Soul. (He is) attributeless, distinct from and superior to *Prakṛti*. He manifests (himself) inside and is self-luminous. The universe, thereby, becomes illuminated.

4. This all-pervading Lord, of his own free will, has accepted the subtle, divine Prakṛti constituted of three *guṇas* as a part of his *līlā* (sport).

5. He was here immediately infatuated[796] with *Prakṛti*

---

*(i) VR. explains : *Puruṣa* is *jīva*. As he illuminates himself as well as other things, he is regarded as self luminous. But unlike *jaḍa* (non-sentient) lamp, his light (knowledge) is useful for himself in becoming conscious of himself and others. He is distinct from *Prakṛti* i.e. its products like the body, sense-organs, mind, vital breaths etc. Hence he is free from *Sattva* and other *guṇas* of Prakṛti. He has pervaded all the universe by entering into gross and subtle bodies from god Brahmā to a blade of grass.

(ii) VJ. states: The Supreme Soul is eternal (lit. is beginningless and endless). He is not caused (created) by anything. He is *Puruṣa*—i.e. the bestower of perfect bliss. Or he is within all but unrelated to *guṇas*. He is beyond Prakṛti. He lives in the lotus called *Abhi-mukha*. He is illuminated by his own light. He has pervaded the world of movables and immovables.

(iii) SD. interprets: He is beginningless, i.e. He existed before the creation and is the cause of everything else He enters all and controls them and confers on the *jīvas* the fruits of their *Karmas*. He is the shelter and controller of *Prakṛti*. He is devoid of *guṇas* and governs the sentient and non-sentient universe. Being self-luminous he has pervaded all the universe.

(iv) VB. construes it differently: He being devoid of attributes (*guṇas*) and being their cause, is himself uncreated by anyone. He is distinct from and unrelated to *Prakṛti*. He is the self-knower and self-luminous and is thus distinct from *ahaṁkāra*. Thus he is Ātman—free from body, *guṇas*, Prakṛti and Kāla. His self-luminosity is his extraordinariness (*alaukikatvaṁ*).

(v) ŚR. tells us that the adj. *pratyag-dhāmā* refutes the Buddhist doctrine of momentariness and the adjectives—*nirguṇa* and *svayaṁ-jyoti* refute the Mīmāṁsaka and Prabhākara's views about the nature of the Soul.

796. *mumuhe*: (i) identified himself with Prakṛti—VR.

(ii) VJ. credits Hari for deluding the *jīvas* by his will or Prakṛti which obscures the knowledge of *jīva*.

(iii) *Jīva* forgot his own real nature by the *vṛtti* of *Prakṛti* known as *avidyā*. *Jīva* had this knowledge before the creation (during the Deluge) but forgot it after creation.

which covers (obscures) knowledge and which creates various wonderful beings similar in attributes (*guṇas*).

6. In this way, due to his wrongly presumed identification with Prakṛti, Puruṣa regards the authorship of *karmas* (as vested) in him when (actually) the *karmas* are being done by the *guṇas* of Prakṛti.

7. Though the Lord is (really) actionless, an unconcerned witness and blissful by nature, it involves him in *saṁsāra* (cycle of births and deaths), bondage and reduces him to a stage of dependence.

8. They (wise people) know that Prakṛti is the cause of the effect (i.e. the body assumed by Puruṣa in an embodied state), means (organs of senses) and the doership (the presiding deities of sense-organs). In reality, Puruṣa is distinct and beyond —superior to—Prakṛti; (but) he is the cause of all pleasures and pains as the experiencer, due to his identification with Prakṛti.[797]

Devahūti said:

9. Oh best among men, please tell me the characteristics of Prakṛti as well as of Puruṣa. They are the cause of this universe, which consists of both gross and subtle products.

The Lord said:

10*. They (the knowers) call that as *Prakṛti* which is *Pradhāna*—(the chief, ultimate first principle). It consists of

---

797. Cf.
kārya-kāraṇa-kartṛtve hetuḥ prakṛtir ucyate|
puruṣaḥ sukha-duḥkhānām bhoktṛtve hetur ucyate| BG. 13.20.

VJ. explains the 2nd half: They know that it is Viṣṇu who is superior to Prakṛti, is the cause of Jīva's experience of pleasure and pain. VC. endorses the same.

*According to ĪSK this *mūla-Prakṛti* is *avyakta* (3) and *Pradhāna* (11, 57 etc.). It appears that the original doctrine of eight-fold Prakṛti (probably related to levels of yogic awareness, vide *Kaṭha*. 3.10-11) was represented later as 'vertical' evolution with *Prakṛti* as the first Principle. The characteristics of the *Prakṛti* are enumerated in ĪSK as follows:

Hetumad anityam avyāpi sakriyam anekam āśritam liṅgam|
Sāvayavaṁ paratantraṁ vyaktaṁ viparītam avyaktam || 10||

:Avyakta is the opposite of *vyakta* which is caused, finite, non-perva-

three *guṇas* (*Sattva*, *rajas* and *tamas*). It is (by itself) unmanifest and eternal. It is of the nature of both cause and effect. It is, by itself, undifferentiated and without any specialities, but it is the basis of (and hence possesses) specialities or attributes.

11. The learned know Brahman as comprising of the effects of Pradhāna—a collection of twentyfour principles, viz. five *tanmātrās* (subtle potentials of elements), five elements (*mahā-bhūtas*), four[798] internal organs, viz. *manas*, *buddhi*, *ahaṁkāra* and *citta*) and ten (sense-organs consisting of five cognitive and five conative organs).

12. There are only five gross elements (*mahābhūtas*), viz., earth, water, fire (heat-light), air and the sky (space).

---

sive, active, plural, supported, emergent, composite and dependent'. The next *Kārikā* (11) further describes *Prakṛti* as 'characterised by three *guṇas* undiscriminated, objective, general (*sāmānya*), non-conscious and productive.

A reference to the Bh. P. (supra I. 10, II.5, III.5, III.7 etc.) will show that the *Prakṛti* is not an independent real as is presumed in the ĪSK. God, in his desire to realize himself, reflects himself in the Prakṛti which is his own power, and it is through this impregnation of himself in his own power, that Prakṛti is enlivened by consciousness, and he appears as individual Souls suffering from the bondage of Prakṛti. It is through his creative effort called Kāla (Time) that the equilibrium of the *guṇas* of Prakṛti is disturbed and categories (or 'Principles') are evolved. Later (infra XI.13, XI. 22 etc.) an extreme idealistic monism practically effaces Sāṁkhya realism, as the Bh. P. holds that ultimate reality is one and that all differences are merely in name and form. Prakṛti and its manifestations are due to the operation of the Māyā power of God. This Māyā is defined as that which manifests non-existent objects but is not manifested itself (Bh. P. II.9.33).

It will thus be found that the concepts of Prakṛti in the ĪSK and in the Bh. P. are not the same. (For Kapila's Philosophy in the Bh. P. vide Dasgupta—*Hist. Ind. Philo*. Vol. IV. 24. 24-48).

A systematic comparative study of the *Sāṁkhya* in the Bh. P. and the classical *Sāṁkhya* is beyond the scope of such foot notes.

798. I enumerated these on the basis of verse No. 14 below. But VR. states them as *manas*, *ahaṁkāra*, *mahat* and *avyakta* (*caturbhir mano'haṁkāra-mahad-avyaktair*). He later (verse 14) admits that if the four aspects of mind enumerated in this verse are counted as independent, the number of categories will be twenty-seven.

The subtle objects of these (elements)[799], viz., smell and others, i.e. taste, colour-form, touch and sound are also the same in number according to me.

13. The sense-organs are ten: the ear, the skin, the eye, the tongue and the nose. (These are the cognitive organs). The organs of speech, the hands, the feet, the organ of generation and the anus is called (enumerated) as the tenth. (These are conative organs).

14. The internal organ has four aspects viz. *manas*, *buddhi*, *ahaṁkāra* and *citta*. (This) fourfold distinction is observed through its characteristic functions.[800]

15. This much is the list of the enumerated principles of Brahman as conditioned by *guṇas* as explained (to you) by me. What is called 'Time' (*Kāla*) is the twenty-fifth principle.

16. Some regard Time (*Kāla*) as the super-human power of God (Īśvara) whence comes fear (death, *saṁsāra* etc.) to the *jīva* who is possessed by Prakṛti, and thereby is deluded by I-ness (*ahaṁkāra*) in identifying himself with the body.

17. Oh Manu's daughter, that divine power is designated as *Kāla* which sets commotion in the undifferentiated *guṇas* of *Prakṛti* which were (originally) in a state of equilibrium.

18. He is the glorious Lord who dwells within all beings as a controller and yet is unaffected, and outside of them as Kāla[801].

---

799. *tanmātrās* : These are not included in old lists of evolutes in the BG. and Mokṣadharma (MBH). I believe that the Bh. P. is following BG. and MBH. in enumerating the objects of senses under *tanmātrās*. In the classical Sāṁkhya the objects of senses are left out of the list of *tattvas*. In it the *tanmātās* are the products of *ahaṁkāra* and serve as subtle potential of gross elements (*Mahābhūtas* vide ĪSK. 38.) G. J. Larsen writes : 'The subtle elements function somewhat like *manas*. . . They are products of self-awareness and yet they in turn come in contact with or generate the external world'.—*Classical Sāṁkhya*, pp. 205-6.

800. VJ. and VD. state the functions as follows: *Buddhi* leads to conclusions; *manas* entertains doubt ; *ahaṁkāra* creates pride; *citta* is the cause of remembrance.

801. ŚR. concludes: Thus there are twenty-four categories of Prakṛti. The twenty-fifth is the jīva (individual Soul) and Supreme Soul (Īśvara) which are identical.

19. The Supreme Man deposited his energy into his Prakṛti whose *guṇas* were disturbed and agitated by the *adṛṣṭa* (unseen-destiny) of *jīvas*. She gave birth to the principle called *Mahat* which was resplendent (as if made of gold).

20*. That cause of the universe which is unchangeable (eternal), wished to manifest the universe which was lying within it in a subtle form. It drank up (dispelled) by its lustre the thick darkness (of the time of deluge) which was capable of covering it. (*Mahat* was absorbed in Prakṛti at the time of *Pralaya*).

21. (It is well known in the *āgamas*) that *Mahat* which is characterised by *sattva-guṇa*, pure, free from passions (like love, hatred etc.) and the place of the Supreme Lord, is the *citta* which is called Vāsudeva and it is composed of *Mahat Tattva*[802].

It will thus be seen that the Bh. P. presents three aspects of Time : God, Power of God and Time-sequence. In this chapter, the Bh. P. deals with the first two aspects. Time is a supra-phenomenal reality. Its characteristic feature is to disturb the equilibrium of Prakṛti and set in motion the process of creation. It thus pre-exists creation. It is God's power, dynamism and effort, as it is a force driving the cosmic process to materialize into subtle and gross creation. Kāla pervades the mind of man as his inner controller and the external universe as time. When Bh. P. enumerates Time as the twenty-fifth category of Sāṁkhyas, it refers to the concept of Time as God. When it takes Time as the power of Puruṣa, it refers to the second aspect. For details Bhattacharya PSB. I.247-259.

*VR. takes this with reference to God: The Lord, the cause of the universe which is unchangeable, wanted to manifest the universe which was lying absorbed in Prakṛti within him. By his lustre (knowledge in the form of his will to create) he drank up (destroyed) the darkness (ignorance, the attribute *tamas*) which obscured (restricted the knowledge of) *jīvātman*.

802. ŚR. explains : From this verse the concept of the four *vyūhas* and how to worship them is given. Here what is considered from the causal or *adhibhūta* point of view is *Mahat*, the same is called *citta* from the point of *adhyātma* (relation to the body). It has Vāsudeva as an object of meditation (*upāsya*) and *kṣetrajña* as the presiding deity (*adhiṣṭhātṛ*).

It is a sort of a synthesis between the Sāṁkhya and the Pāñcarātra *āgama*. The four aspects of *antaḥkaraṇa* of the Sāṁkhyas are connected with the *vyūhas* (manifestations of God) of the Pāñcarātras as follows :

Sāṁkhya		*Pāñcarātra*	
as *adhyātma* (relating to body)	*adhibhūta*	*upāsya* (object of meditation)	*adhiṣṭhātṛ* (Presiding deity.)

1.	Citta	Mahat	Vāṣudeva	Kṣetrajña (the Soul, occupant of the body)
2.	ahaṁkāra	Aggregate of *bhūtas*, senses and mind	Saṅkarṣaṇa	Rudra
3.	manas	manas	Aniruddha	Candra
4.	buddhi	buddhi (intellect)	Pradyumna	Brahmā

The Peñcarātra idea of *Vyūha* is briefly as follows :

Vyūha is derived from √*ūh* with *vi*—'to push, to remove, to thruts' (Apte PSD 307). At the end of *mahāpralaya*, the following six attributes of God are manifested : *Jñāna* (knowledge), *aiśvarya* (power), *śakti* (prowess), *bala* (supremacy), *vīrya* (energy) and *tejas* (splendour). (They may be approximately rendered as : 1. Knowledge—pure consciousness, 2. Independence of activity, 3. Potency to become the material cause of the world, 4. Fatiguelessness and power to sustain, 5. Unaffectedness, 6. Selfsufficiency, splendour. These six *guṇas* form the material of pure creation. The *Vyūhas* have a cosmological function while *avatāras* are concerned with the *līlās*.

The *Vyūhas* are four : Vāsudeva, Saṅkarṣaṇa, Pradyumna and Aniruddha, each having some cosmic functions. Their traditional representation may be summarised in the following table (vide the *Sāttvata Saṁhitā* 5, 9-18).

1:	*Vyūha* :	*Vāsudeva*	*Saṅkarṣaṇa*	*Pradyumna*	*Aniruddha*
2.	*Prominent attributes*	1. *Jñāna*	1. *Jñāna*	—	—
		2. *aiśvarya*	2. *aiśvarya*	—	—
		3. *Śakti*	—	1. *Śakti*	—
		4. *bala*	—	2. *bala*	—
		5. *Vīrya*	—	—	1. *Vīrya*
		6. *tejas*	—	—	2. *Tejas*
3.	*Complexion*	Moon-white	Red-lead	The Sun's rays	Collyrium-dark (like *añjanādri*)
4.	*Colour of Garment*	Yellow	Blue	Red	White
5.	Weapons etc. in 4 hands	All *Vyūhas* show *abhaya-mudrā* (assurance of protection) by the fourth hand and hold a conch in one.			
		1. a Discus	1. a Plough	1. a bow	1. a sword
		2. a Mace	2. a Pestle	2. arrows	2. a Club
6.	Emblem on the banner	*Garuḍa* (an eagle)	*Tāla* (a palm tree)	*Makara* (a crocodile)	*Mṛga* (a deer)

22. The definition of *citta* is given with reference to its attitudes (abiding states) such as clearness (capability to bear the reflection of the Lord), changelessness (absence of *laya* and *vikṣepa*) and tranquillity (freedom from passion). It is just like water in its pure state (before it comes in contact with the earth), changeless (free from foam, ripples etc.), sweet, transparent and clean.

23. The Principle called Mahat which was born out of the potentiality of the Lord, began to undergo modifications. From this *Mahat* was produced ego (*ahaṁkara*) of three kinds. It (*ahaṁkāra*) possessed potentiality to do active work.

24. (The three kinds of *ahaṁkāra* are) *Vaikārika*, *taijasa* and *tāmasa* (according as it is characterised by the *sattva-guṇa*, *rajo-guṇa* and *tamo-guṇa* respectively). From these is the creation of mind (*manas*), sense-organs and great elements (*mahābhūtas*).

25. (Herein the *vyūha*—manifestation of God—to be meditated is) the Puruṣa called Saṅkarṣaṇa. He has actually a thousand heads and is designated as Ananta (endless). He is of the form of aggregate of *bhūtas* (elements), *indriyas* (sense-organs and the mind.

26. The *ahaṁkāra* is characterised as being the doer (as *devatā*), the instrument (as the sense-organs) and the effect or product (as the *bhūtas*). Or it may be characterised by serenity (with *sattva-guṇa*), vehemence (with *rajo-guṇa*) and dullness (with *tamo-guṇa*).

27. The principle called mind (*manas*) was created from *sāttvika* or *vaikārika ahaṁkāra* undergoing modifications. It is characterised by thinking and special meditation and is the source of desire[803].

28. The wise persons know it by the name Aniruddha, the Supreme Master of sense organs. He is bluish in complexion like blue lotus in the autumn. He is to be gradually propitiated by *yogins* (as it is difficult to propitiate him).

29. Oh pious lady, from the *taijasa ahaṁkāra* undergoing modifications was created the principle called *buddhi* (which as distinguished from *citta*) is characterised by intelligence or

803. *kāma-sambhava*—The son of Kāma, i.e Pradyumna.

special knowledge of understanding reality and the power to favour sense-organs.

30. From the point of its aspects, it is separately characterised by doubt, misapprehension, correct determination, memory and sleep (or unconscious state).

31. All the sense-organs (*indriyāṇi*) classified as the conative and cognitive organs, are created from the *Taijasa ahaṁkāra* only. For conation (activity) is the power of Prāṇa (who directs the organs of action). And cognition or the power of understanding and knowing is the power of *Buddhi* (which controls the cognitive organs). —Both Prāṇa and Buddhi being products of the *Taijasa ahaṁkāra*, all the sense-organs are also the products of the *Taijasa ahaṁkāra*.

32. From the *Tāmasa ahaṁkāra* which was prompted by the Power of the Lord, was produced the *tanmātrā* called Sound ('the sound-potential'). Thence came forth the *Mahābhūta* (gross-element) called Space (*ākāśa*) whence was evolved the sense of hearing which receives sound.[804]

33. The wise people know the characteristic of Sound to be the capacity to convey meaning or ideas, to serve as an index of the seer (or the speaker), and to work as the subtle-potential of the space (sky).

34*. With reference to its functions, the characteristics of the space (*ākāśa*) are to provide space for beings, to pervade them within and without, to afford support (abode) to Prāṇa, sense-organs and the mind.

35. Out of the Space (*ākāśa*) characterised by its subtle-potential sound, while undergoing modifications by the force of *Kāla* (Time), there arose the subtle-principle of Touch. From it evolved the Vāyu (wind) and thence the Skin (*tvac*) the sense-organ of touch which gathers i.e. comprehends touch.

36. The chief characteristics of the Touch (*sparśa*) are softness, hardness, cold and heat. It is the subtle principle of Vāyu (wind).

804. Cf. supra III. 5. 32.

* ŚR., VR. remark that in this way the following verses consist of groups of three, the first describing the creation of the gross-element, the second verse giving the characteristic of that *tanmātrā* and the third the characteristic of the *mahābhūta*.

37. From functional point of view, Vāyu is characterised by movement (of branches of trees), collecting together (of grass etc.) reaching (of things), carrying of particles (e.g. fragrance to the nose) and sound (to the ear) and giving strength to all sense organs.

38. When Vāyu with its characteristic subtle principle touch, was impelled by Destiny, was evolved the *tanmātra* (subtle principle) called *Rūpa* (Form—colour). Out of it arose *Tejas* (heat—light) and the eye which is the sense to grasp *Rūpa* (Form—colour).

39. Oh good lady, to give form to a substance, to be its attribute, to be co-extensive (and co-existent) with the substance as well as to be *Tejas* (heat-light) itself, are the abiding characteristics of the *tan-mātra* Rūpa.

40. To illuminate, to cook (food), to intoxicate, to destroy cold, to dry, to make one feel hungry and thirsty—these are the effects of *Tejas*.

41. When *Tejas* with its subtle principal(*tanmātra*) *Rūpa* (Form—colour) was undergoing modifications by being incited by Fate (*daiva*), the *tanmātra* called *rasa* (taste) was evolved. From it was produced water and the Tongue (the sense of taste) which grasps (apprehends) taste.

42. Due to the effect of substances mixed with it, *rasa* (taste), though only one, becomes distinguished as many, such as astrigent, sweet, bitter, pungent, sour (and salty).

43. Moistening, making adhesive, giving satisfaction, sustaining life, refreshing by satisfying thirst, softening, removing heat and exhaustion, abundance (unfailing continuous supply) or the preponderance (of water in the constitution of body)—these are the characteristic properties of water.

44. When water along with its subtle principle *rasa* was impelled by Destiny (*daiva*) and was undergoing modification, the subtle principle Smell was evolved. Thence was formed the earth, and the Sense of Smell (nose) which cognises smell.

45. Due to the different proportions of mixing up of particles of substances, the smell, though one, is distinguished as mixed smell, bad odour, strong fragrance, mild fragrance (as of a lotus), strong smell (as of garlic), acid smell and others.

46. The characteristic functions (and properties) of *Pṛthvī* are formation into an image of Brahman, independent stability in a position (without the support of *jala* etc.), supporting other objects (like water), to be the means of making distinction in *ākāśa* (such as *ghaṭākāśa*, *maṭhākāśa* etc.), to help distinctions in all beings and their qualities.

47. That is called the ear (the sense of hearing) of which the special characteristic is the apprehension of sound (*śabda*), the special attribute of the Space (*ākāśa*). They (the learned ones) know that to be the sense of Touch, the speciality of which is apprehension of touch, the special characteristic of Vāyu.

48. That is called the sense of seeing (eye) of which the object of perception is *Tejas* (Form—colour), the special quality of *Tejas* (Heat—Light). The wise know it to be the sense of taste (Tongue), the special object of which is *rasa* (taste) which is the special characteristic of Water. That is called the sense of smell (nose), the principal object of which is smell, the special characteristic of the earth.

49. The property of the cause is inherently found in the effect. Hence cumulatively, all the characteristics (of all elements) are found in the earth.

50. When the seven[805] principles such as Mahat and others remained separate (there was no creation of the universe so) the creator of the universe along with Kāla (Time), *karma* (action or *adṛṣṭa*) and *guṇas* entered into them.

51. Out of those principles synthesised and (thrown into commotion by him,) thre came forth the inactive, unintelligent Egg of the universe. From it arose the *Virāṭ-puruṣa*.

52. This Egg of the universe is called *Viśeṣa*. It is surrounded by (elements such as) water and others, each ten times bigger than the previous one. (All of them) are covered on the outside by *Pradhāna*. Here this extensive world is the body of Lord Hari.

53*. The Supreme God (giving up inactivity) rose from

805. viz. *Mahat*, *ahaṁkāra* and *bhūtas*. As per older tradition *tanmātrās* are subsumed under *bhūtas*.

* VJ. takes the Abl. in *hiraṇmayad ... kośāt* in the sense of Acc. and interprets : The great God Hari made the golden Egg of the universe lying in the water to rise above it. He entered it and also the body of *Virāj*

the golden egg, lying on the water. After entering (=controlling) it, he pierced the vacant space[806] therein in various ways.

54. From this[807], at first was evolved the mouth. From the Mouth came forth the speech. Along with speech the Fire (*Vahni*) came out. Then were evolved two nostrils. Out of them was issued the sense of smell along with Prāṇa (vital breath).

55. From the sense of smell was evolved Vāyu. (Then) two eyes were formed and thence the sense of seeing. From this (sense) was evolved the Sun (*Sūrya*). (Then) were formed the ears. Thence issued the sense of hearing from which came forth the (presiding deities of) directions.

56. Then was evolved the Skin to *virāj*. Thence grew hair, beard, mustaches etc. from which were produced herbs and plants. Afterward was evolved the organ of generation (the penis).

57. Thence came forth the semen out of which was evolved water. Then was produced the anus whence the *Apāna*. From Apāna came forth Death which causes fear to the world.

58. (Thereafter) were formed the hands from which came forth strength. From them came forth Indra (*Svarāṭ*). (Then) were evolved the feet from which came forth locomotion or movement. Thence came forth Hari.

59. The blood vessels were then formed in him. From them was produced blood from which were issued rivers (goddesses presiding over rivers). Then was evolved the stomach.

Puruṣa who was born of him. Dwelling within, he made space (*ākāśa* in the form of the space in mouth (and other organs), differentiated and manifest.

VB. states : When Hari woke up from sleep, the sense organs were differentiated and evolved for enjoyment of the various *aṁśās* of God.

806. *kham*—(1) a hole,—ŚR. (iii) The conative and cognitive sense-organs which were undifferentiated in his four-foced body (was differentiated by him into different sense organs).

807. *asya* : VR. takes this gen. in the Abl. sense and interprets : God Brahmā's body is an aggregate considered to be made up of parts each of which is consubstantially the same with the whole. From the mouth of this Brahmā's aggregate body the mouths of individual gods were issued. From the mouth was differentiated the speech, and thence Fire, its presiding deity.

60. From it arose hunger and thirst. From them came forth (the presiding deity of) the ocean. Then the heart was evolved in him. From the heart came forth the mind.

61. From the mind was born the Moon. Then Intelligence (*buddhi*) was evolved. From it came forth the Lord of Speech (Brahmā). Then (was evolved Ego (*ahaṁkāra*). Thence was evolved *citta* from which was born *Kṣetrajña*.

62. These gods (with the exception of *Kṣetrajña*—the individual Soul) who have arisen, were unable to make him rise (and to activate him). (Therefore) in order to rouse him (into activity) they, one by one, entered into their own spaces (appointed sense-organs).

63. God Agni (Fire) entered the mouth along with the speech, but the Virāṭ was not roused thereby. When Vāyu (Wind) entered the nostrils along with the sense of smell, but thereby the Virāṭ did not rise.

64. The Sun entered the eyes along with the sense of vision, but even then the Virāṭ did not rise. When the (deities presiding over) directions (along with the sense of hearing entered the ears, the Virāṭ did not get up.

65. When the gods presiding over herbs and plants entered the skin along with hair, the Virāṭ did not rise. When the (presiding deity of) water entered the organ of generation along with semen, the Virāṭ was not roused.

66. The god of Death entered the anus along with *Apāna* but the Virāṭ was not activated. Indra along with strength entered the hands but the Virāṭ remained inactive.

67. Viṣṇu, along with power of movement, entered the feet but the Virāṭ was not roused. Goddesses of rivers entered the blood vessels along with blood, but the Virāṭ was inactive.

68. The (god of the) ocean entered the stomach along with hunger and thirst, but the Virāṭ remained unaroused. The Moon entered the heart along with the Mind, but the Virāṭ was not roused.

69. Even Brahmā entered the heart along with intelligence (*buddhi*) but the Virāṭ did not get up. When Rudra along with *ahaṁkāra* entered the heart, (still) the *Virāṭ* was not-roused.

70. But when Kṣetrajña (the intelligent individual

Soul), the master of *citta* entered the heart, the *Virāṭ Puruṣa* immediately was roused and got up from water.

71. Just as *Prāṇa* (vital breath), sense organs, mind and intelligence are not able to wake up the (body of a) sleeping person by their own power without his (*kṣetrajña's*) help (so was the case with Virāṭ Puruṣa).

72. By devotion unto God, (leading to) non-attachment to anything else, and with mind inclined to and concentrated by *Yoga*, and the knowledge obtained by it, one should meditate on the Soul (*Pratyagātman*) within oneself as different from it (from the chain of causal-relations)*.

CHAPTER TWENTY-SEVEN

(*The Sāṁkhya Philosophy—Prakṛti and Puruṣa*)

1.** Though Puruṣa (the Soul) resides in the body (which is a product of *Prakṛti*), he is not affected by the *guṇas* of Prakṛti (such as pleasure, pain etc.), just as the Sun (in the sky) reflected in the water (is not affected by the qualities or changes in the water). For the Puruṣa is destitute of *guṇas*; hence his freedom from action and the consequent changelessness.

---

* GD. makes explicit the process implied above by ŚR : The first stage is devotion (*bhakti*) of nine kinds. When the heart is purified by devotion, there arises non-attachment to pleasures or worldly things. Then comes the knowledge about the distinction between Prakṛti, Puruṣa and Īśvara. By that knowledge, understanding the individual Soul (*Pratyagātman*) to be different and distinct from the body which is an aggregate of cause and effect, one should, with mind trained for concentration by *yoga* discipline, meditate on the Kṣetrajña or *Pratyag-ātman*.

** (i) VR. : Jīva, though abiding in a body (a product of Prakṛti) is not affected by the *guṇas* of *Prakṛti* such as the form of existence as a god or a man or pleasure, pain etc. For the real nature of jīva does not undergo any change by his birth as a man or god. He is not the doer of the activities of his body, and is free from *guṇas* like *sattva* etc. He is like the image of the Sun in the water—the real remaining unaffected by changes in the reflecting medium. Jīva and the body have thus no connection

2* When this (*jīva*) is attached to the *guṇas* of *Prakṛti*, he becomes deluded by *ahaṁkāra* and regards himself as the doer (through false attribution).

3. Due to that (*Ahaṁkāra*), he loses his independence and blessed state. By the force of the (detrimental) effects of *karmas* due to the association with Prakṛti, he gets involved in *saṁsāra* in some form of existence, good (as a god), bad (as a sub-human being) or mixed (as a man).

4**. (The Soul being the non-doer), the real bondage of *karmas* does not exist. But *saṁsāra* does not cease to be till

---

(*viprakarṣa*) from the point of place (*deśa*); time (*Kāla*) and nature (*svabhāva*).

Alternatively VR. interprets *Prakṛti dharma* as a birth in the from of existence as a man or a god, and states these *dharmas* do not belong to the jīva. His appearance as a man or a god is a false impression (*bhrānti*).

(ii) VJ : The Supreme Being and the *jīva* reside in the same body. But Viṣṇu being perfect is not affected by pleasure, pain, birth, death etc. for he is not affected by the six *vikāras* (changes such as birth, growth etc.). He is not dependent for his action on anybody, and hence an absolute agent. He is free from *guṇas* e.g. *sattva* etc. He is like the Sun, unaffected by the changes in the water wherein he is reflected.

(iii) JG., VC. follow ŚR. in general.

(iv) VB. : Although jīva is found in a body, he is merely reflected in the Prakṛti like the Sun in the water. He is not 'greased' by the *guṇas* like *sattva* etc. for there is no *vikāra* (change) in him. He has no *adṛṣṭa* and hence no action.

* (i) VR: The Soul is different from Prakṛti. But his (false) identification of himself with the body obscures his real essential nature. When he is attached to the *guṇas* of Prakṛti (like sound, taste etc.), he becomes egoistic that he is the independent doer and gets the bondage.

(ii) VJ : When the jīva is attached to the *guṇas* i.e. his body which is composed of *guṇas*, he is deluded by Ego. Consequently he forgets the essential nature of the Lord and his own limits as a dependent doer.

(iii) SD : Though the Soul is really free, he wrongly identifies himself with *guṇas* and out of egoism he gets deluded to regard himself as a man or a god and considers himself as the agent.

(iv) VB : *guṇas* cannot do anything independently. The Soul being *cetana* (sentient), transfers his own attributes to them (just as the Sun makes water hot though it is cool by nature). After thus controlling *guṇas* he becomes deluded by identifying himself with the *guṇas*, and (wrongly) thinks that he is the door.

**(i)VR : The forms of a man, god etc. are not real forms of the Soul. But as long as he thinks about objects of senses, this calamity

he is brooding over the objects (of senses), just as one experiences misfortunes in a dream (even though it is unreal).

5. Therefore, the mind which is attached to the wicked path of sensual enjoyment, should be gradually brought under control by the *Bhakti yoga* (path of devotion) and intense non-attachment (to worldly objects).

6-11. He who practises meditation by the paths of *yoga* characterised by *aṅgas* (stages) like *yama*, *niyama* etc., is full of faith (in me) by real, sincere love to me, and by listening to stories about me, looks upon all beings as equal, renouncing all attachment and company; hates nobody, practises celibacy and observes silence, follows his own duties which are powerful on account of his offering them to God, that sage who is satisfied with whatever he gets by chance, is moderate in eating, resorts to solitude, is serene and friendly to all and self-controlled, does not entertain false attachment (like 'me' and 'mine') to his body and its dependents or property, has the knowledge whereby one can realize the truth about Prakṛti and Puruṣa, has superseded the stages like wakefulness, sleep etc., and hence has ceased to see other things except God. The self-seer sage realizes his Soul (*Ātman*) by his Self (conditioned by ego) just as one sees the Sun (in the sky) by the eye which is also a modified Sun, (such a sage) attains to that non-dual (absolute) Brahman which is completely distinct and free from the subtle-body (*liṅga-śarīra*) and which appears as real in unrealities like *ahaṁkāra* which is the friend, i.e. the support of Pradhāna; which is like an eye to the *Asat* (i.e. which sheds light on *Mahat* etc.) and which is woven fully into all causes and effects.

12. Just as the reflection of the Sun in the water is seen by its reflection on the (wall inside the house on the) shore

---

of *saṁsāra* persists just as in a dream he experiences pain etc. though his body in the dream is unreal.

(ii) VJ. thinks the God's grace is essential for the cessation of *saṁsāra*.

(iii) VC. : Even though *karmas* are unreal, the Soul due to his *ahaṁkāra* as being the doer broods over the objects (and gets bound in *saṁsāra* by the actions done by his body).

(at first)[808] and just as (thereafter the real Sun in the heaven) is noted due to its reflection in the water.

13* Similarly *ahaṁkāra* of three kinds as typified by three *guṇas* is seen as the reflection of *Sat* by the images of *ātman* which are conditioned by the *bhūtas* (body), *indriyas* (sense-organs) and the mind. By the reflection of the *ātman* in *ahaṁkāra*, the real *ātman* whose essential nature is knowledge, is realized.

14. When, due to sleep, the *bhūtas*, their subtle principles (*tanmātras*), sense-organs, the mind, intelligence and others (such as *ahaṁkāra*) are completely absorbed in the unmanifest *Prakṛti*, that which remains awake and free from *ahaṁkāra* (in the dead-like sleeping body) is the Soul.

15. In that state, when the *ahaṁkāra* is dormant (lit. lost), the Seer (the *jīva*), though himself is not lost, wrongly thinks that he is lost, like a man stricken with grief at the loss of his fortune, feels (about himself).

16. In this way, having thoroughly thought over (this distinctness of the *ātman*), he realizes the Soul which is the basis and the illuminator of all the matter (or combination of cause and effect) including *ahaṁkāra*.

Devahūti said:

17. Oh Lord, Brahman, as both (*Prakṛti* and *Puruṣa*) are interdependent (for their manifestation) and eternal, Prakṛti never leaves the Puruṣa.

18. Just as the existence of smell and the earth (the smelling substance) or of taste and water cannot be mutually separate, *Prakrti* and *Puruṣa* cannot be logically discontinuous (i.e. cannot exist separately).

---

808. VJ. adds one more interpretation: Just as the reflection of the face in water indicates the real face (person) standing on the bank, similarly the reflection of the Sun in the water leads to the knowledge of the real Sun in the sky.

* VJ. gives a totally different meaning : Śeṣa is the presiding deity of three types of *ahaṁkāra* (according to three *guṇas*). He is seen through his reflections viz. the presiding deities of *bhūtas*, *indriyas* (sense organs) and the mind (*manas*). By the reflection called Śeṣa, the fourfaced Brahmā is perceived, and through the reflection called Brahmā is seen Lord Nārāyaṇa, the knower of the reality.

19. How can there be emancipation (lit. alone-ness) from Prakṛti when the *guṇas* of Prakṛti are in existence. These *guṇas* form bondage of *karmas* to Puruṣa who is (essentially), inactive.

20. Sometimes the terrible fear (of *saṁsāra*) may seem (practically) receded by careful reflection about the Principles (considered above). But as its cause (viz. the *guṇas* of Prakṛti) is not destroyed, the fear appears again.

21-23. By performance of one's duties (according to one's *Varṇa*—caste—and *āśrama*—stage in life) without any desire for its fruit, by pure mind, and by devotion intensified by hearing the stories of Hari for a long period, by knowledge which has comprehended the reality, by a very strong aversion to the world, by *yoga* accompanied with asceticism, and by intense concentration (of the mind) on the Soul (*ātman*), *Prakṛti*, being consumed day and night, gradually disappears in this very birth like the piece of *Śamī* wood (from which fire is enkindled), the source of fire, (is burnt down by fire).

24. *Prakṛti* which has been abandoned after enjoying her (products), and whose evil effects are always seen, does not bear anything inauspicious (like the bondage of *karma*) to the Supreme Lord who is established in his magnificence.

25. Just as a dream presents a great many of calamities to a man who is not awakened (but is dreaming in sleep), but the same (dream) is not capable of deluding him when he is awake.

26. Similarly Prakṛti never causes any harm to one who has realized the Truth, and who has set his heart upon me, and who is delighted in realizing the Self (*ātman*).

27. When a sage is delighted in his own Self (*ātman*), and after going through many births is unattached and averse to everything upto (i.e. including) the region of Brahmā.

28-29. (and being) my devotee has realized the true Self, by my grace, he easily attains to his essential state, as distinct from his physical body,—a state of final beatitude called *Kaivalya*. The wise man who has cut asunder all doubts (i.e. pseudo-knowledge) by his vision of the Self (*ātma-jñāna*) goes by my grace to the state attained after the destruction of the subtle body (*liṅga-śarīra*) and from which state there is no reversion (to *saṁsāra*).

30. Oh mother, when the mind of the *Siddha* (the emancipated sage) is not attached to the miraculous powers born of *yoga* and obtained through yogic practice, then only is attained the ultimate state pertaining to me—a state where even the death cannot laugh (is powerless).

CHAPTER TWENTY-EIGHT

(*Exposition of the Aṣṭāṅga-Yoga* (*the eightfold Path of Yoga*)

The Lord said :

1. Oh Princess, I shall explain to you the nature of the *sa-bīja*[809] type of Yoga, by practising which only, the mind becomes tranquil and pure, and goes to the path (leading) to Brahman[810].

2*. Performance of one's religious duties according to one's capacity, aversion to irreligion, contentment in what one obtains by the Lord's grace (or one's fate); worshipping the feet of those who have realized the Soul (*ātman*).

3. Abstention from duties pertaining to *dharma*, *artha* and *kāma* (the first three common goals in life), devotion to duties leading to *mokṣa* (liberation), eating pure food in moderation and permanent stay in a safe, secluded place.

4. Non-violence, truthfulness, non-stealing, acceptance of only the bare necessities of life, celibacy, penance, purity,

---

809. *sabīja* : The Yoga is of two types ; *sabīja* and *nirbīja*. *Sabīja* requires an object for meditation (ŚR.) which is according to VJ. & VD. Viṣṇu. The *nirbīja*-yoga consists of curbing the wavering mind and subjugating it solely to the Self as prescribed in the BG. 6.26 (VB.).

810. *sat-patham*—(i) The path of *bhakti* (RR.); (ii) The path leading to the realization of *ātman* (VB.) or of the Lord (VB., SD.).

* Although the commentators label the virtues enumerated in these (2-6) verses as *yama* and *niyama*, the first two *aṅgas* of Yoga, it is an elucidation of Ys. 2.30-32. Cf. the list of virtues in BG. 16.1-3; 17.7-11, 17.14-16 as 'means to knowledge' as the *daivī sampad* and as moral discipline (*tapas*)

study of Vedas (or *Śāstras*), (ritualistic) worship of the Supreme Man.

5. Silence, ever-firmness in bodily posture and steadiness, gradual control of breath, mental withdrawal of senses from their objects into the heart.

6. Concentration of the mind and the breath in one of the plexuses (like the *mūlādhāra cakra*), constant meditation of the *līlās* (sports, actions) of Lord, and concentration of the mind on God.

7. By these and other means (such as observance of vows, giving donations) one should attain control over his breath, and deliberately and without slackness, direct the mind to the right path—mind which has become polluted by going to the path of worldly enjoyment.

8*. Having firmly fixed his seat in a clean holy place, he should (firstly) get (thorough) control of his bodily posture. He should comfortably[811] be seated on that seat, and keeping his body erect, he should practise (breath-control).

9. He should purify the passage (path) of the breath (the respiratory system) by systematic inhalation, retention and exhalation of breath or vice versa, so that the mind becomes quiescent and steady.

10. The mind of a *yogin* who has mastered his breathing, becomes pure immediately just as gold melted by the blast of wind and fire, gives up the dross mixed with it.

11. One should burn one's impure humids in the body by breath-control, the sins by *Dhāraṇā*[812], the attachment to objects of senses by *Pratyāhāra*[813] and undivine qualities by meditation.

12. When one's mind becomes pure and properly steady

---

*. This is practically a quotation from BG. 6.11-13.

811. *svasti* : ŚR. reads *svastikam āsīnam* and interprets : 'in the bodily posture called *svastikāsana*'. He quotes a verse describing this posture. VR., VC., SD., VB. follow ŚR.

812. *Dhāraṇā*—'Fixed attention' is binding the mind to a place like a plexus (*cakra*) in the body—YS. 3.1.

813. *Pratyāhāra—sva-viṣayāsamprayoge cittasya svarūpānukāra ivendriyāṇāṁ pratyāhāraḥ* / YS. 2.54. '*Pratyāhāra* (withdrawal of the senses) is as it were the imitation of the mind-stuff itself on the part of the organs by disjoining themselves from their objects'. Wood—YSP. 197-98.

(poised), by *Yoga*, one should meditate on the form of the Supreme Lord, with his eyes fixed at the farthest end (the tip) of his nose.

13*-18. The Yogin should meditate on the complete form of God, till his mind is completely fixed on God; whose lotus-like face is kindly (i.e. gracious); whose eyes are reddish like the interior of a lotus; whose complexion is dark-blue like the petals of a blue lotus; who is holding (in his hands) a conch, a disc (*Sudarśana-cakra*) and a mace (*Kaumodakī gadā*) whose silk garments are yellow like the bright (shining); filaments of a lotus; whose chest bears the mark of *Śrīvatsa*; who wears the resplendent jewel *kaustubha* around his neck; who is garlanded by a *vanamālā* about which intoxicated bees are humming sweetly; who is adorned with invaluable necklace, bracelets, crown, armlets (*aṅgada*) and anklets; whose waist (lit. hips) is engirdled by a lustrous belt; whose seat is in the lotus-like hearts (of his devotees); who is the most beautiful, serene, delighting the eyes and the minds (of his devotees); who is extremely charming to look; who is ever bowed (and respected) by all the worlds; who appears like a boy (of fifteen) in age; who is eagerly absorbed in (showering) grace on his servants; whose holy fame deserves to be eulogised; who has enhanced the fame of Bali and other *puṇyaślokas* (persons of hallowed name).

19. With his mind full of pure devotion, he should contemplate the God as standing, walking, sitting, lying, or occupying his heart—Lord whose *līlās* are worth looking.

20. When the sage finds that his mind becomes concentrated on all the members of the body of the Lord as a whole, he should try to fix on the members (of the body of the Lord) one by one.

21. He should reflect (contemplate) the lotus-like feet of the Lord which are enriched by the (lines showing) marks of the Vajra, the goad (*aṅkuśa*), the banner (*dhvaja*) and the lotus, and the lunar rays emanating from whose group of prominent, reddish, refulgent (toe-) nails have dispelled the dense darkness in the hearts (of his devotees).

---

* From this verse, the author gives the different mental representations of Viṣṇu on which the Yogin should meditate in a serial order.

22. One should contemplate for a long time the lotus-like feet of the Lord—Feet, the waters washing which flowed forth and became a great river, the Gaṅgā. God Śiva bore the sacred waters (of the Gaṅgā) on his head and became supremely auspicious. (One should meditate on) those feet which are like a thunderbolt discharged against the mountain of evils (sins) in the mind of the meditator (or the feet which detonate the Vajra, the mark on his feet, against the mountain of evils).

23. One should contemplate in one's heart (the pair of the shanks and) knees of the All-pervading Lord who liberates from *saṁsāra*—the knees which are placed on her thighs and are gently served (pressed and massaged) with her brilliant sproutlike hands by Lakṣmī of lotus-eyes, who is the mother of god Brahmā, the creator of all the worlds.

24. (One should meditate in one's hearts on) the thighs of the Lord which appear superbly beautiful on the shoulder of Garuḍa, and which are the source (or reservoir) of strength, and are like *Atasikā* (linseed) flower in complexion. He should further contemplate his waist or round hips which are encircled (lit. embraced) with a girdle which belts his yellow garment (*Pītāmbara*) reaching upto his ankles.

25. (One should contemplate) his deep lake-like navel on the stomach which is like a cave accommodating all the worlds and from which sprouted forth the lotus which was the seat of God Brahmā and the abode of the universe. One should meditate on his pair of emerald-like nipples which appear bright and white by the rays of the shining wreaths of pearls.

26. One should then contemplate in one's heart the chest of the great God (Hari) which is the resting place of his Supreme Power (goddess Mahā-lakṣmī), and which brings great joy to men's minds and eyes. Next, one should meditate upon the neck of Lord Hari who is bowed down by all the worlds—the neck which beautifies the *Kaustubha* jewel.

27. One should then vizualize for meditation his arms, the armlets on which got burnished by the circular movements of the Mandara mountain (while the ocean was being churned for the nectar)—arms which are the support of the *Lokapālas*

(deities protecting the world). (One should then contemplate) the Sudarśana disc of one thousand blades (spokes) of unbearable splendour (and velocity), and the conch which looks like a royal swan in his lotus-like hand (due to whiteness of the conch and the swan).

28. Then one should remember (contemplate) the Lord's beloved mace, Kaumodakī, besmeared with the thick (mudlike) blood of inimical warriors. (Then one should contemplate) the garland (in his neck) which is (as if) resonant with the humming swarm of bees around it. He should (next) meditate on the spotless jewel *Kaustubha* which represents the essential principle of *jīvas* [814] (beings).

29. One should (then) properly contemplate the lotus-like face of the Lord who, with his mind full of compassion for his servants, has assumed a form (incarnation) in this world—(his) face (beautiful) with shapely prominent nose and spotless cheeks illuminated by the oscillations of the refulgent ear-rings of crocodile-like shape.

30*. With close attention, one should contemplate in mind the lotus-like face of Hari which manifests itself in the mind—face looking beautiful due to the locks of curly hair around it, and lotus-like eyes with flashing charming eyebrows, and which thus surpasses in beauty the lotus-abode of Lakṣmī, which, due to its beauty is attended upon (hovered round) by black-bees and resorted to by a pair of fish.

31. With perfect and intense devotion one should contemplate for a long time the glances of the eyes of Hari who is dwelling in the cave in the form of one's heart—glances which are cast with great mercy and favour for soothing the terrible-most afflictions of three types (—*ādhyātmika*, *ādhibhautika* and *ādhidaivika*), and which are accompanied with affec-

---

814. The gem, *Kaustubha* represents the Soul—the *jīva-tattva*—VR., JG. Cf. *Ātmānam asya jagato nirlepam aguṇāmalam |*
Bibharti Kaustubha-maṇi-svarūpaṁ bhagavān Hariḥ ||

—VP. 1.22.68.

'Lord Hari wears on his neck the gem Kaustubha which is a form of the Soul of the living beings. It is destitute of any deposit, *guṇa* or dirt.'

* By clever arguments VB. tries to show that the nine-fold devotion is described in verses 29 and 30.

tionate smile, and which confer abundance of grace (upon his devotees).

32. (One should then contemplate) Hari's most enchanting smile which dries up the sea of tears caused by the intense grief of all the people who bow to him ; (and should meditate on) his circular eyebrows which he has bent by his Māyā to entice and delude the god of love for the sake of sages (whom he—the god of Love—disturbs in their meditations).

33. Viṣṇu manifests himself in the cave of the heart in one's body. With a heart full of (lit. moistened with) devotion, one should contemplate on Viṣṇu's loud laugh as an object of meditation—laugh which exhibits his row of teeth like *Kunda* buds, which appear reddish by the bright glow of his lower lip. Having dedicated one's mind to him, one should not desire to look anywhere else.

34. In this way (of meditating on the Lord) the sage gets the love of Hari engendered in him. His heart is melted with devotion. He finds his hair standing on their ends through ecstatic joy. Due to the tears of joy flowing on account of his ardent love for God, he finds himself frequently submerged in the flood of joys. He gradually disentangles himself from his heart which is like a hook to secure the Lord.[815]

35*. When the mind becomes unattached and with-

---

815. *citta-baḍiśam etc.* (i) The angle in the form of *citta* which hooks up the Lord who is difficult to capture—ŚR.

(ii) He should gradually disengage his mind from the person of the Lord which is to be meditated. He should then meditate on his *pratyag-ātmā* (Soul).—VR.

(iii) The sage who directs the hook of his heart to the Lord—the object of contemplation, disengages it (and enters *samādhi* without any purposeful efforts).—VJ.

This is the method of *sabīja samādhi*.

(iv) The heart of Yogin is hard like a hook. Its touch is troublesome to the Lord. When this hook is removed (disengaged), God confers experience of *Pratyag-ātmā* and Mokṣa on the Yogin but not the experience of the Supreme Soul.

(v) The hook of the mind which is the instrument of grasping worldly objects and turned to meditation etc. which lead to the attainment of Hari. —SD.

*VR.'s explanation may be summarised as follows :

When mind becomes unattached, it becomes destitute of objects of senses like a flame of lamp free from smoke. When the mind ceases to

drawn from the sense-objects, it loses its support (to function as the meditator has no standing in the absence of the object of meditation. It becomes dissolved in Brahman (i.e. its being is transformed into Brahman) just as a flame in the absence of its support (oil, wick etc.) becomes one with the Mahābhūta Fire. In this stage, a man who is free from the flow of *guṇas* i.e. the limitations of the body etc. at once realizes his Soul directly as one (without distinction such as the meditator and the object of meditation).

36. Even he (the devotee or Yogin) becomes dissolved in Brahman which is beyond pleasure and pain. In this last stage attained by the practice of Yoga, his (Yogin's) mind finally withdraws (and becomes free from *avidyā*). Tha Yogin thus realizes the essential nature of the Soul and transfers from himself the agency of the pleasure and the pain to *ahaṁkāra* (ego), known as *asat* which is the produce of *avidyā*.

37. Just as an addict, blind with the intoxication of wine, is not conscious of the existence of the garment he has worn, the perfect Siddha who has reached the final stage (described above) is not conscious whether his body is sitting or standing or is removed to another place or has returned by the will of the destiny, because he (the *siddha*) has reached (realized) his real self.

38. So long as the *karma* which is the cause of the body is effective (and not exhausted) till that period the body along with the sense-organs which is at the mercy of the fate does definitely exist. But he who has mastered the Yoga upto the *Samādhi* and who has realized the thing (i.e. the Soul) does not again accept the body along with its attendants (the *Prapañca*) as if it is an appearance in a dream. (He becomes

---

think about these and rises above the contemplation of forms etc., it abandons its external activities. Then the individual Soul loses attachment to his body and the idea of being absolutely independent and directly finds himself to be a part or attribute of the Supreme Self.—VR.

VC.: When mind becomes unattached and free from *viṣayas* (objects of senses), it loses its stay or support, (as it has nothing to think about). Hence it naturally attains to *nirvāṇa* like the flame of lamp when deprived of its wick and oil. In this stage of dissolution of mind, *jīva*, directly experiences the identity of the pure Soul and individual Soul (jīva). Thenceforth he never returns to *saṁsara*.

free from the *ahaṁkāra* regarding his body, his relatives, belongings etc.).

39. Just as a man is found to be different from his son or wealth, even though they are accepted as his own, similarly the Soul is distinct from his body (and things in association with it, though they are regarded as his self).

40-41. Just as the (real) fire is different from the firebrand or from the sparks (emanating from it) or the smoke (issuing from it) or the burning wood is regarded as the fire, so also the Seer is different and distinct from *bhūtas*, sense-organs and the mind (*antaḥ-karaṇa*); the Brahman is different from what is designated as *jīva*, and the Lord (Supreme Soul) is different from *Prakṛti*.

42. Just as all types of beings (whether born from the womb or from the egg or from perspiration or germinating from seeds as plants) are identical from the point of their constitution from Mahābhūtas, similarly one should see (the identity of) the Soul (*ātman*) in all beings and of all beings in the *ātman*.

43. Just as the fire, though one, appears to be different according to the difference in the quality of its source (i.e. the shape, size and quality of the wood burnt by it)—similarly the embodied Soul appears different according to the difference in quality of its body (whether human, divine etc.).

44. Therefore, after conquering this incomprehensible Prakṛti, God Viṣṇu's own power, which is of the form of cause and effect (*sat* and *asat*), one remains in one's own (original, pure) form.

CHAPTER TWENTY-NINE

(*The Path of Bhakti* (*Bhakti-Yoga*) *and The Power of Time*)

Devahūti said:

1-2. Oh Lord, the accurate description of the *Mahat* and other principles and of the Prakṛti and Puruṣa as described in the Sāṁkhya-Śāstra has been narrated—the accurate description by which the real nature of these (Sāṁkhya) principles is correctly understood. It is said to be the source of the Bhakti Yoga. Please tell (explain) to me in details thes path of the *Bhakti-yoga*.

3. Oh revered Kapila, please tell me the different types of births (existences) of this world of living beings, by hearing which a man becomes free from attachment to everything (and everywhere) in the world.

4. Please tell me about the nature of your all-powerful Kāla or Time. He is regarded as the controller of the great (gods like Brahmā). It is because (of the fear of) Time that people take to good actions.

5. You have certainly manifested yourself as the Sun shedding light on the Yoga, in order to awaken the people who are ignorant and hence full of *ahaṁkāra* (pride) about unreal objects (like their body etc.) and are exhausted due to the attachment of their minds to actions (*karmas*) and are hence fast asleep for a long time in the unending darkness of *saṁsāra*.

Maitreya said :

6. Oh prominent Kuru! The great sage hailed with joy the beautiful speech of his mother. Being pleased with her and out of compassion (for her), he spoke to her.

The Lord said :

7. Oh mother, the path of *Bhakti* is regarded as having many branches; for the objects of men differ according to their natural dispositions and attributes (like *sattva* etc.)

8. He who becomes my devotee with the intention of doing injury (to others) or out of hypocrisy and jealousy or under the influence of anger or with an outlook full of differences (or with incorrect outlook of things), is called a *Tāmasa* type of devotee.

9. He who, with a desire of worldly pleasures or of fame or authoritative power, worships me in my images and entertains notions of difference, is a devotee of *rājasa* type.

10* He who wishes to purge all (his) *karmas*, or desires

---

* ŚR. and later SD. and GD. state that there are 81 types of *saguṇa-bhakti*. ŚR. details them as follows : 1-3 *Tāmasa bhakti*—actuated by injury (*hiṁsā*), religious hypocrisy (*dambha*) and jealousy (*matsara*); 4-6 *Rājasa*

to dedicate them to the Supreme Lord or worships the Lord with the simple objective of worship (and expecting no return for it) but entertains the idea of difference[816], is called a devotee of the *Sāttvika* type.

11-12. Just as the waters of the Gaṅgā continuously flow into the sea, similarly by merely listening to (the description of) my qualities the mind incessantly flows to me who reside in the hearts of all (beings). This close and intimate devotion to the Lord (Puruṣottama), without any ulterior motive, is definitely regarded as the characteristic of the *nirguṇa* type of *Bhakti.yoga*.

13. Even if the kinds of liberation (*muktis*), viz. residence in the same region with me (*sālokya*), equality in wealth, power and glory like me (*sārṣṭi*), staying near me (*sāmīpya*), similarity of form like me (*sārupya*) and even union with God (*ekatva*) are offered to these persons (the *nirguṇa-bhaktas*) they do not accept anything except my service.

14. That only is called the absolute[817] (and the highest) *Bhaktiyoga* whereby one transcends the trinity of *guṇas* (and the *saṁsāra* caused by them) and attains to my state (Brahmahood).

15. The mind of the man (my *nirguṇa* devotee) becomes purified by careful performance of daily religious duties without any motive, by performance of disinterested worship with ardent faith (as prescribed in the Pañcarātra *āgama*) without involving the least injury to beings[818].

16. by beholding at my image, by touching, worshipp-

---

bhakti—motivated by the desire for objects of enjoyment, for reputation and for authority; 7-9 *Sāttvikī bhakti* –generated by a desire to purge all sins, to dedicate *karmas* to God and to worship as a duty with no ulterior motive. Each of these is subdivided into nine according to the ninefold path of *bhakti* consisting of *Śravaṇa*, *Kīrtaṇa* etc.

816. VR. & VS. read *a-pṛthag-bhāva* : (i) The knowledge that he is like the body of the Lord (VR); (Who sees identity or oneness in my forms.

817. *ātyantika*—That which takes place finally, i.e. *sāyujyatā* (absorption into God).

818. *nātihiṁsreṇa*—Some *hiṃsā* (injury) to subtle beings is inevitable while washing the temple, cooking food for offering to God, collecting flowers and fruit etc. for worship. But this injury is condonable.—VC.

ing praising and bowing to me, by regarding me (as residing) in all beings, by firmness or fortitude and non-attachment.

17. by paying great respect to the great, by showing compassion to the afflicted, by friendliness towards one's equals and by observance of *yama* and *niyama*.

18. by listening to the philosophic discourses about *ātman*, by eulogizing the name (of God), by straightforwardness and by association with the noble (Souls) and by giving up *ahaṁkāra*.

19. As soon as such a devotee listens to (the description of) my attributes, he is easily attracted to me.

20. Just as fragrance being carried by (the chariot in the form of) the wind from its source (reaches the nose) and captures the smelling organ, similarly the mind which is constant and unperturbed and absorbed in *yoga*, attains to (and realizes) the *ātman*.

21. I am always abiding in all beings as their Soul (*antaryāmin*). A man who disregards me (the *antaryāmin*) performs a sham idol-worship.

22. He who foolishly neglects me, the controller of the world dwelling as a Soul (*ātman*) in all beings, and worships merely the images, is (as if), offering oblations in ashes (instead of in the fire).

23. The mind of a man who possesses *ahaṁkāra* (about his body identifying it with the Soul) and who hates me in another body regarding me as different (in every person) and contracts enmity with other beings, never attains tranquillity.

24. Oh sinless, I am not at all pleased with a person who slights all beings (even though) I am worshipped as an image by him, with (ritualistic) offerings of various articles (like sandle-paste, flowers, fruits etc.).

25. So long as a man does not realize in his heart that I, the Supreme Lord, am present in all beings he should perform his religious duties and worship me in an idol.

26* If a person makes even a slight difference between

---

* JG. & VC. take *udara*=stomach. JG., VC. : One should treat a hungry man like himself and feed him properly.

VJ. : Mṛtyu in the from of Nṛsiṁha creates great fear (viz. throwing a man in the darkest hell) for the man who regards all the *antaryāmins* (inner Souls of beings) as different.

himself and the Supreme Self (*Paramātman*)[819], I, who am Death, create a big fear for him who entertains the idea of difference.

27. Hence he should worship me by gifts and respectful behaviour, friendliness and equality of outlook—me who dwell in all beings as their Soul.

28. Oh auspicious mother, sentient beings are superior to non-sentient ones. Those who bear Prāṇa (have vital functions of respiration etc.) are superior to the sentient beings. To them are superior the possessors of *citta*. Those who possess the function of the sense organs are higher than the possessors of mere *citta* (mind).

29. Even amongst the possessors of sense-organs those who possess the sense of taste are higher than those who possess the sense of touch. To these are superior those who possess the sense of smell. Higher than these are the possessors of the sense of hearing.

30. Beings which know the difference in colour and forms (i.e. have the eyes) are higher than those possessing the sense of hearing. To these are superior, the beings who have teeth in the lower and upper jaws. Higher than these are the multipeds. Quadruped animals are superior to multipeds and bipeds are higher than the quadrupeds.

31. Among the bipeds, four *Varṇas* (castes) are superior and the Brāhmaṇas are the highest among them (the castes). Among the Brāhmaṇas, the reciters of the Vedas are higher. Superior to these are those who understand the meaning of the Vedas.

32. He who can solve doubts and difficulties (of Vedic interpretation) is superior to him who simply knows the meaning (of the Veda). To him is superior the performer of one's prescribed religious duties. But a person who has renounced all association and does not desire the fruit of his religious acts is higher than the previous one.

33. Superior to him is the man who has dedicated all his actions and body to me and who does not entertain the notion of difference. I do not know anyone superior to a

819. Or : who regards body as coming in between his individual Soul and the Supreme Soul—ŚR.

person who has dedicated his body to me, deposited his *karmas* in me, and has no ego of being the agent of any action and who sees all as equals.

34. One should understand that the glorious Lord himself has entered all beings as their *jīva* (individual Soul) and should pay great respects to them mentally and bow down to them.

35. Oh daughter of Manu, the Bhakti-yoga (the path of Bhakti) and *Yoga* (of eight stages) have been explained to you by me. By following one of them, a man will attain to God (the Supreme Man).

36. This is the form of the glorious Lord, the Supreme Soul, the Brahman. It is both Prakṛti and Puruṣa (and still) is also beyond them. It is the unseen destiny (*daiva*) which is the cause of all *karmas* (in the form of *saṁsāra*).

37. The divine form (of the Lord) which is the cause of the differences in the appearances of things, is called Time. From it, fear is caused to beings, which entertain the notion of difference and which preside over the *Mahat* and others.

38. He enters into all beings (*bhūtas*) and supports them all. He eats them up (annihilates them) by their means. He is called Viṣṇu, presiding deity of sacrifices who confers the fruit of the sacrifice (on the performer). He is the Time, the ruler of rulers.

39. Nobody is dear or inimical to him. He has no friend or relative. He is always alert and enters into the negligent people in order to destroy them.

40. It is out of his (*Kāla's*) fear that the wind blows. It is due to his fear that the Sun shines. God Indra showers (water) out of his fear. Heavenly bodies shine out of his dread.

41. It is due to his fear that trees, creepers, plants and herbs blossom forth and bear fruits in the proper seasons.

42. It is out of his fear that the rivers flow and the sea does not overflow his fixed limits. Being afraid of him, the fire burns and the earth (burdened) with mountains does not submerge (in the sea).

43. It is due to his control that the sky affords space for living (breathing) creatures and the Principle *Mahat* expands its body into the world enveloped in seven sheaths.

44. It is out of his fear that (Brahmā and other) gods who preside over the *guṇas* (like *sattva* etc.) and who can control this mobile and immobile world (creatures), carry out their duties of creation etc. in every *Yuga*.

45. He is endless but puts an end (to all). Time is beginningless but marks the beginning of all. He is immutable. He causes beings to be born of parents and causes the end of *antaka* (god of death) by means of death.

CHAPTER THIRTY

(Saṁsāra and Sufferings in Hell)

Kapila said:

1. Just as a row of clouds does not know the force of the mighty wind even though they are dispersed by it, similarly the people, though at the mercy of Time—*Kāla*—certainly do not know the great prowess of the mighty Time.

2. Whatever object (of pleasure) a man acquires with great efforts for the enjoyment of pleasures, the omnipotent Lord destroys it (lit. shakes it off) and the man grieves over it.

3. For it is out of delusion that an ignorant person regards as permanent that which belongs to this perishable body and its relatives such as the house, lands, money (and other property) which are transitory.

4. In whatever kind of existence (birth) a being is born in this *saṁsāra*, he feels happy in that (particular) birth. He is never disgusted (and unattached) with it.

5. The *Jīva* is so deluded with the *Māyā* of God that even in hell, while he has to subsist on and find pleasure in the products of hell, he verily does not desire to give up his (hellish) body.

6. With his heart deeply rooted in his body, wife, children, house, cattle, wealth and relatives, he regards himself as great and happy.

7. All his body is as if burning with anxiety of supporting these; (and) this ignorant person of evil intentions continuously goes on committing sins.

8. His mind and senses are attracted by the spell of the seductive charms of unchaste women in privacy, and by the sweet indistinct warbling of children.

9. He is prompt and watchful in the householder's life which is characterised by unfair moneydealings leading to a lot of misery. In such houses the householder regards it a pleasure to counteract the miseries.

10 He maintains them with money (and other objects) acquired here and there (in various ways and from any place) with great injury (and trouble to all). He can enjoy (but little of) what is left after their consumption. By (thus) maintaining them, he goes down (to hell).

11. When, despite his fresh attempts to start again and again, his means of livelihood become a failure, he becomes overpowered with greed. Growing weak, he begins to covet after another's property.

12. Being unable to maintain his family, the unfortunate fellow, whose all attempts have ended in failure, becomes destitute of wealth and miserable. Being at a loss to know what to do; the wretch goes on brooding and sighing.

13. Just as miserly farmers neglect old (and hence useless) bulls, his wife and others do not treat him with respect as before, as he has become incapable of maintaining them.

14-15. Even in that stage he does not feel disgust. He is deformed with old age and is approaching death. He is overcome with disease. He eats but little due to loss of appetite. His movements slow down and he is now nourished by those whom he had brought up. He stays in the house like a dog eating what is contemptuously thrown to him.

16. By the (vital) breath which is passing out, he has his eye-balls shot out. Phlegm chokes up the tubular passage (in his lungs). He suffers from extreme difficulty in breathing due to cough and asthema and a gurgling sound is heard in his throat.

17. He lies surrounded by his weeping relatives. He

who is bound down with the noose of Death, does not reply, even though addressed (by his relatives).

18. In this way, a man who has devoted himself completely for the maintenance of his family and has not controlled his sense-organs, loses his consciousness (lit. intelligence, mind) through extreme pain and dies while his relatives are crying.

19. Then he sees two terrible-looking messengers of death with eyes full of anger. At their sight, with terrified heart, he passes on urine and excrement.

20. They perforce shut him (the *jīva*) in a body specially designed to torture him. Fastening a noose round his neck, they drag him along the rout (to the region of death) like the policemen (King's men) do to convicts (persons to be punished).

21-22. His heart is breaking with their threats. He is trembling (with fear). On the way, hellish dogs bite him. Remembering his sins, he feels distressed. He suffers from hunger and thirst. On the road covered with hot sand, he is scorched by the heat of the Sun, forest-conflagration and (hot) blasts of wind. He is severely whipped on the back. Though weak and exhausted, he drags (on the road) where there is neither shelter nor water.

23. Now and then he faints exhausted. He rises again led by the most accursed dark path to the house of Yama (hell).

24. He is dragged within three or two *muhūrtas*[820] on this road of ninety-nine thousand Yojanas and undergoes the sufferings.

25. His body is burnt by surrounding it with firebrands. Sometimes he is made to eat his own flesh cut by himself or by others.

26. While he is alive, his entrails are dragged out by the hounds or vultures in the hell. He is subjected to torments by the biting and stinging of serpents, scorpions, mosquitoes and others.

27. His limbs are chopped off one by one. He is crushed by being trampled by the elephants and such other animals.

---

820. *muhūrta*—A period of 48 minutes.

He is thrown down from the tops of mountains. He is confined and suffocated in caves or under water.

28. Whether a man or a woman, he or she undergoes extreme tortures of the hells called Tāmisra, Andha-tāmisra, Raurava and others as a result of mutual illicit relations.

29. Oh mother, some say that the heaven or the hell is here (in this world) only, because whatever tortures or afflictions are meted out in the hell are seen in this very world.

30. In this way, he who maintains his family or earns his livelihood only, gives up his family and his body, and experiences such kind of fruit for it after death (in the other world).

31. He who has collected only sins as the provision for a journey (in *saṁsāra*) has to give up his physical body which he has maintained by doing wrong to other beings and goes alone to the hell of darkness (*andha-tāmisra* hell).

32. A man who commits sins for feeding his family, experiences in hell their evil consequences brought to him by Destiny. He becomes afflicted like a man who has been robbed of his wealth.

33. The being (*jīva*) who is eager to maintain his family by irreligious behaviour only, goes to the Andha-Tāmisra hell, the lowest region of darkness.

34. He regularly undergoes suffering and miserable types of births (of sub-human beings below, which he has passed through before his rebirth as a human being). He goes through them by degrees and becomes pure and is born as a human being.

CHAPTER THIRTY-ONE

(*Sufferings of the Jīva—The Rājasī Gati*)

The Lord said :

1. The *jīva* is impelled by the force of his Karma which is under the direction and control of God. For the formation of his gross body, he, through the medium of the semen of man enters the womb of a woman.

2. In one night, the mixture of the (man's) semen and (the woman's) blood takes place. In five nights, a circular bubble-like mass is formed. In ten days, it becomes (somewhat) hard like the fruit of the jujube tree (*karkandhu*). Thereafter, it becomes a ball of flesh or an egg.

3. In one month, the head is formed. In two months, the body develops arms, feet and other organs. In three months, nails, hair, bones, skin, the penis and the anus are formed.

4. By the end of the fourth month, the seven essential ingredients of the body are produced. In the fifth month, hunger and thirst are felt. In the sixth month, the foetus is enveloped with an external skin called *jarāyu*, and it begins to make movements in the rightside of the mother's abdomen.

5. He develops the essential ingredients of the body by the mother's intake of food and drinks. The *jīva* stays in an abominable hollow place, full of urine and feces, a breeding place of worms.

6. By the frequent biting of the hungry worms which are there (in the same hollow place), his whole body, being very delicate and soft, is wounded all over. Being extremely tormented, he falls into a swoon at every moment.

7. He is affected by the bitter, pungent, hot, salt, astringent, acidic and such other unbearable substances eaten by the mother, and thereby suffers pain spread all over the body.

8. Enveloped in the womb and surrounded on the outside with the entrails, it lies there with his head protruding towards the stomach and with his back and neck in a bent position.

9. Like a bird (shut up) in a cage, he is incapable of making (free) movements of his body there. As a result of his *karma* in previous births, he recollects his actions (*karmas*) done in the last hundred previous births and suffers the endless pain without a sigh. What happiness can he have (in such a condition).

10. From the seventh month, he gets consciousness. But as he is always moved by 'the winds of delivery' (*sūti-vāta*), he cannot remain in one spot like the worms born in the feces in the same place.

11. The *jīva* who knows both body and the Soul but is bound by seven essential ingredients of the gross body, is afraid. In repentance he folds his hands and in words expressing distress, he praises the Lord who has confined him in the womb. *The jīva* (the Individual Soul) *said* :

12. That the Lord has shown me this condition (made me to experience confinement in the womb) is quite befitting as I am wicked[821]. I, who am of that type, (now) take shelter under the lotuslike feet of the Lord, who fearlessly moves over the earth, after assuming various bodies (incarnations), with the desire of protecting the world, which has submitted to him for refuge[822].

13. I stay as if bound down, here (in the mother's womb), depending on the Māyā in the form (of my body consisting) of five *Bhūtas*, sense-organs and mind (*manas*), and with

---

821. VB., VR. read : *upa-pannam*—(the world) created by him.

822. VC. : "I am ruined by great calamities. But the God has inspired in me such type of mental attitude as is capable of delivering me from this."

VR. : Paramātmā occupies the same body (consisting of bhūtas etc.) as the one occupied by *jīva*. But though he is staying in Prakṛti along with *jīva*, he is untouched by the blemishes of the Prakṛti and hence is extremely pure. He is destitute of changes such as birth, death, grief, delusion, hunger, thirst etc. His knowledge is undiminished. Though he stays in the same impure body as the *jīva* who is subject to *karmas*, he is not at all affected by any impurities. Hence the *jīva* bows to him who manifests in his afflicted heart.

Basing his explanation on *Satyaṁ jñānam anantaṁ Brahma* (Tait. Up. 2.1.1) VJ. states : The Paramātman stays in the body even in the womb as the director of the Prakṛti. But (*tu*) there is extreme difference between the *jīva* and the *paramātman* as he is extremely pure, changeless, of unlimited knowledge. I bow to Hari whose presence in my heart burning with afflictions, is determined by his being free from them.

VC. : I bow to the Lord as we do not know whether he stays in this body to protect us or as a part of his *līlā*. It is proper that as a result of my past sinful actions I am here, but how does he live in this hell as an *antaryāmin* ? His presence due to his dependence on Māyā does not bring any impurity, change or limitation to his knowledge as in my case. He stayed in my heart and gave me the (above) knowledge. Hence I realized this in my heart tormented with affliction.

VB. : This verse describes the absence of blemishes and excellences in the Lord. It describes the blemishes of the *jīva*. And the *jīva* bows to the Lord to remove his weaknesses and faults.

my real nature covered by *karmas*. I bow to the Lord who is being realized in my tormented heart yet is himself unaffected by changes (*avikāra*) as he is extremely pure and unlimited by conditions, and of uninterrupted knowledge.

14.* I who am falsely concealed in a body composed of five *Bhūtas*, am factually unattached to it. I am the *jīva* falsely reflected in the sense-organs, attributes (like *sattva*) and objects of senses. I bow to that Supreme Man whose greatness is not limited[823] by the body—the Supreme Man who is the controller of the Prakṛti and Puruṣa and who is omniscient.

15. By what means can the *jīva* regain for himself his original status[824] without the grace of the Lord by (the power of) whose Māyā he lost his memory (about his true self) and is wandering in this path of *saṁsāra* suffering the afflictions resulting from it and wherein he incurs heavy bondage from actions (committed) due to the three *guṇas*.

16. Which[825] of the gods except the Supreme Being has inspired in me this knowledge of the past, present and future? (It must be the Supreme God as) we *jīvas* follow the course of *karmas* (and are subject to births and deaths). By his *aṁśa*, he has pervaded the mobiles and immobiles (as an *antaryāmin*). We resort to him for the cessation of the three kinds of afflictions (viz. *ādhibhautika*, *ādhyātmika* and *ādhi-daivika*).

17. Oh Lord! this embodied being has fallen into the hollow place full of blood, feces and urine in the cavity in the body of another person (i.e. the mother). His body is extremely scorched by the abdominal fire (of the mother). Being anxious of getting out of this place, he is counting his months.

---

*VR. takes the first half as the description of Paramātman. "Paramātman, though concealed or covered by the body composed of five *bhūtas*, is not at all touched by the defects or blemishes resulting from the contacts with the body. He is the controller of both *cit* and *acit* (sentient and non-sentient) for his body consists of *guṇas*, objects of senses and the sentient principle (*jīva*)".

823. v.l. *avaguṇṭha-mahimānam*—The shroud enveloping whose greatness is destroyed—ŚR.

824. *lokam*—The real knowledge of the self, the means to liberation —VR.

825. *Katamaḥ*—(1) Extremely blessed—VJ. (2) The highest Brahman —VB.

When will this low-minded being be delivered (lit. pushed out of this place)?

18. Oh Omnipotent Lord, you are simply incomparable. By your unbounded mercy, you have blessed a *jīva* of ten months with this knowledge. May that protector of the distressed (i.e. you) be pleased with his (your) own action (of this gift of knowledge). What can anyone do to him (you) except offering one's obeisance ?

19*. This another kind of *jīva*[826] (sub-human beings like birds, beasts) certainly feels physical (pleasures and pains) pertaining to his body. I am blessed by him with intelligence (knowledge and discretion) and gifted by him with a body capable of being disciplined with *śama*, *dama* etc. I can see that eternal, perfect Puruṣa directly both within and without my heart just like a *caitya* (the *jīva* who possesses *ahaṁkāra* and is an enjoyer of pleasure and pain).

20. Oh All-pervading Lord, though I am dwelling in the womb full of many kinds of afflictions, I do not wish to get out of the womb and fall into a dark well (of ignorance) (and be born in this world). (Because, outside) God's Māyā approaches the *jīva* which has fallen into the dark pit (well) of *saṁsāra*. The Māyā is followed by false apprehension (about the identification of the body and the Soul etc.) and this cycle of *saṁsāra*.

21. I have now attained to the feet of Viṣṇu and am

---

* VR. compares the *jīva* in the womb with a Yogī (*damaśarīrī*). I can directly see the Lord in my heart by the power of knowledge (*dhiṣaṇā*) gifted to me. *Caitya*=the eternal god to be grasped by mind purified by Yoga. The *Yogī* has a body of seven sheaths but is different from the body. By the power of seeing, blessed by the Lord, a Yogī visualises the Lord due to his controlled mind and senses.

VC: This *jīva* in the human womb sees by his intelligence the physical pleasures and pains. Another fortunate one becomes a *damaśarīrī* (knower, *jñānī*). Though I am notorious of being evil-minded, I can directly see with the intelligence gifted by him, the Lord—the eternal Puruṣottama, presiding over my mind, both within and without my heart.

826. *sapta-vadhri*: *vadhra*=A leathern strap—ASD 828.

(i) VR. explains it as 'a *jīva* with seven skin sheaths' (i.e. body).

(ii) JG. and VC. : A *jīva* in the womb.

(iii) ŚR., SD, GD. : A *jīva*.

(iv) VJ.: *jīva*, the possessor of seven organs of knowledge.

free from destruction. I shall stay therefore, here (in the womb) only with the help of my mind which is like a friend, I shall soon lift myself up from ignorance. So that the calamity of staying in many holes (wombs at the time of each birth in *saṁsāra*) will not befall me.

Kapila said :

22. In this way, the *jīva* who is ten months old and who has acquired knowledge, makes up his mind. While he is praising the Lord in the womb the wind produced in the womb during the pangs of travail suddenly pushes him with his head downward for his birth.

23. Being thus thrust down by the wind of delivery, the *jīva* gets suffocated and anguished and loses his memory. With great trouble, he is suddenly born with his head downward.

24. He falls on the ground in a pool of blood and urine. He moves about like a worm in feces. (Finding that) he has lost his knowledge and has fallen in the contrary state (of dark ignorance), he frequently cries out.

25. He is being fed by persons who cannot understand the will (and need) of another. If he is presented an unwanted object, he is incapable of refusing it.

26. He is made to lie down (sleep) on a dirty bed rendered troublesome by worms born of sweat. He is unable to scratch his limbs or make movements like sitting, standing or moving.

27. Just as big worms gnaw and bite smaller worms, similarly mosquitoes, flies, bugs etc. bite the soft and delicate skin of the crying child who has lost its (previous) memory.

28. In this way having suffered miseries in childhood and boyhood, (in youth) he becomes down-cast with grief for his inability to obtain the desired object. He flares up with rage out of ignorance.

29. His pride and anger go on increasing with the growth of his body. He, being passionate, fights with other passionate persons like him, and meets his end (ruin).

30. This ignorant, dull-witted embodied being constantly entertains the false notion about this body which is composed of five *bhūtas* to be himself and as belonging to him.

31. He performs action for the sake of the body—the body which gives the *jīva* a great trouble (from birth to death) and which being bound down by *avidyā* (ignorance) and *karmas* (destiny, fruit of actions), always follows him (in the next birth). It is by being bound down to the body that the *jīva* goes to (and is entangled in) the cycle of *saṁsāra*.

32. While on the path of righteousness, if the being comes in contact with and is influenced by the unrighteous who are striving for the gratification of their lusts and appetites and enjoys himself (in those ways), he enters the darkness (of ignorance or hell) as before.

33. (For virtues such as) truthfulness, purity, mercy, silence (control over speech), intelligence or the sense of the highest objective (*puruṣārtha*), affluence, modesty, renown, forbearance, control of sense-organs, control of the mind, prosperity go on diminishing in the company of the evil.

34. One should not form association with those wicked persons who regard the Soul as identical with the body and are devoid of serenity and are ignorant. They are under the influence of women like the domesticated deer with which the women play and hence pitiable.

35. He is not that much affected by delusion and bondage on other occasions as when he is attached to women or to those who are attached to women.

36. The Lord of Creation (Brahmā) was enamoured of the beauty of his daughter when he saw her. When she assumed the form of a female deer, the shameless god assumed the form of a male deer and ran after her.

37. With the exception of the sage Nārāyaṇa who else in this world (and out of the sages like Marīci created by Brahmā and out of sages like Kāśyapa and others born of them and among gods, human beings etc. created by Kāśyapa), is not attracted by the Māyā in the form of woman.

38. Look at the power of my Māyā in the form of the woman. By the mere movement of her eyebrow she tramples under foot (conquers) the conquerors of the quarters (the entire world).

39. He who has attained Self-realization by my service and desires to attain to the highest stage of Yoga, should never

associate himself with women. (For) they (Yogins) call woman as the gate of hell.

40. A woman is the Māyā created by God. She slowly approaches you. You should look upon her as your death, like a deep pit covered by grass.

41. Similarly a woman who wants liberation (should regard as death the Māyā who approaches her in the form of a man and who she thinks to be her husband. The woman is a *jīva* who, due to his attachment to women (in a former birth) has attained the form of a woman which procures for her, wealth, a house and children.

42. Just as the song (sweet notes) of a hunter is a death to the deer, similarly one should understand the Māyā to be the death in the form of the husband, children and home brought to her by Fate.

43. By his *Liṅga-śarīra* surrounding the *jīva*, he wanders from one world to another (from one body to another). While the man enjoys the fruits of actions, he continuously goes on committing actions (*karmas*).

44. The *jīva* i. e. the subtle-body (*Liṅga-śarīra*) closely follows the *ātman* and is conditioned by it. The gross body is the product of the *Bhūtas*, *indriyas* (sense-organs) and *manas* (the mind). The suspension of the use of the gross-body is the Death, and the manifestation of its powers (to produce the effect) is the birth.

45*. When the gross body which is the place (and condition) of the perception of substances becomes incapable in its function of observing them, it is called death. When it (the gross body) is identified with the Self through *ahaṁkāra* and is capable of perceiving the objects, it is called the birth.

---

*VR. states that the change of state is the death of the previous state and the birth of a new one. Here the subtle state (*sūkṣmāvasthā*) wherein a man becomes incapable of perceiving the elemental composition of the gross body, is called the death of that man. But when he sees it with *ahaṁkāra* (It is I), it is his birth.

VJ. agrees with ŚR. : The state in which a man is incapable of taking in the experience of gross objects in relation to the gross body, is called death. When he has the sense of I-ness ('I am this body') with reference to the body and is able to experience gross objects, it is the birth.

46* (For example) when the eyes (the region of visual perception of objects) becomes incapable of seeing the parts of a substance,' it is the incapability of the sensory organ. When the (physical) eyeballs and the sensory organ both cease to function, the seer (the *jīva* that perceives (becomes incapable of seeing. (Thus the *Liṅga-śarīra*—subtle body—becomes incapable of functioning after the incompetence (and cessation of function) of the gross body. But that is not the death of *jīva*, himself).

47. (As there is no birth or death to the *jīva*), the wise man should not get agitated with grief or show niggardliness (or be down-cast with dejectedness in life) nor should get confused. He should understand the nature and the course of *jīva*[827] and should move about (lead his life) without any attachment.

48*. By the power of his intellect capable of properly grasping the truth, and reinforced by the practice of Yoga and non-attachment, he should place his body in this world created by Māyā (i.e. he should give up attachment to his body) and go about the world.

---

*VR. explains: For the creation of the sense of renunciation and to emphasize the distinctness of *ātman* from the body which is created and destroyed, the example of the organ of sight is taken. The physical eye is incapable of seeing the organ of sight and other objects. The organ of seeing is incapable to function when the eye is diseased, even though the object of seeing is present. When a person is absent-minded, he does not see the object though his physical eye and the sense of seeing are healthy and the object is present. Thus it is the intelligent seer (Soul) who sees and he is distinct from the rest. So is the distinction between the Soul and the body.

827. *jīvagati*—The nature of *jīva* as distinct from Prakṛti and Brahman.

*VJ. states that this is the way how *jīvan-muktas* should lead their life here :

The *jīva* is unattached to the body and things pertaining to it. The body of the *jīva* lives in this *karmabhūmi*—the world created by the will of Nārāyaṇa. He should give up attachment, be unmoved like the deep (ocean). He should have correct knowledge and faith. With his intellect strengthened by Bhakti, Yoga and *vairāgya* he should realize Nārāyaṇa, the support of heaven, hell etc. where *jīvas* go. He should lead his life in the service (and meditation) of Nārāyaṇa.

CHAPTER THIRTY-TWO

(*Excellence of the Bhaktiyoga*)

Kapila said :

1. Now, a person who sticks to domestic life and performs the (religious) duties prescribed for householders, obtains from them the two objectives, viz. *kāma* (enjoyment of desired objects) and *artha* (wealth). He continues to perform the same duties again.

2. He also is so much deluded with the objects of enjoyments, that he becomes averse to the *Bhāgavata dharma*. Endowed with earnest faith, he continues to worship the gods and *Pitṛs* (ancestors) by performing sacrifices.

3. The man has his mind completely possessed of faith (in gods and *Pitṛs*). He observes the religious vows (for the propitiation) of manes and gods, and drinks Soma juice (in the Soma sacrifice). Such a man will attain to the heaven presided over by the Moon, (but) will come back (i.e. will be born) again to this world.

4. (But) when Hari who is seated on Ananta (Śeṣa) goes to sleep on the bed of that Lord of serpents (at the time of *Pralaya* at the end of Brahmā's day) those regions (accessible to such householders) are (also) dissolved.

5-7. The wise persons who do not perform their religious duties for obtaining *kāma* (their desired objects) and *artha* (wealth), who are unattached and have deposited (offered) all their religious acts (in God as his worship); who are extremely serene and of pure mind; who are engaged in the *Nivṛtti-dharma*; who have given up the sense of 'mine-ness' (ownership) and I-ness (*ahaṁkāra*)—such wise persons, by their power called 'observance of one's duties' (*Svadharma*), and by thoroughly purified mind, go through the portals of the Sun to the perfect (or omniscient) *Puruṣa* (the Supreme Man), who is the Lord of the universe (of the movables and immovables, the liberated and the unliberated etc.), and who is the material cause of the world, and who causes the creation and the destruction of the universe.

8. Those who meditate upon Hiraṇyagarbha (Brahmā)

as the Supreme Being[828], stay in the *Satyaloka* (Brahmā's region) to the end of the second Parārdha which is the time of god Brahmā's *Pralaya* (the *mahāpralaya* indicating the end of Brahmā's period).

9* When the great god Brahmā enjoys his full span of life called *Parārdha*, he desires to withdraw the universe composed of the gross elements, viz., the earth, water, fire, wind and the sky, the mind, the sense-organs along with their objects and the *ahaṁkāra*. He becomes one with the Prakṛti composed of three *guṇas* and enters the unmanifest Brahman.

10. The Yogins who have controlled their breath and mind and are unattached to worldly objects reach along with Brahmā (Hiraṇya-garbha) to the immortal highest Brahman, the ancient Puruṣa; (for till then) they have not yet shed off their ego (ahaṁkāra) completely.[829]

11. Oh brilliant mother, you devoutly take shelter under him who is enshrined in the lotuslike hearts of all beings and whose glory you have heard (from me).

12. (Even god Brahmā is born again). God Brahmā (who bears the Vedas within him) is the first (i.e. the creator) of the movable and immovable world. Along with sages (like Marīci), great Yogins like Sanatkumāra etc., and Siddhas who have propagated yoga path, even he—

13.** Having attained to the Saguṇa Brahman, the

---

828. *parasya paracintakāḥ* : Yogins who meditate upon the Paramātman —VR.

VC. notes that those who meditate upon Hiraṇyagarbha only are not liberated after Brahmā's liberation.

* VJ. gives a different process of this *saṁhāra* or withdrawal : Brahmā is withdrawn into the unmanifest Lakṣmī along with the deities presiding over all *Tattvas*. He enters Parabrahman through Lakṣmī.

829. *agatābhimānāḥ* : They are proud of being the votaries of Hiraṇyagarbha. Hence they are not completely absorbed in the Supreme Lord. Their dissolution being *prākṛtic* in nature, they are born again—VC.

* VJ. explains : Jīva attains to the Lord (Puruṣa) by proper understanding of the exact differences between Jīva, Īśvara and by complete knowledge that is so essential for Liberation (*mukti*) and by doing actions without any desire even after attainment of knowledge. The Lord is *Brahman*, i.e. full of all excellences. He possesses infinite *guṇas* like know-

foremost among the Puruṣas on account of his actions done without any desire for their fruit, but on account of his notion of being different[830] (from god) as a creator and the (consequent) *ahaṁkāra* about creation,

14. [He] is born again as before at the time of the (next) creation when the balance of three *guṇas* gets disturbed and the *guṇas* get into commotion by the force of Time (Kāla) which is a form of the Lord.

15. They (the sages etc.) also, having enjoyed the divine glories and positions accrued to them by their religious acts, are born again when the universe is created (lit. *guṇas* get mixed up at the time of creation).

16. Those whose minds are attached here to *Karmas*, perform with faith all the daily religious duties as well as those (*kāmya*) actions which are not prohibited by the Dharma Śāstra.

17. Those whose mind has become dull by *rajo-guṇa*, and is attached to enjoyments, have no control over senses. Their heart finds pleasure in domestic life. These (persons) propitiate the *Pitṛs* (ancestors).

18. Those who value only the first three objectives in life (viz. *dharma*, *artha* and *kāma*) set their face against the stories of Hari (the vanquisher of demon Madhu) whose great prowess is worth eulogizing and memory about whom eliminates the *saṁsāra*.

19. They are certainly of accursed fate who leaving aside the nectarlike stories of Hari, listen to the vile accounts just as feces-eating animals feed upon excrement.

---

ledge, power etc. and is *Saguṇa* as the creator of the universe. He assumes Human form for his devotees. Hence he is called *Puruṣa*. He is beyond *kṣara* and *akṣara Puruṣa*. Hence he is called *Puruṣarṣabha*. Brahmā 'enters' into him, that is, gets *sāyujya* type liberation.

830. *bhedadṛṣṭi* : (i) Jīva's ego as being independent and the wrong identification of the body and the Soul—VR.

(ii) The ego of being the creator of the world just as Viṣṇu is the protector—VC.

Even Sanatkumāra and others had the egoistic tinge of being the experiencers of Brahman and they regarded Brahman as 'spotted' with Māyā—VC.

20. They go to the region of *Pitṛs* (ancestors) through the southern path of Aryaman (technically called *dhūmra-mārga*—path of smoke). Those who perform all the prescribed religious rites from the pregnancy—*garbhādhāna*—to the funeral, are born in their own family (lit. of their descendants).

21. Oh pious mother, thereafter when their merit (accrued to them by their religious acts) is exhausted, they are immediately deprived of their means of (celestial) enjoyments by Gods. They being helpless (at the mercy of their *karmas*) fall again to this world.[831]

22. Therefore you adore the Supreme Lord (Viṣṇu) with utmost regard and devotion based on (i.e. felt on account of contemplation of) his excellent attributes. The lotuslike feet of the Lord deserve service.

23. If the *yoga* called devotion to Lord Vāsudeva is intensely practised, it immediately generates desirelessness and knowledge that leads to the realization of Brahman.

24. (As a matter of fact) all objects are equal. But it is when the mind of the devotee becomes fixed and steady in God due to the votary's love for the excellent attributes of the Lord that it does not discriminate (between them) according to the attitude of the senses—as being favourite and agreeable and non-favourite and disagreeable.

25. At that time (in that stage) he realizes the Brahman by his own Self as being free from all attachment, of perfect wisdom,[832] free from acceptability or rejectability (i.e. above merits and demerits) and full of the highest bliss.

26. The Para Brahman is pure knowledge (consciousness). It is described as the Supreme Ātman, the Īśvara and the Puruṣa. The Lord (Bhagavān) is the same who is equally perceived in different capacities (as the seer, the thing-to-be-seen and the act-of-seeing).

27. Perfect non-attachment (to the world) in all respects is the only desired fruit that a Yogin is to get by practising all *yogas* in this world.

---

831. Cf. *Kṣīṇe puṇye martya-lokaṁ viśanti*/ BG. 9.21.

832. *sama-darśana*—(i) One who gives pure knowledge—SD.
(ii) One who knows the reality as it is—VJ.
(iii) One who knows all world as imbued with Brahman—VR.

28*. The Brahman is one (without a second). It is of the nature of knowledge or consciousness and without any attributes. It is an illusion when through outward looking sense-organs it appears as things (like the sky) possessed of sound and other attributes.

29. Just as the one *Mahat* (*-tattva*) appears as *ahaṁkāra* of three types (viz. *sāttvika*, *rājasa* and *tāmasa*) and of five kinds (according to the five *Mahābhūtas*) and eleven kinds (as per ten sense-organs plus the internal organ, viz. the mind), it is from the same principle that the *Svarāj* (jīva), its body and its egg (of the universe) make their appearance.

30. Verily it is only a non-attached person whose mind is composed and serene by faith, devotion and continuous practice of Yoga who realizes this Brahman.

31. Oh mother, I have uptill now explained to you the knowledge that leads to the realization of the Brahman. It is by this knowledge that the real nature of Prakṛti and Puruṣa is clearly understood.

32. The path of knowledge (*Jñāna yoga*) pertains to the attributeless Brahman while the Yoga called *Bhakti* (devotion) is based on firm devotion to me. But both of them have the same objective viz. (the realization of) the Supreme Lord.

33. Just as the same object possessing many attributes is perceived in different forms by the sense-organs with separate functions (lit. doors), (similarly) the Supreme Lord (though absolutely one without a second) is seen in different ways through different *śāstras*.

34. By doing religious acts, by performing sacrifices, by donating gifts, by penance, by the study of the Vedas, by sub-

---

* (i) VR. Quoting BG. 14.27 interprets 'Brahman' as *jīva*. *Jīva* is of the nature of knowledge, destitute of *guṇas* like *sattva*. To regard it as identical with its gross body is illusion. Jīva is conditioned by elements like *Pṛthvī* but the Supreme Soul is beyond these.

(ii) Brahman which incarnated as a Fish, should be understood as possessing non-prākṛtic body. It appears as one endowed with a gross body to the senses which are familiar with gross objects. But that is a delusion.—VJ.

(iii) The Brahman which is of the nature of knowledge appears to outward-looking sense-organs as objects (like the sky) possessing the attribute of sound. It is devoid of rejectable attributes.—SD.

duing the *ātman* and the sense-organs and by renunciation of *karmas*.

35. By means of the *yoga* with (eight) different stages, and by the Path of Bhakti (*Bhakti yoga*), by religious practices both with and without the desire for their fruits, which are called *Pravṛtti* and *Nivṛtti*.

36. By clear knowledge about the nature of the Soul and by firm sense of non-attachment—by means of these, the self-illuminating Lord whether *Saguṇa* or *Nirguṇa* is realized.

37. I have clearly described to you the nature of the four kinds of *Bhakti-yoga* and of *kāla* (Time) whose course is unmanifested but which runs within the beings (to bring about their birth and death).

38. (I have narrated to you) the external courses of *jīva*, which are created by *avidyā* and *karma*. Oh mother, when the Soul enters into these, he does not know its own real nature.

39. This knowledge should not be explained to the evil person nor to one of undisciplined (arrogant) nature, nor to a dullard nor to a man of bad character, nor to a hypocrite.

40. (One should not) advise this to a person of greedy nature, nor to a person whose mind is attached to his house (property etc.), nor to one who is not devoted to me. It should never be taught to the enemies of my devotees.

41. It should be taught to my faithful devotee, who is modest and disciplined and is not jealous of anybody; to one who has formed friendship with beings, and who takes pleasure in serving (his elderly persons or preceptor).

42. It should be expounded to him who is completely unattached internally and externally, who is of tranquil heart, and is not envious of anybody, is pure and to whom I am the dearest of the dear.

43. Oh mother, the man who even once hears this knowledge with faith, or relates this to others with his mind set on me verily attains to my abode.

CHAPTER THIRTY-THREE

(*Devahūti's Enlightenment and Liberation*)

Maitreya said :

1. Having heard the discourse of Kapila, his mother Devahūti, the (beloved) wife of Kardama, got her veil of delusion torn open. She bowed to him and praised him who was the founder (lit. land) of the Sāṁkhya (system of philosophy) which is mainly characterised by the topic—treatment of *Tattvas* (principles).[833]

Devahūti said :

2. Even god Brahmā himself who was born of the lotus in your stomach (could not see your body but mentally) meditated upon your person which was lying manifest in the cosmic waters; which was the cause of the entire universe; which consisted of *bhūtas* (elements), sense-organs and their objects (e.g. fragrance, taste etc.), and the mind, and which has the flow of *guṇas* (Sattva, Rajas, Tamas) in it.

3. It is with your power divided by the flow of your *guṇas* that you (of above description), remaining inactive, bring about the creation, maintenance and destruction of the universe; Your will power is effective; You are the controller of all the *jīvas* (for whose enjoyment you create the universe; Your powers are infinite and beyond comprehension.

4. Oh Lord, how was it possible that you were borne by me in my womb. It was your Māyā, you in whose stomach lay the whole of the universe, and who, at the end of *Yugas*

---

833. *Tattva-viṣayāṅkita-siddha-bhūmim.*

(i) Kapila was the patron of Yogins who are famous for their knowledge of the *Tattvas* viz. Prakṛti, Puruṣa and others—VR.

(ii) Kapila was the supporter of Brahmā and other numerous Siddhas who are devoted to the Tattva, viz., Viṣṇu.—VJ.

(iii) Kapila is so called because he was the past master in the Bhakti-tattva, Sāṁkhya-System, Yoga-tattva etc.—VC.

(iv) Kapila was the asylum of Siddhis which are characterised by Vaiṣṇava-Sāṁkhya the main subject of which are the Tattvas, viz., *cit*, *acit* Brahman.—SD.

(v) Kapila was the preceptor of Siddhas who are characterised by the knowledge of Tattvas, viz., Prakṛti, Puruṣa, Īśvara etc.—GD.

(i.e. after the deluge set in) lay alone on a banyan leaf in the form of an infant sucking its toe.

5. Oh Supreme Lord, you have assumed the corporeal form for the destruction of the wicked sinners and for the prosperity of those who obey your commands. Just as you have your (other) incarnations of Boar etc., this incarnation (of yours) is for showing the path of self-realization.

6. Oh glorious Lord, even a Cāṇḍāla (lit. a dog-eater) immediately becomes worthy (like a performer) of the Soma Sacrifice, if he has but once heard or uttered your name or bowed to you or remembered you. What need be said of a person (like me) who has (directly) seen you?

7. Oh how wonderful it is that even a Cāṇḍāla (the lowest-born person) becomes superior and worthy of respect simply because Your name is on the tip of his tongue. Those persons of noble behaviour who take your name have (the merit of having) performed penance, sacrifices and baths in holy waters, and Vedic studies (Or : It is as a result of doing these meritorious acts in the previous life that they take your name in this birth).

8. I pay obeisance to you, Kapila, who are the highest Brahman, the Supreme Man who are worthy of meditation in mind which is withdrawn from external objects, and who have dried up the flow of *guṇas* by your brilliance and who are Viṣṇu (who holds Vedas within him).

Maitreya said :

9. The Supreme Man called the venerable Kapila who was thus praised and who was affectionate to his mother, spoke thus to her in words deep in significance (Or: with words choked up with emotions.).

Kapila said :

10. Oh mother, I have explained to you the path which is easy to follow. By following this path, you will reach the highest stage (of being liberated while alive).

11. Have faith in my doctrine which has been followed by the knowers of Brahman (or the Vedas). By following

this you will attain to me who am without birth (i.e. eternal). Those who are ignorant about this path go to death (*saṁsāra*).

Maitreya said :

12. The venerable Kapila showed to his pious mother the path leading to Ātman. Having obtained the permission of his mother, who realized the Brahman, Kapila departed (from her hermitage).

13. And in that hermitage which was like a flower-chaplet on the head of the Sarasvatī (river), she adopted Yogic practice in accordance with the guidance of her son, and became composed in mind.

14. She performed ablutions three times a day. Her curly hair became matted and tawny in colour. By severe penance her body became emaciated. She wore bark-garments.

15. The household comforts that were created by Prajāpati Kardama by means of his penance and Yoga were incomparable. They were covetable even to gods.

16. The beds were white and soft like the foam of milk. The ivory couches were chased with gold. The seats of gold were provided with soft cushions (covers).

17. In the walls of transparent crystals and very costly emeralds were shining jewel-lamps along with statues of beautiful damsels made of precious stones.

18. The garden around the house looked beautiful with many blossoming celestial trees, on which couples of birds were warbling and the intoxicated black bees were humming sweetly.

19. Where the followers of gods (Gandharvas) used to praise her when she, fondled by Kardama, entered in the swimming pool fragrant with lotuses.

20. It (the household) was most covetable even to the queens of Indra. But she just abandoned it. Due to the anxiety caused by the separation of her son, she was dejected in appearance.

21. As her husband left for the forest (after renouncing the world) Devahūti, though she realized the Truth (the Sāṁkhya Principles), became overanxious due to the separa-

tion from her son, like a calf-loving cow is fond after her young one.

22. Oh child (Vidura), she meditated upon her child Kapila who was the God Hari. In a short time, she became indifferent to that type of rich household.

23. According to the guide-lines given by her son, she meditated upon the form of the gracious-looking Lord—the object of meditation—by the method of contemplating the complete form followed by concentration on the parts of it.[834]

24. By means of stream or overflow of devotion, by powerful renunciation, and by knowledge which was produced by the proper observances of vows[835] leading to Brahmahood.

25. Her mind became pure. She was then lost in the meditation of all-pervading Ātman who by his essential light removes the limitations of the *guṇas* of Māyā.

26. Her mind became steadied in the glorious Brahman which is the shelter of all the *jīvas*. As she superseded her state of being a *jīva*, all her afflictions were over and she attained to the blessed stage.

27. As she was always engaged in continuous meditation and her delusion due to *guṇas* was dispelled, at that time she did not remember her body, just as an object seen in a dream (is found to be unreal) after waking up.

28. Her body was fed by others (viz. Vidyādhara damsels who were produced by Kardama for attendance upon her). As she was free from diseases, she did not become emaciated. Her body was covered with filth. She looked like a fire covered with smoke.

29. Her mind was so deeply entered (i.e. absorbed) in Vāsudeva that she was not conscious of her body. She had so completely given herself up to penance and Yoga that her hair fell dishevelled and clothes were dropped and she was protected by her previous *karma* (*daiva*).

30. In this way she progressed by the path expounded by Kapila. Within a short period she attained to the Supreme

834. Vide Supra III. 28.12-33.

835. Cf. BG. 6.17.

Soul, the Brahman, the glorious Lord; the stage called Nirvāṇa.

31. Oh warrior (Vidura), the place called Siddhapada where she attained the Liberation became famous as the holiest place in the three worlds.

32. Oh gentle Vidura, her mortal body from which impurities were eliminated by Yoga, was transformed into a river, a prominent one among many rivers. It blesses one with *siddhis* and is resorted to by Siddhas.

33. Even glorious Kapila, the great Yogin, obtained the permission of his mother to depart from his father's hermitage and proceeded to the northern direction.

34. He was praised by multitude of Siddhas, Cāraṇas, Gandharvas, sages and celestial nymphs. He was also respectfully received by the sea and was presented a valuable dwelling place.

35. Kapila stays there practising Yoga. He is highly eulogized by the great teachers of Sāṁkhya School. For the peace and tranquillity of the three worlds, he lives there (absorbed) in meditation.

36. Oh child (Vidura), as per your query I have narrated to you the sacred dialogue between Kapila and Devahūti, Oh sinless one.

37. He who listens to this or narrates this doctrine of the Sage Kapila regarding the secret knowledge about the Ātman, becomes able to concentrate his mind upon the venerable Lord whose banner has the emblem of Garuḍa, and he attains to the lotus-like feet of the glorious Lord.

——ooo——